"Principles of Green HRM"
Strategies & Practices

OrangeBooks Publication

1st Floor, Rajhans Arcade, Mall Road, Kohka, Bhilai, Chhattisgarh 490020

Website: **www.orangebooks.in**

© **Copyright, 2024, Author**

All rights reserved. No part of this book may be reproduced, stored in a retrieval system, or transmitted, in any form by any means, electronic, mechanical, magnetic, optical, chemical, manual, photocopying, recording or otherwise, without the prior written consent of its writer.

First Edition, 2024
ISBN: 978-93-6554-344-5

Principles of GREEN HRM

STRATEGIES & PRACTICES

Miss. Rajeshri P Lasurkar | Dr. Vivek S Kanade

OrangeBooks Publication
www.orangebooks.in

Introduction

This comprehensive reference book on **"Principles of Green Human Resource Management: strategies and practices"** provide practical insights, case studies, and tools for organizations looking to integrate sustainability into their HR practices. From recruitment to performance management, legal compliances to adaptation of technology this book covers all aspects of building a green workforce for a sustainable future.

This book covers aspects of **Sustainable HR practices** focus on encouraging employee well-being, promoting diversity and inclusion, and implementing environmentally responsible policies. By prioritizing ethical recruitment and development, these practices ensure long-term organizational resilience and social responsibility. Green job analysis and design involve identifying roles that contribute to environmental sustainability and incorporating eco-friendly practices into job descriptions and tasks. This approach aims to integrate environmental stewardship into organizational operations while creating meaningful roles that support sustainability goals. Green recruitment and selection strategies prioritize candidates with a commitment to environmental sustainability, ensuring alignment with eco-friendly values and practices within the organization. Environmental training and development programs equip employees with knowledge and skills to adopt and promote sustainable practices within the workplace, fostering a culture of environmental stewardship and responsibility. Performance management in green organizations focuses on aligning employee goals with sustainability metrics, measuring and rewarding contributions to environmental objectives. Green compensation and benefits packages reward employees who contribute to environmental sustainability efforts, reflecting the organization's commitment to eco-friendly practices and values. These incentives aim to attract, retain, and motivate talent dedicated to advancing environmental stewardship within the workforce. Employee engagement in sustainability involves involving employees in green initiatives, encouraging their active participation in reducing environmental impact and promoting sustainable practices within the organization. This fosters a sense of ownership and commitment to environmental responsibility among the workforce. Legal compliance in Green HRM ensures adherence to environmental regulations and standards in all HR practices, including recruitment, training, compensation, and performance management. This approach mitigates risks, promotes corporate responsibility, and enhances organizational reputation in sustainability practices. Diversity and inclusion in sustainable organizations involve fostering a workforce that reflects diverse backgrounds, perspectives, and experiences, which are crucial for innovative and effective sustainability solutions. By promoting inclusivity, these organizations ensure equitable participation in environmental initiatives, enhancing social responsibility and organizational resilience. Green HR metrics and reporting involve measuring and analyzing data related to environmental impact, employee engagement in sustainability initiatives, and compliance with green practices. This enables organizations to track progress, identify areas for improvement, and communicate their environmental performance transparently to stakeholders. Green technology and HR practices involve leveraging eco-friendly technological solutions to enhance HR operations, such as virtual recruitment processes to reduce travel-related emissions or implementing energy-efficient systems in HR offices. These practices aim to minimize environmental footprint while optimizing efficiency and sustainability within HR management.

Preface

In the competitive world of business where environmental issue concerning business practices are increasingly interlinked with corporate strategies, the crucial role of Human Resource Management (HRM) is moving beyond traditional philosophy & boundaries. ***"Principles of Green HRM: Strategies and Practices"*** looks after to witness this transfiguration by exploring the convergence of sustainable development in human resource management.

As businesses encounters increasing pressure to adopt environmental-friendly practices, Human Resource departments are prominent reformer in driving green HR initiatives. This book provides a profound clarity of how HRM can contribute in the culture of environmental sustainability, offering comprehensive insights into HR strategies and practices with real life cases which promote a green workplace.

Through a blend of theoretical view point and practical implementation & applications, this book aspire to equip Human Resource professionals, managers, and academics with the profound knowledge required to integrate environmental control into Human Resource practices. This book focus on innovative approaches for recruiting & selecting green talent encourages a culture of sustainability, and implementing Eco-friendly policies.

Come up with real-world cases and providing actionable frameworks to HR, this book defines the critical & basic role of HR in advancing towards corporate sustainability. As organizations endeavor to balance profitability with environmental responsibility for sustainability, the principles outlined in this book offer a roadmap for attaining both the goals.

Inclusively green HRM, it not only increases organizational performance but also contribute to a greater global initiative towards environmental protection & preservation. This book is a guide to action for Human Resource professionals, managers & Academician to escort by cases and navigate meaningful change in the organization.

Acknowledgements

This book is the outcome of many leanings, experiences, guidance and encouragement by great people, and without their help, this would not have been possible. Some of them, however, deserve special thanks. I owe my deepest gratitude and sincere thanks to my family & mentor.

A special thanks to Orange Book Publication, for their insightful feedback and endless attention to detail. Expertise of their team was played significant role in shaping this book.

Dr. Vivek S Kanade

I would like expressing my gratitude and thanks to my family for their constant support and encouragement. My parents taught me the culture of education in my mind and stood behind me in every life situation. This acknowledgement would not be complete without expressing my heartfelt thank to my mentor Dr. Vivek S Kanade for his endless support and guidance.

Miss. Rajeshri P Lasurkar

Contents

Chapter – 1 1
Green Human Resource Management 1

   1.1 Evolution of HRM to Green HRM 4
   1.1.1 Historical Perspective on the Evolution of Human Resource Management Towards Sustainability 7
   1.1.2 Shift from Traditional HR Practices to Environmentally Conscious Approaches 9
   1.1.3 Emergence of Green HRM as a Strategic Imperative for Organizations 11
   1.2 Importance of Sustainability in HR Practices 13
   1.2.1 Understanding the Significance of Sustainability in the Context of HR Function 18
   1.2.2 Link Between Sustainable HR Practices and Organizational Performance 20
   1.2.3 Benefits of Integrating Environmental Considerations into HR Strategies 22
   1.3 Role of HR in Environmental Management 24
   1.3.1 Responsibilities of HR Professionals in Driving Sustainability Initiatives within Organizations 26
   1.3.2 Collaborating with Other Departments to Promote Eco-friendly Practices 29
   1.3.3 Influence of HR on Forecasting a Culture of Environmental Stewardship among Employee 32

Chapter – 2 35
Sustainable HR Practices 35

   2.1 Implementing Sustainable HR Strategies 38
   2.1.1 Overview of Sustainable HR Strategies and their Importance in Organizational Sustainability 39
   2.1.2 Examples of Organizations Successfully Implementing Sustainable HR Practices 42
   2.1.3 Research Findings on the Impact of Sustainable HR Strategies on Organizational Performance 44
   2.2 Integrating Sustainability into HR Policies 45
   2.2.1 Importance of Incorporating Environmental Considerations into HR Policies 47

2.2.2 Case Studies on Organizations aligning HR Policies with Sustainability Goals 49
2.2.3 Best Practices for Integrating Sustainability into Recruitment, Training, and Performance Management Policies 64
2.3 Building a Green Culture in Organizations 66
2.3.1 Strategies for Fostering a Culture of Environmental Consciousness among Employees 68
2.3.2 Role of HR in Promoting Green Initiatives and Sustainability Awareness 72
2.3.3 Research on the Benefits of a Green Culture in Driving Employee Engagement and Organizational Success 75

Chapter - 3 78
Green Job Analysis and Design 78

3.1 Job Analysis for Environmental Impact 83
3.1.1 Understanding the Importance of Job Analysis in Assessing the Environmental Impact of Different Roles within an Organization 84
3.1.2 Methods and Tools for Conducting a Green Job Analysis, Including Job Description Analysis, Task Analysis, and Competency Mapping 86
3.1.3 Case Studies Showcasing How Organizations Have Utilised Job Analysis to Identify Areas for Improvement in Environmental Sustainability... 92
3.2 Designing Green Job Roles and Responsibilities.................................. 99
3.2.1 The Process of Designing Job Roles and Responsibilities with a Focus on Environmental Sustainability................................. 101
3.2.2 Incorporating Green Principles into Job Design................ 102
3.2.3 Examples of Organizations That Have Successfully Redesigned Job Roles to Align with Sustainability Goals 105
3.3 Green Skills and Competencies Mapping 109
3.3.1 Identifying the Key Skills and Competencies Required for Green Jobs in Various Industries 111
3.3.2 Developing Frameworks for Mapping Existing Skills to Green Competencies and Identifying Gaps for Training and Development....... 115
3.3.3 Research Findings on the Impact of Green Skills Development on Employee Performance and Organizational Sustainability..................... 118

Chapter – 4 122
Green Recruitment and Selection 122

4.1 Attracting Environmentally Conscious Talent 127
4.1.1 Understanding the Importance of Attracting Environmentally Conscious Talent in Building a Green Workforce 130
4.1.2 Strategies for Promoting the Organization's Commitment to Sustainability to Attract Like-minded Candidates................ 133

4.1.3 Leveraging Employer Branding and Corporate Social Responsibility Initiatives to Appeal to Environmentally Conscious Job Seekers............ 136
4.2 Green Recruitment Strategies 142
4.2.1 Implementing Environmentally Friendly Recruitment Strategies, Such as Virtual Recruitment Events and Paperless Application Processes 145
4.2.2 Leveraging Digital Platforms and Social Media to Reach a Wider Pool of Environmentally Conscious Candidates 149
4.2.3 Case Studies Highlighting Successful Green Recruitment Strategies Adopted by Organizations across Industries 152
4.3 Sustainable Selection Processes 159
4.3.1 Designing Selection Processes That Align with Sustainability Goals.. 163
4.3.2 Training Recruiters and Hiring Managers on Green Hiring Practices and the Importance of Diversity and Inclusion in Building a Sustainable Workforce.. 167
4.3.3 Research Findings on the Impact of Sustainable Selection Processes on Employment and Retention Rates... 168

Chapter – 5 173

Environmental Training and Development................................... 173

5.1 Training and Environmental Awareness 179
5.1.1 Understanding the Concept of Environmental Awareness and its Importance in Fostering a Culture of Sustainability within Organizations... 181
5.1.2 Methods for Increasing Employee Awareness about Environmental Issues 183
5.1.3 Examples of Successful Environmental Awareness Training Programs Implemented by Leading Organizations 188
5.2 Developing Green Leadership Skills.. 191
5.2.1 Exploring the Significance of Leadership in Driving Sustainability Initiatives and Promoting Green Practices within the Organization 195
5.2.2 Strategies for Developing Green Leadership Skills in Managers and Executives 200
5.2.3 Case Studies of Organizations That Have Successfully Cultivated Green Leadership Skills Among Their Top Management to Drive Sustainable Business Practices... 205
5.3 Continuous Learning for Sustainability 211
5.3.1 Highlighting the Importance of Ongoing Learning for Sustainability in the Workplace to Adopt to Changing Environmental Trends and Regulations 214
5.3.2 Tools and Resources Available for Continuous Learning on Environmental Issues 221
5.3.3 Research Findings on the Impact of Continuous Learning on Sustainable Practices in Organizations 224

Chapter – 6

Performance Management in Green Organization ... 228

6.1 Setting Sustainable Performance Goals ... 233
6.1.1 Importance of Aligning Performance Goals with Environmental Objectives in Green Organizations ... 237
6.1.2 Strategies for Setting SMART (Specific, Measurable, Achievable, Relevant, Time-bound) Sustainability Goals for Employees ... 239
6.1.3 Examples of Sustainable Performance Goals Related to Waste Reduction, Energy Conservation, and Carbon Footprint Reduction ... 243
6.2 Monitoring Environmental Performance ... 245
6.2.1 Tools and Techniques for Tracking and Measuring Environmental Performance Metrics in Organizations ... 249
6.2.2 Implementing Key Performance Indicators (KPI's) to Monitor Progress Towards Sustainability Targets ... 256
6.2.3 Case Studies of Organizations Using Advanced Monitoring Systems to Track Environmental Performance and Drive Continuous Improvement ... 259
6.3 Feedback and Recognition for Green Initiatives ... 264
6.3.1 Importance of Providing Feedback and Recognition for Employees' Green Initiatives and Contributions to Sustainability Goals ... 265
6.3.2 Strategies for Incorporating Environmental Performance into Regular Performance Reviews and Feedback Sessions ... 269
6.3.3 Examples of Innovative Recognition Programs for Employees who Demonstrate Exceptional Commitment to Sustainability Practices ... 273

Chapteer – 7

Green Compensation and Benefits ... 278

7.1 Designing Eco-Friendly Compensation Packages ... 283
7.1.1 Overview of Incorporating Environmental Considerations into Compensation Structures ... 288
7.1.2 Strategies for Designing Green Compensation Packages, Such as Pay-for-Performance Linked to Sustainability Goals ... 294
7.1.3 Case Studies of Organizations Implementing Eco-friendly Compensation Practices to Motivate Employees towards Sustainability 298
7.2 Incentives for Sustainable Behaviour ... 304
7.2.1 Importance of Incentivizing and Rewarding Sustainable Behaviours in the Workplace ... 308
7.2.2 Types of Incentives for Promoting Green Incentives ... 311
7.2.3 Examples of Successful Incentive Programs that Drive Employee Engagement in Sustainability Efforts ... 317
7.3 Employees Wellness Programs with a Green Focus ... 321
7.3.1 Integrating Environmental Wellness Initiatives into Employee Well-being Programs ... 324

7.3.2 Benefits of Promoting Green Lifestyles and Health-conscious Practices Among Employees 327

7.3.3 Best Practices for Developing and Implementing Employee Wellness Programs with a Green Focus to Enhance Overall Organizational Sustainability.. 334

7.3.4 Examples of Companies That Have Successfully Integrated Environmental Sustainability into Their Employee Wellness Programs .. 337

Chapter – 8 340
Employee Engagement in Sustainability 340

8.1 Engaging Employees in Environmental Initiatives............................. 345

8.1.1 Importance of Engaging Employees in Environmental Initiatives for Organizational Sustainability 346

8.1.2 Strategies for Involving Employees in Green Projects 352

8.1.3 Case Studies Highlighting Successful Employee Engagement in Sustainability Initiatives 357

8.2 Building Employee Advocates for Sustainability 367

8.2.1 Fostering a Culture of Sustainability Advocacy Among Employees 369

8.2.2 Empowering Employees to Become Ambassadors for Sustainable Practices within and Outside the Organization.. 375

8.2.3 Examples of Companies That Have Effectively Built a Network of Employee Advocates for Sustainability 378

8.3 Employee Participation in CSR Activities 380

8.3.1 Encouraging and Facilitating Employee Involvement in Corporate Social Responsibility (CSR) Activities 384

8.3.2 Examples of Impactful CSR Programs 395

8.3.4 Best Practices for Integrating Employees into CSR Initiatives to Drive Meaningful Impact and Enhance Employee Satisfaction 398

Chapter – 9 404
Legal Compliance in Green HRM 404

9.1 Understanding Environmental Laws and Regulations 407

9.1.1 Overview of Key Environmental Laws and Regulations Relevant to HRM 471

9.1.2 Implications of Environmental Legislation on HR Practices 475

9.1.3 Case Studies Illustrating the Impact of Non-compliance with Environmental Laws on Organizations... 482

9.2 Ensuring Compliance with Sustainability 489

9.2.1 Importance of Adhering to Sustainability Standards in HRM......... 497

9.2.2 Strategies for Integrating Sustainability Criteria into HR Policies and Procedure 500

9.2.3 Examples of Organizations Successfully Aligning HR Practices with Sustainability Standards.. 504

9.3 Legal Implications of Green HR Practices.. 510

9.3.1 Examination of the Legal Implications of Implementing Green HR Practices 515

9.3.2 Addressing Potential Legal Challenges in Areas of Green HR Practices 520

9.3.3 Best Practices for Mitigating Legal Risks While Promoting Environmentally Responsible HRM 529

Chapter – 10 534
Diversity and Inclusion in Sustainable Organization 534

10.1 Promoting Diversity in the Green Workplace 538

10.1.1 Importance of Diversity in the Context of Sustainability and Environmental Initiatives 541

10.1.2 Strategies for Recruiting and Retaining a Diverse Workforce in Green Organization 547

10.1.3 Case Studies Highlighting Successful Diversity Initiatives in Sustainable Companies 551

10.2 Inclusive Practice for Environmental Equity 555

10.2.1 Addressing Environmental Justice Issues through Inclusive HR Practices 562

10.2.2 Ensuring Equal Access to Green Opportunities for all Employees, Regardless of Background 566

10.2.3 Best Practices for Creating a Culture of Inclusion in Sustainability Efforts 568

10.3 Empowering Diverse Voices in Sustainability Efforts 571

10.3.1 Leveraging Diverse Perspectives to Drive Innovation and Creativity in Sustainability Initiatives 575

10.3.2 Encouraging Participation and Leadership from Underrepresented Groups in Green Projects 579

10.3.3 Examples of Organizations that have successfully Embraced Diversity and Inclusion in their Sustainability Programs 583

Chapter – 11 588
Green HR Metrics and Reporting 588

11.1 Measuring Environmental Impact of HR Practices 592

11.1.1 Defining and Understanding the Environmental Impact of HR Activities 600

11.1.2 Identifying Key Performance Indicators (KPIs) for Measuring Environmental Impact 606

11.1.3 Methods for Tracking and Quantifying the Sustainability Impact of HR Processes 611

11.2 Reporting on Sustainability Performance 616

11.2.1 Importance of Transparent Reporting on Sustainability Performance in HR 620

11.2.2 Communicating Environmental and Social Impacts to Internal and External Stakeholders... 624
11.2.3 Compliance with Reporting Standards and Frameworks 629
11.3 Using Data for Continuous Improvement... 635
11.3.1 Leveraging HR Metrics to Drive Continuous Improvement in Sustainability Efforts 637
11.3.2 Analysing Data to Identify Areas for Efficiency Gains and Resource Optimization.. 642
11.3.3 Integrating Sustainability Metrics into HR Dashboards and Performance Management Systems 649

Chapter – 12..655
Green Technology and HR Practices.. 655
12.1 Adopting Sustainable Technologies in HR Operations 661
12.1.1 Overview of Sustainable Technologies Applicable to HR Functions.. 663
12.1.2 Implementation Strategies for Integrating Green Technologies in Recruitment, Training, and Performance Management 666
12.1.3 Case Studies Showcasing Organizations that have Successfully Adopted Sustainable HR Technologies 671
12.2 Leveraging Tech for Remote Work and Reduced Emissions............. 684
12.2.1 Role of Technology in Enabling Remote Work and Reducing Carbon Emissions 694
12.2.2 Tools and Platforms for Virtual Collaboration, Communication, and Training 698
12.2.3 Best Practices for Managing Remote Teams Sustainably and Effectively 702
12.3 Future Trends in Green HR Technology 705
12.3.1 Emerging Technologies Shaping the Future of Green HR Practices.. 708
12.3.2 Predictions on the Impact of AI, Block chain, and IoT on Sustainability in HR 712
12.3.3 Opportunity and Challenges in Adopting Cutting-edge Green HR Technologies 715

This comprehensive reference book on Green Human Resource Management provides practical insights, case studies, and tools for organizations looking to integrate sustainability into their HR practices. From recruitment to performance management, this book covers all aspects of building a green workforce for a sustainable future.

Chapter – 1

Green Human Resource Management

Introduction

A modern strategy called "green human resource management" (GHRM) combines environmental sustainability with conventional HRM procedures inside a company. Its foundation is the knowledge that companies have an obligation to the environment in addition to their stakeholders and employees. Adopting projects, policies, and practices that support environmental sustainability and reduce the organization's ecological imprint are all part of GHRM.

Fundamentally, GHRM highlights the necessity of coordinating HR procedures with environmental objectives, encouraging an eco-friendly work culture among staff members, and incorporating green practices into a range of HR duties. This covers things like hiring, development and training, performance monitoring, staff involvement, and even supply chain management.

The concept of "green human resource management," or "GHRM," acknowledges the connection between sustainable environmental practices and company operations, marking a paradigm shift in organizational management. This new strategy emphasizes how important it is for companies to take proactive measures to address environmental issues as they pursue their operational goals. As sustainable practices are not only morally right but also necessary for long-term survival, GHRM promotes the incorporation of eco-friendly concepts into all facets of human resource management.

The idea that human capital is essential to the advancement of sustainability initiatives in a business is at the heart of the GHRM ethos. As a result, GHRM stresses the significance of developing a workforce that is engaged, ecologically conscious, and skilled in addition to being productive. To attract people who share the organization's green goals, it is necessary to include sustainability standards into the hiring process.

GHRM recognizes that partners and suppliers are equally important in attaining environmental sustainability, and it goes beyond the boundaries of internal operations to include the full value chain. As a result, GHRM entails working with stakeholders to create environmentally responsible procurement processes and encourage them across the entire supply chain.

Moreover, GHRM promotes employees' ongoing professional growth via green training and development initiatives, equipping them with the information and abilities needed to implement eco-friendly procedures in their jobs. Performance management systems are also in line with sustainability criteria, which encourages employees to participate in the company's environmentally friendly activities and promotes an accountable culture.

In the end, GHRM stands for an all-encompassing method of managing organizations that acknowledges the intrinsic worth of protecting the environment for coming generations in addition to placing a high priority on financial success. Organizations may reduce their environmental impact, recruit top personnel, improve their reputation, and support the global movement towards a more sustainable future by incorporating environmental sustainability into HR operations.

Meaning

The strength of green human resource management is its all-encompassing approach to sustainability, which acknowledges that workers play a major role in determining an organization's environmental effect. GHRM seeks to strike a balance between achieving business goals and protecting the environment for coming generations by integrating green practices into HR procedures. By incorporating environmental factors into decision-making processes, GHRM goes above and beyond typical HR duties and supports the organization's overall sustainability initiatives.

By recognizing the interdependence of human activity, corporate operations, and the environment, green human resource management (GHRM) signifies a paradigm shift in how businesses approach human resource management. Fundamentally, GHRM represents a dedication to sustainability, understanding that businesses have a critical role to play in protecting the environment while also achieving their operational goals. In actuality, GHRM is a broad umbrella word for a variety of programs, regulations, and practices designed to lessen the environmental effect of corporate operations and promote an environmentally conscious work culture among staff members. It means incorporating environmental factors into all aspects of HR management, including hiring, training, performance reviews, and employee engagement.

GHRM is rethinking standard HR duties from an eco-centric perspective, emphasizing the mitigation of damaging environmental behaviours, the promotion of resource efficiency, and the reduction of waste production. This could entail using green hiring techniques to draw in eco-aware candidates, offering eco-training courses to raise staff members' understanding of environmental issues, and adding green performance measures to performance reviews to reward sustainable behaviour.

In addition, GHRM goes outside the walls of the company to include external relationship management with vendors, clients, and other stakeholders in order to guarantee that environmental sustainability is integrated into the whole value chain. It places a strong emphasis on working together, being open and accountable, and achieving favourable environmental results throughout the organization's larger operating ecosystem.

The fundamental idea behind GHRM is that environmental sustainability and corporate success are inextricably linked. Organizations that adopt GHRM principles can improve their long-term viability and competitive edge as well as make a significant contribution to the global effort to solve urgent environmental issues.

Definition
Green Human Resource Management (GHRM) can be defined as "set of guidelines, practices, and systems that simulate the green behaviour of a company's employees in order to create an environmentally conscious, resource-efficient, and socially responsible organisation."

1.1 Evolution of HRM to Green HRM

The road that Human Resource Management (HRM) took to become Green HRM is complex and illustrates how firms' objectives changed as a result of environmental concerns around the world. At first, HRM gave little thought to environmental issues and instead concentrated mostly on administrative HRM responsibilities including hiring, training, and performance reviews. However, the role that organizations played in tackling these problems came under examination as communities around the world started to cope with urgent crises like pollution, resource depletion, and climate change.

- One way to think about the shift from standard HRM to Green HRM is as a progressive process with several turning points and motivators.

First, corporations were becoming more conscious of how their operations affected the environment. Public pressure, media attention, and scientific study all contributed to this awareness by emphasizing how vital it is for companies to switch to more sustainable methods. HR departments became aware of their responsibility for promoting environmental stewardship in businesses, which set the stage for the incorporation of green practices within HRM.

The evolution of HRM towards sustainability was significantly shaped by the introduction of environmental rules and standards. Organizations were forced to comply with these criteria or face legal and reputational penalties as governments throughout the world imposed stronger environmental laws and regulations. The groundwork for more proactive environmental management was laid by HRM's critical role in making sure that staff members have the necessary tools and training to follow environmental laws.

A more general organizational priority shift toward sustainability and corporate social responsibility (CSR) propelled the evolution of green HRM. Businesses started to understand that environmental sustainability was a source of long-term value creation and competitive advantage in addition to being morally required. HR divisions were essential in coordinating HR strategies with more general business sustainability objectives by incorporating eco-friendly practices into hiring, training, performance reviews, and employee engagement procedures.

In addition, businesses faced pressure to implement more ecologically friendly operations due to the growth of stakeholder activism and customer demand for sustainable goods and services. In order to advance sustainability projects, HRM has become crucial in promoting stakeholder participation and collaboration as well as communication between workers, vendors, consumers, and communities.

Prominent companies began to invent and develop novel strategies for Green HRM, surpassing simple adherence to environmental laws and actively searching for chances for environmental innovation and stewardship. This includes programs like eco-friendly workplace policies, green recruitment techniques, and sustainability-focused employee development that not only lessened their negative effects on the environment but also improved employee morale, engagement, and retention.

Organizations are adopting a culture of continuous improvement and adaptability as they get closer to green human resource management. They are regularly reviewing their HR procedures to find new ways to increase sustainability and lessen their impact on the environment. Green HRM reduces environmental risks and promotes resilience, creativity, and long-term value generation in a world that is changing quickly by integrating environmental sustainability into company culture and operations.

Green HRM, the development of HRM, is a reflection of a larger cultural change toward corporate social responsibility and environmental sustainability. Conventional HRM placed minimal attention on environmental factors and instead concentrated mostly on employee relations, recruitment, and personnel management. But as environmental issues became more widely known, businesses realized they had to integrate sustainability into all aspects of their operations, including human resource management.

❖ **The Transition from HRM to Green HRM can be traced through several key stages:**

1. **Awareness and Recognition:** In the first stage, companies had to admit how their operations affected the environment and how HRM could help with these issues. A change in perspective toward

incorporating sustainability into HR procedures was brought about by this insight.

2. **Compliance and Regulation**: Organizations were forced to abide by environmental laws and standards as environmental regulations grew increasingly strict. In order to ensure that workers received the necessary training and were aware of compliance standards, HRM was crucial in setting the stage for more proactive environmental management.

3. **Alignment and Integration:** Including environmental sustainability in HRM practices and policy was the next step. This entailed integrating green concepts into hiring, training, performance management, and employee engagement procedures, as well as coordinating HR initiatives with more general organizational sustainability goals.

4. **Innovation and Leadership:** As a result of HRM programs, top firms started to look for creative ways to lessen their environmental impact, going beyond simple compliance. This included programs like eco-friendly workplace policies, green recruitment techniques, and employee development with a sustainability focus.

5. **Stakeholder Engagement and Collaboration:** In order to promote a group approach to environmental stewardship, companies began interacting with stakeholders, such as workers, suppliers, and communities, after realizing how interwoven sustainability is. In order to promote cooperation and communication among stakeholders and advance sustainability initiatives, HRM was essential.

6. **Continuous Improvement and Adaptation:** The process of transitioning to Green HRM is characterised by a persistent focus on adaptation and continuous improvement in response to evolving environmental circumstances. Businesses are always reviewing their HR procedures to find new ways to improve sustainability and lessen their negative effects on the environment.

All things considered, the transition from HRM to Green HRM signifies a forward-thinking move in the direction of integrating environmental sustainability into the operations and organizational culture. Organizations that adopt Green HRM practices can use sustainability as a source of long-term value creation and competitive advantage, in addition to reducing environmental concerns.

1.1.1 Historical Perspective on the Evolution of Human Resource Management Towards Sustainability

Many historical, cultural, and environmental factors have influenced the slow but substantial evolution of human resource management (HRM) towards sustainability. HRM has experienced revolutionary changes from its beginnings as a purely administrative function to its current position as a strategic partner in organizational sustainability. These changes have been fuelled by evolving paradigms, laws, globalization, and the growing awareness of the connections between corporate success and social and environmental responsibility.

Early in the 20th century, labour relations and personnel administration were the main areas of concentration for HRM. The Industrial Revolution, which put corporate efficiency and productivity ahead of worker welfare and environmental concerns, defined this era. But as labour movements gained traction and laws like the National Labour Relations Act (NLRA) and the Fair Labour Standards Act (FLSA) were passed, HRM's function grew to encompass workplace compliance and employee rights.

With the advent of the environmental movement and the concept of Corporate Social Responsibility (CSR), the 1960s and 1970s were a watershed in HRM history. Businesses began to realize how crucial it was to balance economic objectives with social and environmental effects. Due to this change, HRM now includes workplace safety, equal opportunity, and diversity into its operations. With the establishment of the Environmental Protection Agency (EPA) in 1970, businesses were even more compelled to address environmental issues, which led HRM to get increasingly involved in sustainability projects.

HRM became a strategic role in the 1980s and 90s when companies realized they could gain a competitive edge by investing in their workforce and implementing sustainable practices. During this time, ideas like Total Quality Management (TQM), which placed a strong emphasis on ongoing improvement and employee interaction, gained traction. This helped to pave the way for HRM to take on a strategic role in organizational development. HRM's approach to sustainability was further shaped by the need to negotiate multiple cultures, labour markets, and regulatory frameworks as a result of globalization brought about by technological and communications breakthroughs.

The first part of the twenty-first century saw a greater assimilation of sustainability principles into HRM procedures. The necessity of striking a balance between profit and the well-being of people and the environment has been highlighted by the introduction of frameworks like the Triple Bottom Line (TBL), which assesses organizational performance based on economic, social, and environmental aspects. In response, HRM integrated sustainability measures into plans for employee engagement, performance reviews, and talent management. Furthermore, the rise of sustainable supply chain management brought attention to the necessity of HRM working with stakeholders and suppliers to guarantee ethical sourcing and responsible procurement procedures.

In the 2010s, public awareness of environmental challenges, social injustice, and corporate misbehaviour increased, leading to a greater focus on business sustainability. As a result of stakeholders such as workers, investors, and customers—holding companies responsible for their deeds, HRM has made accountability, transparency, and moral leadership a top priority. Furthermore, during this time, ideas like Corporate Social Responsibility (CSR), Diversity, Equity, and Inclusion (DEI), and Environmental, Social, and Governance (ESG) criteria gained widespread acceptance and were incorporated into HRM's mission to support long-term organizational cultures.

In the present environment, HRM is still developing toward sustainability in response to difficult problems including resource shortages, population shifts, climate change, and technology disruptions. Businesses are realizing more and more that they must integrate sustainability into their core values, and HRM is a key factor in this shift. Human resource management (HRM) is at the forefront of creating businesses that prosper financially while also making significant contributions to society and the environment. This includes integrating green HR practices and building an innovative and resilient culture.

The transition of HRM towards sustainability is indicative of a wider societal movement towards conscientious corporate conduct. HRM has evolved from its administrative beginnings to its current position as a strategic partner in organizational sustainability. It has done this by expanding and adapting its functions to meet the needs of stakeholders, evolving legal requirements, and shifting norms. HRM will remain essential to promoting sustainable business practices and inclusive, resilient, and accountable cultures in firms as demand to address environmental and social issues mounts.

1.1.2 Shift from Traditional HR Practices to Environmentally Conscious Approaches

A rising understanding of the connection between corporate operations and environmental sustainability is shown in the transition away from traditional HR practices and toward ecologically friendly alternatives. Organizations must make this shift in order to reduce their environmental impact, maintain corporate social responsibility, and adjust to shifting social norms. Let's examine how this change plays out in different HR roles.

1. **Recruitment & Talent Acquisition:** Conventional HR procedures frequently overlook environmental values in favour of concentrating just on skill sets and expertise. However, candidates that show a commitment to and awareness of the environment are given preference by eco-conscious organizations. Job advertisements that highlight sustainability initiatives may draw applicants who share the company's values. In addition, asking environmental interview questions evaluates candidates' perspectives on sustainability and guarantees a harmonious cultural fit.

2. **Employee Training and Development:** Consciousness about the environment demands constant learning and development. By incorporating sustainability courses into employee on-boarding programs, HR departments may promote environmental awareness from the outset. Additionally, providing training in fields like green technology, waste management, and renewable energy gives staff members the tools they need to make a significant impact on the company's environmental objectives.

3. **Performance Evaluation and Recognition:** Environmental sustainability should be included in performance indicators. Assessing workers according to how they contribute to sustainability objectives promotes proactive involvement in environmental projects. Acknowledging and incentivizing eco-friendly conduct strengthens a sustainability culture and encourages staff members to incorporate eco-friendly practices into regular work duties.

4. **Workplace Policies and Procedures:** Green workplace regulations lessen their negative effects on the environment. This could entail taking steps to minimize paper use through digital documentation, implement recycling programs, promote telecommuting as a way to lower carbon emissions from commuting, and embrace energy-efficient practices. HR is essential in spreading awareness of and implementing these rules, guaranteeing that everyone in the company follows them.

5. **Employee Engagement and Communication:** Open communication encourages staff support and involvement in environmental projects. Through forums like town hall meetings, newsletters, and intranet platforms, HR may promote candid criticism and recommendations for enhancing sustainability processes. A sense of shared responsibility is fostered when employees are empowered to take ownership of environmental projects through participation in decision-making processes.

6. **Compensation and Benefits:** Organizational values are reinforced when benefits and compensation are in line with sustainability performance. Employees are encouraged to prioritize sustainability by offering incentives like bonuses linked to meeting environmental targets, health programs that emphasize outdoor activities, or subsidies for eco-friendly transportation. Furthermore, the organization's dedication to environmental stewardship is demonstrated by the inclusion of sustainability criteria in performance-based bonuses.

7. **Supplier and Vendor Relations:** Examining vendors and suppliers for their sustainable business practices is part of extending environmental knowledge outside of internal operations. HR and procurement teams can work together to evaluate suppliers according

to environmental standards like waste management, energy efficiency, and ethical sourcing. Forming alliances with environmentally aware suppliers promotes sustainable business practices and increases the supply chain resilience of the company.

8. **Community Engagement and Social Responsibility:** Environmental stewardship involves the entire community in addition to the workplace. HR can take the lead in organizing community outreach events that highlight sustainable development, conservation, and environmental education. Organizations can show their commitment to environmental stewardship while building goodwill and a positive brand perception by actively participating in community partnerships and activities.

9. **Continuous Improvement and Adaptation:** Organizations can stay at the forefront of sustainable HR practices and drive long-term environmental impact by fostering a culture of continuous learning and innovation. HR departments should regularly assess the effectiveness of eco-initiatives and solicit feedback from stakeholders and employees to identify areas for improvement. Adopting environmentally conscious HR practices requires ongoing evaluation and adaptation.

In conclusion, the transition from conventional human resource techniques to ecologically conscious methods signify a revolutionary path towards sustainable corporate operations. Businesses may maintain their environmental stewardship commitment while promoting a sustainable culture that benefits workers, communities, and the environment at large by incorporating environmental issues into every aspect of HR management.

1.1.3 Emergence of Green HRM as a Strategic Imperative for Organizations

The rise of Green HRM (Human Resource Management) as a strategic requirement for companies can be attributed to the increasing awareness of the relationship between environmental sustainability and business operations. With environmental issues at the forefront of public policy, companies are realizing that incorporating green practices into HRM strategies is essential to long-term success, fostering sustainable development, and improving organizational reputation.

Green HRM is primarily about coordinating HR procedures with environmental sustainability objectives. Recruiting, training, performance management, and employee engagement tactics that place an emphasis on environmental responsibility and awareness fall under this category. Organizations may attract applicants that share their commitment to sustainability and are environmentally conscientious by implementing green criteria into their recruiting processes. Furthermore, offering environmental training and development programs can enable staff members to support sustainable business practices.

The significance of employee engagement and participation in sustainability activities is emphasized by green HRM. Green projects within firms are frequently spearheaded by employees, and by cultivating a culture of environmental responsibility, organizations may use their creativity and innovation to achieve sustainable solutions. Initiatives like green teams, staff volunteer programs for environmental causes, and reward systems for eco-friendly behaviour are examples of this.

In order to implement green HRM, performance management systems must be updated to include environmental performance metrics. Through the establishment of environmental goals and their integration into employees' performance objectives, enterprises can guarantee the efficient implementation of sustainability objectives across the workforce. This holds workers accountable for their environmental impact and motivates them to contribute to environmental sustainability.

Beyond internal procedures, supply chain management and external stakeholders are included in green HRM. Companies are being held more and more responsible for the environmental policies of their partners and suppliers. In order to achieve overall sustainability goals, it is crucial to include green factors into supplier selection procedures and form collaborations with environmentally conscious vendors.

Adopting Green HRM practices can provide firms with several competitive advantages from a strategic standpoint. First of all, it improves the reputation and brand image of the company, which increases stakeholder trust and consumer loyalty. Customers are favouring businesses that show a commitment to sustainability more and more in today's environmentally concerned market. Companies can set themselves apart from rivals and draw in eco-aware clients by putting Green HRM principles into practice.

Secondly, Green HRM can promote cost reductions and operational effectiveness. Organizations can cut operational expenses and increase their bottom line by lowering energy use, waste production, and resource usage. Furthermore, the adoption of sustainable practices can reduce the risks related to environmental rules and compliance, protecting the organization's finances in the process.

Green HRM also helps with staff retention and happiness. Studies have indicated that when workers believe their company is dedicated to environmental sustainability, they become more engaged and motivated. Green HRM methods can boost employee loyalty and morale by fostering a sense of purpose and shared values. This lowers turnover rates and the related expenses of hiring new staff.

In conclusion, the increased understanding of the significance of environmental sustainability in business operations is reflected in the rise of Green HRM as a strategic priority for organizations. Organizations can gain a number of advantages by incorporating green practices into HRM strategy, such as improved employee engagement, operational efficiency, and reputation. Future organizational success will surely depend more and more on Green HRM as environmental issues continue to influence the corporate landscape.

1.2 Importance of Sustainability in HR Practices

In today's business environment, sustainability in human resources (HR) operations has become increasingly important. It includes a range of tactics designed to guarantee that businesses run in an economically viable, environmentally responsible, and socially responsible manner. The process of incorporating sustainability into HR procedures entails matching the workforce management strategy of the company with its social, commercial, and environmental objectives.

❖ **Here's a comprehensive look at why sustainability is crucial in HR practices:**

1. Talent Attraction and Retention: In a world where Gen Z and millennials make up the majority of workers, sustainability plays a big role in drawing and keeping top talent. These generations place a high value on employment with companies that show a dedication to social and environmental responsibility. HR procedures that prioritize sustainability, including introducing diversity and inclusion programs or providing remote work choices to lessen carbon footprint, can improve business branding and draw in socially conscious workers.

2. Employee Engagement and Motivation: Motivation and engagement among employees are enhanced by sustainable HR strategies. Employees are more likely to be dedicated to their work and driven to contribute to the success of the firm when they believe that their organization is positively impacting society and the environment. A sense of purpose and belonging among employees can be fostered by HR initiatives including volunteer programs, green teams, and sustainability training programs.

3. Cost Reduction and Efficiency: Putting into practice sustainable HR practices can save costs and boost productivity. Adopting standards for remote work, for instance, can lower overhead expenses related to *utilities* and office space. Investing in energy-efficient practices and *technologies* can also reduce environmental impact and *utility* expenditures. Organizations can increase their bottom *line* and lessen their environmental impact at the same time by *optim*izing resource utilization and cutting waste.

4. Risk Management and Compliance: HR practices that are sustainable aid organizations in *risk* mitigation and regulatory compliance. This entails following *labour* regulations, encouraging health and safety at work, and *tack*ling challenges related to diversity and inclusion. Through pro*active* management of these facets, firms can protect their long-term *s*tability and sustainability by averting legal conflicts, harm to their reputation, and regulatory penalties.

5. Enhanced Corporate Social Responsibility (CSR): In order to further an organization's CSR goals, HR is essential. HR departments can show their organization's dedication to moral business conduct and corporate citizenship by incorporating sustainability into their hiring, training, performance management, and employee well-being initiatives. This can therefore have a good social impact, strengthen stakeholder trust, and improve the company's reputation.

6. Long-Term Strategic Planning: Sustainable HR practices support long-term strategic planning by encouraging an agile and forward-thinking culture. Future workforce trends, such the increase in remote work or the requirement for up skilling in sustainable technology, can be predicted by HR professionals, who can then create proactive strategies to deal with these issues. Companies may future-proof their workforce and maintain competitiveness in quickly changing markets by coordinating HR policies with the organization's long-term sustainability goals.

7. Stakeholder Relations and Brand Equity: HR practices that incorporate sustainability initiatives have the potential to enhance connections with a range of stakeholders, including as employees, customers, investors, and communities. Building confidence and credibility with stakeholders is facilitated by transparent reporting on sustainability metrics, including as diversity measurements, employee satisfaction scores, and carbon emissions reductions. As a result, all parties involved may benefit from increased investment, strengthened brand equity, and shared value.

8. Building Resilience: Sustainable HR practices provide a culture of support and ethics in the workplace, which strengthens organizational resilience. This can make it easier for organizations to deal with difficulties like environmental catastrophes, economic downturns, and other issues. Organizations that possess resilience are more able to adjust to shifts in the marketplace, laws and regulations, and public expectations. A strong and flexible workforce is created through sustainable practices such comprehensive employee well-being programs, diverse and inclusive efforts, and flexible work schedules. These procedures make certain that employees are ready to deal with unforeseen circumstances and carry on advancing the company.

9. Aligning with Sustainable Development Goals (SDGs): Companies can align their operations with the Sustainable Development Goals (SDGs) of the UN by incorporating sustainability into HR practices. This alignment benefits the company's credibility and reputation internationally while also supporting international initiatives to address pressing challenges like poverty, inequality, and climate change.

10. Reducing Environmental Impact: Reducing the company's overall environmental impact can be achieved through sustainable HR practices. Reduced paper use, recycling programs, and energy conservation in the workplace are a few examples of initiatives that help reduce carbon footprints and foster environmental stewardship. This helps the environment and puts the business in line with international sustainability objectives.

11. Adapting to Changing Consumer Preferences: Companies that include sustainable practices into their HR policies are better positioned to adapt to the shifting attitudes of consumers toward sustainability. Employees may assist lead projects that fulfil these changing demands because consumers are more likely to support businesses that share their beliefs.

12. Driving Market Differentiation: In the marketplace, sustainability can be a crucial point of differentiation. Companies that put sustainability first can set themselves apart from rivals by providing distinctive value propositions that appeal to customers who care about the environment and the community. Gaining a competitive edge, more market share, and client loyalty are all possible outcomes of this distinction.

13. Strengthening Community Relations: Sustainable HR procedures can improve a company's reputation in the society by showcasing its social responsibilities. The company's reputation can be improved and relationships with the local community can be strengthened by taking part in environmental conservation programs, supporting local companies, and getting involved in community-based initiatives. Additionally, this may result in favourable press coverage and a rise in public support.

14. Encouraging Professional Development: Organizations that prioritize sustainability frequently make investments in chances for ongoing education and training in the field. Employees' skills and knowledge are improved as a result, and they are given more authority to support the sustainability objectives of the organization. A culture of innovation and constant improvement can be promoted by offering training on sustainable practices and by rewarding involvement in sustainability initiatives.

15. Boosting Morale and Job Satisfaction: Worker morale and job satisfaction can be greatly increased by implementing sustainable HR strategies. Employees are more likely to be satisfied with their jobs when they believe that their work advances important causes and that their employer values their growth and development. A more positive workplace culture, more productivity, and improved teamwork can all result from this high morale.

16. Long-term Financial Performance: Long-term financial performance is intimately associated with sustainable HR policies. There can be large cost savings through enhanced worker productivity, decreased waste, and efficient resource utilization. Businesses with a solid track record of sustainability are frequently viewed as lower-risk investments, which can increase investor interest in them. Furthermore, innovative goods, services, and business models can result from sustainable practices, creating new revenue streams and market prospects. For example, a sustainability-focused approach might influence the creation of ecologically friendly products that appeal to customers that care about the environment.

17. Promoting Organizational Reputation: A company's dedication to sustainability has a big impact on its reputation in today's market. Companies that are well-known for their sustainability efforts typically have a higher reputation, which can boost client loyalty and strengthen their brand. Due to its favourable reputation in the labour market, the company is favoured by prospective employees. Employees, investors, partners, and consumers who are becoming more aware of how their decisions affect society and the environment are drawn to businesses that are seen as ethical and responsible.

In summary, sustainability is now more than just a catchphrase; it is a key component of HR strategies that has an immediate influence on the resilience and success of organizations. HR departments may promote innovation, accelerate change, and add value for the company and society at large by incorporating sustainability into talent management, employee engagement, recruitment, and CSR efforts. Incorporating sustainability into HR processes is not just a strategic need for companies looking to remain competitive and viable in the long run, but it is also a moral obligation.

1.2.1 Understanding the Significance of Sustainability in the Context of HR Function

Sustainability has emerged as a key priority for businesses all around the world in recent years. Sustainability has expanded to include social and economic issues as well as environmental ones, influencing business operations and strategy. According to this concept, human resources (HR) have a much different role now that they are integral to pushing sustainable practices and cultivating a sustainable culture within firms. The significance and ramifications of the relationship between sustainability and HR functions are examined in this essay.

Understanding Sustainability in HR

Understanding sustainability as a concept is crucial before exploring HR's involvement in sustainability. Meeting current requirements without sacrificing the capacity of future generations to meet their own needs is referred to as sustainability. It entails striking a balance between social justice, environmental integrity, and economic growth. Sustainability in the context of an organization is incorporating these ideas into practices, decision-making procedures, and behaviour.

Integrating sustainability into firms requires HR functions. HR has historically been in charge of things like hiring, training, pay, and employee relations. But as businesses come to understand the value of sustainability, HR's responsibility has grown to include programs that support moral behaviour, inclusiveness, diversity, and the health and welfare of workers as well as environmental stewardship.

Recruitment and Talent Management

HR plays a major role in sustainability through personnel management and recruitment. Employers that are committed to sustainability and share their values are sought after by sustainable businesses. Integrating sustainability criteria into job descriptions, screening procedures, and interviewing approaches is the responsibility of HR experts. They seek out applicants that exhibit social responsibility, environmental awareness, and ethical behaviour in order to cultivate a workforce that is aligned with the organization's sustainability objectives.

Additionally, HR is essential to the retention and development of people. Programs for staff training and development that improve sustainability-related competencies such as environmental management, social impact assessment, and ethical leadership are funded by sustainable businesses. HR supports workers in making significant contributions to sustainability efforts and developing their careers within the company by fostering a culture of ongoing learning and development.

Performance Management and Incentives
Another critical HR job is integrating sustainability into performance management systems. Performance reviews ought to evaluate workers' contributions to sustainability goals in addition to their job-related competencies. In order to achieve sustainability goals like lowering carbon emissions, fostering diversity, or assisting with community involvement projects, HR creates key performance indicators, or KPIs. Human resources (HR) make sure that workers are held responsible for their effects on the company's triple bottom line profit, people, and planet by coordinating performance indicators with sustainability targets.

HR also creates incentive programs that recognize and honour employees for long-term performance and behaviour. Programs for acknowledgment, bonuses, or other types of compensation linked to sustainability performance may fall under this category. Through providing incentives for sustainability, HR encourages staff members to take an active role in projects that further the company's social and environmental goals, resulting in the development of an innovative and engaged culture.

Employee Engagement and Well-being
Sustainability is largely dependent on the wellbeing and engagement of employees. In order to create a work climate where employees feel appreciated, encouraged, and empowered to participate in sustainability initiatives, HR is essential. This includes programs like wellness centres, flexible work schedules, and chances for staff members to participate in sustainability-related decision-making.

HR enables coordination and communication across various departments and levels of the hierarchy to guarantee that sustainability objectives are incorporated into every facet of the company's activities. HR creates trust and alignment around sustainability goals by encouraging open communication, inclusion, and openness. This encourages group action and shared accountability.

Organizational Culture and Leadership Development
Sustainable organizations are built on a culture that upholds moral principles like accountability, creativity, and integrity. Through encouraging diversity and inclusion, advancing ethical leadership, and ingraining sustainability concepts into the organization's core values, HR plays a critical role in forming and sustaining corporate culture.

HR creates leadership development initiatives that foster the knowledge and abilities needed to guide in a dynamic, multifaceted global setting. This entails encouraging moral decision-making, developing a feeling of purpose and social responsibility, and providing leaders with the resources they need to successfully handle sustainability-related issues.

Thus, sustainability is more than just a catchphrase; it is a basic requirement for businesses hoping to succeed in the long run and remain resilient in a world that is changing quickly. Because they develop talent, Mold organizational culture, and coordinate employee behaviour with sustainability objectives, HR services are critical catalysts for sustainability. HR plays a key role in promoting organizational sustainability objectives by incorporating sustainability into people management, performance management, employee engagement, recruitment, and leadership development activities. HR will continue to be in the lead as businesses adopt sustainability as a strategic priority, supporting programs that benefit the company, its workers, and society at large.

1.2.2 Link Between Sustainable HR Practices and Organizational Performance
Organizational performance and sustainable human resource (HR) practices are closely related, with sustainable HR practices being essential to improving the effectiveness, efficiency, and long-term success of

organizations. This connection is based on the knowledge that workers are an organization's most important asset, and that fostering their well-being through sustainable HR practices affects the business's success as a whole.

The idea of employee engagement and happiness is the foundation of successful HR strategies. Employee engagement increases productivity and performance because it increases when workers feel appreciated, supported, and respected. The establishment of a pleasant work environment where employees are motivated to grow professionally, seek out possibilities for advancement, and preserve a healthy work-life balance is a top priority for sustainable HR strategies. Employee commitment and loyalty are thus increased, which lowers turnover rates and the related expenses of hiring and training new staff.

Actions to advance inclusion, equity, and diversity in the workforce are included in sustainable HR practices. Establishing a workplace that is both diverse and inclusive allows firms to capitalize on the distinct views and skills of their workforce, resulting in increased capacity for creativity, innovation, and problem-solving. By doing this, the company not only becomes more adaptable to change but also has a better reputation as an employer of choice, which draws top people and gives it a competitive edge in the market.

Additionally, sustainable HR practices take into account an organization's influence on the larger community and environment in addition to its internal operations. Businesses that put a high priority on sustainability initiatives like cutting back on waste, lowering carbon emissions, and promoting ethical supplier chainsnot only help to conserve the environment, but also improve their standing and attract investors and customers who share that concern. In addition to increasing brand loyalty, this socially conscious positioning draws in partners and investors, bolstering the organization's long-term viability and financial performance.

A culture of trust, openness, and moral behaviour within the company is greatly enhanced by sustainable HR practices, in addition to these obvious advantages. Organizations may improve their reputation and reduce the risk of legal liability and reputational harm by emphasizing ethical decision-making, transparent communication, and equitable pay among its stakeholders. Additionally, this trust-based culture encourages cooperation and teamwork, which helps firms better address difficult problems and grasp opportunities.

The physical and mental health of employees is directly related to sustainable HR practices. Employers that put a high priority on employee wellness efforts, like wellness programs, flexible work schedules, and mental health support services, see improvements in employee retention and satisfaction as well as lower rates of presentee, absentee, and medical expenses. Employee engagement, productivity, and resilience are all increased in well-being, and this positively impacts the organization's overall performance and resilience.

Enhancing company performance in a variety of ways requires sustainable HR policies. Organizations can cultivate a culture of excellence, innovation, and resilience that propels long-term success and competitive advantage by placing a high priority on employee engagement, diversity, equity, and inclusion, environmental sustainability, ethical behaviour, and employee well-being. Consequently, for companies looking to prosper in a world growing more linked and complicated, investing in sustainable HR practices is both a moral and a strategic need.

1.2.3 Benefits of Integrating Environmental Considerations into HR Strategies

Organizations that want to promote sustainability and social responsibility must incorporate environmental factors into their HR policies. The benefits of this integration can go well beyond environmental stewardship and include long-term economic viability, employee engagement, and brand reputation.

Firstly, coordinating HR tactics with environmental objectives improves worker retention and engagement. More and more workers are looking for companies with a clear mission and values that coincide with their own. By exhibiting a dedication to sustainability, companies may draw in and keep talent that is enthusiastic about environmental issues. Involving staff members in environmentally conscious projects also makes them feel proud and fulfilled, which boosts their level of job satisfaction and productivity.

Secondly, including environmental factors into HR plans encourages efficiency and cost reduction. In addition to minimizing their negative effects on the environment, sustainable methods like waste reduction, energy saving, and eco-friendly sourcing also save operating costs. Establishing telecommuting policies, for example, lowers overhead expenses related to office space and utilities while also reducing carbon emissions from transportation. In a similar vein, implementing recycling initiatives and using renewable energy sources lower energy and garbage disposal costs, respectively. Organizations can save a lot of money over time by maximizing resource utilization and reducing waste production.

Thirdly, Brand reputation and attractiveness to stakeholders are improved when environmental sustainability is integrated into HR initiatives. Sustainability is becoming a top priority for customers, investors, and business partners when deciding which businesses to support or work with. Businesses may improve their brand image and set themselves apart from competitors by showcasing their commitment to environmental responsibility through HR initiatives like green procurement, carbon footprint reduction, and employee sustainability training. In addition to drawing clients and investors, this stellar reputation forges closer bonds with partners and suppliers who have similar values.

Furthermore, including environmental factors into HR policies encourages creativity and innovation within the company. Sustainability issues frequently call for creative solutions, which inspire staff members to think creatively and unconventionally while tackling problems. Organizations can encourage staff members to come up with ideas for environmentally friendly goods, procedures, and services by fostering a culture of environmental responsibility and awareness. These inventions boost corporate expansion and give companies a competitive edge in the market in addition to supporting environmental sustainability.

Incorporating environmental factors into HR initiatives also reduces the risk of regulatory and compliance violations. Organizations are under more and more pressure to abide by environmental laws and rules as governments over the world impose stronger environmental regulations and standards. Companies may assure compliance with current requirements and prepare for potential changes by proactively integrating environmental considerations into HR policies and procedures. By taking a proactive stance, the likelihood of non-compliance penalties, legal action, and harm to one's reputation resulting from environmental infractions is reduced.

Moreover, the integration of environmental sustainability into human resource strategies enhances stakeholder connections and cultivates collaborations with environmental associations and community organizations. Organizations honour environmental stewardship and social responsibility by taking part in environmental projects including habitat restoration, beach clean-ups, and tree planting. These cooperative initiatives improve the organization's standing and goodwill in the community in addition to helping the environment. Companies can cultivate trust and loyalty among stakeholders by establishing strong connections, both of which are necessary for sustained corporate success.

In conclusion, organizations can gain a lot from incorporating environmental factors into HR strategy, such as increased stakeholder connections, cost savings, improved employee engagement, improved brand reputation, and regulatory compliance. Businesses can build sustainable workplaces that promote a healthy world, business performance, and resilience in the face of environmental difficulties by coordinating HR practices with environmental goals.

1.3 Role of HR in Environmental Management

The contemporary business environment places a premium on sustainability and corporate responsibility, making the function of Human Resources (HR) in environmental management even more crucial. HR departments are integral to the establishment of policies, employee involvement, and training, as well as the driving and supporting of environmental activities within businesses. The many facets of HR's engagement in environmental management and its importance in developing an organizational culture of sustainability will be discussed in this essay.

The creation and execution of policies is one of HR's main responsibilities in environmental management. HR specialists work with other departments, such legal and operations, to create environmental policies that support the organization's sustainability goals and comply with legal requirements. These policies cover directives for energy saving, waste minimization, emissions control, and other environmental stewardship activities. HR makes sure that all staff members are properly informed about these rules and that they are included into the company's standard operating procedures.

Hiring and keeping people with the abilities and attitude required for efficient environmental management is a major responsibility of HR. This entails adding sustainability standards to job descriptions, vetting applicants based on their knowledge of and familiarity with the environment, and offering chances for training and development to raise staff members' environmental capabilities. HR plays a crucial role in the long-term success of the company's environmental activities by cultivating a workforce that is devoted to and informed about environmental sustainability.

Another important area where HR leads environmental management initiatives is employee engagement. HR specialists try to give workers at all organizational levels a sense of ownership and accountability for environmental sustainability. To encourage staff to adopt environmentally friendly behaviours in the workplace and in their personal life, this may entail planning awareness campaigns, green teams, and other efforts. Additionally, HR provides feedback systems so that workers may share ideas and proposals for enhancing environmental performance and promoting a continuous improvement culture.

HR works with external stakeholders, including suppliers, consumers, and community organizations, in addition to internal initiatives, to further the organization's environmental goals. Engaging customers in sustainability activities, collaborating with suppliers to find ecologically friendly materials and products, and taking part in conservation and community clean-up projects are a few examples of how to achieve this. HR helps to the organization's overall sustainability strategy and strengthens its reputation as a conscientious corporate citizen by cultivating strong partnerships with external stakeholders.

Measurement and reporting of performance are another essential component of HR's role in environmental management. HR establishes key performance indicators (KPIs) for environmental performance and monitors the department's progress toward sustainability targets in close collaboration with other departments. Data collection and analysis on energy use, waste production, greenhouse gas emissions, and other pertinent variables may be required for this. In addition, HR creates reports and disseminates data on environmental performance to both internal and external stakeholders, including as the general public, investors, senior management, and regulatory bodies. Accountability is made possible by transparent reporting, which also shows the organization's dedication to environmental stewardship.

HR is essential to the organization's efforts to promote a sustainable culture. This entails encouraging attitudes and actions that place a high priority on resource efficiency and environmental preservation. HR creates workshops, training courses, and other learning materials to educate staff members about environmental challenges and encourage them to take action. Additionally, HR incorporates sustainability into the corporate culture and basic values of the company, highlighting the significance of environmental stewardship in daily operations and decision-making processes.

Through driving policy development, attracting and keeping environmentally conscious talent, involving staff members and external stakeholders, tracking and disclosing environmental performance, and encouraging a sustainable culture within companies, human resources play a critical role in environmental management. Organizations may improve their environmental performance, reduce risks, and provide long-term value for stakeholders by incorporating environmental considerations into all facets of HR functions. HR will become more and more important in influencing sustainable business practices and promoting favourable environmental results as companies come under greater pressure to address environmental issues.

1.3.1 Responsibilities of HR Professionals in Driving Sustainability Initiatives within Organizations

The task of spearheading sustainability efforts in firms is complex and calls for the participation of multiple departments and individuals, including HR specialists. In order to integrate sustainability into the business culture, policies, and practices, HR is essential. This article provides a thorough analysis of the roles that HR specialists play in advancing sustainability initiatives inside businesses.

1. Policy Development and Implementation: It is the duty of HR specialists to create and carry out policies that support sustainability. This covers guidelines for resource management, diversity and inclusion, employee welfare, and moral business conduct in addition to environmental preservation. HR makes ensuring that all employees are properly informed about these rules and that they are in line with the organization's sustainability goals.

2. Training and Education: In order to empower staff members to take action and increase understanding of sustainability challenges, HR offers training and educational programs. Workshops, seminars, and online courses on subjects including waste management, ethical sourcing, energy efficiency, and sustainable procurement may fall under this category. HR also offers advice on how staff members can integrate sustainability into their regular work schedules.

3. Recruitment and Talent Management: HR incorporates sustainability standards into personnel management and hiring procedures. Finding applicants who share the organization's ideals and show a dedication to sustainability is part of this. In addition, HR creates plans to hold onto top people by encouraging a sustainable culture and providing chances for professional growth.

4. Performance Management and Measurement: HR sets up measuring tools and performance indicators to monitor the organization's advancement toward sustainability objectives. This entails keeping an eye on important metrics including employee engagement, trash production, energy usage, and carbon footprint. HR works with other departments to analyse data, pinpoint areas that need improvement, and create plans of action to deal with sustainability issues.

5. Employee Engagement and Communication: Engaging employees in sustainability efforts and decision-making processes is one way that HR promotes employee engagement. This could entail setting up volunteer programs, creating green teams, and honouring staff members for their efforts to sustainability. Additionally, HR routinely updates staff members on the organization's sustainability objectives, developments, and accomplishments via a variety of platforms, including intranet portals, newsletters, and town hall meetings.

6. Supplier and Partner Engagement: HR works in tandem with the supply chain management and procurement teams to include business partners and suppliers in sustainability initiatives. This could entail evaluating suppliers, establishing sustainable standards for contracts, and offering assistance and direction to suppliers to help them enhance their sustainability performance. Additionally, HR seeks to establish strategic alliances with businesses that have comparable sustainability objectives and principles.

7. Compliance and Reporting: HR makes that the company abides by all applicable laws, rules, and sustainability-related industry standards. This includes keeping track of documents, carrying out audits, and creating reports for internal and external stakeholders regarding sustainability performance. In order to handle any potential risks or problems relating to sustainability, HR also collaborates closely with the legal and compliance departments.

8. Innovation and Continuous Improvement: By promoting a culture of learning, experimentation, and information sharing, HR promotes creativity and ongoing progress in sustainable practices. This could entail creating innovation hubs, putting in place staff suggestion processes, and identifying and rewarding creative concepts and endeavours that advance sustainable objectives.

Finally, by creating and implementing policies, offering instruction and training, incorporating sustainability into hiring and talent management procedures, assessing and tracking performance, involving stakeholders and employees, guaranteeing compliance and reporting, and encouraging creativity and continuous development, HR professionals play a critical role in advancing sustainability initiatives within businesses. HR contributes to building a sustainable future for the company, its workers, and the larger community by carrying out these duties.

1.3.2 Collaborating with Other Departments to Promote Eco-friendly Practices

Promoting environmentally friendly practices within a business through departmental collaboration is a complex endeavour that calls for strategic planning, clear communication, and a dedication to sustainability. Businesses can improve their environmental footprint and also enjoy many advantages like cost savings, enhanced brand recognition, and increased employee satisfaction by encouraging collaboration throughout departments.

While integrating sustainability into HR procedures is crucial, departmental cooperation is needed to create a truly environmentally responsible company. Collaboratively, many divisions can put into practice comprehensive and well-thought-out initiatives that integrate sustainability into the operations and culture of the business.

❖ **Here's how HR can collaborate with other departments to promote sustainability:**

1. Facilities Management
Green Office Initiatives: Facilities management and HR can work together to establish and maintain sustainable workplaces. This entails employing sustainable materials for office furniture, installing energy-efficient lighting, and working toward LEED certification for green buildings.

Waste Reduction Programs: Together, the two departments may implement recycling initiatives, cut back on paper use, and promote digital recordkeeping. They can also encourage the usage of reusable tools and materials for the workplace.

2. Operations
Sustainable Supply Chain: HR and operations can work together to make sure the company's supply chain is sustainable. This entails minimizing waste in the production process, maximizing logistics to lower transportation emissions, and procuring from sustainable sources.

Lean Manufacturing: By offering training courses on lean manufacturing methods that emphasize cutting waste and boosting productivity, HR may assist operations.

3. IT Department

Energy-efficient Technology: By working together, HR and IT can install energy-efficient PCs, servers, and other digital infrastructure, greatly lowering the carbon footprint of the business.

Digital Transformation: Encouragement of paperless offices via digital documentation and cloud services can help cut down on waste and dependency on physical documents. IT can help with the upkeep and application of these technologies.

4. Marketing and Communications

Sustainability Branding: Marketing, communications, and HR can collaborate to create campaigns that showcase the business's sustainable initiatives. By engaging eco-aware customers and employees, these programs can strengthen the company's reputation.

Employee Engagement: One way to encourage employees to actively participate in green practices is through using internal communication channels to create knowledge about sustainability projects.

5. Finance

Green Investments: In order to investigate and implement green investment alternatives, such as sustainability funds or renewable energy projects, HR can collaborate with finance. The company's financial standing and environmental effect may both be enhanced by these expenditures.

Sustainable Budgeting: Working together to determine how much money should be set aside for sustainability projects guarantees that funds will be available for things like employee training, energy-efficient renovations, and sustainability reporting.

6. Procurement

Sustainable Purchasing: HR and procurement can collaborate to create rules that give buying sustainable and eco-friendly goods top priority. This covers furniture, office supplies, and even services.

Vendor Partnerships: Together, the two departments can form alliances with suppliers who share the company's commitment to sustainability, making sure that the company's environmental principles are reflected throughout the supply chain.

7. Product Development

Eco-friendly Products: HR may assist teams working on products by finding candidates with experience in manufacturing and sustainable design. Additionally, they might advocate for training initiatives that instruct current employees on sustainable methods of product development.

Lifecycle Assessments: Work together to carry out assessments of the product lifecycle in order to comprehend and minimize the environmental impact of products from conception to disposal.

8. Legal and Compliance

Regulatory Compliance: To make sure that all sustainability projects abide by national and international laws, HR can collaborate with the legal and compliance departments. This guarantees that the business's procedures are up to par and helps prevent legal problems.

Policy Development: All departments are held accountable and in alignment when they collaborate to establish and execute policies that support sustainability goals across the entire organization.

9. Research and Development (R&D)

Innovative Solutions: HR may help R&D and other departments' works together to find creative solutions that have a less environmental impact. This could involve innovative methods, supplies, or technological advancements that improve sustainability.

Funding and Resources: When HR and R&D collaborate, funding and resources can be allocated for projects and research with a sustainability focus.

10. Sales and Customer Service

Eco-friendly Sales Practices: HR and sales can collaborate to teach and train employees in environmentally friendly sales techniques and language that emphasizes the advantages of goods and services for sustainability.

Customer Education: Work with customer service to increase the overall impact of the company's sustainability initiatives by teaching customers how to utilize items sustainably.

To sum up, working together with other departments to support environmentally friendly practices guarantees a comprehensive approach to sustainability. Working together, the departments can develop a cohesive plan that incorporates sustainability into every facet of the business. Each department contributes special strengths and views to the table. Together with assisting in the accomplishment of environmental goals, this partnership promotes innovation, efficiency, and corporate responsibility.

1.3.3 Influence of HR on Forecasting a Culture of Environmental Stewardship among Employee

All divisions within a corporation must work together to create a culture of environmental stewardship, including human resources (HR). HR has a major impact on encouraging environmental stewardship among employees and plays a crucial role in forming business culture. This essay will look at the ways that HR procedures might help an organization develop an environmentally conscious culture.

HR may, first and foremost, incorporate environmental sustainability into the mission, vision, and values statements of the organization. The tone for the entire workforce is set by HR, who states the organization's commitment to environmental stewardship clearly. By bringing employees' personal beliefs into line with the organization's, this messaging fosters a sense of purpose and camaraderie as they strive toward environmental goals.

Policies and procedures that support environmental sustainability can be created and implemented by HR. This covers programs like energy saving, trash minimization, and environmentally friendly purchasing techniques. HR can set rules for environmentally responsible behaviour in the workplace, like supporting paperless transactions, recycling, and using alternate modes of transportation. HR makes sure that environmental responsibility is integrated into the organization's daily operations by formalizing these policies.

When it comes to teaching and training staff members on environmental challenges and best practices, human resources are essential. To promote environmental stewardship and offer helpful advice for minimizing environmental effect, this may entail planning training sessions, seminars, and workshops. HR enables people to take charge of their environmental impact and make wise decisions in both their personal and professional life by funding employee education.

HR can use reward and recognition schemes to encourage eco-friendly conduct. Employees that show a commitment to sustainability are recognized and rewarded by HR, which promotes a culture that values and celebrates environmental stewardship and reinforces desired behaviours. This can include rewards for taking part in environmental efforts or reaching sustainability targets, such performance bonuses, public recognition, or even additional vacation days.

Environmental factors can be incorporated into the recruiting and recruitment process by HR. HR makes certain that new hires are likely to make a positive contribution to the environmental stewardship culture by looking for individuals who share the organization's values and commitment to sustainability. This may entail asking interviewee questions concerning sustainability and conducting an environmental awareness assessment to determine how well they connect with the company's ideals.

By creating green teams or committees, HR may support employee involvement and engagement in environmental efforts. These groups bring together staff members from various departments within the company to exchange ideas, carry out projects, and track advancement toward sustainability objectives. Through the provision of a forum for cooperation and grassroots advocacy, HR enables staff members to initiate constructive transformations and bolster an environment-conscious culture from the ground up.

HR may use technology to encourage sustainable habits and assist environmental projects. To cut down on paper use and the carbon emissions that come with commuting, this can involve putting digital solutions for document management, communication, and collaboration into place. HR can also make investments in infrastructure and energy-efficient technologies to reduce the company's environmental impact and show that it is committed to sustainability. As a result, HR is essential to developing an organizational culture of environmental stewardship. HR may enable staff members to make environmentally responsible decisions and contribute to a more sustainable future by incorporating sustainability into the organization's principles, policies, and practices. HR may promote positive change and establish a climate in the workplace where environmental stewardship is not only a goal but a shared value that is accepted by all through engagement, incentives, education, and technology.

Chapter – 2

Sustainable HR Practices

In order to promote a positive and mutually beneficial relationship between an organization and its workforce, sustainable HR policies take into account the wider societal and environmental implications of the firm's operations. These impacts can take many different forms. With the ultimate goal of creating workplaces that are not only profitable and productive but also equitable, inclusive, and environmentally sustainable over the long run, these diverse approaches are supported by the values of social responsibility, environmental stewardship, and ethical conduct.

Promoting diversity and inclusion in the workforce is essential to sustainable HR practices because it guarantees that everyone has equal access to opportunities for employment, progression, and growth, regardless of background, identity, or ability. This means actively seeking out and valuing a range of viewpoints, experiences, and abilities as well as fostering an atmosphere where each worker feels appreciated, respected, and empowered to provide their own talents and perspectives to the company.

Sustainable HR practices not only promote diversity and inclusion but also give employees' health and work-life balance first priority. This is because a happy and healthy workforce is crucial for both individual growth and organizational performance. This entails putting in place laws and initiatives that promote mental and physical well-being, promote work-life balance, and give staff members the tools and assistance they need to successfully balance their personal and professional obligations.

Furthermore, as businesses strive to reduce their environmental impact and advance environmental sustainability across their whole operations, sustainable HR practices go beyond the workplace to include broader environmental factors. This could entail taking steps like cutting back on waste and energy use, finding eco-friendly products and materials, and setting up sustainable employee mobility and commuting options.

Additionally, sustainable HR practices include a dedication to funding workers' continuous learning and development, realizing that these endeavours are necessary for both individual fulfilment and organizational resilience in a world that is changing quickly. This could entail creating an environment that values criticism, mentoring, and ongoing development in addition to offering chances for professional growth, education, and training.

Organizations can promote good social change and environmental stewardship on a larger scale in addition to creating more inclusive, supportive, and environmentally sustainable workplaces by incorporating these diverse factors into their HR policies and practices. In the end, sustainable HR practices are about creating value and fostering long-term success for businesses in a world where people are becoming more interconnected and dependent on one another, in addition to doing what is morally right for workers and the environment.

❖ **Sustainable HR practices aim to balance the needs of employees, the organization, and the environment. Here are a few examples**:

1. **Flexible Work Arrangements:** Reducing emissions from commuting and promoting work-life balance are achieved by providing telecommuting, flexible hours, or reduced workweeks.

2. **Green Initiatives:** A dedication to sustainability can be shown in the implementation of recycling programs, the reduction of paper use, and the promotion of energy-efficient practices in the workplace.

3. **Employee Well-being Programs:** Offering exercise programs, mental health services, and wellness initiatives enhances worker productivity and well-being while lowering absenteeism.

4. **Diversity and Inclusion:** In addition to drawing in top talent, embracing diversity and promoting an inclusive workplace atmosphere also boosts innovation and creativity.

5. **Ethical Sourcing:** Making sure suppliers follow sustainable practices lowers the company's carbon footprint and is consistent with corporate ideals.
6. **Community Engagement:** Encouragement of staff members to volunteer or take part in community service initiatives creates a feeling of direction and community while having a beneficial effect outside of the office.
7. **Remote Work Policies:** Long-term use of remote work increases employee flexibility while lowering the carbon impact of office space and transportation.
8. **Green Benefits Packages:** Encouraging sustainable commuting and lifestyle choices can be achieved by providing incentives like discounts on eco-friendly products, bike-to-work programs, or public transportation subsidies.
9. **Leadership Development for Sustainability:** Encouraging managers and executives to adopt sustainable leadership practices through training and tools can help integrate sustainability concepts into decision-making processes across the entire firm.
10. **Training and Development:** In addition to increasing worker satisfaction, investing in training and development initiatives for staff members keeps the company competitive in a world that is changing quickly.
11. **Performance Evaluation Criteria:** A culture of accountability is promoted and employees are encouraged to consider sustainability in their daily work by integrating sustainability goals and KPIs into performance evaluations.
12. **Carbon Offsetting Programs:** An organization's dedication to environmental stewardship is demonstrated by the implementation of steps to offset its carbon footprint, such as tree-planting programs or investments in renewable energy projects.
13. **Supplier Sustainability Assessments:** Aligning suppliers' environmental and social practices with the organization's sustainability goals and values is ensured by conducting assessments.

14. Employee Resource Groups: By creating sustainability-focused employee resource groups, staff members may work together, exchange ideas, and support organizational sustainability objectives.

2.1 Implementing Sustainable HR Strategies

Putting sustainable HR strategies into practice requires a proactive, all-encompassing strategy that goes beyond simply following the law. It entails the purposeful blending of procedures and guidelines that take into account long-term effects on workers and the business as a whole in addition to the workforce's current demands. This complex undertaking involves coordinating HR programs with broad sustainability objectives, which include social responsibility, environmental conservation, and economic feasibility.

The development of a workplace culture that places a high priority on diversity, equity, and inclusion (DEI) is one of the essential elements of sustainable HR strategy. Employers who support DEI not only help their staff members feel like they belong, but they also use the variety of viewpoints and experiences they have on staff to stimulate innovation and creativity. HR departments may use programs like diverse hiring procedures, training on unconscious bias, and employee resource groups which support and advocate for underrepresented groups to accomplish this.

Furthermore, holistic development and employee well-being are prioritized in sustainable HR strategies. This entails offering competitive pay and benefits in addition to fostering an environment at work that supports mental health resources, work-life balance, and chances for both professional and personal development. Employees that have more flexible work arrangements, like remote work choices and flexible scheduling, are more productive and have higher job satisfaction because they are better able to balance their personal and professional obligations.

A crucial component of long-term HR strategy is leadership development. Driving organizational change and developing a sustainable culture require effective leadership. HR departments can fund leadership development initiatives that give managers the abilities and know-how required to guide diverse teams, spur creativity, and resolve difficult moral conundrums. Organizations can initiate a positive ripple effect that spreads throughout the entire organization by giving executives the authority to support sustainability projects within their teams.

Sustainable human resource methods also heavily depend on corporate governance and ethical behaviour. Businesses that place a high value on moral behaviour and openness gain the trust of their stakeholders, including consumers and staff. To make sure that workers feel comfortable coming out with unethical behaviour or wrongdoing, HR departments can set up transparent whistleblower policies and standards of conduct. Furthermore, incorporating ethical issues into performance management procedures can encourage staff members to behave in a way that is consistent with the principles and objectives of the company.

Additionally, environmental sustainability programs that lessen the organization's ecological footprint are included in sustainable HR strategies. This can entail putting in place energy-saving procedures, cutting back on trash and water use, and encouraging environmentally friendly staff transportation choices. Organizations can show their commitment to responsible management of the earth and support global efforts to address climate change by integrating environmental sustainability into their operations.

In summary, putting into practice sustainable HR strategies necessitates an integrated, proactive strategy that takes into account the long-term effects of HR procedures on both the firm and its workforce. Organizations can cultivate a work environment that supports resilience, creativity, and long-term success by emphasizing diversity, equity, and inclusion; putting employee well-being and development first; investing in leadership development; encouraging ethical conduct and corporate governance; and embracing environmental sustainability.

2.1.1 Overview of Sustainable HR Strategies and their Importance in Organizational Sustainability

In order to ensure that a company's human capital is handled in a way that not only fulfils present demands but also takes into account the long-term impact on the environment, society, and economy, sustainable HR strategies are essential for organizational sustainability.

Introduction:

Organizations are realizing more and more how important sustainability is to all facets of their operations, including human resources (HR), in the fast-changing world of today. In order to generate long-term value for the company and society, sustainable HR strategies concentrate on incorporating economic, social, and environmental factors into HR procedures.

❖ Importance of Sustainable HR Strategies:

1. Attracting and Retaining Talent: Employers that show a commitment to sustainability are more in demand from workers, particularly Millennial and Gen Z. Employer branding may be strengthened and top people can be drawn in by implementing sustainable HR practices. Moreover, by encouraging a feeling of purpose and alignment with corporate values, a strong sustainability mindset can enhance staff retention.

2. Cost Reduction: In the long run, sustainable HR initiatives frequently result in cost savings. Lowering operating costs can be achieved, for instance, by implementing energy-efficient techniques like remote work or utilizing digital HR systems to reduce paper usage. Investing in initiatives for the well-being of employees can also lower healthcare expenses and increase productivity.

3. Risk Mitigation: Businesses can lower their risk of lawsuits, reputational harm, and compliance issues by addressing social and environmental hazards in the workforce. Ethical sourcing guidelines and diversity and inclusion programs are two examples of sustainable HR practices that assist reduce these risks and increase resilience.

4. Innovation and Creativity: Adopting a sustainable approach can help the company develop a creative and innovative culture. Sustainable human resource practices foster innovation, problem-solving skills, and a commitment to ongoing development among staff members. This may result in the creation of novel goods, services, and procedures that set the company apart from competitors.

5. Stakeholder Engagement: Customers, investors, and communities are examples of stakeholders who are putting more and more pressure on businesses to show their commitment to sustainability. By demonstrating that the company is accountable and responsible for its social and environmental effects, sustainable HR practices assist in increasing the organization's reputation and confidence among stakeholders.

❖ **Key Components of Sustainable HR Strategies:**

1. Diversity and Inclusion: Encouraging diversity and inclusion in the workplace improves decision-making, creativity, and innovation in addition to creating a sense of belonging. Creating equal opportunity for every employee, regardless of their identity or history, is the main goal of sustainable HR initiatives.

2. Employee Well-being: For HR to be sustainable, employee well-being must be prioritized. This entails offering wellness and health initiatives, encouraging work-life balance, and establishing a welcoming workplace that places a high priority on both physical and emotional well-being.

3. Training and Development: Putting money into employee training and development is essential to developing a team that is knowledgeable and flexible. In order to guarantee that workers have the abilities and information required to prosper in a business environment that is changing quickly, sustainable HR strategies place a high priority on ongoing education and professional development.

4. Ethical Sourcing and Supply Chain Management: Businesses are being held more and more responsible for the effects that their supply chains have on the environment and society. Sustainable HR methods entail collaborating with suppliers who follow human rights, environmental, and ethical labour norms.

5. Community Engagement: Sustainable HR fundamentally involves supporting social causes and interacting with local communities. This can involve charitable endeavours, volunteer projects, and collaborations with charity groups to tackle social concerns and enhance the welfare of the community.

By coordinating HR procedures with social, political, and financial objectives, sustainable HR strategies are essential to promoting organizational sustainability. In an increasingly complex and interconnected world, sustainable HR practices help firms succeed in the long run by recruiting and retaining talent, cutting costs, minimizing risks, encouraging innovation, and involving stakeholders. Adopting sustainability is a smart business move that benefits the company and society at large in addition to being morally required.

2.1.2 Examples of Organizations Successfully Implementing Sustainable HR Practices

❖ Here's an overview of some organizations that have successfully implemented sustainable HR practices:

1. Patagonia:
Patagonia is well known for its dedication to environmental sustainability, and its HR policies reflect this philosophy as well. The organization provides a wide range of perks to its staff, such as comprehensive health and wellness initiatives, paid time off for volunteer work, and on-site child care. In addition, Patagonia promotes work-life balance and offers flexible work schedules including job sharing and telecommuting. Furthermore, the company regularly updates its workforce on its progress in mitigating its environmental impact and is open and honest about its sustainability goals.

2. Unilever:
Global consumer goods giant Unilever has incorporated sustainability as a key component of its business plan. Unilever has put in place HR procedures that support diversity and inclusion, like gender balance targets and training on unconscious prejudice. In an effort to further promote sustainability, the company also provides a variety of staff advantages, including discounts for green employees, eco-friendly transportation choices, and rewards for lowering energy use. Employee contributions to sustainability goals are taken into account when evaluating Unilever employees, and the company's sustainability activities are integrated into its performance management system.

3. Interface:
Interface is a carpet tile manufacturer that has set ambitious sustainability goals, including achieving carbon neutrality by 2020. Interface places a strong emphasis on employee empowerment and involvement in its HR procedures. Examples of such programs include regular sustainability

training sessions and employee-led sustainability teams. Additionally, the corporation provides incentives to staff members who choose to adopt environmentally friendly habits, such carpooling or taking public transportation to work. The company's basic values and guiding principles are infused with sustainability, which demonstrates Interface's dedication to sustainability in the workplace culture.

4. IKEA:

IKEA is renowned for its dedication to sustainability and has put in place a number of HR procedures to help achieve this objective. The organization provides a wide range of training and development options for staff members, including courses on environmental management and sustainability. Through programs like inclusive leadership development and gender-neutral job descriptions, IKEA also encourages diversity and inclusion among its employees. Furthermore, IKEA offers incentives to its workforce to embrace sustainable practices at work and at home, including reduced prices on environmentally friendly goods and financial support for public transit.

5. Google:

Google is a leader in sustainable business practices and has implemented a range of HR initiatives to support its sustainability goals. Employees can take advantage of the company's extensive sustainability training program, which covers subjects including waste minimization, sustainable sourcing, and energy conservation. Incentives like electric vehicle charging stations, solar panel installation subsidies, and bike-to-work programs are among the ways Google encourages its staff to embrace sustainable practices. Furthermore, Google prioritizes the well-being of its employees by providing benefits including on-site wellness canters, nutritious food alternatives, and flexible work schedules that support work-life balance.

These are only a handful of the businesses that have effectively incorporated sustainable HR practices. By making sustainability a top priority in their HR strategy, these businesses are improving employee engagement, motivation, and productivity while simultaneously lessening their environmental effect.

2.1.3 Research Findings on the Impact of Sustainable HR Strategies on Organizational Performance

A wide range of programs and techniques are included in sustainable HR strategies with the goal of fostering an environment at work that prioritizes social, environmental, and financial sustainability. These complex techniques give equal weight to the health of workers as well as the wider effects of organizational decisions on the environment and society. Several studies suggest that businesses that implement these tactics can benefit from increased employee engagement, higher employee retention rates, increased productivity, and ultimately better organizational success.

Patagonia is one striking real-world illustration of how sustainable HR policies can be implemented successfully. Well-known for its steadfast attention to environmental care, Patagonia has created a number of employee-focused policies and initiatives that highlight its commitment to sustainability. These programs cover a wide range of services, from paid time off for volunteer work and environmental advocacy to flexible work schedules and full childcare support. Patagonia has established itself as a leader in corporate sustainability and developed a highly engaged workforce by prioritizing the overall well-being of its employees and actively fostering an environmental conscious culture. This coordinated strategy not only helps to draw in and keep elite talent, but it also strikes a powerful chord with environmentally sensitive customers, thereby fortifying Patagonia's long-term viability and competitiveness in the market.

Unilever's groundbreaking Sustainable Living Plan is another excellent example of sustainable HR practices. This ambitious plan places a strong emphasis on encouraging sustainable living among staff members, clients, and supply chain partners while integrating sustainability within the company's HR framework. Unilever has effectively fostered an innovative, accountable, and inclusive work environment by allocating strategic resources towards employee development and diversity and inclusion programs. As a result, the business has seen measurable increases in employee retention and happiness. In addition, it has encouraged a culture of unrelenting innovation and purpose-driven entrepreneurship. As a result, Unilever's market posture has significantly improved, supported by strong financial results and observable benefits for society as a whole.

In summation, businesses that fully adopt sustainable HR practices stand to benefit from improved organizational performance as well as a critical role in furthering the global sustainability agenda. By supporting programs that put employee well-being first, encourage environmental stewardship, and promote positive social change, these progressive companies are not only securing their own long-term success but also making a significant contribution to a future that is more equitable and sustainable for future generations.

2.2 Integrating Sustainability into HR Policies

Organizations that want to match their practices with their social, economic, and environmental responsibilities must incorporate sustainability into their HR policies. This integration is a proof of a dedication to sustainable development, which includes social justice, economic prosperity, and environmental sustainability. Companies may cultivate a culture of responsibility, improve their reputation, draw in top talent, and contribute to a more sustainable future by incorporating sustainability into HR policy.

First and foremost, hiring and keeping workers who share the organization's values and sustainability commitment is a key component of sustainability in HR practices. This can be done by include sustainability standards in hiring procedures, like testing applicants' familiarity with sustainable practices or awareness of environmental issues. Furthermore, HR policies can guarantee that staff receive continuing education and training on sustainability, maintaining sustainability as a top priority at all organizational levels.

Secondly, by defining standards for resource conservation, waste minimization, and energy efficiency, HR policies can encourage sustainable practices in the workplace. Policies might, for instance, encourage staff members to recycle, use energy-efficient equipment and appliances, and use as little paper as possible. Additionally, HR can help put sustainable initiatives into action, like carpooling incentives or composting programs, to lessen the company's carbon footprint and encourage eco-friendly behaviour among employees.

Thirdly, by encouraging diversity, equality, and inclusion (DEI) activities, sustainability can be incorporated into HR policies. Organizations can harness multiple perspectives and experiences to create creativity and innovation while promoting social equality by cultivating a diverse and inclusive workplace. HR regulations can help DEI initiatives by enforcing equitable recruiting procedures, offering equal chances for professional growth, and fostering a positive work atmosphere where all workers are treated with respect and value.

By guaranteeing adherence to labour regulations, encouraging ethical work practices, and maintaining human rights standards across the supply chain, HR policies can address the ethical and social dimensions of sustainability. In addition to advocating for

equitable pay, secure working conditions, and the wellbeing of employees, this entails tackling problems like child labour, forced labour, and workplace discrimination. Organizations can show their dedication to ethical business operations and corporate social responsibility by giving ethical issues top priority in their HR policies.

Furthermore, thorough strategy that takes into account the interdependence of environmental, social, and economic aspects is needed to include sustainability into HR policy. This involves implementing frameworks to direct decision-making and assess the organization's impact on people, the environment, and profit—such as the Sustainable Development Goals (SDGs) or the triple bottom line. In order to guarantee that sustainability goals are incorporated into every facet of the company's operations and strategic planning, HR policies must to be in line with these frameworks.

In summary, firms must include sustainability into HR practices in order to successfully manage their effects on the environment, society, and economy and to foster an environment of accountability and responsibility. Organizations may create value for stakeholders, reduce risks, and contribute to a more sustainable future for all by integrating sustainability into recruitment, workplace practices, diversity efforts, ethical standards, and strategic planning.

2.2.1 Importance of Incorporating Environmental Considerations into HR Policies

It is not only fashionable, but also imperative in the modern world for HR policies to take the environment into account. The need for businesses to operate responsibly and sustainably is growing, and human resources (HR) departments are essential in spearheading environmental efforts inside companies. The significance of incorporating environmental factors into HR policy will be discussed in this essay, which will touch on a number of topics including hiring, training, employee engagement, and company culture in general.

Attracting and keeping top personnel is a major motivation for incorporating environmental factors into HR practices. In the current competitive labour market, workers particularly millennials and Gen Zare looking for companies that place a high priority on environmental responsibility and sustainability. Organizations may attract eco-aware individuals and improve their employer brand by integrating green initiatives into HR practices. Employee loyalty and morale may increase as a result, and the workforce may become more diverse and talented.

Including environmental factors in the hiring process can help guarantee that new personnel support the sustainability objectives of the company. To gauge a candidate's attitude toward sustainability, HR departments can ask interview questions about environmental ideals and practices. Furthermore, highlighting the company's dedication to environmental stewardship in the hiring process might draw in applicants who have similar ideals, creating a more harmonious and ecologically conscious staff.

Human resource policies have a significant impact on how employees behave and view environmental sustainability. Employers can foster an environmentally conscious culture among their workforce by enacting rules that support eco-friendly behaviours like energy conservation, recycling, and sustainable commuting options. Additionally, training programs can be created to teach staff members the value of sustainability and provide them with the information and abilities needed to make personal and professional decisions that are ecologically friendly.

HR rules have the power to affect not just an individual's conduct but also the procedures and activities of an organization. Organizations can prioritize buying from environmentally friendly suppliers and vendors, for instance, by including environmental factors into their procurement rules. In a similar vein, companies can lessen their carbon footprint and support the fight against climate change by putting in place rules that support telecommuting and virtual meetings. All things considered, including environmental factors into HR policy can result in more environmentally conscious and sustainable business operations.

The potential for cost savings and efficiency advantages is another major reason to include environmental factors in HR policies. In addition to being good for the environment, sustainable practices like resource efficiency, waste reduction, and energy conservation can help businesses save money. Organizations can cut expenses and increase overall profitability by improving resource utilization and minimizing waste production. By offering incentives for employees to adopt sustainable behaviours and including environmental metrics into performance reviews, HR departments can play a significant role in promoting these practices.

Integrating environmental factors into HR practices can assist businesses in meeting legal obligations and reducing the risk of environmental non-compliance. Organizations are under more and more pressure to prove compliance and reduce their environmental impact as governments throughout the world impose harsher environmental restrictions. Organizations can lower the risk of expensive fines and penalties by incorporating environmental issues into HR policies and ensuring that staff members are informed of pertinent laws and processes.

Adopting environmental sustainability can improve a company's reputation and brand image, which will encourage stakeholder participation and customer loyalty. Customers are growing more aware of the effects that the goods and services they buy have on the environment and society in today's connected world. Through showcasing their HR policies and practices, businesses may set themselves apart from rivals and forge closer bonds with investors, clients, and other stakeholders by showcasing their dedication to sustainability.

Additionally, broader societal objectives like environmental conservation and climate action might benefit from the inclusion of environmental issues in HR regulations. Businesses must act to reduce their environmental effect and advance sustainable development as they are significant contributors to greenhouse gas emissions and resource depletion. Organizations can take the initiative to address urgent environmental issues and aid in the shift to a more resilient and sustainable economy by incorporating environmental considerations into HR practices.

In conclusion, companies hoping to prosper in a world growing more intricate and linked must integrate environmental factors into HR practices. Incorporating sustainability into HR operations has several advantages for companies, workers, and society at large, ranging from luring top talent to producing cost savings and efficiency increases. Through putting sustainability and environmental responsibility first, enterprises may build a more resilient and prosperous future for future generations.

2.2.2 Case Studies on Organizations aligning HR Policies with Sustainability Goals

Title: Google: A Case Study in Aligning HR Policies with Sustainability Goals

Introduction:
The technology giant Google, renowned for its cutting-edge goods and services, has also come under fire for its dedication to sustainability. Google has incorporated sustainability into many aspects of its operations, including human resources (HR) procedures, in addition to lessening its environmental impact. This case study examines how Google links its HR practices to sustainability objectives, highlighting the company's initiatives to support social responsibility, employee well-being, and environmental stewardship.

Sustainability Goals at Google:
Google's sustainability objectives cover a wide range of topics, such as social impact, renewable energy, and environmental preservation. The

company wants to show that it is committed to reducing climate change by becoming carbon neutral and running entirely on renewable energy. Google also funds community projects, engages in sustainability efforts, and encourages environmental awareness and education.

❖ Alignment of HR Policies with Sustainability Goals:

Google understands that reaching sustainable goals depends in large part on its workforce. Therefore, in a number of crucial areas, the business has put in place HR policies that support its sustainability goals:

1. Employee Wellness and Work-Life Balance:

Work-life balance and employee well-being are given top priority at Google because of their significance for sustainability. The organization provides all-inclusive wellness programs that include mental health services, nutritious meals, and fitness canters. Google contributes to a more sustainable work environment by increasing productivity and decreasing absenteeism through the promotion of employee health and happiness.

2. Environmental Responsibility:

Google has a number of programs to promote environmental stewardship among its staff members. For example, the corporation offers rewards for choosing environmentally beneficial modes of transportation like walking, bicycling, and public transportation. Google's transportation benefits lessen traffic in nearby areas, encourage environmentally friendly driving practices, and cut carbon emissions.

3. Sustainable Facilities and Operations:

Google incorporates eco-friendly facilities, renewable materials, and energy-efficient elements into the design of its workplace spaces to promote sustainability. The business promotes eco-friendly workplace behaviours among its staff members, including water efficiency, energy conservation, and recycling. Google is a leader in sustainable building methods and its dedication to sustainable facilities is in line with its larger environmental ambitions.

4. Diversity, Equity, and Inclusion (DEI):

Diversity, equality, and inclusion (DEI) are important aspects of Google's sustainability plan that it prioritizes. A culture of belonging is promoted by the organization, making employees from a variety of backgrounds feel appreciated and supported. Recruiting a diverse workforce, offering equal opportunities for professional growth, and putting inclusive policies and procedures into place are all part of Google's DEI goals. Google contributes to long-term sustainability by fostering diversity and inclusion, which improves organizational resilience, creativity, and innovation.

5. Learning and Development:
Google funds employee education initiatives that emphasize environmental responsibility and sustainability. To educate staff members about sustainability challenges, best practices, and solutions, the organization provides training modules, workshops, and resources. Google gives its workers the tools they need to lead good change both inside and outside the company by becoming sustainability champions in their teams and communities.

Impact and Outcomes:
Google's alignment of HR policies with sustainability goals has yielded significant impact and outcomes:

a. **Enhanced Employee Engagement:** Focusing on diversity, environmental responsibility, and employee well-being, Google cultivates a work environment where employees are engaged and dedicated. Workers are inspired to support the company's sustainability initiatives because they feel appreciated, supported, and respected.

b. **Sustainable Work Practices:** Google's efforts to support environmentally friendly transportation, buildings, and operations have decreased carbon emissions and improved resource efficiency and environmental stewardship. For sustainable business practices, both inside and outside the technology sector, the company is a model.

c. **Innovation and Collaboration:** Google encourages innovation and teamwork on sustainability projects among its workers through learning and development activities. Workers use their varied backgrounds, viewpoints, and experiences to come up with original answers to challenging sustainability problems.

Conclusion:

Google is an excellent example of how businesses can make their workforces more resilient and sustainable by coordinating HR practices with sustainability objectives. Google prioritizes sustainability in all facets of its business, as evidenced by its emphasis on diversity, learning and development, employee well-being, and environmental responsibility. Being a pioneer in the digital sector, Google creates a standard for incorporating sustainability into company culture and promoting favourable social and environmental effects.

Title: IKEA: A Case Study in Aligning HR Policies with Sustainability Goals

Introduction:

Known for its furniture and home goods, IKEA is a multinational retailer based in Sweden that has made a name for itself in the retail sector for sustainability. In addition to providing reasonably priced and fashionable goods, IKEA is dedicated to reducing its environmental footprint, encouraging social responsibility, and cultivating a sustainable culture. In order to highlight the company's efforts to incorporate sustainability into its workforce practices and organizational culture, this case study examines how IKEA connects its HR policies with sustainability goals.

Sustainability Goals at IKEA:

IKEA's sustainability objectives cover a wide range of topics, such as social justice, ethical sourcing, and environmental stewardship. By 2030, the company wants to be climate positive, which means that it will cut its greenhouse gas emissions across its whole value chain more than it produces. In addition, IKEA works to advance fair labour practices, circularity, and resource efficiency throughout its supply chain and operations.

❖ **Alignment of HR Policies with Sustainability Goals:**

IKEA understands that its workers are important contributors to sustainability and that they are essential to accomplishing the company's sustainability goals. Therefore, in a number of crucial areas, the business has put in place HR policies that support its sustainability goals:

1. Diversity and Inclusion (D&I):

Diversity and inclusion are important aspects of IKEA's sustainability strategy. The organization encourages a varied and welcoming work environment where staff members feel appreciated, respected, and free to share their special skills and viewpoints. Equal opportunities for career growth, inclusive policies and practices that promote a sense of belonging among employees, and diversity-focused recruitment methods are just a few of IKEA's diversity and inclusion initiatives.

2. Employee Well-being and Work-Life Balance:

Work-life balance and employee well-being are important aspects of IKEA's sustainability initiatives. The organization provides extensive wellness initiatives that focus on mental, emotional, and physical well-being. These initiatives include flexible work schedules, mental health assistance, and access to fitness canters. IKEA promotes employee well-being to increase job happiness, productivity, and retention—all of which help to create a workforce that is more robust and sustainable.

3. Sustainable Sourcing and Supply Chain Management:

IKEA encourages sustainability across its whole supply chain, which includes moral sourcing procedures and conscientious production techniques. Strict environmental and social requirements, such as limiting waste, cutting energy use, and guaranteeing fair labour salaries and conditions, are what the corporation wants from its suppliers. IKEA's HR policies include training, audits, and supplier inspections to make sure sustainability standards are met and to encourage ongoing development.

4. Learning and Development:

IKEA funds employee education and training initiatives that emphasize sustainability and ethical business conduct. In order to educate staff members about sustainability challenges, raise their knowledge of ethical issues, and help them develop the skills necessary to implement sustainable solutions, the organization offers training modules, workshops, and tools. IKEA gives its workers the tools they need to become sustainability advocates in their groups and local communities, which promotes change throughout the company.

5. Community Engagement and Social Impact:

IKEA is dedicated to improving the areas in which it works, and part of this commitment includes sponsoring regional projects, nonprofits, and social issues. The organization supports its workers' involvement in volunteer work, community service initiatives, and extracurricular pursuits pertaining to sustainability. IKEA's human resources policies encourage staff members to participate in outreach initiatives in the community, which is consistent with the company's larger commitment to social responsibility and community development.

Impact and Outcomes:

IKEA's alignment of HR policies with sustainability goals has resulted in significant impact and outcomes:

a. **Enhanced Employee Engagement and Retention:** IKEA cultivates a culture of dedication and engagement among its employees by placing a high priority on learning and development, employee well-being, diversity, and inclusivity. Employee job satisfaction and retention rates are higher when they feel appreciated, supported, and inspired to contribute to the company's sustainability initiatives.

b. **Sustainable Supply Chain Practices:** Throughout its value chain, IKEA has improved environmental and social performance as a result of its emphasis on sustainable sourcing and supply chain management. Through close collaboration with suppliers to maintain sustainability standards, IKEA reduces risks, improves transparency, and encourages ethical business practices throughout its worldwide operations.

c. **Community Collaboration and Social Impact:** Through its community participation programs, IKEA develops trust, fortifies ties with regional stakeholders, and adds value to communities. IKEA exhibits its commitment to social responsibility and makes a positive social impact in the communities it serves by enabling its workers to take part in community outreach initiatives.

Conclusion:

IKEA is a prime example of how businesses can make socially conscious and environmentally conscious hiring practices by coordinating HR practices with sustainability objectives. IKEA shows its dedication to sustainability in all facets of its business by including learning and development, employee well-being, diversity and inclusion, and community involvement into its HR procedures. IKEA, a pioneer in the retail sector, creates a standard for incorporating sustainability into company culture and promoting favourable effects on the environment and society.

Title: Unilever: A Case Study in Aligning HR Policies with Sustainability Goals

Introduction:

The multinational consumer goods corporation Unilever has made a name for itself as a pioneer in sustainability by incorporating social and environmental responsibility into its operations. Beyond just producing goods, Unilever is dedicated to enhancing global health and wellbeing while lessening its influence on the environment. This case study highlights Unilever's initiatives to promote a culture of diversity, inclusiveness, employee well-being, and environmental stewardship by examining how the company links its HR policies with sustainability goals.

Sustainability Goals at Unilever:

Unilever's Sustainable Living Plan lays out the company's sustainability objectives, which include enhancing livelihoods, lowering environmental impact, and improving the health and well-being of one billion people. The organization prioritizes a number of issues, such as social impact, waste reduction, carbon emissions reduction, and sustainable sourcing. Throughout its value chain, Unilever is dedicated to advancing sustainable production and consumption methods while fostering constructive social change.

❖ Alignment of HR Policies with Sustainability Goals:

Unilever acknowledges that its workforce is essential to accomplishing environmental goals and fostering innovation. Therefore, in a number of crucial areas, the business has put in place HR policies that support its sustainability goals:

1. Diversity and Inclusion (D&I):

Diversity and inclusivity are important aspects of Unilever's sustainability strategy. The organization encourages a varied and welcoming work environment where staff members from all backgrounds feel appreciated, respected, and free to share their special skills and viewpoints. Unilever has implemented diversity-focused recruitment procedures, equal career progression opportunities, and training programs that address unconscious bias and cultural competency as part of its diversity and inclusion initiatives. Unilever contributes to long-term sustainability by fostering diversity and inclusion, which improves organizational resilience, creativity, and innovation.

2. Employee Well-being and Work-Life Balance:

Work-life balance and employee well-being are important components of Unilever's sustainability initiatives. The organization provides extensive wellness initiatives that focus on mental, emotional, and physical well-being. These initiatives include flexible work schedules, mental health assistance, and access to fitness canters. Additionally, Unilever exhorts staff members to focus self-care, uphold a positive work-life balance, and assist one another's wellbeing. Unilever contributes to a more resilient and sustainable workforce by enhancing morale, productivity, and retention through investments in employee well-being.

3. Sustainable Sourcing and Supply Chain Management:

As cornerstones of its sustainability strategy, Unilever advocates for ethical supply chain management and sustainable sourcing methods. To ensure that raw ingredients, including as palm oil, soy, and tea, are sourced responsibly, the company maintains tight relationships with its suppliers. In order to maintain sustainable standards and encourage ongoing development, Unilever's HR policies include supplier audits, training initiatives, and certification criteria. Unilever reduces risks, improves transparency, and cultivates long-term relationships with suppliers who uphold ethical standards by placing a high priority on sustainable sourcing.

4. Learning and Development:

Programs for staff learning and development that emphasize ethics, sustainability, and ethical business practices are funded by Unilever. The organization offers workshops, training modules, and other materials to teach staff members about supply chain ethics, environmental concerns, and community involvement. With the help of innovation, advocacy, and education, Unilever workers are empowered to lead their teams and communities as sustainability advocates, bringing about good change. Through the promotion of an environment that values ongoing education and training, Unilever gives its workers the know-how to handle challenging environmental issues and further the company's goals.

5. Community Engagement and Social Impact:

Through social responsibility and community engagement programs, Unilever is dedicated to improving the areas in which it operates. The organization supports its workers' involvement in volunteer work, community service initiatives, and extracurricular pursuits pertaining to sustainability. Employee participation in community outreach initiatives is made easier by Unilever's HR practices, which are in line with the business's larger commitment to social responsibility and community development.

Impact and Outcomes:

Unilever's alignment of HR policies with sustainability goals has resulted in significant impact and outcomes:

a. **Enhanced Employee Engagement and Satisfaction:** Through giving diversity, inclusion, learning and development, employee well-being, and community participation top priority, Unilever cultivates a culture of engagement, teamwork, and dedication among its employees. Employee job satisfaction and retention rates are higher when they feel appreciated, supported, and inspired to contribute to the company's sustainability initiatives.

b. **Sustainable Sourcing Practices:** Throughout its value chain, Unilever has improved environmental and social performance as a result of its focus on sustainable sourcing and supply chain management. Unilever assures the ethical treatment of workers, promotes biodiversity, and supports livelihoods in areas where it operates by collaborating closely with suppliers to uphold sustainability standards.

c. **Community Collaboration and Social Impact:** Through its community engagement programs, Unilever develops trust, fortifies ties with regional stakeholders, and adds value to communities. Unilever exhibits its commitment to social responsibility and has a positive social impact in the communities it serves by enabling its workers to take part in community outreach initiatives.

Conclusion:

In order to develop a more inclusive, socially conscious, and sustainable workforce, Unilever serves as an excellent example of how businesses may match HR practices with sustainability objectives. Incorporating learning and development, employee well-being, diversity and inclusion, and community involvement into HR procedures is one way Unilever shows its dedication to sustainability in all facets of its operations. Leading the consumer products sector, Unilever is a model for incorporating sustainability into company culture and promoting beneficial social and environmental effects.

Title: Interface Inc.: A Case Study in Aligning HR Policies with Sustainability Goals

Introduction:

For many years, Interface Inc., a leading provider of environmentally friendly flooring solutions worldwide, has been at the forefront of environmental sustainability. Interface, a company founded with the goal of leaving no trace on the environment, has incorporated sustainability into all facets of its operations, including its human resources (HR) practices. This case study highlights Interface's dedication to social responsibility, employee well-being, and environmental stewardship by examining how the company connects its HR practices with sustainability goals.

Sustainability Goals at Interface:

Interface's ambitious "Mission Zero" effort, which seeks to eradicate any adverse environmental impact by 2020, embodies the company's sustainability objectives. Throughout its supply chain and operations, the company prioritizes sustainable innovation, biodiversity promotion, resource conservation, and a decrease in carbon emissions. Interface's dedication to sustainability aims to set a good example for the industry and encourage constructive change.

❖ **Alignment of HR Policies with Sustainability Goals:**

Interface is aware that its workers play a critical role in advancing innovation and accomplishing sustainability goals. Therefore, in a number of crucial areas, the business has put in place HR policies that support its sustainability goals:

1. Employee Engagement and Empowerment:

Interface considers empowerment and employee participation to be critical elements of their sustainability plan. Employees are encouraged to submit ideas, engage in decision-making, and take ownership of sustainability projects since the organization promotes a culture of cooperation, openness, and shared responsibility. The HR policies of Interface facilitate open communication, ongoing feedback, and professional growth opportunities, empowering staff members to actively participate in the company's sustainability initiatives.

2. Sustainable Work Practices:

Interface encourages environmentally friendly and worker-friendly sustainable work methods. The organization provides flexible work schedules, such telecommuting and shortened workweeks, in an effort to lower emissions from commutes and encourage work-life balance. In order to create a more sustainable work environment, Interface also employs eco-friendly initiatives, trash reduction tactics, and energy-saving measures in its office facilities. Interface exhibits its dedication to environmental stewardship and employee pleasure by incorporating sustainability into regular work processes.

3. Learning and Development:

Interface funds staff training initiatives with an emphasis on innovation and sustainability. The organization teaches staff members about sustainable principles, best practices, and new trends through training modules, workshops, and other materials. Interface encourages staff members to take part in cross-functional sustainability projects, attend conferences, and obtain certifications. Interface gives staff members the tools they need to promote positive change and come up with innovative solutions to sustainability problems by promoting a culture of constant learning and creativity.

4. Wellness and Health Promotion:

Integral to its sustainability approach, Interface places a high priority on employee well-being and health promotion. The organization provides all-inclusive wellness initiatives that address mental, emotional, and physical health. These initiatives include staff support programs, mindfulness training, and fitness canters. Interface promotes a healthy work-life balance, emphasizes self-care, and fosters a supportive environment for one another's wellbeing. Interface contributes to a more resilient and sustainable workforce by enhancing morale, productivity, and retention through investments in employee wellbeing.

5. Community Engagement and Social Impact:

Through community involvement and social responsibility programs, Interface is dedicated to improving the communities in which it operates. The organization supports its workers' involvement in volunteer work, community service initiatives, and extracurricular pursuits pertaining to sustainability. The HR policies of Interface encourage staff members to participate in outreach initiatives in the community, which is consistent with the organization's larger commitment to social responsibility and community development.

Impact and Outcomes:

Interface's alignment of HR policies with sustainability goals has resulted in significant impact and outcomes:

a. **Enhanced Employee Engagement and Satisfaction:** Interface cultivates a culture of dedication and cooperation within its workforce by supporting employee empowerment, learning and growth, wellness, and engagement. Being employed by a company that places a high priority on sustainability and social responsibility makes employees feel appreciated, inspired, and proud.

b. **Sustainable Work Practices and Operations:** Reduced environmental effect and resource consumption have resulted from Interface's focus on sustainable work practices, which include energy efficiency, waste reduction, and flexible work arrangements. The company encourages positive change among suppliers, partners, and rivals by setting an example for sustainable business practices in the flooring sector.

c. **Community Collaboration and Social Impact:** Through its community engagement programs, Interface develops trust, fortifies ties with regional stakeholders, and adds value to communities. Interface shows its commitment to social responsibility and makes a positive social impact in the communities it works in by allowing its workers to take part in community outreach programs.

Conclusion:

Interface Inc. is a prime example of how businesses can make their workforce more resilient, engaged, and sustainable by coordinating HR practices with sustainability objectives. Interface exhibits its dedication to sustainability in all facets of company operations by including learning and development, wellness, community involvement, employee empowerment, and engagement into its HR procedures. Setting the standard for incorporating sustainability into business culture and promoting positive social and environmental impact, Interface is a leader in the field of environmental sustainability.

Title: Starbucks: Integrating Sustainability into HR Policies

Introduction:

The massive worldwide coffee chain Starbucks is well known for its dedication to sustainability. Sustainability is a key component of Starbucks' business strategy, from using coffee beans that are sourced responsibly to minimizing its environmental effect. This case study explores the ways in which Starbucks links its HR practices to sustainability objectives, resulting in favourable social and environmental effects as well as the promotion of an innovative and responsible culture.

Background of Starbucks:

Starbucks was established in Seattle, Washington, in 1971, and now has hundreds of locations across the globe, making it one of the most recognizable coffee shop chains in the world. The idea that companies can and should have a positive impact on the communities they serve is fundamental to Starbucks' mission. The company's sustainability programs, which cover social responsibility, ethical sourcing, and environmental stewardship, are a reflection of this philosophy.

❖ **Alignment of HR Policies with Sustainability Goals:**

Starbucks has implemented several HR policies that align with its sustainability goals:

1. Employee Education and Training: Starbucks makes significant investments in training initiatives to teach staff members about sustainable business practices. In order to enable them to integrate sustainability into their everyday routines and contacts with clients, baristas and other staff members receive training on subjects including waste reduction, energy saving, and ethical sourcing.

2. Incentives for Sustainable Behaviour: Starbucks uses recognition programs and awards to encourage sustainable behaviour among its staff members. Workers who exhibit outstanding dedication to sustainability—for example, by encouraging the use of reusable cups or cutting waste—may be recognized and given rewards, which will help to cultivate an eco-friendly culture inside the company.

3. Diverse and Inclusive Workforce: Starbucks' sustainability mission includes promoting inclusiveness and diversity among its employees. Starbucks builds a sense of togetherness and belonging by creating a diverse and inclusive work environment where people feel appreciated and respected. This increases employee engagement and boosts organizational success.

4. Health and Wellbeing Programs: Acknowledging the significance of worker well-being for overall sustainability, Starbucks provides its employees with health and wellness initiatives. Starbucks places a high priority on employee wellbeing, offering everything from fitness programs to mental health resources, making sure that its workers are content, healthy, and capable of making valuable contributions to the company's sustainability goals.

5. Community Engagement and Volunteerism: As part of its sustainability plan, Starbucks promotes community involvement and staff volunteering. Employees can get involved in volunteer projects that tackle local environmental and social concerns through programs like the Starbucks Community Service Program. This fosters stronger links with the community and has a positive influence outside of the office.

Impact and Outcomes:

The alignment of HR policies with sustainability goals has yielded significant impact and outcomes for Starbucks:

a. **Enhanced Employee Engagement:** Starbucks has encouraged employee participation and a sense of purpose by incorporating sustainability into HR policy. Workers are inspired to support the company's sustainability objectives, which boosts output, innovation, and loyalty.

b. **Reduced Environmental Footprint:** Starbucks' environmental impact has decreased considerably as a result of its sustainability initiatives. Starbucks is taking significant steps to lessen its environmental effect, from boosting recycling rates to introducing energy-efficient procedures in its locations.

c. **Improved Brand Reputation:** Starbucks' brand reputation and customer loyalty have improved as a result of its HR policies' commitment to sustainability. Customers are drawn to companies that put social and environmental responsibility first, and Starbucks is positioned as a pioneer in sustainable business practices because to its proactive strategy.

d. **Positive Social Impact:** Positive social effect is being driven by Starbucks through the promotion of diversity, inclusivity, and community engagement, both within and beyond the company. Starbucks is using its human resources practices to make the world more sustainable and equitable by helping underserved communities and giving employees the tools, they need to make a difference.

Conclusion:
Starbucks serves as an excellent example of how businesses may successfully match HR practices with sustainability objectives in order to generate value and have a beneficial impact. Incorporating sustainability concepts into its workforce management procedures has allowed Starbucks to lessen its environmental impact while also promoting accountability, creativity, and teamwork. As companies continue to face sustainability-related obstacles, Starbucks' strategy offers insightful information on the critical role that human resources play in promoting sustainability and guaranteeing the long-term success of organizations.

2.2.3 Best Practices for Integrating Sustainability into Recruitment, Training, and Performance Management Policies

It is imperative for firms seeking to connect their operations with environmental and social responsibility goals to incorporate sustainability into their recruitment, training, and performance management strategies. By integrating sustainability into these fundamental HR procedures, businesses may develop a sustainable culture, draw in and keep top personnel, and promote long-term financial success. For each area, the following are some recommended practices:

1. Recruitment:
   i. **Incorporate Sustainability Criteria:** Provide candidate profiles and job descriptions that highlight values, experiences, and abilities related to sustainability. This could be an understanding of environmental laws, familiarity with sustainable methods, or a dedication to social responsibility.
   ii. **Engage with Sustainable Talent Pools:** Engage in active recruitment from sustainability-focused networks and platforms,

such as environmental advocacy groups, job boards, or colleges with robust sustainability curricula.

iii. **Assess Sustainability Competencies:** Incorporate interview questions and scenarios pertaining to sustainability to ascertain candidates' comprehension and dedication to sustainability ideals.

2. Training:

i. **Offer Sustainability Training Programs:** Give staff members the chance to get training on sustainability subjects related to their jobs, such as waste management, energy conservation, and ethical sourcing. Workshops, online classes, or guest lectures by specialists in sustainability could fall under this category.

ii. **Embed Sustainability in On boarding:** Include sustainability objectives and principles in the on boarding process for new employees to make sure they are aware of the company's commitment to sustainability right away.

iii. **Promote Cross-Functional Learning:** Encourage staff members to take part in multidisciplinary training courses in order to promote a comprehensive grasp of sustainability problems and solutions within departments.

3. Performance Management:

i. **Set Sustainability Goals:** Set measurable, precise sustainability goals in line with the organization's overarching sustainability plan. These objectives can have to do with lowering carbon emissions, boosting energy effectiveness, or enhancing social impact measurements.

ii. **Integrate Sustainability Metrics:** Incorporate both conventional and sustainable performance indicators into staff performance reviews. This could entail monitoring team or individual contributions to sustainability projects and how they affect important sustainability metrics.

iii. **Recognize and Reward Sustainability Leadership:** Reward staff members that show outstanding leadership in promoting sustainability inside the company. This could entail prizes, bonuses for performance, or public acknowledgement.

4. Overall Integration:
  i. **Leadership Commitment:** Make sure top leadership is clearly in favour of sustainability and committed to it, as their endorsement is essential to bringing about change across the entire organization.
  ii. **Embed Sustainability in Organizational Culture:** Encourage a culture that views sustainability as essential to the goals and methods of the business. This could entail highlighting sustainability heroes, acknowledging sustainability milestones, and enticing staff members to get involved in sustainability projects.
  iii. **Regular Review and Adaptation:** Review and modify hiring, training, and performance management procedures on a regular basis to align with changing stakeholder expectations, industry best practices, and sustainability concerns.

In conclusion, organizations may successfully incorporate sustainability into their HR procedures by putting these best practices into practice. This will improve employee engagement, performance, and long-term economic success while also producing beneficial social and environmental consequences.

2.3 Building a Green Culture in Organizations

Establishing a green culture in an organization requires a thorough and ongoing effort to instil a dedication to sustainability and environmental care in every aspect of operations. Fundamentally, a green culture is characterized by a commitment to reducing ecological footprints, preserving limited resources, and supporting actions that improve the resilience and overall health of the environment.

An organization's leadership must be steadfast in their commitment to fostering a green culture. Setting sustainability as a top priority for executives not only sets the tone for the entire organization but also sends a strong message to internal and external stakeholders. Leadership demonstrates its commitment to sustainability by taking concrete steps including funding sustainability programs, establishing challenging but doable environmental targets, and incorporating sustainability into general strategic planning procedures.

Engaging employees is another essential component in fostering a green culture. Through granting employees, the authority to engage in and make contributions to sustainability initiatives, companies cultivate a feeling of communal accountability and ownership for environmental care. This empowerment can take many different forms, such as offering thorough instruction and training on environmental issues, rewarding and identifying sustainable behaviour, and cultivating an innovative work atmosphere where staff members are encouraged to suggest and carry out green projects.

The foundation for establishing and sustaining a green culture within the company is effective communication. Fostering awareness, buy-in, and commitment among employees and stakeholders is facilitated by transparent and frequent communication regarding the reasoning behind sustainability programs, the steps taken toward achieving environmental goals, and the obstacles faced along the way. Information flows freely and everyone feels informed and involved in the organization's sustainability journey when a variety of communication channels are used, including town hall meetings, digital platforms, internal newsletters, and sustainability reports.

Concrete sustainability measures serve as the cornerstone around which a green culture is constructed. These programs cover a wide range of tasks, such as putting energy-saving procedures into place, cutting down on waste production, making the best use of water, locating sustainable resources, and encouraging environmentally friendly transportation options. Additionally, organizations can increase their impact by forming strategic alliances with government bodies, non-profits, and companies that share their values in order to intensify their joint efforts and bring about systemic change.

To further ingrain sustainability into the organization's DNA, it is crucial to incorporate sustainability considerations into supply chain management procedures and decision-making processes. To achieve this, it is necessary to carry out thorough lifecycle assessments in order to assess how goods and services affect the environment, to implement sustainable procurement methods, and to work in conjunction with suppliers in order to improve sustainability all the way up the value chain. Organizations can reduce their environmental impact while promoting innovation, resilience, and competitive advantage in a world with limited resources by embracing a comprehensive approach to sustainability.

All things considered, creating a green culture calls for a coordinated and diverse strategy that includes leadership dedication, staff involvement, clear communication, and concrete sustainability projects. Organizations may lower their ecological footprint, inspire positive change, stimulate innovation, and help create a more sustainable and fair future for future generations by adopting sustainability as a guiding concept and incorporating it into all aspects of operations.

2.3.1 Strategies for Fostering a Culture of Environmental Consciousness among Employees

"Strategies for fostering a culture of environmental consciousness among employees" are deliberate methods or initiatives that are intended to create an environment at work where workers are conscious of and actively involved in supporting environmentally friendly practices and behaviours. These tactics usually entail educating staff members, supporting them, and putting initiatives in place that encourage accountability, environmental awareness, and action.

Establishing a climate of environmental awareness among staff members is essential to developing sustainability in a company. This is an all-inclusive approach that includes engagement, education, policy implementation, and acknowledgment, among other things:

1. Education and Awareness:
Promoting environmental sensitivity requires education. Offering training sessions, workshops, or seminars to staff members can assist spread knowledge about sustainability, environmental challenges, and the power of individual actions. These discussions may touch on issues including pollution, depletion of natural resources, biodiversity loss, and climate change. Employees who are well-informed about environmental issues are

more inclined to embrace sustainable practices in both their personal and professional life.

2. Lead by Example:
Organizations need to lead by example. Adopting environmentally friendly procedures in the workplace conveys to staff members the organization's strong commitment to sustainability. This can involve taking steps to cut back on paper use, conserve energy by using energy-efficient HVAC and lighting systems, use less water, and put in place programs for recycling and trash reduction. Employees are more inclined to copy these habits and feel pleased to work for a firm that values the environment when they observe them in action.

3. Encourage Participation:
Getting workers involved in environmental projects promotes a feeling of community and shared accountability. Encourage involvement by giving staff members the chance to volunteer for environmental programs like neighbourhood clean-ups, tree planting campaigns, or habitat restoration projects. Creating green teams or sustainability committees inside the company can also provide staff members the authority to spearhead initiatives and integrate eco-friendly procedures into their divisions or groups.

4. Recognition and Incentives:
Acknowledging and praising staff members who show a dedication to environmental stewardship might encourage others to adopt similar practices by reinforcing positive behaviour. For eco-friendly behaviours like cutting back on trash, saving energy, switching to more eco-friendly modes of transportation, or taking part in environmental education initiatives, think about putting in place incentive schemes or recognition programs. Awards, certifications, bonuses, and public acknowledgement through company-wide communications are just a few ways that recognition can be given.

5. Provide Resources:
It is crucial to make it simple for workers to adopt sustainable practices. Establish infrastructure and resources to encourage eco-friendly working

practices. This can include amenities like composting sites, recycling bins, and spaces set aside for parking bicycles or carpooling. Give staff members access to educational materials, internet tools, and training opportunities to further their knowledge of eco-friendly living and sustainable activities.

6. Incorporate Sustainability into Policies:
Integrating environmental factors into business policies and decision-making procedures guarantees that sustainability will always be a fundamental principle of the company. This may entail creating sustainability targets and goals, incorporating environmental impact studies into project planning and development procedures, or incorporating environmental criteria into procurement strategies. At all organizational levels, prioritizing sustainability increases the likelihood that staff members will see it as a crucial component of their work and decision-making.

7. Communicate Impact:
Establishing a culture of responsibility and establishing trust need open and honest communication about the organization's environmental performance as well as the consequences of employee actions. Provide regular updates on important environmental indicators, like greenhouse gas emissions, waste production, and the use of water and energy. Emphasize accomplishments, difficulties, and areas that could use better. Also, invite staff input and recommendations. When the tangible results of teamwork are shown, employees are inspired to carry on with their environmental stewardship journey.

8. Empowerment:
Giving staff members the freedom to lead environmental projects promotes an innovative culture and a sense of empowerment. Encourage staff members to come up with concepts, put forward solutions, and carry out independent sustainability projects in the spheres of influence that they control. Encourage teamwork, experimentation, and creativity. Also, acknowledge and honour the efforts of individuals and groups who promote positive change. Organizations may leverage employees'

creativity and passion to discover novel solutions to environmental concerns by enabling them to act as change agents.

9. Collaboration:

The impact of environmental efforts can be enhanced and employee participation opportunities can be expanded through collaboration with external organizations, industry partners, and environmental stakeholders. For the purpose of achieving sustainability goals, collaborating with regional non-profits, governmental organizations, or environmental groups can give access to networks, resources, and knowledge. Employees can link with larger sustainability activities outside of the workplace through collaborative projects like industry-wide initiatives, environmental education programs, or neighbourhood clean-up events. This fosters a sense of shared purpose and collective responsibility.

10. Continuous Improvement:

Organizations must constantly assess and enhance their environmental practices since sustainability is a journey. Provide systems for routinely evaluating and tracking environmental performance, gathering employee input, and pinpointing areas in need of improvement. Establish challenging yet attainable sustainability objectives and goals, and then monitor advancement over time. Promote a culture of innovation and ongoing education wherein staff members are motivated to try out novel concepts, tools, and procedures in order to improve environmental performance. Organizations can adjust to changing environmental obstacles and promote long-term beneficial change by cultivating a culture of continuous improvement.

Together, these tactics provide a comprehensive strategy for encouraging an environmentally conscious workplace culture among staff members. Organizations may develop a workforce that is not just conscious of environmental challenges but also actively involved in addressing them, both within and outside of the workplace, by combining education, engagement, empowerment, and continuous improvement.

In summary, developing a culture of environmental consciousness among staff members necessitates a multifaceted strategy that includes collaborations, policy creation, employee involvement, education, leadership commitment, and monitoring. Businesses may lessen their environmental impact and encourage good change in their communities and sectors by incorporating sustainability into every part of their operations.

2.3.2 Role of HR in Promoting Green Initiatives and Sustainability Awareness

In the modern world, encouraging green projects and sustainability consciousness within a company is not simply a trend but also a vital component of corporate responsibility. Driving and maintaining these initiatives is mostly the responsibility of HR departments. Let's examine each of the previously mentioned elements in more detail as well as some more tactics HR can use to advance sustainability awareness and green initiatives:

1. Policy Development:
HR departments engage with management to create policies that integrate sustainability into the structure of the company. Establishing policies for waste management, energy conservation, lowering carbon footprints, and buying environmentally friendly goods are all included in this. While being customized to the unique requirements and purposes of the company, these policies should be in line with more general environmental goals and legal obligations.

2. Training and Development:
HR provides workshops and training sessions to inform staff members about the value of sustainability and to give them useful advice on how to support environmental preservation initiatives. Topics including water conservation, recycling techniques, sustainable transportation solutions, and energy efficiency may be discussed in these sessions. Through the provision of knowledge and skills to employees, HR cultivates a culture of sustainability across the entire organization.

3. Recruitment and On boarding:
HR incorporates sustainability into hiring by looking for applicants that show a strong commitment to environmental responsibility. By emphasizing the company's sustainability activities in job descriptions,

you can draw applicants who share your beliefs. New hires are briefed on the company's sustainability policies, objectives, and expectations throughout the on boarding process. This guarantees that the incorporation of sustainability into the corporate culture starts as soon as new employees join the team.

4. Employee Engagement:
Through a variety of programs and events, HR promotes employee participation in sustainability projects. Creating volunteer opportunities for environmental projects, putting on competitions or challenges cantered around sustainability, and supporting affinity groups or committees led by employees are a few examples of how to do this. HR motivates staff members to actively engage in sustainability projects and have a positive influence both inside and outside the workplace by establishing a sense of ownership and togetherness.

5. Performance Management:
HR makes sure that performance reviews include sustainability targets and indicators so that workers are held responsible for their environmental sustainability contributions. These objectives could have to do with taking personal initiatives like cutting back on paper use, boosting energy conservation, or coming up with creative solutions for environmental problems. Employees that perform exceptionally well in sustainability are acknowledged and rewarded, which promotes ongoing development and serves to emphasize the significance of environmental stewardship.

6. Resource Management:
HR works in tandem with other departments to maximize resource usage and reduce waste production. This could entail putting recycling systems into place, using less energy and water, and looking into more ecologically friendly alternatives for materials and technologies. HR contributes to reducing the environmental effect of operations and may also save expenses by finding areas for improvement and implementing sustainable practices throughout the company.

7. Communication and Advocacy:
Internally and globally, HR plays a vital role in communicating the organization's sustainability initiatives. HR uses a variety of internal

communication tools, including newsletters, intranet portals, and town hall meetings, to share information on sustainability projects, developments, and best practices. HR represents the company outside in partnerships, conferences, and forums pertaining to sustainability, demonstrating its dedication to environmental responsibility and disseminating information to outside stakeholders. HR promotes the organization's sustainability agenda by interacting with internal and external audiences in order to increase awareness, trust, and support for it.

8. Partnerships and Collaboration:

HR may collaborate with corporations, governmental organizations, and environmental groups to increase the effect of their combined knowledge and resources. Joint sustainability projects, forums for exchanging knowledge, and advocacy campaigns are examples of collaborative initiatives that can strengthen an organization's sustainability efforts and promote significant change on a larger scale.

9. Innovation and Continuous Improvement:

By asking staff members for suggestions and comments on how to improve sustainable procedures, HR promotes an innovative and continuous improvement culture. This could entail organizing hackathons with a sustainable theme, invention challenges, or recommendation systems. HR stimulates the creation of fresh ideas and methods to more successfully handle environmental concerns by utilizing the creativity and inventiveness of its workforce.

10. Supply Chain Sustainability:

HR prioritizes partnerships with suppliers who follow sustainable practices and evaluates the environmental impact of suppliers in collaboration with procurement and supply chain departments. This could entail carrying out supplier audits, developing sustainable standards for choosing vendors, and encouraging ethical sourcing practices all the way through the supply chain. HR supports the overarching objective of building a more robust and sustainable global economy by bringing sustainability considerations outside the walls of the company.

11. Community Engagement and Outreach:

HR supports community involvement programs that give workers the opportunity to support environmental conservation outside of the workplace. This could entail planning volunteer days, environmental cleanup events, or instructive seminars in collaboration with neighbourhood associations, non-profits, and schools. Human resources assists workers in taking an active role as positive change agents in their communities by promoting a sense of social responsibility and environmental stewardship.

12. Metrics and Reporting:

HR sets up measurements and key performance indicators (KPIs) to monitor the organization's advancement toward sustainability objectives and to measure the long-term effects of initiatives. These measures could include things like energy usage, waste diversion rates, carbon emissions, and staff engagement levels. HR shows the organization's dedication to measurable outcomes by routinely tracking and reporting on sustainability performance, which demonstrates transparency and accountability to both internal and external stakeholders.

In conclusion, HR has a variety of roles to play in encouraging eco-friendly projects and raising awareness of sustainability inside businesses. HR contributes to the development of an environmental responsibility culture that permeates every facet of the business by incorporating sustainability issues into policies, training initiatives, hiring procedures, and performance management systems. HR promotes significant change and ongoing development in the direction of a more sustainable future via cooperation, innovation, and community involvement.

2.3.3 Research on the Benefits of a Green Culture in Driving Employee Engagement and Organizational Success

Establishing a green culture in the workplace requires a multifaceted strategy that goes beyond following environmental laws or launching ad hoc sustainability projects. Prioritizing environmental stewardship and responsibility in all facets of operations necessitates a fundamental change in the company culture, values, and practices. A number of factors are covered by this all-encompassing strategy, including as supply chain procedures, employee conduct, corporate rules, and community engagement initiatives.

A strong commitment to sustainability principles, which act as a framework for internal decision-making and activity, is at the core of an organization's green culture. These values could be limiting damage to the environment, preserving resources, cutting carbon emissions, increasing biodiversity, and supporting social justice. Organizations can contribute to constructive social change and match their efforts with more general environmental aims by adopting these concepts.

There is no shortage of research on how a green culture may boost employee engagement and corporate success. Several case studies demonstrate the beneficial effects of sustainability programs on workplace dynamics and business outcomes.

Patagonia, a well-known outdoor clothing brand with a strong dedication to environmental responsibility, is one prominent example. Patagonia uses recycled materials in their products and promotes environmental protection as part of its commitment to sustainability. The workplace rules of the company, which prioritize work-life balance through flexible scheduling options and offer paid time off for environmental volunteering, clearly reflect its green culture.

Studies on Patagonia's sustainability strategy have shown how well it works for both business success and employee engagement. In comparison to industry averages, employees at Patagonia reported better levels of inspiration, dedication, and job satisfaction, according to a study published in the Journal of Management Inquiry. The company's strong environmental ideals struck a chord with staff members and encouraged a sense of purpose and pride in their job, which was credited with this increased involvement.

In addition, Patagonia's eco-friendly efforts have improved the company's financial results. Through investments in waste reduction initiatives, supply chain transparency, and energy efficiency measures, the company has improved operating efficiency, boosted its brand, and realized cost savings. For example, Patagonia's "Worn Wear" initiative encourages apparel repair and reuse, which not only lessens its impact on the environment but also fosters consumer loyalty and repeat business.

The advantages of adopting a green culture are also evident in Interface Inc., a multinational producer of modular carpet tiles. Inspired by its founder Ray Anderson's goal of turning Interface into a "restorative enterprise" that gives back more to the environment than it takes, the company set out on a sustainability journey in the 1990s. The business established challenging sustainability targets, such as supporting renewable energy sources, cutting greenhouse gas emissions, and reaching zero waste.

Studies on Interface's environmental initiatives have shown how well they work to increase employee satisfaction and corporate success. The company's sustainability measures have led to increased job satisfaction, commitment, and pride among Interface employees, according to a study published in the Journal of Organizational Behaviour. The mission of Interface motivated staff members and gave them the confidence to support environmental objectives in their day-to-day work.

Furthermore, Interface's dedication to sustainability has produced important financial gains, improved brand recognition, and operational efficiencies. The company has improved profitability and minimized its environmental impact by working with suppliers, revamping products, and streamlining manufacturing processes. For example, Interface saved millions of dollars in material costs and achieved a 90% decrease in trash shipped to landfills thanks to their "Mission Zero" campaign.

In conclusion, actual companies like Interface and Patagonia show how a green culture can improve worker satisfaction and business performance. Incorporating sustainability into their operations has allowed these businesses to lessen their environmental effect while also giving their staff members a feeling of pride, direction, and inspiration. Additionally, their sustainability initiatives have resulted in measurable financial gains, improved brand recognition, and operational efficiencies. These illustrations highlight how crucial it is to foster a green culture in order to achieve desired commercial and environmental results.

Chapter - 3

Green Job Analysis and Design

Introduction to Green Job Analysis:

Organizations are realizing more and more that their workforce planning and employment analysis procedures need to take environmental factors into account in this day of sustainability and environmental consciousness. A process known as "green job analysis" enables firms to pinpoint and specify internal roles that support environmental sustainability objectives and projects.

Green job analysis is the process of assessing current positions or developing new ones with an emphasis on corporate social responsibility (CSR) and environmental sustainability. It seeks to define the competencies knowledge, skills, and abilities needed for roles supporting the organization's sustainability initiatives.

We will examine the main ideas, tenets, and advantages of integrating environmental concerns into job analysis procedures in this introduction to green job analysis. We'll talk about how businesses may utilize green job analysis to encourage environmental stewardship, match workers with sustainability objectives, and produce favourable environmental results.

Organizations can improve their environmental performance and develop a more engaged and motivated workforce by implementing green job analysis practices. The goal of green job analysis is to build a sustainable culture that permeates every area of an organization's operations and to link corporate objectives with environmental ideals. It goes beyond simply describing job roles.

Meaning of Green Job Analysis:

The process of assessing and defining job functions within an organization with an emphasis on corporate social responsibility (CSR) and environmental sustainability is known as "green job analysis." It entails locating and evaluating jobs that support organizational sustainability goals, initiatives, and practices.

Assessing how different work functions affect the environment, finding ways to incorporate sustainability into job responsibilities, and defining the competencies knowledge, skills, and abilities needed for tasks that promote environmental stewardship are the goals of green job analysis. Organizations can use this study to better connect their staff with sustainability goals, encourage eco-friendly behaviour, and produce good environmental results.

Organizations can discover positions like sustainability coordinators, environmental engineers, or renewable energy specialists that directly contribute to environmental sustainability through green job analysis. It also enables companies to assess current employment positions and find ways to incorporate sustainability concerns into duties, responsibilities, and performance standards. All things considered, green job analysis is a crucial tool for businesses looking to integrate environmental factors into their personnel management, organizational growth, and workforce planning initiatives. It assists businesses in developing a workforce capable of tackling environmental issues, advancing sustainable practices, and making a positive impact on the environment in the future.

Definition of Green Job Analysis:

"The process of locating, assessing, and classifying jobs that support resource efficiency, environmental sustainability, and the shift to a low-carbon economy is known as green job analysis."

Introduction to Green Job Design:

A complex strategic approach, "green job design" includes the intentional incorporation of social responsibility and environmental sustainability into the planning and development of career prospects. This proactive approach seeks to create roles and organizational structures that support a strong commitment to reducing environmental impact and advancing conservation initiatives, while also giving priority to eco-friendly methods, renewable resources, and ethical considerations. Businesses and organizations can link their operations with sustainable development goals and help to move towards a more socially just and ecologically balanced economy by adopting green job design concepts. This all-encompassing strategy includes a number of aspects, such as identifying jobs that have a direct impact on environmental sustainability, integrating sustainability principles into current job roles, encouraging equity and inclusivity in the workforce, and developing an environmental stewardship-focused corporate culture. Green employment design paves the way for a more sustainable future for future generations by promoting social cohesion, economic prosperity, and environmental resilience through coordinated efforts.

Meaning of Green Job Design:

A strategic method of creating jobs, "green job design" places an emphasis on social responsibility, environmental sustainability, and economic feasibility. It entails incorporating sustainability concepts into job descriptions, hierarchies, and operational procedures. Fundamentally, the goal of green employment design is to solve the urgent problems caused by resource depletion, environmental degradation, and climate change.

Organizations can lessen their environmental effect while also promoting social progress and economic success by designing jobs with eco-friendly techniques, renewable resources, and ethical issues in mind. This all-encompassing strategy includes a number of aspects, such as the recognition and cultivation of positions that directly support environmental sustainability. Jobs in waste management, green building, sustainable agriculture, and environmental conservation are a few examples of these.

Green job design includes not only the creation of new jobs but also the incorporation of sustainability concepts into current positions in a variety of industries. This may entail putting into effect eco-friendly procedures including waste management plans, energy-saving techniques, and ecologically conscious purchase procedures. Organizations can reduce their ecological footprint, possibly save operating expenses, and improve their reputation as socially conscious businesses by implementing these approaches into job design.

Moreover, green job design highlights how critical it is to advance inclusivity and equity in the workforce. This entails making sure that people from a variety of communities and backgrounds, especially those who have historically been excluded or underrepresented in the labour market, may access green jobs. Organizations can promote increased social cohesion and guarantee that the advantages of environmental sustainability are distributed fairly among all members of society by giving equality in job design top priority.

All things considered, green job design is an aggressive strategy for tackling social and environmental issues while fostering economic growth. A more resilient, egalitarian, and sustainable future for future generations can be built by businesses and policymakers by incorporating sustainability principles into job positions and organizational structures.

Definition of Green Job Design:
"Green job design is the process of creating employment that minimizes its negative effects on the environment and encourages sustainability."

Concept of Green Job Analysis and Design
The process of analysing and designing green employment is complex and involves a thorough evaluation of different work functions in different industries to find ways to integrate ecologically sustainable practices. To fully grasp their environmental implications and possible areas for improvement, this requires digging deeply into the nuances of work activities, resource consumption patterns, waste management techniques, energy utilization, and emissions profiles.

The first stage of this endeavour usually entails performing extensive evaluations of current positions within companies. The purpose of this assessment is to evaluate each role's environmental impact by looking at things like energy use, waste production, raw material use, and greenhouse gas emissions. Businesses can identify opportunities to develop, improve, or extend eco-friendly operations by closely examining these factors.

Additionally, the analysis includes a review of the possible effects of green job redesign on productivity, bottom-line performance, and overall organizational operations. This means taking into account elements including stakeholder perceptions, market competitiveness, efficiency improvements, and cost consequences. Organizations can gain a full grasp of the potential and difficulties related to the shift to greener employment roles by conducting a thorough assessment of these aspects.

The next step is to strategically create green employment roles after the analytical phase has highlighted opportunities for improvement. Creating job descriptions that highlight environmental sustainability while still being in line with overarching company objectives is part of this approach. This could entail developing brand-new job responsibilities specifically for sustainability projects, changing current jobs to include green practices, or incorporating sustainability competencies into already-existing job functions, depending on the unique requirements and circumstances of each firm.

It's essential to take a comprehensive strategy to creating green jobs, taking into account social and economic factors in addition to environmental ones. This means considering the welfare of workers, nearby communities, and the larger ecosystem in which businesses function. Through the cultivation of a mutually beneficial association among environmental conservation, social accountability, and financial success, enterprises can generate enduring value that confers advantages to the environment and the broader community.

A broad range of sectors and work functions are represented by examples of green employment jobs. These could include coordinators of sustainability who oversee and carry out environmental projects for businesses, technicians of renewable energy who install and maintain solar panels or wind turbines, waste reduction experts who devise plans to reduce waste generation and encourage recycling, and environmental compliance officers who make sure rules are followed.

In summary, for businesses looking to embrace sustainability and promote environmental change, analysing and creating green jobs is a strategic requirement. Businesses may reduce their environmental effect, improve their reputation as ethical corporate citizens, and support the group effort to create a more sustainable future for future generations by incorporating eco-friendly practices into different job responsibilities.

3.1 Job Analysis for Environmental Impact

An in-depth investigation of the roles and duties within businesses is necessary to fully grasp the job analysis's substantial effects on the environment. It is a laborious and rigorous process. It comprises determining the activities, responsibilities, duties, and necessary skills connected with each employment post through a thorough and methodical examination in order to determine the direct and indirect consequences on environmental sustainability.

The fundamental goal of job analysis for environmental impact is to locate, assess, and lessen any negative environmental effects that may arise from organizational operations. This is a complex undertaking that involves examining a number of factors, including the use of natural resources, energy consumption patterns, waste generation and management techniques, emissions, and the total environmental impact linked to individual job functions.

Organizations may obtain vital insights into the environmental effects of their operations at the specific job function level by carrying out an extensive job analysis. This makes it possible for them to create focused plans and programs that are meant to lessen adverse effects on the environment and promote sustainable practices in every aspect of their business.

Usually, the process starts with the methodical gathering of information about job tasks and responsibilities using a range of techniques, such as surveys, interviews, observation, and a careful examination of the documentation that already exists. After a thorough analysis of this abundance of data, actions and activities that could have a good or negative impact on the environment are identified.

After identifying possible environmental implications, job analysts carefully evaluate the skills, knowledge, and abilities needed to carry out these duties efficiently. They closely examine if current work positions are in line with the organization's objectives for environmental sustainability. This critical evaluation could include finding knowledge or skill gaps regarding environmental practices and if more training or skill development programs are required.

Moreover, industry standards, best practices for environmental management and sustainability, and legal requirements are all considered while doing a work analysis for environmental effect. This guarantees that job responsibilities are carefully crafted to adhere to pertinent environmental legislation and guidelines and support more general company environmental stewardship goals.

The results of environmental effect job analyses are crucial for many HR tasks, including as training and development, performance management, hiring, and selection. Environmental sustainability-related duties can be specifically included in job descriptions with great care, and applicants with the necessary training and expertise can be given preference throughout the recruitment and selection process.

To evaluate employees' contributions to environmental sustainability, performance management systems can also include precise environmental performance measures and goals. Training and development plans can be carefully crafted to give staff members the information and abilities they need to reduce environmental effects in their jobs.

To summarize, the process of job analysis for environmental impact is a complicated and vital tool that helps organizations fully comprehend and manage the environmental effects of their operations at the individual job level. Organizations can support their sustainability initiatives, reduce adverse environmental effects, and actively contribute to a more environmentally conscious future by carefully assessing employment roles and responsibilities in terms of their environmental repercussions.

3.1.1 Understanding the Importance of Job Analysis in Assessing the Environmental Impact of Different Roles within an Organization

As a comprehensive procedure that is essential to organizational management, job analysis includes a multidimensional investigation of different aspects related to certain tasks in an organization. It entails a methodical examination and assessment of each job's related activities, responsibilities, abilities, knowledge, and environmental impact. When evaluating the environmental impact of various tasks within a company, job analysis becomes a crucial instrument for fully comprehending, measuring, and tackling the ecological footprint that is inherent in every role.

First of all, job analysis carefully dissects jobs and activities into their component parts, delving into the minute details of work functions. Organizations can identify specific behaviours and procedures that have an influence on the environment, either directly or indirectly, by conducting this thorough study. Organizations can identify places where environmental resources, including raw materials, energy, or water, are used, consumed excessively, or possibly wasted by closely examining the components of the task. Organizations receive priceless insights into the exact environmental effects of every employment role through this detailed study, which paves the way for well-informed decisions about resource management plans and sustainability projects.

Secondly, job analysis makes it easier to conduct a thorough evaluation of the abilities, know-how, and skills needed to carry out the work well. Organizations can find ways to include sustainability and environmental consciousness into staff training and development programs by knowing the skill set required to perform job duties. Businesses enable their workforce to embrace eco-friendly practices by raising employee awareness of environmental issues and providing them with the skills and knowledge they need. This creates an environment of environmental stewardship and encourages sustainable behaviour within the company.

An essential first step in finding ways to improve resource efficiency and reduce environmental impact in organizational operations is job analysis. Organizations can find inefficiencies, redundancies, and areas for development that directly impact environmental sustainability by closely analysing job processes, workflows, and procedures. In line with the organization's overall sustainability goals and objectives, this thorough evaluation enables the identification of strategies targeted at maximizing resource utilization, decreasing waste generation, and mitigating adverse environmental effects associated with particular job roles.

Additionally, job analysis makes it easier to create and carry out focused environmental policies, initiatives, and programs that are made to meet the particular environmental opportunities and difficulties connected to certain job functions. Businesses can create and execute policies and processes that encourage environmentally conscious behaviour among employees by knowing the particular environmental implications of each role. Establishing guidelines for sustainable procurement practices, offering incentives for energy conservation efforts, or incorporating environmental performance metrics into employee performance reviews are just a few examples of the many actions that these initiatives may take to promote sustainable and environmentally conscious culture at all organizational levels.

All things considered, employment analysis is essential to developing a sustainable and environmentally conscious culture in businesses. Job analysis helps firms develop and implement policies aimed at lowering ecological footprint, conserving natural resources, and promoting sustainable practices throughout the workforce by offering thorough insights into the environmental impact of various job positions. By taking a proactive stance, companies not only help the environment but also reap concrete advantages like lower expenses, improved public perception, and long-term commercial sustainability. This guarantees their success and sustainability in an increasingly ecologically aware world.

3.1.2 Methods and Tools for Conducting a Green Job Analysis, Including Job Description Analysis, Task Analysis, and Competency Mapping

Organizations that want to incorporate sustainability principles into their workforce and operations must conduct a comprehensive green job analysis. Employers can efficiently hire, train, and develop staff to meet environmental goals by knowing the unique requirements, tasks, and abilities associated with green jobs. I'll go into more detail about each facet of green job analysis, look at some other techniques and resources, and talk about how crucial it is to integrate sustainability concepts into workforce planning and development plans in this longer explanation.

1. Job Description Analysis:
The basis of green job analysis is job description analysis, which sheds light on the duties, responsibilities, and credentials needed for jobs in

environmentally conscious businesses or sectors. Several important factors need to be taken into account when examining job descriptions for green jobs:

i. **Identification of Green Roles:** Start by determining which jobs directly support environmental sustainability or call for particular knowledge of green practices. Jobs in green building, waste management, sustainable agriculture, renewable energy, and environmental conservation might fall under this category.

ii. **Incorporating Sustainability Criteria:** Include sustainability requirements in standard job descriptions, such as familiarity with eco-friendly technologies, understanding of environmental rules, or a dedication to lowering carbon emissions. Emphasize your obligations regarding resource conservation, climate action, and environmental responsibility.

iii. **Alignment with Organizational Goals:** Verify that job descriptions correspond with the organization's overarching sustainability goals and programs. In your job descriptions, stress the value of sustainability and explain how each position fits into the organization's efforts to uphold social responsibility and environmental performance.

iv. **Language and Tone:** Make sure your words and tone convey the organization's dedication to sustainability. Stress the benefits of green jobs and the role that environmental stewardship plays in drawing and keeping great personnel.

Through the application of a green lens to job descriptions, firms can make clear the needs and standards for green occupations, draw in individuals with the necessary training and expertise, and show potential employees and stakeholders how committed they are to environmental sustainability.

2. Task Analysis:

Task analysis is the process of dissecting work roles into discrete actions, processes, and tasks in order to determine how each task affects the environment and determine whether there are any chances to integrate sustainability principles. The following actions can be taken when performing task analysis for green jobs:

i. **Task Identification:** Determine the main responsibilities and duties connected to every position in the company. This could entail going to work and seeing how people work, interviewing or surveying them, and going over records like standard operating procedures.

ii. **Environmental Impact Assessment:** Evaluate each task's environmental impact by taking into account variables including emissions, pollution, waste generation, energy consumption, and resource usage. Ascertain which tasks have the biggest impact on the environment and rank the areas that need improvement.

iii. **Sustainability Integration:** Find ways to incorporate sustainable practices into work duties and procedures. This can entail putting energy-saving technology into practice, using less water, producing less trash, obtaining environmentally friendly products, and choosing environmentally friendly modes of transportation.

iv. **Efficiency and Optimization:** Seek methods to increase work tasks' efficacy and efficiency while reducing their negative effects on the environment. Think of substitute techniques, tools, or strategies that need less energy or produce fewer emissions while producing comparable results.

Organizations can find ways to green their operations, lessen their ecological impact, and encourage environmental responsibility among staff members by undertaking task analysis via a sustainability lens.

3. Competency Mapping:

Competency mapping entails determining the knowledge, skills, and abilities (KSAs) necessary for effective performance in green employment as well as evaluating employees' current competencies to find gaps and areas in need of development. The following actions can be conducted to map competencies for green jobs:

i. **Identification of Green Competencies:** Determine the particular talents needed for green professions, such as technical understanding of sustainability and environmental science, hands-on experience with eco-friendly technology and practices, and behavioural abilities like flexibility, creativity, and teamwork.

ii. **Assessment of Current Competencies:** Evaluate current staff competencies to find gaps, areas of strength, and areas of weakness with regard to green work needs. This could entail performing competency-based interviews, performance reviews, or skills assessments.

iii. **Development of Competency Frameworks:** Create competency models or frameworks specific to green jobs and industries. The key competencies for success in green jobs should be outlined in these frameworks, along with suggestions on how staff members might gradually acquire and exhibit these competencies.

iv. **Training and Development Initiatives:** In order to close competency gaps and improve staff members' knowledge, skills, and talents in green fields, put training and development efforts into action. Formal training courses, seminars, workshops, on-the-job training, and certifications in fields linked to sustainability are a few examples of this.

Organizations may make sure that their staff has the skills and knowledge needed to support environmental sustainability goals and promote positive change within the company and the society at large by investing in employee development and mapping competences for green occupations.

Additional Methods and Tools:

A thorough green job analysis can be carried out using a number of other techniques and instruments in addition to task analysis, competency mapping, and job description analysis:

i. **Environmental Impact Assessments:** To examine how organizational actions, projects, or policies will affect the environment, conduct environmental impact assessments. These evaluations support the identification of possible environmental hazards, areas for development, and methods for reducing adverse effects.

ii. **Life Cycle Assessments (LCAs):** To examine the environmental effects connected to a product, process, or service's whole life cycle, use life cycle evaluations. LCAs offer information on hotspots for environmental issues as well as chances for eco-design, resource efficiency, and waste minimization.

iii. **Sustainability Metrics and Indicators:** Create and apply sustainability metrics and indicators to monitor and assess the advancement of environmental sustainability objectives. Indicators of waste production, energy and water use, greenhouse gas emissions, biodiversity preservation, and social equality are a few examples of these measurements.

iv. **Job Analysis Software:** Employ software tools for job analysis to expedite the procedure of gathering, examining, and deciphering information pertaining to green jobs. To assist in making decisions based on evidence, these software programs may have features like task libraries, competency dictionaries, job description templates, and reporting tools.

v. **Stakeholder Engagement:** Involve stakeholders in the green job analysis process, such as staff members, clients, vendors, government agencies, non-governmental organizations (NGOs), and local residents. In order to guarantee that the analysis takes into account a variety of viewpoints and priorities, solicit input, feedback, and cooperation.

Importance of Green Job Analysis:

Conducting a green job analysis is crucial for organizations for several reasons:

1. Talent Acquisition and Retention: Employers can draw and keep top personnel with a passion for sustainability by establishing green employment roles, responsibilities, and requirements explicitly.

2. Operational Efficiency: Using a sustainability lens to analyse work tasks and procedures can help find ways to cut waste, increase productivity, and save operating expenses.

3. Environmental Impact Reduction: Organizations can reduce their environmental impact and make a valuable contribution to wider environmental conservation initiatives by incorporating sustainability principles into occupational activities and procedures.

4. Compliance and Risk Management: Organizations can detect and reduce compliance risks with regard to environmental rules, standards, and industry best practices by having a thorough understanding of the environmental impact of occupational operations.

5. Corporate Reputation and Brand Image: By using green job analysis to show that a business is committed to environmental sustainability, it can improve its reputation, fortify its brand, and win over stakeholders' trust.

6. Innovation and Adaptation: Green job analysis encourages workers to investigate and use sustainable practices, technologies, and solutions, thereby promoting a culture of creativity and adaptability. Organizations may remain ahead of the curve and promote good change in their sectors by consistently modifying employment responsibilities and procedures to correspond with shifting environmental challenges and possibilities.

7. Supply Chain Resilience: Organizations can find opportunities to improve resilience to environmental disruptions and vulnerabilities by analysing the environmental impact of work activities along the supply chain. Organizations can create a more resilient and sustainable supply chain by working with partners and suppliers to implement sustainable practices and lessen reliance on limited resources.

8. Regulatory Compliance: By verifying that work roles and activities comply with industry guidelines and regulatory criteria, green job analysis helps firms maintain compliance with environmental rules, laws, and standards. Through proactive measures like as job design, training, and monitoring, firms can mitigate the legal risks and harm to their brand that come with non-compliance with environmental regulations.

9. Employee Engagement and Satisfaction: Encouraging work that is meaningful and in line with employees' values and goals is achieved by incorporating sustainability into employment tasks and responsibilities. Organizations can cultivate a sense of purpose, pride, and loyalty among their workforce by enabling employees to make a positive impact on environmental sustainability through their work.

10. Risk Mitigation and Resilience: Green job analysis assists businesses in identifying and reducing environmental risks that could have an impact on their operations, supply chains, and reputation. These risks include pollution, resource scarcity, ecosystem deterioration, and the effects of climate change. Organizations can enhance their ability to withstand shocks and uncertainties in the environment by taking proactive measures to mitigate these risks, such as job redesign, training, and emergency preparation.

11. Community Engagement and Partnerships: Green job analysis gives businesses the chance to interact with academic institutions, government agencies, non-profits, and local communities to solve environmental issues and generate shared value. Organizations can cultivate relationships with stakeholders, promote trust, and strengthen programs by working together on community development, training, and green job creation projects.

12. Market Differentiation and Competitive Advantage: Organizations can get a competitive edge and stand out from the competition by showcasing their dedication to environmental sustainability through green job analysis. Businesses may draw in environmentally concerned partners, investors, and customers by touting their green credentials to stakeholders, investors, and customers. They may also establish a reputation as an ethical and progressive leader in their sector.

In general, firms can use green job analysis as a strategic tool to boost innovation and competitiveness, match their personnel with sustainability objectives, and have a good social and environmental impact. Organizations may help create a more resilient and sustainable future for future generations by investing in green jobs and training a trained and enthusiastic workforce.

3.1.3 Case Studies Showcasing How Organizations Have Utilised Job Analysis to Identify Areas for Improvement in Environmental Sustainability

- Procter & Gamble (P&G) provides an excellent real-life case study of how organizations have utilized job analysis to identify areas for improvement in environmental sustainability:

Case Study: Procter & Gamble (P&G)

Background:
Multinational consumer Products Corporation P&G is well-known for its various brands, including Gillette, Pampers, and Tide. In an effort to be more sustainable, P&G has established high standards for lowering the environmental impact of all of its business processes.

Problem:
P&G recognized the need to step up its efforts to be environmentally sustainable, especially in the areas of supply chain management and manufacturing.

Solution:
In order to comprehend how various jobs and responsibilities contributed to environmental effect and identify areas for improvement, P&G started a comprehensive job analysis program.

Implementation:
1. Job Analysis Process: P&G carried out in-depth job studies across a number of divisions, including operations, supply chain, manufacturing, and research and development. Examining the duties, responsibilities, and conduct of workers at various organizational levels was necessary for this.

2. Identification of Environmental Impact: P&G conducted a job study to pinpoint particular duties and procedures that had a big impact on the environment, like emissions, water and energy use, trash production, and energy use.

3. Opportunity Identification: P&G found ways to enhance environmental sustainability by applying the knowledge gathered from employment analysis. For instance, they found ways to maximize resource efficiency across their processes, decrease waste production, improve energy utilization, and cut down on water consumption.

4. Development of Sustainability Initiatives: P&G created focused sustainability activities to address highlighted areas for improvement based on the job analysis's findings. Among these efforts were the following:

- Equipping production facilities with energy-efficient technologies and procedures.

- Improving packaging designs to cut down on waste and material consumption.

- Increasing supply chain effectiveness to reduce emissions associated with transportation.

- Making investments in green energy to lessen carbon emissions.

5. Employee Training and Engagement: In order to promote a sustainable culture, P&G involved staff members at all levels and incorporated sustainability concepts into training programs for staff members. They promoted staff participation in sustainability projects, offered training on sustainable methods, and honoured and recognized sustainability accomplishments.

Results:

P&G made great strides toward lowering its environmental impact by using employment analysis to pinpoint opportunities for environmental sustainability improvement and putting focused initiatives into action. The business managed to:

- Reduce manufacturing and operational energy use and greenhouse gas emissions.

- Lower water use and increase water efficiency throughout the organization's facilities.

- Reduce the amount of waste produced by using efficient procedures and packaging.

- Increase the sustainability of the supply chain by cutting transportation-related emissions and increasing efficiency.

All things considered, P&G's use of employment analysis to propel environmental sustainability initiatives shows how businesses may take use of insights into work roles and responsibilities to find areas for improvement and make significant strides toward sustainability objectives.

- Here's a case study of how Google utilized job analysis to identify areas for improvement in environmental sustainability:

Case Study: Google

Background:
Leading internet giant Google runs data canters all over the world to support its wide range of online services. Both their energy consumption and environmental impact are huge for these data canters.

Problem:
In order to lower energy costs and lessen its carbon impact, Google realized that improving the environmental sustainability of its data canter operations was necessary.

Solution:
Google initiated a thorough job analysis program to pinpoint opportunities for enhancing environmental sustainability in its data canters.

Implementation:
1. Job Analysis Process: For a number of positions in its data canter operations, including operators, engineers, and technicians, Google performed thorough job studies. This required looking at the duties, responsibilities, and conduct of workers who manage and maintain the infrastructure of data canters.

2. Identification of Environmental Impact: Google conducted a job analysis to determine whether particular tasks and procedures within its data canters contributed to energy consumption and environmental impact. This covered tasks like facility management, server upkeep, and cooling system administration.

3. Opportunity Identification: Google looked for ways to improve environmental sustainability using the information gathered from employment analysis. For instance, they found ways to streamline resource consumption, enhance cooling effectiveness, and optimize energy utilization across the board for their data canter operations.

4. Development of Sustainability Initiatives: Google created focused sustainability initiatives to address highlighted areas for improvement based on the results of the job analysis. Among these initiatives were:

- Putting cutting-edge cooling technology into practice to increase energy economy.

- Reducing energy usage through workload control and server setup optimization.

- Utilizing renewable energy sources, such solar and wind, to power data canter operations.

- Creating cutting-edge data canter designs that put sustainability and energy efficiency first.

5. Employee Training and Engagement: Google engaged the workforce of its data canters and incorporated sustainability principles into employee training programs to encourage an environmentally conscious culture. They recognized and rewarded sustainability accomplishments, encouraged staff participation in sustainability projects, and offered training on energy-saving techniques.

Results:
Google has reduced the environmental effect of its data canter operations by using job analysis to identify areas for improvement in environmental sustainability and implementing focused initiatives. The business managed to:

- Lower energy usage and increase energy efficiency throughout its data canters.

- In order to fuel data canter operations, more renewable energy sources should be used.

- Cut back on water use and make cooling system improvements to lessen your environmental impact.

- Put into effect environmentally conscious and efficient data canter designs and procedures.

All things considered, Google's use of job analysis to propel environmental sustainability initiatives shows how businesses can take advantage of insights into job roles and responsibilities to find areas for improvement and make significant progress toward sustainability objectives, even in extremely specialized and technical settings like data centre operations.

- Here's a case study of how Unilever utilized job analysis to improve environmental sustainability:

Case Study: Unilever

Background:
Multinational consumer goods manufacturer Unilever offers a variety of commodities in the food, personal care, and home care areas. The business is committed to sustainability, seeking to lessen the impact it has on the environment throughout its supply chain and operations.

Problem:
Unilever recognized the necessity of augmenting its endeavours towards environmental sustainability, specifically in relation to its supply chain operations.

Solution:
In order to comprehend how various positions and responsibilities contributed to environmental effect and to discover areas for improvement, Unilever started a comprehensive job analysis exercise.

Implementation:
1. Job Analysis Process: Throughout its supply chain, Unilever performed thorough job analysis in the areas of manufacturing, distribution, procurement, and logistics. This required looking at the duties, responsibilities, and actions of workers engaged in various supply chain phases.

2. Identification of Environmental Impact: Unilever conducted a job analysis to identify particular jobs and processes that had a substantial impact on the environment. These included energy use, trash generation, and emissions related to transportation and logistics.

3. **Opportunity Identification:** Unilever identified areas for environmental sustainability development by utilizing the insights gathered from job analysis. For instance, they found ways to streamline shipping routes, cut down on fuel use, cut down on packaging waste, and support environmentally friendly sourcing methods.

4. **Development of Sustainability Initiatives**: Unilever created focused sustainability efforts to address highlighted areas for improvement based on the results of the job analysis. Among these initiatives were:

   - Putting into practice sustainable sourcing methods to lessen the raw material procurement process's negative environmental effects.
   - Minimizing carbon emissions and lessening environmental impact through distribution and transportation process optimization.
   - Rethinking the materials and designs of packaging in order to minimize waste and encourage recycling.
   - Encouraging partners and suppliers to implement sustainable practices all the way through the supply chain.

5. **Employee Training and Engagement:** In order to promote an environmentally conscious culture, Unilever involved staff members at all levels and incorporated sustainability concepts into employee training initiatives. They promoted staff participation in sustainability projects, offered training on sustainable methods, and honoured and recognized sustainability accomplishments.

Results:

Unilever made great strides in lowering its environmental footprint throughout its supply chain by using job analysis to pinpoint areas for environmental sustainability improvement and putting focused strategies into action. The business managed to:

- Cut down on the carbon emissions that come from distribution and transportation.
- Reduce waste production by using sustainable procurement methods and optimized packaging.

Principles of Green HRM

- Encourage partners and suppliers to follow sustainable practices all the way through the supply chain.

- Encourage a culture of environmental responsibility among staff members to boost involvement and engagement in sustainability programs.

Altogether, Unilever's application of job analysis to environmental sustainability projects shows how businesses can make use of understandings of job roles and responsibilities to find areas for development and make significant strides toward sustainability objectives, especially in the context of intricate supply chain operations.

3.2 Designing Green Job Roles and Responsibilities

The process of creating green employment roles and responsibilities is complex and requires careful planning, analysis, and execution to successfully incorporate sustainable practices into many areas of a business. Developing green jobs has become a critical strategy for governments, corporations, and non-profit organizations alike in the modern world of growing environmental concerns and pressing climate action.

Sustainability Officers and Managers are at the forefront of this initiative; their main duty is to spearhead the creation and implementation of sustainability strategies that are customized to the unique requirements and goals of their company. These experts carry out thorough evaluations of the company's environmental impact, pinpoint areas in need of development, and create workable plans to improve sustainability performance throughout the company's supply chains, operations, and product life cycles. Moreover, they are instrumental in cultivating a climate of environmental consciousness and accountability among staff members, stakeholders, and the general public.

Parallel to this, the move toward clean and renewable energy sources is greatly aided by specialists in renewable energy. Utilizing their technical proficiency, these specialists appraise the viability of renewable energy initiatives, weigh the advantages and disadvantages of each, and offer suggestions for incorporating renewable energy technology into the company's energy mix. To lessen dependency on fossil fuels and reduce greenhouse gas emissions, Renewable Energy Specialists investigate a wide range of renewable energy options, from solar and wind to hydropower and geothermal.

In the context of sustainability, waste reduction managers play a crucial role as well. They work to reduce waste production, encourage recycling and reuse, and maximize resource use across the board. These experts create customized waste reduction plans, work with internal and external partners to adopt sustainable waste management techniques, and carry out thorough waste audits to find inefficiencies and areas for development. Waste Reduction Managers conduct programs including material recovery facilities, composting, and circular economy efforts, among others, to reduce environmental impact while also opening up cost-saving opportunities for the firm.

Eco-design engineers, who specialize in creating infrastructure, buildings, and products with sustainability as a core principle, offer a special combination of technical know-how and creative vision to the table. To reduce environmental effect and optimize resource efficiency, these professionals include eco-design principles, such as life cycle assessment, material efficiency, and integration of renewable energy, into the design and development process. The built environment is significantly shaped by eco-design engineers, who use sustainable materials and provide energy-efficient design solutions to support sustainable development objectives.

By guaranteeing compliance with environmental laws, guidelines, and best practices, environmental compliance analysts complete the range of green employment positions. These experts carry out comprehensive compliance evaluations, keep an eye on regulatory modifications, and offer advice on legal duties and requirements pertaining to sustainability and environmental protection. Environmental Compliance Analysts help reduce legal risks, maintain organizational integrity, and show a commitment to corporate responsibility and environmental stewardship by proactively addressing compliance issues.

To put it briefly, creating green employment roles and responsibilities requires a comprehensive strategy that integrates organizational participation, technological know-how, and strategic planning in order to effectively promote change toward a more sustainable future. Organizations may establish themselves as leaders in sustainability and foster innovation, resilience, and long-term value generation by developing a broad talent pool with the know-how to address environmental concerns.

3.2.1 The Process of Designing Job Roles and Responsibilities with a Focus on Environmental Sustainability

Creating organized frameworks and policies that imbue positions within an organization with a conscious commitment to reducing adverse environmental consequences is a necessary step in designing job roles and duties with an emphasis on environmental sustainability. This means carefully creating detailed job descriptions, task descriptions, and performance expectations that flow naturally from overarching sustainability goals. Every aspect of a job function, from strategic decision-making and managerial responsibilities to procurement and operational tasks, is imbued with sustainability concepts. The primary objective is to cultivate a climate of environmental stewardship in which staff members are aware of and actively involved in promoting sustainable practices, therefore guaranteeing that the company runs in balance with the environment while pursuing operational excellence.

- ❖ **Designing job roles and responsibilities with a focus on environmental sustainability involves several steps:**

Step-1. Assessment: Assess the company's present environmental effect and pinpoint areas that need improvement. This could involve the use of water, electricity, and waste management, among other things.

Step-2. Goal Setting: Set definite targets and goals for incorporating sustainability into job responsibilities. These objectives must be time-bound, meaningful, quantifiable, achievable, and targeted (SMART).

Step-3. Research and Benchmarking: Examine industry best practices and compare yourself to rivals to see how similar businesses are promoting environmental sustainability in their work.

Step-4. Collaboration: Involve pertinent parties, such as staff members, supervisors, specialists in environmental issues, and potentially outside consultants, to obtain a range of viewpoints and knowledge.

Step-5. Job Analysis: Examine current work tasks and responsibilities in detail to find ways to incorporate sustainability issues. Revisions to duties, performance measures, and job descriptions might be necessary for this.

Step-6. Training and Development: To guarantee that staff members have the information and abilities needed to successfully carry out their sustainability-related duties, offer training and development opportunities.

Step-7. Integration: Update job descriptions, include duties and goals relevant to sustainability in performance reviews, and match incentives with environmental goals to incorporate sustainability principles into work roles.

Step-8. Monitoring and Evaluation: Establish systems for tracking the accomplishment of sustainability objectives and assessing the success of redefining work roles and responsibilities. Review often and make adjustments as necessary.

Step-9. Communication and Engagement: Employees and stakeholders should be made aware of the value of sustainability, and they should be actively involved in programs that encourage environmental responsibility in their jobs.

Step-10. Continuous Improvement: To further strengthen environmental sustainability initiatives, cultivate a culture of continuous improvement by asking for feedback, taking lessons from successes and mistakes, and modifying job duties and responsibilities accordingly.

3.2.2 Incorporating Green Principles into Job Design

A complex process, including environmental concerns and sustainable practices into different organizational processes is involved in incorporating green principles into job design. Fundamentally, this idea highlights how crucial it is to advance environmental stewardship, waste minimization, and resource efficiency within the parameters of job tasks and responsibilities. We will examine the need of integrating green ideas into job design, the essential components required, and the advantages it offers to enterprises and the larger ecosystem in this thorough investigation.

Job design is, at its core, the act of arranging and arranging duties, responsibilities, and connections in the workplace in order to effectively and efficiently accomplish particular goals. Historically, the main goals of work design have been to maximize performance, productivity, and employee happiness. Nonetheless, there is a rising understanding of the necessity of incorporating sustainability concepts into work design procedures in light of the mounting environmental difficulties and concerns.

Resource Efficiency

The core of green job design is resource efficiency. Through efficient utilization of resources like energy, water, raw materials, and other inputs, companies can decrease waste, lower expenses, and have a smaller environmental impact. When resource-efficient approaches are integrated into job design, processes are evaluated and redesigned to get rid of waste, optimize workflows, and get the most out of the resources that are available. This can entail putting in place programs for recycling and reuse, integrating energy-efficient technology, and streamlining supply chain operations to utilize less resources.

Waste Reduction

Waste reduction is another key feature of green job design. Traditional production and consumption methods typically result in large waste generation, which raises environmental problems and leads to resource depletion. Organizations may reduce waste at every stage of the value chain by integrating waste reduction tactics into job design. This could entail creating systems for trash segregation and recycling, engineering items to be more robust and recyclable, and encouraging an attitude of waste avoidance and reduction among staff members.

Environmental Stewardship

The dedication to safeguarding and conserving the natural environment is referred to as environmental stewardship. Environmental stewardship in the context of job design is incorporating sustainability concerns into operational procedures and decision-making processes. This entails actively searching out chances to positively contribute to environmental conservation efforts in addition to reducing negative environmental impacts. Encouraging sustainable land use practices, supporting biodiversity conservation programs, and putting green procurement rules into place are a few examples of environmental stewardship measures in job design.

A comprehensive strategy that takes into account the interactions between people, processes, and the environment is needed to include green concepts into job design. It entails coordinating corporate aims and values with sustainability goals, involving staff members at all levels in the shift to more environmentally friendly practices, and encouraging cooperation with outside parties like communities, suppliers, and customers. Organizations may foster a sustainable culture that permeates every part of their operations and spurs innovation and continual improvement by incorporating green concepts into job design.

There are numerous advantages to designing jobs using ecological principles. Initiatives aimed at reducing waste and increasing resource efficiency can also save money by lowering energy and resource consumption, decreasing the cost of disposing of garbage, and improving operational effectiveness. Additionally, companies that show a dedication to environmental stewardship frequently have improved brand value and reputation, which can result in a competitive advantage and higher consumer loyalty.

Green employment design can have major social and environmental benefits in addition to economic ones. Organizations may safeguard ecosystems and natural habitats, improve the wellbeing of local communities, and lessen the negative effects of climate change by supporting sustainable practices and cultivating an environmental responsibility culture. Furthermore, green work design can result in increased job satisfaction, motivation, and retention by placing a priority on employee involvement and well-being. This will eventually drive organizational success.

In conclusion, it is strategically critical for firms to integrate green ideas into job design if they hope to prosper in a world that is becoming more linked and complicated. Organizations may develop workplaces that are more innovative, competitive, and socially responsible in addition to being more sustainable and resilient by placing a high priority on resource efficiency, waste reduction, and environmental stewardship. A more sustainable future is within reach for everyone with the help of green work design, while the world community continues to struggle with urgent environmental issues.

3.2.3 Examples of Organizations That Have Successfully Redesigned Job Roles to Align with Sustainability Goals

1. - Tesla

Known for its creative approach to environmentally friendly transportation, Tesla has revamped positions in a number of departments to better reflect its commitment to sustainability. Here are a few instances:

1. Vehicle Design and Engineering: The engineers and designers at Tesla strive to create electric cars (EVs) that are not only aesthetically pleasing and highly efficient, but also ecologically sustainable. Their main goals are to maximize battery efficiency, decrease weight for increased energy efficiency, and build vehicles using sustainable materials.

2. Manufacturing: Tesla's production teams have reduced waste, used less energy, and increased efficiency in their operations by implementing sustainable practices. This covers actions like recycling materials, maximizing supply chain logistics, and utilizing renewable energy sources in industries in order to reduce their negative effects on the environment.

3. Supply Chain Management: Sustainable sourcing procedures are now the top priority in supply chain management roles at Tesla. This entails encouraging ethical labour standards, lowering the carbon footprint of transportation logistics, and collaborating with suppliers to guarantee responsible mining practices for raw materials used in batteries.

4. Sales and Marketing: The marketing and sales departments at Tesla are vital in encouraging customers to choose environmentally friendly modes of transportation. Their main goals are to inform consumers on the advantages that electric cars have for the environment, emphasize Tesla's dedication to sustainability, and promote the usage of EVs as a way to cut greenhouse gas emissions.

5. Research and Development: The R&D teams at Tesla are always coming up with new ideas to advance EV technology and create new products that help the firm reach its sustainability targets. This covers developments in battery technology, autonomous driving to maximize energy efficiency, and investigation of renewable energy sources including solar energy and energy storage.

The goal of expediting the global switch to sustainable energy is the foundation of Tesla's organizational structure and culture. By redefining work roles throughout the organization with a focus on sustainability, Tesla has become a market leader in electric vehicles and a major factor in the worldwide fight against climate change.

2. - Coca-Cola

Coca-Cola has undertaken several initiatives to align its job roles with sustainability goals:

1. Packaging Design and Innovation: To put a stronger emphasis on sustainability, Coca-Cola changed employment positions in its packaging and innovation departments. This includes creating recyclable materials and plant-based bottles as eco-friendly packaging options to lessen the impact of their products on the environment.

2. Water Stewardship: Coca-Cola has specialized teams that work on water stewardship, preserving water resources and enhancing the quality of the water in the areas where the firm is present. These responsibilities include encouraging responsible water usage throughout the supply chain, supporting regional water conservation initiatives, and installing water-efficient technologies in manufacturing facilities.

3. Supply Chain Management: Redesigned supply chain management responsibilities at Coca-Cola put an emphasis on sustainable sourcing methods. This entails collaborating with suppliers to guarantee ethical ingredient sourcing, cutting carbon emissions in shipping logistics, and encouraging moral labour standards all the way through the supply chain.

4. Recycling Initiatives: Coca-Cola has made employment positions and investments in recycling programs aimed at raising recycling rates and cutting down on plastic waste. This entails funding the development of recycling infrastructure, encouraging recycling among consumers through awareness campaigns, and investing in cutting-edge recycling technologies.

5. Community Engagement: Coca-Cola has devoted groups that work with neighbourhood groups to solve environmental issues and advance sustainable development. In order to carry out environmental projects, promote recycling initiatives, and increase public knowledge of sustainability issues, these responsibilities entail collaborating with non-governmental organizations, governmental bodies, and community organizations.

Coca-Cola is aiming to positively impact society and the environment by incorporating sustainability into its fundamental business activities. Coca-Cola is showing its dedication to ethical business practices and supporting international initiatives to address climate change and environmental sustainability by redefining employment responsibilities to be in line with sustainability goals.

3. - IBM

IBM has put in place a number of efforts to match employment responsibilities with sustainability objectives:

1. Green IT and Data Canter Optimization: With an emphasis on sustainability, IBM has reorganized job positions within its IT services and data canter management teams. These positions entail maximizing the effectiveness of data canters, cutting down on energy usage, and putting green IT strategies like server virtualization and energy-saving cooling systems into practice.

2. Environmental Data Analytics: IBM has created employment positions cantered around environmental data analytics, which entail identifying opportunities for lowering environmental impact and enhancing sustainability performance using data-driven insights. In order to maximize resource efficiency, cut waste, and improve environmental stewardship, these positions take advantage of IBM's capabilities in data analytics and machine learning.

3. Sustainable Supply Chain Management: Sustainable sourcing methods and ethical supply chain management have been given priority in IBM's revamping of supply chain management positions. These responsibilities include encouraging fair labour standards, lowering the carbon footprint of logistics and transportation operations, and collaborating with suppliers to guarantee responsible material procurement.

4. Renewable Energy Integration: IBM has established positions devoted to the integration of renewable energy, entailing the creation and execution of plans to augment the utilization of sustainable energy resources like wind and solar energy. These positions concentrate on locating prospects for the adoption of renewable energy, assessing the viability of renewable energy initiatives, and putting renewable energy solutions into practice throughout IBM's operations.

5. Environmental Consulting and Services: IBM now offers environmental sustainability solutions as part of its broader consulting and service offerings. This entails establishing positions cantered on offering clients environmental consulting services, assisting them in designing and putting into practice sustainability strategies, and tracking and reporting on environmental performance.

By means of these endeavours, IBM is exhibiting its dedication to sustainability and ecological responsibility, concurrently generating novel prospects for novelty and expansion. IBM is incorporating sustainability into its core business operations and supporting worldwide efforts to address climate change and promote environmental sustainability by redefining work responsibilities to match with sustainability goals.

4. - Walmart

Walmart has undertaken numerous initiatives to align its job roles with sustainability goals:

1. Sustainable Sourcing: Walmart has prioritized sustainable sourcing techniques by redesigning job positions within its supply chain management teams. These responsibilities include encouraging fair labour practices, lowering the environmental effect of production processes, and collaborating with suppliers to ensure responsible product sourcing.

2. Energy Efficiency and Renewable Energy: Walmart has established positions cantered on the integration of renewable energy sources and energy efficiency. In order to lower carbon emissions and energy expenses, these jobs entail installing energy-saving equipment in retail spaces and distribution canters, funding renewable energy initiatives like solar and wind power, and streamlining energy management procedures.

3. Waste Reduction and Recycling: Walmart's operations and facilities management teams now have reorganized job positions with an emphasis on recycling and waste reduction. These positions entail putting trash reduction plans into action, encouraging consumers and staff to recycle, and looking into creative ways to manage and repurpose waste products.

4. Sustainable Product Development: Walmart has created positions devoted to innovation and sustainable product development. These positions entail lowering packaging waste, collaborating with suppliers to create eco-friendly products, and designing products and manufacturing procedures with sustainable materials in mind.

5. Community Engagement and Education: Walmart has established positions cantered on educating the public about sustainability issues and engaging the communities. In order to promote sustainable living habits, support community-based environmental projects, and increase public knowledge of environmental sustainability, these responsibilities entail collaborating with regional groups, governmental organizations, and other stakeholders.

Walmart is proving its dedication to environmental stewardship and sustainability through these efforts, which also benefit suppliers, consumers, and communities. Walmart is incorporating sustainability into its core business operations and promoting positive change throughout its supply chain and beyond by redefining job roles to match with sustainability goals.

3.3 Green Skills and Competencies Mapping

A thorough procedure called "mapping green skills and competencies" aims to discover, classify, and evaluate the knowledge and abilities people need to succeed in tasks pertaining to sustainability, environmental protection, and the adoption of green technologies. In a world that is changing quickly and is marked by worries about resource depletion, environmental degradation, and climate change, there is a growing need for people who have the know-how to properly handle these issues.

Fundamentally, environmental sustainability-related employment positions, industries, and sectors are systematically analysed as part of the process of green skills mapping. This study pinpoints the particular abilities, proficiencies, and prerequisites needed for people to succeed in these positions. The term "green skills" refers to a broad range of subjects and disciplines, such as waste management, circular economy practices, renewable energy, energy efficiency, environmental conservation, sustainable agriculture, green architecture design, and adaptation and mitigation measures for climate change.

Finding important companies and sectors that offer chances for sustainable development or have a major influence on the environment is usually the first step in the mapping process. This could encompass sectors like transportation, manufacturing, construction, forestry, agriculture, forestry, water and waste management, and renewable energy (solar, wind, hydroelectric, etc.).

The next stage is to examine the different employment responsibilities within each sector and ascertain the particular skills and abilities needed for these occupations after the primary sectors and industries have been identified. As part of this analysis, employers, educators, industry experts, and other stakeholders will be consulted to gain insights into the best practices, technological breakthroughs, existing and emerging skill demands, and regulatory requirements within each sector.

Technical skills, soft skills, and specialized knowledge areas are the main categories into which the skills and competencies identified through this method can be divided. Technological competencies could include mastery of green building design, water conservation strategies, waste reduction and recycling procedures, energy auditing, renewable energy technology, and environmental monitoring and assessment methods.

Conversely, in the context of sustainability activities, soft skills are crucial for effective problem-solving, leadership, teamwork, and communication. Critical thinking, creativity, flexibility, cooperation, communication, project management, and stakeholder involvement are a few examples of these abilities.

Green skills mapping highlights the significance of specialized knowledge domains that are unique to certain sectors or industries in addition to technical and soft skills. Professionals in the field of renewable energy, for instance, could require in-depth knowledge of grid integration, solar systems, wind turbine technology, energy storage options, and energy policy frameworks.

Following identification, the essential competencies and abilities are usually arranged into competency frameworks or skill matrices that act as reference manuals for employers, legislators, and anyone looking to advance their green skill sets as well as education and training providers. These frameworks offer an organized method for determining skill gaps, creating training curricula, and matching workforce development and education programs to business need.

Furthermore, mapping green talents is a continuous process that changes in response to growing sustainability priorities, technological breakthroughs, shifting market dynamics, and regulatory needs. It is not a one-time exercise. The need for particular skills and abilities may change as new technologies are developed and industries move toward more environmentally friendly practices, requiring regular changes to competency frameworks that are already in place.

To sum up, the mapping of green talents is an essential tool for closing the skills gap that exists between training, education, and employment in the green economy. It helps to guarantee that people have the knowledge and competence necessary to confront urgent environmental concerns and promote positive change towards a more sustainable future by defining and articulating the skills and competencies needed for sustainable development.

3.3.1 Identifying the Key Skills and Competencies Required for Green Jobs in Various Industries

"Identifying the key skills and competencies required for green jobs in various industries" describes the process of figuring out what particular talents, abilities, and attributes people need to have in order to work in roles that are environmentally sustainable across a variety of industries. This entails examining the requirements for green jobs across a range of industries and determining the key abilities and knowledge that applicants need to possess in order to succeed in these positions.

Finding the essential knowledge and abilities needed for green professions in a variety of industries is essential for navigating the ever-changing field of careers that emphasize sustainability. Professionals with specific expertise and skills to handle challenging environmental issues are in greater demand as industries come to understand the need of environmental stewardship. In this thorough investigation, we explore the various facets of green professions, looking at the various industries and the fundamental knowledge and abilities required for success.

1. Environmental Knowledge and Awareness:

A thorough awareness of environmental issues, laws, and sustainability concepts is essential for positions in the green economy. Experts in these positions need to have a deep understanding of biodiversity preservation, climate change dynamics, and ecological systems. The platform for well-informed decision-making and the creation of sustainable practices across industries is provided by this fundamental knowledge.

2. Renewable Energy Expertise:

Being knowledgeable about renewable energy technology is essential for the shift to a low-carbon economy. Experience with the design, installation, and upkeep of renewable energy systems is necessary for green careers in industries like solar, wind, hydro, and geothermal energy. Additionally, promoting innovation in renewable energy solutions requires an understanding of cutting-edge technology, including developments in energy storage and grid integration.

3. Energy Efficiency Optimization:

Using energy resources efficiently is essential to minimizing the effects of climate change and the environment. Energy audits, energy saving methods, and the implementation of these practices in manufacturing processes, transportation networks, buildings, and other sectors are common tasks associated with green employment responsibilities. To maximize energy efficiency, one must possess expertise in demand-side management, energy management, and the application of energy-efficient technologies.

4. Resource Management Skills:

Across industries, efficient resource management is the foundation of sustainability initiatives. Green work professionals need to be adept at managing resources like water, materials, and trash in a way that maximizes resource efficiency and reduces its negative effects on the environment. This covers techniques for cutting down on waste, reusing and recycling materials, conserving water, and acquiring products sustainably.

5. Sustainable Design and Innovation:

Creating infrastructure, buildings, and goods with the least amount of negative environmental impact over the course of their lives requires the integration of sustainable design concepts. Working in green jobs frequently entails incorporating eco-design techniques, life cycle assessments, and the usage of eco-friendly materials and technology into the design process. Sustainable design techniques rely heavily on innovation, which calls for imagination and a forward-thinking outlook.

6. Climate Change Mitigation Strategies:

Proactive steps must be taken to cut greenhouse gas emissions and improve resistance to the effects of climate change. Green occupations include positions that concentrate on mitigating the effects of climate change, such as reducing carbon emissions, utilizing renewable energy sources, planting trees, and restoring ecosystems. To create successful plans for climate action, professionals in these areas need to have a thorough understanding of mitigation technology, policy frameworks, and climate science.

7. Knowledge of Green Building Standards and Certifications:

Green building techniques are a major contribution to the advancement of sustainability made by the real estate and construction industries. Knowledge of green building certifications and standards, such as BREEAM (Building Research Establishment Environmental Assessment Method), WELL Building Standard, and LEED (Leadership in Energy and Environmental Design), is necessary for green work jobs in these industries. To ensure environmental sustainability in the built environment and to obtain green building certifications, one must possess proficiency in sustainable building design, construction techniques, and building performance optimization.

8. Environmental Policy and Regulatory Compliance:
To ensure compliance and promote sustainable practices across a range of industries, it is imperative to adeptly navigate intricate environmental rules and policy frameworks. Advocating for policy changes to support sustainability goals, monitoring regulatory developments, and conducting environmental impact assessments are common tasks associated with green employment jobs. Strong analytical abilities, legal knowledge, and the capacity to interact with stakeholders and policymakers in an effective manner are prerequisites for professionals in these positions.

9. Data Analysis and Decision-Making:
Evaluating environmental performance, monitoring the advancement of sustainability goals, and pinpointing areas for improvement all depend on data-driven decision-making. Proficiency in environmental data analysis, including data collection, interpretation, and visualization, is necessary for green work responsibilities. For the purpose of supporting evidence-based decision-making and maximizing environmental management techniques, expertise in statistical analysis, GIS (Geographic Information Systems), and environmental modelling is beneficial.

10. Collaboration and Stakeholder Engagement:
Due to their inherent complexity, sustainability challenges call for cooperative strategies involving a wide range of stakeholders. In order to create and execute sustainable solutions, green job jobs frequently require collaborative work with diverse teams, governmental organizations, non-governmental organizations, corporations, and communities. To create alliances, forge agreement, and motivate group action toward common sustainability goals, effective communication, stakeholder involvement, and negotiating abilities are critical.

In summary, the recognition of essential proficiencies and abilities needed for environmentally conscious positions across multiple sectors highlights the complex character of vocations cantered around sustainability. To handle complex environmental concerns and promote sustainable development across sectors, workers in green occupations need to possess a varied range of skills, from understanding of the environment and renewable energy to resource management and stakeholder involvement. Giving people the right knowledge and abilities will help us create a robust and sustainable future for future generations.

3.3.2 Developing Frameworks for Mapping Existing Skills to Green Competencies and Identifying Gaps for Training and Development

In the context of shifting to a more sustainable and environmentally conscious economy, mapping current skills to green competencies and identifying gaps for training and development are critical. In order to evaluate their workforce's present capabilities, match them with the skills needed for green occupations, and close any gaps through focused training and development activities, organizations must establish comprehensive frameworks. We'll go more deeply into each stage of this procedure in this expanded explanation, examining its importance and offering helpful advice for putting it into practice.

Step-1. Identify Green Competencies:
Prior to mapping current skills, it's critical to identify the green competencies pertinent to the goals and industry of the firm. A broad range of abilities and subject areas are covered by "green competencies," such as mitigation techniques for climate change, sustainable resource management, renewable energy technology, and environmental laws. These skills are necessary for jobs in a variety of industries, including sustainable agriculture, green building, clean transportation, and renewable energy.

Organizations can determine their green competences by thoroughly researching market trends, legal requirements, and sustainable best practices. Working together with academic institutions, industrial groups, and sustainability specialists can yield important insights into the particular knowledge domains and skill sets that are in demand in the green economy.

Step-2. Assessment of Current Skills:

Assessing the workforce's present skills and capabilities is the next step. Both hard skills necessary for the job and soft abilities like adaptation, communication, and problem-solving should be evaluated. It should also assess how well staff members understand sustainability concepts and how well they can incorporate environmental concerns into their job.

A range of approaches can be used for assessment, including as performance reviews, skill inventories, questionnaires, and interviews. Organizations can acquire a clear picture of their strengths and opportunities for development with regard to green competences by collecting extensive data on employees' skills and competencies.

Step-3. Mapping Skills to Competencies:

The next stage is to map the workforce's present skill set to the recognized green competencies after the skills have been evaluated. The mapping method entails matching the current competencies of individuals with the specialized knowledge and skill sets needed for green jobs. To graphically depict how existing abilities and green competencies connect, a matrix or mapping tool might be created.

Both direct matches—where current skills directly match green competencies—and transferable skills—which can be improved or modified to fit the requirements of green jobs—must be taken into account when mapping skills to competencies. Project management abilities, for instance, can be helpful in carrying out sustainability programs, and technical know-how in renewable energy systems is closely related to green energy capabilities.

Step-4. Identifying Gaps:

The next stage is to find any gaps between the abilities and green competencies that have been mapped out. There could be deficiencies in a number of areas, such as technical proficiency, acquaintance with green technologies, awareness of sustainability practices, and comprehension of legal requirements. In order to prioritize training and development activities to meet the most important areas of need, it is essential to identify these gaps.

Comparative examination of the mapping results, stakeholder discussions, employee input, and performance reviews can all be used to find gaps. Furthermore, comparing the personnel of the company to industry norms and best practices will assist identify any gaps in their knowledge of green capabilities.

Step-5. Developing Training Programs:

Organizations can create focused training and development programs to upskill staff members and fill up the shortages based on the gaps that have been discovered. These courses ought to be created with the intention of giving staff members the information, abilities, and tools required to succeed in environmentally conscious careers and make meaningful contributions to the company's sustainability goals.

There are many different types of training programs, such as on-the-job training, online courses, workshops, seminars, classroom instruction, and mentorship programs. These programs' material ought to be specifically designed to fill in the skill gaps that were found during the mapping process, making sure that it is applicable to the roles and responsibilities of the staff members.

Step-6. Integration with Existing Systems:

Integrating the framework for skill mapping to green competencies with current HR systems and procedures is crucial for the successful execution of training and development programs. This connectivity makes it possible to easily monitor staff development, assess the success of training, and match training initiatives with more general company objectives and plans.

Performance management tools, talent management software, and learning management systems (LMS) can all be used to achieve integration. These technologies can help with training content delivery, employee engagement and completion tracking, and long-term skill development monitoring. Furthermore, the firm may attract and retain personnel with the required green capabilities by including the framework into its recruitment and succession planning procedures.

Step-7. Continuous Improvement:

Ultimately, it is important to see the process of matching abilities to green competencies and filling in skill gaps as a continuous and iterative one. The green economy is always changing as new sustainable practices, laws, and technology comes into being. In order to respond to these developments and guarantee that staff members continue to possess the competencies required to succeed in the green jobs of the future, businesses must periodically assess and update their frameworks and training curricula.

Periodically performing skill evaluations, getting input from stakeholders and staff, keeping an eye on market changes, and making necessary revisions to training materials and delivery strategies are all examples of continuous improvement initiatives. Organizations may remain ahead of the curve and establish themselves as leaders in the shift to a more sustainable future by adopting a culture of constant learning and adaptation.

In summary, creating frameworks to connect current abilities to green competencies and pinpoint areas in need of training and growth is crucial for businesses hoping to prosper in the green economy. Organizations may guarantee that their workforce possesses the necessary knowledge and skills to propel sustainability and innovation by using a methodical approach that includes evaluation, mapping, gap analysis, training, integration, and continuous improvement initiatives. Organizations may effectively address current difficulties and capitalize on future opportunities in the fast-changing fields of sustainability and environmental stewardship by making strategic investments in staff development.

3.3.3 Research Findings on the Impact of Green Skills Development on Employee Performance and Organizational Sustainability

The term "green skills development" describes the process of gaining expertise in environmental sustainability techniques across a range of sectors and industries. These abilities cover a broad range of topics, such as waste management, renewable energy technology, sustainable supply chain management, energy efficiency, and compliance with environmental standards.

Several studies have shown how developing green skills improves employee performance on an individual basis as well as the sustainability of the firm as a whole. A noteworthy discovery is the association between training in green skills and increased job satisfaction among workers. Studies have indicated that workers who are trained in environmentally conscious techniques report feeling more fulfilled and interested in their work because they believe they are making a positive impact on society and the environment. improved levels of employee motivation, dedication, and retention are frequently correlated with improved job satisfaction, which lowers turnover rates and the related recruiting expenses for businesses.

Additionally, there is a correlation between increased levels of innovation in organizations and the development of green talents. Workers who understand the fundamentals of environmental sustainability are better able to spot opportunities for cost-cutting measures, new product development, and process enhancements that support both environmental and economic sustainability. Through the implementation of green skills training, firms may cultivate an innovative culture, remain ahead of their competition, adjust to shifting market demands, and leverage emerging sustainability trends.

The influence of green skills development on worker productivity is another important factor. Studies have shown that workers who are adept in green practices are frequently more productive because they are more effective in their professions. People who have received training in energy-efficient methods, for instance, might put policies in place to cut down on energy use during workdays, which would save the company money. In a similar vein, staff members skilled in sustainable supply chain management could spot chances to improve overall operational efficiency by streamlining logistics, cutting waste, and optimizing resource usage.

Additionally, firms that make investments in the development of green talents frequently see observable gains in terms of resource optimization and cost savings. Organizations can achieve considerable reductions in energy, water, and raw material consumption by providing staff with the necessary information and skills to adopt sustainable practices. Furthermore, the implementation of eco-friendly measures can result in decreased environmental impact and regulatory compliance costs by reducing pollution, waste output, and carbon emissions. These cost reductions and operational improvements boost an organization's standing as a respectable corporate citizen while also supporting its long-term financial viability.

Developing green talents has economic advantages as well as improving organizational resilience and risk management. Organizations can reduce the risks of supply chain disruptions, regulatory non-compliance, resource scarcity, and reputational harm by taking proactive measures to address environmental issues and sustainability challenges. Employees that are aware of environmental opportunities and hazards are also better able to recognize possible threats and create effective countermeasures, which strengthens organizational resilience in the face of unpredictability and volatility.

Additionally, developing green skills helps companies cultivate a corporate social responsibility (CSR) culture, which is crucial for drawing in clients, investors, and skilled workers. Studies reveal that patrons are inclined to endorse companies that exhibit a dedication to ecological sustainability, and investors are progressively incorporating environmental, social, and governance (ESG) factors into their investment choices. In a similar vein, job seekers—millennials and Generation Z in particular—prioritize employment with companies that share their values and have a beneficial social and environmental impact. Organizations can obtain a competitive advantage in the market, recruit top people, and improve their brand reputation by investing in sustainability and green skills development projects.

The development of green skills supports larger social objectives including climate action, sustainable development, and environmental protection. Organizations are essential in tackling global issues like resource depletion, biodiversity loss, and climate change because they equip people with the information and abilities to adopt sustainable practices. Green skills development also fosters social inclusion and equity by giving underrepresented groups, women, and young people access to green jobs and the chance to participate in the green economy.

To sum up, studies have shown time and time again that developing green skills improves worker performance and organizational sustainability. Organizations can contribute to environmental protection and societal well-being while improving employee satisfaction, fostering creativity, increasing productivity, and achieving cost savings through the implementation of green skills training. Building resilient, competitive, and socially responsible firms requires incorporating environmental factors into workforce development initiatives, as sustainability gains prominence in the corporate sector.

Chapter – 4

Green Recruitment and Selection

Introduction to Green Recruitment:

Organizations are realizing the value of environmental sustainability and corporate social responsibility (CSR) in today's fast-paced commercial environment. In an effort to attract and retain talent that supports their environmental values and helps them achieve their sustainability goals, many organizations are adopting green recruitment techniques as part of their commitment to sustainability.

The term **"Green Recruitment"** describes the hiring process that places an emphasis on CSR and environmental sustainability. It entails incorporating environmental factors into the hiring process at every level, from posting jobs and choosing candidates to on boarding and engaging staff. Organizations hope to develop a workforce committed to environmental stewardship, sustainable practices, and the company's efforts to lessen its environmental impact by implementing green recruitment techniques.

The main ideas, tenets, and advantages of implementing green recruitment techniques will be covered in this introduction to the subject. We'll talk about how businesses may successfully incorporate environmental factors into their hiring practices to draw in eco-aware applicants and foster a sustainable work environment.

Organizations can improve their standing as green employers, contribute to beneficial environmental results, and build a more sustainable future for future generations by adopting green recruitment strategies. The goal of green recruitment is to create a workforce that shares the organization's environmental values and is dedicated to changing the world, not only to fill job openings.

Meaning of Green Recruitment:

Hiring staff while taking corporate social responsibility (CSR) and environmental sustainability into account is referred to as "green recruitment." It entails including environmental factors into the hiring process at every level, from job advertisements and candidate selection to on boarding and employee engagement. Green hiring seeks to draw in and keep employees that are dedicated to environmental stewardship, advance sustainable business practices, and improve environmental results. Choosing applicants with environmental experience first, using eco-friendly hiring procedures, and encouraging a sustainable culture at work are a few examples of how to do this. In general, green hiring reflects the company's dedication to sustainability and corporate citizenship and is consistent with its environmental aims and principles.

Definition of Green Recruitment:

The term green recruitment describes the "process of integrating environmentally friendly practices and ideas into an organization's employment and recruitment procedures."

Introduction to Green Selection:

Organizations are realizing the value of corporate social responsibility (CSR) and environmental sustainability in their operations as the world around them changes quickly. Many companies are making the commitment to match their staff with their environmental aims and values by using green selecting methods.

The practice of choosing job candidates while giving consideration to environmental sustainability and corporate social responsibility (CSR) concepts is known as **"Green Selection."** It entails incorporating environmental factors into the hiring process to find candidates who not only meet the organization's sustainability goals but are also highly qualified for the position.

The main ideas, tenets, and advantages of implementing green selection techniques will be covered in this introduction to the subject. In order to create a workforce that is committed to environmental stewardship and supports the company's sustainability initiatives, we will talk about how firms can include environmental factors in their hiring and selection procedures.

In this guide, we'll look at a variety of tactics and methods for putting green selection into practice, such as evaluating candidates' environmental commitment and knowledge, encouraging sustainability values inside the company, and cultivating an environmental responsibility culture among staff members.

Organizations may demonstrate their commitment to being responsible corporate citizens and recruit and retain top people who are passionate about environmental sustainability by implementing green selection methods. Hiring people is only one component of green selection; another is creating a sustainable culture that pervades all facets of the business's operations and helps the world achieve its environmental goals.

Meaning of Green Selection:

The term **"Green Selection"** describes the method of choosing job applicants that has an emphasis on corporate social responsibility (CSR) and environmental sustainability. As with green recruiting, green selection is incorporating environmental factors into the process of choosing applicants in order to make sure they share the organization's environmental values and goals. This could entail evaluating the candidates' familiarity with environmental issues, their dedication to sustainable practices, and their capacity to support green projects inside the company. Green selection seeks to develop a workforce that supports sustainable practices, is committed to environmental stewardship, and helps the firm lessen its environmental impact. All things considered, choosing green products is a part of a larger plan to establish a sustainable culture within the company and show its dedication to environmental responsibility.

Definition of Green Selection:

"The practice of choosing job candidates based on their environmental knowledge, expertise, and dedication to sustainability is known as green selection."

Concept of Green Recruitment and Selection

In recent years, eco-friendly hiring and selection procedures have become essential elements of sustainable corporate practices. Organizations are under increasing pressure to implement eco-friendly practices in all facets of their operations, including human resource management, as the whole community comes to understand the significance of solving environmental challenges. This in-depth conversation will cover the idea of "green recruitment and selection," as well as its importance, implementation tactics, obstacles, and possible advantages.

Fundamentally, environmentally conscious recruiting practices include candidates' qualifications for positions into the hiring process to make sure they share the company's commitment to sustainability. This is known as "green recruitment and selection." This means looking for people who have a sincere interest for environmental concerns, have the necessary knowledge and skills, and will probably have a beneficial impact on the company's environmental objectives.

The understanding that workers are essential to the sustainability of the company is one of the main drivers behind green hiring and selecting practices. Employers may develop a sustainable culture from the inside out by selecting candidates that value environmental stewardship. This will promote creativity, effectiveness, and long-term success.

Incorporating environmental issues into traditional employment criteria is the first step towards implementing green recruitment and selection methods. This could entail changing job descriptions to highlight duties connected to sustainability, such cutting down on waste, preserving resources, or introducing eco-friendly technologies. Companies might also include sustainability-related questions in job interviews to gauge applicants' perspectives, backgrounds, and environmental actions.

Businesses may help green recruitment efforts by utilizing technology. Hiring procedures can be streamlined with the use of digital platforms and tools, which will minimize the environmental impact and eliminate the need for paper-based documentation. Remote hiring can be facilitated by video interviews, virtual job fairs, and online exams, which can help reduce the carbon footprint associated with travel.

Collaborating with academic institutions and environmental organizations is an additional tactic to support green hiring and selection. Companies may access a pool of environmentally conscious talent and create pipelines for hiring people with the necessary skills and expertise by working with universities, schools, and sustainability-focused organizations.

Organizations may have difficulties in implementing green recruitment and selection methods, despite the potential advantages. A challenge is the absence of common standards to evaluate applicants' environmental qualifications. Environmental values and behaviours, in contrast to more conventional credentials like education or work experience, might be more challenging to measure and impartially assess.

Hiring managers and recruiters that value traditional criteria more highly than sustainability factors can be resistant. To overcome this opposition, the organization's leadership must be fully committed, and education must continue to spread the word about the value of sustainability in hiring practices and how they match with the organization's larger objectives.

Employers in sectors like manufacturing or transportation that have a big environmental impact could have more trouble finding applicants who care about the environment. In these situations, businesses need to stress their dedication to sustainability, highlight their efforts to lessen their environmental impact, and draw attention to ways that staff members may help bring about good change.

Despite these obstacles, companies can gain a lot from adopting green hiring and selection practices. Companies may improve their reputation as socially conscientious employers and increase their brand image and competitiveness in the market by attracting and keeping environmentally concerned staff. Furthermore, workers that have a strong commitment to sustainability are probably going to be more engaged, motivated, and productive, which will improve corporate results.

Incorporating sustainability into the employment process can also assist businesses in developing a staff that is inclusive and varied. Organisations can enhance their talent pool and promote creativity and innovation by appealing to a diverse variety of individuals by prioritising environmental values and behaviours in addition to traditional qualifications.

Green hiring and selection not only have internal advantages but also has the potential to further environmental objectives by promoting positive change both within and between industries. Employing people who are dedicated to sustainability helps businesses foster innovation in goods, services, and procedures, which results in more environmentally friendly operations and sustainable business practices.

To sum up, environmentally conscious hiring and selection practices are a critical first step in creating long-lasting businesses in a world that is changing quickly. Companies may promote a culture of environmental stewardship, align their personnel with sustainability goals, and effect good change both inside and outside their walls by including environmental factors into the employment process. Although putting green recruitment strategies into reality could be difficult, for forward-thinking companies that want to succeed in the long run, it might be worth it for the possible gains in environmental impact, employee engagement, and brand reputation.

4.1 Attracting Environmentally Conscious Talent

Drawing in eco-aware personnel is a critical undertaking for contemporary companies hoping to prosper at a time when sustainability is more than just a catchphrase, but an essential requirement for survival. In this thorough investigation, we look into the various tactics and sophisticated ways that businesses may use to draw in, involve, and keep people who are ardently dedicated to environmental stewardship.

Businesses are being asked more and more to take the lead in promoting sustainability and reducing their ecological impact in today's linked world, where environmental deterioration and climate change represent existential risks. Recruiting and retaining environmentally conscious talent—people who are skilled in their professions but who have a strong desire to use their skills to promote positive environmental impact—is essential to the success of this endeavour.

Demonstrating an unshakeable commitment to sustainability across all organizational processes is a fundamental pillar in the drive to attract environmentally conscious individuals. This means incorporating sustainable practices into the company's core values rather than just giving lip service to environmental concern. Businesses need to take concrete steps that demonstrate their commitment to environmental stewardship, from cutting back on waste and energy use to adopting renewable resources and cutting carbon emissions.

Companies may attract environmentally conscious individuals by providing a range of alluring perks and rewards, in addition to implementing eco-friendly policies and practices. One such benefit is the availability of flexible scheduling options or remote work options, which not only encourage work-life balance but also lessen the carbon footprint of employees by reducing the need for daily commuting. Furthermore, encouraging different forms of transportation—like bicycling, carpooling, or using public transportation—through incentives systems or subsidies can emphasize the company's dedication to sustainability even more.

Companies that use carbon footprint offset programs can increase their appeal to talent that care about the environment. These programs entail the business funding initiatives like carbon capture, renewable energy, or reforestation that lessen or counteract the negative effects of employees' activities on the environment. Companies that actively address their ecological footprint not only show their dedication to environmental responsibility, but they also give their workers the tools they need to use their jobs to positively impact the world.

Attracting environmentally conscious people requires the organization to incorporate sustainability into its employer branding and recruitment activities in addition to offering concrete actions and benefits. This means developing an engaging story that emphasizes the company's sustainability objectives, projects, and successes in order to appeal to applicants that place a high value on environmental responsibility. Through a variety of platforms, including job advertisements, career fairs, and recruitment events, companies may set themselves out as the preferred employer for those who care about the environment.

Developing a sustainable culture within the company can greatly increase its attractiveness to individuals who care about the environment. In addition to implementing top-down programs and policies, this entails giving staff members at all levels the authority to promote sustainability in their particular positions. Developing a culture where sustainability is not just a corporate buzzword but a shared value embraced by all can be accomplished in part by rewarding and recognizing employees who show exemplary commitment to environmental stewardship, offering opportunities for professional development in sustainability-related fields, and encouraging innovation and creativity in finding sustainable solutions.

Businesses can use their corporate social responsibility (CSR) programs to draw in talent who care about the environment. Organizations can exhibit their dedication to creating a positive impact that extends beyond their immediate sphere of influence by coordinating their corporate social responsibility (CSR) initiatives with environmental concerns and actively involving workers in volunteer work and community outreach initiatives that prioritize sustainability. This not only gives workers a feeling of pride and direction, but it also improves the company's standing as an environmentally and socially concerned employer.

In order to draw in talent who care about the environment, it's also critical to promote accountability and transparency in sustainability reporting and communication. When deciding whether or not to join an organization, candidates that place a high priority on environmental responsibility are likely to carefully consider the sustainability goals, environmental track record, and advancement towards those goals. Employers may recruit more environmentally concerned candidates by establishing trust and credibility with candidates by giving them clear and thorough information about the company's environmental performance, aims, and activities.

Businesses may improve their sustainability efforts and attract personnel that cares about the environment by utilizing innovation and technology. Whether by implementing smart building systems to maximize energy efficiency, adopting renewable energy technologies, or using data analytics to find opportunities for resource conservation and waste reduction, leveraging technology can help businesses achieve greater environmental sustainability while also demonstrating their dedication to innovation and advancement.

In conclusion, luring talent that cares about the environment takes more than just putting in place token benefits or green washing strategies; rather, it calls for a sincere and comprehensive commitment to sustainability in every facet of organizational operations. Companies can position themselves as employers of choice for environmentally conscious talent by showcasing a steadfast dedication to environmental stewardship, providing alluring perks and benefits, incorporating sustainability into employer branding and recruitment efforts, fostering a culture of sustainability, utilizing CSR initiatives, promoting transparency and accountability, and utilizing technology and innovation. By doing this, they contribute to creating a more sustainable and just future for everybody, as well as improving their competitiveness and resilience in a business environment that is changing quickly.

4.1.1 Understanding the Importance of Attracting Environmentally Conscious Talent in Building a Green Workforce

Building a green workforce requires attracting talent that cares about the environment because they bring a passion and dedication to sustainability that can spur innovation, lessen environmental impact, and strengthen corporate social responsibility initiatives. Their principles coincide with the company's sustainability objectives, which enhances staff engagement and retention and enhances the company's standing with investors and customers who place a high value on environmental responsibility.

Attracting environmentally conscious individuals and fostering a green workforce requires a multimodal strategy that includes employee involvement, company culture, recruitment tactics, and sustainability programs. Let's examine each in more detail:

Recruitment Strategies:
Organizations should include sustainability in their job postings and recruitment message to draw in environmentally concerned talent. Candidates who place a high priority on these principles may be won over by emphasizing the company's dedication to green projects, sustainable practices, and environmental responsibility. Furthermore, it can be beneficial to actively seek for candidates with a strong enthusiasm for environmental stewardship in the fields of environmental science, sustainability studies, renewable energy, and similar fields.

Organizational Culture:

Attracting and keeping talent that cares about the environment requires a corporate culture that appreciates and promotes sustainability. This entails creating an atmosphere at work where decision-making procedures, everyday activities, and the company's broader culture are all infused with sustainability. In order to promote sustainability activities and provide a model for employees to follow, leaders are essential. Organizations may show their dedication to environmental stewardship and attract candidates who care about the environment by supporting eco-friendly activities like recycling, energy conservation, and trash reduction.

Employee Engagement:

Involving staff members in sustainability initiatives improves their connection to the mission and values of the organization while also fostering a sense of pride and ownership. Through a variety of strategies, including volunteer opportunities, sustainability training, green team involvement, and recognition programs for sustainable accomplishments, organizations can promote employee involvement in green efforts. Employers can leverage the energy and creativity of their workforce to effect significant change by allowing staff members to offer ideas and solutions related to sustainability goals.

Sustainability Initiatives:

Strong sustainability efforts are a valuable tool for attracting professionals who care about the environment and show that a company is genuinely committed to environmental responsibility. These projects might include everything from waste management plans and energy efficiency improvements to carbon footprint reduction techniques and sustainable sourcing methods. Organizations can reduce their environmental impact and establish a reputation for sustainability by embracing eco-friendly technologies, investing in renewable energy, and implementing sustainable business practices. This can attract candidates who prioritize environmental concerns.

Benefits of Attracting Environmentally Conscious Talent:

There are numerous benefits to attracting environmentally conscious talent to build a green workforce:

1. **Innovation and Creativity:** Employees that care about the environment frequently provide new insights and creative concepts for sustainable processes and goods, fostering ongoing development and competitive advantage.

2. **Cost Savings:** Using sustainable practices can improve an organization's bottom line by reducing waste, increasing energy efficiency, and optimizing resources.

3. **Enhanced Corporate Social Responsibility (CSR):** An organization's CSR initiatives are strengthened by having a green workforce, which shows a sincere dedication to social responsibility and environmental care. This can improve brand reputation and increase consumer loyalty.

4. **Regulatory Compliance:** Hiring personnel who care about the environment can assist ensure that environmental laws and standards are followed, lowering the possibility of fines, penalties, and reputational harm that come with breaking them.

5. **Talent Attraction and Retention:** Prioritizing sustainability makes an organization more appealing to applicants who care about the environment, which increases employee engagement, satisfaction, and retention rates.

6. **Positive Impact:** Organizations may help the environment, support international sustainability initiatives, and encourage others to follow suit by developing a green workforce.

7. **Risk Mitigation:** Talent that cares about the environment can assist in identifying and reducing environmental risks related to the operations of the company. The firm can lessen the possibility of environmental events, regulatory infractions, and related liabilities by carrying out comprehensive environmental assessments and putting proactive risk management techniques into place.

8. **Brand Differentiation:** Developing a green workforce enables the company to stand out from rivals in the industry. Through the demonstration of its dedication to sustainability by its workers, the company can draw in environmentally concerned customers who

favour companies that share their values, giving it a competitive advantage and a larger market share.

9. **Stakeholder Engagement:** Throughout the value chain, a green workforce may improve stakeholder involvement and collaboration. Employee participation in sustainability programs allows the company to build relationships with vendors, clients, and community members who share its commitment to environmental responsibility. These relationships can result in win-win situations and the production of shared value.

10. **Access to Green Markets:** Hiring personnel that cares about the environment might give the company access to new green markets and prospects. enterprises with a green workforce are better positioned to take advantage of the growing demand for eco-friendly goods, services, and technologies as sustainability becomes more and more important to consumers, governments, and enterprises globally.

In summary, developing a green workforce that fosters innovation, sustains the environment, and raises the bar for corporate social responsibility requires luring in environmentally conscious people. Organizations can attract, retain, and empower environmentally conscious talent to build a more sustainable and brighter future by integrating sustainability into recruitment strategies, cultivating a culture of environmental stewardship, involving employees in green initiatives, and implementing sustainable practices.

4.1.2 Strategies for Promoting the Organization's Commitment to Sustainability to Attract Like-minded Candidates

Showcasing projects like cutting carbon footprints, adopting eco-friendly practices, and supporting environmental causes are some ways to promote sustainability commitments and draw in applicants who share such values. Candidates that share your beliefs may be drawn to your position if you highlight these efforts on social media, in job advertisements, and on the corporate website. Further showcasing your company's commitment to the cause is possible through involvement in partnerships, certifications, and sustainability events.

Strategies that organizations can employ to effectively showcase their dedication to sustainability and appeal to environmentally conscious candidates.

1. Develop a Comprehensive Sustainability Strategy:
Start by developing a comprehensive sustainability plan that details the objectives, programs, and schedule for your company's attainment of environmental targets. Energy efficiency, waste minimization, water conservation, and lowering carbon footprints should all be included in this plan. All sustainability initiatives are built upon a well-defined strategy that also conveys the organization's long-term commitment to environmental responsibility.

2. Incorporate Sustainability into Company Culture:
Encourage staff members at all levels to adopt an environmentally conscious mindset in order to weave sustainability into the very fabric of your business. Promote involvement in energy-saving campaigns, recycling programs, and volunteer opportunities with environmental organizations, among other sustainability activities. Organizations may show their dedication to environmental stewardship and draw in candidates who share these values by fostering a culture of sustainability.

3. Showcase Sustainable Practices:
Emphasize your company's accomplishments and sustainable practices on your website, in your recruitment materials, and on social media. Disseminate case studies, KPIs, and success stories that show the observable results of your sustainability initiatives, including trash diversion rates or decreases in greenhouse gas emissions. Candidates may be more convinced of your dedication to sustainability when they see visual components like images and videos.

4. Leverage Green Certifications and Partnerships:
Acquire pertinent green certifications to demonstrate your company's dedication to sustainability, such as B Corp or LEED (Leadership in Energy and Environmental Design). These certifications can strengthen your reputation as an ecologically conscious employer and act as external validations of your environmental performance. To further show your involvement with the larger sustainability community, collaborate with

industry groups, environmental organizations, and sustainability-focused projects.

5. Integrate Sustainability into Recruitment Messaging:
Include message about sustainability in all of your job postings, career portals, and employer branding initiatives. Give a succinct explanation of your company's principles and sustainability pledges, highlighting chances for applicants to support important environmental projects. Speak in a way that appeals to those who care about the environment and emphasizes the difference they can make by joining your team.

6. Engage Employees as Brand Ambassadors:
Employees can act as brand ambassadors for your company's sustainability initiatives if you give them the chance to share their knowledge and perspectives. Encourage staff members to take part in conferences, industry events, and speaking engagements so they may talk about the company's sustainability efforts and demonstrate its thought leadership in environmental sustainability. Employee advocacy has the power to spread the word about sustainability and draw in candidates who share your enthusiasm for the issue.

7. Offer Sustainability-focused Benefits and Perks:
Integrate eco-friendly incentives and bonuses into your employee offer to draw in and keep talent who cares about the environment. This could involve choices like working remotely to cut down on emissions from commuting, incentives for environmentally friendly transportation, green health initiatives, and volunteer opportunities with environmental organizations. Employer perks that are in line with sustainability principles show your dedication to promoting employees' overall health and environmental responsibility.

8. Provide Training and Development Opportunities:
Invest in education and training programs that provide staff members the know-how and abilities they need to spearhead organizational sustainability initiatives. Provide certifications, workshops, and seminars on sustainable subjects like circular economy principles, renewable energy, and sustainable supply chain management. You may empower

staff members to contribute to the organization's sustainability goals and draw in individuals who are enthusiastic about promoting environmental sustainability by cultivating a culture of continual learning and innovation.

In conclusion, highlighting an organization's dedication to sustainability is critical to drawing in people who share that passion and value environmental responsibility. Organizations can effectively communicate their commitment to environmental stewardship and attract environmentally conscious talent by developing a comprehensive sustainability strategy, integrating sustainability into company culture, showcasing sustainable practices, utilizing green certifications and partnerships, integrating sustainability into recruitment messaging, enlisting employees as brand ambassadors, providing training and development opportunities, and offering benefits and perks that are sustainability-focused. By utilizing these tactics, companies may establish themselves as pioneers in sustainability and draw in applicants who align with their principles, ultimately leading to a more sustainable future for the company and the environment.

4.1.3 Leveraging Employer Branding and Corporate Social Responsibility Initiatives to Appeal to Environmentally Conscious Job Seekers

It's a smart move to use employer branding and corporate social responsibility (CSR) programs to draw in eco-aware candidates. Emphasizing your company's dedication to eco-friendly operations, sustainability, and community service will help you attract applicants that place a high priority on environmental issues. You might highlight programs to reduce your carbon footprint, waste management efforts, promote renewable energy, participation in environmental conservation projects, and volunteer opportunities for staff members that are connected to sustainability. This improves your reputation as a socially conscious employer and draws in talent who care about the environment.

Let's dive deeper into leveraging employer branding and corporate social responsibility initiatives to attract environmentally conscious job seekers.

Attracting top talent in today's cutthroat employment market requires more than just providing competitive pay and perks. A growing number of job searchers are giving consideration to a company's principles and dedication to improving society and the environment. The necessity of integrating environmental sustainability into employer branding strategies and corporate social responsibility activities is thus becoming more and more apparent to firms.

Showcasing a business's dedication to environmental sustainability through employer branding initiatives is a crucial component of this strategy. This entails explaining to prospective recruits the organization's environmental ideals, objectives, and accomplishments in an effective manner. By emphasizing these facets of the business culture and operations, employers can attract candidates that are driven to change the world and are looking for companies that share their beliefs.

- ❖ **To effectively leverage employer branding for attracting environmentally conscious job seekers, organizations can employ several strategies:**

1. Crafting a Compelling Sustainability Narrative: Create an engaging story that conveys the business's dedication to environmental sustainability. The organization's sustainability-related principles, objectives, and projects should be highlighted in this narrative, along with the effects they are having on the local community and the environment.

2. Showcasing Environmental Initiatives: Emphasize the company's particular environmental policies and objectives. This could involve making an attempt to support renewable energy sources, cut down on waste, save resources, and lower carbon emissions. Giving prospective employees specific instances of the company's sustainability projects enables them to gauge the extent of the organization's environmental responsibility commitment.

3. Employee Engagement and Empowerment: Display the ways in which staff members are actively spearheading environmental efforts inside the company. Green teams run by employees, volunteer opportunities for environmental causes, and sustainability champion recognition programs are a few examples of this. Showcasing staff participation in sustainability initiatives not only draws in candidates who care about the environment, but it also makes current staff members feel engaged and proud of their work.

4. Transparency and Accountability: Be open and honest about the company's objectives and environmental performance. Talk about important environmental data, like waste diversion rates, energy efficiency gains, and targets for reducing carbon footprint. Furthermore, exhibit accountability by providing regular updates on the status of sustainability objectives and resolving any obstacles or setbacks that arise.

5. Feature Employee Testimonials: Provide anecdotes and endorsements from staff members who are enthusiastic about sustainability and actively participating in company-wide environmental activities. Emphasize their backgrounds, accomplishments, and the beneficial effects they have had on environmental sustainability. Genuine employee testimonies can speak to prospective employees who care about the environment and show how committed the company is to giving them the tools they need to change the world.

6. Participate in Green Certifications and Rankings: Look for and take part in green rankings, prizes, and certifications that honour businesses for their sustainability and environmental performance. Examples include rankings like the Dow Jones Sustainability Index or the Corporate Knights Global 100 Most Sustainable Corporations, as well as certifications like ENERGY STAR for energy-efficient structures and LEED certification for green buildings. Placing these awards in plain sight can help the company become known as a pioneer in environmentally sustainable practices.

7. Engage in Thought Leadership: Establish the company as a thought leader in environmental sustainability by disseminating sustainability-related thoughts, findings, and best practices. Write about current environmental challenges, creative sustainable solutions, and market trends in articles, whitepapers, and blog postings. Engage in speaking engagements, webinars, and industry conferences to demonstrate the organization's proficiency and dedication to promoting constructive transformation.

8. Offer Green Benefits and Perks: Offer your staff eco-friendly advantages and benefits, such the ability to work from home, flexible work hours to cut down on commuting, rewards for taking the bus or bike, and access to eco-friendly goods and services. These perks enhance worker happiness and wellbeing in addition to showcasing the company's dedication to sustainability.

Connect with professionals and job seekers who care about the environment by actively participating in environmental forums, groups, and networks. Engage in dialogues, distribute pertinent material, and establish connections with people and institutions that support environmental sustainability. Developing connections within the environmental community can assist a company attract talent that shares its values and highlight its commitment to environmental responsibility.

Corporate social responsibility (CSR) programs, in addition to employer branding, are essential for drawing in environmentally conscientious job candidates. CSR is the term used to describe an organization's extracurricular efforts to make a good impact on the environment and society. Employers may show that they are committed to being environmentally conscious employers and good corporate citizens by including environmental sustainability into their CSR programs.

❖ **Here are some ways organizations can leverage CSR initiatives to appeal to environmentally conscious job seekers:**

1. Environmental Philanthropy and Partnerships: Sponsorships, collaborations, and charitable gifts can help support environmental causes and organizations. To solve urgent environmental challenges, this could entail working with environmental NGOs, sponsoring conservation projects, or providing financing for environmental education initiatives.

2. Community Engagement and Outreach: Involve the community in addressing environmental issues and advancing sustainability. This can entail planning environmental conservation education programs, clean-up days, or tree planting events. Organizations can show their dedication to environmental stewardship and cultivate strong bonds with regional stakeholders by actively taking part in community projects.

3. Supplier and Supply Chain Sustainability: Adopt ecologically friendly sourcing strategies and collaborate with vendors who follow eco-friendly corporate procedures. This could entail finding eco-friendly suppliers, cutting back on packaging waste, and encouraging ethical labour practices and environmental standards all the way through the supply chain. Organizations can increase their environmental effect outside of their internal operations by emphasizing sustainability in their supplier relationships.

4. Stakeholder Engagement and Advocacy: Promote environmental sustainability by interacting with stakeholders, including as staff members, clients, investors, and governmental organizations. This could be pushing for legislative adjustments that encourage the use of renewable energy, taking part in industry-wide sustainability programs, or urging consumers to make eco-friendly purchasing decisions. Organizations can become leaders in environmental activism and promote positive change on a larger scale by making the most of their resources and influence.

5. Communicate CSR Initiatives Effectively: It is imperative to effectively convey the organization's corporate social responsibility (CSR) programs and environmental commitments to potential candidates using diverse channels such as the company website, social media platforms, recruitment materials, and employee communications. To demonstrate the organization's commitment to social responsibility and environmental sustainability, highlight particular environmental relationships, accomplishments, and initiatives.

6. Provide Opportunities for Professional Development: Give staff members the chance to advance their knowledge and abilities in environmental sustainability through workshops, training courses, and ongoing educational opportunities. Encourage employees who are enthusiastic about sustainability by offering them the tools and assistance they need to pursue additional training, certifications, or professional development in environmental sectors. Organizations show their dedication to developing and strengthening environmentally conscious talent by funding employee development in sustainability.

7. Demonstrate Authenticity and Transparency: Make sure that the company's CSR efforts are sincere, open, and consistent with its objectives. Steer clear of green washing and exaggerating your environmental accomplishments to attract employers. Rather, concentrate on observable processes, quantifiable results, and ongoing environmental performance enhancement. Genuine dedication to environmental sustainability is demonstrated by the organization's authenticity and openness, which also help to establish confidence and trust with prospective employees.

8. Track and Report Environmental Performance: Establish mechanisms for monitoring, calculating, and informing stakeholders such as staff members, financiers, clients, and government agencies about environmental performance metrics. Use corporate social responsibility disclosures, yearly sustainability reports, and other channels of communication to openly share environmental goals, developments, and accomplishments.

9. Promote Sustainable Events and Practices: Make sure that business gatherings, activities, and events are organized and carried out with sustainability in mind. This can involve selecting eco-friendly locations, offering recyclable or compostable products, and implementing sustainable transportation options for guests in order to reduce waste. Encourage environmentally friendly behaviours in the workplace by educating staff members and organizing awareness campaigns on issues like water efficiency, trash reduction, and energy conservation.

All things considered, companies can draw in and hold on to top personnel who are enthusiastic about having a positive influence on the environment by skilfully utilizing employer branding and CSR activities to emphasize their dedication to environmental sustainability. Organizations have several possibilities to demonstrate their environmental leadership and entice environmentally concerned job candidates, from developing compelling sustainability narratives to carrying out tangible activities and interacting with stakeholders. Organizations may draw in top people and promote beneficial changes for the environment and society at large by emphasizing sustainability in their employer branding and CSR initiatives.

4.2 Green Recruitment Strategies

Green recruitment tactics are the methods and techniques used by businesses to draw in, keep, and develop personnel that are environmentally aware and supportive of the enterprise's sustainability objectives. These tactics incorporate environmental factors into job advertisements, employer branding, candidate selection, on boarding, and other recruitment-related processes. The objective is to create a workforce that supports the company's dedication to environmental sustainability and helps to achieve favourable environmental results. Green hiring practices can involve activities like emphasizing sustainability efforts in employer branding, adding environmental standards to the candidate selection process, providing flexible work schedules to cut down on carbon emissions, and rewarding staff members who support sustainability initiatives. All things considered, green hiring practices help companies not only draw in top candidates but also further their sustainability mission and uphold their standing as ethical employers.

The goal of green recruitment techniques is to integrate the organization's sustainability objectives with the attraction, engagement, and retention of environmentally conscientious talent. These tactics entail bringing environmental factors into play at every step of the hiring process, from candidate selection to employer branding and all in between.

❖ **Here are several key components of green recruitment strategies:**

1. Sustainable Employer Branding:
  i. Create a compelling employer brand that emphasizes the company's dedication to environmental sustainability.

  ii. Use a variety of platforms, such as the corporate website, social media accounts, and recruitment materials, to highlight sustainability objectives, accomplishments, and staff participation in environmental activities.

  iii. Recruiting materials and job ads should include sustainability messaging to draw in candidates that care about the environment.

2. Green Job Descriptions:
   i. Write job descriptions that highlight the position's contribution to environmental goals and the organization's sustainability goals.
   ii. Provide a clear description of any particular sustainability duties or requirements, such as prior experience with sustainable practices or a dedication to minimizing environmental effect, which may be necessary for the position.

3. Environmental Screening Criteria:
   i. Include questions or assessments about sustainable attitudes, experiences, and behaviours in the candidate screening process to incorporate environmental factors.
   ii. Seek applicants who have a sincere interest in environmental matters and a readiness to support the company's sustainability programs.

4. Sustainability Interviews:
   i. Ask questions on sustainability during the interview process to see whether candidates share the organization's environmental principles and culture.
   ii. Inquire of applicants regarding their opinions on environmental issues, their prior involvement in sustainability projects, and their suggestions for promoting sustainability within the company.

5. Employee Referral Programs:
   i. Through referral schemes that reward recommendations in line with the organization's sustainability goals, encourage staff members to recommend applicants who are concerned of the environment.
   ii. Utilize sustainability-focused communities and employee networks to draw in applicants with similar interests and values.

6. Green On-boarding and Training:
   i. During the on boarding process, introduce new hires to the organization's values and sustainability goals.

ii. Employees can better grasp their role in promoting sustainability goals and implementing eco-friendly work practices by receiving training and materials.

7. Flexible Work Arrangements:
i. Provide employees with flexible work arrangements, such reduced workweeks or remote work choices, to lessen their carbon footprint associated with transportation and to encourage work-life balance.

ii. Use technological solutions that facilitate remote collaboration and cut down on travel requirements to further lessen your impact on the environment.

8. Sustainability Recognition and Rewards:
i. Acknowledge and reward staff members who make a significant contribution to the company's environmental initiatives.

ii. Create sustainability awards or recognition schemes to commemorate accomplishments and promote ongoing environmental performance enhancements.

9. Continuous Feedback and Improvement:
i. Ask staff members for their opinions on sustainability-related policies and procedures, and consider their suggestions for continued development.

ii. To make sure that green recruitment tactics are in line with changing sustainability priorities, evaluate and revise them frequently in response to input from stakeholders, employees, and candidates.

Employers can develop their reputation as socially conscientious employers, advance their sustainability goals, and attract, engage, and retain environmentally conscious personnel by putting green recruitment techniques into practice. These tactics support companies in creating a workforce that upholds their environmental principles and also have a positive impact on the environment both inside and outside the company.

4.2.1 Implementing Environmentally Friendly Recruitment Strategies, Such as Virtual Recruitment Events and Paperless Application Processes

Adopting procedures that reduce the hiring process's environmental impact is necessary when implementing eco-friendly recruitment techniques, such as virtual recruitment events and paperless application processes. These tactics make use of technology to expedite the hiring process while cutting back on the use of resources like paper and the carbon emissions brought on by travel. By connecting candidates and recruiters online, virtual recruitment events do away with the requirement for physical locations and cut down on emissions associated with travel. Paperless application procedures automate workflows and recruiting documentation, allowing candidates to electronically submit applications and decreasing the need for paper-based resources.

Reducing the environmental impact of the hiring process while still successfully attracting top talent can be achieved by proactively using eco-friendly recruitment tactics, such as paperless application processes and virtual recruitment events.

❖ **Here's how organizations can implement these strategies:**

Virtual Recruitment Events:

1. Online Job Fairs: Organizers can reach a larger pool of people by holding virtual job fairs instead of using actual locations. Recruiters can engage with prospects through chat or video calls at these events through virtual booths dedicated to various departments or positions. By exploring employment prospects, attending presentations, and networking with recruiters from the comfort of their homes, candidates can lessen the environmental effect of venue leases and travel.

2. Offer Green Networking Opportunities: Give job searchers the chance to network virtually with employers and business experts. Organize online networking events, panel talks, and Q&A sessions cantered around sustainability subjects to attract job candidates who care about the environment.

3. Webinars and Info Sessions: Organizing informational meetings and webinars gives prospective employees a comprehensive understanding of the company's culture, beliefs, and open roles. These online conferences may address subjects like hiring procedures, career development chances, and corporate cultures. Organizations may minimize travel and paper documents while interacting with applicants in real-time, answering their concerns, and offering a more customized experience by utilizing video conferencing solutions.

4. Choose Sustainable Platforms: Choose virtual event platforms that reduce carbon emissions and use renewable energy sources to promote environmental sustainability. Seek for suppliers who offset their carbon footprint and deliver energy-efficient data canters.

5. Reduce Travel Emissions: Organize virtual hiring events to reduce travel requirements and transportation-related carbon emissions. To avoid the need for travel by plane or for commuting, encourage participants to take part from the comfort of their own homes or businesses.

6. Offer Green Networking Opportunities: Give job searchers the chance to network virtually with employers and business experts. Organize online networking events, panel talks, and Q&A sessions cantered around sustainability subjects to attract job candidates who care about the environment.

7. Measure and Offset Carbon Emissions: Determine the energy and platform utilization components of virtual recruitment events' carbon impact. To show guests that the organization is committed to environmental stewardship, invest in verifiable carbon offset initiatives to neutralize carbon emissions.

8. Virtual Tours and Interviews: Organizations can display their facilities and engage with candidates virtually, eliminating the need for in-person encounters, by using video conferencing solutions to conduct remote interviews. While remote interviews allow recruiters to evaluate candidates' talents, qualifications, and cultural fit from any location in the world, virtual tours give candidates an overview of the workspace, amenities, and facilities of the organization. Through the utilization of technology to enable remote communication, establishments can optimize the hiring procedure, minimize the environmental impact of travel, and accept applications from a wide range of geographical regions.

Paperless Application Processes:

1. Online Application Portals: Candidates can send their cover letters, resumes, and other application materials electronically by implementing online application portals, which eliminates the requirement for paper-based applications. By offering candidates a consolidated platform to explore and apply for job positions, follow the status of their applications, and submit supporting documents, these portals can expedite the application process. Organizations can cut down on paper use, administrative burden, and increase the effectiveness of recruitment operations by automating the application process.

2. Track Environmental Metrics: Keep track of and monitor environmental measures, such as paper saves, carbon emissions reductions, and resource conservation, that are associated with paperless recruitment processes. Utilize sustainability reporting instruments or environmental management software to track developments and pinpoint places where paperless hiring procedures need to be improved.

3. Electronic Document Management: Organizations can manage and save information electronically by digitizing recruiting papers including resumes, cover letters, and candidate profiles. This helps them to become less dependent on paper-based records. Recruiters can quickly search, filter, and retrieve candidate information with the help of electronic document management systems, which improves decision-making and communication during the hiring process. Organizations may decrease the environmental impact of paper usage and disposal while streamlining document workflows and cutting costs for printing and storage by switching to electronic document management.

4. Electronic Signatures: Organizations can get legally binding signatures on employment contracts, offer letters, and other recruitment-related documents electronically by utilizing electronic signature software. This eliminates the need for paper copies to be printed, signed, and mailed. Electronic signatures offer a safe and effective means of completing contracts and expediting the on boarding of new employees. Organizations may speed up document turnaround times, cut down on administrative hold-ups, and advance sustainability by cutting back on paper use and waste by implementing electronic signatures.

6. Digitize Recruitment Materials: To reduce the amount of paper used, switch from paper-based to digital formats for recruitment materials. On the company website or recruiting portal, make electronic versions of job descriptions, application forms, brochures, and other recruitment materials available.

❖ **Benefits of Environmentally Friendly Recruitment Strategies:**

1. Reduced Environmental Impact: Organizations can drastically cut down on waste, their carbon footprint, and their environmental effect by adopting paperless application processes and virtual recruitment events. Organizations can limit their usage of paper-based procedures, printed documents, and travel in order to save natural resources, lower greenhouse gas emissions, and promote a more sustainable future.

2. Cost Savings: Employing environmentally friendly hiring practices can also save businesses money by cutting back on travel, venue leases, printing, and document storage costs. Through the use of technology to enable remote communication and optimize administrative procedures, establishments can attain increased productivity and better distribute resources towards other aspects of their hiring endeavours.

3. Enhanced Candidate Experience: The candidate experience is improved overall by providing applicants with more flexibility, accessibility, and convenience through virtual recruitment events and paperless application processes. Organizations can facilitate diversity in the recruiting process and foster inclusivity by offering candidates the ability to electronically submit application materials, engage in virtual events, and access information online.

4. Improved Efficiency and Productivity: Streamlining workflows, decreasing manual chores, and utilizing digital solutions can help firms increase productivity and efficiency in the recruitment process. Additionally, paperless application processes streamline document management and communication, freeing recruiters to concentrate on more important operations and duties. Virtual recruitment events facilitate more effective candidate engagement.

5. Alignment with Corporate Values: Eco-friendly hiring practises reflect a company's values and mission by showcasing its dedication to sustainability and corporate social responsibility. Through the integration of environmental factors into their hiring procedures, companies can strengthen their standing as socially conscious employers and draw in applicants who have comparable objectives and beliefs.

To summarize, there are several advantages for companies, job seekers, and the environment when green recruitment tactics are used, like online events and paperless application procedures. Organizations may save costs, improve candidate experience, minimize environmental effect, increase efficiency and productivity, and show their commitment to sustainability by using technology to streamline workflows, minimize the need for paper, and allow virtual interactions. In addition to attracting great talent, companies may help ensure a more sustainable future for future generations by adopting environmentally conscious recruitment practices.

4.2.2 Leveraging Digital Platforms and Social Media to Reach a Wider Pool of Environmentally Conscious Candidates

Leveraging social media and digital platforms to connect with a larger group of people who care about the environment is a calculated move that takes advantage of the growing popularity of online platforms for networking, communication, and information exchange. Social media platforms, business networking websites, and online communities are essential tools in today's digital world for bringing people and organizations together around common interests and ideals. Organizations may broaden their applicant pool, interact with candidates who value environmental sustainability, and draw in top talent to help with sustainability projects by leveraging the power of digital platforms and social media.

1. Understanding the Landscape:

Organizations must have a thorough understanding of the internet activity and candidate landscape of environmentally concerned applicants before launching their digital recruitment campaigns. Social media sites like Facebook and Twitter, environmental forums and communities, specialized websites devoted to sustainability and green living, and professional networking sites like LinkedIn may all fall under this category.

2. Tailored Messaging and Content:

Effectively reaching and engaging this demographic requires crafting content and messaging that speaks to candidates that care about the environment. Through engaging storytelling, eye-catching graphics, and engaging interactive content, organizations may emphasize their dedication to environmental sustainability, eco-friendly practices, and corporate social responsibility efforts.

3. Engagement on Social Media:

Building relationships and fostering connections on social media platforms requires active engagement with candidates. This entails distributing pertinent content, engaging in dialogue, replying to messages and comments, and enhancing the organization's visibility through sponsored content and targeted advertising.

4. Employee Advocacy:

Encouraging staff members to act as social media evangelists for the company can greatly increase the outreach of recruitment initiatives. Employees can use their personal connections and reputation to draw in prospects who care about the environment by sharing job advertisements, company updates, and sustainability efforts with their networks.

5. Content Marketing and Thought Leadership:

Developing thought-provoking and educational content about environmental and sustainability issues can establish the company as a thought leader in the industry. Organizations can attract applicants that are enthusiastic about making a positive influence on the environment and seeking opportunities to contribute to meaningful change by releasing articles, blog posts, films, and infographics on pertinent themes.

6. Influencer Partnerships:

The organization can reach a larger audience of environmentally minded people and increase the visibility of its messaging by working with thought leaders, bloggers, and environmental influencers. Influencer collaborations offer chances for real interaction and networking with possible prospects through sponsored content, guest blog entries, social media takeovers, and virtual events.

7. Virtual Events and Webinars:

Hosting virtual events and webinars focused on sustainability topics allows organizations to engage with candidates in real-time and provide valuable insights into their environmental initiatives and career opportunities. These events can include panel discussions, workshops, networking sessions, and Q&A sessions, providing candidates with opportunities to learn, connect, and engage with the organization from anywhere in the world.

8. Data Analytics and Targeting:

Organizations can find and connect with candidates who care about the environment by using data analytics and targeting tools found on digital platforms. These tools allow for the identification of candidates based on their online behavior, hobbies, and demographics. Organizations can enhance the efficacy of their outreach and engagement initiatives by customizing their recruitment efforts and message to target audience segments based on data-driven insights.

9. Measurement and Optimization:

Continuously monitoring and analysing the performance of digital recruitment efforts allows organizations to measure the impact of their strategies and make data-driven decisions to optimize their approach over time. Key metrics to track may include engagement rates, website traffic, conversion rates, and candidate quality, providing valuable insights into the effectiveness of recruitment efforts and areas for improvement.

Conclusively, by utilizing digital platforms and social media to access a broader range of ecologically aware applicants, organizations can greatly enhance their recruitment efforts, establish connections with candidates who hold similar environmental beliefs, and draw in top talent to assist with sustainability projects. Organizations may successfully connect with environmentally conscious people and achieve favourable results for their recruitment efforts by putting into practice a comprehensive digital recruitment strategy that includes customized messaging, employee advocacy, content marketing, influencer partnerships, virtual events, and data-driven targeting. Furthermore, companies can make sure that they are effectively contacting and interacting with applicants that care about the environment and making a significant impact on their sustainability initiatives by tracking and optimizing their digital recruitment efforts on a regular basis.

4.2.3 Case Studies Highlighting Successful Green Recruitment Strategies Adopted by Organizations across Industries

❖ Here's a case study highlighting successful green recruitment strategies adopted by The Body Shop:

Case Study: The Body Shop

Background:

Global cosmetics shop The Body Shop is renowned for its dedication to social responsibility, environmental sustainability, and ethical sourcing. Through its campaigns and activities, the company promotes numerous social and environmental concerns and provides a wide choice of natural skincare, cosmetics, and fragrance products.

Challenge:

The Body Shop, a business with a strong foundation in social and environmental activism, aimed to draw applicants who shared its enthusiasm for social justice, ethical consumption, and environmental stewardship by matching its hiring procedures with these principles. Creating a green recruitment approach that would both successfully communicate the company's commitment to sustainability and draw in top individuals who shared its values was the challenge.

Strategy:

The Body Shop launched a green hiring strategy that highlighted the company's social responsibilities, ethical business practices, and sustainability initiatives. The following were the strategy's main components:

1. Values-Based Messaging: The Body Shop promoted its ideals of activism, empowerment, and environmental responsibility in job advertising, recruitment materials, and employer branding initiatives. Seeking applicants who aligned with its principles, the company emphasized its dedication to cruelty-free products, ethical sourcing, and community engagement.

2. Engagement on social media: Via social media sites like Facebook, Instagram, and Twitter, The Body Shop actively engaged with communities and groups that share their concerns about the environment. In an effort to connect with candidates who held similar principles, the company disseminated content about social justice, ethical consumption, and sustainability.

3. Employee Advocacy: Through publishing job openings, corporate news, and sustainability projects on social media, The Body Shop encouraged staff members to act as brand ambassadors. Staff participation and empowerment were highly valued by candidates, and employee advocacy increased the company's reach and exposure within environmentally aware groups.

4. Content Marketing and Thought Leadership: The Body Shop produced thought-provoking and educational content about social effect, ethical sourcing, and sustainability. The company used its website and social media platforms to disseminate information and encourage applicants who were enthusiastic about changing the world. This included blog entries, info-graphics, videos, and articles.

5. Partnerships and Collaborations: The Body Shop engaged with environmentally concerned talent and promoted career prospects by working with environmental organizations, sustainability-focused groups, and educational institutions. The Body Shop was able to reach a larger pool of candidates and tap into well-established networks of environmentally conscious people by partnering with these groups.

Results:
The Body Shop's green recruitment strategy has yielded significant results, including:

i. **Attracting top talent:** Candidates that care about the environment, are enthusiastic about sustainability, and want to work for a firm with a clear mission have been successfully drawn to the company.

ii. **Building a motivated workforce:** The employees at The Body Shop are extremely driven and committed to advancing sustainability programs, promoting moral business conduct, and improving the environment and society.

iii. **Strengthening employer brand:** The Body Shop's dedication to eco-friendly hiring practices has strengthened its standing as an employer that values social responsibility and the environment and draws in applicants who respect sustainability and ethical consumption.

Conclusion:

The Body Shop has been able to draw in top talent who are enthusiastic about social responsibility, ethical consumption, and sustainability thanks to its green recruitment strategy. Through the integration of digital platforms and social media with its recruitment methods, The Body Shop has established a highly engaged staff that is committed to promoting positive social and environmental change, all the while meeting its business goals.

❖ **Here's a case study highlighting successful green recruitment strategies adopted by Cisco:**

Case Study: Cisco

Background:

Cisco is a multinational technology corporation that specializes in telecom equipment, networking gear, and software. Cisco has undertaken a number of measures to lessen its carbon footprint, encourage energy efficiency, and assist environmental conservation efforts as part of its commitment to corporate social responsibility (CSR) and environmental sustainability.

Challenge:

As a preeminent technology business, Cisco aimed to draw applicants who shared its dedication to environmental responsibility and green technology by coordinating its hiring procedures with its sustainability principles. Creating a green recruitment approach that would successfully explain Cisco's sustainability goals and draw in top talent ready to work for a socially conscious company was the challenge.

Strategy:

Cisco launched a green hiring approach that highlighted the company's environmental stewardship commitment, green technology solutions, and sustainability activities. The following were the strategy's main components:

1. Values-Based Messaging: Cisco placed an emphasis on corporate values of innovation, sustainability, and social responsibility in job postings, recruitment materials, and employer branding initiatives. In an attempt to draw in applicants who shared its dedication to sustainability, the corporation emphasized its initiatives to lower carbon emissions, advance energy efficiency, and assist environmental conservation.

2. Engagement on social media: Cisco proactively participated in ecologically concerned communities and organizations on social media sites including Facebook, LinkedIn, and Twitter. The organization disseminated information about green technology, renewable energy, and environmental sustainability in order to initiate dialogues and cultivate connections with prospective employees who had comparable beliefs.

3. Employee Advocacy: Cisco urged staff members to promote the company on social media by notifying their networks about job openings, corporate news, and sustainability programs. Employee advocacy attracted applicants that prioritized employee empowerment and participation, as well as expanding the company's reach and exposure among environmentally concerned communities.

4. Content Marketing and Thought Leadership: Cisco produced thought-provoking and educational content about environmental impact, green technology solutions, and sustainability. The company inspired and educated people who were enthusiastic about using technology to address environmental concerns by posting blog entries, info-graphics, videos, and articles on its website and social media platforms.

5. Partnerships and Collaborations: To increase career possibilities and interact with environmentally conscious individuals, Cisco worked with environmental organizations, sustainability-focused groups, and educational institutions. By collaborating with these groups, Cisco was able to reach a larger candidate pool and gain access to well-established networks of people who share its values.

Results:
Cisco's green recruitment strategy has yielded significant results, including:

i. **Attracting top talent:** The organization has been effective in drawing applicants who care about the environment, are enthusiastic about sustainability, and want to work for a leader in green technology.

ii. **Building a motivated workforce:** The employees at Cisco are extremely driven and committed to advancing green technology solutions, promoting sustainability activities, and improving the environment.

iii. **Strengthening employer brand:** Cisco's dedication to eco-friendly hiring practices has strengthened its standing as an employer that values sustainability and innovation in the workplace and draws in applicants who share these values.

Conclusion:
Cisco has been able to draw in top personnel who are enthusiastic about sustainability, green technology, and environmental responsibility because to its green recruitment approach. By matching its hiring procedures to its sustainability principles and making good use of digital and social media channels, Cisco has developed a driven workforce committed to advancing both corporate goals and constructive environmental and social change.

❖ **Here's a case study highlighting successful green recruitment strategies adopted by Tesla:**

Case Study: Tesla

Background:
Elon Musk founded Tesla, a renowned producer of electric vehicles (EVs) and a clean energy enterprise. By producing solar energy products, energy storage systems, and electric cars, the company hopes to hasten the global shift to sustainable energy. Tesla wants to fight climate change and lessen reliance on fossil fuels in order to build a sustainable future.

Challenge:
Tesla aimed to draw in top people who were enthusiastic about sustainability, renewable energy, and cutting-edge technology because it was a pioneer in the electric vehicle market and a leader in clean energy innovation. Creating a green hiring approach that effectively communicated Tesla's mission and values and drew in candidates who shared its outlook on a sustainable future was the issue.

Strategy:
Tesla implemented a green recruitment strategy focused on promoting its commitment to sustainability, innovation, and environmental stewardship. The key elements of the strategy included:

1. Mission-Centric Branding: Tesla positioned itself as a business with a mission that is dedicated to hastening the switch to renewable energy sources. Candidates that shared the company's goal were drawn in by its emphasis on combating climate change and promoting renewable energy solutions in job ads, recruitment materials, and employer branding initiatives.

2. Engagement on social media: On social media sites like LinkedIn, Instagram, and Twitter, Tesla actively participated in conversations with groups and communities that care about the environment. In an effort to connect with people who had similar principles, the company posted content about sustainability projects, solar energy, and electric car technologies.

3. Employee Advocacy: Tesla urged staff members to act as brand ambassadors on social media by inviting their networks to view job advertisements, corporate news, and sustainability projects. The company's reach and exposure within environmentally concerned communities were enhanced by employee advocacy, which also attracted candidates who valued employee empowerment and involvement.

4. Innovation Showcase: As part of its recruitment campaign, Tesla displayed its cutting-edge goods and technologies, such as solar panels, energy storage systems, and electric cars. To showcase its cutting-edge technology and give candidates a chance to learn about Tesla's contributions to sustainability and sustainable energy, the business arranged events, webinars, and demos.

5. Partnerships and Collaborations: To develop employment possibilities and interact with environmentally concerned personnel, Tesla worked with environmental organizations, sustainability-focused groups, and educational institutions. Through these partnerships, Tesla was able to reach a larger pool of candidates and gain access to well-established networks of people who share its values.

Results:
Tesla's green recruitment strategy has yielded significant results, including:

i. **Attracting top talent:** Candidates that are enthusiastic about sustainability, renewable energy, and cutting-edge technology have been successfully drawn to the organization. The employees of Tesla are extremely driven and committed to advancing the company's goal of hastening the switch to sustainable energy sources.

ii. **Building a diverse workforce:** Tesla has developed a diversified workforce with a wide range of talents and knowledge in fields including engineering, design, manufacturing, and renewable energy thanks to its commitment to green recruitment.

iii. **Strengthening employer brand:** Tesla's green recruitment strategies have contributed to the company's image as a leader in sustainability and clean energy innovation by drawing applicants who respect environmental responsibility and aspire to have a positive global impact.

Conclusion:
Tesla has been able to draw in top personnel who are enthusiastic about sustainability, renewable energy, and cutting-edge technology thanks to its green recruitment approach. Tesla has developed a driven and diverse workforce committed to accelerating the global shift to sustainable energy while promoting the company's goal of driving positive environmental and social change. This has been made possible by the company's effective use

of digital platforms and social media, as well as by matching its recruitment practices to its mission and values.

4.3 Sustainable Selection Processes

A wide range of tactics and ideas are included in sustainable selection procedures with the goal of guaranteeing that the decisions we make now do not jeopardize the welfare of future generations. Sustainability in selection processes is essentially choosing options that are socially, economically, and environmentally responsible while also taking into account the effects of our choices on the environment.

The assessment of environmental impact is a crucial component of sustainable selection procedures. This means choosing solutions that will cause the least amount of harm to the environment by weighing their environmental footprints. For instance, sustainable selection procedures would give preference to recyclable, biodegradable, or renewable materials when selecting building materials, thereby using less energy and water.

Social responsibility is an additional crucial factor to consider. The goal of sustainable selection procedures is to make sure that all parties involved workers, communities, and future generations share fairly in the advantages and disadvantages of decisions. This could entail choosing partners and suppliers who follow ethical labour standards, offer secure workplaces, and offer competitive pay. It also entails taking into account how actions may harm marginalized groups or exacerbate social inequity, among other social ramifications.

Another essential component of sustainable selection procedures is economic viability. In the end, sustainability is about creating value that lasts over time, even if it is frequently linked to higher expenses, especially in the short term. The long-term costs and advantages of various options are considered in sustainable decision procedures, together with variables like resource availability, climate change resilience, and growth and innovation potential. Through a comprehensive analysis of the lifecycle costs of goods and services, companies may make better-informed decisions that strike a balance between immediate profit and long-term sustainability.

Life cycle assessment (LCA) is one method for sustainable selection procedures; it includes assessing a product or service's environmental effects at every stage of its lifecycle, from the extraction of raw materials to disposal. Organizations can find ways to cut back on resource usage, eliminate waste, and lessen environmental contamination by taking into account the environmental effects of every step of the lifecycle. For instance, a business might decide to use locally sourced products to cut down on emissions from transportation or might decide to power its operations with renewable energy.

Sustainable selection procedures may also take into account the circular economy's tenets, which aim to promote resource recovery, recycling, and reuse while minimizing waste. This can entail creating items that are easy to disassemble and reuse, putting in place closed-loop recycling systems, or collaborating with suppliers to collect and reuse products that have reached the end of their useful lives. Organizations may lessen their reliance on finite resources and help create a more sustainable future by closing the loop on material flows.

Sustainable selection procedures also require accountability and transparency. Organizations should take responsibility for the social and environmental effects of their decisions and be open and honest about the methods they use to assess possibilities and make decisions. This may include monitoring and reporting on key performance metrics linked to sustainability, as well as interacting with stakeholders, including staff members, clients, and communities, to get their opinions.

Ultimately, sustainable selection procedures are about making decisions that support the planet's and people's well-being and are consistent with sustainability principles. Through the incorporation of environmental, social, and economic factors into decision-making procedures, entities can generate value that is not only sustainable but also fair and comprehensive. Sustainability needs to be the guiding concept that influences every decision we make, whether we are choosing supplies for a building project, suppliers for a supply chain, or investments.

❖ **Here's a detailed breakdown of the steps involved in a sustainable selection process:**

Step-1. Needs Assessment and Job Analysis:
- To find out the organization's personnel needs and the essential competencies needed for the role, start by performing a comprehensive needs assessment.
- To determine the essential duties, responsibilities, and competencies required for the position, conduct a job analysis.
- To make sure that the job analysis is in line with the organization's environmental and social objectives, think about adding sustainability criteria.

Step-2. Development of Sustainable Job Descriptions:
- Make that the duties, requirements, and expectations of the role are appropriately reflected in the job descriptions.
- Add sustainability-related requirements, if applicable to the position, such as familiarity with environmental laws, prior expertise with sustainable practices, or a dedication to diversity and inclusion.
- Avoid using discriminatory language that could deter candidates from underrepresented groups and instead use inclusive language.

Step-3. Recruitment Strategy:
- Create a hiring strategy that highlights the company's dedication to sustainability and reaches out to a wide range of prospects.
- To draw in a varied candidate pool, use a range of recruitment channels, such as job boards, social media, professional networks, and neighbourhood associations.
- Collaborate with organizations that prioritize diversity and take part in job fairs and activities aimed at underrepresented populations.

Step-4. Application Screening:
- Examine resumes and applications to find applicants who fit the requirements and have the necessary experience and skills.
- During the screening process, take into account credentials relevant to sustainability, such as prior involvement with sustainability projects or a track record of demonstrating a commitment to environmental and social responsibility.

Step-5. Interview Process:
- Conduct organized interviews to evaluate applicants' suitability for the position, qualifications, and skills.
- Incorporate inquiries that delve into the candidates' comprehension of sustainability matters, their methodology for moral decision-making, and their capacity to foster a varied and welcoming workplace.
- Assess candidates' prior experiences and actions in relation to sustainability and social responsibility by using behavioural interviewing techniques.

Step-6. Candidate Assessment and Selection:
- Assess applicants according to their credentials, background, and compatibility with the organization's sustainability objectives and principles.
- Take into account utilizing evaluation instruments or activities, such as role-playing games, simulations, or case studies, that gauge applicants' sustainability competencies.
- In order to guarantee consistency with company aims and values, involve important stakeholders in the selection process, such as recruiting managers, team members, and representatives from pertinent departments.

Step-7. Offer and On boarding:
- Offer positions to chosen applicants, stressing the company's dedication to social responsibility and sustainability.

- Make sure new hires are thoroughly on boarded and informed about the organization's sustainability policies, expectations, and projects.
- To encourage staff members' development and participation, provide chances for continuous training and development on sustainability-related subjects.

Step-8. Performance Evaluation and Feedback:
- Put in place performance evaluation procedures that incorporate social responsibility and sustainability objectives.
- Give staff members regular feedback on how they are contributing to sustainability goals and where they can do better.
- Acknowledge and reward staff members that go above and above in promoting sustainability and making a good impact on the environment and society.

Step-9. Continuous Improvement:
- Evaluate and assess the sustainable selection process on a regular basis.
- To determine strengths, shortcomings, and areas for development, get input from hiring managers, candidates, and staff members.
- As appropriate, modify the procedure to better align it with the objectives and core values of the company and produce better results over time.
- These guidelines can help companies create and execute a sustainable hiring process that draws in top talent, encourages social responsibility and sustainability, and improves social and environmental consequences.

4.3.1 Designing Selection Processes That Align with Sustainability Goals

Organizations that are dedicated to social responsibility and environmental stewardship should take the initiative to design selection procedures that support sustainability objectives, such as adding environmental standards into candidate evaluations. This strategy acknowledges the relationship between human activity and environmental effects and seeks to find and draw applicants who not only have the required training and experience but also exhibit a sincere interest in sustainability.

A crucial element of integrating environmental standards into candidate evaluations is formulating precise and pertinent standards that mirror the company's sustainability objectives and principles. This entails determining the precise environmental sustainability-related knowledge, abilities, and characteristics that are necessary for the position in issue. While positions in other departments may benefit from candidates who show a general awareness of environmental issues and a willingness to learn and adapt, positions in sustainability management, for instance, may require candidates to have a thorough understanding of environmental regulations, climate change mitigation strategies, and sustainable business practices.

Organizations can incorporate the environmental criteria into job ads, applications, interviews, and assessments, among other stages of the selection process, once they have been established. This can be accomplished in a number of ways, such as asking targeted questions or providing prompts about sustainability in job applications; conducting behavioural interviews to gauge candidates' attitudes and prior experiences with sustainability; and assessing candidates' application of sustainability principles in real-world situations through case studies or simulations.

Organizations should consider a candidate's compatibility with the sustainability culture and values of the company in addition to their unique qualities. This entails evaluating candidates' potential to positively impact the organization's sustainability objectives as well as their alignment with the organization's sustainability-related purpose, vision, and values. Interviews for cultural fit, in which prospective hires meet with current staff members who support sustainability, are especially useful for determining a candidate's fit with the company's sustainable culture.

Organizations can also help candidates on their path to sustainability by offering opportunities for education and training. Offering tools like online classes, seminars, or mentorship programs can assist candidates acquire the know-how, abilities, and attitude required to successfully incorporate sustainability into their work. Organizations can show their dedication to promoting a sustainable culture and bolster their ability to tackle environmental issues by investing in the professional development of their workforce.

Organizations that are devoted to social responsibility and environmental stewardship have a moral and strategic obligation to incorporate environmental parameters into candidate assessments. Organizations can create value for society at large as well as for themselves by developing a staff that is dedicated to achieving sustainability goals in addition to being capable and competent. For businesses to succeed over the long run in the linked world of today, where environmental challenges are becoming more pressing and complicated, it is crucial to create selection procedures that support sustainability objectives.

❖ **To effectively incorporate environmental criteria into candidate assessments, organizations can adopt several strategies:**

1. Define Environmental Criteria: To begin, it is necessary to specify the environmental requirements that are pertinent to the organization's sustainability objectives and principles. Examples of these requirements include familiarity with environmental concerns, prior experience implementing sustainable practices, and a track record of environmental responsibility.

2. Integrate Environmental Questions: Employers may include particular questions on environmental sustainability in assessments, interviews, and job applications. These inquiries can evaluate the candidates' knowledge of sustainability concepts, their involvement in environmental projects, and their suggestions for incorporating sustainability into their work.

3. Behavioural Interviews: Interviewing applicants behaviourally might reveal important information about their prior actions and perspectives on sustainability. Organizations can evaluate candidates' commitment to sustainability in a real-world setting by asking them to share instances of how they have solved environmental concerns or implemented sustainable practices in previous employment.

4. Case Studies or Simulations: The selection process might evaluate candidates' capacity to implement sustainability principles in practical contexts by using case studies or simulations. Candidates might be required to evaluate a business case and suggest sustainable solutions, for instance, to show that they have problem-solving abilities and an awareness of environmental issues.

5. Reference Checks: Further confirming a candidate's commitment to sustainability can be done by running reference checks on the accomplishments and environmental experience they claim to have. Candidates' contributions to environmental projects and fitness for employment with environmental responsibility might be better understood by consulting with previous employers or colleagues.

6. Assess Cultural Fit: Organizations should evaluate candidates' alignment with the organization's sustainability culture and principles in addition to their technical skills and qualifications. This can be accomplished through interviews for cultural fit or by including current workers who support sustainability in the hiring process.

7. Provide Education and Training: Through the provision of training and educational opportunities, organizations can assist candidates in their journey towards sustainability. In order to successfully contribute to environmental stewardship programs and incorporate sustainability into their job, applicants may benefit from developing the knowledge, abilities, and mindset that these initiatives require.

8. Evaluate Long-Term Potential: Organizations should evaluate individuals' long-term potential to support sustainability goals in addition to their immediate fit for the position. Assessing candidates' openness to learning, development, and adaptability to changing sustainability opportunities and challenges may fall under this category.

Organizations may develop a workforce that is dedicated to achieving sustainability goals in addition to being knowledgeable and competent by include environmental criteria in applicant assessments. This strategy not only makes the company more capable of handling environmental issues, but it also cultivates a sustainable culture that appeals to stakeholders, consumers, and staff. In the end, creating selection procedures that support sustainability objectives is both strategically and morally necessary in the globalized world of today.

4.3.2 Training Recruiters and Hiring Managers on Green Hiring Practices and the Importance of Diversity and Inclusion in Building a Sustainable Workforce

"Training recruiters and hiring managers on green hiring practices and the importance of diversity and inclusion in building a sustainable workforce" entail putting in place an extensive educational program designed to enhance the awareness, knowledge, and abilities of those in charge of finding new hires for an organization. This comprehensive training program explores two related domains in great detail:

Green Hiring Practices:

Green recruiting practices, as they relate to hiring and employment, comprise a wide range of approaches and techniques intended to reduce the environmental impact of hiring activities within organizations. These procedures cover every stage of the hiring process, from contacting potential candidates to making the final decision and providing on boarding. For example, recruiters may receive training on how to use digital platforms and technology to reduce the number of paper-based materials they use, which would cut down on waste and save natural resources. Additionally, they might learn how to include sustainability factors in candidate assessments and job listings, which would help them find and rank applicants who show a dedication to sustainable practices and environmental stewardship in their work. Organizations can exhibit their commitment to environmental responsibility and establish a reputation as moral and progressive employers among potential employees, clients, and stakeholders by incorporating green hiring practices into their recruitment procedures.

2. Diversity and Inclusion in Building a Sustainable Workforce:

This aspect of the training program highlights the fundamental connection between inclusion and diversity in the workforce and the long-term viability of the company. Diversity is the wide range of individual distinctions among people, including things like age, gender identity, sexual orientation, race, ethnicity, socioeconomic level, and cultural heritage. Conversely, inclusion refers to establishing a work climate in which people with different backgrounds feel appreciated, respected, and free to share their special skills and viewpoints. A workforce that embraces diversity and cultivates a sense of inclusivity and belonging is one that is sustainable. Organizations that embrace diversity and inclusion not only improve their ability to innovate, solve problems, and be creative, but they also help their staff members feel cohesive, respectful, and collaborative. Additionally, inclusive workplaces are better able to draw in and hold on to top talent from a variety of demographic backgrounds, which improves organizational flexibility, competitiveness, and resilience in a constantly changing global economy.

Beyond just theoretical ideas, the training program offers hiring managers and recruiters' real-world tools, resources, and case studies to help them operationalize green hiring practices and advance diversity and inclusion in their particular domains of influence. This could entail creating workshops, learning materials, and training modules specifically suited to the organization's aims and particular needs. Furthermore, the program might include interactive components like group discussions, role-playing, and real-world simulations to help with peer-to-peer learning and collaboration while reinforcing important concepts.

Recruiters and recruiting managers can create a more sustainable and socially conscious staff by investing in training on diversity and inclusion, green hiring practices, and other related topics. They enable their talent acquisition specialists to make well-informed choices that are consistent with the values, objectives, and general expectations of the firm. In addition, they cultivate an environment that values ongoing learning, innovation, and progress, which helps them to remain ahead of new trends and obstacles in a world that is getting more complicated and linked by the day. By doing this, they not only improve their standing as morally and responsibly conducting business, but they also help to build a society that is more just, inclusive, and sustainable for coming generations.

4.3.3 Research Findings on the Impact of Sustainable Selection Processes on Employment and Retention Rates

The results of studies examining how sustainable selection procedures affect employee engagement and retention rates offer important new perspectives on the real advantages of incorporating sustainability concepts into talent acquisition strategies. This topic has been the subject of numerous organizational settings research, which have clarified the favourable relationship between sustainable recruiting strategies and employee outcomes.

1. Increased Employee Engagement: Several studies have shown that when workers believe their company is socially and ecologically conscious, they are more engaged. For instance, a study that was published in the Journal of Business Ethics discovered that when workers believe their company practices environmental responsibility, they are more likely to be devoted to it. This view is fostered in large part by sustainable selection procedures, which give preference to applicants who show a commitment to sustainability. Sustainable selection procedures help to foster a sense of shared purpose and values alignment among employees by choosing applicants who share the organization's social and environmental values. Employee engagement is positively correlated with pro-activity, productivity, and dedication to work, which in turn promotes general well-being and job satisfaction.

2. Enhanced Retention Rates: Studies reveal that companies with robust sustainability programs have reduced employee turnover. Researchers at Cornell University discovered that workers are more inclined to stick with an organization if they believe it to be socially responsible. This is made possible by sustainable selection procedures, which draw applicants who are committed to social and environmental causes and are more likely to be long-term employees of the company. Workers who are committed to the goals and values of their company are less inclined to look for work elsewhere, which gives the company more stability and consistency.

3. Improved Organizational Culture: An organization's positive culture that emphasizes sustainability and social responsibility can be fostered through sustainable selection methods. Studies have indicated that companies possessing robust sustainability cultures are more appealing to workers and enjoy greater levels of employee engagement and retention. Employers may attract individuals who are enthusiastic about sustainability and who are more likely to uphold and advance these principles at work by using sustainable selection procedures. This promotes a collaborative, innovative, and morally-driven culture that strengthens bonds between co-workers and creates a positive work atmosphere that encourages employee engagement and retention.

4. Alignment with Millennial Values: The current generation of workers, known as millennial, place a high value on social responsibility and sustainability while making employment decisions. 64% of millennial think about a company's ethical and environmental goals when choosing where to work, according to a Cone Communications study. This group finds appeal in sustainable selection procedures because they are consistent with their values and provide avenues for them to use their profession to positively impact the world. Organizations can improve employee engagement and retention rates by attracting and retaining millennial talent by giving preference to candidates who exhibit a commitment to sustainability.

5. Positive Employer Brand Image: Employers can improve their employer brand image and attract more candidates by implementing sustainable selecting practices. Even if they were unemployed, 69% of job seekers would turn down a job offer from a company with a poor image, according to a study by the Corporate Responsibility Association. Job seekers have a more positive perception of organizations that practice social responsibility and environmental responsibility, which increases their interest and engagement in the recruitment process. A business can stand out from the competition and use a strong employer brand that is based on sustainability as a potent recruitment and retention strategy.

6. Greater Employee Motivation and Pride: When a firm prioritizes social and environmental responsibility, its employees can feel motivated and proud to work for it thanks to sustainable selection methods. When workers believe their company is changing the world for the better, it inspires them to put in their all to help the business succeed. An enhanced feeling of purpose can result in better job satisfaction, greater spirits, and a more steadfast sense of loyalty among staff members.

7. Enhanced Employee Well-being: Studies have indicated that workers employed by companies that practice social responsibility and environmental responsibility report better levels of general well-being. This is made possible by sustainable selection procedures, which foster an environment at work that is consistent with the values and beliefs of the employees. Workers are more likely to be fulfilled and satisfied in their roles and to have better mental and emotional health if they believe that their organization shares their commitment to sustainability.

8. Positive Impact on Employee Health: Workplace practices that prioritize health and wellbeing, such as encouraging active commuting, granting access to healthy food options, and establishing green places for rest and rejuvenation, are frequently the outcome of sustainable selection procedures. Stress levels are likely to drop, physical health outcomes are more likely to improve, and overall quality of life is more probable for workers in environmentally friendly and health-conscious workplaces.

9. Enhanced Team Collaboration and Innovation: Organizations can cultivate a collaborative and innovative culture by implementing sustainable selection processes. Recruiting workers who are enthusiastic about sustainability and social responsibility allows firms to form multidisciplinary teams that include a range of skills and viewpoints. This variety of perspectives and backgrounds can stimulate innovation, foster creativity, and result in the creation of fresh answers to challenging problems, strengthening the organization's competitive advantage in the market.

10. Positive Impact on Corporate Social Responsibility (CSR) Initiatives: Businesses that put sustainability first when it comes to hiring are better positioned to live up to their corporate social responsibility (CSR) obligations. There is a higher likelihood of active participation in CSR activities, such as volunteer programs, community service projects, and sustainability efforts, among employees recruited using sustainable selection methods. Employee involvement in CSR initiatives improves the company's standing with stakeholders and has a beneficial social and environmental impact on the communities in which it works.

11. Long-term Sustainable Growth: The long-term sustainable growth and performance of organizations are facilitated by sustainable selection processes. Organizations may develop a workforce that is resilient, adaptive, and prepared for the future by luring and keeping workers who share their commitment to sustainability and social responsibility. This workforce will drive continuous growth and profitability for the company by better navigating obstacles and seizing opportunities in an increasingly complicated and linked global environment.

To sum up, studies show that sustainable selection procedures influence employee engagement and retention rates in a variety of ways. Organizations can establish a work environment that promotes employee motivation, well-being, and pride, strengthens corporate social responsibility initiatives, and drives long-term sustainable growth by harmonizing recruitment practices with sustainability principles. These advantages not only help specific firms succeed, but they also have a favourable impact on the environment and society as a whole.

Chapter – 5

Environmental Training and Development

Introduction to Environmental Training:

One essential element of any endeavour to address the numerous environmental issues that our world is currently facing is environmental training. It includes a variety of educational programs intended to raise consciousness, develop understanding, and cultivate abilities linked to sustainability and environmental preservation. Environmental education is essential for enabling all stakeholders from individuals and communities to corporations and governments to comprehend, value, and safeguard the natural world.

Fundamentally, the goal of environmental education is to inform people about the complexity of environmental problems and how they relate to human activity. Participants learn about issues including pollution, resource depletion, biodiversity loss, climate change, and ecosystem health through workshops, seminars, courses, and other educational opportunities. Environmental training builds the foundation for responsible environmental stewardship and informed decision-making by deepening understanding of these concerns.

Participants in environmental training gain the useful skills necessary to apply sustainable practices in a variety of settings. This covers methods for controlling waste, boosting biodiversity, saving energy and water, and lowering carbon footprint. People who receive environmental training are better equipped to adopt eco-friendly behaviours and contribute to positive environmental outcomes, whether in the company, community, or personal sphere.

The significance of environmental leadership and activism is frequently emphasized in environmental training. Participants gain knowledge on how to interact with stakeholders, lobby for changes in legislation that support sustainability, and communicate about environmental issues in an effective manner. Environmental training encourages group action and has an impact on local, national, and international decision-making processes by enabling people to become environmental champions in their areas of influence.

Environmental training not only increases individual competence but also encourages networking and cooperation amongst a variety of stakeholders. Connecting with colleagues, professionals, and organizations involved in environmental sustainability is possible for participants. By exchanging knowledge, working together on initiatives, and fostering partnerships, they may better utilize their combined resources and experience to tackle environmental issues.

To develop a new generation of environmental leaders and professionals, environmental training is crucial. Future generations are motivated and empowered to pursue jobs in environmental science, conservation, policy, and activism by environmental training, which provides educational opportunities for students and young professionals. Young people acquire the information, abilities, and enthusiasm required to significantly contribute to environmental sustainability through formal education programs, internships, and mentorship efforts.

All things considered, environmental education acts as a stimulant for improvement, encouraging people and groups to take an active and environmentally concerned stance. Investing in environmental training is crucial for creating a more resilient and sustainable future in a time when environmental risks are on the rise. Environmental training is essential to safeguarding the environment for present and future generations because it empowers, educates, and mobilizes stakeholders.

Meaning of Environmental Training:
The term "environmental training" describes educational programs and activities intended to raise people's awareness of, familiarity with, and proficiency with environmental issues, sustainable practices, and conservation efforts. It seeks to enable people and institutions to embrace

ecologically conscious actions and behaviours by helping them to comprehend the complexities of environmental issues. Workshops, seminars, courses, online modules, and other educational opportunities cantered around issues like resource management, pollution prevention, biodiversity conservation, climate change, and sustainable development can all be considered forms of environmental training. Promoting environmental stewardship and helping to preserve and safeguard the natural world are the ultimate goals of environmental training.

Introduction to Environmental Development:
Sustainable outcomes for the earth and its inhabitants are the goal of environmental development. It entails putting into action plans, procedures, and initiatives that advance human welfare and socioeconomic development in addition to fostering the preservation and restoration of ecosystems, biodiversity, and natural resources.

Fundamentally, the goal of environmental development is to achieve a balance between socioeconomic development and environmental protection. It acknowledges nature's inherent worth and the significance of protecting ecological integrity for present and future generations. Furthermore, environmental development advocates for strategies that support inclusive and sustainable growth by acknowledging the interconnectedness of social justice, economic prosperity, and environmental health.

Initiatives for environmental development cover a broad spectrum of operations in multiple areas, such as waste reduction, water management, renewable energy, sustainable agriculture, conservation, and climate adaption. Governments, corporations, communities, non-governmental organizations (NGOs), and international agencies may spearhead these programs, all of which support group efforts to solve environmental problems.

The significance of incorporating environmental factors into decision-making processes at all levels, from local to global, is emphasized by environmental development. The statement advocates for the implementation of policies and methods that give precedence to environmental sustainability, foster adaptability to environmental disruptions, and guarantee the just allocation of environmental advantages and drawbacks.

Environmental development understands that in order to make significant progress, various stakeholders must work together and form partnerships. It entails bringing communities, corporations, governments, universities, and civil society organizations together in concert to solve environmental problems and accomplish shared objectives. Environmental development projects can optimize their impact by harnessing expertise, resources, and creativity through the promotion of cooperation and collaborative action.

Environmental development seeks not only to solve environmental problems but also to improve human welfare and quality of life. It acknowledges that vulnerable groups and marginalized communities are disproportionately impacted by environmental deterioration, which exacerbates social inequality and threatens human rights. Environmental development therefore aims to ensure that everyone has access to clean air, water, food, and a healthy environment by promoting environmental justice, equity, and inclusivity.

In general, environmental development is an all-encompassing, multidisciplinary strategy that promotes sustainable socioeconomic growth while tackling environmental issues. Environmental development aims to create a world where people and nature may coexist peacefully by incorporating environmental considerations into practices, regulations, and initiatives. In light of the pressing environmental issues of the twenty-first century, environmental development presents a way forward for creating a future that is more sustainable, egalitarian, and resilient for all.

Meaning of Environmental Development:
The process of promoting sustainable results for both the natural environment and human societies is referred to as environmental development. It entails programs and activities meant to advance human welfare and socioeconomic development while simultaneously supporting the preservation and restoration of ecosystems, biodiversity, and natural resources. In order to strike a balance between environmental preservation, social justice, and economic development, environmental development aims to include environmental factors into decision-making procedures, laws, and practices across a range of industries. The ultimate goal of

environmental development is to build a sustainable, just, and resilient future where people and the environment may coexist together.

Concept of Environmental Training and Development:

Programs for environmental training and development are essential for tackling the urgent environmental issues that our world is currently confronting. The urgency of concerns like resource depletion, pollution, climate change, and biodiversity loss is making it more and more important for people and organizations to understand and implement sustainable practices. In order to provide participants with the knowledge and skills they need to make wise decisions and take action in the direction of environmental stewardship and conservation, these programs provide thorough instruction.

Increasing public knowledge of environmental issues and how they relate to human activity is one of the main goals of environmental training and development. Through the impartation of knowledge regarding the origins and aftermaths of environmental deterioration, these initiatives aid in cultivating a more profound appreciation for the significance of safeguarding natural ecosystems and resources. Participants gain knowledge of important ideas such ecological systems, sustainable development principles, and climate science through engaging workshops, lectures, and multimedia presentations.

Programs for environmental training and development also give people the hands-on experience they need to apply sustainable practices in a variety of settings. This covers methods for sustainable agriculture, waste minimization, water conservation, and energy efficiency. It is possible for participants to gain knowledge about creating sustainability strategies, integrating green technologies into daily operations, and conducting environmental evaluations. Through acquiring practical knowledge and experience, individuals become more equipped to adopt sustainable solutions in their communities, workplaces, and personal lives.

Additionally, the significance of environmental leadership and activism is frequently emphasized in these programs. In order to encourage environmental awareness and action, participants learn about effective communication strategies, stakeholder engagement tactics, and policy advocacy approaches. These programs support larger initiatives to promote positive change and have an impact on local, national, and international decision-making processes by enabling people to take on the role of environmental champions within their businesses and communities.

Programs for environmental training and development not only enhance knowledge and abilities but also offer chances for networking and teamwork. Participants get the opportunity to network with like-minded people, professionals, and organizations involved in environmental sustainability. Together, they can address environmental concerns by exchanging ideas, exchanging best practices, and forming alliances through networking events, cooperative initiatives, and group projects.

Furthermore, programs for environmental leadership and development are essential in forming the next generation of environmental professionals and leaders. Through the provision of educational opportunities, these initiatives encourage and enable the upcoming generation to take on the role of environmental stewards. Young people acquire the knowledge, abilities, and drive to pursue professions in environmental research, conservation, policy, and activism through both official education programs at universities and colleges and informal training efforts.

Programs for environmental training and development also support communities' and organizations' general sustainability and resilience. They lessen the dangers brought on by resource limitations and environmental hazards by developing capability and encouraging an attitude of environmental responsibility. Businesses that engage in environmental training and development can save money, become more efficient, build their brand, and face less risks associated with regulatory compliance. Communities may experience an uptick in social cohesiveness, a rise in resistance to environmental shocks, and an improvement in quality of life.

Programs for environmental training and development can also boost the economy by encouraging innovation and generating green jobs. Through the provision of training in sustainable technology and practices, these programs foster economic expansion and employment opportunities in industries including waste management, green building, eco-tourism, and renewable energy. Additionally, they aid in meeting the increasing need for environmental knowledge across a range of businesses, improving workforce preparedness and competitiveness.

Programs for environmental training and development are crucial instruments for creating a future that is more resilient and sustainable overall. They support the group effort to save our planet for future generations by enlightening, empowering, and inspiring people and groups to take action. These programs—which can be delivered through official education, online learning platforms, community seminars, or workplace training initiatives—have a significant impact on how people think, act, and behave in relation to the environment. Investing in environmental training and development is becoming more and more necessary as we face the difficult environmental concerns of the twenty-first century in order to create a fairer and more sustainable world.

5.1 Training and Environmental Awareness

The goal of environmental awareness training is to foster a deep understanding of the complex interactions that exist between human society and the natural world. It is a complete and dynamic process. It includes a broad range of educational programs, from structured classroom training to opportunities for hands-on learning in natural settings. Fundamentally, environmental awareness training aims to develop a comprehensive viewpoint that acknowledges the inherent worth of ecosystems, the compelling need to address environmental issues, and the part that people and communities play in bringing about positive change.

Learning more about the intricate network of ecological processes that support life on Earth is one of the main goals of environmental awareness training. Investigating ideas like ecological resilience, biodiversity, and the interconnectedness of species within ecosystems are all part of this. Participants develop a greater understanding of the complex relationships that shape the natural world and the significant effects of human activity on ecological systems by exploring the principles of ecology.

Additionally, environmental awareness training provides a forum for explaining the various environmental problems that modern civilization is facing. These issues, which range from pollution and resource depletion to climate change and habitat destruction, pose serious risks to the integrity of the environment and human well-being. Participants receive in-depth instruction and analytical tools via interactive workshops and extensive curriculum, which enable them to understand the underlying causes and far-reaching effects of environmental deterioration.

Beyond merely increasing public awareness, environmental education aims to provide people the knowledge, abilities, and self-determination to actively effect change in their communities. This means developing participants' critical thinking, problem-solving, and decision-making skills so they can recognize long-term solutions to environmental issues and push for their adoption. Environmental awareness training enables people to take part in group action and aid in the shift towards a more just and sustainable society by promoting a feeling of civic duty and environmental stewardship.

Training in environmental awareness also emphasizes the significance of embracing sustainable lifestyles and consumption habits that reduce their negative effects on the environment. This entails encouraging actions like using ecologically friendly items, cutting back on waste, conserving energy, and supporting sustainable transportation. Environmental education encourages people to adopt sustainable habits that help protect natural resources and slow down climate change by motivating them to make thoughtful decisions in their daily lives.

Environmental awareness training frequently includes experiential learning opportunities that let participants get up close and personal with nature, in addition to traditional educational curricula. Field visits to natural areas, practical conservation initiatives, and immersive outdoor experiences that promote a stronger sense of connection and respect for the natural world are a few examples of this. These experiential learning activities cultivate awe, wonder, and reverence for the beauty and complexity of the natural world by offering chances for direct involvement with the environment.

In general, environmental awareness training is essential for influencing environmental attitudes, actions, and values in both the individual and the larger community. Environmental education establishes the foundation for creating a society that is more resilient, peaceful, and environmentally conscientious by encouraging ecological literacy, empowering civic engagement, and supporting sustainable lifestyles. It is impossible to overestimate the significance of environmental awareness training as a catalyst for constructive change in a time of unparalleled environmental concerns.

5.1.1 Understanding the Concept of Environmental Awareness and its Importance in Fostering a Culture of Sustainability within Organizations

Recognizing the importance of knowledge, understanding, and concern about environmental issues among individuals and within organizations is necessary in order to comprehend the idea of environmental awareness. It comprises realizing how closely human activity and the state of the world are related, as well as how crucial it is to adopt eco-friendly habits and behaviours in order to lessen adverse environmental effects.

Encouraging environmental consciousness in organizations involves more than just sharing knowledge; it also involves developing a strong grasp of sustainability and a dedication to it at every level of the organizational structure. It involves fostering a climate in which strategic decision-making and routine working procedures are infused with an awareness of the environment.

Here's a detailed exploration of the significance of environmental awareness within organizations:

1. Informed Decision Making and Strategic Planning: The basis for strategic planning and well-informed decision-making in companies is environmental awareness. Employees and decision-makers are better able to incorporate environmental considerations into business strategy, goals, and policies when they have a thorough awareness of environmental challenges and their repercussions. By taking a proactive stance, companies can effectively position themselves for long-term success by anticipating and responding to environmental concerns like resource shortages, climate change, and regulatory changes.

2. Behavioural Change and Organizational Culture: An organizational culture that prioritizes sustainability can be developed through increasing environmental awareness and encouraging behavioural change. Organizations can encourage employees to adopt more environmentally responsible habits both inside and outside the workplace by raising knowledge of the effects that individual and group activities have on the environment. There are several ways in which this shift in culture toward sustainability can be seen, such as more recycling efforts, lower energy use, the adoption of green procurement procedures, and support for eco-friendly transportation options.

3. Risk Management and Resilience: To effectively manage risks and strengthen organizational resilience against environmental hazards, environmental knowledge is crucial. Organizations can identify vulnerabilities, evaluate the implications of their activities, and create proactive plans to manage risks by having a thorough awareness of the potential environmental threats. This could entail taking steps like putting environmental management systems into place, assessing environmental risks, and creating backup plans in case of natural disasters or unintentional environmental accidents.

4. Cost Savings and Operational Efficiency: Organizations can experience major cost savings and operational efficiencies as a result of environmental awareness. Organizations can save operational expenses and their environmental impact at the same time by investing in energy-efficient technologies, maximizing resource utilization, and reducing waste output. Furthermore, implementing sustainable practices can boost resource allocation, expedite procedures, and improve operational efficiency—all of which will eventually benefit the organization's bottom line.

5. Enhanced Reputation and Stakeholder Relations: An organization's reputation is improved and its connections with consumers, investors, regulators, and local communities are strengthened when it demonstrates environmental awareness. Organizations can gain the respect and confidence of stakeholders by showcasing their dedication to sustainability and environmental management. Gaining a favourable reputation can result in concrete advantages including a bigger market share, stronger brand loyalty, and easier access to funding and investment opportunities.

6. Legal Compliance and Regulatory Adherence: Ensuring compliance with environmental laws, regulations, and standards requires a high level of environmental awareness. Organizations can prevent legal risks, financial penalties, and harm to their brand by remaining up to date on changing regulations and industry best practices. Additionally, upholding a proactive stance toward environmental compliance shows a dedication to moral business conduct and responsible corporate citizenship, which improves the company's reputation with regulators, clients, and the general public.

7. Employee Engagement and Talent Attraction: Within enterprises, environmental awareness campaigns can increase staff morale, happiness, and involvement. Employees are more likely to feel inspired, appreciated, and pleased to work for a company that values sustainability and environmental responsibility. Getting staff members involved in environmental projects, volunteer work, green teams, and sustainability efforts creates a feeling of mission, team spirit, and shared influence. Furthermore, placing a high priority on environmental awareness helps draw in and keep top talent, especially from environmentally conscious workers who are looking for meaningful work and companies that share their values.

To sum up, in order to promote sustainability, resilience, and responsible stewardship of the environment, it is critical for organizations to emphasize environmental awareness. Organizations can gain a lot by putting an emphasis on environmental awareness programs and incorporating sustainability into their operations and organizational culture. Some of the advantages include better risk management, more effective decision-making, cost savings, enhanced reputation, and regulatory compliance, engaging employees, and attracting top talent. Businesses that make environmental awareness a fundamental value will be better positioned to prosper in a world that is changing quickly as environmental concerns continue to evolve and deepen.

5.1.2 Methods for Increasing Employee Awareness about Environmental Issues

Creating a sustainable culture in firms requires raising employee knowledge of environmental issues. Organizations can empower their employees to make environmentally responsible decisions and contribute to beneficial environmental outcomes by educating and engaging them.

Organisations can utilise a range of techniques and approaches, such as seminars, training sessions, communication campaigns, and other efforts, to improve employee understanding regarding environmental issues.

1. Workshops and Training Sessions:
Employees can gain comprehensive knowledge and skills about environmental challenges and sustainable practices through workshops and training sessions. A wide range of subjects can be discussed in these sessions, such as water conservation, recycling, energy conservation, waste reduction, climate change, and sustainable transportation. To keep participants interested and promote learning, workshops may incorporate talks, interactive exercises, case studies, presentations, and hands-on activities. Organizations may guarantee that staff members have the knowledge and tools necessary to make environmentally responsible decisions in both their personal and professional life by providing workshops and training sessions on environmental issues.

2. Communication Campaigns:
Effective communication campaigns can be used to promote sustainability activities within organizations and increase public awareness of environmental challenges. To spread knowledge, share success stories, and highlight best practices, these campaigns may make use of a variety of communication channels, including emails, newsletters, posters, intranet portals, social media, and digital signage. Multimedia content, such podcasts, info-graphics, and videos, can also be used in communication efforts to effectively engage staff members and communicate important messages. Organizations can motivate employees to take action by introducing focused communication initiatives that keep environmental issues at the forefront of their minds.

3. Green Teams and Employee Committees:
Employees who are enthusiastic about sustainability and environmental stewardship form green teams and employee committees. These organizations are essential in spearheading environmental programs and cultivating a sustainable culture. Green teams can plan activities, campaigns, and projects to raise awareness of environmental issues. Some examples of these include community clean-up days, recycling drives,

energy-saving competitions, and Earth Day celebrations. Green teams and employee committees can leverage employees' excitement and ingenuity to accomplish significant outcomes by including them directly in environmental efforts.

4. Environmental Policies and Guidelines:

A framework for directing staff behaviour and environmental decision-making is provided by environmental policies and guidelines. These guidelines may set standards for employee behaviour, specify goals and targets for environmental performance, and describe the company's commitment to sustainability. Environmental guidelines can offer useful suggestions and optimal methodologies for mitigating environmental effect across a range of operational domains, including energy use, waste disposal, procurement, and transportation. Organizations can set an example for environmental responsibility and give staff members the direction they need to match their behaviour with company objectives by putting in place thorough and well-defined environmental policies and standards.

5. Environmental Audits and Assessments:

An organization's environmental performance, procedures, and impacts are systematically evaluated through environmental audits and assessments. To find areas of concern and potential for improvement, these assessments may involve energy, waste, water, and carbon footprint audits. Organizations can collect information, track advancement, and determine the most important areas for change by carrying out environmental audits and assessments. Workers can contribute to the audit process, help with data collecting, and put recommendations into practice. Environmental audits and assessments are useful instruments for raising staff understanding of environmental problems and promoting ongoing development.

6. Partnerships and Collaborations:

Employee understanding of environmental issues can also be raised through partnerships and collaborations with outside groups like government agencies, academic institutions, business associations, and non-profits. Joint projects, activities, and programs aimed at environmental outreach, education, and involvement may be a component of these collaborations. Organizations can increase the scope and effect of their environmental initiatives by collaborating with outside partners and taking advantage of their knowledge, assets, and networks. Employee engagement in volunteer work, community service initiatives, and environmental advocacy can also be facilitated by partnerships and collaborations.

7. Employee Engagement Platforms:

Establishing intranet portals or staff engagement platforms with a focus on environmental sustainability can serve as a single location for information exchange, resource sharing, and success stories. These platforms can have interactive components like polls, discussion boards, forums, and quizzes to promote employee involvement and teamwork. Employee engagement platforms can raise awareness and encourage continuing discussion and learning about environmental issues by making pertinent content easily accessible and creating a feeling of community around these topics.

8. Guest Speakers and Subject Matter Experts:

Bringing in outside speakers and subject matter experts to conduct seminars or lectures on environmental issues can provide staff members with fresh viewpoints and ideas. Environmental scientists, conservationists, sustainability consultants, and business professionals with specialized knowledge in environmental management or sustainability are a few examples of these experts. Invited speakers can motivate staff members to take action by highlighting the value of environmental awareness through case studies, best practices, and real-world examples.

9. Green Certifications and Recognition Programs:

Employers can encourage their staff to actively participate in environmental projects and show their commitment to sustainability by putting in place green certification and award programs. As part of these initiatives, staff members may receive certification training in energy efficiency, waste reduction, or green construction techniques, among other environmental management specialties. Workers who obtain certifications or contribute significantly to environmental goals may be acknowledged and rewarded with rewards, prizes, or public recognition, inspiring others to do the same.

10. Environmental Impact Assessments and Reporting:

Organizations can become more transparent and accountable by carrying out environmental impact assessments and disclosing environmental performance. These evaluations could include monitoring the advancement of environmental goals and targets as well as assessing the effects of operations, supply chains, services, and goods on the environment. Organizations can encourage group action to enhance sustainability practices and increase employee understanding of their environmental impact by routinely providing environmental performance data to staff members.

11. Sustainability Challenges and Competitions:

Encouraging environmentally friendly habits and practices among employees can be achieved through organizing sustainability challenges and competitions that offer interesting and participatory experiences. These challenges could include encouraging staff members to participate individually or in teams in activities pertaining to waste reduction, energy conservation, water efficiency, or sustainable transportation. Organizations can create excitement and momentum for environmental awareness and action by gamifying sustainability efforts and providing incentives or rewards for reaching targets.

12. Continuous Learning and Professional Development:

Employees can be empowered to stay up to date on new trends, technology, and best practices by having access to opportunities for professional development and continuous learning in environmental sustainability. This could entail providing access to webinars, workshops, conferences, and certification programs in the fields of green innovation, sustainability strategy, and environmental management in addition to online courses. Organisations may cultivate an educated and capable workforce that can effect positive change both internally and externally by allocating resources towards employee education and skill development.

To sum up, raising employee knowledge of environmental issues is crucial to developing a sustainable culture in businesses. Employers can enable staff members to become environmental advocates and catalysts for change by putting into practice strategies including training sessions, workshops, communication campaigns, green teams, environmental policies, audits, and partnerships. Organizations have the power to build a more sustainable future for the earth and themselves by involving employees in environmental efforts and equipping them with the information, abilities, and tools necessary to make sustainable decisions.

5.1.3 Examples of Successful Environmental Awareness Training Programs Implemented by Leading Organizations

❖ Here are a few examples of successful environmental awareness training programs implemented by leading organizations:

1. IBM's Sustainability Training Program:

As a leader in innovation and technology worldwide, IBM understands the value of environmental sustainability in the modern world. In order to solve this, the business has created an extensive training program on sustainability with the goal of educating its varied personnel. To engage employees at all levels and departments, this program incorporates a variety of learning modalities, such as online courses, workshops, and hands-on activities.

IBM staff members get knowledge on a variety of environmental concerns, such as biodiversity loss, resource depletion, and climate change, through these training programs. In addition, they acquire the know-how and abilities needed to use sustainable practices in both their personal and professional life. Possible subjects covered include carbon footprint management, sustainable sourcing, waste reduction, and energy conservation.

Additionally, IBM's sustainability training program promotes a collaborative and innovative culture in addition to increasing awareness. Workers are encouraged to exchange ideas, take part in environmental projects, and support the organization's overarching environmental objectives. By providing its employees with the skills and resources they need, IBM is able to effect significant change inside the organization and in the communities, it works with.

2. Google's Green Team Program:

Google, a company renowned for its dedication to sustainability and corporate social responsibility, launched the Green Team program to engage staff members in environmental concerns. Through this initiative, Google staff members have a platform to actively participate in sustainability initiatives both within and outside of the company.

Employees can get involved in environmental issues through a range of activities offered by the Green Team program, such as volunteer work, educational events, and sustainability challenges. Employee education on issues like waste management, renewable energy, water conservation, and sustainable transportation is made possible by these programs. Additionally, they can take part in practical projects that directly support Google's environmental objectives.

The Google Green Team program's emphasis on employee empowerment and grassroots engagement is one of its main advantages. A large number of the program's activities are employee-led and motivated projects rather than top-down initiatives. In addition to encouraging employee ownership and dedication, this bottom-up strategy produces original ideas and imaginative problem-solving.

3. Walmart's Sustainability Leadership Program:

Walmart, one of the biggest merchants in the world, is aware of the profound effects it may have on society and the environment. In order to tackle this issue, the organization has put in place a Sustainability Leadership Program that teaches staff members how to incorporate environmental concerns into their regular workdays.

Walmart's Sustainability Leadership Program aims to provide staff members with the information, abilities, and resources necessary to spearhead sustainability projects throughout the organization. Training courses on subjects like waste minimization, energy efficiency, sustainable sourcing, and supply chain sustainability may fall under this category. Employees learn how to spot areas for improvement, put best practices into practice, and track their progress toward sustainability goals through a combination of in-person instruction, online courses, and practical projects.

Scalability and reach are two of Walmart's Sustainability Leadership Program's main advantages. Frontline staff members through senior executives can participate in the program, as can personnel in all departments and at all levels. This guarantees that everyone in the organization contributes to positive change and that sustainability concepts are ingrained throughout. Walmart's size and power also imply that its sustainability efforts can have a big impact on the corporation as a whole as well as on its extensive network of partners and suppliers.

4. Coca-Cola's Water Stewardship Training Program:

The international beverage giant Coca-Cola understands the value of prudent water management for protecting the environment and assisting local communities in which it does business. In order to do this, Coca-Cola has put in place an extensive water stewardship training program that aims to educate staff members on the opportunities and problems associated with water.

A variety of subjects are covered in the Water Stewardship Training Program, such as community involvement, water risk assessment, watershed management, and conservation of water. Employees are taught the value of water stewardship and their part in safeguarding this essential resource through a combination of in-person instruction, online courses, and field trips. Additionally, they acquire useful abilities for identifying and mitigating hazards associated with water in Coca-Cola's supply chain and operations.

Coca-Cola's training program is unique in that it emphasizes teamwork and partnership. To create and provide the training materials, the organization collaborates closely with local communities, governments, and non-governmental organizations. By working together, we can make sure that the program takes into account the unique requirements and difficulties of every area in which Coca-Cola works, as well as the most recent scientific research and industry best practices.

5. Microsoft's Environmental Sustainability Learning Path:

Leading global technology company Microsoft is dedicated to reducing its environmental effect and promoting sustainability throughout its business. Microsoft has created an Environmental Sustainability Learning Path as part of its commitment to inform staff members about important environmental concerns and provide them with the tools they need to incorporate sustainability into their work.

A number of online courses, webinars, and resources addressing subjects including energy efficiency, lowering carbon emissions, sustainable sourcing, and green building design make up the Environmental Sustainability Learning Path. Through Microsoft's internal learning platforms, employees may access these learning materials and study at their own leisure and pace.

The training program offered by Microsoft is notable for its comprehensive approach to teaching about sustainability. The program promotes values and mentality transformations in addition to imparting technical information and skills to employees. Workers are urged to consider carefully how decisions may affect the environment and to look for ways to innovate and improve. Microsoft wants to continuously advance its sustainability goals by promoting an innovative and environmentally conscious culture.

5.2 Developing Green Leadership Skills

Introduction to Green Leadership:
A complex concept, "green leadership" includes elements of ethical governance, environmental stewardship, and sustainability. Fundamentally, green leadership is encouraging an eco-aware and socially responsible culture within communities and businesses in addition to making decisions that are environmentally mindful. Green leaders put the health of the environment and future generations first by incorporating environmental factors into their decision-making processes, encouraging sustainable lifestyles, and supporting laws that deal with urgent environmental problems. Green leaders inspire others, work with stakeholders to create significant change, and lead by example towards a more equitable and sustainable future for all.

Meaning of Green Leadership:
A diverse and dynamic strategy for pointing people, groups, and communities in the direction of environmentally responsible behaviour is

known as "green leadership." Fundamentally, green leadership is a dedication to developing a thorough awareness of environmental challenges, encouraging environmentally responsible decision-making, and establishing a sustainable culture.

"Leading by example" is a fundamental component of green leadership. Sustainable practices are given priority by green leaders, who show a dedication to environmental responsibility through their activities and attitudes. They set an example for people to follow, whether it is through cutting back on waste, decreasing their carbon impact, or switching to renewable energy sources.

Green leaders support structural change within organizations and communities in addition to taking personal action. This entails adopting green policies and procedures, including environmental factors into decision-making processes, and promoting cooperation amongst stakeholders and departments. Green leaders encourage organizational and societal change toward eco-friendly behaviours by supporting sustainability projects.

Developing a sense of social responsibility and environmental stewardship in followers is another aspect of green leadership. Green leaders encourage sustainability activities through knowledge, resources, and support, enabling others to become change agents. They motivate people to take responsibility for environmental problems and actively engage in group initiatives to find solutions.

Furthermore, green leadership highlights the value of ingenuity and inventiveness in resolving difficult environmental problems in a sustainable manner. Green leaders support research and development in green technologies and practices, welcome new technology, and encourage experimentation. They hope to accelerate the shift to a more resilient and sustainable future by encouraging innovation.

In the end, green leadership is about advancing fairness and comprehensive well-being for all living things, not only environmental preservation. Green leaders work to develop solutions that benefit people, the environment, and prosperity because they understand how interwoven the social, economic, and environmental systems are. Green leaders create positive change and inspire hope for a more sustainable and peaceful society via their imaginative leadership and teamwork.

Definition of Green Leadership:
The term green leadership describes the "approach of managing and leading in a way that values and advances environmental sustainability."

Developing Green Leadership Skills:
Growing as a person, professionally, and with a strong commitment to environmental stewardship are all parts of the journey towards developing green leadership abilities. In the modern world, green leadership is more crucial than ever as environmental issues like pollution, resource depletion, and climate change become more pressing.

❖ **Here are some practical steps you can take to cultivate these skills:**

1. Education and Awareness: It's essential to begin by educating yourself on sustainability principles and environmental challenges if you want to be a successful green leader. This can entail delving into subjects like sustainable development, waste management, renewable energy, and biodiversity preservation. Read books, go to seminars, take online courses, and talk to professionals in the subject to stay informed. Gaining a strong knowledge base will enable you to support sustainable practices and make well-informed judgments.

2. Lead by Example: Green leadership is based on setting a good example for others. You have the chance to motivate people by your deeds as a green leader. This could entail making environmentally beneficial lifestyle choices for yourself, such as cutting back on your carbon footprint, using less water and energy, recycling and composting, and endorsing eco-friendly modes of transportation like public transportation, walking, and biking. In your working life, you can introduce eco-friendly policies, energy-efficient technology, waste reduction, and other sustainable practices into your community or company.

3. Develop Strategic Thinking: To manage the intricacies of environmental concerns and spot chances for positive change, green leadership demands strategic thinking. This entails analysing the long-term effects of choices and actions, balancing the interests of social, political, and economic groups, and creating plans that strike a balance between sustainability and organizational objectives. Anticipating future trends and obstacles, adjusting to shifting conditions, and grasping chances for advancement and expansion are further components of strategic thinking.

4. Build Collaboration and Partnerships: Collaboration is essential to solving environmental issues on a large scale. You can establish alliances as a green leader with a wide range of stakeholders, such as governmental bodies, corporations, nonprofits, educational institutions, and neighbourhood associations. Together, you can make the most of resources, pool knowledge, and carry out collaborative projects that have a significant impact. In addition to promoting individual and group ownership and accountability for environmental stewardship, collaboration produces more lasting and productive results.

5. Communicate Effectively: For sustainability projects to gain traction and garner support, effective communication is crucial. A green leader must be able to explain the value of environmental stewardship, motivate people to take action, and foster agreement on common objectives. This entails customizing your message to appeal to various groups of people, explaining complicated ideas through narrative and visual aids, and making use of a variety of communication platforms to reach a larger audience. You can create trust, increase awareness, and mobilize support for sustainable behaviours through good communication.

6. Empower and Motivate Others: Green leadership involves inspiring and encouraging people to become change agents in addition to leading from the front. This entails establishing a welcoming and inclusive atmosphere where people are encouraged to provide their thoughts, abilities, and skills in support of sustainability objectives. As a green leader, you may assist others reach their full potential as sustainability advocates by offering them chances for leadership development, training, and mentorship. Acknowledge and honour their accomplishments, and promote an environment that values ongoing education and development.

7. Embrace Innovation and Continuous Improvement: The core of green leadership is innovation. You may advance sustainability and create new chances for good change by embracing innovative concepts, methods, and tools. Promote an innovative culture in your company or community were taking chances, being creative, and trying new things are rewarded. To improve results, be willing to try new things, learn from mistakes, and refine your strategy. You can stay ahead of the curve and have a long-lasting effect on the environment by embracing innovation and ongoing development.

8. Measure and Evaluate Progress: Setting specific objectives, benchmarks, and metrics to monitor development over time is crucial to ensuring that your green leadership initiatives are having a significant impact. This could entail establishing precise goals for cutting greenhouse gas emissions, boosting energy effectiveness, raising trash diversion rates, or strengthening initiatives to conserve biodiversity. Keep a close eye on these measures and regularly assess your performance against them. Then, use data-driven insights to pinpoint areas in need of optimization and improvement. You can hold yourself and others accountable, show the results of your work, and promote continual growth in the direction of sustainability goals by tracking and analysing your progress.

In conclusion, a mix of education, action, teamwork, communication, empowerment, creativity, and assessment is needed to create green leadership abilities. Within your sphere of influence, you may significantly impact the advancement of environmental sustainability by setting an example, being dedicated to lifelong learning and development, and taking initiative. Being a green leader gives you the ability to motivate people, effect change, and build a more sustainable future for future generations.

5.2.1 Exploring the Significance of Leadership in Driving Sustainability Initiatives and Promoting Green Practices within the Organization

The claim that "Leadership plays a crucial role in driving sustainability initiatives and promoting green practices within organizations" emphasizes the important role that strong leadership plays in advancing environmental sustainability in the context of establishments, institutions, and other organizational structures.

In this sense, leadership is the capacity of those in positions of power or influence within an organization to inspire, motivate, and lead others toward shared objectives concerning environmental responsibility and sustainability.

The phrase "sustainability initiatives" refers to a broad category of practices and tactics that are intended to reduce negative effects on the environment, preserve natural resources, and advance long-term ecological balance. This could involve taking steps to cut down on waste production, conserve energy and water, adopt renewable energy sources, reduce carbon emissions, and support sustainable supply chain and procurement methods.

"Green practices" are eco-friendly actions, rules, and guidelines that try to reduce negative environmental effects and advance ecological sustainability. This could entail actions like waste reduction and recycling, energy-saving techniques, environmentally friendly product design and production, sustainable transportation options, and natural habitat preservation.

Leadership plays a crucial role in driving sustainability initiatives and promoting green practices within organizations. Here's why:

1. Setting the Tone from the Top: The tone of the entire organization is determined by its leaders. Leadership that places a high priority on sustainability and exhibits a dedication to environmental stewardship communicates that these are significant concerns deserving of attention. When people witness leadership actively promoting sustainability projects, staff members are more likely to support them.

2. Establishing Priorities and Goals: It is the duty of leaders to establish the organization's priorities and goals. Leadership that prioritizes sustainability sends a message to stakeholders and staff alike that the organization's goal and vision are inextricably linked to environmental stewardship. Efficient decision-making at all organizational levels is facilitated by well-defined objectives pertaining to sustainability, such as cutting down on waste, boosting energy efficiency, or lowering carbon emissions.

3. Allocating Resources: When it comes to providing funds to support sustainability efforts, leadership is essential. This comprises monetary resources for the purchase of eco-friendly technology, people resources for capacity building and training, and time and effort to incorporate sustainability into day-to-day operations. When executives give sustainability top priority when allocating resources, it strengthens the organization's dedication to environmental stewardship.

4. Creating a Culture of Innovation: A culture of innovation is fostered by effective leaders, who inspire their staff members to think creatively and experiment with new concepts. Leaders who uphold sustainability as a key principle encourage staff members to come up with creative solutions for pressing environmental issues. This could include creating new goods and services with less of an impact on the environment, streamlining processes to use less resources, or looking into alternate renewable energy sources. Organizations that foster an innovative culture are better able to stay ahead of the curve and promote ongoing sustainability performance improvement.

5. Engaging and Empowering Employees: When it comes to motivating and enabling staff members to take part in sustainability projects, leadership is crucial. Proficient leaders actively involve staff in environmental management decision-making processes, offer chances for education and training, and emphasize the value of sustainability. Employee ownership of sustainability efforts and internal change-driven behaviour are more likely when they feel appreciated and empowered to share their knowledge and ideas.

6. Building Partnerships and Collaboration: Sustainability issues are frequently complicated and call for cooperation across various parties and industries. Building alliances with other businesses, governmental bodies, non-governmental organizations, and community groups allows leaders to pool resources, exchange best practices, and increase influence. Leaders may mobilize collective action towards shared sustainability goals and tackle issues that beyond the purview of individual organizations by cultivating collaboration and cooperation.

7. Measuring and Reporting Progress: The establishment of systems for monitoring, reporting, and measuring sustainability performance is under the purview of leadership. This entails putting in place mechanisms for gathering information on important sustainability indicators, tracking advancement toward objectives, and informing internal and external stakeholders of results. Building trust with stakeholders, holding the company accountable for its environmental impact, and offering chances for ongoing improvement are all made possible by transparent reporting.

8. Leading by Example: Sustainable leadership is exemplified by effective leaders. By acting and behaving in ways that reflect their commitment to environmental stewardship, they not only talk the talk but also walk the walk. Leaders provide a strong example for others to follow, whether it is by lowering their personal carbon footprint, supporting sustainable practices in meetings, or taking part in volunteer clean-up projects. When staff members witness their superiors engaging in sustainable practices, it serves to emphasize the significance of these endeavours and motivates them to follow suit.

9. Fostering Employee Engagement and Buy-In: In order to promote employee involvement and buy-in for sustainability initiatives, leadership is essential. A sense of ownership and pride in sustainability initiatives is fostered when executives include staff members in decision-making procedures, solicit their opinions on sustainability plans, and acknowledge their contributions to environmental stewardship. More innovative ideas, green practices, and active participation in the implementation of sustainability programs are all likely to be adopted by engaged employees, which will increase overall performance.

10. Aligning Sustainability with Business Strategy: Proficient executives understand that sustainability is an essential component of the company's overall business plan, not merely a stand-alone project. Leaders may promote alignment between sustainability goals and business objectives by incorporating sustainability into key company tasks including supply chain management, product development, and marketing. This connection makes sure that sustainability efforts are viewed as crucial components of resilience and long-term success rather than as something apart from the organization's main objectives.

11. Creating a Resilient and Future-Ready Organization: Building resilience and adaptability in the face of shifting market and environmental conditions is a key component of sustainability leadership, which goes beyond merely minimising environmental effect. Prioritizing sustainability allows leaders to foresee and reduce risks related to resource scarcity, consumer preferences, regulatory demands, and climate change. In a world that is changing quickly, leaders can future-proof their businesses and set them up for long-term success by making investments in sustainable practices, technology, and business models.

12. Driving Innovation and Market Differentiation: By inspiring businesses to consider innovative ways to lessen their environmental impact and still provide value to customers, sustainability leadership fosters innovation. Sustainable business practices are a top priority for leaders that push their teams to innovate, find new ways to do things, and stand out from the competition. Through the implementation of sustainable practices such as creating environmentally friendly packaging, initiating renewable energy projects, or embracing circular economy concepts, companies can enhance their competitiveness and seize novel market prospects.

13. Building Trust and Reputation: In today's socially conscious economy, leadership is essential to an organization's ability to establish trust and a positive reputation. Through exhibiting a sincere dedication to sustainability, executives can gain the confidence of clients, financiers, staff members, and other stakeholders. Transparent communication, moral business conduct, and conscientious environmental resource management are the foundations of trust. Perceived leaders in sustainability have an increased ability to draw in clients, hold onto talent, and get funding, all of which contribute to an organization's long-term survival and prosperity.

14. Driving Regulatory Compliance and Risk Management: Ensuring regulatory compliance and controlling environmental risks inside firms require effective leadership. Sustainability-focused leaders keep a close eye on changes in environmental laws, evaluate how they will affect their company's operations, and put compliance measures in place. Organizations can prevent expensive fines, legal conflicts, and brand harm associated with non-compliance by staying ahead of regulatory requirements. To safeguard the resources and reputation of the company, leadership is also essential in detecting and reducing environmental hazards, such as pollution, habitat destruction, and climate-related disasters.

15. Promoting Social Responsibility and Equity: Beyond environmental stewardship, sustainability leadership takes social responsibility and equality into account. Prioritizing sustainability allows leaders to understand how social, economic, and environmental challenges are intertwined and work toward achieving favourable results for both people and the environment. This could entail funding ethical hiring procedures, encouraging inclusivity and diversity, encouraging community involvement, and tackling social justice concerns. Leaders may build more inclusive and equitable organizations that benefit society at large by incorporating social responsibility into sustainability programs.

16. Inspiring Change Beyond the Organization: Good sustainable leadership has the potential to motivate change in the company as well as in the larger industry and community. Advocates for sustainability projects have the power to persuade stakeholders, legislators, and other organizations to follow comparable procedures and guidelines. Sustainability leaders may increase their influence and promote good change on a large scale by exchanging best practices, working together on joint projects, and lobbying for legislative reforms. This knock-on effect has the potential to bring about revolutionary changes that will make everyone's future fairer and more sustainable.

To summarize, the promotion of green practices and sustainability projects within firms is greatly aided by strong leadership. Leaders can help their organizations and communities have a more sustainable future by establishing a culture of innovation, empowering and engaging staff, forming partnerships and collaborations, measuring and reporting progress, and setting the tone from the top.

5.2.2 Strategies for Developing Green Leadership Skills in Managers and Executives

Introduction:
There has never been a greater important need for strong leadership to advance green practices inside companies and drive sustainability projects in the quickly evolving global marketplace of today. Managers and executives have a critical role to play in promoting environmental stewardship as organizations and institutions deal with environmental

concerns such pollution, resource depletion, and climate change. It is imperative that managers and executives acquire green leadership abilities in order to promote a sustainable culture, stimulate innovation, and have a positive environmental influence inside enterprises.

Developing green leadership skills in managers and executives is essential for driving sustainability initiatives and promoting green practices within organizations. Here are some strategies for fostering green leadership development:

1. **Training Programs:**
Provide thorough training courses covering a broad variety of subjects related to environmental sustainability and green leadership. Modules on environmental science, corporate social responsibility, renewable energy technology, climate change, sustainable business practices, and environmental legislation may be included in these programs. Sustainability-focused specialists from the industry, external consultants, or internal subject matter experts can lead training sessions. In order to optimize efficacy, training curricula ought to be customized to the distinct requirements and functions of managers and executives, furnishing them with applicable expertise and competencies that they may utilize in their daily leadership duties.

2. **Mentoring and Coaching:**
Create coaching and mentorship programs that match executives and managers with seasoned leaders who have demonstrated success in spearheading sustainable projects. Mentees can get direction, counsel, and support from mentors as they work through the challenges of green leadership. They can exchange best practices, lessons discovered, and personal experiences incorporating sustainability into leadership roles. Coaching sessions might concentrate on fostering the development of particular competencies and skills associated with green leadership, such as communication skills, strategic planning, stakeholder involvement, and conflict resolution. Mentoring and coaching programs can expedite the development of green leadership skills and enable managers and executives to effect significant change inside their organizations by offering tailored support and feedback.

3. Leadership Development Programs:

Create leadership development initiatives that prioritize sustainability as an essential element of leadership education. These courses can include case studies, workshops, seminars, simulations, and hands-on learning exercises that push managers and executives to consider environmental problems from a different perspective and consider creative solutions. The significance of moral leadership, social responsibility, and environmental stewardship in today's corporate environment ought to be emphasized in leadership development programs. In addition, they ought to give participants the chance to work together with colleagues, exchange ideas and viewpoints, and create a common vision for sustainability leadership in their institutions.

4. Cross-functional Collaboration:

Encourage managers and executives from various departments, business units, and organizational levels to collaborate across functional boundaries. Cross-functional teams may address difficult sustainability challenges and effect significant change by bringing together a variety of viewpoints, skills, and resources. Organizations may create comprehensive and integrated approaches to sustainable leadership by using the knowledge and experience of their staff by dismantling organizational silos and encouraging cooperation. An increased sense of shared accountability and ownership for sustainability projects can be fostered by cross-functional collaboration, which will increase organizational coherence and alignment.

5. Performance Metrics and Incentives:

To encourage managers and executives to adopt more environmentally friendly behaviours and to emphasize the value of green leadership, match performance measures and rewards with sustainability objectives. Key performance indicators (KPIs) pertaining to environmental performance, such as resource conservation, waste reduction, energy efficiency enhancement, and carbon emissions reduction, can be established by organizations. The ability of managers and executives to satisfy these KPIs and meet the organization's sustainability targets can be used to evaluate them. Rewards for green leadership can take the form of tangible items like bonuses, promotions, and recognition when they are linked to sustainability criteria. This promotes a culture of accountability and results-driven action.

6. External Partnerships and Collaborations:
Managers and executives should be urged to participate in professional networks, industry groups, and outside partners that emphasize sustainable leadership. External collaborations can offer beneficial chances for education, networking, and cooperation with groups and individuals who share a dedication to environmental sustainability. Attending conferences, workshops, and forums is an excellent way for managers and executives to network, discuss best practices, and get ideas for advancing sustainability programs inside their own companies. Building trusting connections with outside partners allows organizations to take advantage of outside knowledge, resources, and assistance to hasten the achievement of sustainability objectives and increase their influence.

7. Continuous Learning and Improvement:
Encourage an environment where green leadership abilities are always being learned and improved by offering chances for professional growth, training, and education. Access to webinars, workshops, seminars, and online courses on subjects related to sustainability leadership can be provided by organizations. Additionally, they can help managers and executives pursue advanced degrees, certificates, and certifications in sectors connected to sustainability. Furthermore, companies have the capacity to promote involvement in sustainability-oriented communities of practice, discussion forums, and networking functions. These platforms allow leaders to exchange ideas, gain knowledge, and benefit from one another's experiences. Organizations may guarantee the long-term knowledge, involvement, and efficacy of their leaders in spearheading sustainability projects by allocating resources towards ongoing education and enhancement.

8. Integration into Organizational Culture:
Integrate sustainability into the culture of the company by endorsing attitudes, customs, and actions that give social impact and environmental stewardship first priority. Leaders have the power to provide an example of sustainable conduct, explain the value of sustainability, and recognize

achievements in green leadership. For the purpose of supervising sustainability programs, tracking advancement, and advocating for sustainability efforts, organizations can also form task groups or committees made up of managers, executives, and staff members from various departments. Leaders may foster a common goal and dedication to environmental stewardship at all organizational levels by weaving sustainability into the very fabric of the company.

9. External Certification Programs:

Urge CEOs and managers to enrol in external sustainability leadership certification programs, like GRI (Global Reporting Initiative), ISO 14001 (Environmental Management Systems), and LEED (Leadership in Energy and Environmental Design). These certification programs help improve leaders' credibility and level of sustainability competence by offering organized frameworks for comprehending and implementing sustainable practices inside enterprises. Managers and executives can position themselves as leaders in advancing sustainability programs within their firms and show their dedication to lifelong learning and professional growth in green leadership by gaining external certifications.

10. Innovation and Entrepreneurship Initiatives:

Promote the exploration of innovative and entrepreneurial ideas within the sustainability environment by managers and executives. Eco-friendly product creation, sustainable packaging design, circular economy business models, and sustainability-focused startups are examples of innovation projects that organizations may help. In order to foster creativity, experimentation, and collaboration around sustainability concerns, leaders can establish innovation laboratories, incubators, or accelerators within the firm. Businesses may open up new avenues for long-term expansion and influence the market for the better by cultivating an innovative and entrepreneurial culture.

11. Corporate Social Responsibility (CSR) Programs:

Programs and efforts related to corporate social responsibility (CSR) should incorporate sustainable leadership. A broad range of activities, like as volunteerism, philanthropy, community involvement, and environmental stewardship, can be included in CSR programs. When it comes to developing CSR strategies, establishing priorities, and allocating funds to support sustainability projects that are consistent with the goals and values of the company, managers and executives can take the lead. Organizations may show their dedication to improving society and the environment while also boosting their reputation and brand value by including sustainability into their CSR initiatives.

12. Public Advocacy and Thought Leadership:
Motivate executives and managers to take on thought leadership and public advocacy roles on sustainability-related issues. Leaders have the capacity to fight for laws, rules, and programs that support environmental sustainability and tackle urgent global issues like pollution, climate change, and biodiversity loss by using their platform and influence. In addition, they can take part in conferences, industry forums, and media interviews to exchange knowledge, best practices, and inspirational tales of green leadership. Through vocally advocating for sustainability, leaders have the capacity to motivate people to take initiative and promote positive change on a large scale.

To sum up, training programs, mentoring and coaching, leadership development initiatives, cross-functional collaboration, performance metrics and incentives, external partnerships and collaborations, continuous learning and improvement, integration into organizational culture, external certification programs, innovation and entrepreneurship initiatives, corporate social responsibility programs, public advocacy, and thought leadership are all necessary to help managers and executives develop green leadership skills.

5.2.3 Case Studies of Organizations That Have Successfully Cultivated Green Leadership Skills Among Their Top Management to Drive Sustainable Business Practices

- A case study of Toyota, showcasing how the organization has successfully cultivated green leadership skills among its top management to drive sustainable business practices:

Case Study: Toyota's Leadership in Sustainable Mobility

Background:
The Japanese automaker Toyota is well known for its dedication to environmental protection and sustainability. The company has put in place

a number of programs to encourage sustainable mobility and lessen its environmental impact since it understands how important it is to address environmental issues like pollution and climate change.

Cultivating Green Leadership:

1. CEO Commitment: Toyota's CEO, Akio Toyoda, has made the company's sustainability a primary emphasis. Akio Toyoda has proven to be a formidable leader in the field of sustainable mobility initiatives, having set high standards and accelerated the process of reaching them. His dedication to sustainability has motivated both staff and upper management to give environmental responsibility top priority when making decisions and taking actions.

2. Sustainability Strategy: To reduce its environmental effect and advance sustainable mobility, Toyota has created a comprehensive sustainability strategy. The company's fuel-efficient vehicle development, electric and hybrid vehicle technology investments, and alternative fuel alternatives promotion are all part of its sustainability plan.

3. Employee Engagement: In terms of sustainability, Toyota lays a lot of emphasis on employee empowerment and participation. The organization helps staff members at all levels comprehend the value of sustainability and their part in bringing about good change by offering them resources, education, and training. Workers are invited to submit concepts, recommendations, and projects to enhance sustainability performance in their spheres of influence.

4. Supplier Collaboration: Toyota works closely with its suppliers in order to encourage sustainability along the whole supply chain. The business collaborates with suppliers to raise social and environmental standards, cut emissions, and support ethical sourcing methods. Toyota's upper echelon actively interacts with suppliers in order to establish goals, convey expectations, and promote ongoing sustainability performance enhancement.

5. Innovation and Technology: Toyota uses its technological and innovative know-how to create solutions that tackle environmental issues and advance sustainable mobility. The business makes investments in the development of hydrogen fuel cell vehicles, electric and hybrid vehicle technologies, and fuel-efficient engines. To identify innovative ways to lessen environmental effect and promote sustainable transportation solutions, Toyota's top management encourages experimentation and creativity through innovation.

Impact:

Toyota has significantly impacted both the car industry and the larger transportation sector with its leadership in sustainable mobility. The business has made great strides toward lowering its carbon impact, improving fuel economy, and supporting alternate fuel sources. Toyota's sustainability programs have reduced its negative effects on the environment while simultaneously fostering innovation, cost reduction, and a competitive edge.

In conclusion, Toyota is a great illustration of a company that has developed green leadership abilities within its upper echelons of management in order to promote environmentally friendly business practices. Toyota has shown that integrating environmental responsibility into corporate operations can generate value and promote long-term success. This has been achieved through emphasizing sustainability, involving stakeholders, encouraging innovation, and exhibiting great leadership.

- A case study of IKEA, showcasing how the organization has successfully cultivated green leadership skills among its top management to drive sustainable business practices:

Case Study: IKEA's Commitment to Sustainability

Background:

The Swedish multinational furniture company IKEA is well known for its dedication to environmental responsibility and sustainability. The company has made great progress in this area over the years and has long understood how important it is to include sustainability into its business operations.

Cultivating Green Leadership:

1. Founder's Vision: IKEA's founder, Ingvar Kamprad, had a vision that inspired the company's dedication to sustainability. Ingvar Kamprad has stressed the value of environmental stewardship and ethical business practices from the company's founding. His idea started IKEA on its path toward sustainability and still directs the company's operations today.

2. Top Management Buy-In: The executives and senior leaders of IKEA have a strong commitment to environmental responsibility and sustainability. They are aware of the benefits of sustainability for business and how crucial it is to incorporate sustainability into every facet of IKEA's operations. In order to promote progress towards these goals, top management actively supports sustainability efforts, establishes challenging sustainability targets, and offers guidance and leadership.

3. Sustainability Strategy: IKEA has created an extensive sustainability plan that directs its endeavours to reduce its ecological footprint, preserve natural resources, and foster social accountability. The company's sustainability plan includes a broad range of activities, such as investments in renewable energy, energy efficiency programs, waste reduction campaigns, and sustainable material sourcing.

4. Employee Engagement: When it comes to sustainability, IKEA emphasizes employee empowerment and participation heavily. The organization helps staff members at all levels comprehend the value of sustainability and their part in bringing about good change by offering them resources, education, and training. Workers are invited to submit concepts, recommendations, and projects to enhance sustainability performance in their spheres of influence.

5. Supplier Collaboration: IKEA promotes sustainability throughout its supply chain by collaborating closely with its suppliers. The business works with suppliers to raise social and environmental standards, cut emissions, and support ethical sourcing methods. Top management at IKEA actively interacts with suppliers to establish goals, convey expectations, and promote ongoing sustainability performance improvement.

6. Transparency and Reporting: IKEA constantly updates stakeholders on its sustainability initiatives through annual reports, sustainability reports, and other channels. The company is open and honest about these efforts. Top management of the organization makes ensuring that sustainability reporting is precise, thorough, and compliant with global norms and industry best practices. IKEA promotes greater knowledge and engagement regarding environmental issues and shows its commitment to accountability by sharing information in an open and transparent manner.

Impact:
IKEA has seen notable success as a result of its dedication to sustainability and its initiatives to develop green leadership qualities among its senior management. The business has achieved significant strides in lowering its environmental impact, enhancing resource economy, and encouraging social responsibility. In addition to improving consumer loyalty and brand perception, IKEA's environmental initiatives have increased long-term commercial performance and profitability.

In conclusion, IKEA presents a strong illustration of a company that has effectively developed green leadership competencies throughout its upper echelons of management to promote environmentally friendly business practices. IKEA is a prime example of how sustainability and commercial success can coexist when it comes to stakeholder engagement, environmental responsibility, and sustainability.

- **A case study of Unilever, showcasing how the organization has successfully cultivated green leadership skills among its top management to drive sustainable business practices:**

Case Study: Unilever's Sustainable Living Plan

Background:
In 2010, Unilever, a global leader in consumer goods, introduced its Sustainable Living Plan (USLP), marking the beginning of a revolutionary shift towards sustainability. The USLP is a comprehensive plan designed to improve social well-being throughout Unilever's global operations and decouple growth from environmental impact. To ensure the USLP succeeds, Unilever's top executives must develop green leadership abilities.

Cultivating Green Leadership:

1. CEO Leadership: Sustainable business practices have been Unilever's top priority under CEO Paul Polman's direction. Paul Polman has been a strong supporter of the USLP at Unilever, stressing the role that sustainability plays in fostering long-term corporate growth and value generation. Paul Polman, an outspoken supporter of sustainability, has established the standard for green leadership at Unilever and motivated senior management to give sustainability top priority when making decisions and taking action.

2. Integration into Business Strategy: Unilever has incorporated sustainability into its fundamental business strategy, making sure that all facets of the business' operations take sustainability into account. In order to reduce environmental impact, improve social well-being, and promote sustainable sourcing and production techniques, the company's top management has been actively involved in creating and implementing sustainability programs that are in line with the USLP's objectives.

3. Training and Capacity Building: Unilever has made investments in capacity-building and training programs to give top management the know-how, abilities, and resources they need to lead sustainability initiatives successfully. Sustainability of the environment, social responsibility, moral business conduct, and stakeholder involvement are all covered in training programs. Through these programs, upper management may better grasp the business case for sustainability, spot areas for improvement, and set an example for others by incorporating sustainability into their own spheres of influence.

4. Performance Metrics and Incentives: For the purpose of coordinating top management's activities with the USLP's objectives, Unilever has set performance indicators and rewards. Reducing carbon emissions, increasing water efficiency, and fostering diversity and inclusion are a few examples of sustainability-related key performance indicators (KPIs) that are used to senior management incentive programs and performance reviews. Top management is encouraged to emphasize sustainability and advance sustainability goals by Unilever by linking performance measures to sustainability objectives.

5. External Engagement and Collaboration: NGOs, governments, suppliers, and customers are just a few of the external stakeholders that Unilever actively interacts with in order to advance sustainability and encourage group action on social and environmental challenges. Top management at the organization takes part in partnerships, conferences, and industry forums to share ideas, promote policies that support sustainability goals, and share best practices. Unilever works with outside partners to address difficult sustainability challenges and promote change by pooling resources and expertise.

Impact:
The operations of Unilever and the larger consumer products sector have been greatly impacted by the company's Sustainable Living Plan. The business has made significant strides toward lowering its environmental impact, enhancing social welfare, and supporting environmentally friendly procurement and production methods. The implementation of sustainability measures by Unilever has yielded several benefits, including improved brand reputation and consumer loyalty, as well as sustained commercial performance and profitability.

In conclusion, Unilever is a great illustration of a company that has developed green leadership abilities within its upper echelons of management in order to promote environmentally friendly business practices. Unilever has shown that it is committed to environmental and social responsibility while simultaneously promoting business growth and value creation. This has been accomplished by giving sustainability top priority, incorporating it into business strategy, investing in training and capacity building, coordinating performance metrics and incentives, and interacting with external stakeholders.

5.3 Continuous Learning for Sustainability

Introduction:
One of the main pillars of solving the urgent environmental, social, and economic issues our world is currently experiencing is continuous learning for sustainability. Embracing a culture of lifelong learning that promotes sustainability principles and practices is increasingly important for

individuals, businesses, and communities as we navigate an era of rapid change and uncertainty.

The Need for Continuous Learning:
Continuous learning offers the knowledge, skills, and competencies needed to navigate complex sustainability issues and drive meaningful action. The world is experiencing unprecedented environmental transformations, from pollution and resource depletion to climate change and biodiversity loss. Addressing these challenges requires a deep understanding of sustainability concepts as well as the ability to adapt to evolving circumstances and develop innovative solutions.

- To effectively respond to the ever-changing environmental, social, and economic sustainability problems and possibilities, people, organizations, and communities must engage in continuous learning. Here's why continuous learning is crucial and how it can be implemented:

1. Adaptation to Change: The dynamic and diverse nature of sustainability challenges is driven by a number of factors, including population expansion, urbanization, climate change, and technological improvements. By means of continuous learning, both individuals and organizations can remain up to date with the latest developments in sustainability best practices, technology, and trends. Stakeholders can foresee future issues, spot new possibilities, and modify their strategies and actions by staying up to date with change.

2. Enhanced Problem-Solving Skills: Innovative solutions that strike a balance between social, economic, and environmental factors are frequently needed to address sustainability concerns. Ongoing education helps people become more creative, critical thinkers, and problem solvers, which help them come up with practical solutions for sustainability-related problems. Learning about topics like social fairness, sustainable agriculture, renewable energy, and the circular economy can help people develop integrated, comprehensive solutions that advance sustainability in a variety of fields and businesses.

3. Promotion of Collaboration and Networking: Opportunities for networking and cooperation amongst stakeholders with different backgrounds and specialties are made possible by continuous learning. Individuals can collaborate to achieve sustainability goals by exchanging ideas, sharing experiences, and forming partnerships through learning groups, seminars, conferences, and online forums. By working together, stakeholders can take advantage of one another's perspectives, abilities, and resources to solve sustainability problems in more creative and significant ways.

4. Empowerment and Engagement: People who are engaged in continuous learning are better equipped to take initiative and make decisions that support sustainability. A greater knowledge and comprehension of sustainability concerns makes people more interested in and driven to take part in initiatives that support social justice, environmental preservation, and economic prosperity. Individuals can be empowered to become effective advocates and change agents for sustainable development within their companies and communities through education and training programs that emphasize sustainability literacy, leadership development, and community engagement.

5. Integration into Organizational Culture: The integration of professional development opportunities, knowledge-sharing efforts, and training programs can facilitate continuous learning within an organization's culture. Organizations can enable staff members to generate positive change within their departments and roles and contribute to sustainability goals by cultivating a culture of learning and innovation. Establishing a supportive learning environment that promotes experimentation, collaboration, and ongoing progress in sustainability performance requires the backing of the leadership, the distribution of resources, and the acknowledgment of sustainability accomplishments.

6. Measurement and Evaluation: Continuous learning makes data collection, analysis, and feedback mechanisms easier to use in measuring and evaluating sustainability performance. Through tracking advancements and evaluating the efficacy of sustainability endeavours, people and institutions can pinpoint opportunities for enhancement and formulate evidence-based choices to maximize their influence. Benchmarks, sustainability reporting frameworks, and key performance indicators (KPIs) offer insightful information about the results and effects of sustainability initiatives. They help stakeholders monitor their progress toward objectives, spot patterns, and share findings with both internal and external stakeholders.

7. Lifelong Commitment to Sustainability: By developing beliefs, attitudes, and behaviours that prioritize social responsibility, ethical leadership, and environmental stewardship, continuous learning cultivates a lifetime commitment to sustainability. People who develop a sense of responsibility for the environment and future generations become lifelong supporters of sustainable development. Opportunities for lifelong learning, including online classes, seminars, workshops, and peer-to-peer learning networks, help people stay aware and involved in the latest developments in sustainability concerns, trends, and solutions for both their personal and professional lives.

To put it succinctly, learning never stops. It helps people and organizations become more flexible, improve their problem-solving abilities, collaborate and network, empower and involve stakeholders, integrate sustainability into organizational culture, assess sustainability performance, and encourage a lifelong commitment to sustainability. Stakeholders can invest in programs for continuous learning to develop the abilities, knowledge, and skills required to meet the complex possibilities and challenges of the twenty-first century in a fair and sustainable way.

5.3.1 Highlighting the Importance of Ongoing Learning for Sustainability in the Workplace to Adopt to Changing Environmental Trends and Regulations

❖ Highlighting the importance of ongoing learning for sustainability in the workplace is crucial to adapt to changing environmental trends and regulations. Here's why continuous learning is essential in this context:

1. Adaptation to Changing Environmental Trends:
Due to variables including resource depletion, consumer tastes, and climate change, environmental trends are always changing. Employees that engage in continuous learning are more equipped to recognize areas for development, comprehend the consequences of these trends for business operations, and stay up to date on emerging trends. Organizations

may position themselves as leaders in sustainability and anticipate changes in the market by remaining proactive and knowledgeable.

Employees that engage in continuous learning are able to stay current on cutting-edge developments and technologies that have the potential to reduce environmental impact and enhance sustainability performance. Innovations in waste management, water conservation, energy efficiency, and renewable energy, for instance, might present fresh chances for businesses to lessen their environmental impact and improve their sustainability credentials. Organizations may provide staff with the necessary knowledge and skills to effectively utilize these technologies and affect good change by funding continuous learning efforts.

Moreover, continuous learning encourages employees to experiment and develop new ideas and methods for sustainability within firms by fostering a culture of innovation. Encouraging staff to think outside the box and take calculated risks helps firms find new ways to solve difficult sustainability problems and stay ahead of the curve in a world that is changing quickly.

2. **Compliance with Regulations:**

As countries around the world work to address urgent environmental concerns, environmental restrictions are getting stricter. Employees that engage in continuous learning are guaranteed to be informed about pertinent rules, comprehend their own compliance needs, and possess the skills necessary to successfully adopt sustainable practices. Keeping staff members informed about regulatory developments helps companies stay out of trouble and preserve their standing as ethical businesses.

Continuous learning offers insights into new trends and regulatory developments, which aids firms in navigating the complicated world of environmental rules. Employees can get training on new regulations, guidelines, and standards pertaining to waste management, product stewardship, water quality, and carbon emissions, for instance. Through comprehension of these regulations and their effects on business operations, companies may create proactive plans to reduce risks, maximize compliance efforts, and grab hold of growth prospects that will last.

Additionally, firms can forge solid bonds with trade associations, government agencies, and other parties engaged in establishing environmental policy thanks to constant learning. Employees can exchange best practices, have productive conversations with regulators, and help create fair and effective regulatory frameworks by taking part in training sessions, workshops, and industry events. Organizations can increase their influence and credibility in the regulatory space by showcasing their dedication to cooperation and compliance.

3. Integration of Sustainability into Business Practices:

Sustainability is becoming a key component of business strategy rather than only a corporate social responsibility (CSR) project. Employees that receive continuous learning are better equipped to comprehend the business case for sustainability, incorporate sustainable practices into their everyday tasks, and coordinate their efforts with those of the organization. Organizations can stimulate innovation, increase long-term competitiveness, and improve operational efficiency by cultivating a culture of sustainability.

Employees that receive continuous learning opportunities are better able to comprehend the ways in which sustainability factors relate to different business processes, such as product development, supply chain management, marketing, finance, and stakeholder engagement. Employees that are aware of these intersections might spot chances to develop goods that benefit both the company and society as a whole, such as eco-friendly products, resource optimization, and robust supply networks.

A comprehensive approach to sustainability that takes into account the interdependence of environmental, social, and economic variables is promoted by continuous learning. Organizations can achieve sustainable results throughout the value chain and prevent unexpected consequences by encouraging people to think holistically and long-term impacts of their decisions. Employees can be trained in life cycle assessment (LCA), for instance, to examine how goods and services affect the environment from birth to death, pinpoint areas in need of improvement, and make well-informed decisions to reduce environmental harm.

4. Enhancement of Employee Skills:

Employees that engage in continuous learning acquire the competences, knowledge, and skills necessary to successfully tackle sustainability issues. Through workshops, professional development opportunities, and training programs, employees can gain expertise in areas like sustainable supply chain management, waste reduction, and energy efficiency. Organizations may cultivate a skilled workforce capable of enacting long-lasting change by investing in the skill-building of their workforce.

Employees can gain technical skills like data analysis, environmental modelling, and carbon accounting through continuous learning. These abilities are critical for evaluating sustainability performance, tracking target progress, and spotting areas for improvement. Workers can also acquire soft skills, which are essential for involving stakeholders, encouraging collaboration, and promoting organizational transformation. These abilities include leadership, teamwork, and communication.

Organizations that practice continuous learning encourage their staff to ask for feedback, think back on their experiences, and modify their behaviouras a result. Organizations can attract and retain top talent, boost employee morale and motivation, and create an excellence culture that fosters long-term company success by offering chances for continual skill development and career growth.

5. Strengthening Stakeholder Relationships:

When interacting with organizations, stakeholders such as consumers, investors, and members of the community are giving sustainability a higher priority. Employees that engage in continuous learning are better able to comprehend stakeholder expectations, communicate about sustainability programs with effectiveness, and establish credibility and trust with important stakeholders. Organizations may improve their standing as sustainability leaders and fortify their connections with stakeholders by showcasing a dedication to continuous learning and development.

Employees can have meaningful conversations about sustainability with stakeholders, hear out their worries and suggestions, and work together to co-create solutions that meet common problems and possibilities thanks to continuous learning. Organizations can establish trust and credibility with stakeholders, improve their standing as ethical corporations, and generate shared benefit for society at large by promoting openness, accountability, and communication.

6. Innovation and Creativity:

Ongoing education helps companies cultivate a culture of creativity and invention, which propels the creation of original answers to sustainability problems. Organizations can unleash potential and promote good change by urging staff members to think creatively, try new things, and accept failure as a teaching tool. Employees that engage in continuous learning have the opportunity to investigate novel methods to sustainability, such as regenerative design, bio-mimicry, and circular economy concepts, which have the potential to produce ground-breaking discoveries and competitive benefits.

In a world that is changing quickly, innovation is crucial to solving sustainability concerns. Employees who receive continuous learning are more equipped to think creatively about ways to improve social welfare, lessen environmental impact, and generate revenue all at the same time. Organizations can encourage staff to find creative solutions that go beyond conventional approaches to sustainability by cultivating a culture of experimentation and risk-taking.

Additionally, ongoing education promotes knowledge sharing and collaboration across disciplines, allowing for the interchange of concepts and viewpoints from other professions. Organizations can foster creativity and innovation by bringing together people with diverse backgrounds, specialties, and life experiences. This can result in the development of comprehensive and integrated solutions to challenging sustainability issues.

Employers, consumers, and other stakeholders can contribute ideas through crowdsourcing and collaborative innovation by using digital technology and online platforms. Organizations can leverage the combined knowledge of heterogeneous stakeholders to jointly develop solutions that tackle common sustainability concerns and promote constructive transformation by establishing virtual innovation hubs and online communities.

7. Risk Management and Resilience:

Sustainability risks can have a big impact on long-term viability and business continuity. Some examples of these risks include reputational harm, legislative changes, and supply chain disruptions. Through the provision of knowledge and tools to employees, continuous learning assists firms in effectively identifying, assessing, and mitigating sustainability risks. This allows employees to predict possible hazards and implement proactive strategies. Organizations may enhance their capacity for resilience, adaptability, and agility in the face of uncertainty by integrating risk management principles into sustainability training initiatives.

Organizations can take a proactive approach to risk management by focusing on recognizing and resolving possible sustainability issues before they become crises, thanks to continuous learning. Organizations can reduce the possibility and effect of sustainability-related disruptions on their operations and reputation by equipping staff with the knowledge and tools necessary to perform risk assessments, scenario planning, and contingency planning.

Furthermore, as a result of the interdependence of environmental, social, and economic issues, firms are encouraged by continuous learning to embrace a holistic approach to risk management. Organizations can create comprehensive risk management plans that address systemic vulnerabilities and underlying primary causes by acknowledging the interdependencies between various types of hazards.

Continuous learning makes it easier for businesses to learn and adapt, which helps them take advantage of new opportunities and dangers related to sustainability. Organizations can cultivate a continuous improvement and innovative mentality that empowers them to confidently foresee and overcome future issues by establishing a culture of learning and reflection.

8. Cultural Transformation:

Organizations can move toward more ethical and sustainable business practices by implementing culture change, which is mostly facilitated by ongoing learning. Organizations can foster a sense of unity and identity among their workforce by integrating sustainability principles into their business values, practices, and behaviours. This will encourage staff members to embrace sustainability as a fundamental value. Initiatives for continuous learning, such team-building activities, sustainability seminars, and leadership development courses, can help employees feel more connected to the company, participate in more open communication, and generate a sense of trust.

In order for enterprises to integrate sustainability into their core values and make it a key component of their strategy, operations, and identity, cultural transformation is necessary. Initiatives for continuous learning can support firms in articulating their sustainability vision and values, communicating expectations to staff, and enabling them to live out these values in their day-to-day actions and choices.

Organizations can overcome cultural hurdles and reluctance to change that could impede sustainability efforts by engaging in continuous learning. Organizations may create a culture of psychological safety and trust that empowers people to voice their concerns, share their viewpoints, and actively participate in organizational change initiatives by giving staff members the chance to have candid discussions about sustainability.

A culture of accountability and openness is fostered by continuous learning, wherein staff members are motivated to accept responsibility for their actions and participate in group initiatives to advance sustainability. Organizations can reinforce desired cultural norms and behaviours and establish a positive feedback loop that supports cultural transformation over time by recognizing and rewarding behaviours that are in line with sustainability goals.

In conclusion, it is critical for employees to continuously learn about sustainability in the workplace in order to adjust to evolving environmental laws and trends. Organizations can improve employee skills, fortify stakeholder connections, and incorporate sustainability into their business operations by remaining aware, compliant, and proactive. Employees who engage in continuous learning are better equipped to effect good change and build a more sustainable future for both their companies and society at large.

5.3.2 Tools and Resources Available for Continuous Learning on Environmental Issues

❖ There are numerous tools and resources available for continuous learning on environmental issues, ranging from online courses and webinars to industry conferences and workshops. Here are some examples:

1. **Online Courses:**
a. **Coursera:** Provides a broad choice of environmental courses offered by eminent experts and institutes on subjects like climate change, sustainability, renewable energy, and environmental conservation. These courses allow students to study at their own speed and receive certificates upon completion. They often consist of video lectures, interactive quizzes, and assignments. The platform offered by Coursera also gives students the chance to communicate with one another through group projects and discussion boards, creating a more dynamic and rich learning environment.

b. **edX:** Offers online courses on environmental science, ecology, sustainable development, and environmental policy from universities and other institutions worldwide. In order to improve learning results, these courses frequently incorporate case studies, multimedia content, and real-world applications. They are created in partnership with industry partners. The flexible enrolment options provided by edX's platform enable learners with varying schedules and backgrounds to attend self-paced and instructor-led courses.

c. **Udemy:** Provides industry-trained courses in environmental management, environmental engineering, sustainable agriculture, and other relevant subjects. With the help of Udemy's on-demand video lectures, downloadable materials, and hands-on exercises, students may gain information and abilities that they can use right away for their own or their employer's projects. Furthermore, Udemy regularly runs specials and discounts on course registration, which makes it a cost-effective choice for ongoing education on environmental concerns.

2. **Webinars and Virtual Events:**
a. **GreenBiz Webcasts:** Presents webinars on a variety of sustainability-related subjects, including as sustainable supply chain management, renewable energy, corporate sustainability initiatives, and the circular economy. Thought leaders, business specialists, and practitioners present during these webinars, which are followed by lively Q&A sessions and panel discussions. Webcasts from GreenBiz are available to a worldwide audience and offer insightful information about new trends, industry best practices, and creative ways to advance sustainability in business and other fields.

b. **World Resources Institute (WRI) Webinars:** Arranges webinars on environmental topics, including managing water resources, reducing the effects of climate change, protecting biodiversity, and sustainable urban development. These webinars offer actionable insights and workable solutions for tackling urgent environmental concerns. They feature research findings, policy analysis, and case studies from WRI's global network of experts and partners. Policymakers, practitioners, researchers, and other stakeholders interested in furthering sustainable development goals are welcome to attend WRI webinars.

c. **United Nations Environment Programme (UNEP) Webinars:** Carries out webinars on a range of environmental subjects, such as waste management, air quality, ecosystem restoration, and sustainable production and consumption. These webinars showcase international efforts, policy frameworks, and best practices for achieving environmental sustainability. Presenters include UNEP specialists, government officials, and representatives of civil society. The webinars offered by UNEP facilitate the exchange of knowledge, the development of capacity, and cooperation among stakeholders who are striving for a sustainable future.

3. **Industry Conferences and Workshops:**
a. **Green-build International Conference & Expo:** One of the biggest conferences devoted to sustainable design and green architecture, with networking opportunities, workshops, and instructional events. Architects, engineers, builders, developers, and legislators come together at Green-build to discuss the newest developments, ideas, and

technology in environmentally friendly building and urban planning. The conference provides a forum for professional growth, knowledge sharing, and teamwork, enabling participants to influence good changes in the built environment.

b. **SXSW Eco:** Focuses on social impact, sustainability, and environmental innovation; it includes keynote speakers, panels, and workshops on subjects including sustainable fashion and renewable energy. Entrepreneurs, financiers, activists, and thought leaders come together at SXSW Eco to talk about new developments in technology, disruptive trends, and game-changing approaches to solving global sustainability issues. The conference encourages creativity, innovation, and cross-sector collaboration, motivating attendees to take initiative and promote change both inside and outside of their communities.

c. **Global Climate Action Summit:** Gathers influential figures from the public, private, and non-profit sectors to talk about obligations and solutions for climate change. Includes high-level talks, seminars, and exhibitions. The conference presents cutting-edge strategies for mitigating the effects of climate change and showcasing effective initiatives, laws, and collaborations that are advancing the transition to a resilient, low-carbon future. Networking, information sharing, and global, national, and local action on climate change are all made possible for participants.

4. **Professional Associations and Organizations:**

a. **Association of Environmental Professionals (AEP):** Provides webinars, conferences, and professional development opportunities for environmental professionals employed in governmental, consulting, and academic settings. AEP offers excellent chances for networking, learning, and continuing education through its events, which cover a wide range of issues such as environmental impact assessment, land use planning, regulatory compliance, and environmental justice. In order to promote professional development and career success, AEP also provides mentoring opportunities and certification programs.

b. **Society of Environmental Journalists (SEJ):** Offers conferences, training courses, and materials to journalists that cover environmental topics such as biodiversity, climate change, and environmental justice. Expert panels, field trips, and workshops on investigative reporting, data journalism, and multimedia storytelling are all part of SEJ's activities, which provide journalists the knowledge and abilities they need to write factual, engrossing, and influential articles about the environment. More public knowledge and involvement on environmental issues are promoted by SEJ's conferences, which also let journalists, scientists, policymakers, and communicators network and collaborate.

c. **International Society of Sustainability Professionals (ISSP):** Provides study materials, webinars, training courses, and training programs for professional growth. Members receive savings on courses, have access to an extensive collection of educational materials, and can obtain globally recognized sustainability certifications. In addition, ISSP offers cheap event tickets and networking possibilities through its online community. Members can also take advantage of sponsorship and advertising opportunities inside the ISSP network (ISSP Home) (American Sustainable Business Network) and use the ISSP logo for professional branding.

With the aid of these tools and resources, people may make significant contributions to the fight against global environmental difficulties as well as broaden their networks, knowledge, and expertise in environmental concerns. They can also stay up to date on the most recent advancements and best practices. Continuous learning, whether through publications, webinars, conferences, or online courses, is essential for promoting innovation and increasing capacity for environmental sustainability.

5.3.3 Research Findings on the Impact of Continuous Learning on Sustainable Practices in Organizations

Research findings on the impact of continuous learning on sustainable practices in organizations provide valuable insights into the benefits of investing in employee education and development.

❖ Here are some research findings highlighting the positive outcomes of continuous learning initiatives:

1. Improved Employee Engagement:

According to a Gallup study, companies with high employee engagement levels have 21% higher profitability than those with low engagement levels. Opportunities for ongoing learning, such as skill development projects and training programs, enable people to learn, grow, and progress in their careers inside the company, which raises employee engagement levels. Workers are more likely to be involved in their work, which boosts productivity, creativity, and job satisfaction, if they feel respected and supported by their employers.

Multinational corporations, such as Google and Microsoft, allocate significant resources towards employee development initiatives. These initiatives encompass a diverse array of training options, such as workshops on diversity and inclusion, technical skill training, and leadership development. These businesses understand that keeping people engaged, drawing in top talent, and developing an innovative and collaborative culture all depend on ongoing learning. Organizations can foster a pleasant work environment where workers feel empowered and inspired to give their best efforts towards sustainable practices by giving them access to meaningful and relevant learning opportunities.

2. Reduced Environmental Impact:

According to an International Institute for Sustainable Development (IISD) study, companies that place a high priority on staff sustainability education and training are more likely to encourage ecologically friendly behaviour and lessen their ecological footprint. Green supply chain workshops and environmental management systems (EMS) training are examples of continuous learning efforts that assist staff members in adopting environmentally friendly habits and realizing the value of sustainability. Organizations can minimize resource consumption, waste generation, and greenhouse gas emissions by implementing sustainable practices after providing staff with the necessary knowledge and skills to identify areas for improvement.

Companies such as Unilever and Patagonia, for example, are well-known for their dedication to sustainability and staff training. Ambitious objectives to lessen environmental effect are part of Unilever's Sustainable Living Plan, which covers the company's whole value chain from sourcing raw materials to manufacturing and distribution. To assist staff members in incorporating sustainable practices into their daily work and helping to achieve these objectives, the organization offers sustainability training and resources. Similar to this, the outdoor clothing brand Patagonia provides workshops and environmental training courses to inform staff members on the company's sustainability efforts and encourage them to take initiative in reducing their own environmental effect at work.

3. Enhanced Corporate Reputation:

Companies with robust sustainability programs and a dedication to employee development are seen more favourably by stakeholders, including customers, investors, and employees, according to a survey done by Corporate Responsibility Magazine and Cielo. Initiatives for continuous learning that prioritize ethics, innovation, and sustainability leadership help the company establish a favourable reputation and set itself out as a responsible, progressive leader in its sector. Organizations can establish confidence and credibility with stakeholders by investing in employee education and development as a means of demonstrating their commitment to sustainability and corporate social responsibility.

Firms such as Interface and Tesla, for instance, have established robust brand identities by prioritizing sustainability and fostering employee involvement. A major component of Interface's corporate culture and business plan is sustainability. Interface is a worldwide producer of commercial flooring. By 2020, the corporation wants to completely eradicate its negative environmental effects. Part of this effort includes cutting back on waste, water use, and greenhouse gas emissions. In addition to offering sustainability training, Interface invites staff members to submit concepts and breakthroughs that further the organization's sustainability objectives. In a similar vein, employee development programs at Tesla, the producer of electric vehicles, place a strong emphasis on sustainability and innovation. Opportunities for training and skill development are provided in fields including renewable energy, battery technology, and sustainable mobility.

The results of this study emphasize how crucial it is for businesses to adopt sustainable practices in order to achieve favourable results like higher employee engagement, less environmental effect, and increased brand recognition.

Organizations may empower individuals to drive innovation, contribute to sustainability goals, and create long-term value for the business, the environment, and society by investing in the education and development of their workforce.

Chapter – 6

Performance Management in Green Organization

Introduction to Green Performance Management:

A variety of tactics and procedures are included in the broad approach known as "green performance management," which aims to improve an organization's environmental sustainability. Fundamentally, it entails setting precise goals and measurements to assess resource usage, carbon emissions, and environmental effect. Furthermore, green performance management involves putting policies like waste reduction plans, energy efficiency programs, and sustainable procurement methods into action. Organizations may successfully monitor their progress towards sustainability goals and find areas for improvement by including environmental factors into their key performance indicators (KPIs) and performance evaluation processes. In addition to reducing environmental hazards and adhering to regulations, this proactive approach promotes innovation, builds brand reputation, and increases long-term profitability in a market that is becoming more environmentally sensitive.

Meaning of Green Performance Management:

The goal of green performance management is to assess and improve an organization's environmental performance using a comprehensive framework that includes a variety of approaches, activities, and practices. Fundamentally, it entails defining specific environmental goals and creating pertinent measurements to gauge advancement toward these targets. Implementing tactics like waste reduction plans, carbon footprint tracking, sustainable sourcing policies, and energy efficiency measures are all part of this process. Green performance management allows firms to systematically identify areas for development and drive continual progress towards sustainability targets by including environmental issues into key performance indicators (KPIs) and performance evaluation processes. It also strengthens the business's image as a socially and environmentally responsible organization and cultivates a culture of environmental responsibility and innovation in sustainable operations.

Definition of Green Performance Management:

"The process of assessing and enhancing an organization's sustainability and environmental performance is known as green performance management."

Concept of Performance Management in Green Organisations:

A systematic and multidimensional method to assessing and improving environmental sustainability initiatives in the context of overall company performance is performance management in green organizations. In order to promote positive environmental outcomes while maintaining or improving operational efficiency and effectiveness, it incorporates environmental factors into conventional performance management frameworks. This allows environmental goals to be aligned with larger business objectives.

Setting specific environmental goals is the cornerstone of performance management in green businesses. Usually, the organization's mission, values, and dedication to sustainability serve as the foundation for these goals. A variety of environmental objectives may be included, such as lowering greenhouse gas emissions, cutting down on waste production, protecting natural resources, enhancing the quality of the air and water, encouraging biodiversity, and assisting in the switch to renewable energy sources. Establishing SMART (specific, measurable, attainable, relevant, and time-bound) environmental goals helps organizations track their progress toward desired outcomes and give their sustainability initiatives a clear direction.

Here's a detailed breakdown of how it works:

1. Alignment with Environmental Objectives:
- Green organizations match more general environmental goals with the aspirations of individuals and teams. This guarantees that

each worker is aware of how they fit into the larger picture of sustainability goals.

- Reducing carbon emissions, cutting back on trash production, saving energy and water, and encouraging eco-friendly behaviours across the board are a few examples of possible objectives.

2. **Key Performance Indicators (KPIs):**
   - Environmental performance is measured using certain Key Performance Indicators (KPIs).
   - The decrease of carbon footprint, recycling rates, the use of renewable energy sources, and employee involvement in sustainability programs are just a few examples of the quantitative and qualitative components of sustainability activities that are measured by these KPIs.

3. **Regular Performance Reviews:**
   - Employees are evaluated on their contributions to environmental sustainability through regular performance assessments.
   - Along with typical performance indicators, feedback is given on how well individuals and teams perform in meeting environmental targets.
   - In order to promote continual development, managers provide advice on how to enhance performance in sustainability-related areas.

4. **Training and Development:**
   - Green businesses make training and development program investments to give staff members the know-how and abilities they need to support sustainability projects.
   - Energy conservation, waste reduction, environmentally friendly technology use, and sustainable procurement procedures are just a few of the subjects covered in training.

- Opportunities for ongoing education guarantee that staff members are knowledgeable about cutting-edge approaches to environmental sustainability and best practices.

5. **Recognition and Rewards:**
   - Workers who make contributions to environmental sustainability are acknowledged and rewarded.
   - Incentives might take the form of cash bonuses, job advancements, praise from the public, additional vacation time, or involvement in unique projects.
   - Honouring sustainability achievements encourage staff members to keep up their good work and strengthens the culture of environmental stewardship.

6. **Employee Engagement:**
   - Success in sustainability programs depends on involving employees.
   - Workers collaborate on projects, hold workshops, and conduct brainstorming sessions in order to find areas for development and put creative solutions into practice.
   - Employee engagement results in increased motivation and performance because engaged workers have a sense of ownership and commitment to environmental goals.

7. **Feedback Mechanisms:**
   - Employee feedback on performance management procedures and sustainability initiatives is gathered through feedback systems.
   - Surveys, suggestion boxes, team meetings, and one-on-one conversations with management are all used to gather feedback.
   - Including employee viewpoints increases employee buy-in and guarantees that performance management plans reflect their goals and needs.

8. **Continuous Improvement:**
 - In green organizations, performance management is an ongoing process of development.
 - Based on feedback, lessons learned, and changes in the external environment, organizations review and improve their management processes, performance indicators, and sustainability goals on a regular basis.
 - In order to maintain environmental sustainability, continuous development guarantees flexibility and reactivity to new opportunities and challenges.

9. **Integration with CSR Initiatives:**
 - Initiatives pertaining to Corporate Social Responsibility (CSR) and performance management are strongly related.
 - The organization's reputation and connections with clients, investors, and the community at large are improved when sustainability goals and performance metrics are included in CSR reports and shared with stakeholders.

10. **Leadership Commitment:**
 - In green organizations, strong leadership commitment is necessary for efficient performance management.
 - Sustainability is given top priority by leaders, who also promote environmental stewardship and offer tools and assistance for implementation.
 - The dedication of leaders sets the standard for environmentally friendly operations, inspiring staff members to adopt sustainability and incorporate it into their regular workdays.

To summarize, green organizations' performance management entails setting up KPIs to measure sustainability performance, conducting regular reviews, offering training and development, acknowledging contributions, involving staff, obtaining feedback, fostering continuous improvement, collaborating with CSR initiatives, and exhibiting leadership commitment.

By using these strategies, firms may successfully monitor performance and forward their sustainability goal.

6.1 Setting Sustainable Performance Goals

Introduction:
Establishing sustainable performance objectives is essential for companies who want to support long-term sustainability and match their operations with environmental values. In the contemporary world, characterized by swift transformations and heightened global conversation surrounding environmental issues, enterprises are gradually realizing the significance of incorporating sustainability into their fundamental business strategy. Organizations may lessen their ecological footprint, foster innovation, increase stakeholder trust, and add value to society by establishing specific, attainable targets for their environmental performance.

❖ **Important Things to Remember:**

1. Context of Sustainability: Start by outlining the background and significance of sustainable performance goals in the context of today's corporate environment. Draw attention to the growing public awareness of environmental problems including pollution, resource depletion, and climate change, as well as the part that businesses play in finding solutions.

2. Business Imperative: Describe the reasons that businesses must prioritize sustainability as a strategic requirement in addition to a moral duty. Talk about how incorporating sustainability into business operations may assist companies in risk management, grabbing expansion possibilities, and preserving their social license to operate in a market that is becoming more and more mindful.

3. Benefits of Setting Sustainable Goals: Emphasize the advantages that companies might have by establishing goals for sustainable performance. These consist of increased operational effectiveness, reduced costs via resource optimization, higher brand recognition, ease of access to new markets and clientele, and resistance to changes in regulations and market upheavals.

4. Integration with Corporate Strategy: Talk about how important it is to match the organization's strategic objectives, mission, and vision with its sustainable performance goals. In order to achieve coherence and effectiveness, emphasize that sustainability should be integrated into all facets of business planning and decision-making processes.

5. Stakeholder Expectations: Recognize the influence that stakeholders' investors, clients, staff, regulators, and communities have on the need for sustainable business practices. Describe how meeting stakeholder expectations and developing confidence and trust can be achieved by establishing transparent and unambiguous sustainability goals.

6. Challenges and Opportunities: Acknowledge that obstacles such resource shortages, technology hurdles, and organizational inertia may arise while establishing sustainable performance targets. Reiterate, nonetheless, that these difficulties also offer chances for creativity, teamwork, and competitive edge.

7. Continuous Improvement: Emphasize how crucial it is to keep improving in order to achieve sustainability goals. Emphasize that creating goals is a dynamic process that needs to be reviewed, adjusted, and innovated upon often to remain applicable and efficient in a changing context.

- **Setting sustainable performance goals is essential for aligning organizational objectives with environmental priorities.**
- ❖ **Here's how organizations can establish such goals:**

Step-1. Identify Environmental Priorities:
- ➤ Start by determining which environmental issues are most important for your sector and company.
- ➤ Take into account variables such waste production, pollution, energy and water use, carbon emissions, and biodiversity preservation.

Step-2. Set Specific Targets:
- ➤ Make sure your environmental sustainability goals are measurable, precise, and unambiguous.

- Consider setting goals like a % reduction in carbon emissions, energy efficiency gains, 0% waste to landfills, or the adoption of sustainable sourcing techniques.

Step-3. Use the SMART Criteria:
- Make sure your objectives are SMART: Specific, Measurable, Achievable, Relevant, and Time-bound.
- Specific: Clearly state the objectives that must be met.
- Measurable: Establish standards for monitoring development and achievement.
- Achievable: Make sure your objectives are doable and practical given the resources at hand.
- Relevant: Ensure that goals are in line with the organization's environmental priorities, values, and mission.
- Time-bound: Establish due dates or checkpoints to keep yourself accountable and focused on your goals.

Step-4. Engage Stakeholders:
- Include important parties in the goal-setting process, including as staff members, clients, vendors, investors, and members of the community.
- To make sure that the objectives represent the interests and worries of all stakeholders, gather opinions and comments.

Step-5. Integrate with Business Strategy:
- Align the organization's entire business strategy and objectives with the aims of sustainable performance.
- Make certain that decision-making procedures in all divisions and organizational levels incorporate environmental priorities.
- **Step-6. Consider Life Cycle Assessment:**
- Setting sustainable goals takes the whole life cycle of goods, services, and operations into account.

- To find environmental hotspots and rank areas that need improvement along the value chain, do a life cycle assessment.

Step-7. Benchmark Against Industry Standards:
- Compare performance to peer organizations, best practices, and industry standards.
- Measure and report progress using instruments like sustainability reporting frameworks (like the Global Reporting Initiative) and environmental management systems (like ISO 1401).

Step-8. Encourage Innovation and Collaboration:
- Encourage an innovative and cooperative culture to find fresh approaches to enhancing sustainability.
- In order to achieve sustainable performance targets, encourage staff members to suggest concepts, test projects, and initiatives.

Step-9. Monitor and Evaluate Progress:
- Establish reliable monitoring and assessment mechanisms to monitor the advancement of sustainability objectives.
- Review performance data on a regular basis, look for patterns, and pinpoint any areas that could require extra attention to keep on course.

Step-10. Celebrate Achievements and Learn from Challenges:
- Celebrate accomplishments and turning points along the path to sustainability to acknowledge and incentivize advancement.
- Use obstacles and failures as teaching moments and chances for introspection and growth.

Step-11. Continuously Improve:
- Adopt a philosophy of constant improvement by going over and improving sustainability objectives on a regular basis.
- Goals should be adjusted in response to evolving dangers, new opportunities for innovation, and shifting internal and external factors.

These guidelines help firms build long-term value for stakeholders, improve brand reputation, and develop sustainable performance targets that support environmental stewardship.

To sum up, organizations that are dedicated to promoting environmental sustainability and generating long-term value for their stakeholders must first establish sustainable performance targets. Businesses may take the lead in the shift to a more sustainable future by setting clear goals, including sustainability into corporate strategy, involving stakeholders, and adopting a continuous improvement culture.

6.1.1 Importance of Aligning Performance Goals with Environmental Objectives in Green Organizations

Environmental sustainability has become a crucial factor for businesses all over the world in the modern business landscape. Sustainability is a top priority for green organizations since they are committed to environmental stewardship and social responsibility. The matching of performance targets with environmental goals is essential to their success. This introduction goes into the relevance of this alignment and its far-reaching ramifications for green firms in realizing their sustainability ambitions.

❖ **Key Points to Include:**

1. Rising Environmental Consciousness: Let us start by recognizing the growing consciousness and anxiety over environmental problems such pollution, depletion of natural resources, climate change, and loss of species. Describe how stakeholders are expecting companies to show their commitment to environmental responsibility, which has sparked a global movement towards sustainability.

2. Role of Performance Goals: Talk about how important performance goals are for directing organizational behaviour and setting priorities. Emphasize how performance goals are concrete objectives that direct workers' behaviour, inspire better performance, and gauge achievement. Stress that by coordinating these aims with environmental targets, you can make sure that sustainability becomes an essential component of business success.

Principles of Green HRM

3. Importance of Alignment: Explain why it is critical for green organizations to have performance targets that are in line with environmental objectives. Examine how this alignment guarantees the incorporation of sustainability considerations into all facets of the organization's operations, ranging from daily tasks to strategic planning. Show how it aids in prioritizing actions that reduce their negative effects on the environment and enhance their beneficial benefits to sustainability.

- **Aligning performance goals with environmental objectives is crucial for the success and credibility of green organizations.**

❖ **Here's why it's so important:**

1. Strategic Focus: Strategic focus on sustainability is ensured by green firms through the alignment of performance goals with environmental objectives. As a result, the organization's goal and vision are meaningfully advanced and measures that support resource conservation, environmental protection, and climate mitigation are given priority.

2. Clear Direction: Employees have a clear direction and purpose when performance targets are set in line with environmental objectives. It conveys the company's dedication to sustainability and gives staff members the freedom to operate in a way that promotes environmental stewardship in their day-to-day jobs.

3. Measurement and Accountability: Establishing measurable targets for sustainability improvement is made possible for organizations when performance goals are in line with environmental objectives. This makes it possible to more accurately monitor development over time and hold people and groups responsible for their contributions to environmental goals.

4. Resource Optimization: Efficient resource usage is encouraged when performance targets are set in line with environmental objectives. Workers are encouraged to come up with creative solutions to cut down on waste, save energy and water, and lessen their environmental effect, which lowers costs and improves operational effectiveness.

5. Risk Management: Environmental legislation, the effects of climate change, and reputational harm from environmental incidents are among the dangers that green organizations must contend with. Organizations can proactively manage these risks, improve regulatory compliance, and strengthen their resilience to environmental issues by coordinating performance goals with environmental objectives.

6. Enhanced Stakeholder Trust: Customers, investors, staff members, and communities are just a few of the stakeholders that have increased expectations of businesses about their environmental sustainability. When performance targets are in line with environmental goals, stakeholders will see real progress being made toward sustainability goals, which will increase credibility and trust.

7. Competitive Advantage: Green companies can obtain a competitive edge in the market by successfully coordinating performance targets with environmental aims. They set themselves apart from the competition by being ecologically conscientious, which draws in investors, customers, and workers who want to work for companies that share their beliefs.

8. Innovation and Collaboration: Organizational creativity and teamwork are encouraged when performance targets are in line with environmental goals. To develop and implement long-term solutions that promote continuous improvement, staff members are urged to exercise creativity, try out novel concepts, and work across departmental boundaries.

In conclusion, green organizations must strategically focus their efforts, give employees clear direction, measure progress, optimize resources, manage risks, build stakeholder trust, gain a competitive advantage, foster innovation, and drive collaboration in order to achieve sustainability goals. This can only be done by aligning performance goals with environmental objectives.

6.1.2 Strategies for Setting SMART (Specific, Measurable, Achievable, Relevant, Time-bound) Sustainability Goals for Employees

Introduction to Setting SMART Sustainability Goals for Employees

In the quickly changing corporate environment of today, sustainability has become a crucial area of concern for businesses all over the world. A growing number of businesses are adopting sustainability as a core value as they recognize the significance of incorporating social and environmental responsibility into corporate operations. But in order to lead sustainability efforts successfully, companies need to make sure that their staff members are enthusiastic about and dedicated to these objectives.

Setting SMART goals is a tried-and-true way to motivate staff members and direct their efforts toward sustainability. The term SMART stands for Specific, Measurable, Achievable, Relevant, and Time-bound. It offers a methodical framework for creating goals that promotes responsibility, clarity, and results that can be put into practice.

We will explore how to create SMART sustainability goals that are specific to the roles and responsibilities that people have inside the company in this tutorial. By implementing these tactics, companies can improve their social and environmental impact while simultaneously cultivating an all-encompassing sustainable culture within the workforce.

We will look at real-world examples, insights that can be put into practice, and best practices for creating SMART sustainability goals throughout the guide. This will enable organizations to effect real change and make a beneficial impact on the planet. One SMART goal at a time, let's set out on this journey towards a more sustainable future.

Employee sustainability goals should be SMART (Specific, Measurable, Achievable, Relevant, Time-bound). This is a strategic process that requires careful preparation, employee participation, and alignment with the organization's larger goals. Businesses can effectively leverage the combined efforts of their workers to advance sustainability objectives by adhering to particular tactics.

1. Engage Employees in Goal-Setting: It is essential to involve staff members in goal-setting in order to promote ownership and dedication to sustainability goals. Employees that actively contribute to goal definition feel more accountable and invested in seeing those goals through to completion. Collaborative workshops, team meetings, or surveys that elicit opinions and suggestions from staff members in various departments and levels might help achieve this.

2. Align with Organizational Objectives: Sustainability objectives must to be in line with the organization's main mission, core values, and strategic goals. Businesses may emphasize sustainability as a fundamental value and smoothly incorporate it into their operations by making sure that alignment is maintained. This alignment also fosters a sense of purpose and motivation among employees by assisting them in understanding how their individual efforts contribute to the organization's greater goal.

3. Identify Specific Areas for Improvement: Finding particular areas where changes can be made is considerably easier when an organization's present sustainability practices are thoroughly assessed. Determining which areas to concentrate sustainability efforts on—waste reduction, energy conservation, supply chain process optimization, or ethical sourcing—gives clarity. Because of this precision, businesses are able to establish focused objectives that tackle their most urgent sustainability problems.

4. Establish Measurable Metrics: Tracking the advancement of sustainability goals requires the definition of precise and quantifiable measures. Metrics like cutting carbon emissions by a specific percentage, raising recycling rates, or enhancing water efficiency should be measurable. Measurable metrics give organizations concrete standards for success, enabling them to monitor their advancement, pinpoint areas for development, and recognize milestones along the route.

5. Ensure Goals are Achievable: Maintaining momentum and motivation requires setting realistic goals that can be accomplished in the allotted time. Think about things like the resources at your disposal, the state of technology, and any obstacles that can get in the way of achieving your objectives. Organizations can reduce employee frustration and disappointment and preserve their commitment to sustainability projects by making sure that goals are reachable.

6. Relevance to Employees' Roles: Sustainability goals are meaningful and directly impact employees' daily actions when they are crafted to correspond with their positions and responsibilities inside the company. It is ensured that sustainability efforts are incorporated into multiple departments and functions, for example, by setting waste reduction targets for procurement teams or energy saving goals for facilities management workers. This alignment motivates staff members to actively contribute to accomplishing objectives pertinent to their roles and highlights the significance of sustainability throughout the company.

7. Provide Training and Support: Employees must receive support and training in order to be fully prepared to contribute to sustainability goals with the necessary resources, knowledge, and abilities. Offering workshops on sustainable practices, granting access to pertinent training materials and resources, or designating sustainability champions within teams to offer direction and assistance are a few examples of how to do this. Organizations can empower their workforce to spearhead sustainability projects and act as change agents within their departments by investing in employee development.

8. Set Time-Bound Deadlines: Giving staff members a deadline to meet sustainability goals instils a feeling of urgency and accountability. Time-bound objectives support efficient resource allocation, action prioritization, and goal progress monitoring. Organizations can generate momentum towards accomplishing sustainability objectives and emphasize the significance of prompt action in tackling environmental and social issues by imposing deadlines.

9. Track Progress and Provide Feedback: Ensuring that sustainability targets are tracked and that employees receive regular feedback are critical to sustaining momentum and enthusiasm. Organizations can monitor performance, pinpoint areas for development, and recognize accomplishments along the way by tracking progress. Giving feedback motivates ongoing development, validates workers' dedication to sustainability objectives, and recognizes their efforts. Furthermore, consistent feedback and communication promote openness and trust inside the company, guaranteeing that sustainability stays a top concern for all parties.

Through the integration of these tactics into the goal-setting procedure, companies can enable their staff members to take an active role in sustainability initiatives and effect significant transformations that lead to a future with greater environmental and social responsibility.

6.1.3 Examples of Sustainable Performance Goals Related to Waste Reduction, Energy Conservation, and Carbon Footprint Reduction

- Here are some examples of sustainable performance goals related to waste reduction, energy conservation, and carbon footprint reduction set by organizations:

1. Waste Reduction:

i. Google:

Google, a well-known tech company for its dedication to sustainability, has set high standards for reducing waste in all aspects of its business. A primary goal of Google is to attain zero waste to landfill in all of its offices, campuses, and data canters. This all-encompassing strategy includes programs for recycling, composting, and reuse in addition to waste reduction and trash diversion from landfills. Google hopes to reduce its environmental impact and support a circular economy by instituting strict waste management procedures and encouraging a sustainable culture among its staff.

ii. Unilever:

The global consumer goods corporation Unilever has prioritized waste reduction as a component of its larger sustainability plan. By 2025, Unilever aims to reduce waste related to its products by half, specifically focusing on waste from product disposal. Initiatives to reduce packaging waste, improve product design for recycling, and support recycling infrastructure and education are all part of this comprehensive strategy. In order to promote systemic change in the direction of a more sustainable and circular economy, Unilever collaborates with stakeholders at every stage of the value chain and makes use of its size and power.

2. Energy Conservation:

i. Apple:

As a pioneer in innovation and technology, Apple has set high standards for lowering its environmental effect and switching to renewable energy sources. Apple wants to become carbon neutral throughout its whole product lifecycle and supply chain by 2030 as part of its commitment to sustainability. This include converting its manufacturing partners to renewable energy sources, enhancing product energy efficiency, and funding global renewable energy initiatives. Apple aims to use energy-efficient technologies and embrace renewable energy in order to lessen its carbon impact and pave the path for a more sustainable future.

ii. IKEA:

Global retailer IKEA, well-known for its reasonably priced furniture and household goods, has made notable progress in the use of renewable energy sources and energy saving. By 2025, IKEA wants to have produced as much renewable energy as it used for operations. This audacious goal entails making investments in wind and solar energy projects, mounting solar panels atop retail buildings, and putting energy-saving equipment in its distribution and retail facilities. By adopting energy-efficient practices and renewable energy, IKEA hopes to lessen its dependency on fossil fuels, cut down on carbon emissions, and encourage other companies to do the same.

3. Carbon Footprint Reduction:

i. Microsoft:

Leading computer giant Microsoft has made audacious promises to combat climate change and lessen its carbon footprint. By 2030, Microsoft wants to be carbon negative, which means it will take out more carbon from the environment than it adds. Furthermore, Microsoft wants to eliminate all of the carbon it has released since its establishment in 1975 by the year 2050. Microsoft is investing in carbon capture and storage technology, increasing its usage of renewable energy, and putting energy efficiency measures in place across its businesses in order to meet these lofty goals. Microsoft is leading the way in corporate leadership and promoting innovation in the battle against climate change by proactively reducing its carbon footprint.

ii. Walmart:

One of the biggest merchants in the world, Walmart, understands the significance of lowering greenhouse gas emissions and addressing climate change. Walmart wants to cut its greenhouse gas emissions from its baseline of 2015 by 18% by 2025. This all-encompassing strategy involves cutting emissions from company operations, like energy usage in fleets of vehicles and retail spaces, as well as collaborating with suppliers to cut emissions all the way through its supply chain. Walmart is leading the retail sector and advancing its carbon reduction targets by working with stakeholders and using its size and power to its advantage.

These examples highlight how forward-thinking companies are establishing challenging sustainability targets for lowering their energy use, trash production, and carbon footprint. Through the implementation of focused strategies and a sustainability priority, these organizations are not only lessening their environmental footprint but also promoting innovation, encouraging teamwork, and exhibiting corporate leadership in sustainability.

6.2 Monitoring Environmental Performance

Introduction to Monitoring Environmental Performance:
Nowadays, companies in a wide range of industries are paying more attention to their environmental impact since environmental sustainability is a critical issue. Corporate strategy now includes monitoring environmental performance as a crucial element to make sure businesses not only meet legal obligations but also advance the global sustainability agenda.

What is Environmental Performance Monitoring?
Monitoring an organization's environmental consequences entails measuring, tracking, and assessing them in a methodical manner. This includes a broad range of operations, such as waste management, greenhouse gas emissions, and water and energy consumption. Understanding how organizational operations impact the environment and seeing areas for improvement are the main objectives.

❖ Why is it Important?

1. Regulatory Compliance: Environmental laws and regulations have been enforced by governments and regulatory entities globally. These must be followed by organizations in order to prevent fines and legal problems. Monitoring aids in ensuring that these rules are followed.

2. Sustainability Goals: Many firms have a commitment to sustainability that goes beyond compliance. Companies can establish and accomplish challenging sustainability targets, like cutting carbon footprints, cutting waste, and improving resource efficiency, by tracking their environmental performance.

3. Risk Management: Environmental hazards that can seriously jeopardize corporate operations include pollution and resource depletion. Keeping an eye on these factors enables firms to recognize and address such dangers early on.

4. Cost Savings: Efficiency in the utilization of resources, such water and energy, frequently results in large cost savings. Performance monitoring enables firms to pinpoint inefficiencies and execute economical solutions.

5. Corporate Reputation: Environmental stewardship is becoming more and more valued by stakeholders, including investors and consumers. Strong environmental performance can improve an organization's reputation, foster brand loyalty, and draw in environmentally sensitive investors.

6. Innovation and Competitiveness: Innovation can be stimulated by environmental performance monitoring. Businesses can find innovative, environmentally friendly methods and technology that not only lessen their influence on the environment but also give them a business advantage.

An organization's environmental impact is tracked, assessed, and improved as part of the extensive process of monitoring environmental performance. This strategy promotes corporate responsibility and sustainability in addition to guaranteeing adherence to environmental laws.

❖ **Here is a detailed explanation of the key steps involved in monitoring environmental performance:**

1. Define Environmental Performance Indicators (EPIs):
Particular measures known as Environmental Performance Indicators shed light on the environmental impact of a firm. These indicators fall under a number of categories, including resource efficiency, waste production, energy and water use, and greenhouse gas emissions. The correct EPIs

must be chosen in order for the organization's environmental goals and regulatory obligations to be met. For example, a company that wants to lessen its carbon footprint may monitor energy consumption and CO_2 emissions.

2. Set Performance Targets:
Set specific, quantifiable objectives for each of the EPIs after they have been identified. The organization's sustainability goals, industry standards, and legal obligations should all be taken into consideration while setting these goals. Performance targets can be long-term (multi-year goals) or short-term (annual goals), and they function as a benchmark for assessing progress. For instance, a business may decide to cut its water usage by 20% over the following five years.

3. Data Collection:
Gathering accurate data is essential to tracking environmental performance. This entails collecting data on the specified EPIs using a variety of tools, including audits, sensors, meters, and employee reports. Data might be gathered manually or automatically. IoT sensors and smart meters are examples of automated technologies that lower the possibility of human error while providing real-time data. This information can be enhanced by routine surveys and audits, which will give a complete picture of the organization's environmental performance.

4. Data Analysis:
Understanding the organization's performance in relation to its goals is made easier by analysing the data that has been gathered. Finding trends, patterns, and anomalies in the data is the goal of this research. This process can be aided by advanced analytics software and tools, opening the door to more complex analyses like scenario planning and predictive modelling. Organizations can find possibilities for improvement and identify particular areas where performance is inadequate by analysing the data.

5. Reporting:
Monitoring environmental performance requires transparency. It is crucial to notify stakeholders—such as management, staff, investors, and regulatory agencies—of findings on a regular basis. These reports can be written in-depth, be presented in a graphic dashboard, or be full

sustainability reports, among other formats. In addition to the statistics, effective reporting should outline the steps being taken to rectify any problems and the advancement made toward achieving performance goals.

6. Review and Improvement:
Environmental performance monitoring is an iterative process. Organizations should routinely evaluate their current strategies and procedures in light of the analysis and findings. In order to identify underlying problems and come up with remedies, this review may entail performing root cause analysis. Adopting new technology, boosting staff training initiatives, optimizing operational procedures, or making investments in more environmentally friendly products and procedures are all examples of how to implement changes.

7. Compliance and Certification:
An essential component of environmental performance monitoring is making sure that environmental laws and standards are followed. Companies should keep abreast of pertinent regulations and make an effort to comply with or surpass them. Getting certified for things like ISO 14001 shows that you're serious about having strong environmental management systems. Additionally, these certifications might give the company a competitive edge and improve its standing among stakeholders.

8. Stakeholder Engagement:
Having conversations with stakeholders is a crucial aspect of the monitoring procedure. This include informing the local community, clients, workers, and suppliers about the company's environmental accomplishments and initiatives. Involving stakeholders can help an organization develop a sustainable culture and promote teamwork to enhance environmental performance.

9. Continuous Improvement:
Monitoring environmental performance is a continual process rather than an isolated event. Companies should promote a continuous improvement culture in which frequent strategy updates and feedback loops are standard operating procedures. The firm will be able to adjust to new environmental management opportunities and problems thanks to this dynamic strategy.

In summary, modern enterprises must prioritize environmental performance monitoring as a strategic objective, in addition to being required by law. It helps businesses to manage hazards, save expenses, comprehend their impact on the environment, accomplish sustainability targets, and cultivate a positive brand. Organizations can enhance their operational efficiency and competitiveness, as well as contribute to a more sustainable future, by methodically monitoring and improving their environmental performance.

6.2.1 Tools and Techniques for Tracking and Measuring Environmental Performance Metrics in Organizations

❖ Here is a detailed explanation of the various tools and techniques for tracking and measuring environmental performance metrics in organizations:

1. Key Performance Indicators (KPIs):

KPIs are crucial comparison points for evaluating the environmental performance of a company. These measurements show clearly where improvements are needed and where success has been made when they are well-defined and in line with corporate objectives. Organisations can obtain valuable insights into their environmental footprint and monitor their sustainability initiatives over time by implementing a complete set of KPIs that address many facets of environmental impact, including energy consumption, water usage, waste creation, and emissions. Organizations can discover trends, highlight inefficiencies, and execute focused measures to improve environmental performance by routinely monitoring and evaluating KPI data.

2. Environmental Management Systems (EMS):

Organizations can manage their environmental responsibilities in an organized manner with the use of an Environmental Management System (EMS). Organisations that employ a structured approach to environmental management, whether through custom systems developed to meet their needs or through adoption of existing standards like ISO 14001. Setting environmental goals, carrying out risk assessments, putting controls and procedures in place, keeping an eye on performance, and consistently enhancing processes are just a few of the many tasks that make up EMS. Organizations can improve regulatory compliance, reduce environmental hazards, and promote continuous improvement in environmental performance by integrating environmental issues into their operations through the use of an Environmental Management System (EMS).

3. Life Cycle Assessment (LCA):

A thorough methodology for assessing the environmental effects of goods, procedures, or services over the course of their whole life cycle is called life cycle assessment, or LCA. Throughout a product's life cycle, from raw material extraction to end-of-life disposal, environmental inputs and outputs are carefully analysed via life cycle assessment (LCA). This process yields important insights into environmental hotspots and possible areas for optimization. The outcomes of life cycle assessments (LCAs) can help organizations make decisions, set priorities for sustainability projects, and interact openly with stakeholders. Organizations may reduce their environmental impact and encourage sustainable practices throughout their value chain by incorporating life cycle assessment (LCA) into their supply chain management, procurement, and product development processes.

4. Carbon Footprint Analysis:

The entire amount of greenhouse gas emissions connected to the operations, goods, or services of a company is measured by a carbon footprint analysis. Organizations may see their carbon footprint and find areas where emissions can be reduced by computing emissions from sources like energy use, transportation, trash production, and supply chain operations. Analyzing one's carbon footprint is essential for creating carbon management plans, establishing goals for reducing emissions, and monitoring the journey towards carbon neutrality. By implementing strategies like increasing energy efficiency, embracing renewable energy, and launching carbon offsetting programs, companies can reduce their carbon footprint and support international efforts to tackle climate change.

5. Environmental Audits:

An organization's environmental performance, practices, and compliance with relevant laws, regulations, and standards are all systematically evaluated during an environmental audit. Organizations can identify environmental risks, evaluate regulatory compliance, and promote continuous improvement in environmental management practices by regularly auditing their facilities, operations, and management systems. Environmental audits can address a range of topics, including as resource conservation, waste management, pollution avoidance, and the quality of the air and water. Organizations can improve operational efficiency, boost stakeholder trust, and improve their environmental performance through careful recording, analysis of results, and execution of corrective actions.

6. Environmental Management Software:

With the use of environmental management software (EMS), enterprises can gather, organize, and analyse environmental data with greater efficiency. Features including data tracking, reporting, risk assessment, compliance management, and performance monitoring are provided by these software programs. Organizations can receive valuable insights into their environmental performance, increase data accuracy and integrity, and optimize data gathering operations by centralizing environmental data onto a single platform. Organizations can use environmental management systems (EMS) to improve environmental transparency, accountability, and decision-making throughout their operations. This can be achieved by implementing off-the-shelf solutions or designing software to fit unique requirements.

7. Sustainability Reporting Frameworks:

Organizations can report to stakeholders about their environmental, social, and governance (ESG) performance by using sustainability reporting frameworks, which offer standards and principles. Environmental indicators, goals, initiatives, and performance data can be disclosed using formal frameworks such those provided by the Sustainability Accounting Standards Board (SASB), the Global Reporting Initiative (GRI), and the Carbon Disclosure Project (CDP). Organizations can increase stakeholder trust and involvement by adhering to these reporting guidelines, which will improve the transparency, reliability, and comparability of their sustainability disclosures. Organizations may successfully communicate their environmental commitments, progress, and impacts both internally and publicly by using sustainability reporting.

8. Remote Sensing and GIS:

Geographic information systems (GIS) and remote sensing technologies offer strong instruments for tracking and evaluating environmental changes on a local, regional, and global level. Aerial photography, satellite imagery, and other remote sensing data sources provide important information about environmental trends, vegetation dynamics, land cover, and land use. Organizations can visualize spatial data, locate environmental hotspots, evaluate the health of ecosystems, and make informed decisions about land management by utilizing GIS technology. In order to monitor the environment, organize conservation activities, respond to disasters, and mitigate the effects of climate change, remote sensing and GIS are essential.

9. Benchmarking:

Benchmarking is the process of evaluating an organization's environmental performance against competitors, peers in the industry, or industry best practices in order to find areas for development and promote excellence in performance. Key environmental indicators, such as emissions intensity, waste diversion rates, energy intensity, and water efficiency, can be analysed by enterprises to benchmark performance, set improvement goals, and monitor progress over time. Through benchmarking, companies can take inspiration from top performers in the field, implement cutting-edge procedures, and consistently improve their environmental performance. Collaboration, knowledge exchange, and industry alliances can help businesses move faster toward resilience and sustainability.

10. Environmental Management Standards:

Organizations can efficiently manage their environmental consequences by using the established frameworks and principles provided by environmental management standards. In addition to ISO 14001 and EMAS, firms may also explore alternative standards customized to specific industries or sectors, such as the Forest Stewardship Council (FSC) accreditation for sustainable forestry practices or the Responsible Care program for the chemical industry. These guidelines assist organizations in defining precise environmental goals, putting best practices into action, and proving to stakeholders that they are committed to environmental stewardship.

11. Water Footprint Assessment:

The entire amount of water used or consumed by a company's operations, goods, or services is measured using a water footprint assessment, which accounts for both direct and indirect water use. Identifying water-intensive operations, evaluating water-related hazards, and prioritizing water conservation measures are all made possible for enterprises by examining patterns of water use at various stages of the supply chain, from raw material extraction to product manufacturing and distribution. Organizations can improve water efficiency, lower water-related expenses, and lessen the danger of water scarcity in areas with limited water supplies by conducting a water footprint assessment.

12. Ecological Footprint Analysis:

An organization's ecological footprint is measured by calculating the amount of biologically productive land and water area needed to sustain its operations, taking into account both the resources used and waste produced. Organizations can obtain insights into their ecological footprint and ecological overshoot by evaluating resource use and waste output in relation to ecological carrying capacity. Organizations can discover unsustainable consumption habits, set reduction objectives for their ecological footprint, and shift to more sustainable forms of production and consumption with the aid of ecological footprint analysis.

13. Pollution Prevention (P2):

Instead, then managing pollutants and wastes after they are produced, pollution prevention focuses on finding ways to reduce or eliminate their development at the source. Organizations can lower environmental hazards, increase regulatory compliance, and boost operational efficiency by putting pollution prevention strategies—such as process redesign, technology improvements, and pollution control measures—into practice. By placing more emphasis on pollution prevention than pollution control or repair techniques, pollution prevention promotes a proactive approach to environmental management.

14. Material Flow Analysis (MFA):

Material Flow Analysis (MFA) is a systematic approach to quantify resource inputs, outputs, and losses by tracking the movement of materials across supply chains and industrial processes. Organizations can maximize resource productivity, reduce waste production, and optimize resource utilization by mapping material flows and detecting inefficiencies. By identifying opportunities for material substitution, recycling, reuse, and waste reduction, Material Flow Analysis assists organizations in advancing resource efficiency and the concepts of the circular economy.

15. Biodiversity Impact Assessment:

An organization's possible effects on biodiversity and ecosystem services, such as habitat destruction, species extinction, and ecosystem degradation, are assessed through biodiversity impact assessments. Organizations can create strategies to reduce adverse effects, conserve biodiversity, and improve ecosystem resilience by evaluating the risks and possibilities related to biodiversity. By incorporating ecological factors into decision-making processes, biodiversity impact assessment assists companies in coordinating their efforts with sustainable development and conservation aims.

16. Social Life Cycle Assessment (SLCA):

The Social Life Cycle Assessment (SLCA) assesses how goods and services affect society at large, taking into account factors including human rights, labor conditions, health and safety, and community well-being. Through the evaluation of social risks and possibilities linked to manufacturing processes, supply networks, and consumption patterns, firms can pinpoint areas of social significance, give priority to social responsibility programs, and improve engagement with stakeholders. By offering a comprehensive perspective on sustainability that takes social factors into account in addition to environmental ones, SLCA enhances conventional environmental assessments.

17. Renewable Energy Certificates (RECs):

Renewable energy generation, such as solar, wind, or hydroelectric electricity, has environmental benefits that are represented by Renewable Energy Certificates (RECs). Businesses can purchase Renewable Energy Certificates (RECs) to help finance the development of renewable energy projects and offset the carbon emissions they produce from using power. Organizations can lower their carbon footprint, show their support for renewable energy, and aid in the shift to a low-carbon economy by investing in Renewable Energy Certificates (RECs). With the use of RECs, the transition away from fossil fuels can be sped up and renewable energy development can be encouraged through a market-based system.

18. Circular Economy Principles:

The ideas of the circular economy support a regenerative approach to resource management, which aims to maximize resource efficiency, reduce waste, and encourage patterns of sustainable production and consumption. Organizations can design goods and processes to reduce resource inputs, increase product lifespans, and recover and reuse materials at the end of their useful lives by using the concepts of the circular economy. Implementing closed-loop supply chains, designing durable and recyclable products, and investigating cutting-edge business concepts like product-as-a-service and sharing platforms are all examples of circular economy approaches. The concepts of the circular economy provide a comprehensive framework for attaining social justice, economic prosperity, and environmental sustainability.

19. Carbon Capture and Storage (CCS):

Carbon dioxide emissions from factories or power plants are captured using carbon capture and storage (CCS) technology, which either store the carbon dioxide underground or use it for other uses, such enhanced oil recovery or industrial applications. Through the capture and sequestration of carbon emissions that would otherwise be released into the atmosphere, CCS assists organizations in lowering their carbon footprint and mitigating the effects of climate change. In order to enable the shift to a low-carbon economy and decarbonize high-emission industries like steel, cement, and power generation, carbon capture and storage (CCS) is essential.

20. Environmental Performance Scorecards:

Organizations may successfully manage and communicate their environmental performance with the help of environmental performance scorecards, which provide visual summaries of key environmental indicators, trends, and targets. Dashboards, graphs, charts, and performance indicators that display information on energy use, water use, waste production, emissions, and other environmental measures can be found in scorecards. Scorecards support continuous improvement in environmental management by facilitating decision-making, encouraging accountability, and providing performance statistics in an understandable manner.

In conclusion, monitoring and assessing environmental performance indicators in businesses necessitates a thorough strategy that incorporates a variety of instruments, methods, and approaches. Organizations may improve their environmental management procedures, promote continuous development, and help create a future that is more resilient and sustainable by making efficient use of these technologies.

6.2.2 Implementing Key Performance Indicators (KPI's) to Monitor Progress Towards Sustainability Targets

The goal of sustainability has become essential for enterprises across industries in the quickly changing world of today. Because of their dedication to environmental stewardship, green businesses are progressively incorporating sustainability into their main business plans. Using Key Performance Indicators (KPIs) to track progress toward sustainability targets is an essential component of this integration. The significance of KPIs in monitoring environmental performance and successfully accomplishing sustainability objectives is examined in this introduction.

To successfully track their environmental performance, green businesses must implement Key Performance Indicators (KPIs) to track progress towards sustainability targets. The following is how businesses can accomplish it:

Step-1. Identify Relevant KPIs:
- Start by determining which KPIs are pertinent to the goals and ambitions your company has for sustainability.
- Key environmental factors including energy use, greenhouse gas emissions, water use, waste production, and biodiversity preservation should be included in these KPIs.

Step-2. Set Clear Targets:
- ▲ Based on the sustainability objectives of your firm, set specific, quantifiable goals for each KPI.
- ▲ Setting goals that are both challenging and doable can help to steer progress in the right direction and enable insightful performance evaluation over time.

Step-3. Establish Baseline Data:
- ▲ To provide a starting point for tracking advancement against the selected KPIs, collect baseline data.
- ▲ To measure the present levels of environmental performance, this may entail carrying out audits, assessments, or data collection activities.

Step-4. Implement Monitoring Systems:
- ▲ Establish reliable monitoring mechanisms to continuously measure performance against KPIs.
- ▲ Make use of technology, data management programs, and reporting systems to effectively and precisely gather pertinent data.

Step-5. Regular Reporting and Analysis:
- ▲ Set up recurring reporting periods to assess how well sustainability targets are being met.
- ▲ Utilize insights to guide strategic planning and decision-making by analysing KPI data to find trends, patterns, and areas that need improvement.

Step-6. Benchmarking and Comparison:
- ▲ To evaluate relative performance and pinpoint areas of strength and weakness, compare performance to peer organizations, industry standards, and best practices.
- ▲ Establish aspirational goals and motivate continual improvement initiatives with the help of benchmarking data.

Step-7. Engage Stakeholders:

- Involve all relevant parties in the monitoring process, such as staff, clients, investors, suppliers, and members of the community.

- To guarantee that development is in line with stakeholder expectations and priorities, be open and honest in your communication of it and ask for input.

Step-8. Adaptability and Flexibility:

- Keep your KPIs and targets fluid and adaptive as organizational priorities shift and external conditions alter.

- Review and improve KPIs on a regular basis in light of fresh information, developing patterns, and lessons discovered by monitoring operations.

Step-9. Incentives and Recognition:

- Reward and recognize achievement of sustainability goals that are connected to KPIs.

- Honour accomplishments, give credit where credit is due, and give incentives to people and groups that do exceptionally well in furthering sustainability objectives.

Step-10. Continuous Improvement:

- Adopt a culture of ongoing development by using KPI data to stimulate creativity and efficiency.

- Encourage staff members to use KPI findings to find chances for resource conservation, environmental innovation, and efficiency improvements.

Step-11. Integration with Decision-Making:

- Include KPI data in decision-making procedures at all organizational levels.

- Make informed decisions about investments, resource allocation, operational management procedures, and strategic planning by utilizing KPI insights.

In summary, the use of Key Performance Indicators (KPIs) is essential for tracking green businesses' advancement toward their sustainability goals. KPIs let firms assess their progress, pinpoint areas for development, and show their dedication to environmental stewardship by offering an organized framework for measuring environmental performance. To successfully accomplish their sustainability goals in the future, firms will need to keep improving their KPIs, include sustainability into their business plans, and promote continuous development.

6.2.3 Case Studies of Organizations Using Advanced Monitoring Systems to Track Environmental Performance and Drive Continuous Improvement

- Here are a some of case studies showcasing how organizations have utilized advanced monitoring systems to track environmental performance and drive continuous improvement:

1. Google's Data-Driven Approach to Energy Efficiency:

Overview:
One of the biggest IT firms in the world, Google, has made substantial investments in energy efficiency and sustainable operations. Google installed sophisticated monitoring systems to track energy consumption throughout its data canters and facilities globally as part of its commitment to environmental sustainability.

Implementation:
- Google created "Google Energy Intelligence," a proprietary energy monitoring system that gathers and evaluates real-time data on energy use, equipment performance, and environmental factors in its data canters.
- To monitor energy use at a granular level, pinpoint inefficiencies, and enhance energy management tactics, the system combines sensors, meters, and data analytics algorithms.
- To improve HVAC systems, lighting, and other energy-intensive equipment in its office buildings and campuses, Google also uses predictive analytics and advanced building management systems (BMS).

Results:
- Utilizing data analytics and cutting-edge monitoring systems, Google has significantly improved its environmental performance and energy efficiency.
- In comparison to industry averages, the company's data canter energy intensity has been lowered by more than 50%, leading to significant cost savings and a decrease in carbon emissions.
- Continuous improvement projects like optimizing server configurations, raising cooling efficiency, and introducing cutting-edge cooling technologies like AI-driven cooling optimization have been made possible by Google's data-driven approach to energy saving.

Impact:
- Google has positioned itself as a leader in sustainable business practices and lowered operational costs and environmental effects because to its proactive approach to energy monitoring and control.
- Google's dissemination of best practices and insights from its energy monitoring endeavours has facilitated the industry's wider adoption of energy-efficient devices and procedures.

2. Walmart's Supply Chain Sustainability Program:

Overview:
The world's biggest retailer, Walmart, has reduced its environmental impact throughout its global operations by implementing a comprehensive supply chain sustainability program. The employment of cutting-edge monitoring technology to track important environmental parameters across its supply chain is a crucial component of Walmart's sustainability initiatives.

Implementation:
- Walmart created the Sustainability Index, a thorough monitoring system that assesses a product's social and environmental performance over the course of its life.

- Data on a range of sustainability measures, including as energy use, greenhouse gas emissions, water use, waste creation, and supply chain transparency, are gathered by the Sustainability Index from suppliers.
- Walmart use sophisticated data analytics and supply chain mapping instruments to pinpoint environmental hotspots, rank potential for enhancement, and involve suppliers in sustainability endeavours.

Results:
- Walmart has significantly reduced the environmental consequences throughout its supply chain by utilizing the Sustainability Index and cutting-edge monitoring tools.
- The organization has established high standards for itself in terms of cutting greenhouse gas emissions, getting rid of waste, and sourcing essential products like palm oil, meat, and seafood responsibly.
- Walmart's sustainability initiative has improved brand perception, reduced costs, and increased operational effectiveness while promoting favourable social and environmental effects across its supply chain.

Impact:
- In the retail sector, Walmart's use of cutting-edge monitoring tools to assess environmental performance has established a standard for supply chain sustainability.
- Walmart has sparked greater awareness and action on sustainability challenges throughout the retail industry by openly disclosing its sustainability progress and working with suppliers, NGOs, and other stakeholders.

3. Intel Corporation's Water Stewardship Program:

Overview:
Leading manufacturer of semiconductors worldwide, Intel Corporation, has put in place a thorough water stewardship program to track and control

water use throughout its manufacturing sites. Acknowledging the significance of water conservation and sustainability, Intel has made investments in sophisticated monitoring systems to monitor water usage, detect areas for enhancing efficiency, and reduce risks associated with water.

Implementation:
- The Water Management Information System (WMIS) is a centralized platform created by Intel that gathers data in real time on the amount, quality, and discharge of water from its manufacturing operations.
- In order to track water flows, spot leaks or other irregularities, and enhance the water treatment procedures, the WMIS combines data from sensors, meters, and process control systems.
- In order to minimize water, use and lessen its environmental impact, Intel also uses cutting-edge water management techniques, such as rainwater collection, water recycling and reuse, and water-efficient devices.

Results:
- Intel has significantly decreased water usage and increased water efficiency in its production processes by utilizing cutting-edge monitoring systems and water management techniques.
- Due to the company's implementation of water conservation initiatives, millions of gallons of water are saved annually, which reduces costs and benefits the environment.
- Intel's water stewardship program has improved its standing as a conscientious corporate citizen while assisting in the mitigation of water-related hazards, such as water scarcity and difficulties with regulatory compliance.

Impact:
- Intel is now recognized as a leader in sustainable water management in the semiconductor sector thanks to its dedication to water conservation and utilization of cutting-edge monitoring technologies.

- By disseminating best practices and insights from its water stewardship program, Intel has aided initiatives within the industry to decrease water usage, increase water efficiency, and protect water resources for coming generations.

4. Johnson Controls' Energy Management Solutions:

Overview:

Leading provider of building technologies and energy solutions worldwide, Johnson Controls has created cutting-edge energy management tools to assist businesses in tracking, optimizing, and lowering energy usage in their buildings. With the use of state-of-the-art technologies and data analytics, Johnson Controls gives its clients the ability to monitor energy performance, spot possibilities for energy savings, and promote ongoing improvements in energy efficiency.

Implementation:

- Building automation systems, energy monitoring platforms, and energy efficiency services are just a few of the energy management solutions that Johnson Controls provides to help businesses track and manage energy use in real time.

- These systems identify energy-intensive machinery or processes, gather and analyse energy data from buildings, and put energy-saving measures into place by utilizing Internet of Things (IoT) devices, sensors, and cloud-based analytics.

- Energy performance contracting is another service offered by Johnson Controls. With this service, clients are guaranteed energy savings through the execution of energy-efficient projects such building envelope enhancements, HVAC optimizations, and lighting upgrades.

Results:

- Organizations have significantly reduced energy usage, operational expenses, and environmental impacts by cooperating with Johnson Controls and implementing its energy management solutions.

- Millions of dollars have been saved on energy costs for clients in a variety of industries by Johnson Controls' energy efficiency projects, including commercial buildings, industrial facilities, healthcare facilities, and educational institutions.

- Through constant monitoring, optimization, and performance improvement made possible by the company's data-driven approach to energy management, clients are provided with long-term sustainability and resilience.

Impact:
- Organizations all around the world have transformed their energy performance, decreased their carbon footprint, and increased their competitiveness in the quickly changing energy market because to Johnson Controls' energy management systems.

- Through cutting-edge technologies, knowledgeable analysis, and customized solutions, Johnson Controls enables businesses to fulfil legal obligations, reach energy efficiency targets, and support international initiatives to combat climate change and advance sustainable development.

These case studies show how businesses like Google, Walmart, Intel Corporation, and Johnson Controls have tracked environmental performance, sparked continuous improvement, and produced noteworthy sustainability results by utilizing cutting-edge monitoring technologies. These businesses have shown leadership in sustainable business practices by investing in data-driven methods to resource efficiency and environmental management, and they have also encouraged others to do the same.

6.3 Feedback and Recognition for Green Initiatives

The adoption of green initiatives has become a crucial part of corporate strategy as businesses all over the world prioritize sustainability. These programs cover a broad spectrum of actions meant to lessen their negative effects on the environment, including increasing energy efficiency, cutting waste, conserving water, and cutting greenhouse gas emissions. Although implementing such practices is necessary to promote a sustainable future, how well they are incorporated into the organizational culture will determine how successful and long-lasting green efforts are.

Acknowledgment and feedback are essential instruments in this integration process. They are essential to sustaining and accelerating the pace of environmental initiatives. Giving feedback promotes a culture of ongoing learning and creativity, helps people and teams understand the effects of their actions, and identifies areas for development. By celebrating accomplishments and serving as a strong incentive, recognition, on the other hand, can increase participation and commitment to sustainability goals.

Gaining an understanding of these tools' significance and properly utilizing them may turn green initiatives from stand-alone projects into essential components of an organization's brand, promoting sustainability leadership and long-term environmental stewardship.

Organizations can motivate and empower staff members to embrace sustainability, promote favourable environmental outcomes, and contribute to a more resilient and sustainable future by putting feedback and recognition initiatives into practice. These procedures improve performance and internal involvement while fortifying the organization's standing and connections with outside parties. Positive feedback and acknowledgement turn green projects from stand-alone undertakings into essential components of an organization's brand, promoting sustainability leadership and long-term environmental care.

6.3.1 Importance of Providing Feedback and Recognition for Employees' Green Initiatives and Contributions to Sustainability Goals

Rewarding staff for their green initiatives and contributions to sustainability goals is crucial in today's company environment, when sustainability is a strategic necessity. It is impossible to overestimate the significance of this. These procedures not only assist in accomplishing environmental goals but also cultivate a supportive and active culture inside the company.

- ❖ Here's a detailed exploration of why feedback and recognition are crucial:

1. Enhancing Motivation and Engagement

Motivation:
Acknowledgment and feedback are effective motivators. Employee efforts and dedication to sustainability are strengthened when they receive positive feedback and acknowledgement for their eco-friendly projects. They are inspired to keep making enthusiastic and committed contributions to environmental aims by this encouraging feedback.

Engagement:
A greater sense of involvement is fostered when employees' efforts to sustainability are valued and acknowledged. Employee engagement increases the likelihood that they will take the initiative to find and apply green practices, which will result in a stronger and longer-lasting effort to meet environmental goals. Higher rates of participation in green initiatives and improved teamwork are the results of this engagement.

2. Building a Culture of Sustainability

Cultural Integration:
Rewarding behaviour and constructive criticism contribute to the organizational culture's integration of sustainability. When environmentally friendly accomplishments are regularly recognized, sustainability becomes one of the organization's key values. Employees at all levels are encouraged by this culture shift to focus and incorporate sustainable practices into their everyday work.

Shared Values:
Employees who share these values are drawn to and kept by an organization that prioritizes sustainability. When an organization's beliefs and personal values coincide, job satisfaction and loyalty increase, creating a more dependable and devoted workforce that is committed to long-term sustainability objectives.

3. Fostering Continuous Learning and Improvement

Feedback for Improvement:
Employees receive insights into their performance and areas for growth when they receive constructive criticism. This ongoing feedback loop enables people and groups to improve their strategies, apply more

successful sustainability measures, and learn from their mistakes. Achieving greater sustainability standards and responding to emerging environmental concerns require constant development.

Innovation:
Employees that receive regular feedback are inspired to solve environmental challenges in novel ways. Acknowledging creative concepts and their effective application fosters a culture of exploration and creativity that advances the creation of sophisticated and more effective green practices and technology.

4. Boosting Morale and Job Satisfaction

Recognition and Appreciation:
Employee morale is greatly raised when efforts toward sustainability are acknowledged. Employee well-being and job satisfaction both increase when they perceive that their contributions are valued. Positive work environments, lower turnover rates, and higher production are all associated with high morale.

Sense of Accomplishment:
A sense of pride and success is brought about by receiving comments and acknowledgment. Workers are more likely to have a sense of purpose and belonging in the company when they are appreciated and rewarded for their hard work.

5. Improving Organizational Performance

Performance Metrics:
Aligning individual efforts with corporate goals is facilitated by establishing precise performance indicators for sustainability and by regularly offering feedback on success. By ensuring that everyone is working toward the same goals, this alignment makes it possible to achieve sustainability targets with more coordination and effectiveness.

Accountability:
Feedback systems foster accountability by making sure staff members understand their roles and how their actions affect the organization's sustainability objectives. Consistent performance and adherence to

recommended practices in environmental management are fostered by this responsibility.

6. Strengthening External Relationships and Reputation

Public Recognition:
Acknowledging green accomplishments in public improves the company's standing with partners, investors, and consumers. A company may stand out from the competition and draw in environmentally sensitive stakeholders by demonstrating its commitment to sustainability in an era where environmental responsibility is highly appreciated.

Stakeholder Trust:
Recognition fosters trust with outside parties by showcasing accountability and openness in sustainability initiatives. Establishing strong and trustworthy relationships with stakeholders can facilitate partnerships and collaborations that further improve the environmental effect of the firm.

7. Encouraging Peer Learning and Collaboration

Peer Recognition:
Peer-to-peer recognition initiatives promote a cooperative work atmosphere where staff members can benefit from one other's accomplishments and difficulties. The adoption of best practices is accelerated by this shared learning, which also improves the sustainability of the company as a whole.

Teamwork and Synergy:
Acknowledging collaborative efforts in environmental projects fosters synergy and teamwork. In order to create greater effect, collaborative recognition encourages teams and departments to work together toward shared sustainability goals by utilizing a diversity of viewpoints and skill sets.

In conclusion, it is critical to give employees feedback and acknowledgement for their green initiatives and contributions to sustainability goals in order to engage and motivate them, create a sustainable culture, promote ongoing learning and innovation, raise morale, enhance organizational performance, fortify external relationships, and promote peer learning and collaboration. These procedures not only make sustainability programs successful, but they also help create a resilient and upbeat workplace culture that encourages and honours environmental stewardship. Organizations may guarantee the effectiveness, impact, and long-term sustainability of their green projects by incorporating feedback and recognition into their sustainability plans.

6.3.2 Strategies for Incorporating Environmental Performance into Regular Performance Reviews and Feedback Sessions

Aligning individual contributions with company sustainability goals requires regular performance reviews and feedback sessions that include environmental performance.

❖ Here are detailed strategies to achieve this integration effectively:

1. Set Clear Environmental Goals and Metrics

Define Specific Objectives:
Create measurable, practical environmental goals that are appropriate for each department or job. Reducing energy use, decreasing greenhouse gas emissions, limiting trash, and raising recycling rates are a few examples.

Establish Measurable Metrics:
Establish measurable metrics for every goal. Track progress using data, such as CO_2 emissions decreased, garbage sent to landfills decreased as a percentage, or energy usage reduced in kilowatt-hours.

2. Integrate Environmental Goals into Job Descriptions

Role-Specific Responsibilities:
Job descriptions should mention environmental obligations. By formalizing sustainability into every function, this guarantees that workers are aware of how their actions affect the organization's sustainability objectives.

Alignment with Organizational Goals:
To bring coherence and unity to the organization's overall plan, make sure that each individual's environmental aims are in line with the organization's larger sustainability objectives.

3. Provide Training and Resources

Offer Sustainability Training:
Regularly teach staff members on sustainability strategies that are pertinent to their jobs. Waste management, sustainable sourcing, and energy efficiency are a few examples of possible topics.

Access to Resources:
Make sure staff members have access to energy-efficient equipment, recycling bins, and software for monitoring environmental metrics, among other resources and tools they need to fulfil their environmental goals.

4. Incorporate Environmental Performance into Reviews

Include Environmental Metrics:
Include indicators for environmental performance in the routine performance review procedure. Talk about the progress made toward environmental targets as well as other performance standards, as well as any successes and obstacles.

Use Data-Driven Feedback:
Give comments in accordance with predetermined metrics. Employ graphical tools like graphs and charts to illustrate data about environmental performance and changes over time

5. Regular Feedback and Recognition

Frequent Check-Ins:
To provide continuous feedback on environmental performance, do check-ins on a regular basis. This aids staff members in staying on course and making the required modifications all year long.

Celebrate Successes:
Recognize and celebrate environmental successes in feedback sessions. Verbal compliments, awards, bonuses, and public acknowledgement in business communications are a few examples of this.

6. Encourage Goal Setting and Personal Development

Employee-Driven Goals:
Encourage workers to establish objectives for their own environmental performance. Higher participation and inventiveness in accomplishing sustainability goals may result from this personal investment.

Professional Development Plans:
Professional development plans should include chances for environmental training and growth. This could be going to conferences on sustainability, becoming certified as green, or serving on environmental committees.

7. Link Environmental Performance to Career Advancement

Performance-Based Rewards:
Connect rewards and possibilities for job progression to environmental performance. Reward staff members who show a remarkable dedication to sustainability with promotions, pay raises, or exclusive project assignments.

Incentive Programs:
Create incentive programs that offer incentives, more paid time off, or other benefits to staff members who meet predetermined environmental milestones.

8. Facilitate Cross-Departmental Collaboration

Team Goals:
Establish departmental or team-wide targets for environmental performance. This promotes teamwork and a feeling of shared accountability for sustainability.

Interdepartmental Projects:
Encourage the completion of cross-departmental projects on sustainability activities, like waste reduction plans, energy audits, and the creation of green products.

9. Use Technology and Tools

Environmental Performance Software:
Put into practice software programs that measure and report on environmental performance indicators. Provide useful information for performance assessments by utilizing resources like as carbon footprint calculators, sustainability reporting platforms, and energy management systems.

Automated Feedback Systems:
Give immediate feedback on environmental performance using automated technologies. These tools can notify staff members about their advancement and offer recommendations for development.

10. Embed Sustainability in Corporate Culture

Leadership Commitment:
Make sure the leadership exhibits a strong dedication to sustainability. Green behaviour should be modelled by leaders, and they should get involved in environmental projects.

Communication and Engagement:
Regularly convey, via internal communications, the significance of environmental performance. Encourage staff participation through events, intranet postings, and sustainability publications.

In summary, a thorough methodology is needed to include environmental performance in regular performance assessments and feedback sessions. Environmental issues can be successfully incorporated into performance management processes by firms through the use of data-driven feedback, defined targets and metrics, integration of sustainability into job descriptions, and provision of relevant training and resources. In order to guarantee that environmental performance is a significant factor in employee evaluations, it is imperative to implement several strategies, including regular recognition, personal development opportunities, career advancement connections between performance and performance, collaboration facilitation, technology utilization, and the promotion of a sustainable culture. By means of these endeavours, establishments can propel noteworthy advancements in their sustainability objectives while fostering employee engagement and motivation.

6.3.3 Examples of Innovative Recognition Programs for Employees who Demonstrate Exceptional Commitment to Sustainability Practices

Recognizing employees who demonstrate exceptional commitment to sustainability practices is crucial for fostering a culture of environmental stewardship and encouraging ongoing engagement with green initiatives.

❖ **Here are some examples of innovative recognition programs:**

1. Green Champion Awards
Program Overview:
Annual or Quarterly Awards: Recognize groups or individuals who have significantly advanced sustainability. Energy conservation, waste minimization, water conservation, and innovative sustainability methods are some examples of categories.

Innovative Features:
- **Peer Nominations:** Encourage a culture of respect and acknowledgement among co-workers by allowing employees to suggest their peers.
- **Judging Panel:** Establish a panel of sustainability specialists to examine submissions and choose victors, guaranteeing that the acknowledgement is reputable and valued.

Example:
Google Green Awards: Google's Green Awards recognize staff members who have made noteworthy contributions to the firm's sustainability objectives. These accomplishments are recognized publicly at company events and with awards.

2. Sustainability Innovation Grants
Program Overview:
Grant Funding: Give grants to staff members or groups that come up with creative sustainability project ideas. These initiatives, which might include

everything from process enhancements to new product concepts, should strive to enhance the business's environmental performance.

Innovative Features:
- **Project Implementation:** The funds and materials winners receive to carry out their projects give them a concrete reward and a chance to advance their careers.
- **Public Showcasing:** Projects that are successful are showcased both within and outside, earning praise and motivating others.

Example:
Patagonia Environmental Internship Program: Patagonia supports the professional and personal development of its workers by providing funds to work on environmental projects for up to two months with organizations of their choosing.

3. Eco-Leader Certification Program
Program Overview:
Certification Levels: Establish a certification program with tiers, such as Bronze, Silver, and Gold, to recognize staff members who fulfil various sustainability training requirements and meet predetermined environmental targets.

Innovative Features:
- **Personal Development:** Professional development options, such attending conferences or courses on sustainability, can be linked to certifications.
- **Public Recognition:** At meetings, in newsletters, and on the workplace intranet, Certified Eco-Leaders are recognized.

Example:
IBM's Smarter Planet Initiative: With IBM's Smarter Planet initiative, employees who lead green projects and complete sustainability training are recognized and awarded credentials that are highly valued inside the organization.

4. Green Team Competitions

Program Overview:
Team-Based Challenges: Set goals for teams or departments to compete against one another to see who can reduce waste, energy use, or other sustainability metrics the most during a given time frame.

Innovative Features:
- **Gamification:** Make the competition interesting and enjoyable by incorporating gamification features like leader boards and badges.
- **Incentives:** Give the winning teams meaningful prizes, such extra cash for team outings, more time off, or contributions to the charity of their choice.

Example:
Unilever's Sustainable Living Plan: Offices of Unilever compete in a range of sustainability challenges across the globe. Winning teams are recognized and awarded, and company-wide implementation of their winning projects follows.

5. Sustainability Sabbaticals

Program Overview:
Paid Sabbaticals: Provides paid sabbaticals to staff members who want to work for outside environmental organizations or on company-sponsored sustainability projects.

Innovative Features:
- **Professional Growth:** Workers acquire fresh knowledge and expertise that they can use to their current positions.
- **Community Impact:** These initiatives frequently improve the community or environment significantly, strengthening the company's standing and demonstrating its dedication to sustainability.

Example:
Sales force's Volunteer Time Off (VTO): Sales force offers its workers the opportunity to volunteer for up to 56 hours a year, including time spent

on environmental projects, during their paid time off. Within the organization, exceptional efforts are honoured and acknowledged.

6. Eco-Friendly Rewards and Incentives

Program Overview:

Sustainable Products: Give your staff members environmentally friendly gifts or experiences, like solar chargers, reusable water bottles, or memberships in environmental groups.

Innovative Features:

- **-Green Incentives:** Provide discounts on electric cars, passes for public transit, or energy audits for your home as incentives.
- **Customized Rewards:** Tailor rewards to reflect the interests of staff members and the company's sustainability objectives.

Example:

Intel's Green Benefits: Employees at Intel are eligible for a number of environmentally friendly benefits, such as financial aid for public transit and incentives for buying electric or hybrid cars.

7. Internal Sustainability Conferences

Program Overview:

Annual Conferences: Organize internal conferences cantered around sustainability so that staff members may learn from experts, share best practices, and showcase their initiatives.

Innovative Features:

- **Employee Presentations:** Presentations of work by employees who have made noteworthy contributions to sustainability are invited.
- **Networking Opportunities:** Employees can network with sustainability professionals both inside and outside the organization by attending these conferences.

Example:

- **Microsoft's Green Champions Summit:** Employees who have made significant contributions to sustainability are invited to Microsoft's annual summit, where they can network with peers and share their experiences.

To sum up, introducing creative award schemes for staff members who show outstanding dedication to sustainable practices not only encourages good deeds but also cultivates a climate of environmental care and ongoing development. These initiatives have the power to dramatically raise staff morale, stimulate creativity, and help a company achieve its sustainability objectives.

Companies may motivate their staff to take charge of sustainability activities and have a bigger environmental effect by recognizing and rewarding green initiatives.

Chapteer – 7

Green Compensation and Benefits

Introduction to Green Compensation:
An organization's employee benefits and pay plan might incorporate environmental sustainability through the growing idea of "green compensation." Businesses are implementing green compensation techniques to incentivize their staff to behave sustainably as they become more aware of the significance of sustainability. This strategy not only lessens the company's environmental impact but also fosters a culture of sustainability and accountability by coordinating staff actions with corporate ideals.

Meaning:
The term "green compensation" describes the monetary and non-monetary rewards that businesses give their staff members in order to encourage and recognize environmentally friendly behaviour. These incentives can take many forms, from non-cash benefits like flexible work schedules and recognition programs to bonuses and subsidies for eco-friendly actions.

Definition of Green Compensation:
"The process of integrating environmental factors into a company's rewards and compensation structure is known as green compensation."

Purpose:
- ❖ The primary purpose of green compensation is to:
    - a. **Encourage Sustainable Behaviour:** Encourage staff members to adopt eco-friendly habits in their personal and professional life.

b. **Reduce Environmental Impact:** Utilize renewable resources, cut down on waste, and minimize energy use to assist the organization in reaching its sustainability goals.

　　c. **Enhance Employee Engagement:** Ensure that staff incentives are in line with the company's sustainability values to foster greater job satisfaction and loyalty.

　　d. **Strengthen Corporate Reputation:** Establish the business as a pioneer in sustainability to draw in clients, capital, and elite personnel.

Introduction to Green Benefits:

Green benefits, which include a variety of non-cash bonuses and incentives intended to encourage environmentally friendly behaviour among staff members, are a crucial component of an organization's commitment to sustainability. As businesses place a greater emphasis on environmental responsibility, offering green incentives has become a crucial tactic for coordinating employee behaviour with company goals and promoting a sustainable workplace culture.

Meaning:

The term "green benefits" describes the non-cash advantages and rewards that businesses offer to promote environmentally friendly behaviour and lessen their overall impact on the environment. These perks may include the ability to work from home, encouragement of environmentally friendly transportation options, health and wellness activities that support sustainable living, and award programs for staff members who show exceptional dedication to environmental causes.

Purpose:

❖ **The primary purposes of green benefits are to:**

　　a. **Promote Sustainable Behaviour:** Encourage staff members to establish and uphold eco-friendly practices at work and at home.

　　b. **Reduce Environmental Footprint:** Encourage the company to take steps to reduce waste, energy use, and carbon emissions in order to lessen its impact on the environment.

c. **Enhance Employee Well-Being:** By providing benefits that encourage a healthy, sustainable lifestyle, employers may increase employee happiness and well-being.

d. **Align Corporate and Employee Values:** Ensure that the company's sustainability objectives and its employees' own values are more closely aligned to create a more engaged and motivated workforce.

e. **Boost Corporate Image:** Boost the business's standing as an environmentally and socially conscious enterprise to draw in talent, investors, and clients.

Concept of Green Compensation and Benefits:

Referred to as "green perks" or "sustainable rewards," green compensation and benefits are elements of an organization's reward structure that encourage and facilitate employees' environmentally conscious actions. More and more companies are incorporating green initiatives into their corporate plans as they realize the value of sustainability. By educating employees about environmental responsibility, these programs seek to lessen the company's environmental impact and that of its employees.

Meaning:

Green benefits and compensation include a variety of awards and incentives that motivate staff members to adopt environmentally responsible behaviours in their personal and professional life. These perks improve overall involvement and commitment to the company's environmental aims by bringing employees' personal beliefs into line with the company's sustainability goals.

Green compensation and benefits are more than simply cash inducements; they're a comprehensive strategy for developing a long-term company culture. Companies can improve their sustainability performance, effect significant change, and benefit the environment by incorporating environmental responsibility into their reward systems. This approach is an essential component of contemporary corporate strategy because it benefits not just the environment but also the workers and the organization as a whole.

❖ **Here are the detailed benefits of green compensation:**

1. Promotes Sustainability: Green compensation plans encourage staff members to prioritize and participate in eco-friendly activities. Employees are more inclined to innovate and adopt methods that cut waste, conserve resources, and lessen the organization's carbon footprint when performance criteria are linked to sustainability goals. This can involve taking steps to minimize waste, utilize less energy, and encourage the use of renewable energy sources.

2. Enhances Corporate Reputation: Businesses that are perceived as being environmentally conscious frequently have a more positive public image. A sincere dedication to sustainability is demonstrated by the implementation of green compensation, and this can improve the company's standing with stakeholders, investors, and customers. A company's market share and customer loyalty may rise if it has a solid reputation for being environmentally conscious. This can set it apart from rivals.

3. Increases Employee Engagement and Motivation: Employees are searching more and more for environments at work that reflect their personal values, such as environmental sustainability. Employers can increase work satisfaction and employee morale by implementing green compensation. Employees are more likely to have a sense of purpose and a connection to the company's vision when they see that their efforts toward sustainability are valued and acknowledged. Increased productivity, retention, and engagement may result from this.

4. Regulatory Compliance and Risk Management: Environmental restrictions are strict for a lot of companies. Companies may prevent fines, penalties, and reputational harm by making sure they meet or beyond these regulatory criteria with the use of green compensation. Through proactive management of environmental hazards and employee behaviour incentives, organizations can enhance their regulatory landscape navigation and reduce potential liabilities.

5. Cost Savings: Costs are frequently significantly reduced as a result of sustainable methods. Operational expenses can be decreased, for instance, by maximizing resource efficiency, cutting waste, and reducing energy consumption. Businesses can lessen their environmental effect and reap financial rewards by empowering staff to find and execute cost-saving sustainability projects. Over time, these savings can add up and benefit the bottom line of the business.

6. Innovation and Competitive Advantage: Green compensation encourages employees to come up with innovative ideas for how to improve environmental performance, which in turn promotes an innovative culture. This may result in the creation of brand-new goods, services, and procedures that are more economical, efficient, and environmentally friendly. Businesses that are seen as sustainability leaders typically have an advantage over their competitors in the market because they draw partners and customers that care about the environment.

7. Attraction and Retention of Talent: Sustainability is highly valued by the modern workforce, especially the younger generations. Top personnel who are enthusiastic about having a good influence is more likely to be drawn to companies that place a high priority on environmental responsibility. Additionally, workers are more likely to stick with the company and lower turnover and related recruitment expenses if they believe that their labour advances larger societal goals.

8. Long-term Viability and Resilience: Prioritizing sustainability contributes to an organization's long-term survival. Businesses that choose to overlook environmental hazards may eventually have to deal with serious issues like resource scarcity, changing regulations, and changed consumer preferences. Businesses can position themselves for long-term success and strengthen their resistance to these risks by incorporating sustainability into their compensation plans.

In conclusion, green compensation encourages sustainable activities and behaviours across the entire organization by coordinating employees' financial incentives with the corporation's environmental goals. This strategy benefits businesses in many ways, including improved reputation, higher employee engagement, regulatory compliance, cost savings, innovation, attracting talent, and long-term sustainability, in addition to helping the environment. Companies may build a more prosperous and sustainable future for themselves and their stakeholders by implementing green compensation.

7.1 Designing Eco-Friendly Compensation Packages

Designing eco-friendly compensation packages entails incorporating environmental sustainability ideas into an organization's benefits and employee compensation plan. By supporting and rewarding sustainable habits in the workplace and in employees' personal lives, this strategy seeks to harmonize the company's environmental objectives with employee incentives.

Designing eco-friendly compensation plans requires incorporating sustainability ideas into the conventional framework for perks and compensation. Reducing the company's environmental impact, encouraging ecologically conscious conduct among staff members, and coordinating employee behaviour with corporate goals are the objectives.

❖ Here's a comprehensive and detailed guide to designing such packages:

1. Assessment and Alignment with Corporate Goals

Evaluate Current Impact:
- Make a detailed evaluation of the company's present environmental impact. Analysing energy use, waste generation, water use, carbon footprint, and other pertinent environmental parameters is part of this process.
- Determine the most important areas for improvement, such as cutting back on waste, encouraging environmentally friendly transportation options, and lowering energy consumption in office buildings.

Set Clear Objectives:
- Establish quantifiable, precise sustainability objectives that complement the business's overall environmental plan. Achieving zero waste to landfill, lowering carbon emissions by a specific proportion, or utilizing more sustainable energy sources are a few examples.
- Make sure that all staff members are aware of these objectives and are committed to the company's sustainability mission by properly communicating them to them.

2. Monetary Green Compensation

Performance-Based Green Bonuses:
- Establish a bonus structure based on the accomplishment of sustainability goals. For example, provide monetary incentives to staff members who surpass energy conservation targets or come up with creative ways to reduce waste in the workplace.
- Establish departmental or team-specific objectives to motivate group efforts toward sustainability. This ensures that sustainability becomes a shared responsibility within the firm in addition to encouraging teamwork.

Subsidies and Grants:
- Employees should receive financial support to buy environmentally friendly goods. Subsidies for energy-efficient appliances, electric cars, and household renewable energy projects like solar panels could fall under this category.
- Provide financial aid for the installation of energy-efficient windows, insulation, and smart home energy management systems. These awards can encourage a sustainable culture among staff members while also assisting them in lessening their own environmental effect.

Public Transportation Incentives:
- To incentivize staff members to take buses, trains, or other public transportation instead of driving a car, reimburse the cost of public transportation passes.
- Provide monetary rewards to employees who bike or carpool to work. This can take the form of refunds for mileage, maintenance stipends for bikes, or payments toward the expense of carpooling services.

Green Investment Options:
- Make sure that employee retirement programs offer sustainable investing options. This makes it possible for workers to contribute

to funds that assist environmentally conscious businesses and initiatives that put sustainability first.

- Create green investment funds supported by the corporation that concentrate on companies and technologies committed to environmental sustainability. This gives staff members the chance to invest in environmental change while also bringing the company's financial procedures into line with its sustainability objectives.

3. Non-Monetary Green Benefits

Flexible Work Arrangements:

- To cut down on emissions from commuting, encourage remote work possibilities. Even a few days of remote work per week can make a big difference in the company's total carbon footprint.
- Provide employees with flexible work schedules to help them avoid rush-hour travel, which can lower emissions and enhance work-life balance.

Recognition Programs:

- Establish programs and awards for staff members who make major contributions to sustainability projects. This could take the form of eco-friendly awards, accomplishment certificates, or open recognition during business meetings.
- Create a program called "Green Employee of the Month" to recognise and reward staff members who go above and beyond in their efforts to be environmentally friendly. Non-cash incentives like extra paid time off or presents that promote the environment can be very inspiring.

Health and Wellness Initiatives:

- By offering safe bike storage, restrooms with showers, and changing areas, you can promote biking to work. This lessens the impact of commuting on the environment and encourages a healthy lifestyle.
- Encourage walking meetings and offer rewards for taking part in initiatives that encourage active commuting. Walking meetings

can cut down on the demand for energy-intensive office spaces while increasing creativity and productivity.

Eco-Friendly Office Environment:
- Create workstations with sustainable materials, indoor plants, and natural lighting. This lowers energy use and fosters wellbeing in addition to making the workplace healthier and more enjoyable.
- Make use of environmentally friendly workplace materials including reusable pens, recycled paper, and energy-saving devices. Make sure sustainable goods and services are given top priority in procurement policies.

Educational Programs:
- Provide frequent training courses on environmental awareness and sustainable practices. Possible topics include green living advice, sustainable transportation, waste reduction, and energy saving.
- Create a sustainability committee or green team to spearhead and support environmental activities inside the business. These groups are capable of planning activities, exchanging best practices, and advancing the business's environmental strategy.

Community Involvement:
- Give staff members compensated time off to engage in environmental projects. Along with being good for the environment, projects like planting trees, cleaning up beaches, and restoring habitats also improve relationships within the community and foster teamwork.
- Collaborate with nearby environmental groups to develop cooperative projects that engage staff members. This could be working together on community projects, supporting regional green events, or taking part in environmental education initiatives.

4. Engagement and Communication

Sustainability Challenges and Competitions:
- Hold contests to motivate staff members to embrace environmentally friendly practices, including cutting back on energy consumption or waste reduction. Monitor results and give

prizes to the departments or teams who use the least amount of energy.

- Create sustainability challenges that encourage cooperative problem-solving and friendly competition. Green commute challenges, zero-waste months, and energy-saving weeks are a few examples.

Green Communication Channels:
- To disseminate sustainability advice, success stories, and updates on company-wide projects, create specialized forums, newsletters, or intranet sites. Maintaining constant involvement and keeping sustainability at the forefront are fostered by regular communication.
- Invite staff members to discuss their own eco-friendly ideas and practices. This encourages a feeling of belonging and shared accountability for the environmental effect of the business.

5. Continuous Improvement and Feedback

Regular Review and Adaptation:
- Keep an eye on and assess the success of green benefits and compensation initiatives. To determine whether objectives are being fulfilled and where changes can be made, use metrics and feedback.
- Get input from staff members to learn about their requirements and preferences. Utilize suggestion boxes, focus groups, and surveys to gather feedback and make the required program changes.

Benchmarking and Best Practices:
- Keep up with best practices in the industry and set yourself apart from businesses that have robust sustainability initiatives. Acquire knowledge from colleagues' accomplishments and obstacles to consistently enhance your own initiatives.
- Pay packages should be updated and innovative on a regular basis to meet changing employee expectations and environmental

requirements. By doing this, the business is certain to maintain its position as a pioneer in sustainability and to draw and keep workers who care about the environment.

Companies may effectively cultivate a sustainable culture, recruit and retain environmentally conscious personnel, and make a beneficial impact on the environment by designing eco-friendly compensation packages. This all-encompassing strategy boosts the company's reputation and raises employee happiness while also improving environmental performance. Although putting these techniques into practice takes dedication and continuous work, there are significant long-term advantages for the firm and the environment.

7.1.1 Overview of Incorporating Environmental Considerations into Compensation Structures

The phrase "overview of incorporating environmental considerations into compensation structures" describes giving a general overview or synopsis of the steps involved in integrating environmental considerations into an organization's compensation plans. This entails creating and executing compensation plans that encourage and recognize employees' environmentally conscious behaviour. Organizations seek to match their non-financial and financial incentives with sustainability goals by incorporating environmental factors into compensation systems. This approach promotes corporate responsibility and environmental stewardship.

❖ Comprehensive Guide to Incorporating Environmental Considerations into Compensation Structures

Including environmental factors in pay plans is a calculated move that combines sustainability ideas with the monetary and non-monetary benefits that employers provide to staff. This procedure tries to reward and promote ecologically conscious behaviour, matching employee benefits with the company's sustainability objectives. Here is an extensive and detailed guide to effectively incorporating these considerations into compensation structures:

1. Assessment and Goal Setting

Evaluate Current Impact:

- Make a thorough evaluation of the company's present environmental effects, taking into account water use, trash generation, energy use, and carbon footprint. To find areas that need improvement, use environmental audits and data analytics.

- Involve stakeholders from various areas of the company to get their opinions and views on environmental opportunities and problems.

Define Objectives:

- Set attainable, quantifiable, and time-bound sustainability objectives that complement the organization's overarching environmental strategy and vision. These goals ought to be particular to the size, setting, and industry of the organization.

- Make sure that the company's overall strategic planning process incorporates sustainability goals, and that these goals are successfully conveyed to every employee.

2. Designing Monetary Incentives

Performance-Based Bonuses:

- Establish a rewards structure based on performance that is linked to the accomplishment of predetermined sustainability goals. These goals could be cutting back on energy use, producing less trash, utilizing more renewable energy sources, or enhancing environmental efficiency in general.

- Set up bonuses to recognize and encourage team, corporate, and individual achievement of sustainability goals. This strategy encourages accountability and a sense of group responsibility for environmental care.

Subsidies and Grants:

- Employees should be given financial support or subsidies to purchase environmentally friendly goods and services. This might include financial aid for the purchase of solar panels for homes, energy-efficient appliances, or electric cars.

- Provide incentives like as grants or reimbursement plans to encourage staff members to improve their houses with energy-efficient features or embrace sustainable living habits.

Public Transportation Incentives:
- Put policies in place to promote commuting by bike, walking, public transportation, and carpooling. Offer financial assistance or reimbursement for memberships in bike sharing programs, public transit passes, or other environmentally friendly modes of transportation.
- To encourage the use of alternate means of transportation, provide rewards to car poolers, cyclists, and owners of electric vehicles, such as preferred parking.

Green Investment Options:
- Include sustainable investing options in retirement plans for staff members so they can match their financial objectives with their environmental beliefs. Provide a wide array of investing choices, such as green bonds and socially conscious investment funds.
- Create green investment funds sponsored by the company with the goal of promoting ecologically friendly ideas, innovations, and activities. Give workers the option to make voluntary payroll deductions or employer matching contributions to these funds.

3. Implementing Non-Monetary Benefits

Flexible Work Arrangements:
- Encourage flexible work schedules, telecommuting, and reduced workweeks to improve work-life balance and lower emissions associated with commuting.
- Encourage the use of remote work possibilities by providing technology-enabled virtual meeting tools, remote access to company systems and resources, and collaboration platforms.

Recognition Programs:
- Establish official recognition initiatives to reward and commend staff members who exhibit extraordinary dedication to sustainability. Give credit to the people, groups, and divisions that use creative thinking, proactive actions, or exceptional work to help achieve sustainability goals.

- Give staff prizes, certifications, or other acknowledgment for their contributions to sustainability both within and beyond the office.

Health and Wellness Initiatives:
- Provide health and wellness initiatives that support sustainable lifestyle choices, such as exercise, a balanced diet, stress reduction, and mental health. Provide discounts, prizes, or other inducements to people who engage in wellness activities that benefit the environment and one's own health.

- Make wellness tools, amenities, and services—like on-site exercise canters, wholesome food alternatives, green areas, and mindfulness programs—available to promote sustainable living.

Educational Programs:
- Provide continuing education and training to develop capacity and increase understanding of environmental challenges, sustainable practices, and green technologies. Give staff members the chance to learn about subjects including biodiversity, climate change, recycling, trash reduction, and energy conservation.

- Use webinars, workshops, seminars, online courses, guest lecturers, and other interactive formats to help people learn. Promote involvement in professional development initiatives that enhance environmental competency and literacy.

Community Involvement:
- Encourage staff members to participate in volunteer opportunities and community service initiatives that promote environmental advocacy, conservation, and restoration. Collaborate with nearby nonprofits, environmental groups, educational institutions, and governmental organizations to find worthwhile volunteer

opportunities that complement the goals and values of the business.

- Support and take part in community get-togethers, cleanup efforts, planting campaigns, habitat restoration projects, educational seminars, and public awareness campaigns. Encourage staff members to give back to the community and environment by volunteering their time, talents, and knowledge.

4. Engagement and Communication

Sustainability Challenges and Competitions:

- Organize campaigns, contests, and challenges focused on sustainability to get staff members involved in working together to accomplish environmental goals. Establish goals, monitor advancement, and give participants recognition for their efforts to sustainability projects.

- Create opportunities for staff to work together to solve problems, innovate, and build a sense of camaraderie and friendly rivalry. Encourage ingenuity, initiative, and ongoing development while tackling opportunities and difficulties related to sustainability.

Green Communication Channels:

- Create specialized venues and communication channels to exchange resources, information, updates, and sustainability-related success stories. To communicate with staff members in various departments, locations, and roles, use digital signage, email newsletters, intranet portals, social media platforms, and internal newsletters.

- Give regular updates on the company's achievements, difficulties, opportunities, goals, initiatives, and sustainability performance. Emphasize both individual and group contributions to sustainability initiatives, recognize exemplary behaviour, and commemorate accomplishments.

5. Continuous Improvement and Feedback

Regular Review and Adaptation:

- Continue to track, analyse, and judge the success of green benefits and compensation schemes. To gauge success, pinpoint areas for development, and assist in decision-making, gather and evaluate pertinent data, metrics, feedback, and insights.

- Review, audit, and evaluate sustainability policies, initiatives, and practices on a regular basis. Determine your strengths, weaknesses, opportunities, and threats. Then, use the information you gather to hone your tactics, establish new goals, and modify your plan as necessary.

Benchmarking and Best Practices:

- Keep up to date on sustainability-related industry trends, new developments, best practices, benchmarks, standards, certifications, and laws. Compare yourself to other companies, prominent figures in the field, and proponents of sustainability to gather knowledge from past mistakes and use tested strategies.

- Consult external partners, consultants, experts, and stakeholders who possess specific knowledge and experience in environmental management, sustainability reporting, and corporate social responsibility to obtain advice, direction, and expertise.

In summary, the integration of environmental factors into compensation schemes is a complex and ever-changing procedure necessitating meticulous preparation, strategic coordination, and continuous involvement. Organizations may develop a sustainable culture that benefits workers, the business, and the environment by planning and executing complete and integrated pay plans that recognize and reward ecologically conscious behaviour. Organizations may create shared benefit for stakeholders both now and in the future, establish resilience, and promote good change by empowering employees to make choices that support environmental sustainability.

7.1.2 Strategies for Designing Green Compensation Packages, Such as Pay-for-Performance Linked to Sustainability Goals

The term "strategies for designing green compensation packages, such as pay-for-performance linked to sustainability goals" describes the methods and techniques that businesses employ to incorporate sustainability concerns into their pay plans. In particular, it entails designing pay plans that reward and encourage staff members who meet sustainability goals. One important tactic that was brought up is the direct connection of pay-for-performance to sustainability objectives, whereby workers receive compensation commensurate with their contributions to the organization's environmental sustainability initiatives. By coordinating employee incentives with the business's environmental goals, this strategy seeks to both encourage and involve staff members in sustainability projects and provide favourable environmental results.

❖ Comprehensive Strategies for Designing Green Compensation Packages

Designing green compensation plans entails incorporating environmental factors into an organization's conventional pay schemes. Directly connecting pay-for-performance objectives to sustainability targets is one useful tactic. Here are several comprehensive strategies to achieve this:

1. Pay-for-Performance Linked to Sustainability Goals

i. **Define Clear Sustainability Metrics:** Set SMART (specific, measurable, achievable, relevant, and time-bound) sustainability goals that are in line with the environmental aims of the company. These can be limiting the amount of trash produced, boosting energy efficiency, encouraging sustainable sourcing methods, or cutting carbon emissions by a specific proportion.

ii. **Incorporate Sustainability Targets into Performance Goals:** Include sustainability goals in key performance indicators (KPIs) and staff performance objectives. This guarantees that workers are responsible for their contributions to the company's environmental goals. For instance, salespeople might be judged on their efforts to market eco-friendly goods and services in addition to their ability to generate income.

iii. **Tie Variable Pay to Sustainability Performance:** Assign a percentage of an employee's variable pay, such as bonuses or incentives, based on how well they accomplish sustainability objectives. Give extra money to teams or individuals who surpass sustainability goals. Profit-sharing plans, bonuses based on performance, and stock options linked to environmental performance indicators are a few examples of this.

iv. **Implement Performance-Based Bonus Programs:** Design bonus schemes that are directly linked to reaching sustainability benchmarks. Offer bonuses, for instance, for adopting creative sustainable methods or for achieving appreciable decreases in trash generation or energy use. These bonuses could be set up as recurring incentives for consistent environmental performance or as one-time awards for reaching predetermined goals.

v. **Provide Transparency and Communication:** Make sure staff members understand the connection between sustainability rewards and performance. The importance of environmental stewardship inside the company is reinforced by transparency on the contribution of sustainability goals to compensation. Utilize a variety of communication platforms, including staff training sessions, intranet portals, newsletters, and corporate meetings, to make sure that workers are aware of the relationship between their work and their pay.

2. Non-Monetary Incentives for Sustainable Behaviour

i. **Recognition and Awards:** Create recognition initiatives to honour staff members that show a model dedication to sustainability. Honour groups or individuals that carry out creative environmental projects or regularly demonstrate eco-friendly conduct. This could take the form of recognition events, achievement certificates, or public announcements in business publications.

ii. **Professional Development Opportunities:** Provide training and development courses with an emphasis on sustainability. Give staff members the chance to learn more about topics including environmental rules, sustainable supply chain management, waste reduction, and energy efficiency. Encourage staff members to get sustainability-related professional certificates or credentials, and offer assistance with ongoing education and professional development initiatives.

iii. **Work-Life Balance Initiatives:** Encourage telecommuting choices, flexible work schedules, and alternate transportation benefits to save carbon emissions and improve work-life balance for staff members. Provide incentives like shortened workweeks, flexible scheduling, or the chance to work remotely to motivate staff to embrace environmentally friendly commute methods and lessen their need on single-occupancy cars.

iv. **Wellness Programs:** By providing rewards for engaging in environmentally beneficial activities like biking to work, gardening, or volunteer work for environmental causes, you may incorporate sustainability into wellness programs. Make wellness tools, amenities, and services like on-site exercise canters, wholesome food alternatives, green areas, and mindfulness programs available to promote sustainable living. Encourage staff members to place a high priority on their physical and emotional health while simultaneously encouraging eco-friendly actions.

3. Employee Engagement and Participation

i. **Employee Involvement in Goal Setting:** Include staff members in the process of establishing aims and goals for sustainability. Encourage them to share their thoughts and suggestions for enhancing environmental performance, and give them the authority to lead sustainability projects. Organize focus groups, town hall meetings, or brainstorming sessions to get input from staff members about environmental opportunities, challenges, and priorities. When creating sustainability strategy and action plans, consider employee feedback and give regular updates on accomplishments.

ii. **Team Collaboration:** Encourage departmental and team collaboration to accomplish common sustainability goals. Promote knowledge sharing and cross-functional cooperation to find and apply the best environmental conservation strategies. Provide staff members the chance to work together on sustainability-related projects, campaigns, and events. Also, honour and reward groups that exhibit outstanding cooperation and teamwork. Employee success stories, lessons learned, and creative ideas for enhancing sustainability inside the company should be encouraged to be shared.

iii. **Feedback Mechanisms:** Create feedback channels to collect opinions and recommendations from staff members for enhancing sustainability programs. Encourage candid discussion and communication on environmental issues, and set up avenues for staff members to express their thoughts, worries, and opinions. To get input on sustainability policies, practices, and initiatives, use employee forums, focus groups, suggestion boxes, surveys, and employee forums. Examine feedback data to find areas that need work, resolve issues raised by staff, and increase the impact of sustainability programs.

iv. **Continuous Improvement:** Encourage a culture of continuous improvement by evaluating and revising sustainability objectives and performance indicators on a regular basis. To improve sustainability methods and lessen environmental effect, promote experimentation and creativity. To evaluate progress, spot patterns, and gauge the success of sustainability programs, keep an eye on the key performance indicators (KPIs) pertaining to sustainability and make use of data analytics and performance dashboards. To identify strengths, weaknesses, opportunities, and threats, conduct regular reviews, audits, and evaluations of sustainability practices, policies, and programs. Use the results to inform strategy, establish new objectives, and modify methods as necessary. Honor successes and significant anniversaries, and thank staff members for their contributions to sustainability initiatives. Employees should be encouraged to share best practices, lessons learned, and success stories with their peers.

They should also be given opportunities to collaborate across departments and exchange expertise.

Organizations may successfully incentivise and compensate staff for contributing to environmental sustainability goals by putting these comprehensive ideas for establishing green remuneration packages into practice. In addition to having a good impact on the environment, aligning compensation with sustainability goals also improves employee engagement, encourages innovation, and builds the company's reputation as a socially conscious business.

7.1.3 Case Studies of Organizations Implementing Eco-friendly Compensation Practices to Motivate Employees towards Sustainability

Google: Driving Sustainability through Eco-Friendly Compensation Practices

Background:
Google is a multinational technological corporation that is a division of Alphabet Inc. and is well-known for its cutting-edge cloud computing platform, mobile operating system, and search engine. Google strives to reduce its environmental effect and encourage sustainable practices throughout its operations. It has a strong commitment to sustainability and environmental responsibility.

Eco-Friendly Compensation Practices:
Google has implemented several eco-friendly compensation practices to motivate employees towards sustainability:

1. Financial Incentives for Sustainable Transportation:
Google offers monetary rewards to staff members who select for eco-friendly modes of transportation during their workday commute. This could include financial aid for public transportation passes, payment for bicycle-related transportation costs, or rewards for carpooling. Google fosters ecologically friendly commuting practices and lessens the carbon footprint of its employees by supporting sustainable transportation.

2. Support for Renewable Energy:
Google provides financial support to its employees so they can put sustainable energy systems on their homes, such solar panels. To assist employees in defraying the expense of making the switch to renewable energy, the company may offer financing options, rebates, or subsidies. Google lessens the dependency of its workers on fossil fuels and encourages the shift to a low-carbon economy by encouraging the adoption of renewable energy.

3. Volunteer Opportunities and Paid Time Off:
Google provides paid time off for staff members who volunteer for environmental causes and encourages them to join in conservation, tree-planting, and community clean-up efforts. Google promotes a feeling of purpose and a connection to sustainability among its staff members by giving them chances to participate in worthwhile environmental activities and give back to their communities.

Impact:
Google's eco-friendly compensation practices have had a positive impact on both employees and the environment:

i. **Employee Engagement:** Google encourages employees to participate in sustainability initiatives and cultivates an environmentally conscious culture by providing financial incentives for the adoption of sustainable mobility, backing for the use of renewable energy, and volunteer opportunities.

ii. **Reduced Carbon Footprint:** Google assists staff members in lowering their carbon footprints and encouraging environmentally friendly lives by supporting the use of renewable energy sources and sustainable modes of transportation.

iii. **Enhanced Brand Reputation:** Google has drawn top personnel who share its ideals thanks to its dedication to sustainability and eco-friendly compensation practices. Google shows its commitment to having a positive environmental impact on the world by matching compensation with environmental goals.

Conclusion:

Google has demonstrated its commitment to environmental sustainability and corporate social responsibility through the deployment of eco-friendly remuneration methods. Google helps create a more sustainable future by encouraging employees to volunteer, supporting the use of renewable energy sources, and offering financial incentives for sustainable transportation. Google's endeavours yield benefits not only for its workforce but also for the company's reputation, the environment, and society at large.

Patagonia: Leading the Way in Eco-Friendly Compensation Practices

Background:

Renowned outdoor apparel and equipment manufacturer Patagonia is deeply committed to environmental sustainability. Since its founding in 1973, the company has centred its brand around corporate social responsibility and environmental activism. Patagonia is renowned for its cutting-edge goods, support of environmental causes, and dedication to ethical labour standards.

Eco-Friendly Compensation Practices:

Patagonia has implemented several eco-friendly compensation practices to motivate employees towards sustainability:

1. Paid Time Off for Environmental Volunteering:

Patagonia provides paid time off for staff members to engage in voluntary work related to the environment. This covers chances to participate in cleanup, conservation, and environmental advocacy projects. Patagonia encourages staff members to actively support environmental causes and have a positive influence on their communities by offering paid time off for volunteering.

2. Financial Assistance for Sustainable Transportation:

Patagonia offers cash support to staff members who select for environmentally friendly modes of transportation on a regular basis. This could include financial aid for public transit passes, payment for bicycle commuter costs, or rewards for carpooling. Patagonia fosters ecologically friendly commuting practices and lessens the carbon impact of its employees by supporting sustainable transportation.

3. Wellness Benefits and Eco-Friendly Facilities:
Patagonia provides wellness perks to promote the sustainability and well-being of its workforce. This covers the use of the on-site exercise canters, yoga courses, and wellness initiatives. In addition, the organization offers environmentally friendly amenities like composting programs and organic cafeterias to encourage staff members to lead sustainable and healthful lives.

Impact:
Patagonia's eco-friendly compensation practices have had a significant impact on both employees and the environment:

i. **Employee Engagement:** Patagonia encourages staff involvement in sustainability initiatives and cultivates a sense of environmental stewardship by providing paid time off for environmental volunteer work and financial support for environmentally friendly transportation.

ii. **Reduced Carbon Footprint:** Patagonia encourages environmentally friendly commute practices and lowers employee carbon emissions by supporting sustainable transportation options.

iii. **Enhanced Brand Reputation:** Patagonia has drawn top personnel who share its ideals because to its dedication to sustainability and eco-friendly remuneration practices. Patagonia shows their commitment to having a good environmental impact on the earth by matching compensation with environmental goals.

Conclusion:
Patagonia's adoption of environmentally conscious remuneration methods is a prime example of their dedication to both corporate social responsibility and environmental sustainability. Patagonia encourages employees to engage in meaningful environmental work and contributes to a more sustainable future by offering paid time off for volunteering in the environment, financial support for sustainable transportation, and

wellness perks to support healthy and sustainable lifestyles. In addition to helping its workers, Patagonia's initiatives enhance the company's reputation, have a positive effect on the environment, and advance society.

PepsiCo: Implementing Eco-Friendly Compensation Practices

Background:
Global food and beverage giant PepsiCo is known for a wide range of products, such as Tropicana, Frito-Lay, Quaker Oats, and Pepsi. The corporation employs thousands of people worldwide and has operations in more than 200 countries and territories. PepsiCo has pledged to be sustainable and practice corporate social responsibility in order to lessen its impact on the environment and to improve the health and wellbeing of its consumers and communities.

Eco-Friendly Compensation Practices:
PepsiCo has implemented several eco-friendly compensation practices to motivate employees towards sustainability:

1. Financial Incentives for Sustainable Behaviours:
PepsiCo provides cash rewards to staff members who embrace eco-friendly practices at work and in their personal lives. Employees who install solar panels on their homes, buy energy-efficient appliances, or take part in renewable energy initiatives are eligible for financial aid or reimbursement from the company. These rewards motivate workers to lessen their carbon footprint and make decisions that benefit the environment on a regular basis.

2. Wellness Benefits:
PepsiCo provides wellness benefits to encourage sustainability and employee health. This includes offering wellness initiatives, on-site exercise canters, and workplace cafeterias with a variety of healthy food alternatives. PepsiCo encourages healthy lifestyles and places a high priority on employee well-being in order to support sustainability both inside and outside the workplace.

3. Volunteering Opportunities:

PepsiCo provides paid time off for staff members who volunteer for environmental causes and encourages them to join in conservation, tree-planting, and community clean-up programs. PepsiCo helps its workers feel connected to sustainability and gives them opportunities to give back to their communities and collaborate on important environmental projects.

Impact:

PepsiCo's eco-friendly compensation practices have had a positive impact on both employees and the environment:

i. **Employee Engagement:** PepsiCo has encouraged a culture of environmental responsibility and involved employees in sustainability initiatives by offering volunteer opportunities and supporting sustainable behaviours.

ii. **Reduced Environmental Footprint:** PepsiCo offers cash incentives for energy-efficient appliances and renewable energy initiatives that help staff members lower their carbon footprint and preserve the environment.

iii. **Enhanced Brand Reputation:** PepsiCo has drawn great personnel who share its values because to its dedication to sustainability and corporate social responsibility. PepsiCo has shown that it is committed to having a good environmental impact on the world by matching compensation with environmental goals.

Conclusion:

PepsiCo has demonstrated its commitment to sustainability and corporate social responsibility by implementing eco-friendly remuneration methods. PepsiCo engages employees in meaningful environmental work and contributes to a more sustainable future by offering opportunities for volunteerism, boosting employee wellbeing, and offering incentives for sustainable behaviour. By these initiatives, PepsiCo improves society and the environment in addition to helping its workers and enhancing the reputation of its brand.

7.2 Incentives for Sustainable Behaviour

The term "incentives for sustainable behaviour" refers to a range of tactics and frameworks intended to encourage people, organizations, and communities to embrace socially and environmentally conscious behaviour. These incentives can come in a variety of shapes and sizes, including monetary compensation, legal advantages, educational programs, public acknowledgment, and infrastructure assistance. Encouraging behaviours that lessen their influence on the environment, conserve resources, and create a more sustainable way of life are the objectives.

Aligning economic, social, and environmental goals is the main objective of incentives for sustainable behaviour. Sustainable behaviours including cutting greenhouse gas emissions, conserving water, cutting waste, and enhancing biodiversity are encouraged by these incentives, which work by rewarding good deeds or removing obstacles. A more sustainable society, where economic growth does not come at the price of social or environmental well-being, is the ultimate goal.

Sustainable behaviour incentives are plans and regulations aimed at motivating people, companies, and communities to embrace ecologically and socially conscious activities. These incentives can be of the financial, governmental, technological, educational, social, or infrastructure variety. Policymakers and groups hope to address urgent environmental issues including pollution, resource depletion, and climate change by utilizing these many forms of incentives to encourage sustainability.

❖ Below is an in-depth exploration of these incentives and how they work to foster sustainable behaviour.

- **Financial Incentives**

Since they directly benefit persons who adopt environmentally friendly conduct, financial incentives are among the most effective instruments for encouraging sustainable behaviour.

1. Tax Breaks and Credits: Governments that invest in sustainable practices and technologies often provide credits or tax discounts to individuals and corporations. For example, installing insulation, energy-efficient windows, or solar panels may qualify homes for tax credits.

Similar incentives could be useful for businesses looking to implement sustainable manufacturing practices, energy-efficient equipment, or renewable energy sources. By lowering the initial investment burden, these tax breaks increase the appeal and viability of sustainable investments.

2. Grants and Subsidies: There are several grants and subsidies available for initiatives that improve environmental sustainability. These can include financing for energy-efficient building projects, sustainable agriculture programs like organic farming and soil conservation, and renewable energy projects like wind farms and solar power installations. Grants and subsidies promote the broader adoption of sustainable practices by removing the financial obstacles to putting such projects into action.

3. Rebates: Rebate schemes give customers who buy electric cars, energy-efficient appliances, or make other home upgrades that lower energy use cash back or savings. For instance, utility companies frequently offer incentives for the purchase of equipment with an ENERGY STAR rating or for upgrading homes with energy-efficient fixtures like smart thermostats and LED lighting.

4. Carbon Pricing: The goal of carbon pricing schemes like cap-and-trade programs and carbon taxes is to make greenhouse gas emissions more environmentally expensive. High emissions are financially discouraged by a carbon tax, which levies a price on emitters per tonne of carbon dioxide released into the atmosphere. Cap-and-trade programs essentially create a market for carbon allowances by limiting overall emissions and enabling businesses to buy and sell emission permits. By increasing the cost of pollution, both strategies encourage businesses to lessen their carbon impact.

- **Regulatory Incentives**

Laws and rules that require or promote sustainable practices are known as regulatory incentives, and they are frequently followed by monetary or non-monetary rewards for compliance.

1. Environmental Regulations: Governments enact laws that establish guidelines for waste management, energy efficiency, and pollution control. Regulations could, for instance, enforce recycling programs for companies, place restrictions on the amount of pollution that manufacturers can emit, or set efficiency requirements for cars and appliances. There are instances where financial incentives, such lowered permit costs or tax advantages, are used to encourage compliance with certain requirements.

2. Green Certifications: Buildings that fulfil strict environmental performance requirements are certified by programs such as LEED (Leadership in Energy and Environmental Design). Obtaining these certificates can have a number of advantages, such as tax reductions, higher property values, and a competitive advantage in the marketplace. Builders and developers are encouraged by certification programs to use environmentally friendly designs, energy-efficient technologies, and sustainable materials.

- **Educational and Informational Incentives**

In order to empower people and businesses to make environmentally conscious decisions, education and information are essential elements in promoting sustainable behaviour.

1. Public Awareness Campaigns: The public is intended to be educated by these efforts about the value of environmental stewardship and the advantages of sustainable practices. Awareness campaigns draw attention to topics like recycling, energy conservation, and sustainable consumerism through the media, workshops, and community events. These initiatives encourage people to modify their behaviour and take up more sustainable habits by increasing awareness.

2. Training and Resources: Enabling individuals and businesses to access resources and training programs facilitates the adoption of sustainable practices. This can include online courses on renewable energy technologies, lectures on sustainable agriculture, and workshops on energy efficiency. Stakeholders are guaranteed to be well-equipped to make knowledgeable judgments and execute effective action when they have access to knowledge and experience.

- **Social and Behavioural Incentives**

Social norms and community dynamics are utilized by social and behavioural incentives to encourage sustainable practices.

1. Recognition Programs: Programs for awards and recognition honour companies and individuals who reach important benchmarks in sustainability. For instance, a city may honour businesses who cut their carbon footprint by a specific percentage or towns that demonstrate exceptional trash management. Acknowledgment improves reputation and can result in higher staff satisfaction, client loyalty, and general prestige.

2. Community Initiatives: Promoting involvement in community-based sustainability initiatives cultivates a feeling of shared accountability and involvement. Community gardens, local recycling programs, and neighbourhood clean-up days are examples of initiatives that unite people in the pursuit of shared environmental objectives. These programs foster shared ideals and peer support to promote sustainable behaviour and foster community cohesion.

- **Technological and Infrastructural Incentives**

Making large-scale investments in infrastructure and technology is necessary to support sustainable behaviour.

1. Development of Green Infrastructure: It is essential to provide infrastructure that promotes sustainable living. This entails making investments in bicycle lanes, public transportation systems, and pedestrian-friendly urban architecture. Green infrastructure encourages healthier lifestyles, lessens greenhouse gas emissions, and lessens dependency on private automobiles. For example, towns with robust bike-sharing programs and public transportation networks facilitate people' selection of environmentally friendly forms of mobility.

2. Support for Innovation: For long-term environmental improvement, funding research and development of new sustainable technologies is essential. This may entail funding for the creation of cutting-edge recycling methods, sustainable energy sources, or energy storage systems. Governments and commercial organizations can spur the development of cutting-edge technology that increase the effectiveness and accessibility of sustainable practices by encouraging innovation.

Combining these incentives can be a useful strategy for encouraging sustainable behaviour at all societal levels and in a variety of industries. These incentives encourages the widespread adoption of environmentally friendly behaviour and guarantees a sustainable future by fostering an atmosphere in which sustainable decisions are financially advantageous, socially acceptable, and logistically possible.

7.2.1 Importance of Incentivizing and Rewarding Sustainable Behaviours in the Workplace

Promoting a sustainable culture in the workplace, increasing operational effectiveness, boosting the organization's reputation, guaranteeing regulatory compliance, and stimulating innovation all depend on rewarding and incentivizing sustainable behaviour. Putting policies in place to promote eco-friendly behaviour among staff members has major benefits for the organization as well as the environment.

❖ Below is a comprehensive exploration of the importance of these practices.

- **Promoting a Sustainable Culture**

Integrating eco-friendly practices into the organization's everyday operations and core values is essential to developing a sustainable workplace culture. For both operational performance and long-term environmental stewardship, this cultural shift is essential.

1. **Employee Engagement and Morale:** Employee engagement and motivation are more likely when they perceive that their employer prioritizes sustainability and actively recognizes and rewards efforts to minimize environmental effect. The company's ideals and a feeling of unity of purpose can greatly improve morale and job satisfaction. Workers who believe that what they do advances society at large are frequently more dedicated and effective.

2. **Behavioural Change:** Employees are encouraged to embrace sustainable behaviours by offering incentives, such as recycling, cutting back on energy use, cutting waste, and choosing eco-friendly transit. As a result, the organization develops a long-lasting culture of sustainability. These practices eventually become engrained habits. This transformation in culture may result in a workforce that actively looks for methods to lessen its ecological footprint and is more environmentally conscientious.

- **Enhancing Operational Efficiency**

Sustainable practices frequently result in higher resource efficiency, which can save the company a substantial amount of money. Long-term profitability and the preservation of competitive advantage depend on these efficiency gains.

1. **Energy and Resource Savings:** Promoting energy-saving behaviours can result in significant savings on utility bills and operating expenses. Examples of these habits include turning off lights and appliances when not in use, adjusting heating and cooling systems, and purchasing energy-efficient technology. Furthermore, encouraging the use of digital documents rather than printed ones can cut down on the amount of paper used and related expenses.

2. **Waste Reduction:** Lowering disposal costs and increasing resource efficiency can be achieved by putting recycling systems into place and advocating for waste reduction techniques like composting organic waste and cutting back on single-use plastics. Reducing waste not only lowers expenses but also lessens the environmental impact of the company, supporting overall sustainability objectives.

- **Strengthening Brand Reputation and Competitiveness**

Businesses that put sustainability first can stand out from the competition and draw in a variety of stakeholders, such as partners, investors, and consumers.

1. **Consumer Appeal:** Customers are showing a growing preference for doing business with companies that practice environmental responsibility. Emphasizing sustainability efforts can increase brand loyalty and draw in eco-aware consumers. Examples of these programs include employing renewable energy, cutting emissions, and funding neighbourhood environmental projects. Strong support for sustainability can also result in favourable press coverage and advantages for public relations.

2. **Investor Interest:** Companies that meet Environmental, Social, and Governance (ESG) standards are sought after by a large number of investors. Investors that value sustainable, long-term growth may find a company more appealing if it demonstrates a dedication to

sustainability. Better access to funding and advantageous investment arrangements may arise from this.

- **Regulatory Compliance and Risk Management**

Organizations can reduce environmental impact risks and comply with requirements by using sustainable practices. Maintaining operational stability and safeguarding the organization's reputation depend heavily on keeping ahead of legal requirements and taking proactive measures to manage environmental concerns.

1. **Regulatory Benefits:** Potential fines and penalties can be avoided by adhering to environmental standards. Additionally, businesses who exhibit proactive compliance may receive preferential treatment from authorities, such as accelerated clearances and lessened regulatory oversight. By taking a proactive stance, the company may strengthen its competitive advantage and establish itself as a sustainability leader.

2. **Risk Mitigation:** Sustainable practices can lower the likelihood of environmental accidents, which can result in expensive cleanups, legal penalties, and reputational harm. These occurrences include spills, emissions, and shortages of resources. Organizations can reduce these risks and guarantee long-term operational resilience by implementing sustainable practices.

- **Innovation and Continuous Improvement**

Promoting sustainable practices can spark innovation inside the company, opening up fresh markets and resulting in ongoing efficiency gains.

1. **Creative Solutions:** Workers who are inspired to think sustainably are more likely to generate creative concepts that enhance procedures, goods, and services. This can involve creating eco-friendly product designs, coming up with innovative, more effective production techniques, or figuring out how to reuse waste materials. Such innovation has the potential to create new markets and competitive advantages.

2. **Continuous Improvement:** Establishing objectives, monitoring advancement, and aiming for ongoing development are common components of sustainability projects. An emphasis on sustainability

has the potential to continuously improve effectiveness, reduce costs, and improve the environment. Organizations can keep up with changes in regulations and industry trends by routinely evaluating and refining their procedures.

To sum up, encouraging and rewarding sustainable behaviours at work is critical to developing a sustainable culture, increasing operational effectiveness, boosting reputation, guaranteeing regulatory compliance, and stimulating innovation. Organizations can attain sustainable advantages that bolster their environmental objectives and overall commercial prosperity by putting these methods into effect. An organization can become stronger and more resilient, have a more engaged staff, save expenses, and be more competitive by taking a deliberate approach to rewarding sustainable behaviour.

7.2.2 Types of Incentives for Promoting Green Incentives

Organizational sustainability efforts can be greatly boosted by offering a range of incentives to encourage green practices. There are many more monetary incentives, non-monetary incentives, and recognition programs that can be put into place in addition to the often-used incentives in order to promote a sustainable culture.

- ❖ Here's an expanded exploration of these incentive types and how they can be utilized to create a comprehensive and effective approach to promoting sustainability in the workplace.

- **Monetary Incentives**

To promote eco-friendly practices and accomplish sustainability goals, these incentives entail providing monetary awards or advantages to individuals or groups. Monetary incentives come in many forms: cash bonuses, bonuses linked to particular sustainability goals or targets, cash vouchers or coupons for eco-friendly goods or services, or reimbursement for costs associated with green initiatives like buying energy-efficient appliances for the house or taking public transit to minimize carbon emissions. Monetary incentives, which come in the form of concrete money benefits, are an effective means of encouraging staff members to embrace eco-friendly behaviours and support the company's sustainability initiatives.

❖ These incentives can take various forms to encourage participation and drive substantial improvements in environmental performance:

1. Performance-Based Raises: Granting pay raises in response to an employee's involvement with environmental initiatives. An employee might get a raise, for instance, if they successfully launch a new recycling program or energy-saving project. This kind of incentive makes sure that workers are continuously encouraged to look for and adopt green practices by directly linking monetary rewards to the accomplishment of sustainability goals.

2. Sustainability Contests with Cash Prizes: Setting up competitions with monetary rewards for teams or employees that can produce the best sustainability outcomes, like the most creative green concept or the largest resource reduction. These competitions, which can span a range of sustainability topics from waste management to energy saving, can be hosted on a regular basis and foster innovative thinking and broad involvement.

3. Eco-Friendly Commuting Subsidies: Offering monetary support to staff members who commute sustainably by riding their bikes, carpooling, or taking public transportation. This can involve giving parking privileges for car poolers, subsidizing bus or train passes, or providing incentives for biking to work. In addition to encouraging environmentally friendly modes of transportation, these subsidies also lessen the carbon footprint left by everyday commutes to and from the office.

4. Stock Options or Equity: Giving employees who make major contributions to sustainability initiatives equity shares or stock options. Their financial interests are thus in line with the company's sustainability and long-term development, giving them a stake in its environmental performance. Shareholders are more likely to have a stake in the long-term viability and success of their employer.

5. Green Allowances: Offering bonuses or allowances to staff members so they can buy environmentally friendly goods or services, such reusable office supplies, energy-efficient home equipment, or environmentally friendly vacation possibilities. Employees may use these benefits to enhance the company's commitment to sustainability outside of the office by making more environmentally friendly decisions in their own lives.

6. **Bonuses:** Bonusing workers or groups who reach or surpass predetermined sustainability goals, such cutting energy use, raising recycling rates, or creating environmentally friendly products. These bonuses may be linked to departmental accomplishments or company-wide objectives. For instance, a business might decide to cut energy use by 10% over the course of a year, and the team that hits this objective would receive a bonus. This kind of reward makes the objective more concrete and inspiring for staff members by directly connecting sustainability initiatives to individual financial gain.

7. **Profit-Sharing:** Putting in place a profit-sharing scheme that would provide staff members a share of the savings made possible by sustainability efforts (such lower utility bills or fees for disposing of waste). This directly correlates sustainability with financial performance in addition to rewarding eco-friendly conduct. Because they will personally profit from the savings, employees become more invested in the company's success and are inspired to identify and implement sustainable cost-saving strategies.

- **Non-Monetary Incentives**

Non-monetary incentives, in contrast to monetary ones, offer prizes that add value to participants in other ways without requiring them to pay money up front. Opportunities for professional growth and career progression in sustainability, such as training courses, workshops, or certifications in environmental management or renewable energy technology, can serve as non-monetary incentives for supporting green efforts. Non-cash rewards can also include perks that improve workers' quality of life and work-life balance, such remote work opportunities, flexible scheduling, or membership in wellness programs that support mental and physical health. Organizations can show their dedication to fostering ecologically friendly practices and enhancing the holistic well-being of their workforce by providing non-monetary incentives.

❖ **These incentives can appeal to employees' intrinsic motivations and support their overall well-being:**

1. **Sustainable Office Perks:** Giving benefits that encourage sustainability, including reusable water bottles, environmentally friendly

workplace supplies, or access to a shared garden where staff members can cultivate their own produce. These benefits can improve workplace satisfaction and ensure that daily operations are consistent with sustainability principles.

2. Work-Life Balance Initiatives: Putting in place activities that support work-life balance, like stress management classes, mental health days, and wellness programs that can be linked to involvement in sustainable projects. Employees who commute by bicycle or carpooling, for instance, may accrue points that can be exchanged for extra wellness advantages.

3. Employee Involvement in Decision-Making: Involving employees in decision-making processes related to sustainability, for example, by establishing task forces or committees to create and carry out green policies. When employees see their ideas and efforts directly impacting business processes, it helps strengthen their sense of ownership and dedication to sustainability goals.

4. Recognition and Development Opportunities: Allowing employees to provide internal training sessions on sustainability, participate in environmental projects in the community, and speak on behalf of the company at conferences on sustainability. These opportunities can help employees grow professionally and demonstrate that the company encourages their progress.

5. Sustainable Workspace Enhancements: Using natural light, building a green roof area where workers can unwind and take in the scenery, or adding plants to improve the air quality are examples of sustainable improvements that may be made to the workplace. These improvements have the potential to improve workplace satisfaction and harmonize the built environment with sustainable principles.

6. Extra Time Off: Allowing employees who reach important sustainability objectives to take additional paid time off. Along with a priceless personal advantage, this award recognizes their hard work. An employee could, for example, be rewarded with an extra day off if they oversee a successful energy-saving project.

7. Flexible Working Arrangements: Offering remote work, flexible scheduling, or shortened workweeks to staff members who participate in green initiatives. This can encourage work-life balance and cut down on emissions from commuting. Promoting telecommuting boosts job happiness by giving employees more freedom and contributes to environmental goals.

8. Professional Development Opportunities: providing opportunities for professional growth, such going to training sessions, workshops, or conferences on sustainability. This can strengthen the company's commitment to sustainability while assisting staff in gaining new skills and knowledge. Workers can return with new ideas and insights that advance the company's sustainability programs.

9. Public Recognition: Showcasing staff members' accomplishments in sustainability through company-wide emails, intranet postings, and newsletters. Gaining attention from the public can improve one's reputation and encourage others to do the same. Telling success tales to one another can foster a feeling of accomplishment and camaraderie.

- **Recognition Programs**

Initiatives known as recognition programs are meant to honour and commemorate the accomplishments of people or organizations who support environmental practices within the company and make a positive impact on sustainability goals. Formal award ceremonies, public acknowledgement during team meetings or business events, inclusion in internal newsletters or mailings highlighting sustainability triumphs, or individual letters of gratitude from organizational executives are just a few ways that recognition can be given. Recognition programs, which openly acknowledge and celebrate employees' efforts to sustainability, serve to both reinforce desired behaviours and encourage others to get involved in green activities. Furthermore, recognition initiatives support the development of a positive workplace culture that emphasizes environmental stewardship and group accountability for advancing sustainability.

❖ These programs can foster a sense of accomplishment and inspire others to engage in similar behaviours:

1. Sustainability Champions: Rewarding staff members who set an example and encourage eco-friendly behaviours within their groups by designating them as "Sustainability Champions." Through internal communications, these champions might be acknowledged and assigned specific duties, including spear heading eco-friendly projects or repping the business at sustainability gatherings.

2. Peer Recognition Programs: Motivating staff members to submit nominations for sustainability awards on behalf of their peers. Peer acknowledgment has the added value of coming from peers who see and value the work that is being done. This could promote a cooperative, encouraging work atmosphere where environmental initiatives are recognized and honoured.

3. Eco-Certificates and Badges: Giving employees who finish sustainability training programs or reach particular sustainability milestones awards or digital badges. These serve as public acknowledgements of their accomplishments and competence and can be shown at work or on professional profiles on websites like LinkedIn.

4. Sustainability Ambassadors: designating staff members to serve as the company's sustainability ambassadors and represent it at external forums, conferences, and neighbourhood gatherings. Acknowledging their ambassador positions can help them build their professional networks, open up new career development options, and contribute fresh perspectives and ideas to the company.

5. Storytelling Platforms: Establishing forums for staff members to discuss their sustainability stories and achievements. This could take the form of an internal newsletter, blog, or social media website that highlights both individual and group efforts to promote sustainability. By encouraging people to take part in sustainability projects, sharing success stories can foster a sense of belonging and group accomplishment.

6. Employee of the Month Awards: recognizing each month those employees who have significantly improved sustainability. A mention in corporate communications, together with awards and plaques, might be used to commemorate this. These honours give workers' efforts official recognition, which raises their spirits and inspires others to follow suit.

In conclusion, an organization's sustainability efforts can be greatly boosted by encouraging green initiatives through a range of incentives, including monetary advantages, recognition programs, and non-monetary benefits. These rewards encourage workers to embrace eco-friendly habits while also enhancing workplace morale, streamlining operations, and enhancing brand recognition. Through careful implementation and administration of these incentive schemes, companies can accomplish their sustainability objectives and cultivate a dedicated and enthusiastic workforce. Long-term advantages for the environment and the company result from this all-encompassing strategy for rewarding sustainable behaviour, which guarantees that sustainability becomes an essential component of the organization's identity and operations.

7.2.3 Examples of Successful Incentive Programs that Drive Employee Engagement in Sustainability Efforts

❖ Here are some examples of successful incentive programs that drive employee engagement in sustainability efforts in various organizations:

1. Sales force's Sustainability Cloud and Impact Labs:

Sales force, a prominent provider of customer relationship management software, has exhibited a robust dedication to sustainability by implementing programs like Impact Labs and Sustainability Cloud. With the aid of a carbon accounting tool called Sustainability Cloud, businesses can monitor, measure, and control their carbon emissions, enabling them to take better informed decisions that will lessen their environmental effect.

Sales force engages its own staff through Impact Labs, employee-led sustainability projects designed to promote positive environmental change within the organization, in addition to providing this cutting-edge technology to its clients. These initiatives span a wide range of topics, including sustainable sourcing and transportation methods, waste reduction, and energy efficiency. Sales force encourages a culture of creativity and cooperation while achieving real progress toward its sustainability objectives by giving workers the freedom to take charge of sustainability projects.

Employees who participate in Impact Labs are recognized and rewarded for their efforts; these could be in the form of cash bonuses, public recognition, or chances to progress in their careers. Employee involvement in sustainability initiatives is encouraged by this accolade, which also upholds Sales force's core principles of social responsibility and environmental care.

2. Unilever's Sustainable Living Plan:

The global consumer goods giant Unilever has launched its Sustainable Living Plan, a comprehensive sustainability initiative. Unilever's ambition to generate positive social effect through its operations and products and divorce growth from environmental impact is outlined in this ambitious endeavour. The Sustainable Living Plan places a strong emphasis on Unilever workers actively pushing sustainability changes throughout the organization.

The "One Minute Sustainability" campaign, which encourages staff members to submit brief but useful suggestions for sustainability enhancements that can be put into action in only one minute, is one illustration of Unilever's employee engagement initiatives. These suggestions address many different subjects, such as trash minimization, water efficiency, and energy saving. Workers who have their ideas chosen and put into action are acknowledged and given incentives, which could include bonuses, gift cards, or more paid time off.

Through ideation sessions with staff members across the board and employee recognition for their efforts, Unilever fosters a culture of innovation and ongoing sustainable improvement. Using a bottom-up approach not only helps employees come up with innovative solutions to environmental problems, but it also makes them feel proud of their role in helping Unilever achieve its sustainability goals.

3. Google's Green Team Network:

Renowned for its dedication to innovation and sustainability, Google has created a global network of Green Teams across its locations. These Green Teams are made up of enthusiastic employee volunteers who are committed to leading environmental projects in their local communities and workplaces. Google gives its employees the tools and assistance they need to transform their ideas into reality while also empowering them to take action on environmental concerns through the Green Team Network.

Principles of Green HRM

The programs run by Google's Green Teams are varied and effective; they include energy-saving competitions, waste reduction campaigns, volunteer events in the community, and educational workshops. Green Teams might, for instance, plan recycling campaigns, advocate for environmentally friendly car options, or invite speakers to discuss issues like climate change mitigation and renewable energy.

Employees who take part in Green Team events are acknowledged and rewarded by Google, which may include perks like team trips, certificates of appreciation, or opportunities for professional growth. Google promotes a culture of environmental stewardship and collective responsibility by acknowledging the contributions made by its employees to sustainability initiatives. This aligns with Google's overarching aim to positively impact the world.

4. Patagonia's Environmental Internship Program:

An employee internship program is available for Patagonia, an outdoor gear brand renowned for its dedication to environmental preservation. Through this initiative, employees can work on conservation and sustainability-related projects with environmental organizations during paid sabbaticals. Employees learn important skills and insights while meaningfully contributing to environmental problems through practical experience and immersion in environmental work.

In addition to helping participating employees, Patagonia's environmental internship program upholds the company's principles and objective of using commerce to further good deeds. Through its commitment to employee development and encouragement of their participation in sustainability initiatives, Patagonia fosters a culture of social responsibility and environmental stewardship among its workers.

5. IBM's Corporate Service Corps:

Teams of IBM personnel are deployed to work on projects in poor nations as part of the Corporate Service Corps program, which is managed by the multinational technology and consulting firm. These initiatives span many different fields, such as economic development, education, healthcare, and environmental sustainability. IBM employees can use the initiative to put their knowledge and experience to use in solving urgent social and environmental issues in local communities all over the world.

Employees who take part in the Corporate Service Corps not only get invaluable possibilities for professional growth and cross-cultural experiences, but they also get to positively touch the lives of others. The initiative strengthens IBM's commitment to corporate responsibility and sustainability while giving workers a feeling of purpose and pride through meaningful volunteer work that is in line with the company's values.

6. Interface's Mission Zero Employee Engagement Program:

Mission Zero, a bold sustainability strategy, aims to eradicate Interface's negative environmental effect by 2020. Interface is a global maker of modular carpet tiles. Interface has put in place a thorough employee engagement program that promotes involvement and creativity in sustainability activities in order to include staff members in accomplishing this challenging objective.

A component of Interface's employee engagement program is the establishment of "Green Teams" in each of its locations, whose job it is to find and implement sustainable changes. Additionally, staff members are invited to submit ideas for sustainable innovations via the company's "Idea Portal," where they can get input and encouragement from management and other staff members.

Interface encourages a culture of continuous development and collaboration in addition to recognizing and rewarding employees for their contributions to sustainability. This gives employees the freedom to take charge of sustainability initiatives and promote positive change within the organization. Interface's integration of sustainability into its corporate culture and its engagement of employees across all levels have allowed it to make substantial progress toward its Mission Zero targets and have served as an example for others in the industry.

These examples highlight the different ways that businesses can use the enthusiasm, ingenuity, and knowledge of their workforce to promote positive environmental change. They also show how companies across a range of industries have implemented incentive programs to involve employees in sustainability efforts.

7.3 Employees Wellness Programs with a Green Focus

In order to improve employee health and wellbeing, employee wellness programs have long been a pillar of business strategy. Typically, these programs encompass an array of activities like health exams, mental health counselling, exercise competitions, and dietary advice. But as people become more conscious of environmental issues, there's a growing movement to incorporate sustainability into these wellness programs, which is leading to the emergence of "green wellness programs."

Employees' physical and mental well-being are prioritized in green wellness initiatives, which also aim to encourage environmentally friendly behaviours. The interdependence of environmental health and human well-being is acknowledged by this dual-focus strategy. Businesses may foster an environment-conscious culture and promote the overall health of their employees by incorporating sustainability into wellness initiatives.

- **The Rationale Behind Green Wellness Programs**

In an effort to promote the health of both employees and the environment, green wellness programs include environmental sustainability into employee wellness activities. These programs have a complex rationale that includes cost savings, employee involvement, business responsibility, health benefits, and favourable public perception.

Here's an in-depth look at the reasons driving the adoption of green wellness programs:

1. Holistic Health Perspective

Environmental Impact on Health: The cornerstone of green wellness initiatives is the understanding of the substantial impact that environmental factors have on health. Chronic illnesses, stress, and respiratory disorders are just a few of the health problems that can be brought on by poor air quality, exposure to chemicals, and a lack of green spaces. Businesses can establish better work environments that promote their employees' general well-being by addressing these environmental determinants.

Integrated Wellness: Conventional wellness initiatives frequently concentrate on personal factors including diet, exercise, and mental well-being. Green wellness initiatives broaden this emphasis to encompass environmental health, realizing that maintaining employee health depends on a healthy environment. For instance, utilizing non-toxic materials and adding plants to improve indoor air quality can improve cognitive and physical health.

2. Corporate Social Responsibility (CSR)

Commitment to Sustainability: A lot of businesses have corporate social responsibility (CSR) objectives that highlight ethical and sustainable behaviour. These objectives are supported by incorporating environmental wellness into employee programs, which shows a company's dedication to improving both society and the environment. The company's reputation is improved and stakeholders are shown that it appreciates environmental stewardship and employee welfare.

Ethical Practices: Businesses that place a high priority on sustainability in their wellness initiatives demonstrate a deeper dedication to moral behaviour. This enhances their reputation while also being in line with the principles of investors and consumers who appreciate social responsibility.

3. Employee Engagement and Retention

Meeting Employee Expectations: The younger generation of employees in particular is becoming more aware about environmental issues and expects their employers to be proactive in promoting sustainability. These ideals are reflected in green wellness initiatives, which increase employee engagement and job satisfaction.

Enhanced Job Satisfaction: Employee pride and motivation to work for their organization are positively correlated with perceptions of social and environmental responsibility. Better performance overall, reduced attrition, and more productivity can result from this enhanced job satisfaction.

Attracting Top Talent: Strong green wellness initiatives help businesses draw in talent that is environmentally sensitive and values working for companies that share their values.

4. Cost Savings and Efficiency

Reduced Operational Costs: Putting sustainable methods into practice frequently results in large cost savings. Utility bills and operating costs can be decreased by using energy-efficient lighting, water conservation techniques, and trash reduction programs. The money saved can be used to fund more sustainability and wellness programs.

Resource Management: Reducing expenses and minimizing the environmental impact are two benefits of resource efficiency. Digital solutions, for instance, that cut down on paper use save money and protect the environment.

Long-Term Financial Benefits: While there could be up-front expenses involved in putting green wellness programs into place, over time, these can be offset by the savings on medical bills, decreased absenteeism, and greater productivity.

5. Positive Corporate Image
Reputation Building: Companies that put employee welfare and environmental sustainability first enhance their brand. This kind of reputation may draw in investors, strengthen partnerships with local authorities, and increase customer loyalty.

Market Differentiation: A company can set itself apart from the competition in a competitive market by demonstrating a strong commitment to green wellness initiatives and establishing itself as a pioneer in sustainability and corporate responsibility.

Media and Public Relations: Positive media coverage is frequently generated by sustainable practices and wellness initiatives, which further improves the company's reputation and public impression.

Conclusively, integrating a green perspective into employee wellness initiatives is a novel and significant strategy for promoting overall health and environmental sustainability. Companies may make significant contributions to the health of the world and cultivate a happier, healthier workforce by coordinating personal wellness programs with environmentally responsible operations. In addition to reflecting a contemporary conception of well-being, this strategy establishes businesses as pioneers in sustainability and corporate social responsibility.

Green wellness initiatives provide a strong way forward for companies as they continue to develop and adjust to the demands of the twenty-first century by showing how inextricably interwoven employee well-being and environmental health are. Businesses can make sure they are not only meeting the short-term requirements of their workers but also fostering a sustainable future for all by adopting an all-encompassing strategy.

7.3.1 Integrating Environmental Wellness Initiatives into Employee Well-being Programs

To establish a comprehensive approach to employee well-being, integrating environmental wellness initiatives into employee well-being programs entails fusing conventional health and wellness activities with eco-friendly methods. Employees and the environment both gain from this combination, which not only enhances personal health but also environmental sustainability. Businesses may foster an environment-conscious culture and promote the overall health of their employees by incorporating sustainability into wellness initiatives.

- **Key Elements of Green Wellness Programs**

1. Sustainable Transportation Solutions

One of the main components of green wellness initiatives is encouraging staff members to use sustainable transportation methods. Companies can support this by:

Offering Incentives: Offer rewards for carpooling, bike repair shops, and public transportation subsidies. This lowers traffic congestion and the carbon footprint of commuting while also encouraging physical activity.

Flexible Work Schedules: Reduce the amount of travel, especially during peak hours, by implementing remote work choices or flexible working hours. This can lessen the impact on the environment and help workers maintain a healthier work-life balance.

Infrastructure Support: Installing bike racks, showers, and changing spaces will make it more convenient to walk or ride a bike to work. Employee choice of sustainable and active commuting methods is encouraged by providing these services.

2. Healthy and Sustainable Work Environments

Creating a healthy work environment with sustainable practices can significantly improve employee well-being:

Green Buildings: Make use of sustainable building methods and environmentally friendly materials. To improve air quality and make your workspace more comfortable, add indoor plants, natural light, and adequate ventilation. Green buildings help protect the environment by using less water and energy.

Ergonomic Furniture: To enhance comfort and physical well-being, purchase office furniture that is ergonomic and made from sustainable materials. In addition to increasing worker productivity, ergonomic workstations can lower the risk of musculoskeletal problems.

3. Green Eating Initiatives

Promoting healthy eating habits while supporting environmental sustainability:

Sustainable Cafeterias: Incorporate locally sourced, organic food options into workplace cafeterias. By putting composting and portion control measures into place, food waste can be decreased. The environmental impact of food production and consumption can be reduced by the use of sustainable food practices.

Community Gardens: Encourage staff members to take part in community or corporate gardening initiatives to promote fresh vegetable access and strengthen ties to the natural world. Additionally, gardening helps lower stress and increase physical exercise.

4. Outdoor and Nature-Based Activities

Encouraging outdoor activities can improve physical and mental health while fostering an appreciation for nature:

Walking Meetings: Encourage walking meeting as a way to integrate exercise and productivity. Walking meetings might help people feel less stressed and more creative.

Green Spaces: Establish or maintain outdoor green areas for staff members to unwind, work out, or hold meetings. It has been demonstrated that having access to green areas improves mental health and lowers stress levels.

Volunteer Opportunities: To involve staff in sustainability initiatives, schedule voluntary environmental events that are funded by the company, such as tree planting or neighbourhood park cleanups. Volunteering can strengthen a person's sense of belonging and purpose.

5. Waste Reduction and Recycling Programs

Implementing robust waste reduction and recycling programs can make a significant environmental impact:

Comprehensive Recycling: Clearly marked recycling bins and easily accessible recycling guidelines should be provided. Inform staff members about recyclables to help cut down on contamination. Recycling initiatives that are successful can keep a sizable amount of waste out of landfills.

Reduce Single-Use Items: Promote the usage of reusable water bottles, utensils, and containers. As part of the initiative, give branded reusable products to the staff. The environmental footprint can be greatly reduced by reducing the use of single-use plastics.

Digital Solutions: Encourage digital communication and documentation to cut down on paper usage. Eliminating paper use can cut waste and preserve trees.

6. Green Wellness Challenges and Competitions

Incorporate fun and engaging activities to motivate employees:

Eco-Friendly Challenges: Create challenges that encourage environmentally friendly habits, including biking to work, cutting back on waste, and using less energy. Give out environmentally friendly awards to the winners. A healthy sense of rivalry and the promotion of enduring behaviours are two benefits of challenges.

Team Competitions: Organize friendly competitions amongst teams or departments to determine who can accomplish the greatest wellness or environmental goals. Team competitions can inspire cooperation and foster togetherness.

7. Education and Awareness

Educating employees about the importance of sustainability and how they can contribute:

Workshops and Seminars: Organize frequent seminars and workshops on subjects pertaining to human health and environmental sustainability. Professional speakers can motivate action and offer insightful commentary.

Regular Communication: Post advice, success stories, and updates on sustainability initiatives on bulletin boards, intranets, and newsletters. Employees remain focused on sustainability when there is constant communication.

8. Mental Health and Nature
Connecting mental health initiatives with environmental wellness:

Nature Therapy: Encourage the use of nature therapy approaches, such as nature-based relaxation methods or mindfulness walks in green areas. Stress levels might drop and mental health can improve with nature therapy.

Stress Reduction Programs: Programs for reducing stress should include elements of nature, such as calm spaces with lots of plants for meditation and relaxation. An atmosphere can be made peaceful by using natural ingredients.

To sum up, including environmental wellness programs into employee well-being initiatives is a progressive strategy for business sustainability and health. Businesses may cultivate a culture of holistic well-being, increase employee engagement, and contribute to a sustainable future by endorsing eco-friendly activities. This dual approach shows a thorough commitment to corporate social responsibility by ensuring long-term environmental sustainability in addition to supporting the immediate health advantages for employees.

7.3.2 Benefits of Promoting Green Lifestyles and Health-conscious Practices Among Employees

Encouragement and support of actions and decisions that place a high priority on individual well-being and environmental sustainability are key components of promoting green lifestyles and health-conscious habits among employees, both inside and beyond the workplace. This method seeks to foster a culture of holistic wellbeing and environmental consciousness by acknowledging the connection between human well-being and environmental health.

❖ Here's a detailed explanation of what this entails:

- **Green Lifestyles:**

1. Environmental Awareness: Teaching staff members about environmental concerns in order to increase their awareness of the significance of sustainable living practices, such as pollution, climate change, and resource depletion.

2. Sustainable Commuting: Encouraging staff members to use environmentally friendly modes of transportation, such as walking, bicycling, carpooling, or public transportation, in order to cut down on carbon emissions and increase physical activity.

3. Resource Conservation: Encouraging the economical use of energy, water, and paper resources by putting in place paperless workflows, energy-efficient appliances, and the practice of shutting off lights and electronics when not in use.

4. Waste Reduction: To reduce landfill trash and encourage a circular economy, recycling programs should be put into place, organic waste should be composted, and single-use plastics and packaging should be reduced.

5. Eco-Friendly Purchasing: Motivating staff members to select eco-friendly goods and services, like reusable water bottles, sustainably sourced office supplies, and ethically sourced products.

- **Health-Conscious Practices:**

1. Physical Activity: Encouraging frequent movement breaks and exercise during the workplace to enhance happiness, lower the risk of chronic illnesses like diabetes, heart disease, and obesity, and improve cardiovascular health.

2. Healthy Eating Habits: To promote general health and well-being, wholesome food options should be made available in office cafeterias and vending machines. Additionally, cooking lessons and nutrition instruction should be provided. Mindful eating should also be encouraged.

3. Stress Management: Providing mental health resources, mindfulness meditation classes, and stress reduction programs to staff members can help them become more resilient and manage stress, anxiety, and burnout.

4. Work-Life Balance: Promoting remote work choices, flexible work schedules, and time-off regulations to assist staff in striking a healthy balance between work and personal obligations.

5. Preventive Healthcare: Providing access to wellness examinations, yearly physicals, immunizations, and screenings as preventative healthcare measures to identify and stop health issues before they become serious.

- **Benefits of Promoting Green Lifestyles and Health-Conscious Practices Among Employees**

Encouraging employees to lead environmentally friendly and health-conscious lives has several advantages for the staff as well as the company. These advantages include better health results, increased worker involvement, less of an influence on the environment, financial savings, and a better reputation for the company.

❖ Here's a detailed and expanded look at the benefits:

1. Enhanced Physical Health
   i. **Reduced Exposure to Toxins:** There is a decrease in the amount of hazardous chemicals and pollutants that employees are exposed to when eco-friendly items are used and indoor air quality is improved. Reduced respiratory difficulties, allergies, and even chronic illnesses like asthma or chronic obstructive pulmonary disease (COPD) may result from this.
   ii. **Increased Physical Activity:** Physical activity is encouraged when active commuting options are promoted, such as biking or walking to work. Frequent exercise is linked to a lower risk of developing chronic illnesses like diabetes, heart disease, obesity, and some types of cancer. By offering amenities like showers, changing rooms, and bike racks, workplaces can encourage employees to use more health-conscious modes of transportation.

iii. **Healthier Eating Habits:** Employee eating habits can be improved by limiting processed food alternatives in the office cafeteria and increasing access to organic, locally sourced food. Nutrition workshops and cooking demos can promote healthy eating even further, which can help with weight management, energy levels, and the risk of diet-related illnesses.

iv. **Promoting Regular Health Screenings:** Regular health screenings can be incorporated into wellness programs to aid in the early diagnosis of health problems and to motivate staff to seek prompt medical attention and take proactive measures to maintain their health.

2. Improved Mental Health

i. **Stress Reduction:** Greenery, plants, and outdoor activities bring a sense of nature into the office, which lowers stress and enhances mental health. Having access to quiet areas, daylight, and outdoor views can help people unwind and think well.

ii. **Enhanced Mental Clarity:** Access to natural light and better indoor air quality can enhance mood, mental clarity, and cognitive performance. Workers that operate in areas with good lighting and ventilation are probably more concentrated, imaginative, and productive.

iii. **Mindfulness and Mental Wellness Programs:** Providing mindfulness and meditation training can improve mental health by assisting staff in managing stress and anxiety. These programs may consist of yoga classes, mindfulness seminars, and mental health resource access.

3. Increased Employee Engagement and Satisfaction

i. **Alignment with Personal Values:** Employees that value sustainability is more content and involved with their employers when they hold similar values. This alignment helps to create a sense of pride and purpose, lifts the spirits, and increases job satisfaction and loyalty.

ii. **Sense of Community:** Green activities can improve team dynamics and create a feeling of community among staff members. Examples of these include corporate gardening projects and volunteer environmental events. Engaging in these activities can foster a supportive work environment, improve teamwork, and foster friendship.

iii. **Employee Empowerment:** Including staff members in sustainability initiative decision-making processes empowers them and instils a sense of pride in them. This may result in a greater sense of drive and dedication to the organization's objectives.

4. Higher Productivity and Reduced Absenteeism

i. **Healthier Employees:** Employees who are in better physical and mental health are less likely to be absent from work due to illness. As a result, there are reduced absenteeism rates and a more dependable and effective team. Acute health problems and chronic illness incidence can be decreased with the use of wellness initiatives and preventive health measures.

ii. **Increased Energy and Focus:** Maintaining higher energy levels and improved concentration is made possible by health-conscious behaviours like frequent exercise and a balanced diet. Higher energy workers are more efficient, commit fewer mistakes, and perform better at their jobs.

iii. **Improved Work-Life Balance:** Work-life balance is supported and stress is decreased by flexible work arrangements including telecommuting and flexible scheduling. Workers who successfully manage their home and work life are more likely to be engaged and effective.

5. Environmental Impact

i. **Reduced Carbon Footprint:** Encouraging environmentally friendly transportation, cutting back on energy use, and eliminating waste all help to significantly lower the company's overall carbon footprint. Energy-efficient appliances, smart thermostats, and LED lighting are a few examples of energy-saving strategies that businesses can use to lessen their environmental effect.

ii. **Waste Reduction:** Lowering the quantity of waste dumped in landfills is made possible by extensive recycling systems and efforts to cut back on single-use plastics. By putting waste management techniques like composting and encouraging reusable things into practice, the workplace's environmental impact can be significantly decreased.

iii. **Resource Conservation:** Utilizing resources like electricity and water wisely not only helps the environment but also shows a company's dedication to sustainability. Resources are conserved and environmental health is promoted by energy-efficient systems, water-saving fixtures, and renewable energy sources.

iv. **Promotion of Sustainable Practices:** Companies can improve their environmental effect and encourage employees to embrace these habits in their personal life by encouraging practices like utilizing reusable water bottles, cutting back on paper consumption, and supporting sustainable suppliers.

6. Cost Savings

i. **Lower Healthcare Costs:** Generally speaking, healthier employees pay less for healthcare. Through wellness promotion and chronic disease prevention, businesses can lower their healthcare costs. Overall health cost savings are facilitated by wellness programs that incorporate exercise activities, health screenings, and preventative care measures.

ii. **Reduced Operational Expenses:** Operating expenses can be considerably reduced by implementing waste reduction strategies, energy-efficient techniques, and sustainable resource management. Consider the significant cost reductions that can be achieved by converting to LED lighting, putting energy-saving measures into place, and using less paper.

iii. **Increased Efficiency:** Sustainable approaches frequently result in waste reduction, improved operational efficiency overall, and more effective use of resources. Lean management approaches and process simplification can both increase productivity and cut expenses.

iv. **Incentives and Rebates:** Government grants, rebates, and incentives may also be advantageous to businesses that use green technologies and sustainable practices. These monetary gains have the potential to cover the costs of the original investment and motivate other sustainability projects.

7. Positive Corporate Image

i. **Enhanced Reputation:** Companies that actively support healthy and environmentally friendly activities are regarded as conscientious and progressive. This improved reputation can draw in partners, investors, and customers who care about the environment and society, which will support the expansion and sustainability of the company.

ii. **Attraction of Top Talent:** The organization attracts top talent more readily when it demonstrates a strong commitment to sustainability and employee well-being, especially from younger employees who place a high value on environmental responsibility. A more inventive, involved, and committed workforce may result from this.

iii. **Customer Loyalty:** Customers are picking more and more to support businesses that show a dedication to sustainability. Encouragement of eco-friendly living can increase client loyalty because consumers are more likely to support companies that share their beliefs.

iv. **Media and Public Relations:** Positive media coverage is frequently generated by sustainable practices and wellness efforts, which further improves the company's reputation and public impression. Being regarded as a pioneer in sustainability might set the business apart from competitors.

In summary, encouraging eco-friendly lives and health-conscious behaviours among staff members has many advantages that go beyond improving people's personal health. Improved productivity, greater employee engagement and happiness, and improved physical and mental health are all results of these approaches. They also have a favourable impact on a company's reputation, cost savings, and the environment.

Companies may demonstrate their commitment to environmental stewardship and corporate social responsibility while cultivating a more motivated, healthy, and productive staff by promoting a culture of sustainability and well-being. This all-encompassing strategy boosts the company's competitiveness and long-term profitability while also benefiting the workforce and establishing the business as a leader in sustainability.

Green measures combined with wellness programs will put companies in a better position to satisfy stakeholders, customers, and employees as environmental awareness rises. A better, more sustainable future for all is ensured by this dual focus on sustainability and health, which helps employees immediately and promotes long-term environmental sustainability.

7.3.3 Best Practices for Developing and Implementing Employee Wellness Programs with a Green Focus to Enhance Overall Organizational Sustainability

To create a work environment that prioritizes employee health and well-being while minimizing the organization's ecological footprint, "best practices for developing and implementing employee wellness programs with a green focus to enhance overall organizational sustainability" involve strategically integrating wellness initiatives with environmental sustainability efforts. By recognizing the connections between environmental health, corporate success, and person well-being, this strategy seeks to promote holistic sustainability in all areas of operations.

Creating and executing green-focused employee wellness programs is a strategic endeavour that needs to be carefully planned, carried out, and continuously assessed. Organizations can cultivate a culture of holistic well-being, lessen their environmental impact, and show their commitment to corporate social responsibility by incorporating environmental sustainability into wellness initiatives.

- ❖ Here's an expanded guide with additional best practices for creating impactful programs:

1. Conduct a Comprehensive Needs Assessment:

Holistic Evaluation: In addition to surveys, hold focus groups, interviews, and workshops to acquire a range of viewpoints regarding the requirements and preferences related to sustainability and well-being.

Environmental Impact Analysis: A full assessment of the organization's environmental impact should be conducted by professionals, going beyond simple audits. Analysing carbon footprints and performing life cycle evaluations may be part of this.

2. Establish Clear and Ambitious Objectives:

Strategic Alignment: Make sure the organization's long-term sustainability goals, mission, and values are in line with the wellness and sustainability objectives.

Benchmarking: Examine industry best practices and establish challenging but attainable goals to enhance environmental performance and worker well-being.

3. Design Tailored Wellness Programs:

Customization: Provide a range of health programs and events to meet the requirements, interests, and preferences of your diverse workforce. This could include gardening clubs, mindfulness exercises, fitness competitions, and volunteer opportunities in the environment.

Personalization: Utilize data analytics and technology to tailor wellness suggestions and programs to each person's unique health profile, preferences, and behavioural patterns.

4. Foster Active Participation and Engagement:

Gamification: Use gamification features like leader boards, badges, and awards to encourage involvement, promote healthy competition, and maintain interest.

Social Support Networks: Establish virtual communities, peer assistance organizations, and networks of wellness advocates to promote responsibility, knowledge exchange, and peer-to-peer support.

5. Provide Comprehensive Resources and Support:

Accessible Resources: Make sure staff members can easily access tools, resources, and information about wellness via a variety of channels, including as mobile apps, intranet portals, and digital platforms.

Expert Guidance: Make health coaches, dieticians, exercise instructors, and sustainability specialists available for individualized counselling, advice, and assistance.

6. Cultivate a Culture of Wellness and Sustainability:

Leadership Role Modelling: Urge senior leaders to take an active role in wellness initiatives, exhibit environmentally conscious conduct, and convey the significance of sustainability and well-being.

Empowerment and Autonomy: Enable staff members to take charge of their sustainability and well-being initiatives by giving them the freedom to make their own decisions and the tools they need to put their ideas into action.

7. Measure, Evaluate, and Iterate:

Comprehensive Metrics: Keep track of a wide range of data pertaining to participation rates, health outcomes for employees, environmental performance indicators, and organizational goals including retention and productivity.

Continuous Improvement: To pinpoint achievements, difficulties, and opportunities for development, evaluate programs on a regular basis. You can also do this by collecting participant input and reviewing statistics. Over time, make use of findings to improve and tweak program offerings.

8. Recognize and Reward Excellence:

Incentive Programs: Establish incentive programs, recognition events, and reward systems to recognize and celebrate both individual and group accomplishments in sustainability and well-being.

Non-Monetary Recognition: Provide in-kind incentives like badges, certificates, and public acknowledgement in company newsletters, intranet articles, and social media posts.

9. Foster Collaboration and Partnerships:

Cross-Functional Collaboration: To take use of different knowledge, resources, and viewpoints, break down departmental silos and promote cooperation throughout teams, departments, and business units.

External Partnerships: To increase the scope and impact of the program, establish strategic alliances with other parties such as wellness canters, sustainability advisors, neighbourhood associations, and environmental non-governmental organizations.

10. Promote Long-Term Sustainability:

Integration with Organizational Strategy: Integrate sustainability and wellness programs within the organization's governance frameworks, performance management systems, and strategic planning procedures.

Continuous Learning and Innovation: Foster an environment that values inquiry, trial and error, and creativity by offering chances for continuous education, instruction, and career advancement about health and environmental issues.

Organizations can create and implement green-focused employee wellness programs that benefit people and the environment by adhering to these extensive best practices. These initiatives support corporate social responsibility and overall organizational sustainability in addition to enhancing worker productivity, engagement, and health. In order to succeed over the long run and maintain resilience in a world that is changing quickly, organizations must engage in holistic wellness programs with a green focus as they become more aware of the connections between human well-being and environmental health.

7.3.4 Examples of Companies That Have Successfully Integrated Environmental Sustainability into Their Employee Wellness Programs

Green-focused employee wellness initiatives support sustainable practices that benefit the environment as well as employees' health and well-being.

- ❖ Here are some examples of companies that have successfully integrated environmental sustainability into their employee wellness programs:

1. Johnson & Johnson's Live for Life Program:

One of the main focuses of Johnson & Johnson's "Live for Life" campaign is sustainability and environmental health. Through activities like encouraging walking or biking to work, taking part in neighbourhood clean-up events, and volunteering for the environment on behalf of the company, the program encourages employees to adopt healthier lifestyles. Additionally, Johnson & Johnson provides organic and locally sourced food in their green cafeterias, further highlighting the link between environmental sustainability and individual wellness.

2. Google's Healthy Materials Program:

Google's approach to sustainability and well-being includes the Healthy Materials Program. The program's main objective is to create healthier work environments by guaranteeing that office supplies and furniture are acquired responsibly and are free of dangerous chemicals. For the purpose of enhancing indoor air quality and worker wellbeing, Google offers standing workstations, ergonomic furniture, and indoor plants. Furthermore, by providing incentives like bike repair shops and discounted transit passes, the corporation encourages environmentally friendly modes of transportation including riding a bike to work and taking public transportation.

3. Patagonia's Environmental Internship and Wellness Initiatives:

Patagonia integrates environmental sustainability with employee well-being with programs like its Environmental Internship Program, which permits staff members to take paid time off to work on environmental projects. By encouraging staff members to take part in outdoor sports and spend time in nature, the company also encourages physical exercise and outdoor involvement. Environmental education initiatives are part of Patagonia's on-site child care, helping to instil a sustainable mindset in young children.

4. Adobe's Green Commute and Wellness Programs:

Adobe encourages green commuting as a way to incorporate sustainability into its wellness initiatives. For workers who bike, carpool, or take public transportation to work, the corporation provides rewards. Additionally,

Adobe encourages the usage of electric bikes and offers charging facilities for electric vehicles. Encouraging dietary selections, wellness challenges, and on-site workout canters frequently integrate environmental stewardship themes like cutting back on waste or energy use in daily operations.

5. Aetna's Sustainable Health and Wellness Program:

Initiatives that connect environmental health and personal health are part of Aetna's wellness program. The organization provides rewards to staff members who take part in environmentally friendly events and activities, like recycling competitions, tree planting occasions, and community garden initiatives. In order to lessen the impact of commuting on the environment, Aetna also encourages telecommuting and flexible work hours. Their wellness initiatives frequently incorporate a sustainability component, motivating staff members to lessen their carbon impact while enhancing their well-being.

6. SAS Institute's Green Wellness Program:

The analytics leader SAS Institute offers a holistic health program that includes sustainability. The organization uses green construction ideas in the design of its fitness canter and on-site health care canter. On its campus, SAS has created green areas and trails to promote outdoor recreation. The company provides organic and locally sourced food in its cafeterias, further encouraging sustainable and healthful eating. Workers are urged to take part in voluntary work and educational initiatives that link environmental responsibility with personal well-being.

These examples show how companies can successfully incorporate eco-friendly efforts into their employee wellness programs, resulting in a comprehensive strategy that is advantageous to the environment and employees alike. These initiatives support the development of a culture of environmental stewardship and individual accountability by endorsing sustainable habits in addition to health and wellness.

Chapter – 8
Employee Engagement in Sustainability

Introduction to Employee Engagement in Sustainability:
The concept of employee engagement in sustainability is multidimensional and dynamic, encompassing the dedication and participation of employees in environmental and sustainable practices inside an enterprise. This strategy tries to match workers' efforts with the organization's overall sustainability goals in addition to fostering a stronger bond between workers and their work. Including employees in sustainability projects has become essential to corporate strategy as companies realize more and more how important it is for long-term success.

Meaning of Employee Engagement in Sustainability:
What is meant by employee engagement in sustainability? Basically, it's the level of knowledge, motivation, and active participation that employees have in the company's attempts to lessen its environmental impact. This can include everything from straightforward efforts like recycling and energy conservation to more intricate ones like developing novel sustainable goods and procedures. Employees that are devoted to making good changes that support the company's sustainability plan are aware of how their actions affect the environment.

Engaging employees in sustainability is a potent tactic that advances both corporate success and environmental objectives. Companies may recruit top talent, increase employee satisfaction, boost operational efficiency, and improve their reputation by cultivating a sustainable culture. In the end, attaining significant and long-lasting sustainability results that are advantageous to the company and the environment depends on having engaged people.

The implementation of environmental and sustainable practices inside a business requires employees to be actively involved, motivated, and dedicated. This is achieved through a complete and integrated approach to employee engagement in sustainability. This strategy is necessary to build a business culture that prioritizes environmental responsibility and to meet long-term sustainability goals.

❖ Here is an expanded explanation of the key elements of employee engagement in sustainability, providing a detailed look at each aspect and its importance.

1. Awareness and Education

Making sure that staff members are knowledgeable about sustainability concerns and the company's unique sustainability objectives is a fundamental component of encouraging employee engagement in sustainability. Workshops, seminars, and online courses are examples of educational initiatives that can give staff members a thorough awareness of environmental issues and the significance of sustainable practices. With this knowledge, staff members may make well-informed decisions and make a significant contribution to sustainability initiatives. For instance, training programs on energy-saving methods or the advantages of recycling can assist staff in comprehending how their actions affect the environment and the sustainability goals of the company.

2. Communication

Maintaining sustainability at the forefront of employees' minds requires effective communication. Communicating sustainability initiatives, progress reports, and success stories on a regular basis should take place via a variety of media, including meetings, newsletters, and internal communication platforms. In addition to keeping workers informed, this openness highlights how crucial sustainability is to the success of the company. Sharing quarterly sustainability reports, for example, that highlight accomplishments and potential improvement areas can inspire staff members by demonstrating the observable outcomes of their hard work.

3. Motivation and Incentives

Acknowledging and rewarding staff members for their sustainability-related achievements can greatly increase engagement and motivation. Formal recognition initiatives, such sustainability awards, incentives, and open recognition at business meetings, can help achieve this. Furthermore, offering incentives such as additional vacation days, gift cards, or chances for professional growth can motivate staff members to embrace and advance sustainable methods. Companies can cultivate a culture that values and encourages environmental stewardship by recognizing sustainability champions within the firm.

4. Participation and Involvement

Employee involvement in sustainability projects should be promoted and provided with opportunities. This entails not just doing small-scale things like recycling and energy conservation, but also bigger-scale things like joining sustainability committees, volunteering at environmental events, or spearheading green projects. For instance, staff members can design and carry out a recycling program for the entire company or take part in clean-up campaigns in the neighbourhood. Engaging employees in active involvement cultivates a sense of ownership and responsibility as well as a connection to the company's sustainability aims.

5. Leadership and Support

Establishing a culture of environmental responsibility requires a strong commitment from the leadership to sustainability. Employers are better served and the significance of these programs is emphasized when corporate executives actively support and engage in sustainability initiatives. By taking part in sustainability-related activities, integrating sustainability into corporate plans, and openly supporting sustainability objectives, leaders can show their dedication to the cause. For example, a CEO who consistently updates staff members on the company's sustainability accomplishments and future goals may motivate them to coordinate their efforts with the environmental goals of the company.

6. Integration into Corporate Culture

Sustainability needs to be included into the organization's mission, fundamental values, and daily operations in order to genuinely engage personnel. This entails matching sustainability goals with job descriptions, business rules, operational procedures, and performance measures. For instance, including sustainability standards into promotions and performance reviews helps encourage staff members to give environmental stewardship top priority at work. Furthermore, including sustainability into the mission and strategic goals of the business can assist guarantee that sustainability is an essential component of the company's operations and identity.

7. Empowerment and Ownership

Providing employees with the necessary tools to take charge and make a positive impact on sustainability goals is crucial to developing a sense of accountability and ownership. Giving employees the freedom to decide, offer suggestions for enhancements, and adopt sustainable practices in their areas of responsibility can help achieve this. Employees can be empowered to effect significant change by setting up task forces or green teams with the authority to plan and carry out sustainability projects. Giving employees access to the tools, resources, and technologies they require to succeed is another aspect of empowerment.

8. Collaborative Efforts

Collaboration between many teams and departments is frequently necessary for sustainability initiatives. Promoting collaboration and interdisciplinary projects can help sustainability initiatives become more effective by bringing a variety of viewpoints and expertise to the table. A task force on sustainability, comprising representatives from marketing, operations, and human resources, has the capacity to formulate all-encompassing approaches that tackle many facets of the company's ecological footprint. As employees cooperate to achieve shared sustainability goals, collaborative activities can also cultivate a sense of community and shared purpose.

9. Measurement and Feedback

To keep employees engaged and motivated, it's critical to measure the results of sustainability projects and give them regular feedback. This entails establishing quantifiable, explicit sustainability targets and using key performance indicators (KPIs) to monitor advancement. Employees can better recognize the fruits of their labour and identify areas for development by receiving regular feedback and progress reports. For example, a business can offer monthly or quarterly reports that emphasize accomplishments and areas for development, and use dashboards to display energy usage, waste reduction, and other sustainability measures.

10. Continuous Improvement

Since the subject of sustainability is constantly changing, staying ahead of new opportunities and challenges requires constant progress. Employees should be encouraged by their organizations to keep up to date on the latest developments in sustainability trends, technology, and best practices. They should also be willing to modify and enhance their methods as necessary. This may entail giving continuing education, going to trade shows, and encouraging an innovative and experimental culture. For example, a business can set up a fund for sustainability innovation to assist staff-led initiatives testing novel concepts and technological advancements meant to enhance environmental performance.

Finally, it should be noted that employee engagement in sustainability is a complex process that calls for a thorough plan that includes leadership, cooperation, empowerment, education, communication, motivation, participation, measurement, and ongoing development. Organizations can effectively involve employees in sustainability initiatives, cultivate an environmentally conscious culture, and guarantee that sustainability objectives are incorporated into all facets of the company by concentrating on five essential components.

Employees that are engaged are more likely to promote innovation, increase productivity, and contribute to the overall success of the company in addition to helping to meet sustainability standards. Including employees in these initiatives is crucial for building a sustainable future for the company and the environment in a world where sustainability is becoming more and more critical for long-term commercial success. Businesses may leverage their combined capacity to significantly improve social and environmental results by enabling and inspiring employees to actively engage in sustainability projects.

8.1 Engaging Employees in Environmental Initiatives

Participating employees in environmental efforts is a strategic method that firms have chosen to leverage the workforce's collective strength in order to achieve sustainability goals. This idea, at its core, focuses on actively engaging employees in initiatives to reduce environmental impact, promote eco-friendly behaviours, and cultivate an environment-conscious culture at work. It focuses on making employees feel a feeling of ownership, responsibility, and dedication to environmental sustainability rather than just following environmental standards.

Encouraging participation and involvement in diverse sustainability activities is a crucial element of involving employees in environmental projects. This can take the form of straightforward activities like recycling and energy conservation or more involved projects like promoting environmental laws or putting green technologies into practice. Employers may harness their workforce's power to effect real change and contribute to environmental sustainability by encouraging employees to get involved in these initiatives.

Engaging employees in environmental efforts is mostly dependent on education and awareness campaigns. Giving employees the information and insight they need to make educated decisions and take proactive efforts toward sustainability is essential. Employees learn about the value of environmental preservation and the part they may play in furthering sustainability initiatives through training programs, workshops, and educational resources.

Encouragement of employees to participate in environmental activities also requires leadership backing and role modelling. Employees are strongly informed about the organization's beliefs and priorities when company executives openly show their support and dedication to sustainability projects. Executives and managers can encourage employees to adopt sustainable work practices and incorporate them into their regular workdays by setting a positive example for them.

Getting employees involved in environmental efforts requires giving them a sense of empowerment and ownership. A sense of pride, ownership, and accountability is fostered in employees when they are given the freedom and resources to implement creative solutions, are recognized for their achievements, and are empowered to take ownership of sustainability projects. Employees are more likely to support environmental sustainability and promote positive change within the company when they have a feeling of ownership.

Promoting environmental efforts among employees also requires effective communication and openness. Organizations keep employees informed about sustainability goals, efforts, and accomplishments by maintaining open and transparent communication channels. Employees are more likely to feel engaged in and committed to the organization's sustainability initiatives when they receive regular updates, feedback channels, and dialogue opportunities.

Employee participation in environmental efforts is also significantly influenced by rewards and recognition. Employees are encouraged to continue their efforts when they are formally recognized for their contributions to sustainability through official recognition programs, incentives, and prizes. This also serves to emphasize the significance of environmental stewardship as a fundamental company principle.

Overall, cultivating a culture of sustainability where each employee feels empowered, motivated, and committed to making a positive difference for the planet is more important than just implementing green policies or acquiring eco-friendly technologies when it comes to engaging employees in environmental initiatives. Aside from achieving environmental goals, companies that actively involve their employees in sustainability initiatives also boost employee morale, spur innovation, and fortify their competitive edge in a world where environmental consciousness is growing.

8.1.1 Importance of Engaging Employees in Environmental Initiatives for Organizational Sustainability

Engaging employees in environmental activities is essential to an organization's long-term performance and sustainability in a variety of industries. Businesses can use the combined strength of their workforce to address urgent environmental issues and gain a number of advantages for their operations, employees, and stakeholders by involving employees in initiatives to lessen environmental impact and promote sustainable practices.

❖ Here are the detailed benefits of engaging employees in environmental initiatives for organizational sustainability:

1. Enhanced Environmental Impact:

Collective Action: Organizations can harness the different perspectives, talents, and contributions of their workforce to achieve shared sustainability goals through employee engagement in environmental programs. Employees are crucial in promoting positive environmental change within the company, whether it be through introducing eco-friendly practices, cutting back on waste production, or putting energy-saving measures into place.

Innovative Solutions: Employees who are actively involved in sustainability initiatives frequently come up with creative ideas and methods for dealing with environmental problems. When given the freedom to share their knowledge and ideas, staff members can come up with creative solutions for sustainable operations, pollution avoidance, and resource conservation, which will lead to ongoing improvements in environmental performance.

Cultural Shift: Organizations can cultivate a culture of environmental care and responsibility by including their employees. Businesses can encourage a shared commitment to environmental conservation among employees at all levels by integrating sustainability ideas into the fabric of the corporate culture. This will encourage sustainable behaviours and practices both within and outside of the workplace.

2. Improved Organizational Performance:

Operational Efficiency: Employee engagement-driven environmental efforts frequently lead to increased operational efficiency and cost savings. Organizations can lessen their environmental impact while also increasing productivity, streamlining procedures, and boosting market competitiveness by optimizing resource utilization, minimizing waste, and implementing sustainable technologies.

Risk Management: Organizations can detect and reduce environmental hazards and vulnerabilities by engaging employees in environmental efforts. Businesses can protect their operations and long-term sustainability by adopting a proactive approach to environmental management, which enables them to better predict and solve potential environmental dangers, regulatory compliance challenges, and reputational threats.

Brand Reputation: An organization's market positioning and brand reputation can be improved by a strong commitment to environmental sustainability, which is made possible through employee engagement. Businesses may increase brand loyalty, draw in new business, and stand out in the market by exhibiting environmental leadership and responsibility. They can also establish trust and credibility with investors, customers, and other stakeholders.

3. Boosted Employee Morale and Job Satisfaction:

Sense of Purpose: Employees gain a sense of purpose and fulfilment by participating in environmental efforts. Employees experience a higher sense of job satisfaction and fulfilment when their professional responsibilities are in line with larger sustainability objectives.

Team Cohesion: Employees develop a sense of camaraderie, teamwork, and shared commitment through collaborative participation in environmental efforts. As a result of their shared commitment to sustainability, employees forge closer ties, show each other more respect, and feel more satisfaction in their accomplishments as a group. This boosts morale and team cohesion inside the company.

Professional Development: Participating in environmental programs provides employees with learning, development, and skill-building opportunities. Employees who participate in sustainability projects acquire important skills, knowledge, and experience in fields like renewable energy, environmental management, and sustainable business practices. These skills can help them grow professionally and open up new career opportunities within the company.

4. Talent Attraction and Retention:

Competitive Advantage: A strong approach to environmental sustainability in employee engagement can be an effective means of attracting and retaining talent. Organizations must actively involve employees in environmental initiatives to attract and retain top talent. In today's competitive job market, environmentally conscious candidates are increasingly looking for employers who demonstrate a genuine commitment to sustainability and social responsibility.

Employee Loyalty: A sense of devotion, pride, and loyalty to the company is fostered by getting employees involved in environmental projects. Over time, businesses can improve employee retention by fostering a strong sense of loyalty and belonging among their workforce. This can be achieved by recognizing employees' contributions, allowing them to participate in meaningful sustainability projects, and involving them in decision-making processes.

5. Compliance and Risk Mitigation:

Regulatory Compliance: Participating in environmental projects with employees contributes to the maintenance of environmental laws, rules, and standards. Organizations can protect their operations and reputations by fostering a culture of environmental responsibility and knowledge, which reduces the likelihood of non-compliance penalties, legal liabilities, and regulatory sanctions.

Resilience and Adaptability: Resilience and adaptability to environmental changes and disturbances are improved when employees are actively involved in environmental activities. Businesses may better resist shocks, crises, and uncertainties as well as efficiently negotiate changing regulatory requirements, market demands, and stakeholder expectations in a world that is changing quickly by developing internal capacity, expertise, and preparedness for environmental problems.

6. Stakeholder Engagement and Collaboration:

Customer Expectations: Companies may meet and surpass consumer expectations for sustainable goods, services, and corporate operations by engaging employees in environmental projects. Businesses can improve consumer relations and loyalty by enlisting employees in initiatives to improve product eco-friendliness, lessen environmental effect throughout the supply chain, and address customer concerns about sustainability.

Supplier Relations: Suppliers and business partners can also participate in environmental efforts through employee engagement. Organizations can establish a more sustainable supply chain ecosystem that improves resilience, encourages innovation, and reduces supply chain risks by working with suppliers to implement sustainable sourcing practices, lower emissions, and promote responsible production.

7. Innovation and Creativity:

Employee-driven Innovation: Engaging employees in environmental projects encourages a creative and innovative culture within the company. Organizations may seize new chances for sustainable growth, product creation, and market differentiation, as well as drive continuous improvement and competitive advantage, by enabling employees to investigate and apply creative solutions to environmental concerns.

Cross-functional Collaboration: Employees from many departments and disciplines can collaborate cross-functionally and share information through environmental projects. Organizations may encourage interdisciplinary cooperation, innovative problem-solving, and the co-creation of sustainable solutions that address complex environmental issues holistically by bringing together varied perspectives, experience, and skills.

8. Corporate Social Responsibility (CSR) and Reputation:

Community Impact: Organizations can improve the communities in which they operate by engaging employees in environmental projects. Through encouraging staff participation, community involvement, and environmental conservation-focused charity endeavours, firms can bolster local sustainability initiatives, foster goodwill, and improve their social license to operate.

Stakeholder Trust and Transparency: The organization's dedication to corporate social responsibility (CSR) and transparency is demonstrated by employee engagement in environmental efforts. Organizations can establish long-term relationships with customers, investors, and the community by proactively involving employees in decision-making processes, seeking their feedback on sustainability strategies, and being transparent with stakeholders regarding environmental performance. These actions foster trust and credibility.

9. Regulatory Compliance and Risk Management:

Legal Obligations: Engaging employees in environmental projects contributes to ensuring adherence to ever-stricter environmental laws and guidelines. Organizations can reduce their exposure to regulatory violations, fines, and penalties that could negatively affect their operations and reputation by raising employee awareness of legal requirements, offering training on environmental policies and procedures, and encouraging staff to report potential compliance issues.

Environmental Due Diligence: The organization's capacity to recognize, evaluate, and manage environmental risks and obligations is improved by employee engagement in environmental projects. Organizations can proactively address environmental issues, implement preventive measures, and reduce any harmful consequences on human health, safety, and the environment by undertaking frequent environmental audits, risk assessments, and impact evaluations with employee involvement.

10. Long-term Value Creation and Resilience:

Strategic Alignment: Engaging employees in environmental activities ensures that sustainability objectives and the company's overall strategy are in line. Organizations may generate innovation, build resilience to social, economic, and environmental challenges, and create long-term value by incorporating environmental issues into their strategic planning, decision-making procedures, and performance measures.

Future-proofing: Employee engagement in environmental activities aids in future-proofing the company against new environmental trends and issues. Organizations can position themselves for sustainable growth and success in a world that is changing quickly by cultivating a culture of environmental awareness, adaptability, and resilience. This allows them to anticipate and respond to changing regulatory requirements, market dynamics, and stakeholder expectations.

To sum up, in today's more complicated and linked world, involving staff members in environmental projects is critical to building organizational sustainability, resilience, and success. Businesses can ensure a prosperous and sustainable future for future generations by enabling employees to become proactive change agents. This approach can also improve operational performance, attract and retain top talent, boost employee morale and job satisfaction, and mitigate environmental risks and liabilities.

8.1.2 Strategies for Involving Employees in Green Projects

The terms "strategies for involving employees in green projects" refer to deliberate methods that firms use to actively involve their staff in environmental sustainability initiatives. Examples of these methods include volunteer programs, idea development, and task forces. These tactics seek to leverage staff members' combined expertise, dedication, and knowledge to promote good environmental change both inside and beyond the company. Through the promotion of involvement, creativity, and teamwork, these tactics enable staff members to support environmental projects and make a substantial impact on the advancement of environmental sustainability objectives.

❖ Here's a more comprehensive explanation with additional details:

1. Volunteer Programs:

Diverse Opportunities: Provide a broad variety of volunteer activities to meet the interests and skill levels of your workforce. Putting together beach clean-ups, park restoration initiatives, or volunteer work at local environmental organizations, for instance, enables staff members to select pursuits that directly speak to them, boosting motivation and engagement.

Flexible Scheduling: Recognize that workers have different schedules and obligations outside of the workplace. Offer possibilities for volunteering on the weekends, in the evenings, or virtually for people who are unable to engage in person to give volunteers flexibility. This guarantees diversity and optimizes involvement throughout the labour force.

Recognition and Appreciation: Establish a comprehensive recognition program to acknowledge staff members who donate their time and energy to environmentally friendly projects. This can involve showcasing their contributions in internal communication channels, social media posts, and company newsletters. Additionally, to publicly acknowledge their commitment and influence, think about planning thank-you parties or award ceremonies.

2. Community Partnerships and Outreach:

Local Collaborations: Join forces with local associations, educational institutions, and environmental organizations to collaborate on sustainable projects. Through these community ties, staff members can volunteer, impart knowledge, and gain insights.

Public Awareness Campaigns: Encourage employees to participate or lead public awareness efforts about sustainability. This not only puts the organization in the forefront of environmental campaigning, but it also increases awareness among the community.

3. Idea Generation:

Open Channels for Communication: Provide employees with a free and open platform to express their thoughts and recommendations for green projects. Assist in cultivating an inclusive and transparent culture by providing employees with a means to anonymously or publicly make suggestions and ideas through online forums, suggestion boxes, or dedicated email addresses.

Idea Generation Workshops: Organize thought-provoking meetings or interactive workshops with a special emphasis on environmental sustainability. Encourage participation from employees from different departments and backgrounds, as this frequently results in creative ideas. Assist in guiding discussions and documenting insightful ideas and insights developed throughout the meetings by assigning facilitators or moderators.

Incentives for Innovation: Provide incentives to employees to encourage their creative ideas that advance environmental projects. This could involve incentives like cash bonuses, additional vacation time, or chances for career advancement. Employees whose suggestions are put into action and help the company achieve its environmental goals should be honoured.

4. Task Forces and Working Groups:

Cross-functional Collaboration: Create working groups or cross-functional task forces devoted to particular green initiatives or projects. To promote cooperation and guarantee all-encompassing approaches to problem-solving, make sure that representatives from all departments, seniority levels, and fields of expertise are included. A task force tasked with cutting down on office waste, for instance, might have members from the procurement, facilities management, and employee engagement departments.

Clear Objectives and Responsibilities: Establish precise goals, deadlines, and objectives for every task force or working group to guarantee that they are in line with the overarching corporate sustainability goals. Clearly define each member's tasks and responsibilities, including deliverables, deadlines, and reporting procedures. Throughout the course of a project, maintaining attention and accountability is facilitated by clarity.

Regular Progress Updates: Arrange frequent check-ins or meetings to discuss issues, give updates on the status of the project, and get input from the task force members. These gatherings provide a forum for sharing best practices, talking about achievements, and cooperatively identifying areas that need work. Promote open dialogue and a welcoming environment where members can freely share their thoughts and worries.

5. Corporate Social Responsibility (CSR) Integration:

CSR Programs: Make sure that environmental measures are in line with social and community objectives by incorporating sustainability projects into larger CSR programs. This all-encompassing strategy highlights how crucial sustainability is to the overall goal of the business.

Employee Involvement in CSR Planning: Involve employees in the conception and implementation of CSR initiatives. Their knowledge and practical expertise can lead to more significant and successful environmental initiatives.

6. Training and Development:

Sustainability Training: Provide extensive training and development courses with an emphasis on sustainability in the environment.

Workshops, seminars, or online courses on subjects like waste management, renewable energy, and sustainable supply chain methods may fall under this category. Employees can effectively contribute to green projects and initiatives if given the knowledge and skills they require.

Leadership Development: Invest in leadership development courses that have a strong emphasis on sustainability and environmental care. Provide opportunities for mentorship, coaching, and practical experience leading green projects to up-and-coming leaders in the organization who have a passion for environmental concerns. A culture of accountability and ownership is fostered for sustainability when employees are given the opportunity to assume leadership roles.

Continuous Learning: Encourage a culture of ongoing education and information exchange about environmental sustainability. Make platforms that employees may use to access webinars, articles, publications, and other instructional materials supporting continuous learning and development on themes linked to sustainability. In order to stay up to date on new trends and best practices in environmental sustainability, encourage involvement in peer-to-peer learning opportunities, industry conferences, and networking events.

7. Integration into Core Business Practices:

Sustainable Procurement Policies: Adopt sustainable policies for procurement that give priority to sustainable goods and services. Provide employees a voice in the creation and implementation of these policies to guarantee compliance.

Green Office Certification: Aim for LEED or other green office certifications, and actively involve your employees in the process of reaching and upholding these standards. Encourage employees to offer suggestions for improving the sustainability of their workstations.

8. Communication and Recognition:

Transparent Communication: Openly discuss green ideas and projects, as well as how they affect the environment and the company. Keep employees informed about progress, accomplishments, and impending chances for involvement by providing regular updates through company-wide meetings, newsletters, or intranet portals. In addition to fostering a sense of shared accountability and ownership for environmental sustainability, transparency also creates trust.

Recognition and Rewards: To honour employees' efforts to environmental projects and activities, implement a strong recognition and incentives program. Recognition and reward both individual and group accomplishments with certificates, prizes, or rewards that emphasize their commitment and influence on environmental sustainability. To further emphasize the company's dedication to environmental stewardship, think about adding sustainability measures to performance reviews and award standards.

Celebrate Successes: Celebrate accomplishments and milestones made possible by eco-friendly initiatives to strengthen the company's environmental sustainability culture. To honour accomplishments and acknowledge the teamwork of employees, throw themed parties, team outings, or recognition activities. Disseminating testimonies and success stories encourages others to get involved in green projects and increases the positive effects of employee involvement.

9. Mentorship and Peer Support:

Mentorship Programs: Create initiatives for employees who are enthusiastic about sustainability to mentor other employees. Assisting employees with less experience with more seasoned sustainability advocates promotes higher engagement in sustainability activities, information transfer, and skill development.

Peer Support Networks: For employees working on sustainability projects, establish buddy systems or peer support networks. These networks can help employees communicate problems and solutions pertaining to their green projects by providing direction, inspiration, and a feeling of community.

10. Employee Engagement Platforms:

Digital Engagement Tools: Engage employees in sustainability initiatives by using digital channels. Apps, intranet sites, and online communities are a few examples of tools that can help with idea sharing, measuring progress, and recognizing green initiatives.

Gamification: Add gamification components, such leaderboards, challenges, and badges, to sustainability projects. More employees will participate as a result of how enjoyable and interesting it is made.

11. Sustainability in Performance Metrics:

Incorporate Sustainability into KPIs: Incorporate sustainability measures into performance evaluations and key performance indicators (KPIs). This reaffirms the significance of environmental stewardship and harmonizes individual aspirations with corporate sustainability goals.

Annual Sustainability Reports: Publish yearly sustainability reports that showcase the business's environmental accomplishments and acknowledge staff members' contributions. Accountability and trust are increased by transparent reporting.

Employers can effectively engage employees in environmentally friendly projects and activities by putting these strategies into practice, which will promote a collaborative, innovative, and environmentally conscious culture. Driving sustainable practices and initiatives is a critical function of engaged employees, who also positively impact the environment and the performance of the firm.

8.1.3 Case Studies Highlighting Successful Employee Engagement in Sustainability Initiatives

❖ Here are a few case studies showcasing successful employee engagement in sustainability initiatives:

Case Study: Cisco's Green Team Program

Introduction:
The global technology company Cisco Systems is dedicated to environmental responsibility and sustainability. Cisco created the Green Team Program to leverage the workforce's combined strength to achieve sustainability objectives.

Background:
Cisco started the Green Team Program in 2006 as a part of their efforts to promote corporate sustainability. The program aims to create a corporate

social responsibility and environmental stewardship culture by including employees from all areas of the company in sustainability activities.

Formation of Green Teams:
Dedicated employees from different departments and offices across the globe made up Cisco's Green Teams. These teams were given the authority to spearhead sustainability programs that catered to the specific needs and goals of their local communities within their designated regions.

Goals and Objectives:
The principal goal of the Green Team Program was to mitigate Cisco's environmental impact while advocating for sustainable practices both on the inside and outside the company. Specific objectives included:

- Enhancing operational and facility energy efficiency.
- Cutting back on waste production and raising recycling rates.
- Encouraging environmentally friendly modes of transportation and commuter habits.
- Raising staff involvement and awareness of sustainability projects.

Implementation of Initiatives:
Green Teams spearheaded a wide range of sustainability initiatives, including:

- Energy-saving techniques like power management, HVAC optimization, and lighting enhancements.
- Programs for reducing waste, such as those for recycling, composting, and disposing of electronic trash.
- Encouragement of environmentally friendly modes of transportation such as public transportation, biking, and carpooling.
- Workshops, seminars, and educational initiatives are used to encourage sustainable behaviour and increase awareness among employees.

Measurement and Evaluation:
Cisco created measurements and key performance indicators (KPIs) to monitor the advancement of sustainability objectives. Green Teams gathered information on energy use, trash diversion, transportation emissions, and employee involvement levels in order to periodically review and assess the results of their activities.

Recognition and Rewards:
Cisco recognized and celebrated the achievements of Green Team members through various channels, including:

- Programs and awards that honour exceptional achievements to sustainability.
- Newsletters, intranet features, and internal communications that highlight effective projects and best practices.
- Incentives for outstanding achievement in sustainability initiatives, such as gift cards, bonuses, or additional paid time off.

Results and Impact:
Cisco's Green Team Program has had a good influence and produced notable outcomes over the years, including:

- Decreases in energy use and greenhouse gas emissions achieved by investments in renewable energy sources and efficiency upgrades.
- Higher recycling rates and trash diversion from landfills, which support the ideas of the circular economy.
- Increased morale and staff engagement, with a strong sense of pride in contributing to sustainability efforts and broad participation in them.

Conclusion:
The Green Team Program at Cisco is an excellent example of how employee involvement can propel sustainability efforts inside a major company. Cisco has established a corporate citizenship and environmental responsibility culture that is consistent with its beliefs and objectives by

giving employees the freedom to take charge of sustainability initiatives and by giving them the tools and assistance they need to be successful.

Cisco is a leader in environmental stewardship and fostering positive change in the community and inside the organization via innovative teamwork, collaborative efforts, and a shared commitment to sustainability.

Case Study: Nike's Sustainable Innovation Teams

Introduction:
Nike, a leader in athletic footwear and gear worldwide, has proven that it is strongly committed to environmental responsibility and sustainability. Through its Sustainable Innovation Teams, Nike has been effective in including its employees in sustainability activities.

Background:
As part of their sustainability strategy, Nike created Sustainable Innovation Teams to address environmental issues and promote innovation in product design and production procedures.

Formation of Sustainable Innovation Teams:
Nike assembled employees from a variety of areas, including design, engineering, manufacturing, and sustainability, to form cross-functional Sustainable Innovation Teams.

Goals and Objectives:
The main goal of the Sustainable Innovation Teams is to include sustainability concepts into the processes of product development and production. Specific objectives include:

- Utilizing eco-friendly materials and production processes in Nike's product lines.
- Minimizing the effects on the environment at every stage of the product lifecycle, from sourcing to disposal.
- Promoting innovation in environmentally friendly manufacturing and design processes.

Implementation of Initiatives:
Teams dedicated to sustainable innovation work together to create and carry out projects that advance sustainability objectives, such as:

- Investigating and testing eco-friendly materials, such as plant-based substitutes, recycled polyester, and organic cotton.
- Creating goods with less of an impact on the environment, such sturdy, lightweight shoes made of recycled materials.
- Putting in place environmentally beneficial production techniques, like waste reduction and waterless dyeing.

Measurement and Evaluation:
Nike use life cycle assessment (LCA) methodologies and key performance indicators (KPIs) to examine the environmental effect of its Sustainable Innovation programs.

- Metrics like carbon footprint, water use, trash production, and material efficiency are examples of KPIs.
- From the extraction of raw materials until the disposal of an object at the end of its useful life, life cycle assessments (LCA) evaluate how operations and products affect the environment.

Recognition and Rewards:
Nike recognizes and rewards employees who demonstrate leadership and innovation in sustainability through various channels, including:

- Internal honours and awards that recognize exceptional achievements to sustainable innovation.
- Opportunities for professional growth and career progress in areas related to sustainability.
- Incentives like extra training, bonuses, or events dedicated to recognizing great performance.

Results and Impact:
Nike's Sustainable Innovation Teams have had a beneficial influence and produced noteworthy accomplishments, including:

- Creation of cutting-edge goods with improved functionality and a smaller environmental effect.
- Decreases in water use, waste production, and carbon emissions over the whole supply chain.
- Improvement of consumer confidence and brand reputation through the provision of sustainable products and open environmental reporting.

Conclusion:
Nike's Sustainable Innovation Teams are prime examples of how to successfully involve employees in sustainability efforts by fostering creativity, impact, and teamwork inside the company. Nike not only achieves its environmental goals but also cultivates a culture of sustainability and innovation that is consistent with its fundamental values and mission by enabling employees to incorporate sustainability into product development and production processes. Nike stays at the forefront of sustainable innovation in the sportswear sector, promoting good change for the environment and future generations, thanks to their unwavering commitment and partnership.

Case Study: IBM's Sustainability Ambassadors Program

Introduction:
IBM is a multinational technology and consulting firm that has a long history of environmental responsibility and sustainability. The Sustainability Ambassadors Program is a prime example of IBM's effectiveness in involving its employees in sustainability initiatives.

Background:
As part of its corporate social responsibility initiatives, IBM introduced the Sustainability Ambassadors Program in response to the growing significance of sustainability.

Formation of Sustainability Ambassadors:
As Sustainability Ambassadors, IBM chose employees from a variety of departments and areas. These brand ambassadors were fervent supporters of the company's sustainability initiatives.

Goals and Objectives:
The main goal of the Sustainability Ambassadors Program was to encourage a sustainable culture and provide employees the tools they need to have a good environmental effect. Specific objectives included:

- Increasing IBM employees' knowledge of sustainability-related concerns and best practices.
- Encouraging staff participation in projects and initiatives related to sustainability.
- Integrating sustainable principles into IBM buildings and operations.

Implementation of Initiatives:
Sustainability Ambassadors led various initiatives to promote sustainability within IBM, such as:

- Planning training sessions, seminars, and workshops with an emphasis on sustainability.
- Putting in place recycling programs, trash reduction plans, and energy-saving techniques.
- Encouraging the use of sustainable procurement methods and ethical supply chain management.

Measurement and Evaluation:
IBM employed sustainability-related metrics and key performance indicators (KPIs) to assess the Sustainability Ambassadors Program's effectiveness.

- Metrics including energy savings, trash diversion, carbon emissions reductions, and staff engagement levels were included in the KPIs.
- Regular tracking and evaluation of metrics was done to determine areas for improvement and gauge the degree of progress made toward sustainability goals.

Recognition and Rewards:
IBM recognized and rewarded Sustainability Ambassadors for their contributions and achievements through various channels, including:

- Internal honours and awards for exceptional work on sustainability.
- Opportunities for professional growth and promotion in roles pertaining to sustainability.
- Incentives like extra training, bonuses, or events dedicated to recognizing great performance.

Results and Impact:
The Sustainability Ambassadors Program has had a favourable impact and produced notable results, including:
- Increased participation and awareness of environmental activities among IBM employees.
- Reductions in carbon emissions, waste production, and energy use throughout IBM's activities.
- Improvement of IBM's standing as a pioneer in social responsibility and business sustainability.

Conclusion:
The IBM Sustainability Ambassadors Program serves as an example of how employee involvement may propel sustainability initiatives inside of major corporations. IBM has established a culture of environmental responsibility and corporate citizenship that is consistent with its values and objectives by enabling employees to act as ambassadors for sustainability and by giving them the tools and assistance they require to be successful. IBM is a leader in environmental stewardship and generating positive change for the earth and future generations via collaborative teamwork and leadership commitment.

Case Study: Google's Green Team Program

Introduction:
The global technological giant Google has made sustainability a top priority and a fundamental part of its corporate culture. The Green Team Program at Google is an example of how well the company has included its employees in environmental initiatives.

Background:

As part of its dedication to corporate social responsibility and environmental sustainability, Google established the Green Team Program. The program's goal is to provide employees the tools they need to address sustainability concerns in their communities and places of employment.

Formation of Green Teams:

Passionate employees from different divisions and offices throughout the world came together to form Google's Green Teams. The teams were assigned the responsibility of spearheading sustainability campaigns and encouraging environmentally conscious behaviours in their specific fields.

Goals and Objectives:

The Green Team Program's main goals were to lessen Google's ecological impact and encourage sustainable behaviour among its employees. Specific objectives included:

- Putting in place recycling programs, trash reduction plans, and energy-saving techniques.
- Encouraging environmentally friendly modes of transportation and commuter habits.
- Educating employees about environmental issues and promoting sustainable practices.

Implementation of Initiatives:

Green Teams implemented a variety of sustainability initiatives tailored to their local needs and priorities, such as:

- Putting up workshops, awareness campaigns, and eco-friendly events.
- Implementing zero-waste initiatives into action and offering office composting programs.
- Promoting the use of renewable energy sources and energy-saving techniques.

Measurement and Evaluation:

Google used measurements and key performance indicators (KPIs) linked to sustainability outcomes to assess the Green Team Program's impact.

- KPIs included measures including employee engagement, carbon emissions reductions, trash diversion rates, and energy savings.
- To determine areas for improvement and gauge progress towards sustainability goals, metrics were monitored and assessed on a regular basis.

Recognition and Rewards:

Google recognized and rewarded Green Team members for their contributions and achievements through various channels, including:

- Honours and awards given internally to recognize exceptional work toward sustainability.
- Opportunities for professional growth and promotion in roles pertaining to sustainability.
- Incentives like extra training, bonuses, or events dedicated to recognizing great performance.

Results and Impact:

The Green Team Program has delivered significant results and positive impact, including:

- Reductions in Google's overall energy use, waste production, and carbon emissions.
- Increased participation and awareness of sustainability activities among employees.
- Improvement of Google's standing as a pioneer in social responsibility and corporate sustainability.

Conclusion:

The effectiveness of employee participation in spearheading sustainability measures within a large corporation is exemplified by Google's Green Team Program. Google has established a culture of environmental responsibility and corporate citizenship that is consistent with its values and objectives by enabling employees to become advocates for sustainability and by giving them the tools and support they need to be successful. Google continues to set an example for environmental stewardship and drives good change for the earth and future generations via cooperative effort and leadership commitment.

8.2 Building Employee Advocates for Sustainability

Developing a staff that is ardently dedicated to encouraging environmental stewardship and bringing about good change both inside and outside the company is essential to creating employee advocates for sustainability. It includes a diverse strategy meant to inform, involve, empower, and honour staff members who make significant contributions to sustainability initiatives. Fundamentally, creating employee advocates for sustainability means giving staff members a feeling of pride, accountability, and enthusiasm for sustainability, enabling them to act as change agents for the environment in the workplace and in their local communities.

The first step towards creating employee advocates for sustainability is education. For employees to be knowledgeable about sustainability issues like pollution, resource depletion, and climate change, organizations must offer extensive training and educational programs. Employees can have a greater understanding of the necessity to act and have a good influence by being more aware of the environmental issues that the world is currently facing and the significance of sustainable practices.

Building employee advocates for sustainability also entails encouraging an engaged and participatory culture within the company. It is important to motivate staff members to actively participate in projects, ideas, and solutions that advance sustainability in their day-to-day operations. Mechanisms like employee forums, suggestion initiatives, and cross-functional teams devoted to sustainability can help achieve this. Through employee participation in decision-making procedures and providing them with a voice in developing sustainability plans, firms may leverage their workforce's creativity, knowledge, and enthusiasm to effect significant change.

Establishing employee advocates for sustainability also requires empowerment. Workers should be given the tools, encouragement, and power to carry out sustainable projects and activities in an efficient manner. In addition to fostering an innovative, risk-taking, and experimental culture within the company, this may entail giving sustainability projects access to finance, resources, and training. Employees are more likely to become fervent supporters of environmental sustainability when they feel empowered to take responsibility for sustainability initiatives and make a real difference.

Building employee advocates for sustainability requires rewards and recognition. Employee contributions that exhibit leadership, inventiveness, and a dedication to sustainability should be acknowledged and celebrated by organizations. This can be accomplished by showcasing excellent sustainability initiatives and results through internal awards, recognition, and incentives. Organizations can inspire people to take up the cause of driving environmental change by recognizing and rewarding employee advocacy for sustainability. This not only encourages individuals to keep up their efforts but also serves as an example for others.

Establishing employee advocates for sustainability requires strong leadership backing. Executives and leaders in organizations must show a strong commitment to sustainability and offer projects in this area clear direction, counsel, and support. Encouraging employees to prioritize sustainability and set a good example for others to follow conveys to them the organization's commitment to environmental stewardship and creating a positive effect. Leadership support, in the form of resource allocation, goal-setting, and the establishment of accountability systems for sustainability, also contributes to the creation of an environment that is conducive to employee advocacy.

Moreover, cultivating a culture of continual improvement is necessary to create employee advocates for sustainability. Regularly assessing the success of sustainability programs, getting employee input, and modifying plans to take advantage of new possibilities and challenges are all important for organizations to do. Organizations may guarantee that sustainability initiatives stay pertinent, significant, and responsive to evolving environmental circumstances and stakeholder expectations by cultivating a culture of learning, adaptation, and innovation.

Ultimately, cultivating employee advocates for sustainability requires community participation. By encouraging employees to participate in volunteer work, community-based initiatives, and relationships with nearby groups, employers can help staff members take their sustainability efforts outside the office. Employees that have a positive influence on the larger community not only support social responsibility and environmental preservation, but they also feel more fulfilled and purposeful in their work as sustainability advocates.

To sum up, building employee advocates for sustainability is a comprehensive and diverse process that entails educating, enlisting, empowering, and rewarding people that are enthusiastic about environmental stewardship. Organizations can unlock the potential of their workforce to promote good change and build a more sustainable future for everybody by cultivating a culture of sustainability, leadership commitment, continuous improvement, and community engagement.

8.2.1 Fostering a Culture of Sustainability Advocacy Among Employees

Organizations that are dedicated to environmental responsibility and positive social impact must cultivate an environment where employees at all levels embrace sustainability as part of their core values, practices, and behaviours. This is known as fostering a culture of sustainability advocacy among employees.

❖ **Here's how organizations can foster such a culture:**

1. Leadership Commitment:
- ➤ Senior executives and managers should show a strong commitment to sustainability by taking an active part in initiatives, establishing definite targets, and providing funding to assist sustainability activities.
- ➤ Make sure that sustainability goals are incorporated into the organization's overarching mission and vision by including sustainability into the strategic planning and goal-setting procedures.

➤ Set a good example for others to follow by modelling sustainable habits and highlighting the significance of sustainability for both long-term corporate performance and societal well-being through your choices, actions, and communications.

2. Education and Awareness:

➤ Offer thorough education and training programs on sustainability-related concerns and practices. These should include a wide range of subjects, including resource conservation, climate change, sustainable company operations, and individual sustainability initiatives.

➤ To ensure widespread comprehension and participation, provide online tools, seminars, and workshops that are open to all employees, regardless of their position or level within the company.

➤ Give employees the knowledge and resources they need to address environmental issues both inside and outside of the workplace by educating and empowering them about sustainability.

3. Employee Engagement:

➤ Encourage employees to actively participate in sustainability efforts and decision-making processes by offering them the chance to join cross-functional sustainability teams, employee resource groups, and volunteer programs that promote social responsibility and environmental conservation.

➤ Encourage employees to share their thoughts, ideas, and feedback on sustainability projects. This will help to increase employee ownership and empowerment and ensure that efforts are in line with employee objectives and values.

➤ Give employees a chance to demonstrate their initiative and leadership in promoting sustainability, honouring and celebrating their achievements to bringing about positive change both inside the company and beyond.

4. Recognition and Rewards:

➤ Create official recognition programs and awards to honour employees that lead and innovate in the advocacy for sustainability, recognizing their accomplishments and contributions to the organization's sustainability objectives.

- Encourage other employees to follow in the footsteps of their more sustainable colleagues by publicly recognizing and celebrating outstanding sustainability achievements through internal newsletters, company-wide communications channels, and recognition events.
- To acknowledge and encourage desired behaviours and accomplishments in sustainability advocacy, provide concrete prizes and incentives, such as bonuses, more paid time off, or chances for professional development.

5. Integration into Performance Management:
- Make sure that sustainability advocacy is represented in performance expectations and acknowledged as a crucial part of work responsibilities by incorporating sustainability goals and indicators into staff performance assessments and goal-setting procedures.
- Organize sustainability targets and efforts to match individual performance objectives. This will help employees understand how their contributions to sustainability support the organization's overall mission and strategic aims.
- Create systems for measuring and observing the advancement of sustainability objectives, and offer employees regular feedback and encouragement to assist them succeed in their sustainability advocacy work.

6. Transparent Communication:
- Encourage open lines of communication to discuss sustainability goals, developments, and difficulties. This will offer up chances for discussion and cooperation between various organizational divisions and levels.
- To ensure that information is clear, understandable, and pertinent to all employees, provide regular updates, newsletters, and town hall meetings regarding sustainability-related activities, accomplishments, and possibilities for involvement.

Principles of Green HRM

- Encourage employees to share ideas, ask questions, and offer feedback on sustainability activities in order to foster innovation and continual progress in the sustainability advocacy field. This will help to establish a culture of transparency and accountability.

7. Continuous Improvement:

- Encourage employees to look for ways to improve and innovate their sustainability initiatives by fostering a culture of continual improvement in your advocacy efforts for sustainability.

- To pinpoint opportunities for development and investigate fresh ideas and tactics for achieving sustainability objectives, solicit feedback from employees, stakeholders, and outside partners.

- Encourage employees to experiment, take calculated chances, and look for novel solutions to challenging sustainability problems by fostering an environment where learning comes from both triumphs and failures.

8. Community Engagement:

- Encourage employees to take their sustainability activism outside of the office by participating in volunteer work, community service projects, and alliances with local organizations.

- Encourage staff members to take part in environmental preservation initiatives, community clean-up days, and educational initiatives that encourage sustainability awareness and action. This will improve relationships with the community and increase the influence and scope of sustainability advocacy campaigns.

- Emphasize the benefits of employees' community engagement initiatives and recognize their contributions to changing the world to instil a feeling of pride and purpose in them.

9. Training and Development Opportunities:

- Give employees the chance to learn new skills, expand their comprehension of sustainability principles, and keep current on sustainability best practices and emerging trends through regular training and development opportunities.

- Provide employees with opportunities to learn about sustainability through conferences, webinars, workshops, and certification programs that are relevant to their positions and interests. This will foster their professional development in the field of sustainability advocacy.

10. Cross-Functional Collaboration:
- Encourage cooperation and information exchange between various organizational departments and functional areas to take use of a range of viewpoints, levels of experience, and available resources to further sustainability objectives.
- To foster innovation and increase impact, encourage cross-functional teams to collaborate on sustainability projects by assembling people with complementary backgrounds and expertise.

11. Supplier and Partner Engagement:
- Promote sustainable practices all the way down the supply chain by interacting with vendors, suppliers, and business partners to expand the organization's sustainability advocacy.
- Establish sustainability standards, put environmental management systems in place, monitor progress toward common sustainability goals, and work with partners and suppliers to create a culture of shared accountability and responsibility.

12. Sustainability Reporting and Transparency:
- To inform stakeholders-employees, clients, investors, and the general public-about the organization's sustainability performance, goals, and efforts, publish yearly sustainability reports or corporate social responsibility (CSR) disclosures.
- Allow employees to track progress, observe trends, and participate in data-driven decision-making in sustainability advocacy activities by providing them with access to sustainability data and analytics.

13. Employee Resource Groups (ERGs):
- For employees to connect, work together, and effect change on particular sustainability subjects or challenges, create affinity groups or employee resource groups (ERGs) with a sustainability focus.
- Employees are empowered to lead grassroots efforts and create significant impact within the organization by providing resources, financing, and leadership direction to support ERGs' activities and ideas.

14. Green Office Initiatives:
- Encourage employees to adopt sustainable behaviours and lessen their influence on the environment by implementing eco-friendly workplace practices and green office initiatives.
- To foster a more environmentally conscious workplace culture, support programs like waste reduction efforts, energy efficiency improvements, eco-friendly office design, and sustainable buying techniques.

15. Long-Term Strategic Planning:
- Make sure that sustainability goals and objectives are in line with the organization's overarching vision, mission, and values by including sustainability issues into long-term strategic planning procedures.
- Establish realistic yet challenging sustainability goals and deadlines. Then, periodically assess the progress made toward these objectives to maintain responsibility and promote ongoing sustainability performance enhancement.

Organizations may empower their workforce to drive positive change, encourage environmental stewardship, and build a more sustainable future for future generations by concentrating on five important areas and increasing efforts to cultivate a culture of sustainability advocacy among employees.

8.2.2 Empowering Employees to Become Ambassadors for Sustainable Practices within and Outside the Organization

Giving employees the encouragement, tools, and chances, they need to promote environmental stewardship both inside and outside the company can help them become ambassadors for sustainable practices both inside and beyond the company. This entails educating and training employees on sustainability-related issues, establishing a culture of leadership and innovation, acknowledging and rewarding their achievements, facilitating communication and engagement, and promoting active involvement in community activities. Organizations may generate positive change, promote sustainable practices, and contribute to a more environmentally conscious society by enabling their employees to advocate for sustainability. This allows organizations to utilize their influence and expertise.

Providing employees with the tools they need to become advocates for sustainable practices both inside and outside the company is crucial to bringing about significant change and encouraging environmental stewardship on a larger scale.

❖ Here's how organizations can empower employees to take on this role:

1. Education and Training:
- Offer employees extensive education and training programs so they can acquire the skills and knowledge necessary to comprehend sustainability issues, tenets, and best practices.
- Educate people on issues including climate change, resource conservation, renewable energy, waste reduction, and sustainable business practices through workshops, seminars, and online courses.

2. Leadership Support:
- Encourage a culture of support inside the company where senior leaders embrace sustainability and incorporate it into strategic decision-making.
- Empower Enable managers and supervisors to set a good example for their teams and encourage sustainable practices, emphasizing

the role that sustainability plays in accomplishing corporate objectives.

3. Resource Allocation:
- Give employees the tools, technology, and assistance they need to successfully implement sustainable practices by allocating resources, money, and support for employee-led sustainability initiatives.
- Establish specialized budgets or grant programs to support employee-driven sustainability projects and initiatives, promoting creativity and innovation in the search for long-term solutions.

4. Recognition and Rewards:
- Employees who show initiative and leadership in advancing sustainable practices inside the company should be honoured and recognized.
- Establish official recognition programs, prizes, and rewards to honor employees' achievements to sustainability, both on an individual level and in groups or departments.

5. Communication and Engagement:
- Encourage employees to communicate with you openly and honestly about sustainability projects, developments, and difficulties.
- Encourage communication and cooperation by holding town hall meetings, employee forums, and feedback channels to get opinions, thoughts, and proposals on issues pertaining to sustainability.

6. Training Programs:
- To enable employees to effectively advocate sustainable practices across their teams and departments, provide training programs and materials to assist them enhance their communication and advocacy skills.

- Provide training in storytelling, public speaking, and persuasive communication techniques so that employees can convince others to take action and communicate the benefits of sustainability.

7. Networking Opportunities:
- Provide employees with networking opportunities to engage with like-minded people and organizations that are engaged in sustainability projects.
- Encourage employees to attend sustainability-focused industry conferences, seminars, and networking events to increase their expertise, exchange best practices, and forge connections with outside stakeholders.

8. Community Engagement:
- Encourage employees to volunteer for community projects and initiatives connected to sustainability, such as tree planting, environmental cleanups, or educational programs.
- Provide employees with the resources and encouragement they require to engage with local communities, schools, and charities in order to raise awareness of and inspire action for sustainability outside of the workplace.

9. Continuous Learning and Improvement:
- Encourage an environment where employees are always learning and developing by giving them regular chances to increase their sustainability-related knowledge and expertise.
- Provide employees with access to tools like webinars, industry magazines, and online courses in order to keep them up to date on the latest developments in sustainability trends, technology, and best practices.

10. Role Modelling and Mentorship:
- Encourage employees with a strong commitment to sustainability to mentor and role model for their colleagues, sharing their views, knowledge, and experiences.

➤ Give employees a platform to share their sustainability initiatives and success stories in order to encourage others to take the lead and implement sustainable practices in their own personal and professional life.

Organizations may use their collective influence and advocacy to drive positive change, encourage environmental stewardship, and contribute to a more sustainable future for everybody by enabling employees to become ambassadors for sustainable practices both inside and beyond the firm.

8.2.3 Examples of Companies That Have Effectively Built a Network of Employee Advocates for Sustainability

Several organizations have effectively built networks of employee advocates for sustainability, leveraging their workforce to drive meaningful change and promote environmental stewardship. Here are a few examples:

1. H&M:
Primarily focused on becoming climate positive by 2030, H&M has made sustainability a central component of its business plan. Through programs like the "H&M Conscious Ambassador Program," the corporation encourages employees to advocate for sustainability. Employees who are designated as Conscious Ambassadors receive unique training and materials to share with their peers and clients about recycling, responsible consumption, and sustainable fashion practices.

2. BASF:
Leading chemical giant BASF has incorporated sustainability into both its business strategy and corporate culture. Through initiatives like the "BASF Sustainability Ambassadors Network," the corporation gives its employees the tools they need to become sustainability advocates. In order to encourage sustainability within their departments, teams, and local communities and to raise awareness and action on environmental concerns, ambassadors are provided with training and materials.

3. Patagonia:

Patagonia is well known for its dedication to social responsibility and environmental sustainability. The "Patagonia Employee Activism Fund," which offers financial assistance to employees who are involved in environmental activism, is one program that the corporation uses to promote employee participation. Employees are given the tools they need to make a difference both inside and outside of the office through Patagonia's internship and volunteer programs in the environmental field.

4. Unilever:

The "Unilever Sustainable Living Plan" is one of many initiatives that Unilever has put in place to encourage its employees to advocate for sustainability. In order to meet these ambitious sustainability targets, the company's operations will be held to a high standard, and employees will be encouraged to offer ideas and initiatives. In order to help employees become more knowledgeable about sustainability concerns and promote good change in their teams and communities, Unilever also offers training and development opportunities.

5. Interface, Inc.:

A global producer of modular carpet tiles, Interface, Inc. has a long history of sustainability, which is embodied in its goal to become a "restorative enterprise." By 2020, the corporation wants to have no environmental impact thanks to its "Mission Zero" campaign. Through initiatives like "Green Teams" and "Sustainability Ambassadors," Interface actively engages employees in sustainability activities and gives them the tools they need to spearhead sustainability projects both inside their departments and in the community.

6. Sales force:

Sales force is dedicated to social impact and sustainability, and it has ingrained these values into its corporate culture through programs like "Earth force" and the "Sales force 1-1-1 Model." Earth force is a sustainability program spearheaded by Sales force employees, involving them in community clean-up events, energy saving, and recycling initiatives. In order to promote a culture of sustainability advocacy, the company also offers paid time off to its employees for volunteering for environmental causes.

7. Microsoft:
Microsoft has made great progress toward sustainability, establishing challenging targets to become water positive and carbon neutral by 2030. The corporation uses programs like "Microsoft Green Teams" and "AI for Earth," which provide staff members the tools to use technology to come up with creative solutions to environmental problems, to get employees involved in sustainability activism. For employees who want to incorporate sustainable practices into their daily work, Microsoft also offers materials and training on sustainability.

8. Adobe:
Adobe has prioritized sustainability throughout all aspects of the business, with a goal of becoming carbon neutral by 2025. Through programs like the "Adobe Green Team Network," the corporation engages its employees in sustainability advocacy. Green Teams, made up of zealous employees, oversee sustainability programs in their workplaces and local communities, encouraging environmentally responsible behaviour and fostering good change.

These businesses show how creating networks of advocates for sustainability among employees can encourage environmental stewardship, spur positive change, and lead to a more sustainable future. Organizations can leverage the power of their workforce to address urgent environmental concerns and build a more resilient and vibrant planet by enabling employees to become ambassadors for sustainability.

8.3 Employee Participation in CSR Activities

The active involvement of employees in projects that advance social justice, environmental sustainability, and community development is referred to as employee participation in Corporate Social Responsibility (CSR) activities. This involvement can take many different forms: from giving time and money to spearheading initiatives and promoting business practices that promote environmental and social objectives. The underlying premise of the concept is that companies have an obligation to improve society in addition to being profit-driven organizations. Companies may develop a culture of social responsibility, boost morale among staff members, and improve their standing as ethical businesses by getting their staff involved in CSR initiatives.

Support from the top level and strong leadership are essential for encouraging employee involvement in CSR initiatives. Senior managers and executives create a great example for the rest of the company when they actively support and take part in CSR projects. The dedication of the company's leadership to CSR shows that these initiatives are essential to the organization's goals and principles rather than merely ancillary. A top-down culture of responsibility and participation can be established by leaders who actively participate in CSR initiatives, since this can encourage and inspire staff members to do the same.

One of the most important things that can be done to encourage employee participation in CSR is to implement structured programs and initiatives. Employees can be encouraged to take part in community service projects by designating designated volunteer days at their workplace. Removing obstacles and facilitating employee involvement can be achieved by providing paid time off for voluntary work. Long-term CSR projects also give employees the opportunity to participate gradually, which encourages a sense of continuity and ownership in their work. To guarantee that these initiatives have an impact and are interesting to employees, they should be well-structured, with distinct objectives and roles.

To meet the many interests and skill sets of the workforce, there must be a wide range of engagement options. Employees can select CSR projects that personally connect with them by choosing from a variety of options, including community service, environmental conservation, pro bono work, and educational outreach. Encouraging diversity and inclusivity are also critical; all employees, especially remote workers and those with disabilities, should have access to CSR opportunities. This can include initiatives that accommodate a range of physical abilities or virtual volunteering opportunities to make sure that everyone has the opportunity to participate.

Providing staff with the authority to spearhead their own CSR projects is another successful tactic. Promoting employee initiative and proposal writing encourages creativity and a sense of ownership. Employers ought to encourage these employee-led projects by contributing funds, space, and marketing help, among other essentials. In addition to increasing employee engagement, this empowerment also sparks creative and varied CSR initiatives that may have a big impact.

Employee participation in CSR can be recognized and rewarded, which can encourage greater engagement. Through internal newsletters, social media, and recognition events, it is possible to regularly recognize and honour employee contributions to CSR programs. Giving rewards like prizes, bonuses, or more time off can boost engagement even further and emphasize how important social responsibility is to the business.

Further ingraining CSR initiatives into the corporate culture can be achieved by including them into goal-setting procedures and performance indicators. Setting personal CSR goals as part of annual objectives and incorporating CSR contributions into performance reviews help employees link their ambitions with the company's larger social responsibility mission. This strategy holds employees responsible for their contributions to CSR initiatives in addition to emphasizing the significance of CSR.

Employees can be given the knowledge and abilities necessary to participate successfully through CSR-focused training and development programs. Providing online classes, workshops, and seminars on subjects like social justice, environmental sustainability, and community development can spur employees' interest and enable them to take significant action. A new generation of executives dedicated to social responsibility can also be cultivated through leadership development programs that prioritize corporate social responsibility (CSR).

Keeping employees informed and participating in CSR efforts requires effective communication and engagement. Keeping staff informed about CSR objectives, actions, and results through intranet updates, newsletters, and company-wide meetings promotes open and honest communication. Creating avenues for employee feedback, including suggestion boxes and surveys, gives workers a sense of being heard when it comes to the development and implementation of corporate social responsibility programs.

Collaborations with local organizations, educational institutions, and nonprofits can boost the effectiveness of CSR initiatives and offer priceless resources and knowledge. Through these community ties, employees can volunteer, offer their skills, and gain knowledge. Beyond the office, employees can further the impact and reach of corporate social responsibility (CSR) projects by leading community initiatives or taking part in public awareness campaigns.

Encouraging eco-friendly workplace practices and sustainable commuting can help further incorporate CSR into day-to-day operations. The company's carbon footprint can be decreased by giving incentives for eco-friendly commute choices like biking, carpooling, or public transit, as well as by installing infrastructure like bike racks and electric vehicle charging stations. Promoting environmentally friendly office procedures like energy conservation and recycling aids in ingraining sustainability into the company culture.

Gamification and digital engagement technologies can increase the enjoyment and engagement of CSR participation. Digital platforms have the potential to enhance idea sharing, progress tracking, and acknowledgment. Additionally, gamification features such as challenges and leaderboards can encourage employees to participate.

Sustainable habits among employees can be promoted by behavioural nudges, such as environmentally friendly reminders and comments on the influence on the environment. Building trust and reiterating the significance of CSR initiatives can be achieved by open communication regarding the effects of these initiatives and frequent updates on their status.

Social responsibility is made to feel like a fundamental part of the company's character through the integration of CSR into corporate culture and performance indicators. Building credibility and trust with stakeholders is achieved through publishing sustainability reports that showcase employee contributions and company accomplishments, as well as including thorough CSR sections in annual reports.

To put it briefly, encouraging employee involvement in CSR initiatives entails establishing a welcoming and inclusive workplace where staff members feel empowered, appreciated, and encouraged to share their

Principles of Green HRM

knowledge and skills. Organizations may create a significant social and environmental impact while raising employee engagement and boosting organizational success by incorporating CSR into their basic beliefs, daily operations, and corporate culture.

8.3.1 Encouraging and Facilitating Employee Involvement in Corporate Social Responsibility (CSR) Activities

The term "encouraging and facilitating employee involvement in corporate social responsibility (CSR) activities" describes the intentional actions taken by businesses to motivate and assist their staff members in participating in CSR projects. In order to encourage and facilitate employees' active participation in social, environmental, and ethical concerns, a culture and infrastructure must be established.

Fostering a sense of purpose, dedication, and excitement among employees to contribute to the benefit of society and the environment is necessary to encourage employee involvement in CSR activities. This can be accomplished by emphasizing the value of corporate social responsibility (CSR) and the beneficial contributions that employees can make through their involvement through communication, recognition, and incentives.

Encouraging employees to participate in CSR initiatives requires giving them the tools, encouragement, and chances to do so in a meaningful way. Giving employees the tools to support CSR efforts that correspond with the organization's beliefs and objectives include providing volunteer programs, gift matching schemes, skills-based volunteering possibilities, and educational initiatives.

All things considered, cultivating a culture of corporate citizenship and social responsibility within the company requires supporting and promoting employee participation in CSR initiatives. It improves employee morale, engagement, and happiness in addition to benefiting the community and society at large. This creates a more positive and influential work environment.

- ❖ Facilitating and promoting employee participation in corporate social responsibility (CSR) initiatives can yield substantial advantages for the organization and its staff. Here are some strategies to effectively engage employees in CSR initiatives:

1. Leadership Commitment and Communication

Role Modelling: Leaders should engage in sustainable activities on a regular basis and provide an example for others to follow. This can involve taking small steps, like promoting recycling or using less paper, to demonstrate leadership in this area.

Top-Down Support: Make sure firm executives engage in and openly support CSR initiatives. The employees' participation may serve as an example for others.

Public Commitments: To further emphasize the company's commitment, leadership could publicly commit to CSR targets and report on success in annual reports or public remarks.

Open Dialogues: Organize frequent town hall meetings or Q&A sessions so employees may speak with top management about CSR projects directly, promoting openness and participation.

2. Align CSR with Company Values and Mission

Strategic Integration: Incorporate CSR objectives into the company's strategic plan, making sure that each department has clear CSR goals that are in line with the overarching business objectives.

Corporate Culture: Integrate corporate social responsibility (CSR) themes into firm training programs and on boarding procedures to foster a corporate culture that prioritizes social responsibility.

Employee-Led Initiatives: To give employees a sense of ownership and a concrete influence, encourage departments to design their own CSR projects that complement the company's overarching goal.

3. Create Opportunities for Participation

CSR Days: Set aside particular days for CSR events, like an annual volunteer day for the entire organization, to promote cooperation and teamwork.

Flexible Scheduling: Offer employees with flexible schedule choices so they can engage in CSR initiatives without sacrificing their ability to do their jobs.

Varied Activities: Provide a range of CSR activities, from environmental clean-ups to mentorship programs, to accommodate diverse interests and skill sets. This will guarantee that there are chances for everyone.

4. Recognition and Incentives

CSR Awards: Establish a specific category for CSR awards in the company's yearly awards program to formally acknowledge exceptional accomplishments.

Storytelling: Employers could showcase the positive effects of their workers' CSR efforts by sharing their success stories on social media, the intranet, and business newsletters.

Peer Recognition: In order to promote a helpful community, create a peer appreciation program where employees can nominate their colleagues for their CSR activities.

5. CSR Committees and Ambassadors

Rotating Membership: To encourage more employee participation and to bring in new ideas, rotate committee membership on a regular basis.

Ambassador Training: To provide CSR ambassadors the tools they need to engage peers and effectively promote initiatives, give them specific training.

Cross-Functional Teams: Create cross-functional CSR teams to foster creativity and collaboration by bringing together a variety of viewpoints from various departments.

6. Employee Education and Training

Guest Speakers: Provide staff with motivational guest lectures who are leaders in the non-profit or social entrepreneurship sectors, sharing their perspectives on corporate social responsibility.

Continuous Learning: Provide staff with access to continuing education tools, such books or online courses, to keep them up to date on the latest developments in corporate social responsibility.

Workshops on Impact Measurement: In order to promote a results-oriented approach, hold workshops where staff learn how to measure and report on the impact of their CSR initiatives.

7. Partnerships with Nonprofits

Long-Term Partnerships: Form long-term partnerships with important NGOs to foster more meaningful connections and long-lasting change.

Employee-Nominated Partners: Allow employee nominations and voting on non-profit partners to ensure that the partnerships match their beliefs and interests.

Collaborative Projects: Provide cooperative initiatives so that workers can assist non-profit employees in order to have practical experience and a greater comprehension of social issues.

8. Transparency and Feedback

Impact Metrics: Create and disseminate comprehensive impact measurements that measure the advantages of corporate social responsibility initiatives and provide quantifiable results.

Feedback Loops: To ensure continual progress, establish formal feedback loops where staff members can regularly offer their opinions on CSR activities.

Transparent Reporting: Publicize thorough CSR reports that highlight accomplishments as well as problems and opportunities for development to build responsibility and confidence.

9. Leverage Technology

Digital Platforms: Create a central location for CSR initiatives using digital platforms, where staff members can access information, register for events, and keep tabs on their involvement.

Gamification: To make participation in CSR activities enjoyable and interesting, include gamification components, such leaderboards or challenges.

Mobile Accessibility: Make sure that CSR communications and platforms are responsive to mobile devices so that staff members may easily participate from any location.

10. Integrate CSR into Performance Reviews and Goals

CSR Objectives: Incorporate CSR objectives into employees' performance evaluations to make sure their social responsibility efforts are acknowledged and rewarded.

Professional Development: Connect CSR endeavours to your professional development objectives by emphasizing the skills and career advancements that can be gained via involvement.

Team Goals: Establish goals for your team's CSR to promote cooperation and group efforts toward social responsibility.

11. Develop Internal CSR Champions

CSR Mentors: Find and cultivate internal CSR champions that can mentor others and spearhead projects, igniting passion and information across the company.

Ambassador Programs: Create ambassador programs where motivated employees can offer their time to further corporate social responsibility initiatives inside their divisions.

Leadership Pathways: Offer professional development pathways, such as leadership roles training within CSR projects, to employees who express interest in CSR.

12. Enhance Employee Engagement Through Storytelling and Communication

Impact Stories: To encourage and inspire employees, provide gripping tales about how CSR initiatives have benefited recipients and communities.

Employee Testimonials: Include testimonies from employees who took part in CSR initiatives, emphasizing their personal development and contentment.

Visual Content: To make the impact of CSR initiatives more interesting and accessible, use visual materials like info graphics and movies.

13. Provide Resources and Support

CSR Toolkits: Provide resources, policies, and best practices for employees to use while leading and taking part in CSR initiatives in the form of CSR toolkits.

Budget Allocation: Make sure there are enough funds to support worthwhile programs by allocating a particular budget for CSR activity.

Logistical Support: Provide logistical support for community service initiatives, like organizing group outings or transportation to volunteer locations.

14. Incorporate CSR into Corporate Events
CSR Focused Events: Include CSR events in corporate events. For example, allocate a portion of an annual meeting to volunteer work or a fund-raising event for charities.

Themed Months: Plan themed months with related activities and initiatives that highlight various facets of corporate social responsibility (CSR), such as community health or environmental sustainability.

Employee Competitions: Encourage a culture of rivalry and camaraderie by holding friendly competitions amongst teams or departments to earn money for charities or accomplish CSR objectives.

15. Offer Flexible Participation Options
Remote Volunteering: To ensure inclusivity, offer remote volunteering options to employees who are unable to engage in person.

Family Involvement: Provide family-friendly corporate social responsibility initiatives that facilitate employee participation by enabling them to include their families.

Short-Term Commitments: Provide employees with hectic schedules with opportunities for short-term volunteering so they may make a difference without committing long-term.

16. Encourage Cross-Sector Collaboration
Partnerships with Other Companies: Collaborate with other companies on cooperative corporate social responsibility projects to increase the effect and create a feeling of purpose.

Government and NGO Collaborations: To address more significant societal challenges, collaborate with government agencies and non-governmental organizations (NGOs) to pool resources and expertise.

Employee Exchange Programs: Create employee exchange programs with affiliated companies to exchange knowledge and viewpoints regarding CSR initiatives.

17. Use Data and Analytics

Impact Analysis: Measure the success of CSR programs with data and analytics to show where they are doing well and where they need to be improved.

Employee Engagement Surveys: Take regular surveys to find out how interested and satisfied employees are with CSR initiatives. Utilize the results to improve and customize programs.

Benchmarking: To find areas for development and innovation, benchmark the company's CSR initiatives against best practices and industry standards.

18. Foster a Culture of Giving and Volunteering

Matching Gift Programs: Introduce matching gift programs to double the impact of employee gifts to charity by having the firm match their contributions.

Volunteer Time Off (VTO): Give employees compensated time off for volunteering activities by implementing volunteer time off regulations.

Peer-to-Peer Fundraising: Promote peer-to-peer fundraising campaigns so that employees can contribute to one another's campaigns and causes.

19. Promote Sustainable Practices in the Workplace

Green Teams: Create green teams whose mission is to advance workplace sustainability measures like energy conservation or recycling programs.

Sustainable Workspaces: Integrate eco-friendly designs and practices to create sustainable workspaces that showcase your company's dedication to environmental responsibility.

Awareness Campaigns: Educate employees on how they may contribute to sustainability both at work and at home by running awareness campaigns on issues such as waste management and lowering carbon emissions.

20. Celebrate Milestones and Successes

Milestone Celebrations: Celebrate significant milestones in the company's CSR journey, such as finishing a sizable volunteer project or reaching a significant fundraising goal.

Annual Reports: Publish yearly CSR reports that demonstrate the company's continued commitment by highlighting the year's accomplishments, lessons learned, and future objectives.

Success Stories: To maintain the energy and excitement behind CSR projects, communicate updates and success stories on a regular basis via internal communications.

Through the implementation of these all-encompassing methods, businesses may establish a strong framework that fosters employee participation in CSR initiatives and firmly integrates social responsibility into the operations and culture of the organization. Stronger community links, increased employee happiness, and an improved company reputation can all result from an all-encompassing strategy.

1.3.1 Benefits of Employee Participation in CSR Programs for Both the Organization and Community

"Benefits of employee participation in CSR programs for both the organization and the community" describes the benefits and favourable results that arise from staff members actively participating in CSR (corporate social responsibility) projects.

Employee participation in corporate social responsibility (CSR) programs offers a multitude of benefits for both the organization and the community. Here's a detailed look at these benefits:

- **Benefits for the Organization**

1. Enhanced Reputation and Brand Image

Public Perception and Trust: Companies that put a high priority on CSR initiatives frequently benefit from improved public perception and increased customer trust. Employees who actively engage in these initiatives serve as brand ambassadors for the company's social responsibility efforts, further improving its standing.

Brand Loyalty and Competitive Advantage: Customers are showing a growing preference for brands that exhibit environmental and social responsibility. Strong brand loyalty and a competitive edge in the market can be achieved by employees who are enthusiastic about their company's CSR initiatives.

2. Increased Employee Engagement and Satisfaction

Fulfilment and Meaningful Work: Employees' sense of fulfilment and a deeper sense of purpose beyond their regular work tasks might be enhanced by participation in CSR initiatives. An improvement in engagement and job satisfaction may result from this deeper significance in their work.

Sense of Pride and Belonging: Employees that actively participate in CSR programs frequently experience a greater feeling of pride in their company and a closer bond with their co-workers. Employee morale can rise and a positive work culture can be fostered by this sense of belonging.

3. Talent Attraction and Retention

Attracting Top Talent: Applicants are looking for companies with strong corporate social responsibility (CSR) commitments in today's competitive job market. Companies that actively include their staff in CSR initiatives stand to gain an advantage in luring top personnel, who are driven by a sense of purpose and a desire to have a positive impact on the world.

Retention and Employee Loyalty: Higher levels of employee loyalty and retention might result from actively participating staff members in CSR projects. Employee retention is higher in organizations when employees are empowered to make important contributions and feel valued.

4. Skill Development and Leadership Opportunities

Professional Growth: Employees that engage in CSR initiatives have the chance to advance their careers and acquire new skills. An employee's communication, teamwork, and leadership abilities can be improved through volunteering, fundraising, or project management for corporate social responsibility.

Leadership Development: Employees participating in CSR initiatives frequently have the opportunity to assume leadership roles outside of their regular work duties. This practical expertise in spearheading projects and promoting constructive change can aid in the development of the organization's future leaders.

5. Improved Workplace Culture and Employee Well-being

Positive Work Environment: Collaborative, empathetic, and socially responsible work environments are promoted when employees are actively involved in CSR projects. Mutual respect and support among coworkers are fostered when they feel encouraged to give back to their communities.

Employee Well-being: Employee well-being can benefit from CSR participation since it offers chances for social interaction, personal fulfilment, and a sense of achievement. Employees who actively participate in community service frequently report greater levels of job satisfaction and general well-being.

- **Benefits for the Community**

1. Addressing Social Issues and Needs

Resource Allocation: Corporate Social Responsibility (CSR) initiatives allocate resources, including financial, human, and material resources, to tackle critical social challenges like poverty, healthcare, and education. Organizations can increase their effect and contribute significantly to the community by including their workforce.

Supporting Vulnerable Populations: Supporting marginalized communities and vulnerable populations is a common target of CSR projects. Through proactive employee involvement in these endeavours, firms can effectively tackle systemic disparities and foster constructive societal transformation.

2. Economic Development and Empowerment

Job Creation and Skills Development: Certain corporate social responsibility (CSR) endeavours, like workforce development programs or aiding small businesses in the community, foster economic growth by generating employment possibilities and equipping people with useful skills and education.

Entrepreneurship and Innovation's initiatives that encourage innovation and entrepreneurship have the potential to boost economic expansion and cultivate a creative and entrepreneurial culture within the community.

3. Environmental Sustainability and Conservation

Environmental Stewardship: Recycle programs, renewable energy projects, and habitat restoration are just a few examples of the environmental sustainability and conservation efforts that are the focus of many CSR initiatives. Organizations can support the conservation of ecosystems and natural resources by encouraging employee involvement.

Educational Outreach's initiatives frequently involve educational outreach initiatives designed to spread sustainable practices and increase public knowledge of environmental challenges. Organizations can encourage positive behaviour change and a culture of environmental stewardship by using employees as educators and advocates.

4. Enhanced Social Infrastructure and Community Services

Supporting Community Organizations: Partnerships with local charities, nonprofits, and community organizations are common components of CSR projects. Organizations may improve social infrastructure and assist in providing basic services like healthcare, education, and social assistance by actively involving employees in these collaborations.

Volunteerism and Civic Engagement: Employee involvement in CSR initiatives promotes civic engagement and voluntarism in the community. Organizations foster a culture of service and civic engagement by providing employees with the tools and resources to give back and change the world.

5. Fostering Social Cohesion and Inclusivity

Building Social Connections: CSR initiatives that promote employee involvement strengthen ties and partnerships in the community. Employees and community members form relationships of mutual respect and trust by cooperating toward common aims and ideals.

Promoting Diversity and Inclusion: A more inclusive and equitable society is a result of CSR programs that place a high priority on diversity, equity, and inclusion. Organizations can advance social justice and provide opportunity for all community members by actively involving staff members with varying backgrounds and viewpoints.

Companies that cultivate a culture of social responsibility and community engagement improve both their organizational health and make a significant contribution to the well-being of society. In the end, this mutually beneficial partnership results in prosperous communities and sustainable corporate practices.

8.3.2 Examples of Impactful CSR Programs

❖ Here are examples of impactful CSR (Corporate Social Responsibility) programs implemented by notable companies:

1. TOMS One for One Movement (TOMS Shoes):
Program Overview: TOMS distributes a pair of shoes to a child in need for each pair of shoes that is purchased. Through the provision of footwear, this effort seeks to improve the opportunity, health, and education of children living in underprivileged communities.

Impact: Over 100 million pairs of shoes have been distributed by TOMS to children in over 70 countries since the company's founding in 2006. In order to help those in need receive therapies that can save their sight, the initiative has recently grown to include eyewear.

2. Starbucks C.A.F.E. Practices (Coffee and Farmer Equity Practices):
Program Overview: Starbucks' extensive set of social, environmental, and economic rules, known as C.A.F.E. Practices, is intended to guarantee the sustainability of its coffee supply chain. It includes topics including supporting coffee producers, protecting the environment, and sourcing ethically.

Impact: Starbucks has made investments in farmer support canters, given coffee producers access to credit and healthcare, and adopted sustainable farming techniques through its C.A.F.E. techniques program. Globally, the initiative has improved thousands of communities that grow coffee.

3. Microsoft's Technology for Social Impact (TSI):

Program Overview: Microsoft's TSI initiative uses technology to tackle some of the most important social and environmental issues facing the globe today. Its main areas of interest include environmental sustainability, healthcare, education, and humanitarian assistance.

Impact: Microsoft has created cutting-edge solutions like AI for Earth, which applies artificial intelligence to tackle environmental issues, and AI for Accessibility, which leverages technology to empower individuals with impairments. Communities all throughout the world have benefited greatly from these projects.

4. Nike's Reuse-A-Shoe Program:

Program Overview: Nike's Reuse-A-Shoe initiative gathers abandoned athletic shoes and turns them into Nike Grind, a substance that is utilized to make sports facilities including courts, playgrounds, and tracks. The program's objectives are to create recreational areas for communities and encourage recycling in addition to reducing garbage.

Impact: Through the Reuse-A-Shoe program, which the company introduced in 1990, Nike has recycled over 32 million pairs of shoes, resulting in the creation of over 1,000 sports surfaces in communities all over the world. These surfaces offer accessible and secure areas for play and physical activities.

5. Unilever's Sustainable Living Plan:

Program Overview: The Sustainable Living Plan from Unilever is a thorough approach to promote sustainable growth, lessen environmental effect, and enhance social outcomes. Its main objectives are to improve livelihoods, lessen environmental impact, and promote health and well-being.

Impact: Unilever has accomplished notable benchmarks with the Sustainable Living Plan, including procuring all of its agricultural raw materials responsibly, cutting manufacturing waste and water consumption, and supporting projects related to sanitation and hygiene. The ecology and society have benefited from the initiative.

6. Patagonia's "1% for the Planet" Initiative:

Program Overview: Through the 1% for the Planet campaign, Patagonia promises to donate 1% of its sales to environmental groups. The program is in favour of many different environmental concerns, such as biodiversity preservation, climate action, and conservation.

Impact: Patagonia has contributed millions of dollars to environmental organizations all throughout the world since joining 1% for the Planet in 1985. The program has provided funding for initiatives that support renewable energy, protect threatened ecosystems, and slow down global warming.

7. IBM's Corporate Service Corps:

Program Overview: Teams of IBM personnel are dispatched on pro bono consulting assignments by IBM's Corporate Service Corps (CSC) to tackle social and economic difficulties in developing nations. The program's focal points include economic development, education, and healthcare.

Impact: Since the organization's founding in 2008, CSC staff have worked on more than 4,000 projects in more than 40 countries, offering local governments, charities, and community organizations their knowledge and assistance. In underprivileged areas, the initiative has aided in expanding access to healthcare, enhancing educational opportunities, and promoting economic development.

8. Coca-Cola's "5by20" Initiative:

Program Overview: By 2020, 5 million women entrepreneurs should be empowered throughout the Coca-Cola value chain, according to the company's 5by20 strategy. The initiative helps women launch and expand their own businesses by giving them access to resources, financial support, and training.

Impact: 5by20 has trained women entrepreneurs in more than 60 nations in financial literacy, business skills, and leadership development. Through the initiative, women have been able to raise their income, become financially independent, and improve the prosperity of their communities.

9. Walmart's Global Responsibility Program:

Program Overview: Walmart's Global Responsibility initiative is cantered on community involvement, philanthropy, and sustainability.

Initiatives like waste reduction, sustainable sourcing, and funding and volunteer support for local communities are all part of the program.

Impact: Due to Walmart's sustainability initiatives, trash, water use, and greenhouse gas emissions have all significantly decreased throughout the company. Through its charitable endeavours, the corporation has helped communities all over the world with their economic development, education, and disaster relief activities.

10. L'Oreal's "Sharing Beauty with All" Sustainability Program:
Program Overview: The Sharing Beauty with All initiative from L'Oreal establishes challenging sustainability goals for every stage of the company's value chain, from product development to manufacturing and delivery. The program's main objectives include empowering women, encouraging ethical sourcing, and lessening the impact on the environment.

Impact: L'Oreal has been able to lower its waste production, water usage, and carbon emissions while boosting the use of sustainable ingredients and renewable energy thanks to Sharing Beauty with All. Initiatives to advance inclusiveness and diversity inside the organization and philanthropically support social causes are also part of the program.

These illustrations show how businesses may use their resources, knowledge, and clout to effectively implement CSR initiatives that have a positive social and environmental impact. Businesses may help create a more just and sustainable society by coordinating their objectives with those of the environment and local communities.

8.3.4 Best Practices for Integrating Employees into CSR Initiatives to Drive Meaningful Impact and Enhance Employee Satisfaction

The term "best practices for integrating employees into CSR initiatives to drive meaningful impact and enhance employee satisfaction" describes the most efficient and tried-and-true techniques for enlisting staff members in CSR endeavours in a way that benefits the company and its workers in a major way.

Involving staff members actively in the creation, management, and assessment of corporate social responsibility projects and programs is known as "integrating employees into CSR initiatives." This engagement extends beyond simple participation and involves giving staff members the freedom to take charge of CSR initiatives, offer their knowledge and experience, and meaningfully contribute to solving social and environmental issues.

❖ **The goal of integrating employees into CSR initiatives is twofold:**

1. Drive Meaningful Impact: By utilizing the resources and combined efforts of its workforce, the organization hopes to positively impact both society and the environment. An corporation may optimize its influence and effectively tackle major social and environmental challenges by coordinating corporate social responsibility (CSR) programs with the passions, skills, and interests of its workforce.

2. Enhance Employee Satisfaction: Engaging employees in CSR projects can improve their feeling of purpose, job satisfaction, and general health. Employees who actively support important causes, give back to their communities, and try to change the world report feeling happier and more motivated at work. Higher levels of employee loyalty, morale, and retention may follow from this.

In general, implementing best practices for incorporating staff members into CSR projects entails fostering an environment that is encouraging and inclusive, enabling staff members to donate their time, skills, and resources to improving society while simultaneously achieving personal and professional fulfilment.

Effective employee participation in CSR (Corporate Social Responsibility) programs necessitates meticulous preparation and deliberate implementation. Here are some best practices for maximizing employee participation to drive meaningful impact and enhance employee satisfaction:

1. Align CSR Initiatives with Employee Interests and Skills:
Conduct Skill Assessments: To determine whether staff have specialized knowledge and abilities that can be used for CSR projects, conduct

assessments. This can involve abilities like project management, graphic design, marketing, and event organizing.

Offer Skill Development Opportunities: Give employees opportunities for training and development so they can acquire skills related to CSR initiatives. Workshops, webinars, or online courses on subjects like nonprofit management, sustainability, or community participation may be part of this.

Match Skills to Projects: Assign skills and interests to jobs in certain CSR projects or to employees working on such projects. To assist with identifying opportunities and gaps for skill utilization across various activities, think about developing a skills matrix.

2. Promote Leadership and Ownership:

Establish Mentorship Programs: Assign employees with a track record of leading CSR efforts to seasoned mentors within the company. As employees negotiate their leadership duties, this mentorship can offer direction, assistance, and encouragement.

Encourage Innovation: Establish an environment that inspires employees to think creatively and innovatively about CSR projects. Urge them to come up with and oversee creative solutions to new environmental or societal problems.

Recognize Leadership Potential: By using formal leadership development programs or succession planning initiatives, employers can identify and develop employees who have the potential to be leaders. Give top-potential employees the chance to participate in CSR projects at progressively higher levels of responsibility.

3. Provide Training and Resources:

Offer Experiential Learning Opportunities: Give employees the chance to participate in community service projects, volunteer work, or CSR-related fieldwork to obtain practical experience. Their comprehension of and dedication to social responsibility may grow as a result of this hands-on education.

Create Knowledge-Sharing Platforms: Create online discussion boards, intranet portals, or lunch-and-learn events where employees can impart expertise, best practices, and takeaways from their experience with CSR projects. Promote interdepartmental cooperation and education.

Partner with External Experts: Work along with other organizations, consultants, or subject matter experts to offer resources and specialized training on subjects related to corporate social responsibility (CSR) efforts. Workshops on corporate generosity, diversity and inclusion, and environmental stewardship may fall under this category.

4. Recognize and Reward Participation:

Implement Peer Recognition Programs: Create peer appreciation programs so that employees can recognize their co-workers for their contributions to CSR projects. Peer-to-peer acknowledgment like this fosters a culture of gratitude and cooperation.

Provide Public Acknowledgment: Through internal newsletters, social media posts, or company-wide meetings, publicly acknowledge the contributions made by employees to CSR projects. Emphasize their accomplishments and the beneficial effects they have had on the community and the organization.

Offer Professional Development Opportunities: Give employees who actively engage in CSR programs chances for professional growth, such as conference attendance, certification pursuits, or leadership development courses.

5. Foster Collaboration and Teamwork:

Facilitate Interdepartmental Collaboration: Make it possible for departmental employees to work together on CSR projects. This kind of cross-functional cooperation can encourage originality, variety of opinion, and joint initiative ownership.

Encourage Mentorship and Peer Support: Encourage employees to mentor and support one another as they participate in CSR projects. Create buddy systems to offer direction and encouragement, or pair seasoned employees with recent hires.

Celebrate Team Achievements: Celebrate the achievements of teams engaged in corporate social responsibility endeavours by organizing team-building exercises, remote getaways, or award ceremonies. Recognize the influence of teams and their combined efforts in bringing about positive change.

6. Communicate Transparently and Regularly:

Host Town Hall Meetings: Organize frequent town halls or forums where employees may voice concerns, offer suggestions, and get firsthand information from management about forthcoming CSR projects. Encourage honest communication and openness about the objectives and advancements of CSR.

Provide Updates Through Multiple Channels: Use a range of platforms, such as email newsletters, intranet updates, bulletin boards, and digital signage, to keep employees informed about CSR initiatives. Make sure the material is readable and easily accessible.

Solicit Employee Input: Use suggestion boxes, focus groups, or questionnaires to actively solicit feedback and input from employees on CSR activities. Include employees in decision-making processes and take their views and ideas into consideration when developing and implementing programs.

7. Encourage Work-Life Integration:

Offer Volunteer Time Off (VTO): Provide employees a specific time off so they can volunteer while they are at work. This shows how dedicated the company is to helping its employees give back to the areas in which they live.

Promote Flexibility: It is recommended that managers provide flexible work arrangements, such remote work choices or modified schedules, to allow employees to participate in corporate social responsibility projects. Recognize the time and obligations that employees have outside of work.

Highlight Personal Benefits: Stress the advantages of participating in CSR projects for yourself, including better health, more job satisfaction, and better opportunities for professional growth. Assist employees in determining how their involvement fits with their objectives and personal values.

8. Measure and Communicate Impact:

Collect Feedback and Evaluation: Through focus groups, surveys, or post-project assessments, find out what the employees involved in CSR projects have to say. Utilize this input to determine areas that require improvement and to evaluate the success of efforts.

Share Impact Metrics: Share regular updates, reports, or dashboards that highlight important data and results with employees to let them know how CSR initiatives are doing. Demonstrate to employees how their efforts are affecting the world for the better.

Celebrate Milestones: Celebrate key milestones and accomplishments in CSR endeavours with employees, such as meeting financial targets, finishing volunteer work, or getting praise from outside partners. Emphasize the influence that employees' combined efforts have on the community and the difference they are making.

Organizations can enhance employee engagement and satisfaction while delivering substantial internal and external impact by putting these best practices into practice and successfully integrating employees into CSR projects.

Chapter – 9

Legal Compliance in Green HRM

Introduction to Legal Compliance in Green HRM:
Green HRM, or "green human resource management," incorporates eco-friendly techniques into HR procedures and guidelines to encourage environmental responsibility in businesses. Businesses are starting to understand how important sustainability is, so it's critical to coordinate their efforts with the law. Ensuring that an organization's attempts to become more environmentally friendly are in line with local, national, and international laws and regulations is known as legal compliance in Green HRM.

Meaning of Legal Compliance in Green HRM:
Legal compliance, as it relates to Green HRM, is the observance of laws, rules, and guidelines controlling environmental practices in an organization's HR department. It basically entails making sure that all HR initiatives, rules, and practices concerning environmental responsibility and sustainability comply with local, state, federal, and international legal obligations. This implies that companies' effects on the environment are governed by particular environmental rules and regulations, which they must abide with. These rules frequently cover topics like resource sustainability, energy conservation, pollution control, and waste management. In order to guarantee that workplaces are safe and healthy for employees, legal compliance in Green HRM also includes adhering to Occupational Health and Safety (OHS) requirements. In order to protect worker well-being and reduce legal risks, this involves controlling environmental dangers, preserving indoor air quality, and handling hazardous products appropriately. Compliance also requires the firm to adopt sustainable rules and procedures. To ensure they adhere to legal

norms and rules, this entails developing and enforcing policies that support green activities like as sustainable procurement, energy efficiency, waste reduction, and sustainability. Legal compliance in Green HRM also includes following labour and employment laws, which may contain provisions pertaining to safe working conditions, anti-discrimination, and fair labour practices. This ensures that sustainability initiatives do not violate the legal rights or protections of employees. In the end, firms that practice Green HRM must adhere to the law in order to conduct business morally, reduce legal risk, and favourably impact social responsibility and environmental preservation.

Key Components of Legal Compliance in Green HRM

In Green Human Resource Management (HRM), legal compliance refers to a wide range of essential elements that guarantee businesses follow the law while encouraging sustainability and environmental responsibility. These elements serve as the cornerstone for incorporating green practices into HR policies and initiatives while keeping them compliant with regional, federal, and worldwide legal requirements.

Here's an expanded explanation of each component:

1. Adherence to Environmental Laws and Regulations:

Organizations implementing green HRM must cross a challenging terrain of environmental rules and regulations that control their environmental impact. Waste management, pollution control, energy conservation, and the preservation of natural resources are only a few of the topics covered by these regulations. Organizations that abide by these standards are guaranteed to conduct business ethically, reducing their ecological imprint and promoting environmental sustainability. Organizations can show their dedication to environmental stewardship and reduce their risk of fines or penalties from the law by following environmental standards.

2. Alignment with Occupational Health and Safety (OHS) Standards:

A key component of green human resource management is ensuring the health and safety of employees. To achieve safe and healthy workplaces, this entails coordinating HR procedures with OHS guidelines.

Environmental variables covered under OHS standards include exposure to hazardous products, air quality, and ergonomic considerations. Adherence to these guidelines shields the company from lawsuits and workers' compensation claims in addition to protecting employees from working dangers. Organizations can cultivate a good work environment and enhance employee well-being by placing a high priority on staff health and safety.

3. Implementation of Sustainable Policies and Practices:

Green HRM is creating and putting into effect sustainable practices and policies that encourage environmental responsibility across the entire company. Numerous topics are covered by these rules, such as energy efficiency, waste reduction, sustainable procurement, and green activities. Organizations can incorporate environmental considerations into their daily operations and decision-making processes by incorporating sustainability into HR policies and practices. In addition to assisting businesses in meeting legal obligations, this proactive approach to sustainability promotes ongoing advancements in environmental performance.

4. Compliance with Labour and Employment Laws:

Green HRM must abide by labour and employment laws that regulate workplace practices and employee rights in addition to environmental standards. Fair labour practices, equal job opportunities, anti-discrimination, and safe working conditions are all covered under these regulations. Ensuring compliance with labour regulations guarantees the implementation of sustainability projects in a way that respects the rights of employees and fosters justice and equity in the workplace. Green practices that comply with labour standards help firms cultivate an inclusive, diverse, and respectful culture.

5. Transparency and Reporting:

Legal compliance in Green HRM depends on open reporting of environmental activities and sustainability initiatives. It is imperative for organizations to truthfully reveal to regulatory agencies, stakeholders, and the general public their environmental effect, sustainability objectives, and performance measures. By being transparent, the company demonstrates its commitment to ethical business practices and environmental responsibility and gains credibility and accountability. Following reporting frameworks and standards like ISO 14001 or the Global Reporting Initiative (GRI) helps firms improve their reputation and promote greater accountability and transparency in the sustainability space.

To summarize, adhering to labour laws, implementing sustainable policies and practices, managing environmental regulations, maintaining openness in reporting, and aligning with OHS requirements are all part of legal compliance in Green HRM. Organizations can encourage environmental responsibility, successfully incorporate sustainability into HR initiatives, and reduce the legal risks associated with non-compliance by addressing five essential components.

9.1 Understanding Environmental Laws and Regulations

Since environmental rules and regulations control how businesses affect the environment and direct their sustainability initiatives, they are an essential component of green human resource management, or green HRM. These laws include a broad variety of actions intended to safeguard the environment, stop pollution, and encourage environmental preservation. Organizations must comprehend these rules in order to guarantee compliance and successfully include environmental responsibility into their HR procedures.

Here's a detailed exploration of environmental laws and regulations:
- **Environmental Laws:**

Governments at all levels-local, national, and international-enact environmental laws as legal legislation to address environmental problems and control human activity that has an influence on the environment. These legal measures support sustainable behaviours, stop pollution, and safeguard the environment. Environmental laws usually address a broad variety of issues, such as energy efficiency, biodiversity conservation, waste management, land use, and air and water quality. To guarantee accountability and compliance, they provide rules, guidelines, and sanctions for people, businesses, and governmental bodies. The Resource

Conservation and Recovery Act (RCRA), the Endangered Species Act, the Clean Air Act, and the Clean Water Act are a few examples of environmental laws. These laws are essential for forming public policy, directing judgment, and encouraging environmental stewardship.

Environmental Regulations:
Regulatory bodies create environmental regulations as guidelines, standards, and orders to carry out and uphold environmental legislation. These rules include comprehensive instructions and specifications for meeting environmental statutes and attaining particular environmental goals. Regulatory agencies, such as the Environmental Protection Agency (EPA) in the United States, are responsible for developing, enforcing, and overseeing environmental regulations. Construction, manufacturing, transportation, energy generation, agriculture, and other sectors are all covered by environmental rules. Permit requirements, emission limitations, pollution control strategies, reporting and monitoring specifications, and enforcement procedures are a few examples of these. Organizations must abide with environmental standards in order to reduce their negative effects on the environment, safeguard ecosystems and public health, and stay out of trouble with the law.

❖ **Key Legislations in Environmental Laws and Regulations:**

   a. **Environmental Protection Acts:** These laws govern how the companies uses resources, manages trash, and emits pollution.

   b. **Occupational Health and Safety (OHS) Regulations:** They provide healthy and safe working environments, encompassing environmental factors like air quality and exposure to dangerous materials.

   c. **Labour Laws:** They might contain clauses pertaining to eco-friendly facilities and fair labor policies, among other sustainable activities.

   d. **Clean Air Act:** Controls automotive and industrial emissions into the air to safeguard public health and air quality.

e. **Clean Water Act:** Ensures the safety of drinking water and aquatic habitats by regulating the flow of contaminants into water bodies and establishing water quality standards.

f. **Resource Conservation and Recovery Act (RCRA):** Governs the management and disposal of both hazardous and non-hazardous solid waste, as well as recycling and waste minimization policies.

g. **Comprehensive Environmental Response, Compensation, and Liability Act (CERCLA or Superfund):** Focuses on cleaning up hazardous waste sites and imposes penalties on those who pollute the environment.

h. **Endangered Species Act:** Protects endangered and threatened species and their habitats, prohibiting actions that may harm them.

i. **Energy Policy Act:** Encourages the use of alternative fuels, renewable energy sources, and energy efficiency to lessen the need for fossil fuels and slow down global warming.

❖ **Here's a detailed explanation of key legislations in Environmental Laws and Regulations:**

1. The Environmental Protection Act, 1986

An important legislative achievement in India is the Environmental Protection Act of 1986, which established a thorough framework for environmental management and protection. After the Bhopal Gas Disaster in 1984, this Act was passed, emphasizing how critical it is to safeguard the public's health and the environment against industrial and environmental risks. The Act, its main clauses, its methods of implementation, and its influence on environmental governance in India are examined in detail below.

- **Key Provisions of the Environmental Protection Act, 1986**

Objectives

Ensuring the preservation and enhancement of the environment is the principal goal of the Environmental Protection Act of 1986. This covers pollution control, prevention, and mitigation of the environment. The Act gives the national government the authority to implement the required changes to safeguard and improve the environment.

Authority and Powers

The Act grants extensive powers to the central government, enabling it to:

- Set guidelines for the environment's quality in all of its facets.
- Provide protocols and safety measures for managing dangerous materials.
- Organize the efforts of state agencies, authorities, and governments.
- Develop and implement national initiatives aimed at preventing, controlling, and reducing environmental contamination.
- Limit the placement of industries and the way that pollutants are handled.

Rules and Regulations

The central government can make rules and regulations to control pollution, which include:

- Establishing guidelines for the discharge and emissions of contaminants into the environment from different sources.
- Controlling the use and removal of dangerous materials.
- Ensuring adherence to environmental regulations at industrial sites.
- Defining protocols for accident avoidance and cleanup strategies for polluted areas.

Environmental Clearance

The Environmental Impact Assessment (EIA) requirement is one of the Act's key features. The Ministry of Environment, Forests and Climate Change (MoEFCC) approval is required for projects and activities that are expected to have a major environmental impact. A detailed evaluation of potential environmental effects and the deployment of mitigation strategies are two steps in the EIA process.

Penalties

The Act stipulates stringent penalties for non-compliance, which include:

- Imprisonment for a maximum period of five years.
- Fines that might total one lakh rupees.
- Fees in addition for ongoing violations.
- More significant infractions may result in harsher punishments, such as larger fines and lengthier jail sentences.

Key Features of the Act

Comprehensive Coverage

Pollution of the air, water, and soil is just one of the many environmental issues covered under the Environmental Protection Act of 1986. In order to stop environmental degradation, it deals with the control of companies and the handling of dangerous materials.

Preventive Measures

The Act places a strong emphasis on taking precautions to stop environmental damage. This comprises instructions for industrial operations to reduce environmental impact, limits for emissions, and laws on the management and disposal of hazardous materials.

Environmental Impact Assessment (EIA)

The Act's implementation of the EIA is a big step in the direction of sustainable development. Before a project is approved, the EIA process makes sure that any potential environmental effects are taken into account and minimized. To ensure openness and public involvement, public consultations are a crucial component of the EIA process.

Public Participation

The Act promotes public participation in environmental decision-making. Environmental clearance projects are required to include public hearings and consultations, which give local populations an opportunity to voice their concerns and recommendations.

Implementation Mechanisms

Central Pollution Control Board (CPCB)
State Pollution Control Boards (SPCBs) and the CPCB are essential to the Act's implementation. Setting environmental standards, ensuring compliance, and offering technical support to SPCBs are all under the purview of the CPCB. The CPCB also offers statistics and carries out research on environmental quality.

State Pollution Control Boards (SPCBs)
State-level Act enforcement is the responsibility of SPCBs. They check industrial facilities, keep an eye on pollution levels, and make sure environmental regulations are being followed. SPCBs are also essential in approving the establishment and operation of industrial facilities and guaranteeing that environmental regulations are followed.

Environmental Monitoring
In order to make sure that environmental criteria are being followed, the Act requires routine reporting and monitoring systems. This covers the handling of hazardous materials, soil pollution, and the monitoring of the quality of the air and water. Regulations and policy decisions are informed by data gathered through monitoring.

Amendments and Notifications
The Environmental Protection Act, 1986, has been supplemented with various notifications and amendments to address specific environmental issues. Notable amendments and notifications include:

Hazardous Waste (Management and Handling) Rules: These rules govern the management and disposal of hazardous waste to prevent environmental contamination.

Coastal Regulation Zone (CRZ) Notification: Regulates activities along India's coastline to protect coastal ecosystems and prevent erosion.

Bio-Medical Waste Management Rules: Ensures the safe handling and disposal of medical waste to protect public health and the environment.

Challenges and Criticisms

Enforcement
Enforcing the Act effectively continues to be a major concern. Even with the extensive framework, enforcement operations are frequently hampered by a lack of funding, infrastructure, and technical know-how. Ensuring industry and local body compliance is an ongoing challenge.

Compliance
Environmental standards are not always followed by the industrial sector. Many industries lack the knowledge and resources necessary to adhere to strict environmental requirements, especially those in the unorganized sector. Widespread non-compliance and environmental damage result from this.

Public Awareness
There is a lack of public understanding regarding environmental challenges and the Act's requirements. To guarantee that environmental laws are implemented and enforced effectively, there must be increased public participation and education.

Impact on Environmental Governance
India's environmental governance has been significantly impacted by the Environmental Protection Act of 1986. As a result, regulatory agencies have been established, environmental standards have been developed, and monitoring and compliance systems have been put in place. Additionally, the Act cleared the path for later environmental laws and policies that prioritize sustainable development.

Conclusion
A pillar of Indian environmental law, the Environmental Protection Act, 1986 offers a strong foundation for environmental enhancement and protection. The Act has made a substantial contribution to increasing public knowledge of environmental issues and encouraging sustainable activities, even though difficulties with enforcement and compliance still exist. To achieve the Act's goals and protect India's environmental future,

continuous efforts are needed to improve implementation, increase public involvement, and guarantee industrial compliance.

2. Occupational Health and Safety (OHS) Regulations

In India, legislation pertaining to Occupational Health and Safety (OHS) are essential for guaranteeing the welfare, safety, and health of workers in several industries. These rules include a variety of legislation and directives aimed at preventing risks at work, shielding employees from occupational illnesses, and establishing secure working conditions. This is a thorough rundown of the main OHS laws, together with information on its elements, methods of implementation, and difficulties in India.

Key Legislations and Their Provisions
- **Factories Act, 1948**

Scope: Applicable to factories employing ten or more workers with power and twenty or more without power.

Health Provisions:
Maintenance of cleanliness and hygiene in the workplace

Adequate ventilation, lighting, and temperature control.

Provision of safe drinking water

Proper sanitation facilities including toilets and washing areas

Safety Provisions:
Fencing of machinery and proper maintenance

Use of safety gear and personal protective equipment (PPE)

Installation of safety devices like fire extinguishers and alarm systems

Regular safety training and drills

Welfare Provisions:
First aid appliances and emergency medical care

Canteens, restrooms, and crèches for women workers

Welfare officers to address workers' grievances and welfare needs

- **Mines Act, 1952**

Scope: Covers the mining industry.

Health and Safety Provisions:

Ensuring safe working conditions in mines

Mandatory health and safety training for workers

Regular medical examinations and health monitoring

Provision of safe drinking water and sanitation facilities

Measures to prevent accidents, such as proper ventilation, dust control, and safety gear

Availability of rescue equipment and emergency response plans

- **Employees' State Insurance Act, 1948**

Scope: Applies to factories and other specified establishments.

Provisions:

Medical Benefits: Comprehensive healthcare services for insured workers and their dependents, including hospitalization and specialist care.

Sickness Benefits: Cash compensation during periods of certified sickness.

Maternity Benefits: Financial support and medical care for pregnant women.

Disability Benefits: Compensation for temporary or permanent disability due to workplace injuries or occupational diseases.

Dependent Benefits: Financial support to dependents in case of the insured worker's death due to employment injury.

- **Building and Other Construction Workers (Regulation of Employment and Conditions of Service) Act, 1996**

Scope: Regulates the employment and conditions of service of construction workers.

Provisions:

Safety Measures: Safe scaffolding, harnesses, helmets, and protective footwear.

Health Provisions: Regular health check-ups, medical care, and hygienic working conditions.

Welfare Measures: Provision of temporary housing, sanitation, drinking water, and first-aid facilities at construction sites.

Training: Safety training and awareness programs for workers.

- **The Dock Workers (Safety, Health, and Welfare) Act, 1986**

Scope: Ensures the safety, health, and welfare of dock workers.

Provisions:

Safe Working Conditions: Proper maintenance of docks and equipment, and safe handling of cargo.

Health Measures: Regular health check-ups and medical facilities.

Welfare Measures: Provision of restrooms, canteens, and sanitation facilities.

Training: Health and safety training programs for dock workers.

- **Implementation and Enforcement**

Directorate General Factory Advice Service and Labour Institutes (DGFASLI)

Role: Provides technical advice and training, conducts safety audits and inspections.

Activities: Develops safety standards, conducts research, and disseminates information on OHS practices.

Directorate General of Mines Safety (DGMS)

Role: Ensures safety regulations in the mining industry.

Activities: Conducts inspections, investigates accidents, and ensures compliance with safety standards and regulations.

State Labour Departments
Role: Enforce OHS regulations at the state level.

Activities: Conduct workplace inspections, ensure compliance with safety laws, and address worker complaints and grievances.

Specific Standards and Guidelines
Bureau of Indian Standards (BIS)
Role: Develops national standards for OHS.

Standards: Includes standards for safety equipment, industrial safety practices, and occupational health guidelines.

National Institute of Occupational Health (NIOH)
Role: Conducts research on occupational health hazards and diseases.

Activities: Provides technical support, training, and guidance on occupational health issues.

Challenges and Areas for Improvement
Compliance
Issues: Ensuring compliance with OHS regulations remains a significant challenge, particularly in the informal sector and small industries.

Needs: Regular inspections and stringent enforcement are required to improve compliance rates and adherence to safety standards.

Awareness and Training
Issues: Lack of awareness and inadequate training programs on OHS for both employers and employees.

Needs: Continuous education and skill development programs to enhance understanding and implementation of safety practices and regulations.

Infrastructure and Resources
Issues: Inadequate infrastructure and resources for effective implementation of OHS regulations.

Needs: Investment in safety equipment, medical facilities, and emergency response systems to ensure worker safety and health.

Recent Developments and Reforms

Code on Occupational Safety, Health, and Working Conditions, 2020

Scope: Consolidates and amends various existing laws related to occupational safety, health, and working conditions.

Provisions:

Comprehensive coverage of all establishments employing ten or more workers

Enhanced safety measures and working conditions.

Better health facilities, including provisions for medical examinations and monitoring.

Increased penalties for non-compliance

Introduction of a single registration and licensing mechanism for employers

Impact on Occupational Health and Safety Standards

Improvement in Safety Culture

Observations: Increased focus on safety training and awareness programs has led to an improved safety culture in many industries.

Benefits: Reduced incidence of workplace accidents and occupational diseases, leading to a healthier and safer work environment.

Technological Advancements

Observations: Adoption of new technologies and automation has enhanced safety measures and reduced human error.

Benefits: Improved efficiency and safety in industrial operations, leading to better compliance with OHS standards.

Conclusion

In India, occupational health and safety laws are essential to guaranteeing a secure and healthy working environment for all employees. Promoting occupational safety and health requires the broad framework that major laws like the Factories Act, Mines Act, and other specialized acts provide.

Nonetheless, issues including proper infrastructure, compliance, and efficient enforcement continue to exist. To achieve the intended results, ongoing initiatives to improve awareness, training, and investment in safety infrastructure are crucial. Occupational health and safety standards in India will be greatly enhanced by enforcing OHS legislation more strictly and implementing best practices, which would enhance worker productivity and general well-being.

3. Labour Laws

India's labour laws comprise a vast range of legislation aimed at safeguarding workers' rights and well-being, guaranteeing equitable treatment, and promoting harmonious relationships between employers and employees. Numerous facets of employment are covered by these regulations, such as compensation, social security, working conditions, dispute resolution, and workplace safety. A comprehensive framework to cover a variety of employment circumstances is created by the combination of central and state legislations that characterize the Indian labour law environment. This is a thorough examination of India's main labour laws, including its provisions, methods of application, most recent revisions, and difficulties.

- **Key Labour Laws in India**
- **The Factories Act, 1948**

Scope: Applies to manufacturing units employing 10 or more workers with power and 20 or more without power.

Health Provisions:

Ensures workplace cleanliness, proper ventilation, and adequate lighting

Provides for the safe disposal of wastes and effluents

Mandates the provision of safe drinking water and sanitation facilities

Safety Provisions:

Requires fencing of dangerous machinery and safety devices

Implements measures against fire hazards, including fire fighting equipment and emergency exits.

Stipulates regular maintenance of machinery and equipment to prevent accidents

Welfare Provisions:
Establishes restrooms, canteens, and crèches for children of women workers

Ensures the availability of first-aid boxes and emergency medical care

Requires appointment of welfare officers in large factories

Working Hours:
Sets maximum working hours, daily and weekly limits

Provides for overtime pay and compulsory weekly holidays

- **The Industrial Disputes Act, 1947**

Scope: Regulates industrial disputes and provides mechanisms for resolution.

Provisions:
Dispute Resolution: Establishes mechanisms for resolving disputes through conciliation, arbitration, and adjudication.

Layoffs and Retrenchment: Defines procedures and compensation for layoffs, retrenchments, and closures.

Worker Rights: Protects workers' rights during strikes and lockouts, ensuring that industrial actions are conducted legally.

- **The Minimum Wages Act, 1948**

Scope: Applies to scheduled employments.

Provisions:
Wage Fixation: Empowers the government to fix minimum wages for different sectors and regions.

Periodic Revision: Requires periodic review and revision of minimum wages to account for inflation and cost of living increases.

- **The Payment of Wages Act, 1936**

Scope: Ensures timely payment of wages to employees.

Provisions:

Timely Payment: Mandates payment of wages without unauthorized deductions.

Wage Period: Fixes wage periods (monthly, fortnightly, or weekly) and permissible deductions for absences or damages.

- **The Employees' Provident Funds and Miscellaneous Provisions Act, 1952**

Scope: Covers establishments employing 20 or more workers.

Provisions:

Provident Fund: Requires contributions from both employer and employee to a provident fund.

Pension Scheme: Provides pension benefits to employees' post-retirement.

Insurance Scheme: Offers life insurance benefits through the Employees' Deposit Linked Insurance (EDLI) scheme.

- **The Employees' State Insurance Act, 1948**

Scope: Applies to factories and establishments with 10 or more employees.

Provisions:

Medical Benefits: Provides comprehensive medical care to insured employees and their families.

Sickness Benefits: Offers cash benefits during periods of certified sickness.

Maternity Benefits: Ensures financial support and medical care during maternity leave.

Disability and Dependent Benefits: Compensates for workplace injuries, disabilities, and supports dependents in case of death.

- **The Child Labour (Prohibition and Regulation) Act, 1986**

Scope: Prohibits employment of children under the age of 14.

Provisions:

Prohibition: Bans child labour in hazardous occupations and processes.

Regulation: Regulates working conditions in non-hazardous sectors, including working hours and health measures.

- **The Maternity Benefit Act, 1961**

Scope: Applies to women workers in factories, mines, and plantations.

Provisions:

Maternity Leave: Provides paid maternity leave for a specified period (26 weeks for the first two children).

Other Benefits: Includes nursing breaks, prohibition of dismissal during maternity leave, and provision for additional medical bonus.

- **The Payment of Bonus Act, 1965**

Scope: Applicable to factories and establishments with 20 or more employees.

Provisions:

Bonus Payments: Mandates payment of bonuses to employees based on profits or productivity.

Minimum Bonus: Ensures a minimum bonus is paid regardless of profit or loss.

- **The Contract Labour (Regulation and Abolition) Act, 1970**

Scope: Governs establishments employing 20 or more contract labourers.

Provisions:

Registration: Requires mandatory registration of establishments and contractors.

Welfare Measures: Ensures provision of canteens, restrooms, and first-aid facilities.

Abolition: Allows for the abolition of contract labouring certain conditions where it is found to be exploitative.

- **Recent Reforms and the New Labour Codes**

The Government of India has combined 29 core labour laws into four extensive labour codes in an attempt to modernize and streamline labour legislation. The objectives of these reforms are to improve worker welfare, facilitate compliance, and streamline the regulatory environment.

- **Code on Wages, 2019**

Combines: The Payment of Wages Act, Minimum Wages Act, Payment of Bonus Act, and Equal Remuneration Act

Provisions:

Universal Minimum Wage: Ensures a minimum wage across all sectors, linked to living standards.

Timely Payment: Mandates the timely disbursement of wages.

Equal Remuneration: Enforces equal pay for equal work, preventing gender-based wage discrimination.

- **Industrial Relations Code, 2020**

Combines: The Industrial Disputes Act, Trade Unions Act, and Industrial Employment (Standing Orders) Act.

Provisions:

Dispute Resolution: Simplifies mechanisms for resolving industrial disputes.

Trade Union Recognition: Standardizes processes for the recognition of trade unions.

Layoff and Retrenchment: Streamlines procedures for layoffs, retrenchments, and closures, balancing employer flexibility and worker security.

- **Code on Social Security, 2020**

Combines: The Employees' Provident Funds Act, Employees' State Insurance Act, Maternity Benefit Act, and others.

Provisions:

Comprehensive Coverage: Extends social security benefits to all workers, including those in informal sectors and gig economy.

Unified Registration: Simplifies registration processes for employers.

Improved Benefits: Enhances various social security schemes, including pensions, insurance, and maternity benefits.

- **Occupational Safety, Health and Working Conditions Code, 2020**

Combines: The Factories Act, Mines Act, Dock Workers Act, and others

Provisions:

Health and Safety: Strengthens provisions for occupational health and safety.

Working Conditions: Improves working conditions, including regulations on working hours, leave policies, and welfare facilities.

Welfare Facilities: Enhances welfare measures, ensuring better living and working conditions.

- **Implementation and Enforcement**

Central and State Government Roles

Central Government: Formulates labour policies, enacts laws, and oversees major industrial relations.

State Governments: Implement and enforce labour laws within their jurisdictions, conduct inspections, and resolve disputes at the state level.

Labour Commissionerate's

Role: Enforce labour laws, address worker grievances, and ensure compliance.

Activities: Conduct inspections, handle worker complaints, facilitate dispute resolution, and ensure fair labour practices.

- **Specific Standards and Guidelines**

Bureau of Indian Standards (BIS)
Role: Develops national standards for labour safety and welfare.

Standards: Includes standards for safety equipment, industrial safety practices, and occupational health guidelines.

National Institute of Occupational Health (NIOH)
Role: Conducts research on occupational health hazards and diseases.

Activities: Provides technical support, training, and guidance on occupational health issues.

- **Challenges and Areas for Improvement**

Informal Sector
Issues: High prevalence of informal employment with limited access to formal labour protections.

Needs: Policies to formalize employment, extend labour protections, and improve working conditions in the informal sector.

Enforcement
Issues: Inconsistent enforcement of labour laws across different states and sectors.

Needs: Strengthened enforcement mechanisms, increased inspectorate resources, and better compliance monitoring.

Awareness and Education
Issues: Low awareness of labour rights among workers, particularly in rural and informal sectors.

Needs: Enhanced worker education programs, widespread dissemination of information on labour rights, and capacity building for trade unions.

- **Impact on Labour Standards**

Improvement in Safety and Welfare

Observations: Enhanced safety protocols and welfare measures have led to better working conditions in many sectors.

Benefits: Reduced incidence of workplace accidents and occupational diseases, leading to improved health and safety for workers.

Technological Advancements

Observations: Adoption of new technologies and automation has improved efficiency and safety in industrial operations.

Benefits: Minimizes human error and enhances compliance with safety standards, leading to better labour practices.

- **Conclusion**

The labour laws of India offer a thorough framework to safeguard the welfare and rights of employees, guarantee equitable treatment, and promote harmonious workplace relationships. A major step toward streamlining and updating labour laws has been taken with the recent consolidation of labour laws into four labour codes. To fully realize the benefits of these regulations, though, more awareness must be raised and measures addressing the issues in the unorganized sector must be implemented. Consistent endeavours to augment infrastructure, education, and compliance will elevate labour standards and augment the general welfare and efficiency of the Indian labour force.

4. Clean Air Act, 1981

The Air (Prevention and Control of Pollution) Act, 1981, is one of the most important laws India has passed to address air pollution. The cornerstone of India's legal system for reducing and regulating air pollution is this Act, together with later changes and new initiatives. This is a comprehensive analysis of the Indian Clean Air Act, covering its provisions, methods of implementation, obstacles, and latest advancements.

Background and Need

Major Indian cities often record air quality levels that are dangerous to human health, making air pollution a serious environmental and public health concern. The problem has gotten worse due to the quick industrialization, urbanization, and rise in vehicle emissions; strict laws and efficient enforcement methods are now required. Strong legal frameworks and policy initiatives are desperately needed to alleviate the impacts of air pollution, which are linked to respiratory ailments, cardiovascular disorders, and premature deaths.

- **Key Provisions of the Air (Prevention and Control of Pollution) Act, 1981**

Objectives

Prevention, Control, and Abatement: The Act aims to prevent, control, and reduce air pollution to protect and improve the quality of air.

Establishment of Boards: Establishes Central and State Pollution Control Boards (CPCB and SPCBs) to implement and enforce the provisions of the Act.

Regulatory Framework

Ambient Air Quality Standards: Empowers the CPCB to set national ambient air quality standards.

Emission Standards: Authorizes the establishment of emission standards for industries, vehicles, and other sources of air pollution.

Permits and Licensing: Requires industries to obtain consent from the SPCBs before establishing or operating facilities that discharge pollutants into the air.

Monitoring and Inspections: Grants powers to the CPCB and SPCBs to monitor air quality, inspect industrial plants, and enforce compliance with emission standards.

Action Plans: Mandates the creation of air quality management plans for regions with high pollution levels, outlining specific measures to be taken to improve air quality.

Penalties and Enforcement

Non-Compliance: Prescribes penalties for industries and individuals who fail to comply with the standards and regulations.

Legal Actions: Allows the pollution control boards to initiate legal proceedings against defaulters.

Polluter Pays Principle: Implements the 'polluter pays' principle, ensuring that polluters bear the cost of pollution control and remediation measures.

Public Participation

Public Awareness: Promotes public awareness and education on the effects of air pollution and the importance of air quality.

Citizen's Right: Empowers citizens to report violations and file complaints regarding air pollution.

Community Involvement: Encourages community involvement in air quality monitoring and improvement initiatives.

Implementation Mechanisms

Central Pollution Control Board (CPCB)

Role: Formulates policies, sets standards, and provides technical assistance to SPCBs.

Activities: Conducts nationwide air quality monitoring, research, and development activities related to pollution control.

Data Management: Maintains a comprehensive database on air quality, sources of pollution, and trends to inform policy decisions.

State Pollution Control Boards (SPCBs)

Role: Implement and enforce the regulations set by the CPCB within their respective states.

Activities: Issue permits, conduct inspections, and monitor air quality at the state level.

Local Initiatives: Develop and implement state-specific action plans to address unique air quality challenges.

National Air Quality Monitoring Program (NAMP)

Objective: Monitor ambient air quality across India to assess pollution levels and trends.

Network: Operates a network of monitoring stations in urban, industrial, and rural areas to collect air quality data.

Reporting: Publishes regular reports on air quality status, trends, and compliance with standards.

Challenges and Issues

Enforcement and Compliance

Resource Constraints: SPCBs often face financial and human resource constraints, limiting their ability to effectively enforce regulations.

Industrial Resistance: Industries sometimes resist compliance due to the cost of implementing pollution control technologies.

Coordination Issues: Lack of coordination between various government agencies and departments hampers effective implementation.

Corruption: Corruption and bureaucratic inefficiencies can undermine enforcement efforts.

Data and Monitoring

Insufficient Coverage: The existing network of monitoring stations is insufficient to cover the entire country comprehensively.

Data Quality: Issues with data accuracy, consistency, and real-time availability hinder effective decision-making.

Technological Gaps: Limited use of advanced monitoring technologies and real-time data analytics.

Public Awareness and Participation

Awareness Levels: Low levels of public awareness and participation in air quality management activities.

Engagement: Limited mechanisms for meaningful public engagement and input into policy-making processes.

Behavioural Change: Challenges in promoting behavioural change towards pollution reduction practices.

Recent Developments and Initiatives

National Clean Air Programme (NCAP)

Launch: Launched in January 2019 as a comprehensive strategy to tackle air pollution.

Goals: Aims to achieve a 20-30% reduction in particulate matter (PM10 and PM2.5) concentrations by 2024.

Strategies: Includes city-specific action plans, strengthening monitoring networks, enhancing public awareness, and promoting research and development.

Funding and Support: Provides financial and technical support to states and cities to implement air quality improvement measures.

Graded Response Action Plan (GRAP)

Objective: Provides a set of emergency measures to be implemented during severe pollution events.

Phases: Outlines different levels of actions based on the severity of air quality, ranging from restrictions on vehicular movement to the shutdown of construction activities.

Implementation: Coordinated implementation involving multiple agencies, including traffic police, municipal corporations, and pollution control boards.

National Green Tribunal (NGT)

Role: Judicial body established to address environmental issues, including air pollution.

Actions: Issues directives and orders to enforce compliance with air quality standards and penalizes defaulters.

Public Interest Litigation: Allows individuals and groups to file petitions for environmental justice, promoting accountability.

Bharat Stage Emission Standards (BSES)

Implementation: Gradual implementation of stringent emission standards for vehicles to reduce vehicular pollution.

Bharat Stage VI: The latest and most stringent standards, implemented nationwide from April 2020.

Impact: Significant reduction in vehicular emissions, particularly of nitrogen oxides (NOx) and particulate matter (PM).

Comprehensive Action Plans for Non-Attainment Cities

Target Cities: Focuses on cities that consistently fail to meet national air quality standards.

Measures: Includes interventions such as improving public transportation, promoting cleaner fuels, regulating industrial emissions, and enhancing green cover.

Monitoring and Evaluation: Regular assessment of action plan implementation and effectiveness.

Sector-Specific Interventions

Industrial Pollution Control

Technological Upgradation: Encourages industries to adopt cleaner technologies and best practices.

Emission Control: Mandates the installation of pollution control devices and adherence to emission standards.

Compliance Monitoring: Regular inspections and audits to ensure compliance with environmental regulations.

Vehicular Pollution Control

Fuel Quality Improvement: Introduction of cleaner fuels like compressed natural gas (CNG) and Bharat Stage VI compliant fuel.

Electric Mobility: Promotion of electric vehicles (EVs) through incentives, subsidies, and infrastructure development.

Public Transport Enhancement: Expansion and modernization of public transport systems to reduce reliance on private vehicles.

Agricultural Pollution Control
Crop Residue Management: Promotion of alternatives to crop burning, such as in-situ management, use of crop residue for bio-energy, and mulching.

Farmer Support: Providing financial and technical support to farmers for adopting sustainable agricultural practices.

Residential Pollution Control
Clean Cooking Solutions: Promotion of cleaner cooking technologies, such as LPG and electric stoves, to reduce indoor air pollution.

Energy Efficiency: Encouraging the use of energy-efficient appliances and lighting to reduce household emissions.

International Cooperation and Assistance

Bilateral and Multilateral Agreements
Collaborations: Partnerships with international organizations and countries to share knowledge, technology, and best practices for air quality management.

Funding and Support: Access to international funding and technical assistance for implementing air pollution control measures.

Global Environmental Initiatives
Participation: Active involvement in global initiatives such as the United Nations Environment Programme (UNEP) and the World Health Organization (WHO) to combat air pollution.

Compliance: Commitment to international environmental agreements and protocols aimed at reducing air pollution.

Conclusion
India has a strong legislative framework to tackle air pollution thanks to the Clean Air Act, principally implemented by the Air (Prevention and Control of Pollution) Act, 1981. Enforcing and implementing regulations effectively are still difficult tasks in spite of the extensive provisions and regulatory framework. Encouraging recent measures to improve air quality include the Graded Response Action Plan (GRAP), the National Clean Air

Programme (NCAP), and strict automobile emission requirements. To manage air pollution, however, the necessary measures of increased public participation, improved coordination, improved resource allocation, and persistent efforts are required. To guarantee purer air and a better environment for India's future generations, aggressive policy-making, stringent enforcement, and ongoing monitoring will be essential.

5. Clean Water Act, 1974

The Water (Prevention and Control of Pollution) Act, 1974, primarily governs India's legal framework for controlling water pollution. The cornerstone of India's attempts to control and lessen water pollution is this act, together with later revisions and new policies. The Act intends to create pollution control boards to supervise the application of its provisions, prevent and regulate water pollution, and maintain or restore the wholesomeness of water. This article provides a thorough analysis of the Indian Clean Water Act, including its provisions, methods of implementation, difficulties, and most current changes.

Background and Need

In India, the contamination of rivers, lakes, groundwater, and coastal waterways by wastewater has emerged as a serious threat to both the environment and public health. A significant amount of water body contamination has resulted from rapid industry, urbanization, agricultural runoff, and poor wastewater treatment. Significant health concerns, biodiversity, and economic activities like fishing and tourism are all threatened by the deterioration of water quality. Addressing these issues and advancing environmentally friendly water management techniques was the goal of the 1974 Water (Prevention and Control of Pollution) Act.

- **Key Provisions of the Water (Prevention and Control of Pollution) Act, 1974**

Objectives

Prevention, Control, and Abatement: The Act aims to prevent, control, and abate water pollution to protect and improve the quality of water.

Establishment of Boards: Establishes Central and State Pollution Control Boards (CPCB and SPCBs) to implement and enforce the provisions of the Act.

Regulatory Framework

Effluent Standards: Authorizes the setting of standards for the discharge of pollutants into water bodies from various sources, including industries, municipal bodies, and agriculture.

Permits and Licensing: Requires industries to obtain consent from the SPCBs before discharging any effluents into water bodies.

Monitoring and Inspections: Grants powers to the CPCB and SPCBs to monitor water quality, inspect facilities, and enforce compliance with discharge standards.

Pollution Control Areas: Designates specific areas as pollution control zones where stringent regulations are applied to control water pollution.

Penalties and Enforcement

Non-Compliance: Prescribes penalties for industries and individuals who fail to comply with the standards and regulations.

Legal Actions: Allows the pollution control boards to initiate legal proceedings against defaulters.

Polluter Pays Principle: Implements the 'polluter pays' principle, ensuring that polluters bear the cost of pollution control and remediation measures.

Public Participation

Public Awareness: Promotes public awareness and education on the effects of water pollution and the importance of clean water.

Citizen's Right: Empowers citizens to report violations and file complaints regarding water pollution.

Community Involvement: Encourages community involvement in water quality monitoring and improvement initiatives.

- **Implementation Mechanisms**

Central Pollution Control Board (CPCB)
Role: Formulates policies, sets standards, and provides technical assistance to SPCBs.

Activities: Conducts nationwide water quality monitoring, research, and development activities related to pollution control.

Data Management: Maintains a comprehensive database on water quality, sources of pollution, and trends to inform policy decisions.

State Pollution Control Boards (SPCBs)
Role: Implement and enforce the regulations set by the CPCB within their respective states.

Activities: Issue permits, conduct inspections, and monitor water quality at the state level.

Local Initiatives: Develop and implement state-specific action plans to address unique water quality challenges.

National Water Quality Monitoring Programme (NWQMP)
Objective: Monitor water quality across India to assess pollution levels and trends.

Network: Operates a network of monitoring stations in rivers, lakes, groundwater, and coastal areas to collect water quality data.

Reporting: Publishes regular reports on water quality status, trends, and compliance with standards.

- **Challenges and Issues**

Enforcement and Compliance
Resource Constraints: SPCBs often face financial and human resource constraints, limiting their ability to effectively enforce regulations.

Industrial Resistance: Industries sometimes resist compliance due to the cost of implementing pollution control technologies.

Coordination Issues: Lack of coordination between various government agencies and departments hampers effective implementation.

Corruption: Corruption and bureaucratic inefficiencies can undermine enforcement efforts.

- **Data and Monitoring**

Insufficient Coverage: The existing network of monitoring stations is insufficient to cover the entire country comprehensively.

Data Quality: Issues with data accuracy, consistency, and real-time availability hinder effective decision-making.

Technological Gaps: Limited use of advanced monitoring technologies and real-time data analytics.

- **Public Awareness and Participation**

Awareness Levels: Low levels of public awareness and participation in water quality management activities.

Engagement: Limited mechanisms for meaningful public engagement and input into policy-making processes.

Behavioural Change: Challenges in promoting behavioural change towards pollution reduction practices.

- **Recent Developments and Initiatives**

National Mission for Clean Ganga (NMCG)

Launch: Launched as part of the Namami Gange Programme to rejuvenate the Ganges River.

Goals: Aims to achieve effective abatement of pollution, conservation, and rejuvenation of the Ganges.

Strategies: Includes River surface cleaning, sewage treatment infrastructure development, riverfront development, and public awareness campaigns.

Funding and Support: Provides financial and technical support for various projects under the mission.

Swachh Bharat Abhiyan (Clean India Mission)

Objective: A nationwide campaign to clean the streets, roads, and infrastructure of India, indirectly contributing to water pollution control.

Initiatives: Promotes the construction of toilets, solid waste management, and elimination of open defecation, which helps reduce contamination of water bodies.

Public Participation: Encourages citizen participation in maintaining cleanliness and hygiene, thereby reducing water pollution.

Jal Shakti Abhiyan

Launch: A time-bound, mission-mode water conservation campaign.

Focus Areas: Emphasizes rainwater harvesting, groundwater recharge, and reuse of treated wastewater.

Community Involvement: Engages local communities, NGOs, and other stakeholders in water conservation activities.

National Water Mission (NWM)

Objective: Part of the National Action Plan on Climate Change (NAPCC), focusing on the conservation of water, minimizing wastage, and ensuring more equitable distribution.

Strategies: Enhances water use efficiency, promotes integrated water resources management, and ensures sustainable development of water resources.

Research and Development: Supports R&D activities to develop innovative technologies for water conservation and pollution control.

- **Sector-Specific Interventions**

Industrial Pollution Control

Effluent Treatment Plants (ETPs): Mandates the installation of ETPs in industries to treat wastewater before discharge.

Common Effluent Treatment Plants (CETPs): Encourages the establishment of CETPs for clusters of small-scale industries to collectively treat their effluents.

Zero Liquid Discharge (ZLD): Promotes the adoption of ZLD technologies in highly polluting industries to ensure no discharge of untreated wastewater.

Agricultural Pollution Control

Nutrient Management: Promotes the use of balanced fertilizers and integrated nutrient management practices to reduce agricultural runoff.

Pesticide Control: Regulates the use of pesticides and promotes organic farming to minimize chemical runoff into water bodies.

Irrigation Efficiency: Encourages the adoption of efficient irrigation techniques such as drip and sprinkler irrigation to reduce water wastage and contamination.

Urban and Municipal Wastewater Management

Sewage Treatment Plants (STPs): Mandates the establishment of STPs in urban areas to treat municipal wastewater before discharge into water bodies.

Decentralized Wastewater Treatment: Promotes decentralized wastewater treatment systems in smaller towns and rural areas.

Reuse and Recycling: Encourages the reuse and recycling of treated wastewater for non-potable purposes such as irrigation, industrial processes, and landscaping.

Groundwater Management

Aquifer Mapping and Management: Implements aquifer mapping and management plans to sustainably manage groundwater resources.

Groundwater Recharge: Promotes groundwater recharge through rainwater harvesting, recharge wells, and managed aquifer recharge (MAR) techniques.

Regulation and Monitoring: Strengthens regulations and monitoring of groundwater extraction to prevent over-exploitation and contamination.

- **International Cooperation and Assistance**

Bilateral and Multilateral Agreements

Collaborations: Partnerships with international organizations and countries to share knowledge, technology, and best practices for water quality management.

Funding and Support: Access to international funding and technical assistance for implementing water pollution control measures.

Global Environmental Initiatives

Participation: Active involvement in global initiatives such as the United Nations Environment Programme (UNEP) and the World Health Organization (WHO) to combat water pollution.

Compliance: Commitment to international environmental agreements and protocols aimed at reducing water pollution.

Conclusion

A strong legislative framework for addressing water pollution is provided by India's Clean Water Act, which is mainly represented by the Water (Prevention and Control of Pollution) Act, 1974. Effective implementation and enforcement continue to be difficult despite the extensive laws and regulatory instruments. Water quality has improved significantly as a result of recent initiatives like the Jal Shakti Abhiyan, Swachh Bharat Abhiyan, and National Mission for Clean Ganga (NMCG). To achieve the intended results in water pollution prevention, however, requires persistent efforts, improved resource allocation, improved coordination, and greater public participation. To guarantee cleaner water and a healthier environment for future generations in India, tough enforcement, proactive policy-making, and ongoing monitoring will be essential.

6. Resource Conservation and Recovery Act (RCRA)

The Resource Conservation and Recovery Act (RCRA) of the United States do not have a direct equivalent in India. To handle hazardous waste, encourage resource conservation, and guarantee material recovery and recycling, India has created its own set of laws and regulations. The Hazardous and Other Wastes (Management and Trans-boundary Movement) Rules, 2016, the Environment (Protection) Act, 1986, and other relevant regulations provide the main legislative framework that governs waste management and resource conservation in India. This thorough explanation describes India's policies for material recovery, resource conservation, and hazardous waste management.

Background and Need

A substantial amount of waste, particularly hazardous waste, has been generated as a result of India's quick industrialization and urbanization. To safeguard both human health and the environment, this waste must be managed effectively. To ensure resource conservation and advance sustainable development, the legislative framework attempts to control the handling, transportation, treatment, and disposal of hazardous waste.

Key Legislation and Regulations

- **Environment (Protection) Act, 1986**

Objectives: Provides a comprehensive framework for environmental protection, including the management of hazardous waste.

Provisions: Empowers the government to set standards, regulate industrial activities, and enforce compliance to prevent environmental pollution.

- **Hazardous and Other Wastes (Management and Trans-boundary Movement) Rules, 2016**

Objectives: Regulates the management of hazardous and other wastes, ensuring their safe handling, treatment, and disposal.

Provisions: Establishes guidelines for the generation, collection, storage, transportation, recycling, and disposal of hazardous waste.

- **Key Features of the Hazardous and Other Wastes (Management and Transboundary Movement) Rules, 2016**

Waste Classification

Categories of Waste: Classifies hazardous waste into different categories based on their physical, chemical, and biological characteristics.

Hazardous Waste: Includes waste materials that pose a significant risk to health and the environment.

Generator Responsibilities

Authorization: Requires waste generators to obtain authorization from the State Pollution Control Boards (SPCBs) for handling hazardous waste.

Management Plans: Mandates the preparation and implementation of waste management plans by generators.

Record Keeping: Obligates generators to maintain records of waste generation, storage, transportation, and disposal.

Transportation and Storage

Transport Regulations: Sets standards for the safe transportation of hazardous waste, including packaging, labelling, and documentation requirements.

Storage Guidelines: Specifies conditions for the safe storage of hazardous waste to prevent contamination and accidents.

Treatment, Disposal, and Recycling

Treatment Facilities: Regulates the establishment and operation of hazardous waste treatment facilities.

Disposal Methods: Defines acceptable disposal methods, including landfilling, incineration, and other approved technologies.

Recycling and Recovery: Encourages the recycling and recovery of materials from hazardous waste to promote resource conservation.

Import and Export Regulations

Trans-boundary Movement: Controls the import and export of hazardous waste to ensure compliance with international conventions, such as the Basel Convention.

Approval Process: Requires prior approval from the Ministry of Environment, Forest and Climate Change (MoEFCC) for the trans-boundary movement of hazardous waste.

- **Implementation Mechanisms**

Central Pollution Control Board (CPCB)
Role: Formulates policies, sets standards, and provides technical assistance for hazardous waste management.

Activities: Monitors compliance, conducts research, and promotes best practices in waste management.

State Pollution Control Boards (SPCBs)
Role: Implement and enforce hazardous waste regulations at the state level.

Activities: Issue authorizations, conduct inspections, and monitor waste management practices.

- **Challenges and Issues**

Compliance and Enforcement
Resource Constraints: SPCBs often face financial and human resource constraints, limiting their ability to effectively enforce regulations.

Industrial Non-Compliance: Some industries resist compliance due to the cost of implementing waste management technologies.

Coordination Issues: Lack of coordination between various government agencies hampers effective implementation.

Corruption: Corruption and bureaucratic inefficiencies can undermine enforcement efforts.

Data and Monitoring
Insufficient Coverage: The existing monitoring network is insufficient to cover the entire country comprehensively.

Data Quality: Issues with data accuracy, consistency, and real-time availability hinder effective decision-making.

Technological Gaps: Limited use of advanced monitoring technologies and real-time data analytics.

Public Awareness and Participation

Awareness Levels: Low levels of public awareness and participation in hazardous waste management activities.

Engagement: Limited mechanisms for meaningful public engagement and input into policy-making processes.

Behavioural Change: Challenges in promoting behavioural change towards waste reduction and proper disposal practices.

- **Recent Developments and Initiatives**

Extended Producer Responsibility (EPR)

Concept: Holds producers responsible for the entire lifecycle of their products, including end-of-life management.

Implementation: Requires producers to establish systems for the collection, recycling, and disposal of their products, particularly electronic waste (e-waste) and plastic waste.

Swachh Bharat Abhiyan (Clean India Mission)

Objective: A nationwide campaign to clean the streets, roads, and infrastructure of India, indirectly contributing to better waste management.

Initiatives: Promotes the construction of toilets, solid waste management, and elimination of open defecation, which helps reduce contamination of land and water bodies.

National Green Tribunal (NGT)

Role: A specialized judicial body to address environmental disputes and enforce environmental regulations.

Activities: Adjudicates cases related to hazardous waste management, ensuring compliance with legal standards and penalizing defaulters.

- **Sector-Specific Interventions**

Industrial Waste Management

Effluent Treatment Plants (ETPs): Mandates the installation of ETPs in industries to treat wastewater before discharge.

Common Effluent Treatment Plants (CETPs): Encourages the establishment of CETPs for clusters of small-scale industries to collectively treat their effluents.

Zero Liquid Discharge (ZLD): Promotes the adoption of ZLD technologies in highly polluting industries to ensure no discharge of untreated wastewater.

E-Waste Management
E-Waste (Management) Rules, 2016: Provides a framework for the management of electronic waste, including collection, recycling, and disposal.

Producer Responsibility Organizations (PROs): Facilitates the collection and recycling of e-waste through authorized organizations.

Plastic Waste Management
Plastic Waste Management Rules, 2016: Regulates the manufacture, sale, and disposal of plastic products.

Ban on Single-Use Plastics: Implements a phased ban on single-use plastic items to reduce environmental pollution.

Biomedical Waste Management
Biomedical Waste Management Rules, 2016: Provides guidelines for the segregation, collection, treatment, and disposal of biomedical waste generated by healthcare facilities.

Treatment Facilities: Ensures the establishment of adequate treatment facilities to manage biomedical waste safely.

- **International Cooperation and Assistance**

Bilateral and Multilateral Agreements
Collaborations: Partnerships with international organizations and countries to share knowledge, technology, and best practices for hazardous waste management.

Funding and Support: Access to international funding and technical assistance for implementing waste management measures.

Global Environmental Initiatives

Participation: Active involvement in global initiatives such as the United Nations Environment Programme (UNEP) and the World Health Organization (WHO) to combat hazardous waste pollution.

Compliance: Commitment to international environmental agreements and protocols aimed at reducing hazardous waste pollution.

- **Conclusion**

Although not exactly the same as the US RCRA, India's legal framework for hazardous waste management, resource conservation, and recovery offers a strong basis for tackling the nation's waste management issues. A number of laws and regulations, including the Environment (Protection) Act of 1986 and the Hazardous and Other Wastes (Management and Trans-boundary Movement) Rules of 2016, provide detailed guidelines for the safe handling, processing, and disposal of hazardous waste. Challenges including enforcement, compliance, data veracity, and public awareness still exist despite tremendous efforts and advancements. Improving waste management procedures requires recent initiatives like the National Green Tribunal (NGT), Swachh Bharat Abhiyan, and Extended Producer Responsibility (EPR). Ensuring sustainable waste management, resource conservation, and environmental protection in India would require vigilant policymaking, stringent enforcement, and ongoing monitoring.

7. Comprehensive Environmental Response, Compensation, and Liability Act (CERCLA or Superfund)

India has created a framework for handling environmental pollution, hazardous waste management, and polluter responsibility, but it lacks a direct counterpart to the United States' Comprehensive Environmental Response, Compensation, and responsibility Act (CERCLA), popularly known as Superfund. The Public Liability Insurance Act of 1991, the Hazardous and Other Wastes (Management and Trans-boundary Movement) Rules of 2016, and the Environment (Protection) Act of 1986 are just a few of the laws and regulations that make up this framework. This explanation offers a thorough analysis of India's strategy for handling environmental liabilities and contamination.

Background and Need

India's fast urbanization and industrialization have created serious environmental problems, such as dangerous material contamination of the air, water, and soil. In order to safeguard both the environment and public health, these contaminated sites must be properly managed and cleaned up. The legal system in India seeks to control the management of dangerous materials, maintain accountability, and encourage the remediation and rehabilitation of contaminated areas.

Key Legislation and Regulations

- **Environment (Protection) Act, 1986**

Objectives: This Act provides a comprehensive framework for environmental protection, including the regulation of hazardous substances.

Provisions: It empowers the government to set environmental standards, regulate industrial activities, and enforce compliance to prevent and control pollution.

- **Hazardous and Other Wastes (Management and Trans-boundary Movement) Rules, 2016**

Objectives: These rules regulate the management of hazardous and other wastes to ensure their safe handling, treatment, and disposal.

Provisions: They establish guidelines for the generation, collection, storage, transportation, recycling, and disposal of hazardous waste.

- **Public Liability Insurance Act, 1991**

Objectives: This Act provides immediate relief to persons affected by accidents involving hazardous substances.

Provisions: It mandates that industries handling hazardous substances maintain insurance policies to cover potential liabilities arising from accidents.

National Green Tribunal (NGT) Act, 2010

Objectives: This Act establishes the National Green Tribunal to handle cases related to environmental protection and conservation of forests and other natural resources.

Provisions: The NGT is empowered to adjudicate disputes related to environmental laws, including those concerning the remediation of contaminated sites.

- **Key Features of India's Approach to Environmental Contamination and Liability**

Identification and Assessment of Contaminated Sites

Survey and Inventory: Conducting nationwide surveys and maintaining an inventory of contaminated sites.

Risk Assessment: Performing risk assessments to evaluate the extent of contamination and its potential impact on human health and the environment.

Liability and Responsibility

Polluter Pays Principle: Holding polluters financially responsible for the contamination they cause, including the costs of cleanup and restoration.

Strict Liability: Imposing strict liability on industries and entities that handle hazardous substances, ensuring they are accountable for any environmental damage.

Cleanup and Remediation

Remediation Standards: Establishing standards and guidelines for the cleanup and remediation of contaminated sites.

Remediation Plans: Requiring responsible parties to develop and implement remediation plans to restore contaminated sites to acceptable standards.

Government Intervention: Allowing government agencies to intervene and undertake cleanup activities if responsible parties fail to do so.

Financial Mechanisms and Funds

Environmental Relief Fund: Creating funds to provide financial assistance for the cleanup of contaminated sites, particularly in cases where the polluter is unknown or unable to pay.

Public Liability Insurance: Mandating insurance policies for industries handling hazardous substances to cover potential liabilities and ensure compensation for affected parties.

- **Implementation Mechanisms**

Central Pollution Control Board (CPCB)
Role: The CPCB formulates policies, sets standards, and provides technical assistance for the management of hazardous substances and contaminated sites.

Activities: The CPCB monitors compliance, conducts research, and promotes best practices in environmental management.

State Pollution Control Boards (SPCBs)
Role: SPCBs implement and enforce hazardous waste regulations at the state level.

Activities: SPCBs issue authorizations, conduct inspections, and monitor waste management practices.

National Green Tribunal (NGT)
Role: The NGT is a specialized judicial body to address environmental disputes and enforce environmental regulations.

Activities: The NGT adjudicates cases related to environmental contamination, ensuring compliance with legal standards and penalizing defaulters.

- **Challenges and Issues**

Identification and Assessment
Data Gaps: There is a lack of comprehensive data on the extent and nature of contamination at various sites.

Technical Expertise: Limited availability of technical expertise and resources for conducting thorough site assessments.

Enforcement and Compliance
Resource Constraints: SPCBs and other regulatory bodies often face financial and human resource constraints, limiting their ability to enforce regulations effectively.

Industrial Resistance: Some industries resist compliance due to the cost of implementing cleanup and remediation measures.

Coordination Issues: Lack of coordination between various government agencies hampers effective implementation.

Funding and Financial Mechanisms

Insufficient Funding: Limited financial resources for the cleanup and remediation of contaminated sites, particularly in cases involving orphan sites where the polluter is unknown or insolvent.

Insurance Coverage: Ensuring adequate insurance coverage for all industries handling hazardous substances is a challenge.

Public Awareness and Participation

Awareness Levels: There are low levels of public awareness and participation in environmental management activities.

Engagement: There are limited mechanisms for meaningful public engagement and input into policy-making processes.

- **Recent Developments and Initiatives**

National Clean Air Programme (NCAP)

Objective: This nationwide initiative aims to improve air quality and reduce air pollution, which indirectly contributes to reducing contamination from airborne pollutants.

Initiatives: The NCAP includes measures to control industrial emissions, vehicular pollution, and promote the use of cleaner technologies.

Swachh Bharat Abhiyan (Clean India Mission)

Objective: This nationwide campaign aims to clean the streets, roads, and infrastructure of India, indirectly contributing to better waste management and reduction of environmental contamination.

Initiatives: The campaign promotes the construction of toilets, solid waste management, and elimination of open defecation, which helps reduce contamination of land and water bodies.

Extended Producer Responsibility (EPR)

Concept: EPR holds producers responsible for the entire lifecycle of their products, including end-of-life management.

Implementation: Producers are required to establish systems for the collection, recycling, and disposal of their products, particularly electronic waste (e-waste) and plastic waste.

- **Sector-Specific Interventions**

Industrial Contamination

Effluent Treatment Plants (ETPs): Industries are mandated to install ETPs to treat wastewater before discharge.

Common Effluent Treatment Plants (CETPs): The establishment of CETPs for clusters of small-scale industries is encouraged to collectively treat their effluents.

Zero Liquid Discharge (ZLD): The adoption of ZLD technologies in highly polluting industries is promoted to ensure no discharge of untreated wastewater.

E-Waste Management

E-Waste (Management) Rules, 2016: These rules provide a framework for the management of electronic waste, including collection, recycling, and disposal.

Producer Responsibility Organizations (PROs): PROs facilitate the collection and recycling of e-waste through authorized organizations.

Plastic Waste Management

Plastic Waste Management Rules, 2016: These rules regulate the manufacture, sale, and disposal of plastic products.

Ban on Single-Use Plastics: A phased ban on single-use plastic items is implemented to reduce environmental pollution.

Groundwater Contamination

Central Ground Water Authority (CGWA): The CGWA regulates the extraction and use of groundwater to prevent over-exploitation and contamination.

Aquifer Mapping: The CGWA conducts aquifer mapping to identify contaminated groundwater sources and plan remediation activities.

- **International Cooperation and Assistance**

Bilateral and Multilateral Agreements

Collaborations: India has partnerships with international organizations and countries to share knowledge, technology, and best practices for environmental management.

Funding and Support: India accesses international funding and technical assistance for implementing environmental cleanup measures.

Global Environmental Initiatives

Participation: India actively participates in global initiatives such as the United Nations Environment Programme (UNEP) and the World Health Organization (WHO) to combat environmental contamination.

Compliance: India is committed to international environmental agreements and protocols aimed at reducing environmental pollution and contamination.

Conclusion

Although it is not a straight replica of the US CERCLA, India's legislative structure for controlling environmental contamination and guaranteeing accountability offers a strong basis for tackling the nation's environmental issues. A number of laws and regulations, including the Environment (Protection) Act of 1986 and the Hazardous and Other Wastes (Management and Trans-boundary Movement) Rules of 2016, provide detailed guidelines for the safe handling, disposal, and treatment of hazardous materials. Challenges including enforcement, compliance, data veracity, and public awareness still exist despite tremendous efforts and advancements. Improving environmental management practices requires recent initiatives like the National Green Tribunal (NGT), Swachh Bharat Abhiyan, and Extended Producer Responsibility (EPR). In order to guarantee sustainable environmental management and protection in India, stringent enforcement, proactive policymaking, and ongoing monitoring would be necessary.

8. Endangered Species Act, 1973

The conservation of many endangered species is a concern for India, a country known for its vast biodiversity, as they are at risk from habitat destruction, poaching, and conflicts between humans and wildlife. The nation has created a strong legislative framework and carried out a number of conservation efforts to safeguard its wildlife, even though it does not directly mirror the United States' Endangered Species Act, 1973 (ESA). This extensive exposition explores India's strategy for the preservation of endangered species, emphasizing significant legislation, conservation initiatives, obstacles, and contemporary advancements.

- **Legal Framework**

Wildlife Protection Act, 1972

The cornerstone of India's efforts to conserve wildlife is the Wildlife Protection Act, 1972. It assigns different schedules to different species, providing differing levels of protection. In addition to providing measures for habitat protection and species recovery, the Act forbids the shooting, poaching, and trading of endangered species included in Schedule I.

Biological Diversity Act, 2002

The objectives of this Act are to control access to genetic resources and preserve biological variety. It creates procedures for the preservation of biodiversity, their sustainable use, and the just distribution of the advantages that result from their usage.

Forest Conservation Act, 1980

The Forest Conservation Act restricts the use of forest land for uses other than forests in order to reduce habitat loss and fragmentation. It protects important habitats by requiring prior consent from the federal government for any such diversion.

Environment (Protection) Act, 1986

The central government is given the authority under this Act to take the required actions for environmental protection, including the preservation of wildlife. It offers a framework for legislation to control actions that could endanger wildlife and their ecosystems.

- **Conservation Initiatives**

Species Protection and Management

Programs for the conservation of particular species are carried out by India; examples are Project Elephant for elephant conservation and Project Tiger for tigers. To protect endangered species, these programs emphasize habitat management, anti-poaching measures, and community involvement.

Wildlife Crime Prevention and Enforcement

The Wildlife Crime Control Bureau (WCCB) is one of the specialized organizations that fights crimes involving wildlife and works to stop poaching and the illegal wildlife trade. Initiatives to increase capacity help law enforcement organizations become more adept at preventing wildlife-related crimes.

International Cooperation

India works with foreign organizations and other nations to address trans-boundary conservation challenges. In order to control the international trade in endangered animals and their goods, it upholds the terms of international accords like CITES.

Research and Monitoring

Data from scientific studies, monitoring programs, and routine surveys are crucial for conservation planning and management. The application of technology, such as video traps and GPS tracking, fortifies conservation interventions and improves monitoring operations.

- **Challenges and Issues**

Habitat Loss and Fragmentation

Numerous species are at risk of extinction due to habitat loss and fragmentation brought on by urbanization, infrastructural development, and deforestation. Populations become more isolated due to fragmentation, which lowers genetic diversity and makes them more susceptible to extinction.

Human-Wildlife Conflict

Where habitats overlap, human-wildlife conflicts intensify, resulting in retaliatory deaths and habitat loss. The requirements of local communities for a living must be balanced with conservation objectives in order to address human-wildlife conflict.

Poaching and Illegal Wildlife Trade
Poaching and the illegal trade in endangered species and their components are motivated by the ongoing demand for wildlife items. The smuggling and trafficking activities of organized crime syndicates present serious obstacles to the conservation of wildlife.

Inadequate Funding and Resources
Implementing conservation measures and enforcement activities is hampered by a lack of funds and human resources. The ability to successfully solve conservation concerns is hampered by limited resources and a lack of skilled workers.

- **Recent Developments and Initiatives**

National Mission for Clean Ganga (Namami Gange)
The 2014 launch of Namami Gange is part of an initiative to restore the Ganga River ecosystem, which includes protecting aquatic species that are in danger of extinction, like the Gangetic dolphin and gharial. It consists of community involvement, riverfront development, biodiversity preservation, and pollution management strategies.

Great Indian Bustard Conservation Project
The Great Indian Bustard Conservation Project was started by the government in 2019 in an effort to preserve the severely endangered bird species. The project's main goals are to reduce risks to the species and guarantee its future through habitat restoration, captive breeding, and community involvement.

National Biodiversity Authority (NBA)
The NBA is essential to the preservation of biodiversity and the control of access to biological resources. It supports biodiversity research, conservation efforts, and the implementation of ABS agreements to guarantee fair benefit sharing.

- **Conclusion**

India has used many strategies to protect endangered species, including international cooperation, conservation programs, legislation, and enforcement methods. Even with the tremendous progress that has been done, problems including habitat degradation, poaching, conflict between humans and wildlife, and resource scarcity still exist. The government's dedication to biodiversity protection is exemplified by recent measures; nonetheless, coordinated efforts from stakeholders are necessary to guarantee the survival of endangered species and the conservation of India's natural heritage for posterity.

9. Energy Policy Act, 2005

The energy policy framework of India comprises a wide range of policies, initiatives, and regulations that are designed to tackle the nation's energy requirements, encourage sustainability, and improve energy security. India has developed a comprehensive set of policies and programs to direct its energy sector, even though it lacks a direct counterpart to the US Energy Policy Act, 2005. This comprehensive study examines India's energy policy environment, emphasizing important programs, difficulties, current events, and future directions.

Context and Significance:

India, one of the biggest and fastest-growing economies in the world, is confronted with serious energy-related issues as a result of its quickening industrialization, urbanization, and population expansion. Sustainable development critically depends on meeting the nation's expanding energy needs while lowering carbon emissions, guaranteeing universal access to electricity, and boosting energy security. India's energy transition and solutions to these intricate problems are greatly influenced by the country's energy policy environment.

- **Key Policy Initiatives:**

National Action Plan on Climate Change (NAPCC):

The NAPCC is a comprehensive approach to mitigating and adapting to climate change. It consists of eight national missions that support low-carbon development by concentrating on energy efficiency, sustainable agriculture, renewable energy, water conservation, and other important sectors.

National Solar Mission (NSM):
NSM uses aggressive goals, monetary rewards, and encouraging legislation to hasten the installation of solar power in India. It is essential for promoting renewable energy technology, lowering reliance on fossil fuels, and diversifying the energy mix.

Ujwal DISCOM Assurance Yojana (UDAY):
UDAY seeks to improve service delivery, reduce financial losses, and streamline operations in order to transform India's electricity distribution industry. To rejuvenate the infrastructure for the distribution of energy, it focuses on demand-side management, operational enhancements, and financial restructuring.

Energy Efficiency Initiatives:
India has put in place a number of energy-efficiency programs, such as the Standards and Labelling program and the Perform, Achieve, and Trade (PAT) scheme. The aim of these projects is to lower energy consumption and carbon emissions by improving energy efficiency in houses, vehicles, appliances, and industry.

Renewable Energy Targets:
India has set high goals for the use of renewable energy, aiming to reach 175 GW of capacity by 2022 and 450 GW by 2030. The production of renewable energy from sources including solar, wind, biomass, and hydropower is encouraged by the government through the use of incentives, subsidies, feed-in tariffs, and competitive bidding procedures.

- **Challenges and Issues:**

Energy Access and Equity:
Millions of people in India still lack access to clean cooking fuels and consistent energy, despite tremendous advances in this area. Programs for energy access, off-grid alternatives, and rural electrification are crucial for addressing energy poverty and advancing socioeconomic development.

Energy Security and Dependence on Imports:
India's excessive dependence on imported fossil fuels, especially gas and oil, puts both economic stability and energy security at risk. In order to

reduce reliance on imports and geopolitical risks, it is imperative to diversify the energy mix, encourage domestic production, and invest in alternative fuels.

Environmental Sustainability:
India is confronted with environmental issues such as water scarcity, air pollution, and the effects of climate change. It is imperative to shift towards more environmentally friendly energy sources, enhance energy efficiency, and implement sustainable practices in order to prevent environmental degradation and protect public health.

Infrastructure and Financing:
Access to reasonably priced financing and investment capital is necessary to meet the enormous investment requirements in energy infrastructure, transmission networks, and renewable energy projects. To close the financial gap for infrastructure, public-private partnerships, increased project bankability, and domestic and international financing mobilization are crucial.

- **Recent Developments and Initiatives**

Atmanirbhar Bharat Abhiyan (Self-Reliant India Initiative):
Initiated in reaction to the COVID-19 epidemic, Atmanirbhar Bharat seeks to encourage indigenous production, lessen reliance on imports, and increase self-sufficiency in a number of areas, including energy. To strengthen economic sovereignty, it places a strong emphasis on supply chain resilience, local production, and technological advancement.

Green Hydrogen Mission:
The goal of India's Green Hydrogen Mission is to encourage the production and application of green hydrogen as a clean energy source. The goal is to drive down prices and accelerate adoption while focusing on creating infrastructure, technologies, and the capacity for producing green hydrogen.

Climate Resilient Infrastructure Development Facility (CRIDF):
CRIDF promotes the construction of climate-resilient infrastructure in India, with an emphasis on sustainable transportation, water management, and renewable energy. To improve resilience and sustainability, it offers climate-resilient infrastructure projects financial support, capacity building, and technical support.

- **Conclusion**

India has a dynamic and diverse energy policy landscape that reflects the nation's various energy needs, socioeconomic interests, and environmental requirements. Even while energy efficiency, renewable energy, and power sector reform have advanced significantly, there are still many obstacles to overcome. For India's energy transition, addressing energy availability, lowering reliance on imports, minimizing environmental effects, and raising capital are vital goals. Navigating the intricacies of India's energy landscape and achieving resilient, inclusive, and sustainable energy systems for the future will need sustained policy innovation and stakeholder involvement.

❖ **Components of Environmental Laws and Regulations:**

1.) Scope of Environmental Laws:
The scope of environmental laws includes a broad range of statutes and regulations designed to mitigate pollution, conserve natural resources, and safeguard the environment. These laws are intended to control human actions that may have an influence on the environment as well as to address a variety of environmental challenges. Environmental regulations have a wide range of applications and scope, covering areas such as:

Air Quality:
The main goal of environmental regulations pertaining to air quality is to control the amount of pollutants released by automobiles, factories, and other sources. These regulations specify permissible air pollution limits; mandate emissions control devices, and mandate monitoring programs in an effort to safeguard public health.

Water Quality:
The goal of water quality laws is to prevent pollution of groundwater and surface water. These laws define water quality standards, control the release of contaminants into bodies of water, and mandate storm water management and wastewater treatment. They also deal with matters like the preservation of wetlands, aquatic habitat protection, and drinking water safety.

Waste Management:
Solid and hazardous waste generation, handling, treatment, and disposal are covered by environmental laws pertaining to waste management. These regulations encourage recycling, trash minimization, and appropriate disposal techniques in an effort to lessen the negative effects of waste on the environment. They also control the handling, storage, and transit of dangerous goods in order to avoid contamination and safeguard the environment and public health.

Land Use and Conservation:
Sustainable development, the preservation of biodiversity, and the protection of natural environments are the goals of land use and conservation laws. Land development, deforestation, habitat damage, and wildlife management are all governed by these rules. To protect ecosystems and natural resources, they also set up conservation easements, protected areas, and zoning laws.

Energy Efficiency and Conservation:
Reduced energy consumption, the promotion of renewable energy sources, and the mitigation of climate change are the goals of environmental regulations pertaining to energy efficiency and conservation. These regulations could include mandates for renewable energy incentives, appliance standards, automobile fuel economy, and energy-efficient building design. They also back projects like energy audits, energy saving programs, and the advancement of renewable energy sources.

Pollution Prevention and Control:
The goal of laws pertaining to pollution prevention and control is to reduce the number of pollutants released into the environment and lessen the

negative consequences that they have. These regulations control things like noise pollution, chemical use, industrial pollutants, and agricultural runoff. These could consist of emission standards, programs for preventing pollution, technologies for controlling it, and guidelines for reporting and monitoring.

International Cooperation:
International accords and treaties intended to address global environmental concerns are also included in the category of environmental laws. These accords make it easier for nations to work together to address problems including trans-boundary pollution, ozone depletion, biodiversity loss, and climate change. The Convention on Biological Diversity, the Kyoto Protocol, the Montreal Protocol, and the Paris Agreement are a few examples.

In conclusion, environmental laws include a broad spectrum of human activities and environmental challenges. Their scope is vast. At the local, state, and federal levels, these laws are essential in advancing environmental preservation, protection, and sustainability.

2.) International Environmental Agreements:
International environmental agreements are a cornerstone of efforts to solve urgent environmental issues and promote sustainable development practices globally. These legally binding frameworks, sometimes known as treaties or conventions, are agreements reached and ratified by nations in order to work together to address trans-boundary environmental concerns that cross national boundaries. They are vital tools in the global coordination and harmonization of efforts to conserve the environment, reduce pollution, and safeguard natural resources.

- ❖ **Here's an in-depth exploration of international environmental agreements:**

Purpose and Objectives:
- ❖ There are multiple main goals in mind while crafting international environmental agreements:

Mitigating Global Environmental Issues: They seek to address pressing global issues like depletion of natural resources, deforestation, marine pollution, biodiversity loss, and climate change.

Facilitating Cooperation and Collaboration: International environmental accords encourage cooperative action and mutual assistance in tackling common environmental issues by promoting communication, information exchange, and resource mobilization among nations.

Promoting Sustainable Development: These agreements make sure that human activities are carried out in a way that maintains ecological integrity and promotes intergenerational justice by attempting to harmonize environmental preservation with socioeconomic development goals.

Ensuring Equity and Fairness: The concepts of common but differentiated responsibilities and respective capabilities (CBDR-RC) are highlighted; these principles take into account the diverse capacities and vulnerabilities that different nations have when it comes to tackling environmental concerns, and they assign obligations accordingly.

❖ **Examples of International Environmental Agreements:**

a. Paris Agreement: The Paris Agreement, which was adopted in 2015 under the auspices of the United Nations Framework Convention on Climate Change (UNFCCC), is a historic agreement that aims to keep global warming well below 2 degrees Celsius above pre-industrial levels, with efforts to keep the increase in temperature to 1.5 degrees Celsius. It creates a framework for open reporting and accountability and urges all nations to take aggressive mitigation and adaptation measures.

b. Montreal Protocol: The 1987 adoption of the Montreal Protocol marked the beginning of an innovative international agreement to gradually phase out the manufacture and use of compounds that deplete the ozone layer, or ODSs, including halons and chlorofluorocarbons (CFCs). The protocol has been extremely effective in preventing catastrophic ozone depletion and has established a standard for international collaboration in the resolution of trans-boundary environmental issues.

c. Kyoto Protocol: The Kyoto Protocol was enacted in 1997 and was annexed to the UNFCCC. It imposed enforceable emission reduction targets for industrialized nations (Annex I parties) between 2008 and 2012. In an effort to encourage affordable mitigation strategies for climate change, it instituted market-based systems like emissions trading, the clean development mechanism (CDM), and joint implementation (JI) that facilitate emissions reductions.

d. United Nations Convention on the Law of the Sea (UNCLOS): UNCLOS is a historic treaty that was ratified in 1982 and provides the legal foundation for managing the world's oceans and seas. It covers a number of topics related to the preservation of the marine environment, such as marine pollution, resource management and conservation, and biodiversity preservation.

e. Convention on Biological Diversity (CBD): The CBD is a comprehensive international treaty that was signed during the 1992 Rio de Janeiro Earth Summit with the goals of preserving biodiversity, encouraging the sustainable use of biological resources, and guaranteeing a fair distribution of the benefits resulting from genetic resources. It demands the creation of protected areas, plans for conserving biodiversity, and methods for sustainable development.

❖ **Implementation and Compliance:**

International environmental agreements require efficient implementation and systems for monitoring compliance. Regular reporting of progress, peer evaluations, capacity-building programs, financial support for developing nations, and dispute resolution procedures are common components of these mechanisms. Achieving the goals of international accords and preserving the integrity of the framework for global environmental governance depend on compliance. Failure to comply may lead to diplomatic problems, harm one's reputation, and obstruct the achievement of common environmental objectives.

To sum up, global collaboration and solidarity in tackling urgent environmental concerns are greatly enhanced by international environmental agreements. These agreements assist both the welfare of the current and future generations as well as the ecological integrity of our world by offering a framework for cooperative action and mutual support. To meet their goals and promote the sustainability of the environment worldwide, compliance with international environmental agreements is essential.

3.) Regulatory agencies

Governmental organizations known as regulatory agencies are in charge of creating, carrying out, and upholding policies and regulations in particular fields or industries. When it comes to environmental governance, regulatory agencies are essential in monitoring environmental quality, ensuring that businesses and individuals follow environmental standards, and supervising compliance with environmental laws and regulations. They also have the responsibility of preserving the public's health, preserving natural resources, and promoting sustainable practices.

❖ Here's an in-depth exploration of regulatory agencies in the environmental sector:

Role and Responsibilities:

1. Development of Regulations: Regulations governing the preservation and protection of the environment are created and implemented by regulatory agencies. These regulations, which offer comprehensive instructions and requirements for compliance, are frequently based on legislation passed by legislative bodies.

2. Implementation of Policies: Regulatory agencies are responsible for putting regulations into effect and upholding them after they have been established. To make sure that environmental standards are met, this entails carrying out inspections, issuing licenses, and pursuing enforcement actions against non-compliant entities.

3. Enforcement of Regulations: Regulatory agencies are able to impose fines, penalties, injunctions, and license revocations among other enforcement measures in order to implement environmental regulations. To discourage non-compliance and hold offenders responsible for their conduct, enforcement measures are implemented.

4. Monitoring and Compliance: Regulatory agencies use a variety of techniques, including data collection, reporting requirements, and environmental monitoring programs, to monitor environmental quality and evaluate compliance with regulations. In order to confirm compliance and resolve infractions, they could also carry out audits and investigations.

5. Public Education and Outreach: Regulatory agencies conduct outreach and public education programs to increase public knowledge of environmental issues, laws, and best practices. They offer tools and information to assist communities, corporations, and people in realizing their environmental obligations and embracing sustainable practices.

Types of Regulatory Agencies:

1. Environmental Protection Agency's (EPA):
Government organizations in charge of managing environmental regulation and protection at the federal level are known as environmental protection agencies. They are essential in creating and implementing environmental laws and policies that protect the land, water, air, and public health. The US Environmental Protection Agency (EPA) is one example; it conducts research, establishes and enforces environmental regulations, and offers advice on environmental matters.

2. State/Provincial Environmental Agencies:
Many nations have decentralized systems for governing the environment, with separate environmental agencies in each state or province. These organizations are in charge of putting regional policies and initiatives into action that are suited to the particular environmental issues and goals under their purview. To guarantee uniformity and adherence to broad environmental goals, state or provincial environmental authorities frequently collaborate with federal or national agencies.

3. Local Environmental Departments:
To handle environmental challenges unique to their domain, local governments may set up environmental departments or agencies. The management of regional environmental resources, handling of pollution issues, and encouragement of sustainable community projects are the main objectives of these municipal environmental departments. They frequently supervise tasks like trash management, obtaining environmental permits, and keeping an eye on the condition of the air and water.

4. Sector-Specific Regulatory Bodies:
Sector-specific regulatory bodies exist in addition to general environmental agencies, and they are in charge of monitoring specific sectors or activities that have a substantial influence on the environment.

These regulatory bodies create and implement sector-specific regulations, guaranteeing adherence to environmental norms and tackling industry-specific issues. Examples include:

Nuclear Regulatory Commission (NRC): In charge of overseeing the security and safety of nuclear materials and facilities as well as nuclear energy regulation.

Federal Aviation Administration (FAA): Oversees all aviation-related operations, such as noise pollution, emissions from aircraft, and environmental control at airports.

5. International Environmental Organizations:

International environmental organizations are vital in establishing environmental standards and norms on a worldwide scale, even though they are not regulatory authorities in the conventional sense. International guidance, scientific evaluations, and coordination on environmental issues are provided by organizations like the World Health Organization (WHO), the United Nations Environment Programme (UNEP), and the Intergovernmental Panel on Climate Change (IPCC). They support the execution of international environmental agreements, foster knowledge sharing, and enable international cooperation.

❖ **Challenges and Considerations in Regulatory Agencies:**

1. Resource Constraints:

Regulatory agencies frequently deal with resource limitations, such as inadequate funds, a lack of employees, and antiquated facilities. These limitations may make it more difficult for them to properly carry out their duties, carry out inspections, and enforce laws. Agencies' capacity for research, data gathering, and analysis may be restricted by a lack of resources, making it more difficult for them to keep up with new developments in the environmental field.

2. Political Interference:

Political pressure or meddling by outside parties, such as interest groups, elected politicians, and lobbyists for the business, may be experienced by regulatory agencies. The impartiality and independence of regulatory decision-making processes can be compromised by political interference, which can result in regulatory capture, reduced enforcement, or delays in regulation. Sustaining public trust and confidence in regulatory agencies necessitates upholding regulatory independence and integrity.

3. Complexity of Regulations:

Understanding and adhering to environmental regulations can be difficult for both regulatory agencies and regulated organizations since they are sometimes complicated and open to interpretation. Regulations' complex nature can make them unclear, inconsistent, and difficult to comply with, especially for small enterprises or sectors with little funding for legal advice or regulatory compliance specialists.

4. Emerging Environmental Issues:

Climate change, emerging contaminants, and ecosystem degradation are just a few of the new environmental concerns that regulatory agencies must address. Regulations addressing these problems might need to be creative, grounded on research, and progressive. Developing adaptive management techniques, updating regulations, and incorporating new scientific discoveries are all necessary to stay up to date with the ever-evolving dangers to the environment.

5. Enforcement Challenges:

Due to jurisdictional difficulties, legal loopholes, and a lack of enforcement resources, enforcing environmental legislation can be difficult. Detecting infractions, gathering evidence, and pursuing enforcement proceedings against non-compliant firms may provide challenges for regulatory agencies. Environmental legislation compliance and deterrence may also be compromised by insufficient penalties or enforcement measures.

6. Coordination and Collaboration:

Coordination and cooperation between regulatory bodies, business, academia, non-governmental organizations (NGOs), and the general public are necessary since environmental regulation frequently encompasses numerous parties, jurisdictions, and levels of government. Different stakeholder priorities, mandates, and institutional cultures might make it difficult to collaborate effectively. To effectively manage complex environmental concerns, regulatory agencies must encourage collaboration, information exchange, and stakeholder engagement.

7. Technology and Data Management:
Technological and data management advancements bring regulatory agencies both opportunity and challenges. Technology advancements can improve monitoring, data analysis, and enforcement capacities, but they also drive agencies to change and make investments in new infrastructure, tools, and training. Effective regulatory oversight and decision-making depend on data systems being interoperable, secure, and reliable.

In summary, regulatory agencies create, carry out, and uphold laws that safeguard the environment and public health, which is an essential part of environmental governance. Through their efforts, environmental stewardship, sustainable development, and the preservation of natural resources are all advanced. The intricacy of environmental standards, political meddling, and resource limitations are some of the difficulties that regulatory agencies must deal with. To overcome these obstacles, cooperation, ingenuity, and a dedication to efficient environmental legislation and management are necessary.

4.) Compliance Requirements:
Compliance requirements are the set of requirements, standards, and practices that people, organizations, and entities must follow in order to abide by the laws, rules, and policies that are relevant to them. Compliance requirements, as used in environmental regulations, cover a broad spectrum of actions intended to guarantee that companies, sectors, and other interested parties conduct their operations in a way that reduces their environmental impact and complies with set environmental standards.

- ❖ **Here's a detailed overview of compliance requirements in environmental regulation:**

1. Permitting and Licensing: Regulatory authorities must grant permissions or licenses for a number of actions that may have an influence on the environment. Permissions for resource extraction or land development, hazardous waste, air emissions, and water discharge are a few examples of these permissions. Applications must usually be submitted, requirements must be met, and regulations pertaining to emissions, discharges, and environmental management practices must be followed in order to obtain permits.

2. Environmental Management Systems (EMS): Organizations can voluntarily implement an Environmental Management System (EMS), such as ISO 14001. This will help them manage their environmental responsibilities more systematically and achieve better environmental performance. An environmental management system (EMS) offers a framework for determining environmental risks, establishing goals and objectives, putting controls and procedures into place, and keeping track of and assessing environmental performance. An organization's dedication to environmental stewardship and ongoing improvement is demonstrated by its certification to ISO 14001 or equivalent EMS standards.

3. Reporting and Monitoring: Reports detailing the environmental performance, emissions, discharges, and regulatory compliance of regulated enterprises are frequently needed to be sent on a monthly basis to regulatory bodies. Data on waste creation and management, chemical use, pollution control methods, and air and water quality monitoring may all be subject to reporting requirements. Transparency, accountability, and regulatory oversight all depend on timely and accurate reporting.

4. Pollution Prevention and Control: In order to reduce pollution and lessen its negative effects on the environment, some industries are obliged to create and carry out pollution prevention plans. The methods, technologies, and best practices for cutting emissions, preserving resources, and enhancing environmental performance are described in these plans. Reducing sources of pollution, recycling, increasing energy efficiency, and implementing clean technologies are a few examples of pollution prevention strategies.

5. Training and Education: Achieving compliance with environmental standards requires making sure that staff members have received the necessary training and are aware of their environmental duties. Topics include waste management, emergency response protocols, pollution avoidance, and industry-specific regulations may all be included in training programs. In addition to enhancing compliance and preventing environmental mishaps, well-trained employees can foster an environmental responsibility culture in businesses.

6. Compliance Audits and Inspections: To find out if regulated companies are following environmental laws and regulations, regulatory bodies may do compliance audits or inspections. Audits can be planned or unexpected, and they can look at a number of environmental compliance-related topics, such as waste management, emissions, discharges, and operational procedures. If an audit finds non-compliance, there may be penalties, enforcement actions, or corrective activities taken.

To sum up, environmental regulations' compliance requirements cover a wide range of actions meant to guarantee that companies and sectors function in a way that preserves the environment and public health. Meeting compliance standards is crucial for reducing environmental impacts, guaranteeing regulatory compliance, and encouraging sustainable practices. This includes everything from acquiring licenses and reporting environmental data to putting pollution control measures into place and performing compliance audits. Organizations can show their dedication to environmental stewardship and help create a more sustainable and healthy future by following compliance regulations.

5.) Penalties for Non-compliance:

Penalties for non-compliance with environmental regulations are actions taken by regulatory bodies or authorities to hold people, groups, or companies responsible for breaking environmental laws and standards. These fines are intended to ensure that environmental protection policies are properly implemented, discourage non-compliance, and encourage adherence to legislation.

❖ **Here's a detailed overview of penalties for non-compliance with environmental regulations:**

Administrative Penalties:

1. Fines and Monetary Penalties: If an organization is discovered to be in breach of environmental standards, regulatory agencies are empowered to levy fines or other financial penalties. The gravity of the infraction, the harm done to the environment, and the applicable regulations may all affect how many fines are imposed. Penalties for severe or recurring transgressions can range from hefty penalties to modest amounts for small infractions.

2. Civil Penalties: In order to remedy environmental infractions, civil penalties may be levied through administrative procedures or civil lawsuits. Fines, compensation for environmental harm, and injunctive relief to mandate corrective measures or adherence to legal requirements are a few examples of these sanctions. Compensation for environmental harm, deterrence of future violations, and encouragement of environmental restoration and rehabilitation are the three main goals of civil fines.

Regulatory Enforcement Actions:

3. Permit Revocation or Suspension: Regulatory bodies have the authority to suspend or cancel permits given to non-compliant firms in the event of severe or persistent infractions. Revocation or suspension of a permit may make it illegal to carry out any actions that endanger the environment or cause harm to it, and it may necessitate stopping operations until compliance is obtained.

4. Compliance Orders: Regulatory bodies have the authority to issue compliance orders, which mandate particular measures to be taken by non-compliant entities in order to resolve environmental problems and comply with regulatory standards. Orders for compliance may include requirements for pollution control methods, timelines for corrective actions, and obligations for environmental reporting and monitoring.

Criminal Sanctions:

5. Criminal Prosecution: Regulatory bodies or law enforcement agencies may seek criminal charges against people or companies that violate environmental regulations in circumstances of flagrant or deliberate non-compliance. People convicted of environmental offenses may face jail time, fines, probation, reparations, and probationary sentences.

6. Corporate Liability: If their employees or agents violate the environment, firms and entities may face criminal charges in certain jurisdictions. Organizations found culpable for environmental misconduct may face fines, penalties, and harm to their reputation as a result of corporate accountability.

Other Remedial Measures:

7. Injunctive Relief: Regulatory agencies have the legal right to request court orders for injunctive relief in order to stop ongoing environmental infractions, stop additional environmental harm, and enforce regulatory compliance. An injunction may mandate the stopping of operations, the application of pollution control strategies, or the repair of environmental harm.

8. Community Service or Environmental Remediation: Non-compliant entities may be forced to carry out community service or environmental repair projects as part of enforcement actions or settlements in order to lessen the environmental effects of their infractions. Participating in habitat restoration, public education, or environmental cleanup projects are examples of community service.

In order to ensure accountability, deterrent, and preservation of the environment and public health, penalties for breaking environmental legislation are crucial enforcement measures. Regulating agencies work to encourage compliance, encourage good environmental stewardship, and protect natural resources for current and future generations by enforcing penalties, taking enforcement measures, and implementing criminal consequences. Maintaining ecosystems, reducing environmental harm, and promoting sustainable development all depend on adherence to environmental standards.

9.1.1 Overview of Key Environmental Laws and Regulations Relevant to HRM

The term "Overview of Key Environmental Laws and Regulations Relevant to HRM" describes a thorough analysis or synopsis of the major environmental laws, rules, and filing obligations that affect how Human Resource Management (HRM) is practiced in businesses. The main environmental laws, rules, and standards that HRM professionals must be aware of and make sure their jobs are compliant with are listed and explained in this overview.

To put it simply, it entails describing the legal framework that surrounds sustainability and environmental protection and how it interacts with HRM functions like supply chain management, workplace policies, employee health and safety, training, and awareness campaigns. Giving HRM professionals this kind of overview is meant to give them the information and comprehension they need to incorporate environmental factors into their everyday operations, policies, and decision-making procedures.

1. Occupational Safety and Health Act (OSHA):

OSHA is a federal law in the United States that establishes guidelines to guarantee employees have safe and healthy working environments. OSHA laws cover environmental dangers in the workplace, such as exposure to hazardous chemicals, air contaminants, and poisonous compounds, even though its primary focus is occupational safety. To safeguard the health and welfare of their workforce, HR managers are required to make sure that OSHA regulations are followed.

2. Chemical Management Regulations:

The use, handling, and disposal of chemicals in the workplace are governed by chemical management rules, such as the Registration, Evaluation, Authorization, and Restriction of Chemicals (REACH) regulation in the European Union and the Toxic Substances Control Act (TSCA) in the United States. Chemical safety regulations, including as chemical inventory management, safety data sheet (SDS) management, and employee training on chemical dangers, must be complied with by HRM professionals.

3. Environmental Protection Laws:

A number of environmental protection laws, including the Resource Conservation and Recovery Act (RCRA), the Clean Water Act, and the Clean Air Act, set down rules to manage hazardous waste, preserve natural resources, and ensure the purity of the air and water. By putting in place waste management procedures, environmental monitoring programs, and pollution control strategies at work, HRM specialists help to ensure that these rules are followed.

4. Environmental Impact Assessment (EIA) Regulations:

Before beginning new developments, construction projects, or industrial activities, businesses and projects are required under environmental impact assessment regulation to evaluate and mitigate any environmental repercussions. To reduce negative environmental consequences, HRM specialists working in project management, site planning, or regulatory compliance must make sure that EIAs are carried out and that mitigation strategies are put in place.

5. Hazardous Materials Transportation Regulations:

Hazardous materials handling, packing, labelling, and transportation requirements are set forth in regulations controlling the transportation of hazardous items, such as the Hazardous Materials Regulations (HMR) in the United States. HRM specialists who work in supply chain management, logistics, or staff development must make sure that these rules are followed in order to avoid mishaps, spills, and environmental contamination when doing transportation-related business.

6. Sustainability Reporting Requirements:

Reports on environmental performance and sustainability initiatives are becoming more and more mandatory for businesses as a component of corporate governance and transparency standards. In order to prove compliance with sustainability reporting standards and regulations, HRM experts may be involved in gathering, evaluating, and reporting data on environmental indicators, including as energy usage, greenhouse gas emissions, trash generation, and recycling rates.

7. Renewable Energy Standards and Incentives:

To encourage the use of renewable energy sources including solar, wind, and hydroelectric electricity, several governments have set renewable energy standards and incentives. To support the organization's shift to clean energy and lower its carbon footprint, HRM professionals may need to manage regulatory regulations relating to renewable energy procurement, incentive programs, and renewable energy credits (RECs).

8. Environmental Compliance Audits:

Organizations can reduce environmental risks, guarantee conformity to environmental rules, and identify and remedy possible environmental compliance concerns by conducting environmental compliance audits. HRM specialists may oversee or take part in environmental audits to determine whether relevant rules and regulations are being followed and to carry out any necessary corrective action.

9. International Environmental Agreements:

International environmental agreements, such as the Basel Convention on hazardous waste and the Paris Agreement on climate change, impose obligations and promises on governments to solve global environmental issues. HRM specialists that work in supply chain management, foreign operations, or corporate sustainability are required to monitor adherence to international environmental treaties and provide assistance for activities aimed at mitigating cross-border environmental impacts.

10. Environmental Training and Awareness Programs:

Environmental laws, regulations, and best practices can be taught to employees through the development and implementation of environmental training and awareness programs by HRM specialists. These initiatives seek to encourage workplace adoption of sustainable practices, environmental responsibility, and compliance with regulations.

11. Eco-Friendly Workplace Practices:

To reduce the organization's environmental effect, HRM experts can develop eco-friendly workplace practices like waste reduction programs, energy saving measures, and sustainable procurement strategies. These procedures promote the company's commitment to sustainability and corporate citizenship while also complying with environmental standards.

12. Stakeholder Engagement and Collaboration:

HRM specialists can work together on environmental projects, exchange best practices, and tackle shared environmental concerns with external stakeholders including industry associations, community groups, regulatory agencies, and non-governmental organizations (NGOs). Sustainable business practices can be promoted and environmental compliance efforts can be strengthened by forming alliances and encouraging communication with stakeholders.

13. Green Building and Facilities Management:

Facilities management HRM specialists may be in charge of sustainability initiatives and green construction projects to lessen the environmental impact of company buildings. In order to comply with environmental standards and save operating expenses, this may involve incorporating energy-efficient technologies, green building certifications (such as LEED), and sustainable building practices.

14. Supply Chain Sustainability Management:
Environmental factors can be incorporated into supplier selection, procurement procedures, and supplier performance reviews by HRM specialists working in supply chain management. This involves making certain that suppliers follow environmental laws, use sustainable sourcing methods, and reduce their negative effects on the environment at every stage of the supply chain.

15. Environmental Health and Wellness Programs:
To improve worker well-being and lower occupational health risks related to environmental hazards, HRM experts can create environmental health and wellness programs. These programs could address environmental elements that affect worker productivity and health, such as ergonomic examinations, indoor air quality assessments, and health promotion campaigns.

Conclusion:
When it comes to environmental rules and regulations that are important to workplace sustainability, health, and safety, HRM professionals are essential. HRM specialists support the company's commitment to environmental stewardship and corporate social responsibility by comprehending and putting into practice environmental compliance requirements. This helps to create safe, healthy, and environmentally conscious work environments for employees.

9.1.2 Implications of Environmental Legislation on HR Practices

The implications of environmental legislation on HR practices are significant, as environmental regulations and policies have a direct impact on how organizations manage their human resources.

❖ **Here are some key implications:**

1. Recruitment and Selection:

The hiring of employees with particular skills, knowledge, and attitudes toward environmental sustainability is mandated by environmental legislation, which has an impact on HR processes in recruitment and selection. HR departments must adjust their recruitment strategies to draw in candidates with experience in environmental management, renewable energy, green technology, and sustainable business practices as companies work to comply with environmental regulations and lessen their ecological footprint. It could be necessary to update job descriptions and hiring procedures to clearly incorporate requirements for sustainability and environmental compliance. Additionally, in order to determine the skills and credentials needed for positions like environmental engineers, sustainability specialists, or compliance officers that directly support the organization's environmental goals, HR professionals may need to work with recruiting managers.

2. Compensation and Benefits:

When it comes to rewarding and incentivizing employees for their efforts to environmental sustainability, compensation and benefits policies are influenced by environmental regulations in firms. To integrate financial rewards with environmental objectives, HR departments can incorporate sustainability targets and environmental performance measures into performance-based incentive programs, bonus plans, and performance-based compensation systems. Employees may be eligible for cash bonuses, profit-sharing plans, or recognition prizes if they do very well in areas like waste reduction, energy efficiency, or carbon footprint reduction. Employees may also be eligible for additional environmental perks and advantages from their employers, such as incentives for embracing sustainable lifestyle practices, telecommuting alternatives, and subsidies for environmentally friendly transportation. Organizations can encourage employees to actively participate in sustainability projects, promote good environmental change, and contribute to the overall success of the company by tying compensation and benefits to environmental outcomes.

3. Training and Development:

To ensure that employees have the information, skills, and competences necessary to comply with regulatory standards and support the organization's environmental objectives, extensive training and development programs are required to execute environmental legislation. Training programs that emphasize environmental awareness, adherence to pertinent rules and regulations, and the adoption of sustainable workplace practices are designed, implemented, and evaluated in large part by HR departments. A wide range of subjects are covered in training, such as handling hazardous products, energy conservation, waste management, pollution avoidance, and sustainable purchasing. In order to accommodate employees' varied learning preferences and styles, HR managers can also make use of a variety of learning modalities, including webinars, workshops, e-learning modules, and hands-on exercises. Providing employees with chances for ongoing learning and development is crucial to promoting an environmentally conscious culture and keeping them updated on new regulations, environmental challenges, and sustainable best practices.

4. Performance Management:

The integration of environmental goals, objectives, and metrics into employee performance assessments and key performance indicators (KPIs) is mandated by environmental legislation, which has consequences for performance management techniques in enterprises. In order to set quantifiable goals for environmental sustainability, HR departments work with pertinent stakeholders to develop measures like cutting carbon emissions, limiting waste production, preserving natural resources, or boosting the usage of renewable energy sources. In order to gauge how much these environmental KPIs have contributed to reaching sustainability goals, they are then included into employees' performance goals and assessment criteria. Performance reviews give managers and employees the chance to talk about how they are doing in terms of environmental stewardship, where they can make improvements, and where they are excelling. Organizations can strengthen a culture of accountability, openness, and ongoing environmental performance improvement by coordinating performance management procedures with environmental goals.

5. Employee Engagement and Communication:

When it comes to encouraging employee engagement and communication around environmental sustainability projects, HR departments are essential. Organizations must effectively communicate environmental policies, procedures, and objectives to their employees in order to comply with environmental legislation. HR professionals use a variety of communication platforms, including employee forums, town hall meetings, email newsletters, and intranet portals, to spread knowledge, increase awareness, and get input on environmental issues. To actively involve employees in environmental projects, employer education programs, volunteer opportunities, sustainability challenges, and green initiatives can all be organized. Additionally, HR specialists can help organize employee-led environmental committees or green teams to spearhead sustainability initiatives, generate concepts, and introduce eco-friendly procedures throughout the company. HR departments may enable staff members to take on the role of environmental sustainability champions and advocates for good change in the community and at work by promoting candid communication, teamwork, and involvement.

6. Compliance and Risk Management:

Organizations must adhere to regulatory standards and comply with environmental legislation, which means HR departments must have strong compliance and risk management procedures. To make sure that HR policies, methods, and practices comply with environmental laws and regulations, HR professionals work closely with legal counsel, compliance officers, and environmental health and safety specialists. Conducting routine audits, evaluations, and reviews of HR procedures may be necessary in order to spot non-compliance issues or possible environmental hazards. Human resources departments bear the responsibility of formulating and executing policies and procedures aimed at fostering environmental compliance. These may include training initiatives focused on environmental issues, channels for reporting environmental events or infractions, and guidelines for managing hazardous items or trash. Additionally, HR specialists could be crucial in making sure that workers understand their legal rights and obligations with regard to the environment and get the help and training they need to carry them out. HR departments can minimize legal liabilities, protect the organization's brand, and maintain its dedication to environmental stewardship and regulatory compliance by placing a high priority on compliance and risk management.

7. Employee Wellness and Health:
Regulations designed to protect the health and well-being of employees at work are frequently included in environmental legislation. Ensuring adherence to these regulations is imperative for HR departments in safeguarding employees against environmental dangers and fostering a salubrious work environment. This entails carrying out risk analyses to pinpoint possible environmental hazards, putting policies in place to lessen employee exposure to toxins or dangerous chemicals, and giving them the necessary instruction and personal protective equipment (PPE). Furthermore, HR experts may work with health and safety specialists to create wellness initiatives that tackle issues related to environmental health, including indoor air quality, ergonomic risks, and environmental stressors that cause psychological distress. Prioritizing employee wellness and health can help employers establish work environments that are safer, more supportive, and encourage employee productivity, satisfaction, and retention.

8. Data Management and Reporting:
Organizations are frequently required by environmental legislation to gather, handle, and report data on their environmental performance to stakeholders, regulatory bodies, and the general public. When it comes to managing data and reporting procedures pertaining to environmental sustainability, HR departments are essential. This entails creating procedures for gathering data, putting tracking systems in place, and guaranteeing the confidentiality, integrity, and correctness of environmental data. In order to measure the environmental impact, HR professionals can engage with cross-functional teams to identify key performance indicators (KPIs), create reporting frameworks and templates, and analyse and interpret environmental data for use in strategy and decision-making. Employee engagement with data management and reporting initiatives can take many forms, such as taking part in data collection tasks, providing comments to improve the quality of the data, and attending training sessions to increase data literacy and comprehension. Organizations may foster stakeholder trust, drive

continuous improvement in environmental performance, and demonstrate openness, accountability, and progress towards environmental goals by efficiently handling and reporting environmental data.

9. Supplier and Vendor Management:

Environmental laws frequently impose accountability on suppliers and vendors in addition to the corporation itself. Throughout the supply chain, HR departments are essential in ensuring that vendors and suppliers follow sustainability guidelines and environmental legislation. This could entail working with suppliers to adopt sustainable practices, incorporating sustainability standards into contracts and procurement procedures, and doing assessments of suppliers to gauge their environmental performance. HR specialists can also encourage cooperation between employees and suppliers to promote continuous improvement in environmental performance, facilitate supplier training programs, and increase employee awareness of supply chain sustainability issues. Organizations can improve their reputation, reduce environmental hazards, and support larger initiatives to advance sustainability across industries by using sustainable supply chain strategies.

10. Corporate Governance and Ethics:

Environmental laws have an impact on company policies, practices, and decision-making processes through their intersection with ethical standards and corporate governance principles. By integrating environmental principles and considerations into the organization's culture, policies, and practices, HR departments play a critical role in fostering ethical behaviour and corporate responsibility. This entails developing moral leadership, encouraging accountability and transparency in environmental decision-making, and making sure that moral and legal requirements pertaining to environmental sustainability are met. HR specialists can help with ethics education and training programs to help employees become more conscious of environmental ethics and values, offer advice on moral conundrums and decision-making, and reaffirm the organization's dedication to moral behaviour. Organizations may maintain their good name, gain the trust of stakeholders, and help promote sustainable business practices by encouraging a culture of environmental ethics and accountability.

11. Community Engagement and Relations:

Environmental laws frequently promote corporate participation in local environmental projects in order to solve regional environmental issues and forge closer bonds with stakeholders. When it comes to organizing employee involvement in community engagement initiatives like environmental clean-up days, conservation campaigns, and educational outreach initiatives, human resources departments are essential. This could entail planning volunteer opportunities, offering assistance and resources for projects headed by employees, and cultivating alliances with local and environmental organizations. Employee participation in environmental community activities enhances the company's standing as a conscientious corporate citizen while also helping the local community by solving environmental challenges. Through employee engagement in community environmental initiatives, firms can cultivate a feeling of pride, identity, and direction among staff members, bolster corporate social responsibility, and generate favourable social and environmental outcomes beyond the workplace.

12. Legal Compliance and Due Diligence:

Organizations are required by law to abide by environmental laws, rules, and permits that are relevant to their operations. This is known as environmental legislation. In order to detect, evaluate, and reduce legal risks associated with environmental compliance, HR departments must take due diligence. These activities are crucial to guaranteeing compliance with environmental laws. This entails working with legal counsel and regulatory specialists to comprehend and interpret environmental rules, creating and putting into practice policies and processes to guarantee compliance, and educating employee about their legal responsibilities. In order to monitor compliance with environmental laws and regulations, handle non-compliance issues, and put remedial measures in place to reduce legal risks, HR experts may also supervise internal audits and assessments. Organizations can reduce legal liabilities, protect themselves from possible fines, penalties, and lawsuits, and show their dedication to environmental stewardship and regulatory compliance by placing a high priority on legal compliance and due diligence.

In conclusion, environmental laws have a significant impact on HR practices. Companies must include environmental factors into all facets of

HR management, including hiring, training, performance evaluation, and employee involvement. Organizations can maximize their positive environmental effect while fostering a culture of sustainability and ensuring compliance with environmental laws by coordinating HR practices with environmental goals and regulations.

9.1.3 Case Studies Illustrating the Impact of Non-compliance with Environmental Laws on Organizations

- ❖ Here's a case study of the Volkswagen (VW) Diesel Emissions Scandal illustrating the impact of non-compliance with environmental laws on organizations:

Case Study: Volkswagen Diesel Emissions Scandal

Background:
One of the biggest automakers in the world, Volkswagen (VW), was charged in September 2015 with manipulating emissions testing for its diesel cars marketed in the US. According to an investigation, Volkswagen had put "defeat devices," or illicit software, in millions of diesel cars in order to manipulate emissions test results and get around rules governing nitrogen oxide (NOx) emissions.

Non-Compliance with Environmental Laws:
Volkswagen purposefully installed defeat devices in its diesel vehicles to evade emissions testing procedures, in violation of stringent environmental standards governing vehicle emissions. These computer programs adjusted engine performance to artificially lower NOx emissions when they recognized that a car was going through an emissions test. But when driving normally, the cars released more toxins into the air than was permitted, which hurt the environment and increased air pollution.

Impact on Volkswagen:
1. Reputational Damage: The Volkswagen emissions scandal damaged the company's standing as a reliable and ecologically conscious carmaker. Customers, regulators, and stakeholders began to doubt the company's legitimacy and integrity due to its longstanding commitment to sustainability and innovation. Volkswagen's reputation suffered further due to unfavourable media coverage, public scrutiny, and social media

criticism, which increased the harm to the company's image and reduced its brand equity.

2. Legal and Regulatory Consequences: Volkswagen's involvement in the emissions issue came with serious legal and regulatory repercussions. The corporation paid billions of dollars in fines, penalties, and settlements from legal actions taken by government prosecutors, class-action lawsuits filed by impacted customers, and civil fines imposed by regulatory bodies. In order to eliminate the unlawful defeat devices and apply software updates to lower emissions, VW also had to recall millions of cars.

3. Financial Fallout: Volkswagen had severe financial consequences as a result of the emissions scandal, including a drop in its market value, stock price, and profitability. Customers lost faith in the company and became less loyal, causing irreversible harm to its reputation and brand image. VW experienced a drop in sales and market share, which reduced shareholder value and resulted in revenue losses. The expenses of recalls, repairs, and settlements associated with the emissions crisis severely hurt the company's bottom line.

4. Market Access and Regulatory Compliance: Due to Volkswagen's disregard for environmental rules and regulations, it was subject to import bans, market access limitations, and regulatory scrutiny in a number of international jurisdictions. Regulators from several nations, including the US, Europe, and Asia, launched investigations against the corporation and imposed penalties and punishments. Volkswagen's resources and operational capabilities were stressed by compliance costs, litigation expenditures, and regulatory compliance activities, which had an impact on the company's competitiveness and market position.

5. Leadership and Governance Crisis: Volkswagen experienced a leadership and governance crisis as a result of the emissions scandal, which led to management changes, boardroom reforms, and executive resignations. As a result of the CEO and other senior executives of the corporation coming under fire and investigation for their involvement in the scandal, efforts were made to restructure the organization and replace the leadership in an effort to rebuild accountability and trust.

Long-Term Implications:

The Volkswagen Diesel Emissions Scandal had a significant impact on the company's reputation, growth, and sustainability going forward. The episode made clear how crucial it is for company governance and business operations to prioritize ethical behaviour, openness, and regulatory compliance. Volkswagen had to implement a number of significant changes in order to regain market confidence, credibility, and trust. These included a shift in corporate culture, the establishment of moral leadership, and the incorporation of sustainability into company operations.

Conclusion:

A lesson about the repercussions of breaking environmental laws and regulatory requirements can be learned from the Volkswagen Diesel Emissions Scandal. The incident brought to light the dangers of business misbehaviour, regulatory avoidance, and unethical actions in the name of quick money. Volkswagen's experience highlights the necessity for businesses to place a high priority on corporate responsibility, ethical behaviour, and environmental stewardship in order to maintain their commitment to sustainability and legal, financial, and reputational risks as well as to minimize them.

- ❖ Here's a case study of the Amazon rainforest illustrating the impact of non-compliance with environmental laws on organizations:

Case Study: Deforestation of the Amazon Rainforest

Background:

The Amazon rainforest, sometimes known as the "lungs of the planet," is the biggest tropical rainforest in the world and an essential ecosystem that regulates the planet's water cycles, biodiversity, and climate. But deforestation caused mostly by mining, infrastructure development, agricultural expansion, and illicit logging has posed serious challenges to the Amazon.

Non-Compliance with Environmental Laws:

The Amazon rainforest has seen extensive destruction despite strict environmental regulations and protected zones set aside for conservation. This is because environmental laws are not followed and enforcement measures are insufficient. Millions of hectares of virgin forest are lost annually as a result of illegal land clearing practices like logging and slash-and-burn farming.

Impact on Organizations:

1. Regulatory Penalties: Companies that violate environmental rules risk legal and regulatory repercussions, fines, and other consequences from the government. Businesses that are found guilty of unlawful deforestation may be subject to regulatory enforcement actions, criminal and civil prosecutions, and the suspension or revocation of licenses and permits that are essential to their business operations.

2. Reputational Damage: Companies involved in deforestation in the Amazon region risk serious harm to their reputations as well as public outrage from advocacy groups, environmental organizations, and customers. The reputation and brand image of businesses involved in deforestation can be damaged by negative media coverage and social media campaigns, which can result in protests, boycotts, and a decline in customer loyalty and confidence.

3. Market Access and Trade Barriers: Concerned about the environmental impact of their products, foreign markets and trading partners may apply trade barriers, import restrictions, and certification requirements on companies engaged in deforestation. Market access and competitiveness in international markets may be hampered by non-compliance with sustainability standards and certification programs, such as the Forest Stewardship Council (FSC) or the Roundtable on Sustainable Palm Oil (RSPO).

4. Investor Scrutiny: When evaluating company risk and making investment decisions, investors and financial institutions are taking environmental, social, and governance (ESG) aspects into account more and more. Investors, shareholder activists, and sustainability-focused funds may scrutinize companies involved in deforestation, which could result in divestiture, shareholder resolutions, and pressure to enhance environmental performance and sustainability standards.

5. Financial Risks: Litigation expenses, fines, court settlements, and compensation payments for environmental damage are among the financial hazards connected with breaking environmental rules in the Amazon. Due to reputational harm and regulatory scrutiny, companies may also suffer financial losses via disruptions to supply chains, investor trust, and market access.

Long-Term Consequences:
Violation of environmental rules in the Amazon can have long-term effects such as amplification of climate change, loss of biodiversity, irreversible ecological harm, and disruption of ecosystem functions. Deforestation accelerates global warming and environmental degradation by causing habitat loss, animal extinction, soil degradation, and loss of carbon storage capacity.

Conclusion:
Deforestation in the Amazon rainforest serves as an example of how breaking environmental regulations has a significant negative influence on ecosystems, organizations, and the sustainability of the planet. To protect the ecological integrity of the Amazon, slow down climate change, and advance sustainable development, effective environmental governance, law enforcement, and corporate responsibility are crucial. Prioritizing environmental stewardship, accountability, and transparency can help companies prevent the negative effects of illegal deforestation and support the preservation and restoration of the most ecologically critical and bio-diverse ecosystems on Earth.

- ❖ **Here's a case study of the BP Deepwater Horizon Oil Spill illustrating the impact of non-compliance with environmental laws on organizations:**

Case Study: BP Deepwater Horizon Oil Spill

Background:
One of the greatest marine oil spills in history occurred in April 2010 as a result of a catastrophic explosion at British Petroleum's (BP) Deepwater Horizon offshore drilling rig in the Gulf of Mexico. Millions of barrels of crude oil leaked into the Gulf of Mexico as a result of the explosion, which also claimed the lives of 11 workers and forced the rig to sink.

Non-Compliance with Environmental Laws:

The Deepwater Horizon rig owned by BP was not adhering to several critical safety and environmental criteria at the time of the explosion, despite the strict environmental rules that regulate offshore drilling operations. A number of systemic shortcomings were found throughout investigations, including poor emergency response procedures, broken equipment, and insufficient risk evaluations. The U.S. Department of the Interior's offshore drilling safety requirements, as well as the Clean Water Act and the Oil Pollution Act, were among the numerous environmental laws and regulations that BP was found to have broken.

Impact on BP:

1. Environmental Devastation: The Gulf of Mexico's wildlife, coastal habitats, and marine ecosystems all suffered significant environmental harm as a result of the Deepwater Horizon oil disaster. Millions of barrels of crude oil leaked into the environment, contaminating marshes, sea life, beaches, and waterways. This resulted in long-term ecological devastation, a decline in biodiversity, and disruptions to ecosystem services. Local communities and businesses suffered financial losses as a result of the spill's negative effects on the region's tourism, recreational opportunities, and fisheries.

2. Operational Disruption and Risk Management: BP was compelled by the Deepwater Horizon oil leak to review its corporate governance procedures, risk management guidelines, and operational procedures. The disaster revealed flaws in BP's emergency response protocols, safety standards, and risk assessment procedures. As a result, the firm strengthened its operational oversight, implemented changes, and improved safety standards. The goals of BP's endeavours to enhance operational excellence and risk management were to avert future mishaps, regain the trust of stakeholders, and reconstruct its image as an accountable energy enterprise.

3. Legal and Regulatory Consequences: BP's involvement in the Deepwater Horizon oil spill resulted in legal and regulatory ramifications. A class-action lawsuit filed by impacted individuals and businesses, criminal and civil charges brought by government authorities, and settlements with federal and state governments were among the billions of dollars in fines, penalties, and legal settlements that the corporation had to pay. Due to BP's accountability for the oil spill's effects on the environment, the economy, and public health, protracted legal actions and compensation payments were necessary.

4. Reputational Damage: The Deepwater Horizon oil spill damaged BP's standing as a leading company in the industry and a responsible corporate citizen. Following criticism of the company's environmental stewardship, safety record, and corporate culture, there was a response on social media and media as well as public indignation. BP's credibility, reliability, and social license to operate were undermined by negative press, public relations difficulties, and stakeholder criticism, which intensified the reputational harm.

5. Financial Fallout: BP suffered severe financial consequences as a result of the Deepwater Horizon oil leak, including a drop in its market value, stock price, and profitability. The company's brand image and reputation were irreversibly damaged, which resulted in a decline in market trust, investor confidence, and shareholder value. The financial performance of BP was significantly impacted by the expenditures associated with the oil spill, including cleanup, legal fees, and compensation payments. This led to financial losses and impairment charges amounting to billions of dollars.

Long-Term Implications:
The Deepwater Horizon oil disaster affected BP's business operations, stakeholders, and the environment in significant and lasting ways. The event served as a reminder of how crucial safety procedures, environmental stewardship, and regulatory compliance are in the oil and gas sector. BP's reaction to the oil disaster necessitated continued dedication, investment, and cooperation with local communities, environmental organizations, and government agencies. This included cleanup operations, compensation payments, and environmental restoration projects. As a warning about the dangers and repercussions of breaking environmental laws and regulations, the company's experience served to emphasize the importance of strong risk management, crisis preparedness, and corporate responsibility in the energy industry.

Conclusion:

The disastrous effects of breaking environmental laws and regulatory norms on businesses, ecosystems, and communities are glaringly evident in the aftermath of the BP Deepwater Horizon oil spill. In order to avert environmental catastrophes and promote sustainable practices in the oil and gas sector, the incident emphasizes the significance of proactive risk management, safety culture, and environmental stewardship. In resolving the fallout from environmental disasters, corporate accountability, openness, and a commitment to environmental sustainability are essential. BP's reaction to the oil spill, which included legal settlements, environmental restoration efforts, and stakeholder engagement, exemplifies this.

9.2 Ensuring Compliance with Sustainability

Implementing and maintaining procedures that meet environmental, social, and governance (ESG) standards set by international organizations, industry associations, and regulatory agencies is necessary to ensure compliance with sustainability requirements. By ensuring that an organization runs sustainably, ethically, and responsibly, this thorough procedure ultimately makes a positive impact on both society and the environment. The process of becoming compliant and keeping it that way is complex and calls for a thorough integration of sustainability into every part of corporate operations.

❖ Here is an in-depth exploration of what this entails:

1. Understanding Sustainability Standards

Sustainability standards refer to comprehensive rules and benchmarks that are intended to assist firms in reducing their environmental impact, promoting social responsibility, and strengthening their governance procedures. These guidelines cover a number of topics, such as:

Environmental Impact: Guidelines for cutting back on waste, conserving energy, controlling water use, and limiting greenhouse gas emissions.

Social Responsibility: Fair labour practices, employee well-being, diversity and inclusion, community involvement, and human rights are all covered by these standards.

Governance: Principles for corporate governance, accountability, openness, and moral business conduct.

The Sustainable Development Goals (SDGs) of the United Nations, the Global Reporting Initiative (GRI) for sustainability reporting, and ISO 14001 for environmental management are a few examples of internationally recognized sustainability standards. Following these guidelines enables firms to fulfil stakeholder and societal expectations in addition to legal responsibilities.

2. Developing Policies and Objectives

Policy Development

Complying starts with developing thorough sustainability policies. The organization's commitment to sustainability should be outlined in these policies, along with the precise steps and approaches taken to meet goals related to governance, the environment, and society. International standards, regional laws, and the fundamental principles of the organization should all be reflected in policies.

Objective Setting

Establishing precise and well-defined sustainability goals is essential. These goals ought to be Specific, Measurable, Achievable, Relevant, and Time-bound or SMART goals. For example, a goal could be to expand the usage of renewable energy sources by 50% within ten years, achieve zero trash to landfill by three years, or cut carbon emissions by 30% over the course of five years. Well-defined goals offer guidance and standards for gauging advancement, guaranteeing that the company's endeavours are concentrated and efficient.

Stakeholder Engagement

It is essential to include stakeholders in the creation of sustainability goals and policies. Employees, clients, suppliers, investors, regulators, and the community are examples of stakeholders. By involving these groups, the organization can make sure that the policies are thorough, pertinent, and endorsed by the people who both benefit from and contribute to its sustainability initiatives. Public consultations, workshops, focus groups, surveys, and consultations with stakeholders can all be used to engage stakeholders.

3. Implementing Robust Management Systems

Sustainability Management System

Organizations could use more comprehensive frameworks like ISO 26000 for social responsibility or structured management systems like the Environmental Management System (EMS) based on ISO 14001 to manage and track sustainability initiatives. These systems guarantee that sustainability is included into business operations and decision-making by offering a methodical approach to planning, implementing, monitoring, and reviewing sustainability policies.

Integration with Business Processes

It is crucial to include sustainability concerns into fundamental business procedures. This covers product design, manufacturing, logistics, and procurement. To lower carbon footprints, companies might, for instance, design goods with energy efficiency and recyclability in mind, acquire materials from suppliers who follow sustainable practices, and streamline logistics. Because of this comprehensive integration, sustainability is guaranteed to be a fundamental part of corporate strategy rather than an afterthought.

Continuous Improvement

Create systems for ongoing improvement, including as feedback loops, management reviews, and frequent audits. Utilize the information gathered from these efforts to continuously improve processes, policies, and procedures. By encouraging creativity and resilience, continuous improvement makes sure that the company adjusts to new sustainability possibilities and challenges.

4. Training and Capacity Building

Employee Training

It is essential to hold frequent training sessions to inform staff members about best practices, compliance needs, and sustainability standards. All employees, from frontline staff to top management, should receive training that is specifically designed to meet their needs and help them understand how they fit into the larger picture of sustainability. Topics including waste minimization, energy efficiency, sustainable purchasing, and moral corporate conduct can all be included in training programs.

Leadership Development

Create programs for sustainability leadership that will enable executives and managers to support organizational sustainability goals. To promote a sustainable culture and make sure that sustainability is given top priority when making strategic decisions, leadership commitment is essential. Participation in sustainability forums and networks, workshops, seminars, and mentoring are all components of successful leadership development programs.

Supplier Training

Give suppliers assistance and training so they can fulfil sustainability requirements. Workshops, webinars, and resource materials that instruct vendors on best practices in social responsibility, environmental management, and governance are examples of this. Organizations may make sure that their sustainability initiatives are expanded and strengthened by strengthening the capabilities of the supply chain.

5. Monitoring and Measuring Performance

Data Collection

Establish mechanisms for gathering and evaluating information on important sustainability indicators, such as water use, waste production, energy consumption, and greenhouse gas emissions. To assure accurate and timely reporting and to streamline data administration, use digital tools and software. Sturdy data gathering systems give you the data you need to monitor developments, spot trends, and come to wise judgments.

Performance Metrics

Create key performance indicators (KPIs) to monitor the achievement of sustainability goals. Review and report on these indicators on a regular basis to spot trends, areas that need work, and achievements. KPIs might include the amount of waste diverted from landfills, the amount of carbon footprint reduced, or the quantity of community engagement projects finished. This data-driven strategy aids in holding the company responsible and improving continuously.

Third-Party Verification

Acquire certification or third-party verification of sustainable performance to show stakeholders your dedication and build confidence. A company's efforts can be verified and external parties' trust can be increased by obtaining certifications such as Fair Trade, BREEAM (Building Research Establishment Environmental Assessment Method), or LEED (Leadership in Energy and Environmental Design). Claims about sustainability are verified by a third party to make sure they are reliable and adhere to accepted guidelines.

6. Engaging in Transparent Reporting

Sustainability Reporting

Regularly release sustainability reports outlining the organization's progress toward sustainability goals and requirements. Adhere to established reporting frameworks, such as the Task Force on Climate-related Financial Disclosures (TCFD), the Sustainability Accounting Standards Board (SASB), or the Global Reporting Initiative (GRI). Stakeholders can easily understand the organization's sustainability efforts and results by reading thorough sustainability reports.

Transparency and Accountability

Admit both the good and bad things that have happened in your sustainability endeavours. Give stakeholders frank and transparent reports on areas that require improvement as well as progress. Transparency shows an organization's dedication to transparency and ongoing development while also fostering trust. Organizations can communicate their sustainability journey through a variety of communication platforms, such as websites, social media, annual reports, and stakeholder meetings.

Stakeholder Communication

Engage stakeholders in conversations about sustainability, solicit their opinions, and promote an accountable and transparent culture by using a variety of communication platforms. Public forums, social media, newsletters, and stakeholder gatherings can all be examples of this. Stakeholders who are educated, involved, and supportive of the organization's sustainability objectives are guaranteed by effective communication.

7. Fostering a Culture of Sustainability

Corporate Culture
Integrate sustainability into the organization's basic values to instil it in the corporate culture. Internal campaigns, sustainability awards, and recognition schemes that honoursustainable actions and accomplishments can help achieve this. In addition to promoting a sense of pride and accountability, a strong sustainability culture encourages staff members to incorporate sustainable practices into their daily work.

Employee Involvement
Give staff members the chance to get involved in environmental projects through volunteer programs, green teams, and innovation contests. Encourage staff members' suggestions and ideas to promote sustainability gains and cultivate a feeling of accountability. Increased engagement in sustainability initiatives and creative problem-solving can result from employee involvement.

Leadership Commitment
Make certain that senior leadership exhibits a strong commitment to sustainability. Leadership should convey the value of sustainability, actively engage in projects, and provide the resources required to meet sustainability objectives. A company's commitment to sustainability is reaffirmed and staff members are motivated to participate when there is visible leadership commitment.

8. Leveraging Technology and Innovation

Sustainable Technologies
Invest in technology that enhances sustainability performance, such as water-saving appliances, waste-reduction technologies, energy-efficient equipment, and renewable energy systems (solar, wind). Technological developments can greatly improve an organization's capacity to minimize its environmental impact and achieve sustainability standards.

Innovation
Encourage the creation of sustainable goods, services, and procedures to promote innovation. Work together with industry partners, research institutes, and start-ups to discover novel approaches and remain ahead of sustainability trends. Innovation propels development and aids in an

organization's ability to adjust to shifting sustainability opportunities and requirements.

Digital Tools
Make use of digital platforms and technologies to manage, track, and report on sustainability data. The efficacy and precision of sustainability initiatives can be improved by technologies such as artificial intelligence (AI), big data analytics, and the Internet of Things (IoT). Real-time insights and data-driven decision-making are supported by digital tools.

9. Collaborating with External Partners

Industry Collaboration
Participate in coalitions, networks, and industry associations that are devoted to sustainability. Work together with other groups to create standards, exchange best practices, and promote advancements in the sector. Engaging in programs such as the World Business Council for Sustainable Development or the United Nations Global Compact can help to promote group action and increase the effect of sustainability projects.

Government and NGOs
Collaborate with governmental bodies, non-profit organizations, and local associations to bolster environmental programs and legal compliance. Form public-private partnerships to tackle shared sustainability issues and capitalize on pooled resources and knowledge. Working together with outside partners helps the organization accomplish its sustainability objectives and have a beneficial social and environmental impact.

Supply Chain Management
Build trusting relationships with partners and suppliers to make sure they follow sustainability guidelines. Adopt sustainable procurement procedures, carry out supplier audits, and provide suppliers with assistance and training to help them adopt sustainable practices. A sustainable supply chain guarantees that the company's environmental initiatives reach beyond its daily operations and support more general environmental objectives.

10. Risk Management and Compliance

Risk Assessment

To identify and reduce potential risks associated to sustainability, such as those related to regulations, the environment, and society, conduct frequent risk assessments. Assess the possibility and impact of hazards using risk management frameworks, then create mitigation plans. By taking proactive steps to control risks, a business can make sure it is ready for any eventualities and can react appropriately.

Compliance Audits

Conduct routine compliance audits to make sure that legal requirements and sustainability standards are being followed. In order to stop non-compliance from happening again, take immediate corrective action. Compliance audits give reassurance that the company is fulfilling its legal and sustainability commitments.

Crisis Management

Create and update crisis management plans to handle possible crises pertaining to sustainability, including product recalls, civil unrest, or environmental spills. To effectively manage crises and limit their effects, be sure that these plans include clear roles, duties, and communication channels. Efficient crisis management safeguards the organization's image and guarantees a prompt reaction to sustainability issues.

11. Corporate Governance and Ethics

Ethical Practices

Encourage honesty and moral conduct in all facets of company operations. Create and implement rules of behaviour that address ethical and sustainable issues, and make sure that partners and staff are aware of and follow these guidelines. Ethical behaviour fosters stakeholder trust and advances long-term sustainability objectives.

Board Oversight

Ascertain that the board of directors is in charge of the sustainability strategy and results. Establish committees devoted to ESG matters and include members with experience in sustainability to offer governance and strategic guidance. The organization's dedication to sustainability is reaffirmed by board monitoring, which also makes sure that it is included into the broader business plan.

Stakeholder Interests

When making decisions, take into account the interests of all parties involved, including communities, investors, staff, and customers. Make an effort to use sustainable business strategies that are advantageous to all stakeholders in order to achieve shared value and positive effect. Stakeholder interests must be balanced in order for sustainability initiatives to be inclusive and all-encompassing.

In summary, a thorough and integrated strategy that includes policy creation, management systems, training, performance monitoring, transparent reporting, cultural shift, technology, cooperation, risk management, and corporate governance is needed to ensure compliance with sustainability standards. Organizations can meet regulatory obligations, foster long-term business success, improve their reputation, and contribute to a more sustainable future by implementing these measures. This all-encompassing strategy makes sure that sustainability is ingrained in the organization's culture, encouraging innovation, resistance to social and environmental concerns, and continual improvement. Organizations may contribute significantly to the global sustainability goals and have a long-lasting positive influence on both the environment and society with committed efforts.

9.2.1 Importance of Adhering to Sustainability Standards in HRM

Human resource management (HRM) sustainability standards are important in a number of ways, all of which have an impact on an organization's overall performance, standing, and long-term viability.

Adhering to sustainability standards in Human Resource Management (HRM) is crucial for a multitude of reasons, encompassing environmental, social, and economic dimensions. The growing recognition of sustainability by organizations makes the incorporation of these concepts into HRM processes a strategic necessity.

❖ **Here are several key reasons why adhering to sustainability standards in HRM is essential:**

1. Enhanced Reputation and Employer Branding: Companies that embrace sustainability frequently find that they are more appealing to potential employees, especially from younger generations who highly value social and environmental responsibility. It may be simpler to draw in and keep top personnel as a result of this improved reputation, which can also strengthen the employer brand. In a competitive labour market, companies that are seen as moral and progressive can set themselves apart.

2. Increased Employee Engagement and Morale: Employees are more likely to feel inspired, involved, and devoted when they work for an organization that shares their values, especially those of sustainability. Increased productivity, improved job satisfaction, and lower turnover rates can result from this alignment. Workers who feel that their efforts advance a larger cause are frequently more dedicated and will go above and beyond in their work.

3. Regulatory Compliance and Risk Management: Organizations can comply with an increasing number of environmental and social restrictions by following sustainability guidelines. The possibility of fines, penalties from the law, and harm to one's reputation from non-compliance is decreased by this compliance. Adhering to sustainability norms proactively also puts businesses in a better position to foresee and adapt to future regulatory changes, reducing interruptions and guaranteeing smooth operations.

4. Operational Efficiency and Cost Savings: Utilizing resources more effectively can result in considerable cost savings when it comes to sustainable HRM practices. For example, lowering power costs and operating expenses can be achieved by supporting energy-efficient workplace designs, encouraging waste reduction, and putting in place regulations for remote work. Innovation in technologies and processes is frequently sparked by sustainable practices, which further boost productivity and cut expenses.

5. Social Responsibility and Ethical Leadership: Companies that adhere sustainability guidelines show that they value moral leadership and social responsibility. Relationships with a variety of stakeholders, such as clients, investors, and the community, can be improved by this commitment. Businesses that put sustainability first are generally regarded as dependable and trustworthy, which promotes goodwill and improves their reputation.

6. Innovation and Long-term Viability: Adopting sustainable practices and innovative thinking can boost resilience and long-term corporate growth. Long-term viability of companies is ensured by sustainable HRM practices, which aid in adapting to shifting market situations. In an ever-changing business environment, firms may maintain their competitive edge and stay ahead of the curve by cultivating a culture of innovation and continuous development.

7. Health and Well-being of Employees: A common focus of sustainable HRM practices is on employees' health and wellbeing. A more supportive work environment is the result of initiatives like guaranteeing safe and healthy working conditions, encouraging work-life balance, and giving access to wellness programs. Prioritizing well-being lowers healthcare expenses and absenteeism while simultaneously increasing employee happiness.

8. Talent Development and Retention: Organizations that put sustainability first are probably going to make investments in their employees' ongoing training. Providing employees with chances for sustainability-related training and development can improve their knowledge and abilities, increasing their value to the company. Talent development is an investment that can increase retention rates since employees are more likely to stick with organizations that support their professional development.

9. Global Competitiveness: A major distinction in an international economy is becoming sustainability. Businesses that set the standard for sustainability are better positioned to compete in global marketplaces where partners and customers are calling for more and more ethical business practices. Thus, implementing sustainable HRM practices can boost a business's ability to compete globally and create new business prospects.

10. Contribution to Broader Sustainability Goals: Organizations can support more general societal and environmental objectives, including the

Sustainable Development Goals (SDGs) of the United Nations, by incorporating sustainability into HRM. An organization's legitimacy and support from the larger community can be improved by this alignment with global sustainability activities, which can have a positive feedback loop of influence.

To conclude, the incorporation of sustainability principles into HRM is not only a fad but a strategic imperative. It improves an organization's standing, increases worker satisfaction, guarantees legal compliance, promotes innovation, and increases operational effectiveness. Additionally, it promotes employee health and wellbeing, helps retain and develop talent, increases global competitiveness, and advances larger societal objectives. Organizations can succeed in the long run and have a good effect on the environment and human population by adopting sustainable HRM practices.

9.2.2 Strategies for Integrating Sustainability Criteria into HR Policies and Procedure

Incorporating environmental, social, and governance (ESG) concepts into the various facets of human resource management within a business is the process of integrating sustainability standards into HR policies and processes. For sustainability to be ingrained in all HR-related choices, procedures, and projects, HR practices must be matched with sustainable company goals and principles. Recruitment, training, employee engagement, performance management, organizational culture, rules and regulations, reporting and communication, compliance and governance, community involvement, technology and innovation, and financial and resource management are all included in this integration.

By incorporating sustainability standards into HR policies and practices, companies support long-term economic success while giving employees, the environment, and society top priority. In the end, this strategy leads to a more resilient and socially conscious firm by fostering a work environment that values sustainability, encourages employee involvement, improves the organization's reputation, and stimulates innovation.

Environmental, social, and governance (ESG) concepts are ingrained in all facets of human resource management when sustainability standards are integrated into HR policies and processes. In addition to improving organizational performance, this strategic integration creates a sustainable, moral, and accountable work environment.

❖ **Here are several detailed strategies to achieve this:**

Recruitment and Hiring

1. Sustainable Job Descriptions: Firstly, job descriptions should include expectations and tasks connected to sustainability. Emphasizing the organization's dedication to sustainability might draw applicants who share similar ideals. Give candidates a clear understanding of the role's contribution to the organization's sustainability goals from the outset by outlining how it helps with these activities.

2. Diverse and Inclusive Hiring Practices: Make sure that the hiring procedures you use foster inclusiveness and diversity, as these are essential elements of social sustainability. Adopt anti-bias measures, like employing standardized interview questions and blind hiring methods. Seek for applicants with a variety of backgrounds in order to create a more diverse staff.

Training and Development

3. Sustainability Training Programs: Create thorough training programs that inform employees of sustainable business practices and the organization's unique sustainability objectives. Mandatory workshops, seminars, and online courses on subjects like waste management, social responsibility, and energy saving can fall under this category.

4. Continuous Learning Opportunities: Provide employees with access to industry conferences, seminars, and certifications to encourage them to pursue ongoing education in sustainability. Provide employees with incentives or financial support to further their education in sustainability-related disciplines.

Performance Management

5. Sustainability KPIs: Include sustainability key performance indicators (KPIs) in performance reviews for staff members. Metrics on energy use, trash reduction, involvement in community activities, and other sustainability efforts are examples of these KPIs. The motivation of employees to contribute to sustainability goals will increase when performance appraisals are linked to sustainability criteria.

6. Recognition and Rewards: Employees that actively support sustainability projects should be recognized and given incentives. This can involve official recognition schemes, including sustainability awards, bonuses for meeting predetermined sustainability goals, and acknowledgement of work in public.

Employee Engagement and Well-being

7. Work-life Balance Policies: Adopt work-life balance-promoting policies, such as those that allow for remote work, flexible scheduling, and extensive wellness initiatives. These regulations promote social sustainability by improving worker satisfaction and lowering turnover.

8. Employee Involvement: By establishing green teams or sustainability committees, encourage employees to take part in sustainability efforts. By spearheading company-wide initiatives, planning events, and putting up fresh sustainability projects, these groups can promote a climate of shared accountability.

Organizational Culture

9. Sustainability Mission and Values: It is imperative that the company's mission, vision, and values effectively convey its dedication to sustainability. All employees, even those in upper management, should incorporate these values into their everyday work and ensure that they are reflected in the organizational culture.

10. Leadership Commitment: Make sure executives in the organization take an active role in promoting and engaging in sustainability efforts. To promote cultural change and show that sustainability is a top business goal, leadership commitment is essential.

Policies and Procedures

11. Green Office Practices: Adopt office procedures that reduce their negative effects on the environment, such as paperless workflows, recycling initiatives, and energy-efficient lighting. Encourage eco-friendly modes of transportation for transportation, such as public transportation, biking, and carpooling.

12. Ethical Sourcing and Procurement: Create procurement guidelines that give suppliers and contractors who follow ethical and sustainable practices priority. This entails picking partners who uphold sustainable supply chains, promote fair labour practices, and employ eco-friendly materials.

Communication and Reporting

13. Transparent Reporting: Report on the company's sustainability performance on a regular basis, outlining both its successes and its shortcomings. To keep all stakeholders informed and involved, use sustainability reports, corporate social responsibility (CSR) reports, and internal communications.

14. Employee Feedback Mechanisms: Provide employees with reliable channels to offer input on sustainability projects and make suggestions for enhancements. Utilize suggestion boxes, surveys, and frequent meetings with a sustainability focus to collect and address employee feedback.

Compliance and Governance

15. Adherence to Standards: Make sure that local and international sustainability certifications and standards, such ISO 14001 for environmental management, are followed. Review and update policies frequently to keep them in line with best practices and increasing sustainability standards.

16. Ethical Governance: Create and implement a thorough code of ethics with a focus on sustainable development and ethical business practices. Make sure that ethical behaviour, accountability, and openness are supported by governance structures, which will emphasize the significance of sustainability at all organizational levels.

Community and External Engagement

17. Community Involvement Programs: Initiate sustainability and community service projects with your employees. Employees can give back to the community and strengthen their ties to sustainability efforts by collaborating with local organizations on social and environmental projects.

18. Stakeholder Collaboration: Work together with other partners, like as suppliers, consumers, and local communities, to achieve common sustainability objectives. Participate in relationships and conversations that advance sustainable practices all throughout the value chain.

Technology and Innovation

19. Sustainable Technology Use: Use technology to further sustainable practices. Use digital tools and platforms to facilitate distant communication, cut down on paper use, and simplify sustainable practices. Invest in renewable energy sources and energy-efficient technologies for your business's operations.

20. Innovation for Sustainability: Encourage an innovative culture that prioritizes sustainability. In order to lessen the company's environmental effect and increase its social impact, encourage employees to come up with fresh concepts. Create labs or innovation hubs devoted to investigating sustainable solutions.

Organizations can weave sustainability into the very fabric of their operations by incorporating these methods into HR policies and practices. This all-encompassing strategy improves the organization's general performance, reputation, and resilience in addition to helping the environment and society. Companies have the ability to establish a work environment that is effective and motivating for all parties involved, in addition to being sustainable, by means of persistent dedication and purposeful action.

9.2.3 Examples of Organizations Successfully Aligning HR Practices with Sustainability Standards

Integrating sustainability criteria into HR policies and procedures has become a critical objective for many forward-thinking organizations. These companies understand that incorporating environmental, social, and governance (ESG) concepts into HRM not only improves their brand but also fosters resilience and long-term success.

❖ Here are detailed examples of organizations that have successfully aligned their HR practices with sustainability standards, setting benchmarks in the industry:

1. Microsoft

Microsoft has committed to being carbon negative by 2030 and has integrated this goal into its HR and overall business strategy:

Employee Involvement: Through initiatives like Microsoft Sustainability Champions, Microsoft actively engages its employees in environmental stewardship. Through this effort, the organization cultivates an environmental stewardship culture by empowering employees to lead and take part in sustainability projects.

Sustainability Education: Employees are encouraged to incorporate sustainable practices into their work and the corporation offers considerable training on sustainability-related themes. The workforce that results from this education is better prepared to fulfil Microsoft's aspirational sustainability goals.

Sustainable Facilities: Microsoft has integrated sustainable materials and renewable energy sources into the design of its buildings to make them energy-efficient. In order to lessen the impact that commuting has on the environment, the organization now offers remote work choices.

2. Patagonia

Patagonia, the outdoor clothing company, stands out for its deep commitment to environmental sustainability and social responsibility, reflected in its HR practices:

Employee Engagement: Employees at Patagonia are encouraged to take part in environmental advocacy. Through its Environmental Internship Program, the corporation provides employees with an annual maximum of two months of paid leave to work for environmental causes. This policy encourages a sense of purpose and involvement among employees in addition to supporting the company's environmental mission.

Work-Life Balance: The organization encourages work-life balance by offering daycare services on-site and flexible work schedules. Patagonia supports the personal life and well-being of its employees by offering family-friendly practices including on-site childcare at company offices, which raises employee retention and workplace happiness.

Sustainability Training: Patagonia often offers training sessions to its employees on environmental issues and sustainable business methods. The company's sustainability goals can be actively contributed to by employees, thanks to these efforts that guarantee their knowledge.

3. Cisco

Cisco, a global technology leader, integrates sustainability into its HR practices and corporate strategy:

Green Teams and Employee Initiatives: Employees that oversee and take part in sustainability programs have formed Cisco's Green Teams. These groups are in charge of grassroots sustainability activities and involve all employees in environmental work.

Sustainability Goals and Reporting: Cisco reports on its efforts on a regular basis and establishes explicit sustainability goals. By providing chances for participation in sustainability projects and open lines of communication, the company engages its employees in these efforts.

Training and Development: Cisco provides training courses with an emphasis on ethical business conduct and sustainability. Employees that participate in these programs gain a better understanding of the sustainability objectives of the organization and how they may help achieve them.

4. Unilever

Unilever, a global leader in consumer goods, has embedded sustainability into its HR policies and corporate strategy through its Sustainable Living Plan:

Sustainable Living Plan: Unilever's Sustainable Living Plan is a comprehensive approach designed to increase the company's positive social effect while decoupling its growth from its environmental impact. HR procedures have a strong integration with this plan.

Diversity and Inclusion: Diversity and inclusion are important to Unilever's initiatives towards social sustainability. The organization has set high goals to increase ethnic diversity and gender parity at all levels. The HR rules of Unilever guarantee objective hiring procedures, assistance for a variety of employee resource groups, and continuous training on unconscious bias.

Employee Development: Unilever makes significant investments in training programs for staff members that prioritize sustainability. These courses cover sustainable business practices, sustainability leadership, and innovation workshops aimed at developing sustainable goods and services. In addition to improving skills, this helps employees match their job to the company's sustainability goals.

5. Nestlé

Nestlé, a global food and beverage company, integrates sustainability into its HR practices through its "Creating Shared Value" approach:

Sustainability Training and Awareness: To help its employees become more knowledgeable and conscious of sustainability, Nestlé offers training courses. A variety of subjects are covered by these initiatives, such as sustainable sourcing, waste reduction, and water conservation.

Employee Involvement in Community Projects: Participation in community programs that advance sustainability and social responsibility is encouraged by the corporation among its employees. Employees' sense of belonging and sense of purpose are strengthened by their participation.

Sustainable Workplace Practices: In the workplace, Nestlé encourages sustainable practices like waste minimization, energy efficiency, and ethical material procurement. These methods are backed by extensive policies and procedures and incorporated into day-to-day operations.

6. Google

Google, a global technology giant, has made significant strides in aligning its HR practices with sustainability standards:

Green Workplace Initiatives: The design of Google's offices prioritizes sustainability. The corporation has strong recycling programs, employs renewable energy, and gives priority to energy-efficient structures. In addition, Google offers sustainable and healthful food options in its cafeterias to lessen its environmental impact and enhance employee wellbeing.

Employee Benefits: In order to encourage sustainability, Google provides a number of incentives, including carpooling rewards, public transit subsidies, and electric vehicle charging stations at company headquarters. Through these programs, employees are encouraged to adopt sustainable practices and the carbon footprint of their commutes is lessened.

Sustainability Goals: By include these objectives in performance evaluations and establishing clear guidelines for contributions to sustainability projects, Google encourages employees to take part in its sustainability ambitions. This strategy makes sure that everyone in the company shares accountability for sustainability.

7. IKEA
IKEA, the multinational furniture retailer, integrates sustainability into its HR practices through a strong focus on environmental and social responsibility:

Sustainability Training: For its employees, IKEA offers extensive training programs on sustainable practices. This covers instruction on waste minimization, sustainable sourcing, and energy conservation. Workers are urged to include these procedures into their regular workdays.

Ethical Sourcing Policies: Sustainability and ethical sourcing are given first priority in IKEA's buying practices. Through frequent audits, the organization makes sure that its suppliers follow stringent environmental and social requirements.

Employee Engagement: Through its "People & Planet Positive" policy, IKEA involves its employees in environmental activities. Workers are encouraged to share their thoughts, get involved in community outreach initiatives, and work on environmental projects. The staff develops a sense of ownership and accountability for sustainability as a result of this involvement.

8. Sales force
Sales force, a leading cloud-based software company, has embedded sustainability into its corporate culture and HR practices:

Sustainability Goals: Sales force has set high standards for sustainability, such as employing only renewable energy sources and reaching net-zero greenhouse gas emissions. These objectives are incorporated into the HR guidelines and the company's overall business plan.

Employee Programs: Employees are encouraged to adopt sustainable habits by a number of programs offered by Sales force. These include sustainability challenges, volunteer opportunities cantered around environmental causes, and internal competitions that honour creative sustainable ideas.

Transparency and Reporting: Sales force is dedicated to providing clear reporting on its performance in terms of sustainability. Through initiatives for involvement and transparent communication, the company frequently publishes comprehensive sustainability reports and includes employees in these endeavours. Employee participation in continuing sustainability initiatives is encouraged, and they are constantly updated on the company's success.

9. Interface

Interface, a global leader in modular flooring, has sustainability at the core of its business and HR practices:

Mission Zero: The mission of Interface is to completely eradicate all adverse effects the firm may have on the environment by the year 2020. This challenging objective entails encouraging a culture of environmental responsibility and involving employees in sustainability efforts.

Employee Training: Interface provides thorough training courses with an emphasis on sustainability, promoting creativity and long-term fixes. Workers receive training on the value of sustainable practices and how they may help the business achieve its environmental objectives.

Corporate Culture: The corporate culture of Interface has a strong emphasis on sustainability, which has an impact on staff rewards, performance reviews, and hiring procedures. The organization promotes a work culture in which a shared value and top focus is sustainability.

10. Danone

Danone, a multinational food-products corporation, emphasizes sustainability in its HR practices through its "One Planet. One Health" vision:

Sustainable Sourcing and Fair Trade: Danone makes sure that fair trade and sustainable agriculture are supported by its sourcing policy. Employees are involved in the planning, execution, and oversight of sustainable sourcing efforts as part of the company's HR policies, which demonstrate its commitment.

Employee Engagement and Well-being: Through a number of initiatives that support mental and physical health as well as work-life balance, Danone works to improve employee well-being. These initiatives are a part of a larger initiative to establish a helpful and long-lasting workplace.

Environmental Education: Employees are encouraged to embrace and support sustainable practices both at work and in their personal lives via the company's continual education and training programs on environmental sustainability.

These companies are excellent examples of how HR policies and procedures that are in line with sustainability standards may improve corporate operations, employee satisfaction, and the environment and society. These businesses foster a more resilient, engaged, and progressive staff in addition to supporting global sustainability goals by integrating sustainability into their HR practices. Their dedication to ESG principles and strategic initiatives establish a standard for incorporating sustainability into the fundamentals of human resource management.

9.3 Legal Implications of Green HR Practices

There are a number of legal implications associated with implementing green HR practices, which incorporate environmental sustainability into human resource management. legislation pertaining to corporate governance, labour legislation, environmental rules, and compliance standards are among the many legal domains from which these implications arise. Understanding and negotiating these legal aspects is vital for firms to ensure that their green HR programs are not just effective but also legally sound.

❖ **Here are some of the key legal implications of green HR practices:**

1. Compliance with Environmental Regulations

Organizations implementing green HR practices need to make sure that local, federal, and international environmental laws are followed. This may consist of:

Environmental Reporting Requirements: Companies are required by law in many jurisdictions to record their environmental effect, which includes resource utilization, waste management, and carbon emissions. When using environmental performance measures in HR procedures, these reporting guidelines must be followed.

Sustainable Practices Mandates: Certain sustainable measures, like energy efficiency guidelines, waste minimization procedures, and pollution controls, may be required by regulations. These legal obligations must be complied with by HR policies that support these practices.

2. Labour Laws and Employee Rights

It is important to carefully analyse the potential legal ramifications of implementing green HR practices in order to avoid breaking labour laws and employee rights.

Health and Safety Regulations: Enhancing workplace health and safety through improved environmental practices is a common component of green HR initiatives. Adherence to occupational health and safety regulations is crucial, especially in cases where modifications impact the tangible work environment.

Fair Labour Practices: Regarding fair wages, working hours, and employee treatment, labor regulations must be complied with by any modifications made to work practices or conditions in the name of sustainability. To cut down on carbon emissions, for instance, telecommuting must be allowed while maintaining equitable pay and working conditions.

Non-discrimination: It is crucial to make sure that green HR programs do not unintentionally discriminate against any employee category. For example, advantages such as subsidies for public transportation ought to be available to all employees on an equal basis, irrespective of their location.

3. Corporate Governance and Fiduciary Duties
Green HR practices must be integrated within the broader framework of corporate governance:

Board Oversight: The board of directors must frequently provide its approval and supervision for the implementation of sustainability measures. The company's fiduciary duties, which include acting in the best interests of shareholders while taking into account broader environmental and social implications, must be complied with by the directors.

Disclosure Obligations: Companies may be required by law to inform shareholders and authorities about their sustainability initiatives and results. This covers the truthful and open reporting of sustainability programs and their effects on the environment.

4. Contractual Obligations and Agreements
Green HR practices can impact various contractual relationships within and outside the organization:

Employment Contracts: Employment contracts may need to be updated in order to reflect changes made to HR policies to include green practices. For example, employment agreements may need to explicitly state policies about telecommuting, flexible work schedules, or new performance measures pertaining to sustainability.

Supplier and Vendor Agreements: Companies Businesses frequently include their supply networks in their sustainability standards. Renegotiating contracts with vendors and suppliers to make sure they adhere to environmental requirements may be necessary for this. Making sure these contracts are enforceable and adhere to trade laws is one of the legal ramifications.

5. Intellectual Property and Innovation
Green HR practices can foster innovation and the development of new sustainable technologies or processes:

Intellectual Property (IP) Protection: Patents or other intellectual property rights are required to safeguard innovations resulting from sustainability activities, such as innovative technologies for waste reduction or energy-saving procedures. Maintaining appropriate intellectual property protection helps boost competitive advantage and stop illegal use.

Confidentiality Agreements: To safeguard confidential information and trade secrets pertaining to green advances, employees working on sustainability projects may be required to sign confidentiality agreements.

6. Privacy and Data Protection

Green HR practices, particularly those involving data collection and monitoring, must comply with privacy and data protection laws:

Employee Monitoring: Privacy standards must be followed by initiatives that track energy use or travel habits of employees in order to monitor their environmental impact. This entails securing data security and getting employee consent.

Data Reporting: Gathering and evaluating personal data may be necessary for reporting environmental parameters. Employee privacy rights must be protected by adherence to data protection rules, such as the General Data Protection Regulation (GDPR) in the EU.

7. Environmental Litigation Risks

Organizations engaging in green HR practices can face legal challenges if their initiatives are perceived as insufficient or misleading:

Green-washing Claims: Companies Businesses need to make sure the promises they make about sustainability are true and supported. Deceptive statements may result in legal action from shareholders, consumers, or regulators. Green washing charges, for instance, can arise from marketing goods or procedures as ecologically friendly without providing sufficient evidence.

Regulatory Enforcement: Fines, penalties, and other legal repercussions may arise from breaking environmental laws and regulations. In order to stay out of legal hot water, it is imperative that all green HR practices adhere to regulatory requirements.

8. Employee Relations and Collective Bargaining

Green HR practices can influence employee relations and interactions with labor unions:

Collective Bargaining Agreements: Negotiations with labour unions may be necessary when making changes to workplace procedures for sustainability-related objectives. Agreements on new work procedures, benefits, or health and safety protocols pertaining to green efforts fall under this category.

Employee Representation: Early employee representative involvement in the implementation of green HR initiatives can assist guarantee that the changes are accepted and consistent with the law. By being proactive, you can avoid conflicts and promote cooperation.

9. Training and Development Requirements

Green HR practices often involve training employees on new sustainable practices and technologies:

Mandatory Training: Labour laws pertaining to required training sessions, including equitable pay for employees' time and observance of working hours requirements, must be followed when implementing sustainability training programs.

Certification and Accreditation: Employees may need to earn special certificates in order to participate in some sustainability efforts. It is essential to make sure that these certifications adhere to legal requirements and are accepted by the appropriate authorities.

10. Employment Law Considerations in Green Practices

Changes to HR policies to incorporate sustainability may impact employment law aspects:

Equal Opportunities: Every green HR project needs to be planned with equal opportunity for all staff members in mind. Policies that promote the use of electric vehicles, for instance, must to take into account the possibility that some employees do not have access to them.

Flexible Working Arrangements: Legal requirements for working hours, breaks, and telecommuting laws must be followed while implementing flexible work arrangements to lessen their negative environmental effects.

11. Sustainability Reporting and Auditing

Transparency and accuracy in reporting sustainability efforts are legally significant:

Regulatory Requirements: Regulatory agencies may demand that businesses provide comprehensive sustainability reports. To adhere to legal requirements, these reports have to be truthful and substantiable.

Third-Party Audits: To help avoid potential legal problems connected to erroneous reporting; using third-party auditors to evaluate sustainability claims can offer legal confidence and credibility.

To sum up, incorporating green HR practices necessitates navigating a challenging legal environment that touches on a variety of topics, including corporate governance, labor law, environmental law, and data protection. Businesses need to make sure that their sustainability programs comply with all applicable regulatory obligations in addition to being in line with their strategic goals. This entails proactive interaction with all stakeholders; including regulatory bodies and employee representation, thorough training for staff, open reporting, and ongoing monitoring of legal developments.

Organizations Businesses that successfully integrate sustainability principles into their HR practices while taking into account and handling any related legal ramifications can improve not only their standing and operational effectiveness, but also make a beneficial impact on the environment and society. This well-rounded strategy guarantees the long-term viability of green HR efforts, promoting a strong and ethical business model that is advantageous to all parties involved.

9.3.1 Examination of the Legal Implications of Implementing Green HR Practices

Integrating environmental management concepts into human resources strategy and policies is a necessary step in putting green HR practices into effect. These strategies seek to improve corporate social responsibility, reduce environmental effect, and promote sustainable business operations.

Green HR practices come with a complicated range of legal ramifications, even though they can have many positive effects, such as strengthening employee morale, enhancing corporate image, and generating cost savings through efficiency gains. Organizations must comprehend these legal aspects in order to manage compliance, reduce risks, and guarantee successful implementation. Here, we look at the legal ramifications for a number of areas, including data protection, environmental law, health and safety laws, and employment law.

1. Employment Law Compliance

Workplaces, job descriptions, and operational protocols are frequently altered as part of green HR initiatives. Projects like telecommuting to save carbon emissions, encouraging remote work, and offering flexible work schedules to cut energy use, for example, must be carefully aligned with current employment regulations. The labour laws pertaining to work hours, rest breaks, and overtime compensation must not be violated by these adjustments, and employers must make sure of that. Telecommuting regulations, for instance, must abide by laws regulating working hours to guarantee that employees receive pay for overtime work and that their rights to breaks and time off are upheld. Litigation, employee complaints, and even fines could result from noncompliance.

2. Health and Safety Regulations

The health and safety of employees should never be jeopardized when implementing green practices. When implementing new machinery or procedures to lessen their impact on the environment, organizations must make sure they adhere to occupational health and safety regulations. For instance, in order to prevent workplace mishaps and injuries, safety requirements should be followed when installing energy-efficient gear or changing workspace layouts to improve natural illumination. Employers are required by law to maintain a safe workplace, and breaking health and safety laws can expose a business to serious legal risks, financial penalties, and reputational harm. Maintaining compliance and ensuring the wellbeing of employees depends on regular safety assessments and employee training.

3. Data Protection and Privacy

Innovative technologies that track and control energy consumption, telecom systems, and other sustainability measures are frequently used in green HR projects. These technologies have the capacity to gather large volumes of information about the whereabouts, actions, and behaviours of employees. Strict adherence to privacy and data protection rules is necessary for organizations to avoid misuse and illegal access to personal data. It is imperative to adhere to laws like the California Consumer Privacy Act (CCPA) in the US and the General Data Protection Regulation (GDPR) in the EU. To prevent legal ramifications and safeguard employee privacy, businesses should put strong data protection measures in place, transparent data usage rules, and acquire informed consent from employees.

4. Environmental Legislation

Organizations need to make sure that their green HR policies abide by all applicable environmental rules and regulations on a local, national, and worldwide level. For instance, encouraging telecommuting or public transit to lower carbon footprints needs to be in line with regional transportation and environmental laws. Companies can also need to seek certifications for their sustainability initiatives or meet strict environmental regulations. There may be penalties, legal action, and reputational harm for breaking environmental laws. Retaining compliance and improving the efficacy of green HR practices need active engagement with environmental specialists and keeping up of legislative changes.

5. Discrimination and Equal Opportunity

In order to prevent prejudice and guarantee equal chances for all employees, green HR policies must be developed. Initiatives such as carpooling or cycling to work incentives need to take into account employees who might not be able to participate because of personal circumstances, limitations related to location, or impairments. Employers are responsible for making sure that no specific employee group is inadvertently left out or treated unfairly by their rules. To maintain inclusivity and adherence to equal opportunity regulations, this involves offering substitute options or adjustments. Ignoring these problems can result in lawsuits, allegations of discrimination, and a detrimental effect on inclusion and diversity in the workplace.

6. Contracts and Agreements

Contractual changes resulting from green initiatives, like policies allowing remote work or flexible work schedules, should be made explicit in employment agreements. This guarantees that the rights and obligations of the employer and the employee are clearly defined and enforceable by law. Remote working agreements ought to outline several aspects such as working hours, performance standards, data security protocols, and provisions for equipment and technical assistance. It is helpful to define these phrases precisely in order to avoid confusion, disagreements, and even legal problems. To maintain continued compliance with employment regulations and to reflect changes in green HR practices, employers should review and revise contracts on a regular basis.

7. Union and Labour Relations

Significant adjustments to work procedures pertaining to green HR efforts in unionized workplaces need to be discussed and agreed upon with labour unions. In order to support new green efforts, this may involve retraining programs, changes to employment positions, and modifications to working circumstances. To obtain agreements that strike a balance between the rights and interests of employees and organizational sustainability goals, employers and unions must negotiate in good faith. Labour relations issues, legal challenges, and industrial action may result from improper negotiation of these modifications. The effective adoption of green HR practices requires cooperative strategies and open lines of communication with unions.

8. Employee Incentives and Benefits

Offering incentives for sustainable behaviour, such as bonuses for taking public transportation, financial aid for buying eco-friendly cars, or recognition for taking part in company-sponsored environmental initiatives, is one way that green HR practices can be implemented. To make sure that these incentives don't inadvertently put employees in violation of current compensation regulations or cause tax problems for them, they must be handled properly. Non-cash incentives, such as more leave or flexible work schedules, should be designed in a way that complies with employment laws and tax laws. When creating incentive programs, employers should consult legal and tax professionals to minimize any potential financial and legal issues.

9. Intellectual Property

Intellectual property rights must be taken into account when implementing creative green HR solutions, such as creating exclusive sustainability training curricula or distinctive environmental management systems. By securing these ideas via patents, trademarks, or copyrights, the company can keep its competitive edge and keep rivals from using them without authorization. Employers are responsible for making sure that all intellectual property produced as a result of green HR efforts is correctly recorded, registered, and safeguarded by applicable intellectual property regulations. Working with intellectual property lawyers can assist in navigating the challenges of safeguarding and utilizing these assets.

10. Reporting and Transparency

Green HR practices frequently include more transparency in reporting on sustainability initiatives. Businesses are required to submit accurate and thorough reports on their sustainability efforts, environmental performance, and advancements made toward green objectives. For these reports to be free from legal ramifications pertaining to inaccurate or misleading information, they must adhere to both financial and non-financial reporting criteria. Reporting that is accurate and honest improves a company's reputation, fosters confidence with stakeholders, and shows that it is genuinely committed to sustainability. To preserve transparency and credibility, employers should set up strong reporting procedures, carry out frequent audits, and guarantee that reporting requirements are being followed.

To sum up, there are a lot of advantages to adopting green HR practices, such as better employee engagement, a stronger company reputation, and possible cost savings. To guarantee a successful and compliant implementation, enterprises must navigate a complicated terrain of legal ramifications. To reduce risks and stay out of trouble, it's important to carefully analyse employment law, health and safety laws, data protection, environmental laws, and other legal matters. Green HR practices cannot be implemented effectively and sustainably without the assistance of legal specialists, stakeholder engagement, and proactive legal compliance. Organizations can fulfil their legal and ethical obligations while achieving their sustainability goals by addressing these legal aspects.

9.3.2 Addressing Potential Legal Challenges in Areas of Green HR Practices

Adopting green HR practices presents a number of legal issues that call for careful consideration in order to guarantee adherence to pertinent rules and legislation. This extended analysis includes the following topics: green performance management, green employee engagement, green training and development, green remuneration and benefits, green employee relations, and green recruiting and selection. Organizations can reduce legal risks, advance sustainability, and uphold an equitable and law-abiding workplace by giving these areas careful attention.

1. Green Recruitment and Selection

Legal Challenges:

i. **Discrimination:** Ensuring that there is no discrimination in green hiring practices based on protected traits including age, gender, ethnicity, handicap, or religion.

ii. **Job Descriptions:** Drafting job descriptions that truthfully represent environmental obligations without unintentionally targeting particular applicants.

iii. **Background Checks:** Following the law when it comes to background checks in order to protect applicants' right to privacy and maintain impartial employment procedures.

iv. **Equal Employment Opportunity (EEO):** Respecting EEO regulations to avoid discrimination in recruiting choices and procedures, even when giving preference to green credentials.

v. **Candidate Privacy:** Maintaining candidate privacy and adhering to data protection laws including the California Consumer Privacy Act (CCPA) and the General Data Protection Regulation (GDPR).

vi. **Diversity and Inclusion:** In order to improve workforce participation and prevent accusations of discriminatory behaviours, the green recruitment process should encourage diversity and inclusion.

Strategies for Mitigation:
   i. **Training:** Educating hiring managers in-depth on fair green recruitment procedures, unconscious bias, and EEO regulations.
   ii. **Standardized Processes:** Putting in place uniform procedures for candidate evaluations, interviews, and job listings in order to promote equity and uniformity in the green hiring process.
   iii. **Green Criteria:** Establishing precise, impartial standards for green credentials that are pertinent to the position and do not unjustly reject applicants.
   iv. **Diversity Initiatives:** Putting diversity initiatives into practice, such as diversity goals in green recruitment measures, diversity training for recruiters, and focused outreach to underrepresented groups.
   v. **Candidate Feedback:** In order to encourage openness and justice in the green hiring process, feedback should be given to candidates regarding the status of their applications and the reasons they were not chosen.
   vi. **Legal Review:** Reviewing green hiring procedures on a regular basis from a legal perspective in order to spot and resolve any possible compliance problems.

2. Green Compensation and Benefits

Legal Challenges:
   i. **Fair Labour Standards:** Implementing green incentives while guaranteeing adherence to the Fair Labour Standards Act (FLSA), related state legislation, and minimum wage, overtime compensation, and other related rules.
   ii. **Pay Equity:** Eliminating pay discrimination on the basis of gender, ethnicity, or other protected characteristics by regularly

auditing pay equality and resolving any discrepancies, particularly when presenting incentives or bonuses that are environmentally friendly.

iii. **Green Benefits:** Ensuring that green employee benefits programs support sustainable practices while adhering to pertinent legislation, such as the Affordable Care Act (ACA) and the Employee Retirement Income Security Act (ERISA).

iv. **Employee Classification:** Adhering to rules governing independent contractors and temporary workers in green roles, as well as correctly categorizing personnel as exempt or non-exempt under wage and hour standards.

v. **Wage Theft Prevention:** Putting in place safeguards against wage fraud, such as keeping precise records of the hours worked and paying salaries in line with the law, which includes tracking green incentives.

Strategies for Mitigation:

i. **Regular Audits:** Identifying and resolving any possible compliance issues, such as salary discrepancies and benefit plan violations, by regularly auditing green compensation and benefits practices.

ii. **Training:** Educating managers, payroll specialists, and HR personnel on wage and hour regulations, pay equality concepts, and managing green benefits.

iii. **Legal Review:** seeking legal advice to make sure that green benefits and compensation plans abide by all relevant laws and rules, such as ERISA, the ACA, and state-specific mandates.

iv. **Green Incentives:** Creating wage and hour law-compliant green incentive and reward systems and making sure they are implemented equitably and consistently.

v. **Employee Communication:** To encourage knowledge and compliance, it is important to be open and transparent in discussing green benefits and pay policies, including any updates or adjustments, with employees.

3. Green Employee Relations

Legal Challenges:
i. **Wrongful Termination:** Preventing accusations of wrongful termination by making sure that decisions about termination, including those pertaining to green performance, are made for justifiable reasons and do not contravene anti-discrimination or employment contracts.
ii. **Employee Grievances:** Addressing complaints from employees about green efforts in compliance with business guidelines and applicable labour regulations to avoid legal issues.
iii. **Workplace Investigations:** Addressing claims of harassment, discrimination, or wrongdoing pertaining to green practices by carrying out exhaustive and unbiased workplace investigations.
iv. **Employee Privacy:** Protecting the right to privacy of workers during workplace investigations and making sure that the rules controlling employee monitoring and surveillance are followed, especially when following green practices.
v. **Union Relations:** Navigating collective bargaining agreements and union relations to prevent unfair labour practice claims and guarantee compliance with labour regulations, particularly while launching green initiatives.

Strategies for Mitigation:
i. **Clear Policies:** Establishing clear policies and procedures for managing employee relations matters, such as resolving complaints, taking disciplinary action, and terminating employees in connection with green projects.
ii. **Documentation:** Maintaining records of all communications with employees, including complaints, inquiries, disciplinary actions, and decisions on termination, in order to demonstrate adherence to legal requirements.
iii. **Training:** Giving managers and HR employees training on how to handle employee relations issues pertaining to green initiatives

in a way that complies with the law, as well as effective communication and dispute resolution techniques.

iv. **Legal Consultation:** To guarantee compliance with applicable laws and regulations, legal counsel should be consulted when conducting workplace investigations, dealing delicate employee relations issues, or managing union ties.

v. **Employee Engagement:** To promote teamwork and lessen resistance or complaints, involve employees in the creation and execution of green initiatives.

4. Green Performance Management

Legal Challenges:

i. **Objective Evaluation:** Ensuring that, in order to prevent accusations of discriminatory treatment, green performance criteria are quantifiable, objective, and legally defended.

ii. **Consistency and Fairness:** Ensuring uniform application of green performance metrics throughout the organization to avoid accusations of partiality or prejudice.

iii. **Legal Compliance:** Ensuring that green performance management techniques abide by labour rules and anti-discrimination laws, among other employment requirements.

iv. **Employee Rights:** Preserving employee rights and refraining from taking harsh action against those who disobey voluntary green efforts.

v. **Transparency:** Ensuring transparency in the development, communication, and implementation of green performance measures to prevent disagreements and misinterpretations.

Strategies for Mitigation:

i. **Clear Performance Metrics:** Creating measurable, verifiable green performance metrics that are in line with company objectives and effectively conveyed to all employees.

ii. **Training for Managers:** Educating managers on how to fairly and consistently evaluate green performance in order to guarantee impartial and objective evaluations.

iii. **Regular Reviews and Feedback:** Putting in place frequent performance reviews with constructive feedback sessions and green performance metrics.

iv. **Documentation:** Maintaining thorough records of feedback and performance reviews to show that green performance metrics are applied fairly and consistently.

v. **Employee Involvement:** To achieve alignment and buy-in with reasonable and doable goals, involve employees in the creation of green performance indicators.

5. Employee Engagement in Green Initiatives

Legal Challenges:

i. **Voluntary Participation:** Making sure that involvement in green programs is entirely voluntary in order to prevent accusations of pressure or forced engagement.

ii. **Work-Life Balance:** Regulations pertaining to work-life balance and environmental measures should be balanced, particularly when the former call for greater effort or time outside of usual business hours.

iii. **Inclusivity:** Creating initiatives for employee green involvement that are accessible and inclusive, including to employees with impairments or from diverse cultural backgrounds.

iv. **Privacy Concerns:** Managing data protection laws and tracking employees' involvement in environmental projects while taking privacy considerations into consideration.

v. **Incentives and Rewards:** Putting in place compensation and benefit plans for green initiative involvement in a way that respects wage and hour regulations and prevents discrimination.

Strategies for Mitigation:

i. **Voluntary Programs:** Creating initiatives for green engagement that prioritize voluntary involvement and make it abundantly evident that not participating will not have a detrimental effect on employees' chances or assessments.

ii. **Balanced Work Arrangements:** Ensuring that green projects are planned to accommodate regular work schedules or provide flexible options that adhere to laws governing work hours.

iii. **Inclusive Programs:** Creating inclusive engagement programs that are accessible to all employees, taking into account their various needs, and making sure they adhere to inclusion criteria.

iv. **Privacy Protections:** Strictly adhering to data protection regulations, including the CCPA and GDPR, when collecting information on employees' involvement in environmental projects and protecting such information.

v. **Legal Review of Incentives:** Seeking legal advice to make sure that awards and incentives for being environmentally conscious adhere to relevant regulations and do not unintentionally put people in danger of legal action.

6. Green Training and Development

Legal Challenges:

i. **Compliance Training:** Ensuring that all pertinent regulatory requirements such as those pertaining to worker safety and the environment are included in the training on green practices.

ii. **Accessibility:** In accordance with the Americans with Disabilities Act (ADA) and related requirements, providing employees with disabilities with access to green training programs.

iii. **Intellectual Property:** Preventing illegal use or disclosure of the company's intellectual property in green training materials.

iv. **Employee Development:** Encouraging employees to learn green practices while adhering to company policy and equal opportunity requirements.

v. **Training Recordkeeping:** recording participation in green training programs by employees accurately in order to show adherence to regulatory regulations and industry standards.

Strategies for Mitigation:
  i. **Comprehensive Training Programs:** Creating comprehensive green training courses that address the relevant legal and regulatory aspects of green activities.
  ii. **Accessibility Standards:** Ensuring compliance with disability discrimination legislation and promoting diversity by adhering to accessibility requirements for training materials.
  iii. **Copyright Protection:** Copyright safeguards are being put in place for green training materials to prevent unlawful use or dissemination.
  iv. **Tracking Participation:** Tracking employee participation in eco-friendly training initiatives and keeping track of program completions to prove adherence to regulatory obligations and industry norms.
  v. **Employee Feedback:** Employee feedback on green training efforts is sought after in order to pinpoint areas for development and guarantee that training programs satisfy employees' requirements and expectations.

7. Workplace Health and Safety in Green Initiatives

Legal Challenges:
  i. **Regulatory Compliance:** When putting green initiatives into practice, making sure that OSHA and other health and safety laws are followed.
  ii. **Risk Management:** Recognizing and reducing any hazards to health and safety that may arise from using eco-friendly products or technologies or other green initiatives.
  iii. **Health Programs:** Carrying out green initiatives-related health programs in accordance with HIPAA and other regulations pertaining to health privacy.

Strategies for Mitigation:
  i. **Safety Audits:** Identifying and addressing possible risks for green initiatives through routine safety audits and risk assessments.

ii. **Employee Training:** Provide training on green initiative-specific workplace health and safety procedures.

iii. **Health Programs:** Ensuring compliance with privacy and health information requirements for health programs associated with green initiatives.

iv. **Legal Consultation:** Consulting with legal professionals to ensure that green initiative-related health and safety measures abide by relevant laws and regulations.

8. Diversity and Inclusion in Green Initiatives

Legal Challenges:

i. **Compliance with Anti-Discrimination Laws:** Ensuring that anti-discrimination laws are followed and that no employee group is left out of green efforts.

ii. **Equal Opportunity:** Giving all employees an equal opportunity to engage in and gain from green projects.

iii. **Inclusive Policies:** Creating policies that encourage inclusion in green projects without excluding any group due to protected traits.

Strategies for Mitigation:

i. **Diversity Training:** Providing training on diversity and inclusion that is especially suited to green projects.

ii. **Inclusive Policies:** Making policies that assure adherence to legal requirements and encourage inclusion in green activities.

iii. **Monitoring and Reporting:** Ensuring inclusivity through regular reporting of progress and monitoring of diversity measures connected to green initiatives.

In conclusion, a thorough and proactive strategy to guarantee compliance with laws and regulations is required to handle any legal difficulties in green performance management and employee engagement. Organizations can reduce legal risk and provide a just, inclusive, and encouraging work environment by putting standard operating procedures into place, offering comprehensive training, carrying out frequent audits, speaking with legal professionals, and keeping lines of communication open. HR procedures can successfully support sustainability goals while adhering to legal and ethical norms by making these efforts.

9.3.3 Best Practices for Mitigating Legal Risks While Promoting Environmentally Responsible HRM

Best practices for mitigating legal risks while promoting environmentally responsible Human Resource Management (HRM) refer to the strategies and procedures that organizations can implement to ensure their environmental sustainability initiatives within HRM are both effective and legally compliant. By using these best practices, companies can reduce their risk of legal liability by striking a balance between their sustainable aims and the need to adhere to legal requirements.

Encouraging environmentally conscious human resource management (HRM) is a calculated move that will increase employee engagement, lower expenses, and improve sustainability. Nonetheless, it's imperative to control the legal risks connected to these projects. Below are detailed best practices for mitigating these risks:

1. Compliance with Employment and Environmental Laws

Stay Updated on Legislation: Updates on employment legislation and environmental restrictions at the local, state, and federal levels should be regularly followed. Join professional groups, go to pertinent seminars, and subscribe to legal bulletins.

Regular Audits: To make sure that laws are being followed, conduct internal and external audits. This includes checking for legal compliance in contracts, working conditions, and HR procedures.

Policy Reviews: Review and update HR policies frequently to take into account modifications to employment and environmental legislation. Engage legal counsel in these assessments to guarantee complete adherence.

2. Develop Clear, Comprehensive Policies

Policy Documentation: Create thorough written policies for every green HRM project. Give a clear explanation of the goals, protocols, and standards pertaining to environmental sustainability.

Employee Handbook: Include green HR guidelines in the handbook for employees. Make sure it is simple for all staff to access and comprehend.

Internal Communication: Use internal portals, meetings, and emails to effectively communicate policies so that all staff members are aware of them and know their roles in these efforts.

3. Stakeholder Consultation and Engagement

Inclusive Policy Development: Include a wide range of employees and interested parties in the formulation of the policy. This guarantees that the regulations are workable and broadly embraced.

Feedback Mechanisms: To gather continuing feedback, set up anonymous channels like suggestion boxes or online questionnaires.

Regular Updates: Frequently inform stakeholders on the state of green HR efforts and the ways in which their input is being taken into consideration.

4. Training and Awareness Programs

Regular Training Sessions: Provide obligatory training courses on environmental sustainability and associated legal ramifications to all employees. Make use of a range of instructional techniques, including workshops, online courses, and practical exercises.

Updated Training Content: Update training materials frequently to take into account new legislative changes and sustainable best practices. Collaborate with outside specialists to deliver current knowledge.

Role-Specific Training: Ensure that training programs are relevant and effective by customizing them to particular jobs within the organization.

5. Non-Discrimination and Fair Treatment

Equal Opportunity: Make sure that green HR initiatives don't result in unfair treatment or discrimination. Equal opportunities for participation in and gain from these activities should be extended to all employees.

Inclusive Practices: Adopt ecologically friendly procedures while taking into account the various requirements of all employees. Employees with impairments and individuals from diverse cultural backgrounds are both accommodated in this.

Regular Monitoring: Monitor how different employee groups are affected by green HR initiatives to make sure they are equitable and inclusive.

6. Thorough Documentation

Detailed Records: Ensure that all green HR activities, including as stakeholder meetings, training sessions, and policy drafting, are meticulously documented.

Audit Trails: For each and every sustainability project, create and keep an audit trail. This illustrates compliance efforts and aids in the defence against any legal claims.

Data Security: Make sure that every paperwork is safely kept and safeguarded, particularly if it includes confidential employee data.

7. Dedicated Compliance Team

Formation of a Compliance Team: Create a dedicated team that is in charge of making sure that the legal criteria for green HR practices are met. Personnel from the legal, HR, and environmental departments should be on this team.

Regular Compliance Checks: Verify that all green HR policies are complying by conducting routine audits and reviews. This covers both external and internal reviews.

Continuous Training: To keep the compliance team informed about legislative changes and sustainable best practices, provide regular training.

8. Legal Counsel Involvement

Consult Legal Experts: Consult legal guidance while creating and implementing green HR practices. Legal professionals can offer perceptions into possible dangers and assist in creating policies that lessen them.

Legal Review Process: Establish a procedure whereby legal counsel reviews all green HR initiatives prior to their implementation. This offers suggestions for risk reduction and assists in locating potential legal issues.

Ongoing Legal Advice: To receive ongoing assistance and guidance on new legal matters, keep up a connection with legal counsel.

9. Transparency and Accountability

Open Communication: Encourage an environment of open communication so that staff members are comfortable raising issues with green HR efforts. Regular town hall meetings, anonymous feedback platforms, and open-door guidelines can help with this.

Clear Reporting Mechanisms: Provide precise guidelines for reporting and resolving issues with green HR practices. Make sure that all employees are aware of these guidelines, and that any reports are handled fairly and immediately.

Public Reporting: Report openly on the company's green HR strategies and how they're working in sustainability reports. This strengthens the organization's reputation and encourages accountability.

10. Continuous Monitoring and Improvement

Regular Reviews: Evaluate and evaluate green HRM activities on a regular basis. Utilize metrics and key performance indicators (KPIs) to assess how these initiatives are affecting the organization's sustainability objectives.

Adapt and Improve: Green HR policies should be regularly improved and adjusted in light of review results and input. Remain adaptable and mindful of new regulatory needs as well as developing sustainable best practices.

Benchmarking: In order to find areas for development and implement best practices, compare your green HR activities with those of other firms.

11. Aligning with Corporate Social Responsibility (CSR) Goals

CSR Integration: Align green HR initiatives with overarching corporate social responsibility (CSR) objectives. Make sure the company's commitment to sustainability and moral behaviour is reflected in its HR policy.

Public Reporting: In CSR reports, openly discuss the company's green HR activities and their results. This fosters accountability while also improving stakeholder trust and the organization's reputation.

Employee Involvement in CSR: Motivate employees to take part in environmental sustainability-related CSR initiatives. This can be helping out at community cleanups or taking part in environmental initiatives supported by the business.

12. Risk Assessment and Management

Risk Identification: To find possible legal concerns related to green HR efforts, do a complete risk assessment. This involves assessing the potential interactions between new policies and current legal requirements as well as employee rights.

Mitigation Strategies: Create and put into action plans to reduce hazards that have been identified. This could entail making changes to the policies, offering more training, or stepping up oversight in particular areas.

Contingency Planning: Make backup measures in case you face legal difficulties. Having a plan for handling future legal challenges or compliance difficulties is part of this.

Organizations can effectively promote environmentally responsible HRM while lowering legal risks by adhering to these complete best practices. A more ethical, compatible with the law, and sustainable workplace might result from carefully and legally implementing green HR activities.

Chapter – 10

Diversity and Inclusion in Sustainable Organization

Introduction to Diversity and Inclusion in Sustainable Organizations:

As businesses strive to strike a balance between social responsibility, economic growth, and environmental care, sustainability has become a critical area of concern. The values of inclusion and diversity are essential to reaching these sustainability targets. These values improve innovation, judgment, and general effectiveness in addition to improving the organizational culture.

When disparities exist in a certain environment, it's referred to as diversity. These differences can be of many different kinds, including those related to race, ethnicity, gender, age, sexual orientation, disability, socioeconomic status, and educational background. Diversity is seen as a vital resource in sustainable businesses because it offers a range of viewpoints, experiences, and abilities.

Conversely, inclusion entails actively engaging every member of the organization and making sure that everyone's voice is heard and taken into consideration during decision-making processes. It goes beyond simply having a diverse workforce; inclusion also involves cultivating a culture that supports diversity and allows for meaningful contributions from all of its diverse members.

Meaning of Diversity and Inclusion in Sustainable Organizations:

Diversity and inclusion (D&I) are essential to creating a work climate in sustainable businesses where a range of viewpoints, experiences, and backgrounds are not just welcomed but actively used to further long-term sustainability objectives. An in-depth examination of these ideas and their importance is provided below:

- **Diversity**

Diversity refers to the representation of a wide array of characteristics and experiences within an organization. These characteristics can be categorized into several dimensions:

a. **Race and Ethnicity:** This involves the workforce's representation of various racial and ethnic groupings. Employing people from a range of racial and ethnic origins enables a varied organization to better understand and serve the demands of a multicultural society.

b. **Gender and Gender Identity:** Inclusion of all genders is a component of diversity, as it acknowledges the distinct contributions made by men, women, and non-binary people. Promoting gender fairness and making sure that all gender identities are accepted and encouraged are further aspects of gender diversity.

c. **Age:** A business with a varied age range benefits from a blend of generational viewpoints. While older employees provide expertise and historical perspective, younger employees could offer new ideas and technological know-how.

d. **Sexual Orientation:** Employers who are inclusive welcome people of all sexual orientations, making LGBTQ+ staff members feel appreciated, comfortable, and respected.

e. **Disability:** This entails including individuals with a range of mental and physical challenges. All employees are more likely to participate fully in the workplace when it is accessible and meets their various demands.

f. **Cultural Background:** Understanding and valuing the practices, values, and traditions that people from other cultures contribute to the workplace is a necessary step towards acknowledging and valuing cultural diversity.

g. **Socioeconomic Status:** Individuals from different economic origins can contribute because of the diversity of socioeconomic backgrounds, which fosters empathy and broader viewpoints within the firm.

h. **Educational Background:** Recognizing the distinctive contributions that various academic and training paths can make to creativity and problem-solving entails valuing a variety of educational experiences.

i. **Work Experience:** Including people with different professional experiences and backgrounds broadens the organization's knowledge base and fosters creativity.

- **Inclusion**

Creating an atmosphere where everyone feels appreciated, respected, and capable of making a full contribution to the company is the goal of inclusion. Diversity is all about the "who" and "what," whereas inclusion is about the "how." Important elements of inclusion in long-term organizations consist of:

a. **Equity:** Ensuring that everyone receives equal treatment, opportunities, and growth. This entails locating and removing obstacles that have traditionally prevented members of particular groups from participating. Beyond equality, equity recognizes and responds to the unique demands and difficulties that each person faces.

b. **Belonging:** To foster a sense of belonging, an environment where each employee feels like a vital member of the team must be established. Open communication, inclusive practices, and a culture that values individual differences can all help achieve this.

c. **Voice:** Every voice is given equal weight and attention when it is included. This entails providing venues and chances for various viewpoints to be voiced and taken into account during the decision-making process.

d. **Support:** It is critical to provide all employees with the support and resources they require to succeed. This can include tools for career and personal advancement that are inclusive of a range of needs and experiences, professional development opportunities, and mentoring programs.

e. **Engagement:** Actively involving people from diverse backgrounds in the activities and operations of the organization. Everyone who is engaged has a stake in the organization's success and helps it achieve its sustainability objectives.

- **Intersection with Sustainability**

Tailoring sustainability strategies to diversity and inclusion improves an organization's capacity to address environmental, social, and economic issues holistically:

a. **Social Sustainability:** Social justice and equity are advanced by diversity and inclusion. By ensuring that their sustainability projects benefit all facets of the community, especially those who are frequently disenfranchised or disadvantaged, sustainable organizations aim to establish a just and equitable society.

b. **Economic Sustainability:** Innovation, efficiency, and resilience are fuelled by the utilization of many talents and viewpoints. Diverse teams are more likely to solve difficult challenges in novel ways, which promotes economic growth and more sustainable business practices.

c. **Environmental Sustainability:** Teams that are inclusive and diverse are better able to comprehend environmental concerns and take a multifaceted approach to solving them. Using a comprehensive strategy result in more long-term and efficient environmental solutions.

In summary, integrating diversity and inclusion into sustainable enterprises is a strategic requirement that stimulates creativity, improves decision-making, and cultivates employee engagement, in addition to being a matter of social obligation. Sustainable organizations may better address the complex challenges of today's world by fostering settings where different opinions are welcomed and included. This will result in solutions that are more equitable and resilient for all stakeholders. By using a comprehensive approach, sustainability programs are guaranteed to be efficient, all-encompassing, and genuinely good for the environment and society.

10.1 Promoting Diversity in the Green Workplace

In order to actively promote diversity in the green workplace, firms that prioritize sustainability and environmental goals must actively cultivate an inclusive environment. It entails making certain that individuals of varying racial, gender, age, and ethnic backgrounds, as well as diverse sexual orientations, abilities, and socioeconomic backgrounds, are acknowledged, respected, and afforded equal chances in the workplace.

❖ **Here's a detailed breakdown of its meaning:**

Embracing a Wide Range of Perspectives

Including different points of view facilitates a more efficient approach to challenging environmental issues. Diverse life experiences and cultural origins can inspire creative thinking and better decision-making. People from different parts of the world, for instance, may have distinctive perspectives on how their communities address environmental concerns, which can be applied to international sustainability initiatives. This diversity of opinion can also be useful in pointing up possibilities for innovation and development that were previously unnoticed. Employees with a range of backgrounds can also aid in the creation of more complete solutions and a more thorough grasp of environmental issues.

Ensuring Equal Opportunities

It is essential to establish procedures and regulations that guarantee all workers have equal access to opportunities for professional growth, hiring, and promotions. This entails removing institutionalized prejudices and obstacles that could impede particular populations. Levelling the playing field can be achieved, for instance, by standardizing interview procedures to reduce unconscious prejudice and offering training courses customized to the requirements of marginalized groups. In order to provide equal chances, excluded groups must actively work to identify and remove institutional impediments that impede their advancement inside the company. Companies who follow this practice not only adhere to legal requirements but also develop a workforce that is more driven and efficient.

Building an Inclusive Culture
It is crucial to create an environment at work where everyone feels appreciated, valued, and included. This entails encouraging a feeling of community and making certain that each person's opinion is heard and taken into account when making decisions. Various measures, including diversity training, inclusive policies, and proactive promotion of a culture of respect and empathy, can foster an inclusive culture. An inclusive environment can also be strengthened by promoting candid conversations about diversity and inclusion concerns and by commemorating milestones in diversity and cultural events. Organizations may lower attrition, boost employee satisfaction, and draw in top talent from a variety of backgrounds by fostering such an atmosphere.

Enhancing Social Responsibility
Fostering diversity is consistent with the values of equity and justice, as green workplaces are frequently dedicated to more expansive social and environmental objectives. It demonstrates a dedication to both social and environmental sustainability). Organizations can improve their social license to operate by making sure that sustainability activities take into account and benefit all societal sectors. For instance, there is a greater chance of public support and long-term success for projects that benefit diverse people and incorporate community engagement. Furthermore, socially conscious businesses frequently find it simpler to establish alliances with other institutions that respect sustainability and diversity, which increases their beneficial influence.

Improving Innovation and Performance
Teams with a diversity of perspectives and methods to problem-solving tend to be more creative and innovative. Higher performance and a more robust capacity to address environmental challenges can result from this. It has been demonstrated time and time again that companies with diverse teams perform better financially and innovate more than their less diverse peers. This is so that fresh opportunities can be recognized and taken advantage of. Diversity also promotes a critical thinking environment and

a vibrant interchange of ideas. This refers to creating creative and more efficient solutions to sustainability issues in the framework of the green workplace, which can eventually spur the success and influence of the company.

Reflecting the Community

Making sure that the staff is as diverse as the community it serves helps improve the organization's reputation and relationships with many stakeholders, such as partners, consumers, and the general public. Employee loyalty and dedication are more likely to be felt when they perceive themselves as represented in the company. Additionally, diversified teams are better able to comprehend and cater to the needs of a wide range of clientele. Stronger ties with community partners and increased customer satisfaction and loyalty are two benefits of this alignment. Furthermore, exhibiting a dedication to diversity can improve the company's standing and attract investors who are becoming more and more interested in social responsibility while making investment decisions.

To put it succinctly, encouraging diversity in the green workplace entails actively fostering a more welcoming and fairer workplace within the sustainability industry, which is advantageous to the company as well as the larger community. In order to foster creativity and problem-solving, it entails embracing a broad range of viewpoints, guaranteeing equitable opportunity for all workers, creating an inclusive culture that respects and encourages diversity, and strengthening social responsibility through alignment with larger environmental and social goals. Furthermore, showcasing the community's variety fosters credibility and fortifies ties with a range of stakeholders.

A more dynamic, creative, and resilient company that is well-positioned to take the lead in the pursuit of sustainability and environmental stewardship is the result of these activities taken together. Green companies promote diversity in order to achieve both their own goals and make the world a more sustainable and just environment for everyone.

10.1.1 Importance of Diversity in the Context of Sustainability and Environmental Initiatives

Enhancing the efficacy, inventiveness, and inclusion of environmental and sustainability projects is contingent upon diversity. Diverse teams can better address complex environmental concerns and guarantee that the benefits of sustainability initiatives are distributed fairly by bringing in a wide range of viewpoints and experiences.

❖ **Here's an in-depth look at the importance of diversity in this context:**

1. Enhanced Problem-Solving and Innovation

Diverse Perspectives: Our difficulties are complex and frequently entwined with social, economic, and cultural factors when it comes to sustainability and environmental projects. Teams with a diversity of backgrounds and experiences contribute a multitude of perspectives. People from indigenous groups, for instance, might provide traditional ecological knowledge to supplement modern information, resulting in creative methods for resource management and conservation.

Cultural Insights: Around thousands of years, cultures all around the world have formed a variety of interactions with their surroundings. Bringing these cultural insights into sustainability initiatives can result in more useful and contextually appropriate solutions. For example, in water management projects, understanding local practices and attitudes about water use can help design infrastructure and policies that support sustainability while upholding community values.

Cross-Disciplinary Collaboration: Interdisciplinary solutions that cut across conventional departmental and professional lines are frequently needed to address sustainability concerns. Collaborative groups comprising of scientists, engineers, economists, policymakers, social scientists, and community stakeholders can utilize their specialized knowledge to provide comprehensive and inventive solutions for environmental issues. Organizations can access a wider range of resources and knowledge by promoting cross-disciplinary collaboration, which increases the possibility of successful outcomes.

2. Inclusivity and Equity in Sustainability Efforts

Equitable Distribution of Benefits: Marginalized groups are disproportionately affected by environmental degradation, which exacerbates already-existing inequities. Diverse teams are better able to recognize these differences and can create and carry out programs that give disadvantaged communities' needs first priority. For instance, fair access to clean energy resources for low-income households can help reduce energy poverty and advance social and environmental justice in renewable energy initiatives.

Representation and Advocacy: Developing policies and programs that serve the many needs and goals of communities requires inclusive decision-making procedures that appreciate multiple perspectives. It is important to have diverse representation not only in terms of demographics but also in terms of perspectives and life experiences. Through proactive inclusion of stakeholders from varying backgrounds in decision-making procedures, businesses can cultivate collaboration, establish credibility, and provide more impactful solutions that align with their target audiences.

Inter-sectionality: The concept of inter-sectionality recognizes that people with intersecting identities such as race, gender, class, sexual orientation, and ability experience both privilege and many types of oppression at the same time. An intersectional approach acknowledges the intricate interactions of social, economic, and environmental concerns in the context of sustainability and aims to address the particular difficulties encountered by oppressed groups. Organizations may create more equitable and comprehensive sustainability strategies by addressing intersecting disparities and elevating the perspectives of underrepresented communities.

3. Improved Decision-Making

Comprehensive Understanding: Weighing trade-offs and taking the long-term effects on ecosystems, economies, and communities into account are common components of sustainability decisions. Teams with a diversity of backgrounds and experiences are better able to take into account a greater number of variables and possible outcomes. Organizations can make more informed decisions that strike a balance between social justice, environmental preservation, and economic sustainability by considering a variety of points of view.

Cognitive Diversity: The term "cognitive diversity" describes the variations in how people view, think through, and resolve issues. Organizations can promote new solutions to challenging challenges, question preconceived notions, and inspire creative thinking by bringing together individuals with different cognitive styles. For instance, whilst some team members might be particularly skilled at analytical reasoning, others might be more adept at creative or intuitive problem-solving. Through the utilization of varied thinkers' complimentary skills, businesses can augment their ability to innovate and adapt.

Decentralized Decision-Making: Decision-making procedures that are inclusive enable people at all organizational levels to share their knowledge and viewpoints. Organizations can use the combined knowledge of various teams, as opposed to only top-down instructions, to recognize new opportunities, foresee hazards, and adjust to changing conditions. Organizations can promote a culture of accountability, ownership, and continuous improvement by decentralizing decision-making authority.

4. Strengthened Community Engagement

Building Trust: Establishing a relationship of trust and promoting cooperation with the communities impacted by environmental projects is crucial to the long-term viability and sustainability of the efforts. Diverse teams are more suited to recognize and honour the cultural norms, values, and priorities of many populations, which promotes more genuine and fruitful interaction. Building trust, fostering collaborations, and encouraging ownership of sustainability projects are all possible for organizations through carefully listening to community problems, utilizing local knowledge, and co-designing solutions with community members.

Cultural Competence: The term "cultural competence" describes the capacity to communicate and work well with individuals from various origins and cultures. Cultural competence is crucial for interacting with diverse populations, comprehending their needs and viewpoints, and forming deep connections in the context of sustainability. By providing their employees with cultural competency training, organizations can improve their ability to communicate across cultural boundaries, prevent miscommunications, and cultivate polite and inclusive relationships with community stakeholders.

Participatory Approaches: Participatory approaches to community engagement enable locals to directly influence environmental initiative direction and decision-making processes. Organizations can gain access to local expertise, develop capacity, and make sure that projects are responsive to community needs and goals by incorporating community members in project planning, execution, and evaluation. In addition to enhancing social capital and community cohesion, participatory initiatives can help cultivate a sense of pride and ownership in local natural assets.

5. Greater Organizational Resilience

Adaptability: Since risks and possibilities change over time in response to shifting ecological, social, and economic situations, environmental sustainability is by its very nature unpredictable. Because diverse companies are better able to foresee, adjust to, and capitalize on new trends and disruptions, they are more resilient in the face of uncertainty. Organizations may develop a resilient culture that helps them prosper in a world that is changing quickly by encouraging variety of opinion, experience, and viewpoint.

Innovation Ecosystems: Diversity fosters the development of dynamic ecosystems where ideas can interact, cross-pollinate, and evolve. Diversity is a catalyst for innovation. Organizations can cultivate an environment that is conducive to innovation by promoting an inclusive culture that is receptive to varied viewpoints. Through the cultivation of innovation ecosystems that value diversity, companies can produce innovative responses to intricate environmental problems, capitalize on new possibilities, and sustain a competitive advantage in a quickly changing market.

Learning Organizations: The capacity of learning organizations to continuously adjust and advance in response to input and experience is one of their defining characteristics. Diverse organizations offer a rich tapestry of viewpoints, insights, and experiences that may be drawn from, making them naturally more favourable to learning. Organizations may leverage the collective knowledge of varied teams, spot emerging trends and best practices, and modify their plans and tactics by cultivating a culture of ongoing learning and experimentation.

6. Addressing Global Challenges

Global Perspective: Environmental issues that affect populations all over the world, spanning geopolitical lines, are global in nature and include pollution, climate change, and biodiversity loss. By utilizing knowledge and skills from many areas, disciplines, and cultures, diversified businesses are better able to comprehend and handle these issues from a global viewpoint. Through cross-border collaboration and knowledge sharing, organizations may create more inclusive and effective solutions to urgent global environmental problems.

Transdisciplinary Collaboration: Across disciplines, sectors, and stakeholder groups, cooperation is needed to address complex environmental concerns. By embracing transdisciplinary approaches to problem-solving, diverse organizations can take advantage of the complimentary qualities and viewpoints of several disciplines to create comprehensive and integrated solutions. Organizations can close knowledge gaps, uncover synergies, and spark revolutionary change in the quest of sustainability by dismantling organizational silos and encouraging cross-disciplinary collaboration.

Global Citizenship: Various groups possess an exceptional chance to serve as role models and advocates for global citizenship, emulating the principles of compassion, unity, and joint accountability for the Earth and its inhabitants. Organizations can show their global commitment to social and environmental justice by embracing diversity and cultivating inclusive cultures. Diverse organizations have the power to encourage others to embrace diversity, fairness, and sustainability as cornerstones of a more just and equitable world via their advocacy and activities.

7. Enhanced Public Image and Credibility

Corporate Social Responsibility: A company's reputation among stakeholders, such as customers, investors, and staff, is enhanced when it emphasizes diversity, equity, and inclusion in its sustainability initiatives. Through openly exhibiting their dedication to diversity and sustainability, companies can improve their brand recognition, foster customer loyalty, and draw in support from investors and socially concerned consumers. Organizations that put sustainability and diversity first are better positioned to stand out from the competition and obtain a competitive edge in a market that is becoming more and more competitive.

Stakeholder Engagement: Diverse organizations are more suited to interact with various stakeholders, such as government agencies, commercial companies, community organizations, and non-governmental organizations (NGOs). The establishment of trust, promotion of collaboration, and maintenance of environmental initiatives' long-term viability and sustainability all depend on effective stakeholder engagement. Through proactive stakeholder involvement in decision-making procedures, firms can establish mutual understanding, pinpoint common objectives, and utilize combined knowledge and assets to tackle intricate environmental problems.

Brand Authenticity: In brand management, authenticity is becoming more and more crucial as stakeholders and customers expect firms to be transparent, honest, and accountable. Through really exhibiting diversity, fairness, and inclusion values in their sustainability endeavours, organizations can establish credibility and confidence with their intended audiences. More than simply lip service, authenticity demands sincere dedication, responsibility, and action. Organizations can establish genuine relationships with stakeholders, including employees and customers, by being consistent in their actions and words. This approach enhances the organization's reputation and brand.

8. Compliance and Funding Opportunities

Regulatory Compliance: Organizations are being forced by legal frameworks to show that diversity, equity, and inclusion are important components of their corporate social responsibility and sustainability programs. Organizations can guarantee legal compliance and reduce the risk of legal liability by making diversity and inclusion a priority in their organizational practices and policies. Organizations that actively promote diversity and inclusion are also better equipped to handle legislative changes and foresee new developments in the regulatory field.

Access to Funding: Impact investors, charitable foundations, and government agencies are just a few of the financing organizations that give priority to initiatives that show a dedication to diversity, equity, and inclusion. Organizations can improve their eligibility for financing and assistance by enhancing their project ideas and grant applications with diversity and inclusion. Additionally, by incorporating diversity and inclusion into their corporate culture and procedures, businesses can improve employee engagement and productivity, draw in and hold onto top talent, fortify their position as market leaders, and appeal to funders and investors more.

Social Impact Investing: In the financial sector, social impact investment is becoming more and more popular as investors look for ways to supplement their financial gains with beneficial social and environmental effects. Socially conscious investors see companies with a strong emphasis on diversity, equity, and inclusion to be more appealing investment options. Through the alignment of sustainability activities with investor priorities, organizations can expand their resource pool and discover new funding options to further advance their goals and missions.

In conclusion, diversity is essential to improving environmental and sustainability projects' inclusion, inventiveness, and efficacy. Organizations can improve decision-making, foster community engagement, increase organizational resilience, guarantee equitable benefit distribution, foster innovation and problem-solving skills, and embrace diversity of thought, experience, and perspective. Organizations can also better address global environmental concerns, build their reputation and public image, and get access to more funding sources by promoting diversity. Promoting diversity in sustainability initiatives is ultimately both the morally and ethically correct thing to do as well as the strategically astute thing to do, since it results in more comprehensive, inclusive, and practical environmental solutions that are good for the environment and for people.

10.1.2 Strategies for Recruiting and Retaining a Diverse Workforce in Green Organization

The term "strategies for recruiting and retaining a diverse workforce in green organizations" refers to the intentional and proactive methods used by businesses with an emphasis on the environment or sustainability to draw in, hire, and keep workers from a range of backgrounds, including those who have historically been underrepresented in the workforce. With the help of these tactics, an egalitarian and inclusive workplace culture where diversity is accepted, valued, and used as a source of creativity and strength is hoped to be established.

While retention strategies concentrate on building an environment that promotes the growth, development, and long-term engagement of employees from varied backgrounds, recruitment strategies deal with methods to widen the candidate pool and draw diverse talent to the firm. Green organizations can leverage the distinct perspectives and abilities of individuals from diverse backgrounds to generate environmental and social impact by assembling a staff that reflects the diversity of the communities they serve via the implementation of successful recruitment and retention methods.

❖ **Here are some effective strategies:**

Recruitment Strategies:

1. Diverse Job Postings: Employ inclusive language in job advertisements to draw applications from a diverse pool of applicants. Stress the company's dedication to diversity and inclusion by showcasing programs and employee resource groups that, among other things, show off an inclusive and friendly work environment. To further highlight the organization's varied culture, think about incorporating employee testimonials and diverse pictures.

2. Targeted Outreach: To increase the reach of your recruitment efforts, establish alliances with community organizations, academic institutions, professional associations, and diversity-focused organizations. Attend conferences, employment fairs, and events designed especially with underrepresented groups in the green industry in mind. Work together with affinity groups and diversity networks to access their networks and find possible candidates.

3. Unbiased Hiring Practices: Use blind hiring strategies, such as making resumes anonymous during the first screening phase, to reduce unconscious prejudice and encourage impartial judgment based on credentials and experience. Recruiters and hiring managers should receive training on identifying and reducing bias during the employment process. To guarantee uniformity and equity, provide established evaluation criteria and systematic interview procedures.

4. Diversity Training for Recruiters: Provide hiring managers and recruiters with diversity, equality, and inclusion (DEI) training sessions. Give them the resources and information necessary to detect, confront, and actively seek out diverse talent when making recruiting decisions. Encourage an accountable culture in which recruiters are judged on their capacity to draw in and hold on to a broad pool of prospects.

5. Employee Referral Programs: By rewarding successful referrals, employers can encourage staff members to recommend qualified applicants from a variety of backgrounds. Provide incentives or acknowledgement for recommendations that lead to employment, and make sure that all staff members may utilize the referral procedure. Employees should be given tools and direction on how to promote diversity in their networks and solicit recommendations from underrepresented groups.

6. Internship and Mentorship Programs: Establish internship programs that give students from underrepresented backgrounds the chance to gain practical experience in the green industry. Collaborate with academic institutions and community associations to find diverse interns. Assist interns in navigating their career pathways in the environmental area by matching them with mentors who can offer advice, encouragement, and networking opportunities.

Retention Strategies:
1. Inclusive On boarding: Develop an inclusive on boarding procedure that acclimates recent workers with a range of backgrounds to the culture of the company. Give new hires resources to feel connected and supported, such as information on employee resource groups and diversity training materials. Assign friends or mentors to help during the transition and to offer continuing support.

2. Employee Resource Groups (ERGs): Encourage the creation and expansion of Employee Resource Groups (ERGs) for staff members from a range of backgrounds, including women in sustainability, LGBTQ+

workers, and members of racial and ethnic minorities. Give these organizations resources and leadership support so they can plan events, workshops, and networking opportunities. Encourage involvement from all staff members, irrespective of their cultural background, in order to promote mutual understanding and cooperation.

3. Leadership Development Programs: Provide personnel from underrepresented groups with leadership development programs that offer avenues for career growth and skill development. Give people the chance to be sponsored, mentored, and exposed to high leadership positions. Instead of upholding ingrained prejudices, establish a fair and transparent promotion procedure that honours ability and merit.

4. Flexible Work Arrangements: To meet the varied demands of your workforce, consider implementing flexible work arrangements like reduced workweeks, flexible hours, or telecommuting choices. Acknowledge that depending on their unique situation such as caring obligations or health issues people may require varying work-life balance. Set strict attendance standards aside in favour of productivity and performance, letting staff members handle their workload whichever best meets their needs.

5. Diversity Training and Workshops: Provide regular diversity education and workshops to all staff members to improve their knowledge, comprehension, and appreciation of various viewpoints. Talk about subjects including allyship, cultural competency, unconscious prejudice, and inclusive communication. Give staff members the chance to converse, exchange stories, and gain knowledge from one another in a secure and encouraging setting.

6. Regular Feedback and Recognition: Provide systems for regularly recognizing and giving feedback to staff members from a variety of backgrounds, recognizing their achievements and worth to the company. Celebrate diversity by showcasing the accomplishments of members of underrepresented groups through company-wide events, awards, and recognition programs. Make sure that the procedures for providing feedback are just, open, and equal in order to promote an inclusive and welcoming atmosphere.

7. Fair and Transparent Policies: Organizational policies and procedures should be reviewed and updated to make sure they are equitable, inclusive, and available to all staff members. Take action against any institutionalized prejudices or hurdles that could prevent people from different backgrounds from advancing. Make sure that all hiring, promotion, pay, and performance review procedures are administered equally and without bias. Ask staff members for their opinions on procedures and regulations in order to pinpoint areas that need work and encourage responsibility.

8. Cultivate Inclusive Leadership: Foster and enable leaders who promote inclusion, equity, and diversity in the workplace. Give coaching and leadership development on inclusive leadership skills like empathy, active listening, and cultural competency. Hold leaders responsible for fostering an inclusive workplace where all workers experience a sense of worth, respect, and empowerment to provide their best efforts. Promote an environment of transparency, cooperation, and respect for one another while encouraging leaders to set a good example.

Green companies can establish inclusive workplaces where workers from all backgrounds feel respected, empowered, and inspired to contribute to the company's mission of environmental sustainability and social responsibility by putting these all-encompassing strategies for attracting and keeping a diverse workforce into practice. These initiatives not only boost worker productivity, happiness, and engagement, but they also make the company more capable of enacting constructive change in the environmental field.

10.1.3 Case Studies Highlighting Successful Diversity Initiatives in Sustainable Companies

❖ **Here's a case study highlighting successful diversity initiatives at Microsoft, a sustainable company:**

1. Case Study: Microsoft
Background: The Windows operating system, Office suite, and Azure cloud services are among the software products that Microsoft Corporation, a multinational technology firm, is well-known for. The corporation has projects cantered on carbon reduction, renewable energy,

and sustainable business practices as part of its commitment to sustainability and environmental responsibility.

Diversity Initiative:

1. Diverse Hiring Practices: Microsoft places a high value on diversity in its hiring procedures in an effort to draw in and keep talent from a wide range of backgrounds. To find applicants from underrepresented groups, the corporation collaborates with diversity-focused associations like the Society of Hispanic Professional Engineers and the National Society of Black Engineers. In order to encourage diversity in STEM sectors, Microsoft also provides coding boot camps, internships, and scholarships.

2. Inclusive Workplace Culture: Every person at Microsoft is encouraged to feel appreciated, respected, and empowered to make a contribution in an inclusive work environment. To assist employees from a variety of backgrounds in their professional growth, the organization provides mentorship opportunities, employee resource groups, and diversity training programs. In order to promote candid communication and teamwork, Microsoft also organizes seminars and events cantered on diversity and inclusion issues.

3. Supplier Diversity Program: Microsoft is promoting economic prospects for diverse-owned businesses through the implementation of a supplier diversity initiative. The business aggressively searches for suppliers from small and underprivileged businesses, women-owned, veteran-owned, and minority-owned businesses. Microsoft's supplier diversity initiative supports various groups and works to make the supply chain more inclusive.

Impact: A more varied and inclusive workforce as well as a deeper sense of community and belonging within Microsoft have resulted from the company's diversity and inclusion programs. The business has been honoured for its achievements, winning accolades like Diversity Inc.'s "Top Companies for Diversity" designation. The goal of Microsoft is to enable every individual and organization on the earth to achieve more by fostering innovation, creativity, and social impact. This commitment to diversity is in line with this goal.

Conclusion: Microsoft has demonstrated its commitment to fostering a more inclusive and equitable workplace culture through its successful diversity programs. By emphasizing diversity in hiring, creating an inclusive workplace, and assisting different suppliers, Microsoft is advancing good social change and solidifying its standing as a pioneer in corporate responsibility and sustainability.

- ❖ **Here's a case study highlighting successful diversity initiatives at The Coca-Cola Company, a sustainable company:**

2. Case Study: The Coca-Cola Company

Background: The Coca-Cola Company is a multinational beverage conglomerate well-known for its iconic brands, which include Sprite, Dasani, and Coca-Cola. With projects cantered on water stewardship, packaging sustainability, and climate resilience, the organization is dedicated to sustainability and environmental stewardship.

Diversity Initiative:

1. Diverse Leadership: Diversity in the leadership team is a top priority for The Coca-Cola Company, which strives for gender parity and the inclusion of people from a range of backgrounds. The organization has established goals for broadening the diversity of its leadership ranks and holds executives responsible for achieving these objectives. James Quincey, the CEO of The Coca-Cola firm, has made it known that the firm would prioritize diversity and inclusion as strategic goals.

2. Inclusive Recruitment Practices: To attract and hire diverse people, The Coca-Cola Company has created inclusive recruitment policies. The corporation seeks applicants from underrepresented groups by collaborating with educational institutions and diversity-focused organizations. In order to guarantee fair and equitable recruiting practices, The Coca-Cola Company also offers unconscious bias training to recruiters and hiring managers.

3. Employee Development and Support: The Coca-Cola Company provides its varied workforce with development opportunities and support systems. To support staff members in advancing in their careers, the organization offers mentoring, coaching, and leadership development opportunities. In addition, The Coca-Cola Company provides work-life balance support through parental leave programs and flexible work schedules.

Impact: The diversity and inclusion programs of The Coca-Cola Company have improved employee engagement and retention while also fostering a more inclusive workplace culture and a more varied workforce. Diversity Inc.'s "Top 50 Companies for Diversity" award is only one of the accolades the company has received for its efforts. The principles of inclusion, honesty, and respect that underpin The Coca-Cola Company's commitment to diversity are in line with the company's mission to revitalize the globe and improve the communities it serves.

Conclusion: The Coca-Cola Company has demonstrated its commitment to fostering a more inclusive and fair workplace culture through its successful diversity programs. The Coca-Cola Company is leading positive social change and solidifying its position as a pioneer in sustainability and corporate responsibility by promoting diversity in leadership, embracing inclusive recruitment processes, and encouraging employee growth.

❖ **Here's a case study highlighting successful diversity initiatives at Unilever, a sustainable company:**

3. Case Study: Unilever

Background: Multinational consumer goods manufacturer Unilever makes a variety of goods for the home and personal hygiene. The corporation has programs aimed at lessening its impact on the environment and enhancing community well-being as part of its commitment to sustainability and social responsibility.

Diversity Initiative:

1. Diversity Targets and Accountability: Goals have been set by Unilever to diversify its workforce, especially in leadership roles. The organization monitors these goals' development and holds executives responsible for the results of diversity and inclusion. Alan Jope, the CEO of Unilever, has made it known that the company would prioritize diversity and inclusion as strategic goals.

2. Inclusive Hiring Practices: Unilever has developed inclusive hiring practices to attract and choose a diverse workforce. Through partnerships with educational institutions and diversity-focused organizations, the corporation actively pursues applicants from underrepresented groups. Moreover, Unilever provides unconscious bias training to recruiters and hiring managers to ensure fair and equitable employment practices.

3. Employee Development and Support: Unilever provides its diverse workforce with development programs and support systems. To support staff members in advancing in their careers, the organization offers mentoring, coaching, and leadership development opportunities. Additionally, Unilever provides work-life balance support through parental leave programs and flexible work schedules.

Impact: Employee engagement and retention have grown as a result of Unilever's diversity and inclusion initiatives, which have also resulted in a more varied workforce and inclusive workplace culture. With honours like the "Diversity & Inclusion Leadership Award" from the Society for Human Resource Management, the company has been acknowledged for its achievements. Unilever's dedication to diversity is consistent with its core principles of accountability, honesty, and respect, as well as its goal of establishing sustainable living as the norm.

Conclusion: Unilever has demonstrated its commitment to fostering a more inclusive and equitable workplace culture through its successful diversity programs. Through the implementation of inclusive hiring processes, prioritization of diversity targets, and support for staff development, Unilever is fostering good social change and consolidating its leadership position in sustainability and corporate responsibility.

10.2 Inclusive Practice for Environmental Equity

Environmental equity ensures that everyone has equal access to a healthy environment and equal protection from environmental threats, irrespective of their colour, ethnicity, income, or geographic location. Engaging various groups, tackling systemic inequities, and guaranteeing a fair allocation of environmental benefits and responsibilities are all components of inclusive approaches for fostering environmental equity.

Ensuring that all people and communities, particularly those who have been historically marginalized or disadvantaged, have equal access to a healthy environment and are involved in decision-making processes that impact their environment is known as inclusive practices for environmental equity.

❖ **This concept encompasses several key principles:**

1. Equitable Distribution of Environmental Benefits and Burdens: Ensuring equitable access to clean air, water, green spaces, and other environmental benefits for all communities, while simultaneously preventing any community from being disproportionately burdened by environmental issues like pollution or hazardous waste.

2. Intersectionality: Recognizing and addressing the ways in which different social categories like age, gender, colour, and class intersect and affect how people experience environmental challenges. This strategy aids in making sure that solutions are customized to meet the various demands of every community member.

3. Addressing Historical Inequities: identifying historical injustices and making amends for them, especially in cases where communities of colour or low-income groups have been disproportionately impacted by environmental risks and have not received the benefits of the environment. Correcting these disparities requires focused investments and activities.

4. Inclusive Decision-Making: including a variety of communities in the planning, policy-making, and implementation processes, especially those most impacted by environmental challenges. This entails aggressively soliciting feedback from marginalized communities and making certain that their opinions are acknowledged.

5. Sustainable Development: Encouraging development that ensures that social and economic advancement does not come at the price of environmental health, while still meeting the requirements of the present without endangering the ability of future generations to satisfy their own needs.

6. Building Community Capacity: Empowering local communities to effectively advocate for their environmental rights and adopt sustainable practices by providing them with information, tools, and assistance.

Giving people the knowledge and resources they need to fully engage in environmental decision-making is part of this.

Incorporating these concepts, inclusive methods for environmental equity seek to build a more equitable and sustainable society where all people can take part in the care of natural resources and enjoy a healthy environment.

❖ **Here are some key inclusive practices:**

1. Community Engagement and Participation

Inclusive Decision-Making: It is imperative to involve community members in the decision-making process to guarantee that environmental policies and projects accurately represent the interests and concerns of all relevant parties. This can be accomplished by holding public comment periods, focus groups, and advisory councils where community feedback is actively sought out and appreciated. Recognizing and resolving power disparities that may exist within communities is another aspect of inclusive decision-making, ensuring that marginalized views are emphasized rather than ignored.

Public Meetings and Forums: Having open, accessible meetings is crucial to encouraging meaningful engagement. This entails deciding on convenient times and venues, arranging childcare to lower barriers for parents, and translating and interpreting for non-native English speakers. To reach a wide audience, meetings should be well-publicized through a variety of media. Materials should also be made available in a variety of languages and formats (such as large print or Braille) to suit all attendees.

2. Capacity Building and Empowerment

Training Programs: Community members can be encouraged to participate actively in environmental justice initiatives by offering training courses on sustainable practices, policy participation, and environmental activism. Everyone should be able to participate in these activities, even those with low formal education or language obstacles. A local organization partnership can assist in customizing training to the needs and circumstances of the community.

Support for Community Organizations: When it comes to promoting environmental justice, grassroots organizations are frequently essential. By giving these organizations financial and technical help, you can increase their ability to successfully solve local challenges. Grants, access to legal counsel, and instruction in grant writing and fundraising are a few examples of this support.

3. Equitable Policy Development

Inclusive Policy Frameworks: Policies that take into account systemic and historical injustices that have resulted in disproportionate environmental burdens must specifically address the concerns of marginalized populations. This involves making certain that social and health effects on communities that are susceptible are taken into account in environmental impact assessments. To make sure community leaders' opinions are heard and their issues are taken into consideration, policymakers should interact with them at every stage of the policy-making process.

Environmental Justice Screening Tools: The EPA's EJSCREEN tool, among others, can be used to identify populations that are disproportionately impacted by environmental hazards. These instruments integrate demographic and environmental data to identify problem regions and direct focused responses. To make sure these tools continue to be reliable and efficient in identifying populations that are at risk, they must be updated and improved on a regular basis.

4. Education and Awareness

Environmental Education Programs: Creating specialized educational initiatives can aid in increasing public knowledge of environmental problems and how they affect various populations. These initiatives ought to be tailored to the unique requirements of different age groups, including seniors, adults, and children, while also being culturally appropriate. These programs can be delivered in collaboration with local groups, community canters, and schools to guarantee that environmental education is accessible to all.

Outreach Campaigns: A complex strategy utilizing several media platforms, such as social media, local newspapers, radio, and community bulletin boards, is necessary for effective outreach. Campaigns should make use of imagery and messaging that speaks to the target audience's culture. Involving influential people and community leaders can help increase the reach and effect of these initiatives and guarantee that important information regarding resources and threats related to the environment is shared broadly.

5. Access to Resources and Services

Affordable Green Technologies: Encouraging low-income communities to have access to renewable energy options, including solar panels and energy-efficient appliances, can greatly lessen their financial and environmental burdens. Low-interest loans, grants, and subsidies from the government can increase the accessibility of these technologies. Programs for schooling can also assist locals in comprehending the advantages and upkeep of these technologies.

Infrastructure Investments: Improving environmental quality in underprivileged communities requires funding for infrastructural upgrades. This includes implementing air quality monitoring systems, enhancing waste management procedures, and modernizing water and sewage infrastructure. To ensure that infrastructure projects satisfy local requirements and do not unintentionally create further harm, community involvement should be sought during the planning stage.

6. Legal and Policy Advocacy

Advocacy for Stronger Regulations: Robust rules and stringent enforcement are necessary for effective environmental protection. The main goals of advocacy should be to close regulatory gaps, bolster current environmental legislation, and guarantee the efficiency of enforcement procedures. Public campaigns, lobbying, and grassroots organizing can aid in advancing legislative changes that safeguard marginalized populations.

Legal Support: Many communities impacted by environmental injustices are underequipped to handle the complexities of the legal system. By giving these communities legal support, we can protect their environmental rights, hold polluters responsible, and help them contest damaging practices. Pro bono services, legal clinics, collaborations with advocacy groups and law schools, and other measures can all be considered forms of legal help.

7. Data Collection and Transparency

Community-Led Research: Encouraging community-led research projects gives locals the ability to gather and examine data about their surroundings. Environmental mapping, health impact assessments, and air and water quality monitoring are a few examples of this. Participation of the community in research guarantees that data gathering concentrates on locally pertinent topics and that locals trust and act upon study findings.

Transparent Reporting: Establishing transparency in the dissemination of environmental data and research outcomes is crucial in fostering confidence and facilitating well-informed decision-making. In order to make complex material understandable, reports should be provided in accessible formats with clear language and visual aids. Transparency can be further increased with frequent updates and public discussion platforms for research findings.

8. Collaborative Partnerships

Multi-Stakeholder Collaborations: Coordinated actions across multiple sectors are frequently necessary to address environmental justice challenges. Creating alliances between governmental organizations, nonprofits, educational institutions, and community associations can take advantage of a variety of resources and areas of expertise. Collaboration may be improved and comprehensive approaches to environmental justice can be ensured through regular meetings, cooperative projects, and common goals.

Private Sector Engagement: Systemic change requires involving the commercial sector in sustainability initiatives. Companies can invest in community development initiatives, embrace eco-friendly practices, and work with regional groups on environmental projects. Programs for corporate social responsibility can also concentrate on lessening how much of an influence business have on the environment and aiding regional initiatives for environmental justice.

9. Resilience Planning

Climate Resilience Initiatives: Planning for resilience is crucial because vulnerable communities are disproportionately affected by climate change. This include making strategies for emergency preparedness, improving infrastructure to endure severe weather, and establishing buffer zones to fend off storms and flooding. Involving the community in resilience planning guarantees that strategies are customized to the requirements and conditions of the local area.

Sustainable Land Use Planning: Encouraging sustainable land use practices can guarantee fair access to green places and stop environmental degradation. This entails putting in place zoning regulations that save natural areas, promoting green building techniques, and maintaining parks and community gardens. Prioritizing the needs of marginalized people in sustainable land use planning will guarantee that they enjoy green areas and are shielded from environmental risks.

10. Sustainable Economic Development

Green Job Training: Developing job training programs in energy efficiency, sustainable agriculture, renewable energy, and other green fields can open up business prospects for neglected areas. All people should be able to participate in these programs, which offer routes to steady, well-paying occupations that support environmental sustainability. Collaborations between educational institutions and local businesses can improve the efficacy of these training initiatives.

Community Development Projects: Putting money into community-driven development initiatives can raise standards of living and encourage sustainability. Urban gardening, local renewable energy projects, and habitat restoration are a few examples of possible projects. Participation of the community in the planning and execution of these initiatives guarantees that local needs and priorities are met.

Incorporating these all-encompassing and inclusive methods will enable us to achieve environmental equity with notable progress. It takes consistent work, cooperation, and dedication from all facets of society to guarantee that all communities, particularly those who have been historically marginalized, have the chance to live in a healthy and sustainable environment.

10.2.1 Addressing Environmental Justice Issues through Inclusive HR Practices

Making sure that hiring, training, and workplace regulations take environmental equity and fairness into account and promote it is a necessary step in addressing environmental justice challenges through inclusive HR practices. This could entail hiring people with a variety of backgrounds, offering environmental education, making sure all workers are treated fairly regardless of their affiliations or concerns about the environment, and encouraging a sustainable and environmentally conscious culture within the company.

The fair treatment and meaningful participation of all people in the creation, application, and enforcement of environmental laws, rules, and policies regardless of their race, colour, national origin, or income is referred to as environmental justice. Its goal is to ensure that no community is subjected to pollution or environmental hazards to an excessive degree.

Encouraging fairness, sustainability, and community involvement both inside and outside the workplace requires addressing environmental justice through inclusive HR policies. Ensuring equitable access to a healthy environment for all populations, irrespective of their ethnicity or socioeconomic level, is the goal of environmental justice. Organizations may make a major contribution to a more equitable and sustainable world by incorporating these ideas into their HR operations.

❖ **Here's an expanded approach to how HR can lead these efforts:**

1. Diverse Hiring and Promotion Practices:
Equitable Recruitment: Adopt hiring practices that proactively aim to incorporate applicants from underrepresented communities and a range of socioeconomic backgrounds. Partnerships with various colleges, universities, and community organizations can help achieve this. Use blind hiring procedures to get rid of prejudices based on origins, gender, or names.

Inclusive Job Descriptions: Craft job descriptions that emphasize the organization's commitment to environmental justice, equity, and diversity while avoiding prejudiced wording. Make sure that applicants from a variety of backgrounds are not unnecessarily excluded by the job requirements.

Promotion and Retention: Establish fair and transparent promotion criteria. Offer career development programs and guidance to disadvantaged groups to guarantee equitable possibilities for their progress. Examine promotion data on a regular basis to spot and correct inequalities.

2. Creating an Inclusive Workplace Culture:

Employee Resource Groups (ERGs): Encourage and support the creation of environmental justice and sustainability-focused ERGs. For employees who are enthusiastic about these topics, these organizations can act as think tanks for new initiatives and a support system.

Open Dialogue: Establish safe spaces for open communication so employees can share their perspectives on environmental justice and diversity. To collect and act upon employee feedback, hold town hall meetings, suggestion boxes, and frequent surveys.

3. Employee Training and Education:

Environmental Justice Education: Provide thorough training programs that teach employees about environmental justice, covering the background information, present difficulties, and the organization's responsibility in resolving these concerns. Include case studies from the actual world and schedule talks by specialists.

Cultural Competency: To ensure that employees recognize and appreciate other viewpoints and experiences, provide continuing cultural competency training. This may contribute to the development of a more welcoming and respected work environment for all employees.

Sustainability Practices: Train employee sustainable techniques that they can use to their daily life and work. Encourage green credentials and ongoing learning about sustainability.

4. Equitable Health and Safety Standards:

Safe Working Conditions: Ensure that all employees have a safe and healthy work environment, especially those in roles with greater risk. Conduct routine safety audits and take immediate action to resolve any dangers found. Make certain that all employees have access to the appropriate safety gear.

Health Programs: Provide all employees with inclusive, all-inclusive health and wellness programs. Recognizing that vulnerable communities can be disproportionately affected by environmental stressors, offer resources and support for mental health.

5. Community Engagement and Partnerships:

Community Outreach: Develop and participate in community service initiatives that tackle regional environmental justice problems. Participate in community education programs on sustainability and urban gardening with your employees.

Partnerships with NGOs: Work together with non-profit groups that prioritize environmental justice. By participating in volunteer programs, making donations, and working together on collaborative initiatives that enhance the environment in marginalized areas, you can help these groups.

Local Hiring and Supplier Diversity: Make hiring locals a priority, and collaborate with local vendors, especially those from marginalized areas. This guarantees that the advantages of your company are felt more broadly and boosts the local economy.

6. Transparent Reporting and Accountability:

Regular Reporting: Report on the company's environmental effect and advancements made toward environmental justice objectives on a regular basis. These reports ought to be open and honest, outlining both the accomplishments and the room for development.

Accountability Mechanisms: Provide accountability systems to ensure the successful execution of environmental justice programs. Establishing an oversight committee, conducting frequent internal audits, and hiring outside experts are a few examples of this.

7. Sustainable Workplace Practices:

Green Office Policies: Establish office policies that support sustainability by eliminating waste, encouraging recycling, and cutting down on energy use. To lessen the carbon footprint, set up programs like carpooling incentives, bike-to-work programs, and virtual meetings.

Sustainable Supply Chain: Make sure the supply chain for your business complies with social and environmental regulations. This entails carrying out routine audits to verify compliance and collaborating with vendors who use sustainable methods.

8. Policy Advocacy and Leadership:

Advocating for Change: Leverage the organization's influence to advocate for policies that promote environmental justice. This can involve promoting laws that shield disadvantaged groups from environmental harm, supporting efforts to use renewable energy sources, and fighting for tougher environmental restrictions.

Industry Leadership: Adopt best practices for justice and environmental sustainability to lead by example in the industry. Openly communicate your accomplishments and difficulties to inspire other businesses to do the same. Engage in coalitions and business groups cantered upon environmental justice and sustainability.

9. Holistic Benefits and Compensation:

Fair Compensation: Make certain that each employee receives fair compensation and perks that promote their wellbeing for all employees. This can include paid time off, retirement plans, and health insurance.

Supportive Policies: Adopt measures to meet employees' unique needs and promote work-life balance, such as flexible work schedules, parental leave, and assistance for those impacted by environmental challenges.

10. Employee Empowerment and Engagement:

Encouraging Innovation: Give employees the freedom to develop creative answers to environmental problems. Provide employees with a venue to present their ideas and the means or money to make them a reality.

Engagement Activities: Plan eco-friendly competitions, instructional workshops, and sustainability challenges to include employees in environmental justice projects.

Organizations can significantly contribute to the resolution of environmental justice concerns by incorporating these all-encompassing strategies into HR procedures. The organization's sustainability initiatives, reputation, and general success are all strengthened by this all-encompassing strategy, which also helps employees and the communities they live in.

10.2.2 Ensuring Equal Access to Green Opportunities for all Employees, Regardless of Background

In order to promote diversity, equity, and inclusion in enterprises, it is imperative that all employees, regardless of background, have equal access to green opportunities. This can be accomplished by having open hiring procedures, offering mentorship opportunities, training and development courses, and aggressively fostering an inclusive workplace atmosphere. Furthermore, putting in place laws that deal with institutional prejudices and hurdles can help level the playing field and guarantee that everyone has the opportunity to support and profit from sustainability projects.

❖ **Here's an expanded explanation with additional detail:**

1. Facilitating Inclusive Participation Platforms: Create platforms where employees from all backgrounds can actively participate in sustainability projects to promote inclusive engagement. This could entail establishing task forces, green committees, or employee resource groups tasked with spearheading sustainability initiatives and projects. Organizations can leverage the varied abilities and viewpoints of their workforce to generate inventive solutions for environmental problems by establishing areas dedicated to collaboration and idea exchange.

2. Education and Awareness Initiatives: Develop extensive education and awareness campaigns to improve all employees' comprehension of and participation in sustainable practices. To provide accessibility for people with varying learning preferences and schedule restrictions, these programs should include a variety of learning modalities, including workshops, seminars, online courses, and interactive sessions.

Organizations may empower their employees to make educated decisions and actively participate in green projects by offering a variety of educational opportunities.

3. Accessible Resources and Support Services: Make sure that all employees, irrespective of their backgrounds or talents, have access to the resources and support services associated with green possibilities. To encourage people to participate in sustainable activities, provide them with training modules in many languages, accessible guide materials, and accommodations for people with disabilities. Providing customized support services, like childcare or transportation help, can help lower participation barriers and advance inclusivity.

4. Transparent and Inclusive Communication Channels: Provide open lines of communication throughout the entire organization to spread knowledge about green options. Reach employees from all departments and backgrounds by utilizing a variety of communication tools, such as interactive forums, social media groups, intranet portals, and company publications. Employees can express their opinions and preferences through open communication and feedback requests, which promotes inclusivity and a sense of ownership over sustainability initiatives.

5. Proactive Barrier Identification and Mitigation Strategies: Determine and remove any obstacles that can prevent particular groups of employees from taking advantage of green opportunities in a proactive manner. Implement focused tactics to reduce potential hurdles, such as language challenges, cultural differences, or budgetary limits, after conducting routine evaluations to identify potential roadblocks. To encourage employee involvement in sustainability projects, this may entail setting up financial aid programs, offering flexible schedule alternatives, or providing language interpretation services. Organizations show their dedication to fostering an equal and inclusive work environment where all employees can flourish and contribute to sustainability goals by removing obstacles to access.

6. Equitable Recognition and Rewards Systems: To recognize the contributions of all employees to sustainability projects, implement fair recognition and rewards systems. Acknowledge accomplishments and landmarks in an open, merit-based manner while keeping in mind the many roles and responsibilities that employees have within the organization's various divisions and levels. Organizations encourage a culture of inclusivity and sustain employee involvement with green projects by recognizing the teamwork of employees.

7. Career Development Opportunities: Provide employees from all backgrounds equal access to professional growth opportunities by creating pathways for career development and promotion in jobs or initiatives relevant to sustainability. Provide employees with networking opportunities, skills development workshops, and mentoring programs to help them advance their careers in sustainability. Organizations build an inclusive culture and enable individuals to pursue fulfilling careers that are in line with their interests and objectives by investing in the professional development of all employees.

By implementing these strategies, businesses can cultivate an inclusive culture and ensure that all employees have the chance to actively participate in green initiatives, thereby generating favourable environmental effects and furthering sustainability goals both inside and outside the workplace.

10.2.3 Best Practices for Creating a Culture of Inclusion in Sustainability Efforts

The term "best practices for creating a culture of inclusion in sustainability efforts" describes the most efficient and tried-and-true techniques or approaches for guaranteeing that sustainability projects are planned and carried out in a way that is equitable, inclusive, and takes into account the various needs and contributions of all key players. The goal of these best practices is to create an atmosphere in which everyone is encouraged to take part in and profit from sustainability initiatives, and feels appreciated.

Creating a culture of inclusion in sustainability efforts is crucial for fostering diversity of thought, maximizing employee engagement, and driving meaningful impact.

❖ Here are some best practices to achieve this:

1. Leadership Commitment and Accountability: Clearly state that company leadership is committed to incorporating diversity, equity, and inclusion, or DEI, into sustainability activities. It is imperative for leaders to express the significance of diversity in fostering creativity and guaranteeing the applicability and efficacy of sustainability initiatives. By conducting regular progress assessments, being open and honest about their reporting, and recognizing their accomplishments, they should also hold themselves and others accountable for pursuing DEI goals within sustainability initiatives.

2. Equitable Opportunities: Make certain that, when it comes to training programs, career development pathways, and leadership possibilities within sustainability projects, all employees have equitable access. Provide employees from underrepresented groups with sponsorship, growth opportunities, and mentoring in order to help them advance into jobs and initiatives connected to sustainability.

3. Equitable Access to Resources and Opportunities: Make sure all employees have equal access to the tools, chances, and assistance they need to take an active part in sustainability initiatives. Ensure that employees with varying learning styles, abilities, and language preferences can access training, educational materials, and skill-building activities. Provide employees from underrepresented groups in jobs and projects relevant to sustainability with mentorship, coaching, and networking opportunities to assist their professional development and advancement. Organizations may foster a more inclusive and empowered workforce capable of effecting long-term change by investing in the development and success of all employees.

4. Continuous Learning and Improvement: Encourage an environment where employees are always learning and growing by giving them the chance to learn more about diversity, equity, and inclusion concerns in sustainability and by giving them regular opportunity to do so. In order to achieve diversity and inclusion goals within sustainability efforts, provide training, workshops, and tools that foster cultural competency, empathy, and understanding. Additionally, encourage employees to actively engage in self-reflection, debate, and action. Establish forums where employees may discuss their triumphs, struggles, and experiences in advancing diversity and inclusion in sustainability. You should also recognize accomplishments that help to foster an inclusive and fair work environment.

5. Diverse Representation in Decision-Making: Ensure that groups that make decisions about sustainability, like advisory boards, task forces, and committees, have a broad presence. Actively look for and include employees from underrepresented groups, such as individuals with varying racial, ethnic, gender, age, socioeconomic, and cultural backgrounds. Through the integration of many viewpoints in the process of making decisions, establishments can steer clear of blind spots, recognize inventive resolutions, and bolster the legitimacy and credibility of sustainability campaigns.

6. Cultural Sensitivity and Respect: Recognize and recognize various cultural viewpoints, customs, and values in order to cultivate an environment where cultural diversity is respected and valued within sustainability initiatives. When planning and executing sustainability projects, keep cultural nuances in mind and make sure that the efforts are inclusive of a range of cultural practices and beliefs. Encourage employees from diverse cultural backgrounds to engage in cross-cultural communication, teamwork, and educational opportunities that advance empathy, understanding, and unity. Organizations may create stronger, more resilient sustainability projects that represent the needs and ambitions of various populations by embracing cultural diversity as a source of innovation and strength.

7. Inclusive Communication and Engagement: Encourage a culture of inclusive communication and open discussion so that all employees feel free to voice their opinions, worries, and suggestions regarding sustainability initiatives. Make use of a range of communication channels to get feedback from different stakeholders and make sure their opinions are respected. Some examples of these channels are employee forums, town hall meetings, surveys, and internet platforms. Give employees the chance to take part in sustainability planning, implementation, and assessment procedures so they may use their special knowledge, perspectives, and abilities to promote change.

8. Collaborative Partnerships and Stakeholder Engagement: Establish cooperative alliances with outside organizations, community associations, and other stakeholders who have a range of sustainability-related viewpoints and interests. To make sure that sustainability programs represent the interests and objectives of all stakeholders and contribute to beneficial social and environmental outcomes for different populations, engage in meaningful discourse, co-creation, and shared decision-making processes. Collaborating with a range of stakeholders allows organizations to take use of their combined knowledge, assets, and connections to tackle intricate sustainability issues and create enduring effects on a local, national, and international scale.

Employers may foster an inclusive work environment where employees feel empowered to fully engage in and contribute to sustainability initiatives, resulting in favourable social, environmental, and financial consequences for all parties involved by putting these best practices into effect.

10.3 Empowering Diverse Voices in Sustainability Efforts

The intentional endeavour to incorporate and amplify the opinions, experiences, and contributions of people from different backgrounds, identities, and communities in environmental and sustainability projects is known as "empowering diverse voices in sustainability." This strategy acknowledges that different perspectives offer distinctive ideas and answers to sustainability problems, and that promoting inclusivity is crucial to developing all-encompassing, just, and successful sustainability plans.

Empowering diverse voices in sustainability practically means giving members of marginalized groups the chance to actively participate in leadership positions, decision-making processes, and project execution within sustainability efforts. It also means giving people from all backgrounds the tools and chances they need to effectively contribute to sustainability initiatives. These include training, resources, and support.

Organizations can foster innovation, creativity, and problem-solving skills as well as equality, justice, and social responsibility in environmental projects by elevating the voices of various people in sustainability. This method aids in making sure that sustainability plans are all-encompassing, sensitive to the requirements of various communities, and able to promote beneficial social and environmental change on a larger scale.

In order to promote innovation, equity, and efficacy in tackling environmental concerns, it is imperative that various voices be given voice in sustainability initiatives. It entails establishing an atmosphere in which individuals from all backgrounds feel appreciated, welcomed, and empowered to provide their special viewpoints, experiences, and abilities to sustainability projects. Organizations may access a wider range of ideas, insights, and solutions by embracing diversity and fostering inclusivity, which will eventually produce more significant and long-lasting results.

❖ **Here's an extensive explanation on empowering diverse voices in sustainability efforts:**

1. Leadership Commitment and Advocacy: Promoting diversity, equality, and inclusion (DEI) in sustainability initiatives requires strong leadership. Organizational leaders must advocate for the inclusion of various perspectives in all sustainability-related decisions and projects, set clear objectives and expectations, and exhibit a visible commitment to DEI principles. Through exemplary leadership and the incorporation of DEI into sustainability plans, leaders can foster an environment that values and celebrates diversity.

2. Inclusive Decision-Making: Make sure there is diversity and inclusivity in the decision-making bodies that develop sustainability programs and strategies. This entails deliberately seeking out individuals with a range of professional expertise, cultural viewpoints, and demographic backgrounds. Diverse teams are able to provide a wider range of viewpoints and ideas, which can result in more creative and practical solutions to sustainability-related problems. Furthermore, all employees' sense of ownership and belonging is fostered by participatory decision-making procedures, which raises engagement and dedication to sustainability objectives.

3. Equitable Access to Opportunities: Grant equal access to opportunities for all employees, irrespective of their identity or background, to engage in sustainability initiatives. This covers project responsibilities, leadership positions, and chances for professional growth.

Businesses should recognize and eliminate any obstacles that could keep underrepresented groups from fully engaging, such as by introducing mentorship programs, allowing flexible work schedules, or extending financial support for professional growth. Organizations may develop a diversified pool of talent and sustainability-related skills by encouraging equal access to opportunities.

4. Training and Education: Provide thorough instruction and training with an emphasis on cultural competence, DEI, and sustainability. The aforementioned programs ought to impart knowledge and skills necessary for employees to interact inclusively, bring environmental justice issues to the attention of staff members, and teach them the value of diversity in sustainability. Workshops on unconscious bias, cultural sensitivity, inclusive communication, and allyship are a few examples of training initiatives. Organizations can enable employees to handle challenging sustainability issues with tact and empathy by providing training and development opportunities.

5. Open and Transparent Communication: Establish an environment where employees are empowered to voice their thoughts, concerns, and opinions about sustainability initiatives by fostering an environment of open and transparent communication. Establish avenues for employee feedback, such as town hall meetings, suggestion boxes, and surveys, and make sure that the leadership takes the time to hear what the staff has to say and acts upon it. Open communication encourages employees to feel like they belong and develops trust, which in turn motivates them to actively participate in sustainability projects.

6. Recognition and Reward Systems: Put in place processes for rewards and recognition that highlight the contributions made by a variety of voices to sustainability. Recognize accomplishments with honours, statements made in public, and other methods that draw attention to the work of employees from diverse backgrounds. Organizations can promote inclusivity and encourage more involvement by recognizing and appreciating varied contributions to sustainability in a public way.

7. Community and External Partnerships: Form alliances with outside organizations, community groups, and other stakeholders who have a range of sustainability-related viewpoints and interests. Work together with these organizations to make sure sustainability projects are inclusive and sensitive to the needs of many populations. External collaborations can expand the scope and effect of sustainability initiatives by bringing in fresh perspectives, assets, and networks. Community involvement also promotes a feeling of shared accountability and ownership for sustainability objectives, which encourages group action and constructive change.

8. Continuous Improvement and Accountability: Establish metrics and benchmarks to assess how well diverse perspectives are being empowered in sustainability initiatives. Review and assess these KPIs on a regular basis, get input from stakeholders and employees, and make necessary adjustments to your plans. Accountability and transparency frameworks show a dedication to DEI values and promote ongoing sustainability practice improvement.

9. Fostering a Culture of Inclusion: Create an environment at work where diversity is valued and respected in all of its manifestations. Honour cultural diversity, encourage inclusive conduct, and incorporate DEI concepts into workplace norms, policies, and procedures. A culture of inclusion encourages employees to bring their complete selves to work and actively participate in sustainability initiatives by fostering a sense of belonging and psychological safety among them.

10. Supportive Infrastructure: Establish the infrastructure and resources required to enable a range of participation in sustainability initiatives. This could involve accommodating diverse abilities or learning styles, providing language help for non-native speakers, and creating accessible meeting formats. Organizations may foster a culture where different voices are respected and given the tools, they need to effectively contribute to sustainability efforts by making sure all employees have the resources necessary to engage fully.

In conclusion, increasing the representation of various perspectives in sustainability initiatives is critical to fostering influence, equity, and innovation in the face of environmental issues. Organisations have the potential to foster a more resilient, adaptable and sustainable future for everybody by embracing diversity and encouraging inclusivity.

10.3.1 Leveraging Diverse Perspectives to Drive Innovation and Creativity in Sustainability Initiatives

Leveraging diverse perspectives to drive innovation and creativity in sustainability initiatives refers to the deliberate gathering of people with various experiences, backgrounds, and points of view in order to jointly discover solutions for social and environmental concerns. This strategy is based on the understanding that a broad range of viewpoints greatly increases the originality and efficacy of sustainability initiatives.

❖ Here is a comprehensive explanation of what this means, why it is crucial, and how it can be effectively implemented:

Bringing Together Varied Experiences:

Diverse viewpoints originate from people with various professional, cultural, and educational backgrounds; these people each bring special insights and ideas to the table. These distinctions are important because they make it possible to find creative solutions that might not be found in a more homogeneous group. For instance, a group of engineers, social scientists, business experts, environmental scientists, and community leaders can approach sustainability problems from several perspectives, producing more thorough and practical answers.

Enhancing Problem-Solving Capabilities:

Due to the complexity and diversity of sustainability issues, concurrent attention to the environmental, social, and economic facets of the problem is necessary for finding solutions. A wider variety of experiences and information are brought to bear by diverse teams, aiding in the comprehension and resolution of these issues. By taking a comprehensive approach, problems are ensured to be fully examined, resulting in solutions that are more durable and resilient.

Fostering Creativity:

Innovation frequently flourishes in the nexus of disparate concepts and viewpoints. Collaborating with individuals from different backgrounds exposes them to new approaches to problem-solving and thought processes. In a more homogeneous group, it would be impossible to generate fresh concepts and inventive methods without this exposure. For example, innovative and successful sustainability solutions can be achieved by fusing traditional ecological knowledge with contemporary technological breakthroughs.

Improving Social Equity:
Incorporating a range of viewpoints into sustainability endeavours facilitates the development of equitable and comprehensive solutions. This strategy recognizes the significance of attending to the needs and difficulties of various populations, especially those that are frequently marginalized or underrepresented. Sustainability projects can advance social equity and justice by taking into account a variety of perspectives, which helps to ensure that the advantages and disadvantages of these initiatives are shared more equally.

Increasing Buy-In and Acceptance:
The involvement of numerous stakeholders in the creation of sustainability projects increases the chances of attaining greater acceptance and support. This inclusiveness guarantees that the initiatives are more sensitive to the interests and preferences of diverse groups and strengthens their credibility. As a result, these programs' execution and long-term viability are greatly enhanced.

- **Practical Implications**

a. **Team Composition:** Building diverse teams that each offer a unique viewpoint to the table is crucial. By actively seeking out people with different cultural, educational, and professional backgrounds, it is possible to achieve this diversity. Moreover, incorporating individuals with diverse life experiences and guaranteeing gender parity can enhance the team's viewpoint.

b. **Collaborative Processes:** Leveraging various viewpoints requires inclusive decision-making procedures and open discourse. This entails establishing a polite, comfortable environment where each team member is respected and feels heard. This free flow of ideas can be facilitated by methods like design thinking workshops, brainstorming sessions, and collaborative platforms.

c. **Community Engagement:** It is crucial to actively involve stakeholders and local communities in sustainability projects to make sure that their needs and opinions are taken into account. Community gatherings, participatory research techniques, and constant communication with stakeholders can help achieve this. Sustainability projects can be adapted to the local environment and win the cooperation and support of individuals who will be directly impacted by them by interacting with the community.

d. **Interdisciplinary Approaches:** To address sustainability concerns in novel ways, it is essential to integrate methodologies and information from several sectors. Interdisciplinary cooperation can help dismantle silos and promote idea cross-pollination. For instance, integrating knowledge from the social sciences, engineering, economics, and ecology can result in more comprehensive and successful sustainability solutions.

e. **Training and Education:** Developing a culture where different perspectives are respected and utilized requires training in cultural competency and inclusive behaviours. Providing chances for ongoing education and training on sustainability-related subjects can also assist team members in keeping up with industry trends and best practices.

- **Extended Benefits of Diverse Perspectives**

a. **Enhanced Innovation:** Creative and inventive solutions are more likely to be produced by diverse teams. The diversity of opinions facilitates the exploration of novel ideas and the challenge of the status quo. For example, combining concepts from industrialized and developing nations into product design for sustainability might result in goods that are efficient and suitable to all markets.

b. **Adaptability and Resilience:** Teams with a variety of perspectives are better able to adjust to shifting conditions and unforeseen difficulties. The team can more quickly pivot and identify different solutions because of the wide range of experiences and abilities among its members. In sustainability programs, where conditions and requirements might change quickly, this adaptability is essential.

c. **Broader Skill Sets:** A team with diverse backgrounds has access to a greater pool of knowledge and experience. The crew is better equipped to handle many facets of sustainability initiatives thanks to this wide range of skills. A team comprising engineers, scientists, economists, and social workers, for instance, can fully address the technological, financial, social, and environmental aspects.

d. **Holistic Approaches:** Sustainability efforts that leverage multiple perspectives tend to adopt more holistic methods. Diverse teams are better able to create solutions that address several problems at once by taking into account how various systems are connected. For example, a project focused on increasing water sustainability might also take economic development, community health, and agricultural practices into account.

e. **Strengthened Partnerships:** Stronger partnerships with stakeholders can be facilitated by a diversity of perspectives. Stakeholders are more inclined to get involved and support projects when they see that the efforts represent their needs and viewpoints. This spirit of cooperation can produce more fruitful and long-lasting results.

- **Strategies for Implementation**

a. **Inclusive Leadership:** Within their teams, leaders need to promote inclusivity and diversity. This entails establishing specific diversity objectives, aggressively seeking out varied talent, and fostering an inclusive culture where all opinions are respected and heard.

b. **Cultural Competence:** Teams should receive cultural competency training so that they can recognize and value the diversity among their members. This training aids in reducing misinterpretations and optimizing the advantages of different viewpoints.

c. **Structured Collaboration:** Harnessing the power of diversity can be facilitated through the use of organized collaboration strategies including multi-stakeholder forums, co-creation workshops, and cross-functional teams. These frameworks offer a forum for exchanging and incorporating various ideas within the project.

d. **Monitoring and Evaluation:** It can be helpful to regularly monitor and assess how diversity affects innovation and creativity in order to improve tactics and make sure that the advantages of different viewpoints are fully realized. This entails establishing measurements to gauge diversity's influence on project results.

e. **Policy and Frameworks:** Developing policies and frameworks that promote diversity and inclusion can institutionalize these practices. Adopting diversity charters, establishing goals for varied representation, and putting inclusive practices into practice are all options available to organizations.

f. **Feedback Mechanisms:** Encouraging team members to provide feedback mechanisms that facilitate the exchange of ideas and experiences can improve the efficacy and inclusivity of sustainability projects. This continual conversation aids in refining the strategy for utilizing a variety of viewpoints.

Conclusion:

The phrase "leveraging diverse perspectives to drive innovation and creativity in sustainability initiatives" refers to the process of making greater use of human experience and expertise in order to boost the efficacy of sustainability initiatives. Diverse viewpoints are essential for creating innovative, fair, and significant sustainable solutions because they combine a range of experiences, improve problem-solving skills, encourage creativity, improve social fairness, and increase buy-in and acceptance. This strategy not only encourages innovation but also makes sure that solutions are stronger, more resilient, and have broader support, which eventually results in a more equitable and sustainable world. Incorporating a variety of viewpoints into sustainability projects is not only advantageous but also necessary for tackling today's complex problems in a thorough and efficient way.

10.3.2 Encouraging Participation and Leadership from Underrepresented Groups in Green Projects

"Encouraging participation and leadership from underrepresented groups in green projects" refers to the proactive engagement and empowerment of people from a range of underprivileged backgrounds in order to facilitate their involvement in, contribution to, and leadership of environmental sustainability initiatives. The goal of this endeavour is to guarantee that green projects gain from a variety of viewpoints and experiences, encouraging inclusivity and equity.

Encouraging disadvantaged groups to lead and participate in green projects entails putting in place a variety of strategic measures that support empowerment, equity, and inclusivity. The intention is to make sure that initiatives towards sustainability take into account the diversity of our communities and make use of the special abilities and viewpoints of people from all walks of life. This all-encompassing strategy contributes to the development of a more just and successful sustainability movement.

❖ Here are detailed strategies and explanations on how to achieve this:

1. Targeted Outreach: Raising awareness about potential in green projects requires actively engaging marginalized communities. Local groups, social media, community events, and educational institutions can all help with this. Organizations may successfully communicate the prospects and advantages of sustainability projects by leveraging platforms that these communities trust and interact with.

2. Partnerships: Creating alliances with groups that have a history of working with underrepresented groups is a great method to gain credibility and confidence. These collaborations can help increase awareness and guarantee that green projects are inclusive right from the start. Partnerships with influential people and community leaders can help sustainability initiatives reach a wider audience and have a greater effect.

3. Skill Development Programs: Bridging skill gaps and preparing people for active involvement in green initiatives can be achieved by providing training programs and seminars that are specifically designed to meet the requirements of underrepresented groups. Project management, community organizing, and technical skills in renewable energy are just a few of the topics these programs might cover.

4. Mentorship Programs: The establishment of mentorship programs can offer individuals from underrepresented groups vital assistance and direction. Assisting them in forming networks, advancing their careers, and honing their leadership abilities is achieved by matching them with seasoned sustainability industry professionals. By providing guidance, support, and encouragement, mentors may make the transition into sustainability jobs less intimidating and more approachable.

5. Diverse Hiring Practices: It's crucial to put in place hiring procedures that value inclusion and diversity. This includes establishing diversity objectives, training interviewers on bias, and deploying diverse recruiting panels. Companies should make an effort to hire a workforce that is representative of the community's diversity so that different viewpoints are heard during the decision-making process.

6. Equitable Pay and Benefits: In order to remove financial barriers that may keep underrepresented groups from participating in green projects, it is imperative to ensure equitable compensation and benefits for all participants. Sustainable careers can become more appealing and accessible through fair compensation systems, extensive benefit plans, and financial assistance for education and training.

7. Safe Spaces: Promoting a respectful and inclusive work environment is essential to promoting diverse participation. This entails establishing safe spaces where people feel free to discuss their opinions and concerns and where all voices are respected and heard. Organizations ought to foster a climate of mutual respect, tolerance, and cooperation in which people of all backgrounds are valued and encouraged to participate.

8. Recognition and Visibility: Bringing attention to the accomplishments of underrepresented people in project reports, advertising collateral, and public gatherings can increase visibility and morale. The accomplishments of these people can be highlighted through recognition programs, honours, and public acknowledgements, encouraging others and showcasing the organization's dedication to diversity and inclusion.

9. Participatory Planning: Participating in green project planning and decision-making with community people guarantees that their needs and viewpoints are taken into account. This collaborative method promotes trust-building, teamwork, and the development of more pertinent and useful solutions.

10. Feedback Mechanisms: Organizations can continuously modify and enhance their initiatives based on community feedback by setting up channels for ongoing feedback. Consistent feedback sessions, surveys, and public forums can facilitate the identification of obstacles, collection of recommendations, and maintenance of project responsiveness to community needs.

11. Funding Opportunities: Underrepresented groups can benefit from grants, scholarships, or other financial aid when they engage in green projects. Financial assistance can be used to pay for start-up fees, education, training, and other charges, which makes it simpler for people to get involved in sustainability initiatives.

12. Resource Canters: Underrepresented communities can be strengthened by setting up resource canters that provide knowledge, resources, and encouragement for green projects. These facilities can give users access to resources, knowledge, and connections that are essential for taking part in sustainability projects successfully.

13. Leadership Training: Providing courses that concentrate on enhancing leadership abilities relevant to environmental and sustainability initiatives can enable members of marginalized groups to assume leadership positions. In order to successfully prepare individuals for leadership, these programs may include strategic thinking, project management, advocacy, and public speaking.

14. Pathways to Leadership: Establishing well-defined career trajectories in the context of green projects guarantees that marginalized individuals can develop and assume leadership positions. This may entail succession planning, leadership pipelines, and organized career development strategies.

15. Awards and Recognition: It is possible to encourage and uplift others by establishing awards or recognition programs that emphasize the accomplishments of underrepresented groups in sustainability initiatives. In addition to recognizing personal achievements, public success celebrations increase awareness of the value of diversity in sustainability.

Green initiatives can become more inclusive and take advantage of the many skills and viewpoints of the community by putting these best practices into effect. This all-encompassing strategy fosters social justice and the well-being of communities while producing more inventive, resilient, and successful sustainability results. A more inclusive and sustainable future for all is fostered by the involvement of underrepresented groups in leadership positions, which further guarantees that sustainability initiatives are equitable and representative of the larger community.

10.3.3 Examples of Organizations that have successfully Embraced Diversity and Inclusion in their Sustainability Programs

Numerous entities from diverse industries have effectively integrated diversity and inclusivity into their sustainability initiatives. These organizations have put in place programs that guarantee leadership and varied involvement in their environmental endeavours.

❖ **Here are some notable examples:**

1. The Nature Conservancy (TNC)

Diversity, equality, and inclusion (DEI) has been successfully incorporated by the international environmental NGO the Nature Conservancy (TNC) into its sustainability initiatives. TNC understands that attaining its conservation objectives depends on having a diverse workforce and an inclusive culture. The "Diversity and Inclusion" project of the organization seeks to establish a hospitable atmosphere that appreciates varied viewpoints and encourages cooperation across all levels of the organization.

Several DEI training programs have been put in place by TNC to inform staff members about implicit biases and the value of inclusivity in environmental work. To support the several underrepresented communities inside the business, including as women, people of colour, LGBTQ+ persons, and veterans, they have formed Employee Resource Groups (ERGs). TNC makes certain that its conservation efforts are fair and representative of the communities they serve by actively striving to guarantee diverse representation in project teams and leadership.

2. Environmental Defence Fund (EDF)

One of the top nonprofits that put a strong emphasis on inclusiveness and diversity in its sustainability initiatives is the Environmental Defence Fund (EDF). The organization's operations and environmental strategies are integrated with these ideals by a dedicated Diversity, Equity, and Inclusion team that EDF has developed. The goal of EDF's "Environmental Justice & Health Program" is to involve and assist underprivileged groups that are disproportionately impacted by environmental problems.

In order to identify and address environmental health hazards in underrepresented areas, EDF collaborates closely with local organizations and leaders in the community. The company's efforts to diversify its staff, board members, and leadership demonstrate its dedication to DEI and guarantee that a variety of viewpoints are considered when making decisions. Through endorsing laws that advance environmental and social justice, EDF works to build a more diverse and equitable sustainable movement.

3. Interface

The multinational producer of modular flooring, Interface, is well known for its steadfast dedication to inclusivity and sustainability. The company's Mission Zero sustainability goals, which seek to achieve zero environmental impact by 2020 and beyond, include DEI. Through programs for employee involvement and inclusive hiring, Interface supports diversity. The business makes sure that a variety of communities, especially those who have been historically marginalized, benefit from its sustainability programs.

The goal of Interface's "Climate Take Back" campaign is to reverse global warming by promoting varied involvement in their environmental initiatives. The organization works with a broad range of partners, such as vendors, clients, and community associations, to provide creative solutions that tackle environmental and social issues. Interface shows how companies may set an example in advancing inclusion and sustainability through these initiatives.

4. Unilever

The global consumer goods corporation Unilever has integrated diversity and inclusivity into its sustainable business practices. The "Sustainable Living Plan" of the organization highlights the significance of diversity, inclusivity, and gender equality in attaining sustainable growth. In their communities and supply chains, Unilever actively supports initiatives that foster diversity and actively works to build inclusive work environments.

Unilever's commitment to DEI is demonstrated in its various programs and collaborations targeted at empowering women, helping minority-owned businesses, and promoting social fairness. Through its "Opportunities for Women" program, the corporation hopes to increase women's economic empowerment at every stage of its value chain, from procurement of raw materials to retail. Unilever hopes to positively affect people and the environment by include a variety of viewpoints in its sustainability initiatives.

5. Patagonia

Outdoor apparel and equipment brand Patagonia is well-known for its inclusive style and environmental activism. The corporation helps grassroots environmental organizations, many of whom target underrepresented populations, in order to incorporate DEI into its corporate culture and sustainability initiatives. Patagonia also pushes for laws that improve social and environmental justice and encourages diverse leadership within its own ranks.

Patagonia's "Worn Wear" campaign, which encourages customers to repair, reuse, and recycle their clothing, is a clear example of the company's commitment to diversity. Through job training and employment possibilities, this program benefits communities while simultaneously promoting sustainability. In addition to promoting social justice, climate action, and the preservation of public lands, Patagonia's activism makes sure that its environmental initiatives are inclusive and helpful to all communities.

6. IKEA

IKEA has worked very hard to make sure that all people may participate in its sustainability projects. In order to have a positive effect on both people and the environment, the company has committed to diversity and inclusion as part of its "People & Planet Positive" strategy. In order to provide sustainable solutions that tackle social and environmental problems, IKEA works with local communities, making sure that underrepresented groups are included in both the dialogue and the solutions.

IKEA's community outreach initiatives, which prioritize helping low-income families, refugees, and other vulnerable populations, are a reflection of their inclusive business model. Through its "Better Shelter" project, which it developed in collaboration with the UN Refugee Agency, the company offers displaced individuals secure and sustainable accommodation. IKEA serves as an example of how companies can effects positive social and environmental change by incorporating DEI into their sustainability initiatives.

7. Ceres

A non-profit organization called Ceres collaborates with businesses and investors to foster leadership and advance economic solutions. In order to ensure that climate and sustainability policies are inclusive and fair, Ceres places a high priority on incorporating DEI into its advocacy work. They collaborate with a broad coalition of interested parties to advance laws and corporate conduct that benefit all communities, but especially those that are most at risk from climate change.

The "Climate Justice Working Group" at Ceres seeks to address how low-income and minority communities are disproportionately affected by climate change. Through active participation in frontline communities and the promotion of just climate policy, Ceres guarantees that sustainability initiatives are fair and inclusive. The work of the group emphasizes how crucial intersectionality is to solving environmental problems.

8. Microsoft

Microsoft's environmental initiatives now include a strong diversity and inclusion component. The company's AI for Earth program makes sure that a variety of communities have access to these technological solutions in addition to using them to address environmental concerns. The sustainability programs of Microsoft are intended to be inclusive, encouraging diverse leadership and guaranteeing fair access to opportunities and resources.

Microsoft's supplier diversity program, which attempts to expand economic possibilities for women- and minority-owned businesses, is another example of the company's dedication to DEI. Microsoft makes sure that its sustainability initiatives are extensive and advantageous to a variety of stakeholders by cultivating an inclusive environment. The company's strategy shows how technology may be used to advance social justice and the environment.

These organizations provide as excellent examples of how incorporating inclusivity and diversity into sustainability initiatives may result in more fair and productive environmental consequences. By giving DEI first priority, they make sure that their sustainability initiatives assist a variety of groups and make use of a range of viewpoints to foster resilience and creativity. Their inclusive strategies help to build a more equitable and sustainable world where social and environmental objectives are simultaneously achieved.

Chapter – 11

Green HR Metrics and Reporting

Introduction to Green HR Metrics and Reporting

The emphasis on sustainability in today's corporate environment has permeated many aspects of organizational operations, going beyond traditional environmental conservation measures. Human resources (HR) are one crucial area where this integration has a particularly big influence. In order to support the organization's overall sustainability goals, green HR metrics and reporting offer a systematic way to incorporate environmental sustainability into HR practices and policies.

Meaning of Green HR Metrics and Reporting

Green HR metrics and reporting pertain to the methodical procedures and instruments employed in a business to gauge, monitor, and disseminate the environmental consequences of its human resource-related operations. By incorporating sustainability into HR's fundamental duties, these methods hope to make sure that the company's human resource plans complement its environmental objectives.

Data derived from green HR measures are collected, analysed, and shared as part of green HR reporting. Providing clear, accurate, and thorough information regarding the organization's environmental effect in relation to HR activities is the main goal of green HR reporting.

Understanding Green HR Metrics

Green HR metrics are measurements, both quantitative and qualitative, that assess how well an organization's HR policies support environmental sustainability. These measures, which include energy use, paper use, employee travel habits, and participation in green programs, offer a thorough picture of how successfully a company incorporates sustainability into its HR operations. Organizations can use these measures to track their progress, pinpoint areas for improvement, and assess the success of their sustainability initiatives.

The Role of Green HR Reporting

Data on green HR indicators are systematically gathered, analysed, and disseminated as part of green HR reporting. Green HR reporting's main goal is to inform internal and external stakeholders such as staff members, managers, investors, and clients about the company's sustainability performance. Good reporting demonstrates the organization's dedication to sustainable practices by ensuring openness, encouraging responsibility, and fostering trust.

Green HR Metrics and Reporting: A Comprehensive Overview

Modern human resource management places a strong emphasis on measuring and communicating HR practices that promote environmental sustainability within a business, and green HR metrics and reporting are an essential part of this. These indicators play a crucial role in monitoring the success of green HR programs and in supplying information that can be utilized to improve environmental performance.

❖ **Key Green HR Metrics**

1. Energy Consumption

Metrics on energy consumption are used to track how much energy is used in HR processes. This covers the energy used by data canters, the electricity used in offices, and the power needed for online meetings. Organizations can pinpoint areas for improvement by monitoring these indicators, such as installing energy-efficient lighting, utilizing energy-efficient office equipment, and promoting behaviours that minimize energy usage when working remotely.

2. Paper Usage

Measuring the quantity of paper used for HR tasks like printing, photocopying, and document handling is part of the process of tracking paper usage. Adopting double-sided printing guidelines, promoting electronic communication, and making the switch to digital documentation are some of the steps being taken to cut down on the amount of paper used.

Cutting back on paper use saves a lot of money and has a positive effect on the environment.

3. Employee Commuting
The carbon footprint resulting from employees' commutes to and from work is measured by employee commuting metrics. Carpooling, public transportation, biking, and telecommuting are examples of sustainable mobility options that organizations can support. Businesses may drastically lower their overall carbon footprints by monitoring and rewarding these actions.

4. Green Training Programs
Green training programs are educational endeavours designed to increase staff members' consciousness of environmental issues. The quantity of training sessions held, employee engagement rates, and the success of these initiatives in encouraging sustainable habits are some of the metrics in this field. Good training may encourage people to embrace eco-friendly practices at work and at home, fostering a culture of sustainability.

5. Sustainable Talent Acquisition
Examining the environmental effects of hiring procedures is a key component of sustainable talent acquisition. This includes conducting interviews virtually, using digital onboarding procedures, and minimizing the need for in-person travel. Organizations can streamline the employment process and reduce their environmental impact by utilizing technology.

6. Workplace Sustainability Initiatives
These measurements monitor how much staff members participate in environmental activities like energy-saving campaigns, recycling campaigns, and green office regulations. Organizations can evaluate the success of these initiatives and find areas for improvement by keeping an eye on participation rates and results.

7. Employee Engagement in Sustainability
Measures of staff involvement and attitudes toward sustainability projects are determined through surveys and feedback systems known as

engagement metrics. Elevated degrees of involvement signify a robust company sustainability culture, which has the potential to stimulate more advancements and creativity in ecological methods.

Green HR Reporting

Green HR reporting entails gathering metrics in a methodical manner and disseminating them to different stakeholders. Effective reporting encompasses several key elements:

1. Regular Reports

Reports on sustainability metrics should be released by organizations on a quarterly or annual basis. These reports include updates on the status of environmental goals and point out areas of achievement as well as areas that could use improvement.

2. Transparency

Being transparent about the procedures and information utilized to gather and examine sustainability measures is a key component of transparency in reporting. By doing this, stakeholders' trust is increased and the veracity of the information reported is guaranteed.

3. Stakeholder Communication

Reports must be customized for each stakeholder, including consumers, investors, management, and staff, in order to facilitate effective communication. Reports should emphasize pertinent sustainability initiatives and accomplishments in accordance with the specific interests and concerns that each group may have.

4. Benchmarking

Benchmarking is the process of evaluating an organization's green HR metrics versus competitors or industry norms. This aids in evaluating results and locating best practices that can be implemented to enhance sustainability initiatives.

5. Integrated Reporting

An extensive understanding of the company's environmental impact can be obtained by incorporating green HR measures into more general corporate social responsibility (CSR) or sustainability reports. This all-encompassing strategy illustrates how HR supports the organization's overarching sustainability objectives and projects.

11.1 Measuring Environmental Impact of HR Practices

Introduction to Measuring Environmental Impact of HR Practices

Sustainability is becoming a key element of business strategy in the modern corporate world, rather than being a secondary concern. By incorporating sustainable practices into their daily operations, human resource (HR) departments play a crucial role in this transition. The process of evaluating and quantifying the ecological footprint of different HR activities is a necessary step in measuring the environmental impact of HR practices. For businesses looking to lessen their environmental impact, adhere to rules, and show that they are committed to corporate social responsibility, this procedure is essential.

Meaning of Measuring the Environmental Impact of HR Practices

The methodical evaluation and quantification of the environmental impact of human resource (HR) procedures is known as "measuring the environmental impact of HR practices." To ascertain the extent of their influence, this entails pinpointing particular HR procedures and functions that exacerbate environmental degradation and monitoring pertinent indicators. By doing this, companies can put plans into place to lessen negative effects, improve sustainability, and coordinate with more general environmental objectives.

❖ **Importance of Measuring Environmental Impact in HR**

1. Enhancing Corporate Sustainability

Organizations can find opportunities to cut waste, conserve resources, and cut emissions by measuring the environmental impact of their HR operations. This aids international efforts to tackle climate change and advances more general company sustainability aims.

2. Regulatory Compliance

Businesses are under increasing pressure from governments and regulatory agencies to report on their sustainability initiatives and to comply with environmental regulations. Organizations can assure compliance with regulations and prevent penalties by measuring their environmental impact.

3. Cost Savings
Significant cost savings are frequently achieved by implementing sustainable HR practices. Operational costs can be decreased by, for instance, cutting back on paper use, increasing energy efficiency, and minimizing travel.

4. Employee Engagement and Retention
Nowadays' workers, particularly the younger ones, place a high value on employment with environmentally conscious businesses. Organizations may increase retention rates, draw in top talent, and raise employee morale by emphasizing sustainable HR practices.

5. Corporate Image and Competitiveness
An organization's reputation among stakeholders, including investors and customers, is improved by showcasing a dedication to sustainability. Additionally, it might give you a competitive advantage in the market since more partners and customers want to work with environmentally responsible companies.

Measuring Environmental Impact of HR Practices
Organizations looking to integrate sustainability into their core operations must measure the environmental impact of their HR practices. Through the process of determining and measuring the ecological footprint of human resources operations, businesses can enhance their sustainability tactics, track advancements, and exhibit their dedication to ecological responsibility. This all-inclusive strategy entails tracking and enhancing environmental performance by using precise measurements and looking at every facet of HR operations, from waste management to energy consumption.

❖ **Key Areas and Metrics for Measuring Environmental Impact**

1. Energy Consumption
Office Energy Use
Measurement: Keep tabs on how much electricity and other energy is used in HR departments. This covers the energy consumed for running office equipment, heating, cooling, and lighting.

Metrics: total energy used for HR operations, energy consumption per square foot of office space, and kilowatt-hours (kWh) consumed per employee.

Tools: Utility bills, energy management software, and smart meters.

Techniques: Putting energy-saving measures into place, like using natural light, transitioning to LED lighting, and urging staff to turn off equipment when not in use.

Data Canter Usage

Measurement: Keep an eye on the amount of energy being consumed by data canters that support HR tasks, including virtual meeting platforms, payroll systems, and HR information systems (HRIS).

Metrics: Carbon emissions from data canter operations, energy efficiency ratings (Power Usage Effectiveness, or PUE), and kWh used by servers connected to HR.

Tools: Cloud service provider reports, data canter energy management systems.

Techniques: Implementing virtualization to lower hardware requirements, adopting energy-efficient servers, and utilizing renewable energy sources for data canters.

2. Paper Usage

Documentation

Measurement: Determine how much paper is consumed for HR-related tasks such as printing employee messages, performance reviews, employment contracts, and compliance paperwork.

Metrics: Annual total reams of paper consumed, amount of paper used by each employee, and gradual decrease in paper use.

Tools: Digital document management systems, purchase records, and print management software.

Techniques: Increasing the use of digital signatures, encouraging double-sided printing, and making the switch to electronic documentation and storage systems.

Communication

Measurement: Monitor the transition of HR departments from paper-based to digital communication methods.

Metrics: Use of electronic signatures, ratio of digital to paper communications, and decrease in printed newsletters.

Tools: Analytics for email and communication platforms, software for document signing.

Techniques: Putting in place intranets and other internal communication platforms; utilizing email for formal correspondence; and offering instruction on digital tool usage.

3. Employee Commuting

Transportation Emissions

Measurement: Determine the carbon footprint that employees' commutes to and from work have, taking into account the different forms of transportation and the distances they cover.

Metrics: The percentage of workers who use sustainable transportation options, the average commute distance for each employee, and the total amount of CO_2 emissions from commuting.

Tools: Carbon footprint calculators, commute apps, and employee questionnaires.

Techniques: Encouraging remote work rules, carpooling, walking, bicycling, and public transportation; offering incentives for environmentally friendly commuting.

Flexible Work Schedules

Measurement: Analyse how flexible work schedules, including telecommuting and shortened workweeks, affect the emissions from commuting.

Metrics: Total number of days per employee that they work from home, decrease in days spent commuting, and variations in transportation-related emissions.

Tools: Employee time logs and tools for tracking remote work.

Techniques: Implementing telecommuting guidelines, providing flexible work schedules, and advocating for a hybrid work paradigm that blends remote and in-person work.

4. Recruitment and on boarding

Travel for Interviews

Measurement: Keep track of the distance that candidates must travel for interviews as part of the hiring process.

Metrics: The number of in-person versus virtual interviews, the distance travelled and emissions resulting from applicant travel, and the financial savings associated with virtual recruitment.

Tools: Travel expense reporting, video conferencing analytics, and applicant tracking systems (ATS).

Techniques: Decreasing the need for in-person meetings, completing online exams, and using video conferencing more frequently for interviews.

On boarding Materials

Measurement: Examine the changeover of on boarding materials from print to digital format.

Metrics: Employee input regarding the efficacy of digital on boarding, the quantity of printed on boarding materials and the number of digital on boarding sessions.

Tools: Digital content management systems, employee surveys, and on boarding software.

Techniques: Establishing a thorough digital on boarding procedure that includes electronic handbooks, virtual orientation sessions, and online training modules.

5. Training and Development

In-Person Training

Measurement: Keep an eye on the energy and resources utilized for in-person training sessions, such as the cost of the venue, travel, and lodging.

Metrics: Travel-related emissions, the number of in-person versus virtual training sessions, and the financial savings from virtual training.

Tools: Tools for managing expenses, travel, and learning management systems (LMS).

Techniques: Increasing the number of online training options available, making use of web-based training tools, and reducing the need for travel for training.

Training Materials
Measurement: Monitor the adoption of printed versus digital training materials.

Metrics: The quantity of paper utilized for instructional materials, the quantity of online training courses, and participant comments on online courses.

Tools: LMS, platforms for digital publication.

Techniques: Incorporating multimedia resources into training programs, employing e-books and digital manuals, and offering interactive online training content.

6. Workplace Sustainability Initiatives

Green Office Practices
Measurement: Examine how well green office initiatives like recycling programs and energy-efficient lighting are being implemented and working.

Metrics: recycled material volume, energy savings from energy-efficient lighting, and staff involvement in environmental initiatives.

Tools: Employee engagement surveys, office management tools, and sustainability tracking software.

Techniques: Putting in place energy-efficient equipment, implementing extensive recycling programs, and cutting back on single-use plastics in the workplace.

Employee Engagement Programs

Measurement: Evaluate the extent of staff involvement in sustainability projects and activities.

Metrics: The impact of employee-led green projects, employee participation rates in green initiatives, and the quantity of proposals made by employees linked to sustainability.

Tools: Reports on sustainability programs, suggestion boxes, and employee involvement platforms.

Techniques: Promoting the creation of "Green Teams," setting up sustainability seminars, and honouring staff members for their environmental initiative accomplishments.

7. Waste Management

Recycling Programs

Measurement: Monitor the success of recycling initiatives in HR departments.

Metrics: Quantity of waste kept out of landfills, the proportion of waste that is recycled, and advancements in waste management techniques.

Tools: Data from recycling service providers and waste audit reports.

Techniques: Expanding the availability of recycling bins, training staff on appropriate recycling techniques, and monitoring recycling rates to pinpoint areas in need of improvement.

Electronic Waste

Measurement: Keep an eye on how electronic waste, or "e-waste," produced by HR operations is disposed of and recycled.

Metrics: The quantity of recycled electronics, adherence to e-waste laws, and collaboration with approved e-waste recyclers.

Tools: Software for tracking e-waste and procurement documents.

Techniques: E-waste recycling initiatives, collaborations with approved e-waste recyclers, and encouraging the conscientious disposal of electronic gadgets.

8. Sustainable Procurement

Green Procurement Policies

Measurement: Examine whether sustainable procurement practices have been adopted for HR-related items and services.

Metrics: The percentage of green office supplies bought, adherence to green procurement guidelines, and financial benefits from sustainable purchasing.

Tools: Software for procurement and supplier evaluations.

Techniques: Buying recycled or environmentally friendly products, giving preference to suppliers with solid environmental credentials, and promoting sustainable procurement practices across the entire company.

Vendor Selection

Measurement: Examine the sustainability records of partners and vendors that the HR department has chosen.

Metrics: The quantity of certified sustainable vendors, the proportion of money spent with eco-friendly suppliers, and the sustainability standards met by the vendors.

Tools: Sustainability audits and vendor management systems.

Techniques: Putting in place a procedure for evaluating vendors that takes environmental factors into account, encouraging enduring relationships with eco-friendly suppliers, and routinely comparing the performance of vendors to sustainability benchmarks.

9. Health and Well-being Programs

Promoting Sustainable Lifestyles

Measurement: Evaluate the effects of wellness initiatives that promote eco-friendly living among staff members.

Metrics: Rates of wellness program participation, the quantity of workers implementing eco-friendly habits, and enhancements in workers' health and happiness.

Tools: Systems for managing wellness programs, employee questionnaires.

Techniques: Providing rewards for eco-friendly actions, such planting a garden, planning outdoor exercise programs, and encouraging mindfulness exercises that stress being in tune with the natural world.

10. Corporate Social Responsibility (CSR) Integration
Aligning HR with CSR Goals
Measurement: Assess how well HR initiatives align with overarching corporate social responsibility (CSR) objectives.

Metrics: The quantity of CSR projects headed by HR, employee involvement in CSR initiatives, and the effect of HR efforts on overall CSR performance.

Tools: Software for CSR reporting and surveys of employee engagement.

Techniques: Supporting community programs cantered on sustainability, encouraging employee participation in environmental projects, and making sure HR regulations are in line with the company's CSR goals.

In summary, tracking energy use, paper use, commute emissions, and other significant areas is just one step in the complex process of evaluating the environmental impact of HR practices. Organizations can discover areas for development and obtain important insights into their environmental footprint by putting strong metrics and monitoring systems in place. These metrics not only support the attainment of sustainability objectives but also improve the company's standing, motivate staff, and guarantee adherence to environmental laws. Incorporating green HR measurements and reporting into organizational strategy is not only advantageous but also necessary for long-term profitability and environmental stewardship, as sustainability becomes an increasingly important factor in economic success.

11.1.1 Defining and Understanding the Environmental Impact of HR Activities

Introduction
In today's business environment, sustainability has become a top priority. Environmentally conscious practices must be integrated into all aspects of an organization's operations, including human resources (HR), as more

and more businesses realize. Defining and understanding the environmental impact of HR activities entails determining and evaluating the several ways that environmental deterioration is caused by HR operations. Developing solutions that improve sustainability, lessen an organization's ecological footprint, and support international environmental goals requires an awareness of these concepts.

The Role of HR in Environmental Sustainability

Traditionally, human resources departments have concentrated on managing the staff of an enterprise. But they also have a major influence on how sustainability projects are carried out. HR has the power to shape employee conduct, promote environmental responsibility, and put rules in place that help with sustainable operations. Achieving sustainability integration into HR's fundamental functions begins with an understanding of the environmental impact of HR operations.

Meaning

Although managing the workforce has always been the primary goal of human resource (HR) operations, they also have a big environmental impact. The different ways that HR operations either exacerbate or lessen environmental degradation are included in the environmental impact of HR activities. Organizations dedicated to sustainability must comprehend and manage this impact. This all-encompassing method entails analysing several aspects of HR operations, including as energy use and hiring procedures, and putting strategic plans into place to reduce their environmental impact.

❖ **Key Areas of Environmental Impact in HR Activities**

1. Energy Consumption

Office Energy Use: HR departments are usually located in office buildings that use electricity for equipment powering, lighting, heating, and cooling. Lowering energy use in these areas can help a company's carbon impact considerably. A significant impact can be achieved by taking steps like installing energy-efficient lighting, improving HVAC systems, and promoting energy-saving behaviours among staff members.

Virtual Operations: The move to remote work and digital platforms increases our reliance on data canters, which use a lot of energy. This effect can be lessened by employing energy-efficient servers and switching to renewable energy sources for data canters, among other effective IT resource management techniques.

2. Paper Usage

Documentation: Employment contracts, performance reviews, and compliance paperwork are just a few examples of the substantial paperwork that HR functions frequently entail. Overuse of paper products adds to waste and deforestation. Putting digital document management systems in place can significantly cut down on the amount of paper used.

Communication: To cut down on paper usage, digital alternatives can be used in place of conventional paper-based communication techniques like newsletters and memos. This transformation is further supported by promoting digital forms and electronic signatures.

3. Employee Commuting

Transportation Emissions: Employees' daily commutes add to greenhouse gas emissions, particularly if they utilize single-occupancy cars. Reducing this environmental impact can be achieved by encouraging carpooling, biking, public transportation, and telecommuting. Furthermore, encouraging employees to take use of eco-friendly transportation options might increase involvement.

Flexible Work Schedules: Reducing the number of days spent traveling can be achieved by allowing flexible work schedules or reduced workweeks, which will lower overall emissions.

4. Recruitment and On boarding

Travel for Interviews: The carbon footprint is increased when conducting interviews in person, especially in large firms with global operations. Interviews conducted via video conferencing can cut down on emissions associated with travel considerably. Furthermore, digital portfolios and online tests can reduce the necessity for in-person evaluations.

On boarding Materials: Physical resources and written documents are frequently used in traditional on boarding processes. Using digital on boarding procedures reduces the amount of resources used. Physical handbooks and training sessions can be substituted with online orientation sessions and e-learning modules.

5. Training and Development

In-Person Training: Organizing conferences and training sessions in physical spaces demands energy for facilities, lodging, and transportation. With less travel and resource use, online workshops and training modules provide a more environmentally friendly option.

Training Materials: Offering training materials in digital format as opposed to print can help cut down on waste and usage of paper. E-books and interactive web platforms work well in place of traditional printed manuals.

1. Workplace Sustainability Initiatives

Green Office Practices: The organization's environmental footprint is directly impacted by the implementation of policies like waste reduction programs, energy-efficient lighting, and recycling programs. Sustainability initiatives can be strengthened by fostering behaviours like utilizing reusable cookware, cutting back on plastic consumption, and encouraging a paperless workplace.

Employee Engagement Programs: Encouraging staff members to take part in sustainability initiatives helps to cultivate a culture of environmental consciousness and group effort. Sustainability champions or "Green Teams" are two programs that can motivate people and guarantee ongoing participation.

2. Waste Management

Recycling Programs: Office recycling programs that are successful can drastically cut down on the quantity of waste that ends up in landfills. Having recycling bins that are clearly marked and training staff on correct waste segregation are essential elements.

Electronic Waste: Electronic garbage, or "e-waste," needs to be disposed of and recycled properly because HR departments frequently work with a variety of digital devices. Working with approved e-waste recyclers guarantees that obsolete equipment is disposed of securely and sustainably.

3. Sustainable Procurement

Green Procurement Policies: Reducing environmental effect can be achieved by ensuring that office goods and services that the HR department purchases are sustainable. Buying recycled paper, energy-saving machinery, and environmentally friendly office supplies are all examples of this.

Vendor Selection: Selecting partners and suppliers who follow sustainable standards helps the company's environmental efforts even more. It is proactive to assess suppliers according to their sustainability certifications and environmental policies.

Measuring and Managing Environmental Impact

❖ To effectively manage the environmental impact of HR activities, organizations need to adopt a structured approach that includes the following steps:

1. Assessment and Metrics

Conducting Audits: The key area of environmental effect is identified with the assistance of routine audit of energy use, paper consumption and commute habits. These audits offer a starting point for gauging advancements and locating inefficiencies.

Setting Metrics: Setting up quantifiable, precise measures for energy use, paper use, and other pertinent areas establishes a starting point for monitoring advancement. Metrics should have both short- and long-term objectives and be in line with the organization's broader sustainability aims.

2. Implementation of Sustainable Practices

Digital Transformation: Making the switch to digital procedures for hiring, training, communication, documentation, and recruiting can save a lot of resources. Using collaborative tools and cloud-based solutions increases productivity while reducing environmental impact.

Remote Work Policies: Reducing office energy use and emissions from commuting can be achieved by promoting or requiring remote work whenever feasible. The combination of remote and in-office work in hybrid work models also helps to lessen the impact on the environment.

Sustainable Office Practices: Putting in place procedures in office premises for resource conservation, waste minimization, and energy efficiency. Using recycling stations, installing motion-sensor lights, and cutting back on single-use plastics are a few examples.

Employee Engagement and Training

Awareness Programs: Teaching staff members about how their actions affect the environment and encouraging sustainable practices both within and outside of the workplace. Staff members are informed and involved through workshops, seminars, and frequent updates on sustainability projects.

Incentive Programs: Providing benefits for eco-friendly behaviours, such carpooling or taking public transportation. Programs for rewarding staff members who actively participate in sustainability initiatives can help increase engagement and motivation.

3. Monitoring and Reporting

Continuous Monitoring: Keeping a regular eye on the defined indicators in order to assess development and pinpoint opportunities for enhancement. This procedure can be streamlined by using sustainability management software, which also offers real-time data insights.

Transparent Reporting: Sharing with stakeholders the organization's accomplishments and sustainability initiatives on a regular basis will promote accountability and ongoing development. Stakeholder meetings, intranet updates, and annual sustainability reports are useful platforms for this kind of communication.

❖ Advanced Initiatives for Reducing Environmental Impact

1. **Carbon Offsetting:** Organizations can fund carbon offset initiatives, such as reforestation, renewable energy, or community programs that lower greenhouse gas emissions, to offset their inevitable emissions.

This strategy aids in offsetting the negative environmental effects of crucial HR operations.

2. **Green Conferences and Meetings:** Sustainable event planning entails selecting environmentally friendly locations, cutting waste, and promoting online involvement. It's practical to offer digital materials, use reusable decorations, and find local, organic caterers.

3. **Aligning HR with CSR Goals:** Sustainable practices are approached holistically when HR initiatives are integrated with overarching CSR objectives. Through the facilitation of employee volunteer programs cantered on environmental projects and the promotion of ethical corporate practices, HR can support CSR initiatives.

4. **Promoting Sustainable Lifestyles:** HR can implement wellness initiatives that support sustainable living, like plant-based diets, physical pursuits like cycling that lessen carbon emissions, and mindfulness exercises that highlight a connection to the natural world.

In conclusion, a major component of an organization's overall sustainability footprint is the environmental impact of HR activities. Organizations can lower their environmental footprint, improve sustainability, and reap advantages for the environment and company by identifying and comprehending these impacts. In addition to lowering emissions and saving natural resources, implementing green HR practices helps ensure regulatory compliance, enhance employee engagement, and improve a company's reputation. In a time when environmental stewardship and long-term performance are highly dependent on sustainability, incorporating green HR measurements and reporting into organizational goals is not only advantageous but also crucial.

11.1.2 Identifying Key Performance Indicators (KPIs) for Measuring Environmental Impact

Organizations must select and monitor particular Key Performance Indicators (KPIs) in order to quantify and manage the environmental impact of Human Resource (HR) activities. These KPIs offer quantitative measurements that assist firms in evaluating the success of their sustainability activities, comprehending their environmental impact, and pinpointing areas in need of improvement. Organizations may achieve ongoing improvements in environmental performance and make informed decisions by concentrating on these metrics.

Energy Consumption

1. Office Energy Use (kWh per Employee)

Description: This KPI calculates how much electricity is used for lighting, heating, cooling, and office equipment use per employee in HR departments.

Importance: Organizations can find inefficiencies and ways to cut energy use by tracking office energy use. Reduce the environmental effect and operating expenses by putting energy-saving devices and procedures into place, such as smart thermostats, energy-efficient lighting, and encouraging staff to turn off equipment when not in use.

2. Data Canter Energy Efficiency (PUE - Power Usage Effectiveness)

Description: The ratio of the overall energy consumed by the data canter to the energy used by the IT equipment alone is called Power Usage Effectiveness, or PUE, and it is used to evaluate the efficiency of data canters that support HR functions.

Importance: More effective data canters are indicated by lower PUE values. Organizations can lower overall energy consumption and related greenhouse gas emissions by using renewable energy sources, virtualizing servers, and optimizing cooling systems to improve data canter efficiency.

Paper Usage

3. Paper Consumption (Reams per Employee)

Description: This KPI monitors the amount of paper utilized by each employee for HR-related tasks, such as printing forms and other paperwork.

Importance: Organizations can find areas for reduction and identify excessive paper use by keeping an eye on paper use. Making the switch to digital communication and documentation can drastically cut expenses, lessen the environmental effect of paper manufacturing and disposal, and reduce the amount of waste paper generated.

4. Digital Adoption Rate (Percentage of Digital Documents)

Description: This KPI calculates the percentage of HR communications and documents that are exchanged online as opposed to on paper.

Importance: A greater rate of digital adoption signifies advancements in the direction of a paperless workplace. Businesses can lessen their dependency on paper by using digital forms, electronic signatures, and online communication tools more frequently. This will cut down on paper waste and deforestation.

Employee Commuting

5. Average Commute Distance (Miles per Employee)
Description: This KPI determines the typical commuter distance, which sheds light on the effects of commuting on the environment.

Importance: Organizations can evaluate the potential advantages of remote work rules and the environmental impact of employee travel by having a thorough understanding of commute distances. Encouragement of telecommuting, remote work, and flexible scheduling can help reduce emissions associated with commuting and minimize carbon footprints.

6. Green Commute Rate (Percentage of Employees Using Sustainable Transport)
Description: This KPI calculates the percentage of workers who commute to work using environmentally friendly modes of transportation like public transportation, carpooling, biking, or walking.

Importance: Encouraging environmentally friendly modes of transportation lowers traffic and greenhouse gas emissions. Companies can encourage the use of environmentally friendly transportation by offering rewards for taking public transportation, building bike-friendly infrastructure, and starting carpooling initiatives.

Recruitment and on boarding

7. Travel Emissions for Recruitment (CO2 Emissions per Candidate)

Description: This KPI monitors the carbon emissions related to travel for hiring-related activities, such as travel for interviews and on boarding by recruiters and candidates.

Importance: In order to minimize the environmental impact of HR activities, it is imperative to reduce travel emissions for recruitment. Carbon emissions can be greatly reduced by holding virtual on boarding sessions, using video conferencing for interviews, and reducing the amount of time spent travelling.

8. Digital On boarding Completion Rate (Percentage of New Hires Using Digital On boarding)

Description: The percentage of newly hired employees who finish the on boarding process online is tracked by this KPI.

Importance: Higher completion rates for digital on boarding are a sign of successful digital process adoption, which lowers the requirement for travel and printed materials. By using less resources, digital on boarding promotes environmental sustainability, reduces expenses, and increases efficiency.

Training and Development

9. Virtual Training Participation Rate (Percentage of Training Conducted Online)

Description: This KPI calculates the percentage of virtual versus in-person training sessions.

Importance: Participation in virtual training increases when fewer people need to travel and attend in-person meetings, which lowers related emissions and resource consumption. While promoting sustainability objectives, online training platforms provide accessible and adaptable learning possibilities.

10. Digital Training Materials Usage (Percentage of Digital Training Materials)

Description: This KPI monitors how often digital resources like e-books, online courses, and digital manuals are used for training.

Importance: By eliminating the requirement for printed documentation, using digital training materials helps cut down on wasteful paper use. Training methods that are effective and long-lasting are encouraged by the easy distribution and updating of digital resources.

Waste Management

11. Recycling Rate (Percentage of Waste Recycled)

Description: This KPI calculates the percentage of trash produced overall by HR-related operations that is recycled.

Importance: High recycling rates are a sign of efficient waste management techniques. Deploying thorough recycling programs, setting up appropriate waste segregation infrastructure, and teaching staff members about recycling can all help cut down on landfill waste and its negative effects on the environment.

12. E-Waste Recycling Rate (Percentage of Electronic Waste Recycled)

Description: This KPI monitors the percentage of HR-generated electronic garbage (e-waste) that is appropriately recycled.

Importance: To avoid contaminating the environment, electronic trash needs to be disposed of and recycled properly. By collaborating with approved e-waste recyclers, you can assist environmental sustainability by ensuring that outdated gadgets are handled and recycled safely.

Sustainable Procurement

13. Sustainable Procurement Rate (Percentage of Eco-Friendly Purchases)

Description: The percentage of office supplies and services that HR purchases that satisfy sustainability standards, such as being recyclable, energy-efficient, or ecologically friendly, is measured by this KPI.

Importance: Sustainable procurement practices lessen the impact that goods and services have on the environment. Prioritizing environmentally friendly goods and services helps businesses promote green markets and use fewer resources.

14. Supplier Sustainability Score (Average Sustainability Rating of Suppliers)

Description: This KPI evaluates the environmental policies and practices, such as sustainability certifications and adherence to green standards, of vendors the HR department uses.

Importance: Selecting vendors with a solid track record in sustainability guarantees that the products and services you purchase have the least negative impact on the environment. Assessing and choosing sustainable suppliers encourages ethical procurement and advances overarching business sustainability objectives.

To sum up, by recognizing and monitoring these key performance indicators (KPIs), businesses may quantify the environmental impact of their HR initiatives in a methodical manner. Organizations can enhance their environmental performance over time by implementing sustainable initiatives, understanding their ecological footprint, and concentrating on specific, quantitative indicators. These KPIs assist with cost-cutting and regulatory compliance, but they also help create a sustainable organizational culture and a positive business image. Integrating these KPIs into HR procedures is crucial for long-term success and environmental stewardship in a time when environmental responsibility is becoming more and more important.

11.1.3 Methods for Tracking and Quantifying the Sustainability Impact of HR Processes

Tracking and Quantifying the Sustainability Impact of HR Processes

Organisations that are dedicated to achieving environmental, social, and governance (ESG) objectives must consider the sustainability implications of HR procedures including hiring, training, and employee engagement. Various techniques and instruments must be integrated into a holistic approach in order to track and quantify this influence efficiently.

❖ **Below is a detailed explanation of these methods.**

Recruitment

1. Diversity Metrics:

Tracking Diversity: Keep an eye on how diverse the candidates, interviewees, and hiring are in terms of age, gender, ethnicity, handicap status, and socioeconomic background. Applicant Tracking Systems (ATS) can be used to collect and examine this information.

Benchmarking: To assess your current situation and establish goals for progress, compare the diversity metrics of your company with those of the industry or with the demographics of the area.

2. Sourcing Channels:

Sustainable Sourcing: Examine the carbon footprint of recruitment channels in order to determine how sustainable they are. To cut down on emissions associated with travel, give precedence to virtual job fairs and internet platforms over in-person gatherings.

Supplier Assessment: Examine the platforms' and third-party recruitment agencies' sustainable practices. Those with solid certificates and credentials in sustainability are preferred.

3. Candidate Experience:

Feedback Mechanisms: Use post-application questionnaires to get candidate opinions about how inclusive and fair the hiring process was. Examine this input to find any prejudices or obstacles.

Digital Transformation: Reduce the amount of paper used by switching to digital on boarding and application procedures. Monitor the decrease in the usage of paper and other resources due to digitization.

4. Inclusive Job Descriptions:

Language Analysis: Utilize technological tools to examine job descriptions for inclusion and gender-neutral wording. Maintain job postings up to date with industry standards to draw in diverse candidates.

Training

Training Completion Rates:

Tracking Participation: Track the percentages of participants and programs completion in sustainability-related training. To gather information on course completion, attendance, and feedback, uses learning management systems (LMS).

Continuous Improvement: Update training materials frequently in response to participant comments and emerging sustainability trends. Examine how these modifications have increased student satisfaction and completion rates to gauge their efficacy.

1. **Learning Outcomes:**

Pre- and Post-Training Assessments: Measure the effectiveness of the training and the retention of the material by conducting assessments both before and after the sessions. To assess the training's effectiveness, monitor score changes.

Performance Reviews: Perform reviews that take sustainability competencies into account. Evaluate staff members' adherence to sustainability concepts in their work and monitor their progress over time.

2. **Carbon Footprint:**

Virtual Training: Encourage online training courses to reduce emissions from travel. Determine and contrast the carbon impact of online versus live instruction.

Energy Efficiency: Make the most of energy efficiency in training facilities by using energy-efficient heating, cooling, and lighting systems. Monitor energy use and advancements.

3. **Resource Utilization:**

Minimize Waste: Monitor the training materials' consumption and make an effort to employ reusable and digital resources to cut down on waste. Track the decrease in consumables such as paper and plastic.

Employee Engagement

Employee Surveys:

Regular Surveys: Take staff commitment, awareness, and engagement with sustainability projects via questionnaires on a regular basis. Assure consistency and comparability of data by using standardized survey instruments.

Actionable Insights: Examine survey data to pinpoint areas of strength and room for development. To improve engagement, create action plans based on these insights.

1. Participation Rates:

Tracking Involvement: Track the percentage of people who participate in sustainability projects, volunteer programs, green teams, and committees. To evaluate the impact and reach of these programs, use participation statistics.

Impact Measurement: Analyse the observable results of sustainability initiatives, such as the quantity of garbage recycled, the energy saved, or the influence volunteer hours have on the community.

2. Recognition Programs:

Incentives and Rewards: Put in place recognition initiatives that honour staff members for long-lasting actions. Keep track of the quantity of awards and nominations, as well as the rise in sustainable behaviours that follows.

Case Studies: To encourage best practices and serve as an inspiration to others, create case studies that showcase the accomplishments of honoured staff members.

3. Sustainable Practices:

Adoption Metrics: Monitor the implementation of environmentally friendly work practices, like recycling, energy saving, and eco-friendly transportation. To gather data, make use of instruments like energy meters and waste audits.

Continuous Improvement: Review and update sustainability practices and policies on a regular basis. Monitor the advancement of these changes by observing quantifiable results like decreased energy usage and waste.

General Methods

1. Benchmarking:

Industry Standards: Compare the sustainability KPIs of your company to industry norms and best practices. Make use of this comparison to pinpoint areas in need of improvement.

Peer Comparison: Assess your performance against that of similar firms to determine your relative advantages and disadvantages.

2. Key Performance Indicators (KPIs):

Specific KPIs: Provide particular sustainability-related KPIs for every HR procedure. The percentage decrease in paper use, the number of hours spent on sustainability-related training, employee engagement levels, and the carbon footprint of HR operations are a few examples.

Regular Monitoring: Report these KPIs to stakeholders on a regular basis. Utilize data visualization and dashboard tools to make the information usable and accessible.

3. Reporting and Analytics:

HR Analytics Tools: To collect, examine, and report on sustainability data, use HR analytics technologies. Make dynamic dashboards to track developments and spot patterns.

Integrated Reporting: Make sure sustainability measures are incorporated into overall business performance evaluations by including them in monthly HR reports.

4. Certifications and Standards:

Sustainability Certifications: Go for pertinent certifications in sustainability, including ISO 14001 for environmental management. To guarantee optimal practices, align HR procedures with these criteria.

Continuous Compliance: To keep up with sustainability certifications and requirements, policies and procedures should be reviewed and updated on a regular basis.

5. Stakeholder Feedback:

Multi-Stakeholder Engagement: Get input from a variety of sources, such as staff members, applicants, instructors, and outside partners. Gather a range of viewpoints through interviews, focus groups, and surveys.

Feedback Loop: Create a feedback loop to guarantee that HR procedures consistently take stakeholder insights into account. Keep an eye on updates and enhancements based on these comments.

In summary, for businesses devoted to achieving ESG objectives, tracking and quantifying the sustainability impact of HR processes is crucial. Organizations can obtain important insights into their sustainability performance by combining techniques like employee engagement surveys, sustainable sourcing, training evaluations, and diversity measures. Continuous improvement is further enhanced by regular benchmarking, KPIs, and the incorporation of sustainability data into HR reporting. Organizations can cultivate a sustainable culture and make a significant effect by actively involving stakeholders and coordinating HR procedures with sustainability requirements.

11.2 Reporting on Sustainability Performance

Introduction to Reporting on Sustainability Performance

A key component of contemporary corporate governance is reporting on sustainability performance, which shows an organization's adherence to environmental, social, and governance (ESG) standards. Transparent and thorough reporting is now crucial for fostering confidence, proving accountability, and promoting ongoing progress in sustainable practices as stakeholders including investors, clients, staff, and regulators prioritize sustainability more and more.

Meaning of Reporting on Sustainability Performance

The process of reporting on sustainability performance entails the methodical gathering, examination, and distribution of information about the environmental, social, and governance (ESG) activities and consequences of a company. Through this procedure, firms can inform investors, consumers, employees, regulators, and the general public about their sustainability initiatives, successes, and difficulties.

Reporting on Sustainability Performance

In corporate governance and strategic management, "sustainability performance reporting" is essential for firms that are committed to sustainability. Information on an organization's environmental, social, and governance (ESG) impacts are systematically gathered, analysed, and disseminated. Organizations can fulfil stakeholder and regulatory expectations, lead to continual improvement in their sustainability initiatives, and exhibit transparency and accountability through effective sustainability reporting.

❖ Key Elements of Sustainability Reporting

1. Materiality Assessment

The sustainability concerns that are most important to a company and its stakeholders are determined and prioritized through a materiality assessment. This procedure guarantees that the sustainability report concentrates on the most significant and pertinent problems. Organizations can maintain alignment with stakeholder goals and new sustainability trends by regularly conducting materiality assessments.

2. Performance Metrics and KPIs

Key Performance Indicators (KPIs) and precise, quantitative measurements that monitor performance in areas including energy use, greenhouse gas emissions, waste management, water use, and social consequences should be included in sustainability reports. These indicators give a clear picture of the organization's success in terms of sustainability and its advancement toward its objectives.

3. Data Collection and Analysis

Reliable and accurate data collection is essential to producing sustainability reports that are effective. It is recommended that organizations establish resilient systems and procedures for collecting data on sustainability performance. After then, this data is examined to evaluate developments, spot patterns, and highlight areas in need of improvement.

4. Stakeholder Engagement

An essential component of reporting on sustainability is interacting with stakeholders. To understand their worries and expectations regarding sustainability, this entails getting feedback from stakeholders like as employees, consumers, investors, regulators, and others. Stakeholder priorities and information demands are taken into account in the sustainability report through effective stakeholder interaction.

5. Reporting Frameworks and Standards
Sustainability reports are reliable, consistent, and comparative when they follow established reporting frameworks and standards. The Task Force on Climate-related Financial Disclosures (TCFD), the Sustainability Accounting Standards Board (SASB), and the Global Reporting Initiative (GRI) are examples of common frameworks. Following these guidelines enables organizations to generate excellent reports that satisfy stakeholders.

6. Narrative and Context
Sustainability reports should include narratives that explain the context of performance indicators, highlight accomplishments, and define problems and future goals in addition to quantitative data. This makes the organization's sustainability journey and the larger context of its sustainability initiatives more understandable to stakeholders.

7. Integration with Financial Reporting
A comprehensive understanding of the performance of the company is possible through the integration of sustainability and financial reporting. This integration shows how sustainability activities contribute to the overall profitability and long-term value generation of the business by highlighting the linkages between financial and non-financial performance.

❖ **Steps in Sustainability Reporting**

Step - 1. Planning and Scoping
The sustainability report's scope and goals should be defined. Determine the most important subjects and measurements to address based on stakeholder feedback and a materiality assessment. Provide resources and a schedule for the reporting process.

Step - 2. Data Collection
Gather sustainability performance data through the use of established data gathering procedures and systems. Make that the information is correct, comprehensive, and adheres to reporting guidelines. Obtaining information from several departments, vendors, and partners may be necessary for this.

Step - 3. Data Analysis
Analyse the gathered information to gauge performance, spot trends, and gauge advancement toward sustainable objectives. Make use of this information to highlight important accomplishments and areas that require improvement in the report's narrative.

Step - 4. Stakeholder Engagement
Effective stakeholder engagement helps to create trust and ensures the report is relevant and meaningful. It can involve surveys, interviews, and public consultations to gather feedback, resolve problems, and make sure the report satisfies their information needs.

Step - 5. Report Preparation
Prepare the sustainability report, taking into account both qualitative and quantitative information. To guarantee that the report is thorough and reliable, adhere to established reporting frameworks and criteria. When communicating important points, choose language that is easy to understand and comprehend.

Step - 6. Review and Assurance
To make sure the report is accurate and comprehensive, conduct an internal review. If you want to increase the report's credibility, think about getting external confirmation from a third party. External assurance shows the organization's dedication to accuracy and transparency by offering an impartial confirmation of the information provided.

Step - 7. Publication and Communication
Publish the sustainability report and communicate the findings to stakeholders through a range of channels, such as the company's website, social media pages, and stakeholder events. Use a range of media, including print and digital, to reach a big audience.

Step - 8. Feedback and Improvement
Aim to enhance future reporting procedures by getting stakeholder feedback on the report. Improve the processes for gathering, analysing, and reporting data on a regular basis to improve the caliber and

significance of sustainability reports. Make more ambitious goals by using feedback to find new chances for sustainability projects.

To sum up, the foundation of ethical corporate governance and sustainable business practices is strong sustainability performance reporting. Organizations can improve transparency, satisfy stakeholder and regulatory requirements, and promote continuous development by methodically monitoring, evaluating, and sharing their sustainability initiatives. In addition to showcasing an organization's dedication to social and environmental responsibility, sustainability reporting helps strategic decision-making and cultivates an eco-friendly organizational culture. In a time when sustainability is becoming more and more significant, establishing long-term success, boosting reputation, and fostering trust all depend on thorough and open reporting.

11.2.1 Importance of Transparent Reporting on Sustainability Performance in HR

Importance of Transparent Reporting on Sustainability Performance in HR

Transparent reporting on sustainability performance in Human Resources (HR) is essential to building business reputation, promoting trust, and propelling achievement inside the organization. It guarantees that all interested parties may obtain precise and thorough information regarding an organization's sustainability initiatives, especially those concerning its personnel and internal procedures.

❖ **Here are key reasons why transparent reporting in this context is crucial, with expanded points:**

1. Building Trust with Stakeholders

Employee Trust and Engagement: Employee trust is increased when sustainability performance is reported transparently. A culture of trust and involvement is promoted when HR is transparent in disseminating information regarding sustainable practices, such as equitable work environments, diversity and inclusion programs, and health and safety protocols. Workers are more likely to feel devoted to the company and respected. Trust creates a positive feedback loop that benefits the entire organization by boosting morale, lowering turnover, and increasing productivity.

Investor Confidence: ESG considerations are becoming more and more important to investors when making decisions. By lowering risks and increasing long-term value, transparent reporting reassures investors that the company is managing its human capital sustainably and ethically. Investors that value long-term stability above quick profits may be drawn to transparent and thorough reports.

2. Enhancing Corporate Reputation

Positive Public Perception: A positive public perception is bolstered by transparent reporting on sustainability performance connected to HR. Public perception, customer satisfaction, and prospective employee loyalty are all positively impacted by organizations that publicly share their efforts to establish a sustainable workplace. Increased revenue, improved brand value, and client loyalty can all result from this favourable view.

Competitive Advantage: Businesses that set the standard for sustainability reporting can set themselves apart from rivals. Reputation for accountability and transparency may draw excellent talent, devoted clients, and thoughtful investors. Furthermore, organizations with strong reporting processes are better positioned to gain market share and enter new markets as sustainability becomes an increasingly important priority for both consumers and enterprises.

3. Meeting Regulatory and Stakeholder Expectations

Compliance with Regulations: Organizations must disclose all of their sustainability practices, including HR-related ones, under many jurisdictions. By guaranteeing adherence to these rules, transparent reporting helps to prevent fines and other consequences. Gaining a strategic edge can also come from proactively implementing detailed reporting methods in order to stay ahead of regulatory developments.

Responding to Stakeholder Demands: Stakeholders are calling for more openness from organizations regarding their activities, including customers, workers, and advocacy groups. These expectations are met in part via transparent reporting, which shows that the company recognizes and honours stakeholder concerns. Involving stakeholders through open reporting can encourage cooperation and motivate group efforts to achieve sustainability objectives.

4. Driving Continuous Improvement

Benchmarking and Goal Setting: Organizations can establish specific, quantifiable targets for progress and compare their performance to industry standards thanks to transparent reporting. This cycle of continuous improvement is necessary to advance HR's sustainability goals. The organization is kept motivated to reach higher standards of sustainability through regular benchmarking against peers and industry norms.

Identifying Areas for Improvement: Organizations can find areas for improvement and areas for weakness by transparently sharing performance data. Accountability is promoted by transparency, which also inspires internal stakeholders to aim for improved performance. Frequent audits and feedback loops guarantee that effective procedures are expanded and strengthened, and that areas for improvement are immediately addressed.

5. Supporting Strategic Decision-Making

Informed Decision-Making: Leaders can obtain precise and all-inclusive information regarding HR sustainability performance through transparent reporting. Making strategic decisions that are in line with the organization's sustainability objectives requires having access to this information. Making well-informed decisions lowers risks, improves operational effectiveness, and guarantees efficient resource allocation.

Resource Allocation: Efficient allocation of resources to sustainability efforts with the most impact is made possible by transparent reporting that identifies the areas of greatest need. Allocating resources strategically maximizes the return on investment in sustainability initiatives by ensuring that the organization's sustainability activities are both cost-effective and successful.

6. Fostering a Sustainable Organizational Culture

Cultural Integration: Integrating sustainability into organizational culture is facilitated by open reporting on HR sustainability practices. All staff accept sustainability as a fundamental value when it is freely expressed and integrated into daily operations. This integration synchronizes individual behaviours with organizational objectives and cultivates a feeling of shared purpose.

Employee Empowerment: Employee participation in sustainability efforts is empowered by transparency. Employees are more likely to offer creative solutions and take charge of sustainability initiatives when they are informed about the organization's objectives and performance. An organization can become more dynamic and resilient by empowering its employees to spearhead grassroots initiatives that improve sustainability performance overall.

7. Enhancing Employee Well-being and Retention

Workplace Satisfaction: Increased employee satisfaction stems from open reporting on sustainability measures, including work-life balance programs, wellness initiatives, and ethical labour practices. Employees that are happy with their jobs are more productive, engaged, and inclined to stick around. Elevated levels of contentment additionally diminish absenteeism and enhance the general morale at work.

Talent Attraction and Retention: Top talent is drawn to organizations that are recognized for their sustainability and openness. Transparent reporting helps organizations demonstrate their beliefs, which is something that attracts and retains employees. An organization's ability to maintain a high reputation for sustainability can help it become a preferred employer, which lowers hiring expenses and increases staff retention.

To sum up, transparent reporting on sustainability performance in HR is critical to fostering continuous improvement inside businesses, boosting reputation, and fostering trust. It guarantees adherence to legal mandates, fulfils stakeholder expectations, and facilitates strategic decision-making. In addition, it promotes a long-lasting company culture, raises employee satisfaction, and strengthens the recruitment and retention of talent. By adopting reporting transparency, companies can show that they are committed to ethical behaviour while also setting themselves up for long-term success and resilience in a world where sustainability is becoming more and more important.

11.2.2 Communicating Environmental and Social Impacts to Internal and External Stakeholders

Introduction to Communicating Environmental and Social Impact to Internal and External Stakeholders

Sustainability is becoming a key element of strategic planning and stakeholder engagement in today's business environment, going beyond simple compliance. Building trust, improving reputation, and promoting long-term success are all dependent on firms' ability to effectively communicate their environmental and social effects to internal and external stakeholders. In order to effectively communicate how an organization's operations, goods, and services impact society and the environment, it must emphasize both its successes and shortcomings.

The Role of Transparency in Sustainability Communication

Effective communication about sustainability starts with transparency. It entails disclosing information regarding an organization's social programs, governance frameworks, and environmental policies in an open manner. Being transparent is essential to building confidence and trust with stakeholders, who are calling for more transparency and responsibility from businesses when it comes to their sustainability initiatives.

Internal Stakeholders: The effective implementation of sustainability programs is contingent upon the involvement of internal stakeholders, such as management and employees. Aligning the organization's actions with these goals is made easier with clear communication about its sustainability goals and progress. Active engagement in sustainable activities is encouraged since it cultivates a sense of accountability and ownership.

External Stakeholders: External parties with a stake in an organization's sustainability performance include investors, clients, suppliers, regulators, and the community. By ensuring that these groups are aware of the company's social and environmental impacts, effective communication helps the firm further its commitment to sustainable development.

Communicating Environmental and Social Impact to Internal and External Stakeholders

A key component of contemporary organizational practice is successfully communicating environmental and social consequences to internal and external stakeholders. It entails methodically disseminating data regarding the effects that an organization's operations have on society and the environment. Establishing trust, improving reputation, stimulating engagement, and guaranteeing adherence to market and regulatory standards all depend on this openness. This is a thorough examination of its significance and meaning.

Building Trust and Transparency

Whether it's with employees, clients, investors, or the community at large, trust is the bedrock of each successful relationship. An organization's commitment to integrity and accountability is demonstrated by transparent communication addressing environmental and social impacts. Knowing that their organization is committed to sustainable practices can boost morale, loyalty, and engagement among employees. Employees are more inclined to trust management and feel more deeply a part of the organization's mission when they observe that the business is open about its impact.

Transparency has a big impact on how external stakeholders, including consumers and investors, see you. Environmental, social, and governance (ESG) factors are being considered by investors more and more when making decisions. Organizations may draw in and keep socially conscious investors who value long-term value creation over short-term profits by effectively conveying sustainability activities and benefits. In a similar vein, clients who are aware of a business's dedication to sustainability are more likely to become brand loyalists and promote the business, which improves client retention and satisfaction.

Enhancing Reputation and Brand Value

One of an organization's most important assets is its reputation. A solid reputation for sustainability can help a business stand out from the competition in today's market. Organizations can create and maintain a positive public image by conveying the environmental and social implications in an effective manner. This entails being open about both achievements and difficulties. Even while it could be easy to focus only on the positives, admitting when there is room for improvement demonstrates a dedication to openness and ongoing development, which can further boost trust and reputation.

Reputation for sustainability draws top talent as well as customers. Nowadays, more and more job searchers especially those from younger generations are searching for companies that share their beliefs. Highly qualified employees who are driven by factors other than money can be drawn to companies that are known for their social and environmental responsibility.

Driving Stakeholder Engagement and Support

Clear communication with stakeholders promotes their support and involvement in sustainability activities. This could entail developing programs that actively involve internal stakeholders, like employees, in sustainability activities, including recycling campaigns, energy-saving campaigns, or volunteer opportunities. Employees can be kept informed and involved with regular updates via corporate newsletters, intranet portals, and town hall meetings.

Customers, investors, and the community are examples of external stakeholders that are vital. Public events, press releases, company websites, social media platforms, sustainability reports, and press releases are all useful means of reaching these audiences. Stakeholders are given reliable information about the performance of the company through comprehensive and transparent sustainability reports that follow established frameworks such as the Sustainability Accounting Standards Board (SASB) or the Global Reporting Initiative (GRI).

Meeting Regulatory and Market Expectations

One essential component of communication about sustainability is adhering to regulations. Disclosures of the effects on the environment and society are becoming more and more required by governments and regulatory agencies. By ensuring that organizations comply with these legal requirements, transparent reporting helps them avoid fines and other legal problems. Companies can gain a competitive edge by proactively implementing comprehensive reporting standards, which establish them as leaders in sustainability.

Expectations from the market are also significant. Companies have to change to meet the increasing demands of stakeholders, investors, and customers for increased openness. Meeting these expectations is facilitated by effective communication, which shows that the company appreciates and honours stakeholder concerns. Increased support from important stakeholder groups and greater connections may result from this responsiveness.

Driving Continuous Improvement
Encouraging continual growth is another goal of transparent communication, in addition to discussing past accomplishments. Organizations can use transparency as a tool to advance their sustainability activities by comparing against industry norms and establishing specific, quantifiable targets. Frequent audits and feedback loops guarantee that areas in need of improvement are found and dealt with right away.

For example, sharing comprehensive performance data enables firms to identify gaps and create plans to close them. Accountability is promoted by transparency, which also inspires internal stakeholders to aim for improved performance. Improved overall performance, cost savings, and operational efficiencies can result from ongoing sustainability practice improvement.

Supporting Strategic Decision-Making
Leaders who communicate effectively are able to gather the information required to make well-informed strategic decisions. Thorough and precise data regarding the effects on the environment and society facilitates the alignment of company plans with sustainable objectives. This alignment guarantees the organization's ability to efficiently allocate resources, effectively manage risks, and take advantage of possibilities for innovation and progress.

Efficient allocation of resources to sustainability efforts with the most impact is made possible by transparent reporting that identifies the areas of greatest need. The implementation of a strategic approach to resource allocation guarantees the effectiveness and cost-efficiency of sustainability programs, hence optimizing return on investment.

Fostering a Sustainable Organizational Culture

An organization can be considered sustainable if its employees support sustainability and it is ingrained in all day-to-day operations. The incorporation of sustainability initiatives into the organizational culture is facilitated by transparent reporting. Employees are more likely to embrace these values and apply them into their daily actions when sustainability goals and accomplishments are clearly shared.

Transparency also encourages employees to participate actively in environmental projects. Employees are more inclined to suggest creative solutions and take charge of sustainability initiatives when they are aware of the organization's objectives and performance. This sense of ownership can spur community-based projects that improve an organization's overall sustainability performance and make it more resilient and dynamic.

Enhancing Employee Well-being and Retention

Employee happiness and organizational success are directly related. Employee satisfaction can be greatly increased by openly disclosing sustainability measures, such as work-life balance programs, wellness initiatives, and ethical labour practices. Employees that are happy with their jobs are more productive, engaged, and inclined to stick around. Elevated levels of contentment additionally diminish absenteeism and enhance the general morale at work.

Top talent is also drawn to organizations that are well-known for their sustainability and openness. Employers who share the same values as the job seeker are more in demand, and open reporting is one way to show this. An organization's ability to maintain a high reputation for sustainability can help it become a preferred employer, which lowers hiring expenses and increases staff retention.

To sum up, trust, reputation, and engagement can only be achieved through effectively informing internal and external stakeholders about environmental and social consequences. In addition to supporting strategic decision-making and fostering a long-lasting organizational culture, transparent, unambiguous, and consistent communication helps firms meet regulatory and market requirements. Organizations can show their dedication to ethical behavior, draw and keep top talent, and set themselves up for long-term success and resilience in a world where sustainability is becoming more and more important by embracing transparency.

11.2.3 Compliance with Reporting Standards and Frameworks

Organizations seeking to improve transparency, accountability, and credibility in their sustainability reporting must adhere to established reporting standards and frameworks, such as the Sustainability Accounting Standards Board (SASB), the Global Reporting Initiative (GRI), and the Carbon Disclosure Project (CDP). By offering systematic approaches for revealing environmental, social, and governance (ESG) performance, these frameworks make sure that interested parties are given accurate and thorough information.

- **Global Reporting Initiative (GRI)**

One of the frameworks for reporting sustainability that is most frequently utilized is the Global Reporting Initiative (GRI). with order to assist firms with disclosing a wide range of ESG consequences, it offers comprehensive recommendations.

❖ **Key Features of GRI:**

1. Comprehensive Scope:
Governance, economic performance, environmental implications, labor standards, human rights, and social repercussions are just a few of the many subjects covered by GRI. This wide focus makes sure that every important facet of sustainability is covered.

2. Stakeholder Inclusiveness:
The necessity of including stakeholders in the reporting process is emphasized by GRI. In order to make sure that the report takes into account the aspirations and concerns of diverse groups, organizations are urged to recognize and take into account the interests of their stakeholders.

3. Materiality:
GRI's notion of materiality calls for concentrating on problems that most significantly affect the organization and its stakeholders. Issues that have the potential to significantly affect stakeholder evaluations and decisions are considered relevant.

4. Standardized Reporting:
GRI offers uniform reporting guidelines and disclosures, facilitating uniformity and comparison among various companies and sectors.

❖ **Benefits of GRI Compliance:**

1. Enhanced Transparency:
Adherence to GRI guidelines guarantees that the sustainability report is thorough and lucid, furnishing stakeholders with an unbiased and lucid image of the organization's ramifications.

2. Stakeholder Trust:
Providing thorough and open reporting fosters trust among all parties involved, including regulators, employees, consumers, and investors.

3. Comparability:
Reports that comply with GRI standards enable stakeholders to evaluate and benchmark performance by comparing it across industries and companies.

4. Reputation and Brand Value:
Adopting GRI standards shows a company's dedication to sustainability and ethical business practices, which improves the organization's reputation and brand value.

- **Carbon Disclosure Project (CDP)**

The Carbon Disclosure Project (CDP) is primarily concerned with the effects on the environment, especially those caused by climate change. It promotes the measurement, sharing, handling, and disclosure of important environmental data by organizations.

❖ Key Features of CDP:

1. Environmental Focus:
The three main environmental issues that CDP focuses on are deforestation, water security, and climate change. Reports from organizations detail their use of water, greenhouse gas emissions, and deforestation prevention techniques.

2. Scoring and Benchmarking:
A scoring system is employed by CDP to assess the quality and completeness of responses. Scores serve as a baseline for comparison and show the organization's environmental performance and advancement.

3. Investor and Market Influence:
Investors and market analysts frequently use CDP's data to help them make well-informed judgments. Corporate policy and investment strategies may be impacted by disclosure via CDP.

❖ Benefits of CDP Compliance:

1. Investor Confidence:
Investor trust is bolstered by CDP compliance, which shows proactive management of environmental risks and opportunities.

2. Risk Management:
Organizations can detect and control hazards related to deforestation, water scarcity, and climate change by disclosing environmental data through CDP.

3. Market Differentiation:
An organization can stand out in the market by demonstrating its leadership in environmental sustainability with high CDP scores.

4. Regulatory Preparedness:
By reducing the risk of non-compliance, CDP compliance helps firms get ready for both present and future environmental standards.

- **Sustainability Accounting Standards Board (SASB)**

Companies can report financially important sustainability information to investors with the use of industry-specific guidelines developed by the Sustainability Accounting guidelines Board (SASB).

❖ **Key Features of SASB:**

1. Industry-Specific Standards:
SASB guidelines are industry-specific, emphasizing sustainability issues that are most pertinent to each sector's financial success.

2. Materiality Focus:
The disclosure of material information that may affect an investor's decision-making and financial performance is emphasized by SASB.

3. Integration with Financial Reporting:
The integration of SASB standards with conventional financial reporting offers a more complete picture of an organization's performance.

❖ **Benefits of SASB Compliance:**

1. Investor Relevance:
Sustainability reports are more useful when revealed information is relevant to investors, thanks in part to SASB standards.

2. Financial Integration:
Organizations can combine financial data with sustainability information to get a comprehensive picture of performance by utilizing SASB's materiality-focused approach.

3. Strategic Insight:
Strategic decision-making is informed by SASB compliance, which assists firms in identifying and managing sustainability concerns that are vital to their financial success.

4. Enhanced Decision-Making:
Clear knowledge of the relationship between ESG elements and financial performance is made possible by comprehensive and reliable sustainability data, which facilitates better decision-making.

- **Integrating Multiple Frameworks**

Many businesses decide to combine different reporting formats in order to present a thorough picture of their sustainability performance. For instance, a company may use SASB for financially significant sustainability information, CDP for specific environmental disclosures, and GRI for wide sustainability reporting.

❖ **Advantages of Integrating Frameworks:**

1. Holistic Reporting:
By combining frameworks, businesses can handle a variety of sustainability concerns and have a comprehensive understanding of their effects.

2. Enhanced Credibility:
Sustainability reports can be made more credible and thorough by following several established standards.

3. Stakeholder Engagement:
The requirements and interests of diverse stakeholder groups are satisfied by employing several frameworks, even though different stakeholders may prioritize different aspects of sustainability.

4. Regulatory Compliance:
Organizations are guaranteed to comply with a wide range of legal mandates and stakeholder expectations thanks to many frameworks.

- **Challenges and Best Practices**

Challenges:

1. Resource Intensity:
It can take a lot of resources to comply with numerous frameworks; it takes time and effort to collect information, create reports, and guarantee correctness.

2. Complexity:
It can be challenging to navigate the requirements of many frameworks, especially for firms with little background in sustainability reporting.

Best Practices:

1. Stakeholder Engagement:
Make sure your reports cover the most pertinent topics by interacting with stakeholders to learn about their expectations and objectives.

2. Materiality Assessment:
To determine the most important sustainability concerns for your company and stakeholders, do frequent materiality assessments.

3. Data Management:
Put in place reliable data management mechanisms to guarantee the dependability and correctness of sustainability data.

4. Continuous Improvement:
Continuously enhance reporting procedures by using peer comparison and stakeholder input.

5. Third-Party Verification:
To increase credibility and confidence, think about having sustainability reports certified or verified by a third party.

6. Clear Communication:
Make sure sustainability reports are understandable to all stakeholders, free of jargon, and include graphics to help illustrate difficult data.

In conclusion, successful sustainability communication depends on adherence to reporting systems and standards like SASB, CDP, and GRI. These frameworks improve transparency, credibility, and comparability by offering organized methods for revealing impacts on the environment, society, and governance. Organizations can address the different needs of stakeholders and promote long-term value development by meeting their sustainability performance through the integration of multiple frameworks. Notwithstanding the difficulties, upholding these standards is a calculated investment that can have a big impact on reputation, trust, and competitive advantage.

11.3 Using Data for Continuous Improvement

Introduction to Using Data for Continuous Improvement

Continuous improvement is an essential ideology for companies committed to steadily improving their procedures, goods, or services over time. A factual foundation for decision-making, opportunity identification, progress measurement, and sustainable growth are all made possible by efficiently utilizing data in this environment, which fundamentally changes the way business's function. This methodology, which is commonly represented by Lean, Six Sigma, and the Plan-Do-Check-Act (PDCA) cycle, utilizes data to facilitate small-scale yet significant modifications, promoting a continuous improvement and innovation culture.

Meaning of Using Data for Continuous Improvement

If a company wants to enhance its services, products, and processes over time, using data for continuous improvement is essential. This strategy is based on the methodical gathering, processing, and use of data to support decision-making, spot areas for development, track advancement, and guarantee sustainable growth. Fundamentally, continuous improvement is about making modest, gradual improvements that add up to make big advances, informed by factual data instead of gut feeling or anecdotal evidence. Organizations may more quickly adapt to changes, better manage the complexity of today's marketplaces, and promote an innovative and high-achieving culture by integrating data into every aspect of their operations.

Making objective decisions is key to utilize data for continuous improvement. Data offers a solid foundation for comprehending present performance levels, establishing reasonable objectives, and projecting the results of prospective changes. This decreases biases that might influence decision-making and lessens reliance on subjective judgment. Organizations can increase the probability of success by ensuring that their strategies are in line with current needs and conditions by firmly establishing data as the foundation for their operations. Additionally, since the reasoning behind decisions is transparent and easily shared within the company, data-driven decisions encourage accountability and openness and support a cohesive approach to improvement initiatives.

Analysis and measurement are essential to this strategy. By setting up key performance indicators (KPIs), businesses can measure a range of operational elements, including productivity, quality, and customer happiness. These measurements offer a standard by which advancement can be evaluated. Regression analysis, statistical analysis, control charts, and other analytical tools and procedures aid in the interpretation of this data to find patterns, trends, and the underlying causes of problems. This in-depth knowledge is necessary to provide accurate diagnoses and come up with workable treatments. Moreover, sophisticated analytical techniques such as prescriptive and predictive analytics help firms anticipate future performance and suggest the best course of action, which improves strategic planning.

A feedback loop is a fundamental idea in data-driven continuous improvement. It entails keeping a close eye on the results of adjustments made to make sure the intended advancements are being made. This continuous gathering and processing of data makes it possible for methods to be modified and improved in response to real-time input. Planning, carrying out, assessing, and fine-tuning in an iterative cycle guarantees that improvements are sustained throughout time. Frequent monitoring facilitates the swift resolution of any deviations from anticipated results and sustains the impetus towards ongoing improvement.

Using data for continuous improvement not only increases operational quality and efficiency but also fosters an accountable and transparent culture. Open data sharing inside the company fosters a culture where everyone is aware of performance indicators, obstacles, and successes. Employee engagement and sense of responsibility are increased as a result of this shared awareness, which motivates them to actively participate in initiatives for change. Accurate performance data also encourages a dedication to excellence by holding people and groups responsible for their contributions.

This method has numerous industry applications in practice. To improve efficiency and lower defects, manufacturing companies evaluate data on production rates, defect rates, and equipment downtime to find bottlenecks and quality issues. In the medical field, readmission rates, patient satisfaction surveys, and patient outcomes all offer valuable information that helps providers improve patient care and produce better health outcomes and happier patients. Data on student performance and participation in the classroom are used to create focused interventions that raise academic attainment. Sales information, consumer preferences, and inventory levels are utilized in retail to improve customer happiness and sales success by customizing marketing campaigns and optimizing stock management.

To sum up, the process of utilizing data for continuous improvement involves integrating a methodical, data-oriented methodology into the core of organizational procedures. In addition to gathering and evaluating data, it also entails using the conclusions drawn from analysis to promote continuous development. This methodology guarantees well-informed, transparent, and accountable decision-making, resulting in long-term improvements in productivity, calibre, and overall effectiveness. In today's quickly changing business environment, firms may maintain their agility, innovation, and competitiveness by cultivating a culture of continuous improvement.

11.3.1 Leveraging HR Metrics to Drive Continuous Improvement in Sustainability Efforts

A thorough plan that unifies human resource procedures with sustainability activities is needed to leverage HR metrics to drive continuous improvement in sustainability efforts. This strategy makes sure that sustainability is woven throughout the entire firm, encouraging employee participation and a culture of continuous improvement.

❖ **Below is an expanded framework to guide this integration:**

1. Identify Key HR Metrics Relevant to Sustainability

Finding the important metrics that support your sustainability objectives is crucial if you want to use HR analytics to effectively promote sustainability. These metrics will track developments and identify areas that want improvement.

Recruitment and Retention:
Employee Turnover Rates: Excessive turnover can be expensive and inconvenient. Through engagement that is motivated by sustainability,

firms can lower attrition and increase employee happiness and loyalty. Sustainable practices frequently align with the personal beliefs of employees, resulting in a stronger sense of loyalty to the company.

On boarding and Training Costs: New hires who receive effective on boarding that incorporates sustainability training are better able to comprehend the organization's sustainability objectives right away. This guarantees that workers are prepared to contribute to sustainability projects from day one and lowers training expenditures over time.

Employee Engagement:

Employee Engagement Scores: The degree to which employees feel a connection to their work and the company's objective is indicated by engagement scores. Since engaged workers are more willing to go above and above in their roles, high engagement frequently equates with a strong commitment to sustainability.

Participation in Sustainability Programs: Monitoring the number of workers taking part in sustainability projects or programs can provide insight into the degree of support and zeal for these endeavours. A strong organizational sustainability culture may be indicated by high involvement rates.

Performance and Productivity:

Sustainability-related KPIs: Include particular sustainability goals in performance evaluations. Set goals to decrease waste, energy use, or support recycling programs, for instance. Monitoring these KPIs can encourage staff members to match their everyday actions with more general sustainability objectives.

Innovation Metrics: Count the number of projects and ideas linked to sustainability that staff members come up with and carry out. Promoting sustainability innovation can result in important advancements and fresh, effective methods that are advantageous to both the company and the environment.

Health and Well-being:

Absenteeism Rates: Reduced absenteeism rates may be a sign of a wholesome, encouraging, and long-lasting work environment.

Absenteeism can be directly impacted by initiatives like offering wellness programs and encouraging a good work-life balance.

Employee Health Metrics: Monitor involvement in wellness initiatives, which are frequently a component of the business's larger sustainability initiatives. Healthy workers are more engaged and productive, which helps the company achieve its overall sustainability goals.

2. Set Clear Sustainability Goals

Setting attainable sustainability targets that complement the broader business plan is essential for HR metrics to drive sustainability. These goals should be specific, measurable, achievable, relevant, and time-bound (SMART).

Carbon Footprint Reduction: Set goals to cut back on emissions of greenhouse gases. This could entail taking steps to increase energy efficiency, encourage the use of renewable energy sources, and lower emissions associated with travel.

Waste Reduction: Set objectives to cut the amount of waste the business produces. This could involve making efforts to use less paper, encourage recycling, and decrease packaging.

Energy Efficiency: Establish goals for enhancing workplace energy efficiency. This could entail encouraging staff members to adopt energy-saving practices, encouraging the adoption of energy-efficient office equipment, and updating to energy-efficient HVAC and lighting systems.

Social Impact: Set objectives to enhance social sustainability. This could entail programs that encourage diversity and inclusion, assist community development, and guarantee fair labour practices all the way through the supply chain.

3. Implement Sustainability-focused HR Practices

It is crucial to put sustainability-focused HR strategies into effect when goals have been established. By using these procedures, the organization's daily operations and culture are guaranteed to incorporate sustainability.

Training and Development: Include environmental awareness in your training courses. Inform staff members about the value of sustainability and their own role in it. Training on waste management strategies, sustainable procurement methods, and energy conservation measures may fall under this category.

Performance Management: Incorporate sustainability objectives into performance reviews of staff members. Acknowledge and honour eco-friendly behaviour. Employees that successfully cut waste or use less energy in their departments, for instance, could receive bonuses or praise from the public.

Employee Involvement: Provide your staff with avenues for participation in environmental projects, including as volunteer programs, green teams, and suggestion boxes. Increasing employee involvement has the potential to boost creativity and fortify adherence to sustainable objectives.

4. Collect and Analyse Data

To monitor development and pinpoint areas for improvement, it is essential to routinely gather and evaluate data on designated HR indicators. Refining sustainability initiatives and making well-informed judgments are aided by data analysis.

Data Collection: To collect information on training participation, employee turnover, engagement, and other pertinent metrics, use HR information systems (HRIS). Make that the procedures used to collect data are reliable and accurate.

Trend Analysis: Analyse trends across time to comprehend the effects of sustainability programs. Examine how staff engagement levels have changed, for instance, before and after a new sustainability program is put into place.

Benchmarking: Compare your sustainability indicators to best practices and industry standards. By doing so, you may determine which sectors your company is leading or trailing in and modify your strategy accordingly.

5. Report and Communicate Progress

Sustaining momentum and involving stakeholders requires effective progress communication.

Internal Reporting: Regularly update staff members on sustainability objective progress. Meetings, dashboards, and mailings can all be used for this. Open communication fosters trust and informs staff members of how their work fits into the larger picture of sustainability objectives.

External Reporting: Share sustainability reports and corporate social responsibility (CSR) reports with stakeholders to highlight accomplishments in sustainability. Emphasizing accomplishments and continuous endeavours can improve the company's standing and draw in partners and investors who share those goals.

6. Continuous Improvement

The foundation of successful sustainability initiatives is continuous improvement. Provide systems for continuing to assess and improve sustainability practices.

Feedback Loops: Provide feedback channels so that staff members can offer ways to make sustainability projects better. Promote open communication and aggressively solicit opinions from staff members across the board.

Iterative Processes: Make constant improvements to sustainability objectives and HR procedures based on gathered feedback and data. As new opportunities and difficulties present themselves, modify your approach to meet them.

Kaizen Approach: Embrace the Kaizen method, which places an emphasis on little, gradual adjustments that result in ongoing development. Encourage staff members to find small changes that, when taken together, can make a big impact on sustainability.

7. Foster a Sustainable Culture

Long-term success requires fostering a culture that recognizes and supports sustainability. This entails incorporating sustainability into daily operations and the company ethos.

Leadership Commitment: Make certain that the leadership has a clear commitment to sustainability. Leaders' ought to actively promote sustainability projects and provide an example for others to follow. Their dedication may serve as an example for staff members who wish to incorporate sustainability into their own job.

Recognition Programs: Honour and commend workers and groups that make major contributions to sustainability initiatives. Awards, incentives, and public recognition can encourage staff members to adopt sustainable practices.

Inclusive Environment: Encourage an inclusive workplace environment where all employees feel empowered and accountable to contribute to sustainability. Promote variety of opinion and cultivate an atmosphere where staff members feel appreciated for their contributions to sustainability.

Finally, leveraging HR metrics, organizations can drive continuous improvement in their sustainability efforts is how it is done methodically. This strategy raises organizational effectiveness and total employee involvement in addition to improving sustainability performance. When sustainability is included into HR procedures, workers are more engaged and productive because they are in line with the organization's sustainability objectives. In the end, this all-encompassing strategy promotes an innovative and continuous improvement culture within firms while assisting them in meeting their sustainability goals.

11.3.2 Analysing Data to Identify Areas for Efficiency Gains and Resource Optimization

The complex process of analysing data to identify areas for efficiency gains and resource optimization necessitates a thorough comprehension of the operational context in which the data is used as well as the data that is readily available. Organizations can find chances for major improvements that boost productivity, cut waste, and optimize resource utilization by methodically gathering, processing, and analysing data. This all-encompassing strategy aids in guaranteeing that every facet of the company is functioning to the fullest extent possible.

❖ **Here is a detailed framework to guide this analysis:**

1. Define Objectives and Scope

Objectives:
Clearly state your objectives for using data analysis. Actionable goals should be set, such as cutting operational expenses by 15%, increasing

production efficiency by 20%, eliminating waste by 10%, or using resources optimally to cut down on idle time by 25%. Well-defined goals serve as a focus for the investigation and offer quantifiable benchmarks for monitoring advancement.

Scope:
By selecting the precise departments, procedures, or systems that will be examined, the scope of the analysis may be determined. This could apply to certain departmental workflows or the whole operations of the company. It is ensured that the analysis is manageable and pertinent to the main areas of interest by clearly defining the scope.

2. Collect Relevant Data
Collect data from different organizational sources. Make sure the information gathered is precise, pertinent, and thorough in order to offer a strong basis for analysis.

Types of Data:
Operational Data: Contains data on supply chain KPIs, inventory levels, machine use, downtime, and production rates. This information aids in locating inefficiencies in the manufacturing process as well as potential over- or underuse of resources.

Financial Data: Includes the price of supplies, labour, energy, and other running costs. To determine cost-saving options and evaluate the financial effects of inefficiencies, financial data is essential.

HR Data: Includes information on employee productivity, absenteeism, attrition rates, and training efficacy. HR data sheds light on the human elements that influence productivity and resource use.

Environmental Data: Includes data on emissions, water use, trash production, and energy consumption. To find ways to improve sustainability and lessen the environmental impact of operations, environmental data is crucial.

Data Sources:
Internal Systems: To gather data, use financial management systems, HR Information Systems (HRIS), Manufacturing Execution Systems (MES),

and Enterprise Resource Planning (ERP) systems. These systems offer a thorough understanding of how organizations operate and use their resources.

External Sources: To offer context and comparative insights, incorporate supplier performance data, market trends, and industry standards. Best practices and areas where the company can outperform its rivals are identified with the aid of external data.

3. Data Cleaning and Preparation

Make sure the data is clean and ready for analysis before proceeding. In order to guarantee correct insights and prevent misleading outcomes, this step is essential.

Data Cleaning:

Remove Duplicates: Remove duplicate entries to avoid biased outcomes.

Correct Errors: Find any errors or discrepancies in the data and fix them.

Handle Missing Data: To preserve data integrity, treat missing data appropriately. You can do this by discarding incomplete records or imputing values based on available data.

Data Preparation:

Aggregate Data: When required, combine data to give a clearer picture of trends and patterns (e.g., monthly totals).

Normalize Data: To compare various metrics on a comparable scale and facilitate the identification of correlations and trends, normalize your data.

Segment Data: Divide data into appropriate categories, such as departments, time periods, or product lines, to offer in-depth research and make targeted analysis easier.

4. Conduct Data Analysis

Make use of a range of analytical methods to find trends, connections, and opportunities for development. The type of data and the particular goals of the research will determine which analytical techniques are used.

Descriptive Analytics:

Trend Analysis: Analyse past data to find patterns and trends. Track manufacturing output over time, for instance, to identify long-term growth trends or seasonal changes. Analysing trends makes it easier to spot recurring patterns and comprehend how operational performance has changed over time.

Benchmarking: To determine whether the company is leading or trailing the industry, compare internal KPIs with benchmarks from the sector. Benchmarking indicates areas that could use improvement and offers a relative assessment of performance.

Diagnostic Analytics:

Root Cause Analysis: Examine the root causes of any inefficiencies that you find. For example, examine machine maintenance logs, operator performance, and process workflows to identify particular problems if production downtime is excessive. By addressing issues at their root rather than just treating their symptoms, root cause analysis can help.

Variance Analysis: Analyze performance variations from the intended ranges. Determine why actual performance differs from projected or budgeted results, and investigate the variables that may be causing these differences. Variance analysis aids in the development of strategies to close performance disparities and an understanding of their causes.

Predictive Analytics:

Forecasting: To forecast future trends, use data from the past. For example, to optimize inventory levels, anticipate future demand using historical sales data. Planning for changes in advance is made easier with the aid of forecasting.

Regression Analysis: Determine the connections between the variables. For example, ascertain the effects of labour level changes on production output. Regression analysis is a useful tool for identifying the main efficiency drivers and quantifying the effects of various factors on performance.

Prescriptive Analytics:

Optimization Models: Create models to determine the optimal path of action. For instance, to optimize resource allocation and production schedules, apply linear programming. Models of optimization aid in determining the most effective means of achieving goals.

Scenario Analysis: Examine several situations in order to determine possible results. Examine how introducing new technology affects production efficiency, for instance. Using scenario analysis, one can determine the optimal course of action by comprehending the possible outcomes of various choices.

5. Identify Areas for Improvement

Determine the precise areas where resource optimization and efficiency benefits can be realized based on the analysis. This stage entails converting analytical findings into practical suggestions.

Operational Efficiency:

Process Bottlenecks: Locate and remove production process bottlenecks. Reduce waste and streamline processes by putting lean manufacturing principles into practice. Value stream mapping, for instance, can be used to find and remove non-value-added tasks.

Resource Utilization: Maximize the efficiency of labour, materials, and machinery. Make sure that resources are distributed wisely in order to fulfil production requirements. Predictive maintenance, for example, can be used to increase utilization rates and decrease equipment downtime.

Financial Efficiency:

Cost Reduction: Determine high-cost areas and put cost-cutting strategies in place. This can entail renegotiating contracts with suppliers, cutting back on energy use, or enhancing the procurement procedure. For instance, buy materials in bulk to cut costs or make an investment in energy-efficient machinery to save electricity expenditures.

Budget Allocation: Allocate funds as efficiently as possible by analysing the cost-benefit ratios of different initiatives and projects. Make ensuring that funds are allocated to high-impact projects with the best potential returns on investment.

Workforce Efficiency:

Training Programs: Determine areas of weakness in skills and put in place focused training courses to increase worker output. Offer instruction on novel technology or procedures that improve productivity, for instance.

Employee Engagement: Improve engagement and lower attrition by addressing the causes of discontent among employees. Implement programs for employee appreciation, career growth possibilities, and flexible work schedules.

Environmental Efficiency:

Energy Management: Adopt energy-saving measures in accordance with consumption trends. This can entail replacing outdated equipment with more energy-efficient models, improving HVAC systems, or promoting energy-saving practices among staff members. Installing motion-sensor lighting is one way to cut down on energy consumption.

Waste Reduction: Determine the sources of trash and put recycling or waste minimization plans into action. Examine waste streams to identify areas that can be reduced or reused. For example, start a zero-waste program to enhance resource efficiency and lower landfill contributions.

6. Implement Recommendations

Create a thorough action plan to put the recommended changes into practice. Timelines, accountable parties, explicit activities, and performance measures should all be included in this strategy.

Action Plan:

Define Actions: Give a clear description of the actions needed to make the improvements. Make sure the actions are realistic and doable. For instance, list the procedures for replacing equipment, introducing fresh procedures, or educating employees.

Assign Responsibilities: Assign tasks to particular people or groups of people. Make sure that tasks are owned and accountable for. Assign a project manager, for example, to supervise the adoption of a new procedure or technology.

Set Timelines: Set reasonable timelines for putting changes into effect. Think about any resource limitations or dependencies. Establish benchmarks, for instance, for finishing the purchase, installation, and training phases of a project.

Monitor Progress: Assess progress against the action plan on a regular basis. Key performance indicators (KPIs) can be used to gauge progress and make necessary corrections. Monitor the decrease in energy usage, enhancements in manufacturing effectiveness, or realized cost savings, for instance.

7. Continuous Monitoring and Improvement

Provide a mechanism for continuing monitoring and improvement. Review performance data on a regular basis to make sure that gains are maintained and new opportunities are found.

Monitoring System:

Dashboards: Use dashboards that update in real time to track important indicators. Ascertain that pertinent data is accessible to stakeholders. For instance, use a dashboard to monitor energy usage, cost savings, and manufacturing efficiency in real time.

Regular Reviews: Conduct performance assessments on a regular basis to evaluate advancement and deal with any new problems. Have quarterly review meetings, for instance, to talk about performance, find new areas for growth, and make any necessary adjustments to strategy.

Feedback Mechanisms: Invite employees and other stakeholders to provide comments. Utilize these suggestions to make incremental changes. Establish a recommendation system, for instance, whereby staff members can provide suggestions for enhancing productivity and optimizing resources.

In conclusion, a crucial step for every business looking to improve performance and sustainability is data analysis to pinpoint areas for resource optimization and efficiency benefits. Through methodical data collection, analysis, and action, businesses can gain insightful knowledge and apply focused enhancements that lead to sustained performance. This strategy not only improves operational effectiveness but also advances goals related to workforce, finances, and environmental sustainability.

Organizations may better understand their operations, make well-informed decisions, and foster a continuous improvement culture with the aid of a strong data analytic framework. Consequently, this results in enhanced resource allocation, decreased expenses, increased output, and a more robust market position. The capacity to efficiently analyse data and allocate resources will continue to be essential for success and sustainability as organizations grow and encounter new difficulties.

11.3.3 Integrating Sustainability Metrics into HR Dashboards and Performance Management Systems

The complete strategy of integrating sustainability metrics into HR dashboards and performance management systems links individual and team performance with company sustainability goals. Encouraging a culture of sustainability, promoting continual improvement, and guaranteeing that every employee is involved and responsible for the company's sustainability initiatives all depend on this integration.

❖ **Here's a detailed guide on how to effectively achieve this integration:**

1. Identify Relevant Sustainability Metrics

Finding the indicators that are most pertinent to the organization's sustainability objectives is the first step in incorporating sustainability measures into HR systems. These measurements must to be quantifiable, significant, and in line with the strategic goals of the business.

Environmental Metrics:

Carbon Footprint: To comprehend the organization's environmental impact and find areas for reduction, measure and monitor its greenhouse gas emissions.

Energy Consumption: Track the amount of energy used in each facility to discover high-energy consumption regions and encourage energy savings.

Water Usage: Monitor water usage to find areas for conservation and to advance environmentally friendly water management techniques.

Waste Management: Calculate the quantity of waste produced and the percentage that is recycled or kept out of the landfill.

Social Metrics:

Employee Health and Well-being: To encourage a healthy workforce, keep an eye on employee health outcomes generally, absenteeism rates, and participation in health and wellness programs.

Community Engagement: To gauge the organization's social contributions, keep track of staff volunteer hours and involvement in community impact projects.

Diversity and Inclusion: To maintain an inclusive workplace, measure employee satisfaction with regard to diversity efforts, monitor inclusion programs, and keep track of workforce diversity.

Economic Metrics:

Sustainable Procurement: Measure the effect of sustainable procurement procedures by keeping track of the proportion of suppliers that satisfy sustainability requirements.

Cost Savings from Sustainability Initiatives: Track the monetary gains attained by sustainability initiatives, such as lower energy and trash disposal expenditures.

2. Integrate Metrics into HR Dashboards

Key performance indicators (KPIs) can be seen and tracked in real-time with the use of HR dashboards. The incorporation of sustainability KPIs into dashboards guarantees ongoing oversight and administration of sustainability initiatives.

Steps to Integration:

Select a User-Friendly Dashboard Platform: Select a platform for your HR dashboard that allows for customisation and multi-source data integration. Make sure it is understandable and available to all pertinent parties.

Data Collection and Integration: Establish reliable procedures for collecting data in order to obtain consistent and reliable sustainability information. Gather data from different operational areas using sensors, IoT devices, and manual reporting systems.

Customize the Dashboard: Create specialized dashboard sections or widgets for sustainability metrics. Utilize visual aids like heat maps, graphs, and charts to show performance and trends in relation to sustainability objectives.

Real-Time Data Updates: Create real-time data feeds so that the dashboard always shows the most recent information. This makes it possible to act quickly and make decisions based on current facts.

3. Embed Sustainability into Performance Management Systems

Setting goals and evaluating employee performance with sustainability in mind is ensured by integrating sustainability into performance management systems.

Goal Setting and Alignment:

Define Clear Objectives: Include particular sustainability targets in your individual and group performance objectives. Achieving a recycling rate objective or cutting departmental energy use by a specific percentage are two examples.

Align with Organizational Goals: Make sure that each person's sustainability objectives are in line with the organization's overall sustainability goals. This establishes a coherent plan and guarantees that every endeavour advances shared goals.

Performance Appraisals:

Incorporate Sustainability Metrics: When evaluating employees, make sustainability performance a primary consideration. Assess staff members according to how well they accomplish sustainability objectives, follow sustainable practices, and contribute to sustainability campaigns.

Feedback and Development: During performance reviews, give constructive criticism on sustainability performance. Determine areas that require improvement and provide chances for training and development to increase knowledge and skills linked to sustainability.

Recognition and Rewards:

Reward Sustainable Practices: Employees that thrive in sustainability projects should be acknowledged and rewarded. Bonuses, honours, public recognition, and other incentives can be used to achieve this.

Encourage Participation: Create incentive schemes to promote broad involvement in environmental initiatives. Reward departments that, for instance, achieve the highest recycling rates or the largest energy savings.

4. Training and Development
The effective integration of sustainability metrics into HR systems depends on raising awareness and educating people. Constant training and development make that staff members are aware of the value of sustainability and know how to make a meaningful contribution.

Training Programs:
Sustainability Workshops: Organise seminars on sustainability issues that are pertinent to your sector. Among other things, topics like sustainable procurement, waste reduction, and energy efficiency might be covered.

E-Learning Modules: Create online training courses that staff members can finish whenever it suits them. The company's sustainability objectives, measurements, and individual obligations should all be covered in these courses.

Leadership Training: Give managers and executives specific training so they can understand how to promote sustainability initiatives and inspire their staff to meet sustainability targets.

Continuous Learning:
Stay Updated: Keep employees up to date on the newest developments in sustainable technology, trends, and practices. To distribute information, make use of internal messaging, webinars, and newsletters.

Knowledge Sharing: Promote departmental cooperation and knowledge exchange. Establish discussion boards or other online spaces where employees may exchange sustainable best practices and ideas.

5. Continuous Monitoring and Reporting
To ensure continuous improvement, make data-driven decisions, and measure progress, sustainability metrics must be regularly monitored and reported.

Monitoring Systems:
Automated Data Collection: Install mechanisms to collect and analyse sustainability data automatically. Accuracy is ensured and less manual labour is needed.

Regular Reviews: Plan on regularly reviewing each person's, team's, and organization's sustainability performance. Examine these reviews to determine your accomplishments, obstacles, and room for development.

Reporting:
Internal Reporting: Reports on sustainability performance should be routinely distributed to staff. All parties are kept informed and involved by this transparency.

External Reporting: Release sustainability reports to update external stakeholders' investors, clients, and the community on your progress. Highlight successes and list aspirations for the future.

6. Foster a Sustainable Culture
Long-term success requires fostering a culture that recognizes and supports sustainability. This entails incorporating sustainability into daily operations and the company ethos.

Leadership Commitment:
Lead by Example: Make certain that the leadership has a clear commitment to sustainability. Leaders' ought to actively promote sustainability projects and provide an example for others to follow.

Communicate Vision: Make sure that every employee understands the organization's sustainability vision and goals. Make sure that everyone is aware of the ways in which their roles advance these objectives.

Employee Engagement:
Involve Employees: Provide your employees with avenues for participation in environmental projects, including as volunteer programs, green teams, and suggestion boxes. Promote involvement and creativity.

Celebrate Successes: Celebrate major victories and accomplishments in sustainability. Tell success stories and provide recognition to people and groups who make substantial contributions to sustainability initiatives.

To sum up, the strategic strategy of integrating sustainability metrics into HR dashboards and performance management systems effectively integrates sustainability into the fundamental operations of organizations. By doing this, businesses may guarantee alignment with more general sustainability goals, promote employee involvement, and drive continuous improvement. This integration aids in the development of a sustainable organizational culture in which each worker is aware of how they contribute to the organization's social, economic, and environmental goals. In the end, this comprehensive strategy promotes the organization's resilience and general growth in addition to driving sustainability performance.

Chapter – 12

Green Technology and HR Practices

Introduction to Green Technology

Green technology, also known as environmental technology or clean technology, is a wide range of procedures, approaches, and inventions meant to lessen the negative effects of human activity on the environment. Green technology is a response to pressing environmental problems such resource depletion, pollution, climate change, and biodiversity loss. Its goal is to develop long-term, economically feasible, and socially responsible solutions. The field encompasses a wide range of industries, including waste management, construction, energy, and agriculture.

Meaning of Green Technology

The term "green technology" describes the use of scientific and technical advancements meant to reduce the adverse effects of human activity on the environment and natural resources. The pressing need to mitigate climate change, cut pollution, and preserve natural resources for coming generations is what is driving the development of green technology. In addition to being crucial for protecting the environment, innovations in this area also assist the economy by lowering operating costs and generating green jobs.

❖ **Green technology is characterized by several core principles and goals, which include:**

Sustainable Development: Fundamentally, green technology encourages sustainable development that satisfies current needs without jeopardizing the capacity of future generations to satiate their own. To ensure long-term sustainability, this entails developing technologies and procedures that strike a balance between social, economic, and environmental issues.

Resource Efficiency: The focus of green technology is on using natural resources as efficiently as possible to cut down on waste and the ecological footprint. Reusing and recycling materials, conserving water, and improving energy efficiency are all essential to achieving this aim. Energy-efficient appliances, water-saving gadgets, and circular economy models which reuse resources and goods continuously are examples of these technologies.

Pollution Reduction: Reducing pollution and dangerous material emissions into the environment is a key goal of green technology. This includes developments in pollution control technologies, waste management strategies, eco-friendly industrial processes that reduce environmental contamination, and clean energy production.

Renewable Energy: The development and use of renewable energy sources, such as solar, wind, hydro, and geothermal power, is one of the most important fields of green technology. In addition to offering fossil fuel substitutes that are sustainable, these renewable energy sources are essential for lowering greenhouse gas emissions and halting climate change.

Technological Innovation: Green technology encourages the advancement of both new and current technologies to improve their performance in the environment. This includes enhanced recycling techniques that maximize resource recovery and decrease waste, electric vehicles (EVs) for lowering transportation-related emissions, green construction materials for increased energy efficiency, and smart grid technologies for effective energy distribution.

Introduction to HR Practices

Organizations utilize a wide range of tactics, guidelines, and procedures known as human resource (HR) practices to efficiently manage their personnel. These procedures are necessary to guarantee organizational effectiveness, draw in and nurture exceptional personnel, and accomplish strategic objectives.

❖ Key components of HR practices include:

Recruitment and Selection: One of the main responsibilities of HR is to locate and recruit competent applicants to fill open positions. To hire the best candidates for the company, this includes posting job openings, conducting interviews, administering tests, and going through a selection process.

Training and Development: It's essential to give workers the abilities and information they need to do their jobs well and develop in their professions. This covers leadership development programs, workshops, seminars, continuing education courses, and on-the-job training.

Performance Management: Another crucial HR responsibility is controlling and assessing employee performance to make sure it aligns with company objectives. This entails establishing performance benchmarks, carrying out frequent evaluations, offering constructive criticism, and carrying out plans for performance enhancement.

Compensation and Benefits: The core of HR management is creating and implementing benefit plans and compensation structures to draw in and keep workers. Payroll, bonuses, health insurance, retirement plans, paid time off, and other benefits are all included in this.

Employee Relations: Developing a good working rapport between the organization and its personnel is essential. To ensure employee happiness and engagement, concerns must be addressed, efficient communication must be facilitated, and a positive work environment must be promoted.

Compliance and Legal Issues: An essential HR duty is making sure the company complies with labour laws and regulations. This entails monitoring employee contracts, avoiding discrimination, preserving workplace safety, and managing employment-related legal matters.

Meaning of Green HR Practices

In order to foster sustainability inside the company, green HR practices, also known as sustainable human resource management, incorporate environmental management concepts into conventional HR procedures. These procedures are meant to promote ecologically conscious behaviour among staff members and assist the company's more extensive sustainability plans.

- ❖ **Key aspects of green HR practices include:**

Green Recruitment: A crucial component of green HR practices is hiring people who have the skills required for green jobs and are ecologically concerned. This entails highlighting sustainability in interview questions, job descriptions, and selection standards in order to draw in applicants who are devoted to environmental care.

Green Training and Development: It is essential to provide training courses that emphasize environmental stewardship. These courses may cover subjects including using green technologies, cutting waste, conserving energy, and adopting sustainable work practices. Through employee education on these subjects, companies may cultivate a sustainable culture and guarantee that staff members are equipped with the necessary knowledge to successfully use green practices.

Green Performance Management: Another crucial component of green HR practices is rewarding staff for eco-friendly actions and contributions to sustainability objectives, as well as incorporating environmental standards into performance reviews. This could entail establishing precise goals for environmental performance and rewarding staff members who meet or surpass them.

Green Workplace Initiatives: A key component of green HR is putting policies and procedures into place that lessen the organization's environmental effect. In order to lessen carbon footprints, this involves supporting telecommuting and remote work, adopting energy-efficient technology, boosting recycling initiatives in the office, and lowering paper usage by encouraging digital documentation.

Employee Involvement: Encouraging a sustainable culture and getting workers involved in environmental activities are essential to the success of green HR practices. This can entail setting up environmental awareness campaigns, creating green teams or committees, and motivating staff members to take part in sustainability initiatives both inside and outside the company.

Connection between Green Technology and HR Practices

Organizational sustainability can be improved through a potent synergy that arises from the integration of green technologies with HR practices. The integration of sustainable practices and environmentally friendly technologies into human resource management is the link between green technology and HR practices. This entails fostering a sustainable culture, putting green policies into place, and motivating staff members to act sustainably. Through initiatives like green training programs, hiring for sustainability jobs, and incorporating environmental goals into performance reviews and company policy, HR practices can assist green technology. Organizations benefit from this alignment by lowering their carbon footprint, enhancing CSR, and improving their overall environmental effect.

❖ **Here are several ways in which this integration can be beneficial:**

Enhanced Employee Engagement: Workers that participate in green projects frequently have higher levels of fulfilment and purpose in their work. Through the incorporation of green technology into HR procedures, companies may increase employee dedication and satisfaction. When workers perceive that their company is making significant progress toward sustainability, they are more likely to be engaged and driven.

Improved Organizational Reputation: Businesses may strengthen their reputation as forward-thinking and environmentally conscious by implementing green HR and technology strategies. Top talent wishing to work for companies that share their beliefs may be drawn to this favourable image. Additionally, it can strengthen ties with stakeholders that value sustainability, including as investors, customers, and other stakeholders.

Cost Savings: Because they use less energy, produce less waste, and maximize resource efficiency, green technologies frequently result in cost savings. Green HR procedures can help these technologies by teaching staff members how to use them efficiently and promoting actions that will optimize their advantages. Effective recycling programs, for instance, can cut trash disposal expenses, while energy-efficient HVAC and lighting systems can slash electricity bills.

Compliance and Risk Management: Integrating green technologies and HR procedures can help organizations stay compliant and lower their risk of legal problems as environmental requirements get stricter. By ensuring that staff members are informed about and follow environmental regulations and standards, green HR practices can assist the company avoid the fines and penalties that come with non-compliance.

Innovation and Competitive Advantage: Organizations that use green technologies and HR procedures are frequently regarded as leaders in their industry. By setting them apart from rivals and attracting clients and customers who care about the environment, this can give them a competitive advantage. Green technology innovation can result in the creation of new goods and services that cater to the expanding market for environmentally friendly options.

Cultural Shift: Embracing sustainable practices into HR procedures and green technologies can help an organization's culture change. In order to achieve long-term behavioural and attitude changes, this entails integrating environmental values into the organizational culture. Employee adoption of green practices at work and in their personal lives is more likely when sustainability is ingrained in the company culture.

Long-term Sustainability: Organizations can assure long-term sustainability by fusing efficient HR procedures with green technologies. This all-encompassing strategy tackles environmental stewardship from both a technical and human perspective, strengthening the organization's resilience and enabling it to meet emerging environmental concerns.

In conclusion, green technology and HR practices are complimentary approaches that, when combined, can greatly improve an organization's sustainability initiatives. Organizations can gain significant environmental benefits, increase operational efficiency, and cultivate an engaging and motivating sustainable culture by integrating technical breakthroughs with human resource initiatives. This comprehensive strategy positions the company as a leader in the shift to a more sustainable future by promoting the long-term prosperity and resilience of the enterprise while simultaneously improving the health of the planet.

12.1 Adopting Sustainable Technologies in HR Operations

Adopting sustainable technologies in HR operations is the process of incorporating eco-friendly solutions into many facets of HRM in order to lessen the influence on the environment and encourage sustainability in businesses. The goal of this strategic alignment is to improve overall environmental sustainability, reduce waste production, and maximize resource efficiency by integrating green technologies, practices, and principles into HR procedures.

❖ **Here's an extensive exploration of how organizations can incorporate sustainable technologies into HR operations:**

Digitalization of Processes: Beyond just helping the environment, switching from paper-based to digital HR procedures has several advantages. Implementing electronic document management solutions, digital recruitment platforms, and online training modules improves HR operations while lowering paper usage, printing expenses, and waste generation. Organizations reduce environmental impact, improve accessibility, strengthen data security, and maximize workflow efficiency by digitizing administrative operations like payroll processing, performance reviews, and personnel record-keeping.

Telecommuting and Remote Work Tools: Adopting telecommuting and remote work technologies has several benefits for both people and enterprises, not to mention lowering carbon emissions related to transportation. Employees can work remotely thanks to cloud-based HR management systems, video conferencing, and collaboration tools, which minimizes the demand for physical office space and the carbon footprint of the company. In addition, working remotely fosters a work-life balance, lowers employee stress levels, boosts productivity by saving time and energy on commutes, and strengthens workers' resilience to unforeseen events like pandemics and natural disasters.

Energy-Efficient Office Design: Optimizing energy consumption and mitigating environmental effect in office buildings requires the integration of sustainable design principles and energy-efficient technologies. Energy consumption can be reduced by installing occupancy sensors, smart HVAC systems, and LED lighting. Green building standards and eco-friendly materials can improve interior air quality and foster employee well-being. The need for artificial lighting and heating is further decreased when office layouts that optimize natural light and ventilation are designed, which helps save energy and promotes environmental sustainability while fostering a positive work environment.

Green Procurement Practices: Using eco-friendly goods and services for a range of HR projects is part of implementing green procurement practices in HR operations. This entails choosing locations for events and training sessions that follow sustainable methods, collaborating with suppliers who place a high priority on sustainability, and obtaining eco-friendly office supplies. Organizations may lessen their carbon footprint and promote sustainable business practices all the way through the supply chain by selecting suppliers with open and ecologically conscious supply chains. This helps to create a more sustainable economy.

Eco-Friendly Employee Benefits: Providing eco-friendly employee benefits is a good method to encourage eco-friendly behaviour and encourage employees to work toward sustainability. A more environmentally conscious workplace culture can be created by offering rewards for using the bus, bike, or carpooling to work, giving financial assistance for buying eco-friendly goods, or introducing flexible work hours to cut down on commuting. Furthermore, providing wellness benefits like fitness canters, wellness plans, and mindfulness courses not only enhances employee wellbeing but also supports sustainable, healthy lifestyles that complement company sustainability objectives.

Sustainable Talent Management Solutions: Utilizing sustainable talent management solutions minimizes the impact on the environment while optimizing HR processes. Cloud-based HR software eliminates the need for physical infrastructure. AI-driven recruitment tools improve candidate matching and streamline hiring procedures, resulting in lower resource consumption and carbon emissions. Organizations can maximize talent acquisition, development, and retention strategies while minimizing the impact on the environment and promoting sustainability.

Environmental Education and Training: Employee understanding of sustainability concerns is increased, and they are given the tools to adopt eco-friendly behaviours in their personal and professional life when environmental education and training programs are integrated into HR operations. Providing staff with sustainability certifications, webinars, and workshops gives them the information and abilities they need to make decisions that are less harmful to the environment. Organizations may cultivate a culture of environmental responsibility and enable their workforce to become advocates for sustainability both inside and beyond the workplace by offering chances for continuous learning and development on sustainability-related subjects.

Green Employee Engagement Initiatives: An organizational culture of environmental responsibility is promoted through including employees in sustainability and green activities. Establishing employee-led sustainability committees, planning volunteer opportunities cantered around environmental preservation, and praising and rewarding eco-friendly conduct all serve to stimulate involvement and foster a sense of shared accountability for sustainability. Organizations may leverage the potential of their workforce to achieve good environmental change and contribute to a more sustainable future by integrating employees in decision-making processes and fostering collaboration and creativity.

Organizations can lessen their environmental impact while simultaneously increasing operational effectiveness, boosting employee satisfaction, and solidifying their standing as environmentally conscious employers by implementing sustainable technologies in HR operations. Incorporating sustainability into HR procedures benefits the environment as well as the organization's long-term viability and adaptability in a world where environmental consciousness is growing.

12.1.1 Overview of Sustainable Technologies Applicable to HR Functions

The HR department is undergoing a transformation thanks to sustainable technology, which provide a wide range of creative solutions that balance environmental responsibility with operational efficiency. These solutions cover a wide range of HRM functions, including hiring and choosing employees as well as performance management, training and growth, pay and benefits, employee relations, compliance, and engagement. Organizations may increase productivity, cut waste, and foster a sustainable culture among all members of their workforce by incorporating sustainable technologies into each of these categories.

Green recruiting portals have become indispensable resources in the recruitment and selection process, serving as a bridge between companies that prioritize sustainability and applicants that care about the environment. These platforms match candidates with companies that share their environmental values through the use of sophisticated algorithms, making it easier to hire people who place a high priority on environmental stewardship. Additionally, by automating the processes of candidate screening, assessment, and selection, AI-driven hiring solutions optimize resource usage and reduce the environmental effect of traditional hiring techniques.

The integration of sustainable technologies is bringing about a dramatic revolution in training and development, especially with the implementation of online learning management systems (LMS). These cloud-based systems eliminate the need for physical infrastructure and lower travel-related carbon emissions by offering a single hub for the delivery of instructional materials and training programs. Furthermore, whereas traditional training methods have a greater environmental impact, virtual reality (VR) training simulations minimize that impact and provide immersive learning experiences. Organizations can minimize their carbon footprint and foster ongoing skill development by adopting digital learning solutions.

The use of sustainable technology is revolutionizing performance management, especially with the introduction of digital performance management systems. These systems streamline administrative chores and lessen the need for paper-based documentation by automating goal monitoring, performance evaluations, and feedback procedures. By facilitating continual communication between managers and employees, encouraging accountability, and encouraging a culture of continuous improvement, real-time feedback apps further improve performance management. Organizations may increase employee engagement, cut waste, and maximize efficiency by implementing digital performance management solutions.

The incorporation of sustainable technologies is leading to a shift in compensation and benefits towards environmentally sustainable behaviours. Payroll processing is streamlined by electronic payroll systems, which also cut down on paper use and administrative burden. Furthermore, companies are providing environmentally conscious staff benefits including wellness initiatives emphasizing sustainability and wellbeing, incentives for cycling or carpooling, and subsidies for public transit. Organizations that implement these strategies improve employee satisfaction and well-being in addition to encouraging ecologically sustainable behaviour.

Digital communication tools, which make it easier for employees to collaborate, participate, and share knowledge, are improving employee relations. These systems provide consolidated channels for communication, eliminating the need for emails, documents, and memoranda printed on paper. Moreover, virtual employee assistance programs (EAPs) save carbon emissions related to travel by offering mental health support and counselling services in a digital format, eliminating the need for in-person sessions. Organizations may encourage work-life balance, build a feeling of community, and lessen their environmental footprint by embracing digital communication technologies.

Sustainable technologies are essential for automating regulatory compliance procedures and reducing environmental impact in compliance and legal matters. Organizations may track and manage regulatory obligations with eco-friendly compliance software, which eliminates the need for human data entry and paper-based documentation. Furthermore, employees can receive training content through digital platforms through remote compliance training programs, which minimizes carbon emissions and travel requirements. Organizations can minimize their environmental impact while maintaining regulatory compliance by incorporating sustainable technologies into their compliance operations.

Adoption of sustainable technology fosters high levels of employee engagement, especially when it comes to digital recognition systems and virtual team-building exercises. These platforms facilitate the cultivation of a feeling of appreciation, camaraderie, and belonging among employees, irrespective of their geographical location inside enterprises. Virtual team-building exercises minimize carbon emissions and travel requirements while fostering cooperation and communication. Digital platforms for recognition enable peers and management to recognize and incentivize environmentally conscious conduct, so promoting a sustainable culture within the company. Organizations may strengthen their commitment to environmental sustainability, foster teamwork, and increase employee engagement by implementing these technologies.

To sum up, sustainable technologies are revolutionizing HR roles by providing creative solutions that boost productivity, cut waste, and support environmental sustainability. Utilizing these technologies in a variety of HRM domains allows companies to streamline processes, reduce their environmental impact, and cultivate a sustainable culture among their personnel. Future HR practices will be significantly shaped by sustainable technologies as long as firms maintain their focus on environmental responsibility.

12.1.2 Implementation Strategies for Integrating Green Technologies in Recruitment, Training, and Performance Management

The implementation strategies of green technologies are the planned implements and action plans used to include these eco-friendly technologies in the day-to-day jobs and practices followed in an organization. Thus, through these strategies green technologies are appropriately absorbed and operationalized to accomplish sustainability objectives.

❖ Here's an in-depth exploration of implementation strategies for integrating green technologies in recruitment, training, and performance management:

- **Recruitment**

Green Job Descriptions:
Strategy: Write detailed job descriptions that speak to the larger sustainability connections of the job role.

Implementation: In your job postings, make it clear that your company is environmentally conscious List duties that involve environmental stewardship (i.e., hiring sustainable practices such as waste reduction and energy efficiency or simply making sure that specific environmental regulations are followed). Highlight how the candidate adds value to the company's green objectives through the role. The process is meant to draw in candidates who are qualified, but also excited about sustainability.

Eco-Friendly Employer Branding:

Strategy: Showcase the company's green principles and actions on a variety of media.

Implementation: Create a compelling employer brand that emphasizes your environmental commitment. Showcase sustainable initiatives, such as your usage of renewable energy, recycling programs, or involvement in environmental conservation projects, on your company's website, social media accounts, and job advertisements. Provide case studies and success stories that illustrate how your business affects sustainability. You can draw in candidates who respect and prioritize environmental responsibility by persistently publicizing your green projects.

Green Recruitment Channels:

Strategy: Make use of networks and niche employment portals that are dedicated to sustainability.

Implementation: Join forces with green job boards and sustainability-focused professional associations. You can find applicants that are expressly looking for employment inside green businesses by visiting websites such as Sustainable Business, Green Jobs Online, and other eco-focused platforms. Additionally, to meet possible candidates who are enthusiastic about sustainability, go to job fairs and networking events cantered around environmental careers.

Sustainability in Interviews:

Strategy: In the interview process, assess candidates' sustainability commitment.

Implementation: Inquire about candidates' opinions on environmental issues and their experience with sustainable practices during interviews. "Can you describe a project where you implemented a green initiative?" is one example of a possible question. or "How do you make sustainability a part of your regular workday?" Seek out answers that show a sincere dedication to environmental preservation. Talk about your company's green policies as well, and see how excited the prospect is about helping with these initiatives.

- **Training**

Sustainability Training Programs:
Strategy: Create thorough, ongoing training initiatives with a sustainability focus.

Implementation: Provide required training programs that address a range of sustainability topics, including waste management, energy conservation, and the use of green technologies. To offer this subject, use a combination of lectures, workshops, and e-learning platforms. Make sure that training is a continuous process rather than a one-time occurrence. Update the training materials frequently to incorporate the newest advancements in sustainable practices and green technologies.

Hands-On Experience:
Strategy: Give employees real-world chances to take part in environmentally friendly projects.

Implementation: Create programs that let employees use their sustainability knowledge in practical situations. For example, collaborate with local environmental organizations to organize energy audits, tree planting campaigns, and community clean-ups. Give employees the resources and skills they need to take part in these activities and encourage them to. In addition to strengthening theoretical understanding, this practical method fosters a stronger bond with environmental responsibility.

Continuous Learning:
Strategy: Encourage a culture of ongoing sustainability education.

Implementation: Provide resources including industry conferences, webinars, online courses, and subscriptions to periodicals with a sustainability focus. Encourage employees to keep up with the most recent advancements and trends in green technology. Establish a forum for knowledge sharing within the organization so that employees can exchange sustainability-related ideas and best practices. Give employees who proactively seek out additional training in this area recognition and incentives.

Green Certification Programs:
Strategy: Encourage employees to get certifications in sustainability.

Implementation: Offer employees financial support or incentives to obtain certifications like ISO 14001 (Environmental Management), LEED (Leadership in Energy and Environmental Design), or other pertinent credentials. Emphasize the career rewards and the program's positive influence on the company's sustainability goals to entice employees to participate in these initiatives. To encourage others to follow suit, acknowledge certified employees at business events and in internal communications.

- **Performance Management**

Green Performance Metrics:
Strategy: Include environmental performance metrics in the system of performance management.

Implementation: Establish quantifiable, targeted objectives for sustainability, such cutting back on energy use, cutting waste, or raising recycling rates. Include these measures in the process of evaluating performance. To measure and assess how employees are contributing to the company's green goals, use instruments such as balanced scorecards. Make sure that all employees are informed about these measures and that they are in line with the company's broader sustainability strategy.

Sustainability Goals:
Strategy: For employees, establish attainable and transparent sustainability goals.

Implementation: Align team and personal objectives with the organization's overarching sustainability goals. Establish departmental goals, such as cutting back on paper use, increasing energy efficiency, or introducing new green technologies. Provide the tools and assistance needed to accomplish these goals by breaking them down into precise, doable actions. To guarantee continual improvement, evaluate these targets' progress on a regular basis and make necessary strategy adjustments.

Recognition and Rewards:
Strategy: Employees that excel at promoting sustainability should be recognized and rewarded.

Implementation: Create a formal appreciation program to honour employees who have contributed to the company's environmental initiatives. This could take the form of prizes, incentives, notice in the media, or more vacation time. Think about developing a "Employee of the Month" initiative especially for environmental initiatives. Acknowledge group accomplishments as well to promote cooperation in the pursuit of environmental objectives. Rewarding sustainable conduct helps to instil in the organizational culture the value of environmental care.

Green Performance Reviews:
Strategy: Regular performance appraisals should take sustainability performance into account.

Implementation: Examine employees' accomplishments in sustainability during performance reviews, and offer suggestions for improvement. Discuss how employees may further support the company's green activities during these assessments and use the occasion to set new sustainability targets. Make sure management receive the necessary training to assess sustainability performance objectively and offer helpful criticism.

Employee Engagement:
Strategy: Active employee participation can help to cultivate a culture of sustainability.

Implementation: Form green committees or teams to concentrate on sustainability-related projects. These teams are capable of organizing events, coming up with concepts, and leading the company's adoption of green initiatives. To keep employees informed and inspired, regularly update them on sustainability goal progress and accomplishments. Highlight individual and group contributions to sustainability initiatives by sharing success stories in internal newsletters, workplace meetings, and social media posts.

These all-inclusive tactics can help organizations effectively integrate green technologies and practices into their recruitment, training, and performance management processes. This helps create a workforce that is dedicated to sustainability and guarantees that the firm can meet its environmental targets, increase operational effectiveness, and strengthen its standing as an ethical and progressive business.

12.1.3 Case Studies Showcasing Organizations that have Successfully Adopted Sustainable HR Technologies

Case Study: Accenture's Adoption of Sustainable HR Technologies

Overview:
Sustainability has been given top priority by Accenture, a leading global provider of outsourcing, technology services, and consulting, including human resources (HR) management. Accenture wants to create a sustainable culture within its workforce, improve productivity, and lessen its environmental effect by utilizing sustainable HR solutions.

- **Technologies and Practices:**

1. Virtual Collaboration Tools:
Description: Accenture facilitates remote work and virtual team collaboration through the use of cutting-edge virtual collaboration solutions like cloud-based project management systems, instant messaging platforms, and video conferencing.

Sustainability Impact: Accenture minimizes the need for in-person meetings and travel, which lowers the carbon emissions related to commuting and business travel and leaves a less environmental impact.

2. AI-Powered Talent Management:
Description: Accenture uses data analytics and artificial intelligence (AI) to find, develop, and retain people. Using skills, experience, and

preferences, AI-driven algorithms match employees with appropriate tasks.

Sustainability Impact: The environmental impact of hiring and on boarding new employees is minimized when talent management is done well. Optimized workforce numbers also result in lower waste and resource usage.

3. Sustainable Office Practices:

Description: Accenture carries out eco-friendly office projects, such as waste minimization plans, intelligent lighting systems, and energy-efficient structures. Digital monitoring devices keep tabs on how resources and energy are used in offices.

Sustainability Impact: By reducing energy use, greenhouse gas emissions, and trash production, these procedures help Accenture achieve its environmental sustainability objectives.

4. Remote Work Enablement:

Description: Accenture provides flexible policies and digital infrastructure to accommodate remote work arrangements. In order to carry out their jobs from any location, employees have access to virtual desktop environments, safe VPN connections, and remote work tools.

Sustainability Impact: Because working remotely eliminates the need for daily commuting, there is a huge decrease in the energy and carbon emissions related to running an office.

5. Employee Engagement Platforms:

Description: Accenture facilitates employee involvement, collaboration, and knowledge exchange through the provision of digital platforms and online communities. These platforms offer tools for social interaction, wellness programs, and professional growth.

Sustainability Impact: Accenture supports employee well-being and morale while simultaneously lessening the environmental effect of in-person events and printed materials by encouraging virtual interactions and digital involvement.

- **Outcomes:**

1. Reduced Carbon Footprint:
Impact: Accenture's implementation of remote work policies and virtual collaboration tools has resulted in a noteworthy decrease in carbon emissions associated with business travel and commutes. By reducing trash production and energy usage, sustainable office practices also support environmental sustainability.

2. Improved Operational Efficiency:
Impact: Digital HR solutions and AI-powered talent management systems improve productivity, simplify HR procedures, and cut down on administrative burden. Accenture saves money and uses resources more effectively as a result of this.

3. Enhanced Employee Satisfaction and Retention:
Impact: Accenture's emphasis on work-life balance, professional growth, and employee involvement via remote work choices and digital platforms raises employee retention and job satisfaction. Workers value the support for their well-being and flexibility.

4. Promotion of Sustainability Culture:
Impact: Accenture encourages its employees to practice corporate citizenship and environmental responsibility by incorporating sustainability into HR procedures. This is consistent with Accenture's larger dedication to social impact and sustainability.

Conclusion:
Accenture's implementation of sustainable HR technologies serves as an example of how utilizing cutting-edge techniques and digital tools may promote employee engagement, operational effectiveness, and environmental sustainability. Accenture has implemented sustainable office practises, AI-powered personnel management systems, virtual collaboration tools, employee engagement platforms, and remote work enablement to minimise its environmental impact and increase employee satisfaction and productivity. For businesses looking to include

sustainability into their HR strategy for long-term profitability and beneficial social effect, this case study can be used as a model.

Case Study: Nestlé's Adoption of Sustainable HR Technologies

Overview:

The largest food and beverage corporation in the world, Nestlé, has included sustainability into its HR procedures as part of its all-encompassing dedication to environmental stewardship and corporate social responsibility. Nestlé wants to improve operational effectiveness, lessen its impact on the environment, and promote a sustainable culture among its employees by utilizing sustainable HR solutions.

- **Technologies and Practices:**

1. Digital Recruitment and On boarding:

Description: Digital platforms are used by Nestlé in their hiring and on boarding procedures. This covers digital onboarding programs, electronic document submission, virtual interviews, and job advertisements online.

Sustainability Impact: Nestlé reduces its carbon footprint and resource usage by doing away with the requirement for paper-based documentation and by traveling less for interviews.

2. Remote Work and Flexible Scheduling:

Description: Nestlé has put in place flexible scheduling and regulations for working remotely, backed by powerful digital tools for collaboration like instant messaging, cloud-based project management, and video conferencing.

Sustainability Impact: By eliminating the need for regular commutes, these actions drastically cut greenhouse gas emissions and the energy required to maintain huge office premises.

3. Employee Wellness and Engagement Platforms:

Description: The organization offers online tools for health, well-being, and professional development in order to promote employee wellness and engagement using digital platforms. These platforms include online fitness courses, mental health support services, and e-learning modules.

Sustainability Impact: Nestlé is able to further its sustainability aims by minimizing the requirement for physical infrastructure and travel by encouraging remote access to these resources.

4. Green Office Practices:

Description: Nestlé has introduced green workplace programs that use technology to minimize waste and maximize energy use. This includes waste reduction initiatives backed by digital monitoring and management technologies, energy-efficient HVAC systems, and smart lighting.

Sustainability Impact: In Nestlé's workplace premises, these procedures result in a notable decrease in trash production and energy use.

5. Sustainable Workforce Planning:

Description: Nestlé uses sophisticated data analytics to plan and manage its personnel. This entails forecasting workforce requirements, allocating people as efficiently as possible, and using data-driven insights to manage worker performance.

Sustainability Impact: Effective workforce planning minimizes the negative effects of understaffing and overstaffing, which maximizes resource use and lessens environmental impact.

- **Outcomes:**

1. Reduced Environmental Footprint:

Impact: Nestlé's paper waste and carbon emissions have significantly decreased as a result of its remote work policy and transition to digital recruitment and on boarding. Energy consumption and garbage production are further reduced by using green workplace practices.

2. Enhanced Employee Engagement and Well-Being:

Impact: Employee retention and satisfaction have increased because to digital health and engagement solutions. Flexible work schedules and simple access to tools for professional and health development benefit employees, creating a happy and effective work environment.

3. Operational Efficiency:

Impact: The adoption of digital HR procedures and the application of advanced analytics for workforce planning have simplified operations, decreased manual labour, and increased accuracy. Costs have decreased as a result, and resources have been used more effectively.

4. Promotion of a Sustainable Culture:
Impact: An organizational culture of sustainability has been fostered by Nestlé's dedication to sustainable HR practices. Workers are contributing to Nestlé's larger environmental and social responsibility aims by being more conscious of and involved in sustainability projects.

Conclusion:
The use of sustainable HR technologies by Nestlé is an example of how utilizing digital tools and creative approaches may have a significant positive impact on operations and the environment. By using employee wellness programs, digital hiring and on-boarding, remote work guidelines, green office procedures, and sustainable workforce planning, Nestlé has decreased its environmental impact, raised employee satisfaction, and increased operational effectiveness. This case study serves as an excellent example of how incorporating sustainability into HR procedures may promote both corporate success and a favourable environmental impact.

Case Study: IBM's Adoption of Sustainable HR Technologies

Overview:
IBM has a long history of being a leader in consulting and technology worldwide. This dedication is reflected in IBM's human resources (HR) strategies, which use technology to boost employee happiness, operational effectiveness, and sustainability.

- **Technologies and Practices:**

1. Smart HR Analytics:
Description: IBM optimizes workforce planning and management through the use of advanced data analytics. IBM is able to forecast labour requirements, handle talent more skilfully, and distribute resources more effectively by looking at patterns and trends.

Sustainability Impact: By doing this, waste and inefficiencies in HR procedures are decreased, resulting in the most efficient use of resources and a smaller environmental impact than when human resources are overworked or underutilized.

2. Remote and Flexible Work Programs:

Description: Cloud-based project management platforms, video conferencing, instant messaging, and other digital collaboration technologies have made it possible for IBM to provide strong support for flexible work hours and remote work.

Sustainability Impact: By eliminating the need for commuting, these programs drastically cut carbon emissions and the energy needed to run huge office premises.

3. Sustainable Learning Platforms:

Description: Employees at IBM may now access training and professional development materials from a distance thanks to the company's adoption of online learning and development platforms.

Sustainability Impact: This saves costs and lessens the impact on the environment by eliminating the need for travel, printed materials, and in-person training sessions.

4. Green Data Canters:

Description: IBM runs its HR systems on energy-efficient data canters. Advanced cooling methods, renewable energy sources, and energy-efficient technology are employed in these data canters.

Sustainability Impact: By using these techniques, the energy usage and carbon footprint of maintaining digital infrastructure are decreased.

5. Digital Recruitment and On-boarding:

Description: IBM uses AI-powered recruiting technologies to expedite the entire hiring process, from finding candidates to conducting virtual interviews and providing on-boarding.

Sustainability Impact: As a result, less trash and carbon emissions are produced by eliminating the requirement for paper-based procedures and travel for interviews.

- **Outcomes:**

1. Optimized Resource Use:
Impact: IBM has optimized resource utilization and minimized waste through the application of predictive analytics and astute HR management. Significant cost reductions and improved HR operations are the results of this.

2. Reduced Carbon Footprint:
Impact: The necessity for commuting has been significantly reduced because to regulations supporting remote work and digital collaboration tools, which has decreased carbon emissions. The energy-efficient data canters also support broader sustainability objectives.

3. Enhanced Employee Satisfaction:
Impact: Employee satisfaction and retention have increased because to the flexibility of remote work and the availability of online learning resources. The opportunity for ongoing learning and development as well as the work-life balance are valued by employees.

4. Operational Efficiency:
Impact: Utilizing cutting-edge technologies in HR procedures has enhanced accuracy and efficacy in talent management while streamlining operations and lowering manual labor. Higher productivity and improved alignment between HR activities and business goals are the results of this.

Conclusion:
IBM's implementation of sustainable HR technology serves as an example of how utilizing cutting-edge instruments and procedures can result in major operational and environmental advantages. IBM's sustainability initiatives have been bolstered by the integration of smart analytics, provision of remote work support, and utilization of digital platforms for recruitment and learning. These strategies have also increased overall productivity and employee happiness. In order to implement sustainable HR practices, other firms can use this case study as a model.

Case Study: Microsoft's Adoption of Sustainable HR Technologies

Overview:
Leading technology company Microsoft has integrated sustainability into all aspects of its business, including human resources (HR) procedures. The organization utilizes cutting-edge technologies to promote environmental responsibility, increase operational effectiveness, and improve sustainability.

- **Technologies and Practices:**

AI and Machine Learning in Workforce Management:
Description: Microsoft leverages AI and machine learning to improve talent management, forecast labour trends, and improve HR decision-making. These tools support workforce planning, employee turnover prediction, and candidate selection.

Sustainability Impact: Effective workforce management minimizes the need for regular hiring and training, which saves money and cuts down on waste related to these procedures.

Remote Work Infrastructure:
Description: With powerful online collaboration solutions like Microsoft Teams, SharePoint, and OneDrive, Microsoft facilitates distant work. These solutions make it easier for employees who work remotely to collaborate, communicate, and share documents.

Sustainability Impact: Working remotely minimizes carbon emissions by eliminating the need for daily commuting. It also reduces the number of resources and energy required to maintain huge office spaces.

Sustainable Office Design:
Description: Microsoft has integrated energy-efficient lighting, HVAC systems, and automated energy management systems into its office buildings. These structures are made to minimize waste and maximize energy use.

Sustainability Impact: By significantly lowering energy use and greenhouse gas emissions, these actions help Microsoft achieve its sustainability objectives.

Digital Learning and Development Platforms:

Description: Via services like Microsoft Learn and LinkedIn Learning, Microsoft offers a wealth of online learning and development opportunities. These platforms enable employees to remotely access a vast array of training resources and courses.

Sustainability Impact: Microsoft lessens its overall environmental impact by using digital learning to replace traditional, resource-intensive training techniques. This reduces the need for printed materials and travel.

Cloud-Based HR Systems:

Description: Microsoft manages payroll, benefits, performance reviews, and employee information via cloud-based HR systems. Microsoft's energy-efficient data centres host these systems.

Sustainability Impact: Cloud-based solutions minimize the need for physical data storage and paper-based procedures, which cut down on waste and energy use.

- **Outcomes:**

Reduced Carbon Footprint:

Impact: The increasing use of digital collaboration tools and remote work has resulted in a notable decrease in carbon emissions from business travel and commuting. Microsoft's carbon footprint is further reduced by smart building technologies and energy-efficient workplace designs.

Enhanced Operational Efficiency:

Impact: AI and machine learning have simplified HR procedures, enhanced talent management, and maximized resource usage in workforce management. More operational efficiency and cost savings are the outcome of this.

Improved Employee Engagement and Retention:

Impact: The ability to work remotely, having access to online learning resources, and emphasizing environmentally friendly methods have all improved worker satisfaction and retention. Better work-life balance and opportunities for ongoing professional growth are advantageous to employees.

Promotion of a Sustainable Culture:

Impact: Microsoft encourages a culture of environmental responsibility among its employees through its dedication to sustainable HR practices. This is consistent with the corporate principles and larger environmental goals of the organization.

Conclusion:

Microsoft's adoption of sustainable HR technologies serves as an example of how utilizing cutting-edge digital tools may have a major positive impact on operations and the environment. Microsoft has boosted employee satisfaction, decreased its environmental effect, and increased efficiency using cloud-based HR systems, digital learning platforms, sustainable office designs, strong remote work infrastructure, AI and machine learning in workforce management, and digital learning platforms. This case study illustrates the benefits that can be attained via creative and responsible management, making it an ideal resource for other businesses looking to include sustainability into their HR procedures.

Case Study: Google's Adoption of Sustainable HR Technologies

Overview:

Leading global technology company Google is well known for its dedication to sustainability in all facets of its business, including human resources (HR). Google has successfully incorporated sustainability into its HR procedures by utilizing cutting-edge technologies, which has improved productivity, decreased its environmental effect, and promoted a sustainable culture among its employees.

- **Technologies and Practices:**

Green Data Canters:

Description: Google's HR systems are housed in highly efficient, environmentally friendly data facilities. Advanced cooling methods, renewable energy sources, and energy-efficient technology are employed in these data canters.

Sustainability Impact: As a result, the energy used and carbon emissions produced by maintaining digital infrastructure are greatly decreased.

Cloud-Based HR Systems:

Description: Cloud-based technologies are used by Google to manage its HR functions, including payroll, benefits, performance reviews, and personnel records. Google's energy-efficient cloud infrastructure hosts these technologies.

Sustainability Impact: Systems based in the cloud minimize the need for physical storage and paper-based procedures, which reduces waste and energy usage.

Digital Recruitment and On-boarding:

Description: Google uses digital channels for hiring and on-boarding, such as electronic document submission, virtual interviews, online job advertisements, and digital on-boarding programs.

Sustainability Impact: By reducing the need for travel and paper documentation, these techniques minimize resource use and their carbon imprint.

Remote Work and Flexible Scheduling:

Description: With powerful digital collaboration tools like Google Workspace (previously G Suite), which includes Google Meet, Google Drive, and Google Docs, Google allows remote work and flexible scheduling.

Sustainability Impact: Policies supporting remote work cut down on the necessity of daily commuting, which in turn reduces greenhouse gas emissions and the energy required to maintain large office premises.

Employee Wellness and Engagement Platforms:

Description: Google provides online resources for health, well-being, and professional growth in addition to digital platforms for employee engagement and wellness. These platforms consist of e-learning modules, mental health support services, and virtual fitness programs.

Sustainability Impact: Google contributes to overall sustainability by minimizing the need for physical infrastructure and travel by encouraging remote access to these resources.

Sustainable Office Practices:

Description: Google uses digital monitoring tools, smart thermostats, energy-efficient lighting, waste reduction plans, and other green office practices to monitor and control resource and energy usage.

Sustainability Impact: These methods cut down on trash production, energy use, and greenhouse gas emissions.

- Outcomes:

Reduced Environmental Footprint:

Impact: Paper use, emissions associated with travel, and energy consumption have all significantly decreased as a result of the adoption of cloud-based HR systems, digital hiring and on-boarding processes, and remote work rules. Google substantially reduces its environmental effect with green workplace practices and energy-efficient data canters.

Enhanced Operational Efficiency:

Impact: The use of digital HR technologies has enhanced accuracy and efficiency, minimized administrative burden, and streamlined HR procedures. Costs are reduced and resources are used more effectively as a result.

Improved Employee Satisfaction and Retention:

Impact: Employee retention and satisfaction have increased as a result of flexible work schedules, availability of wellness tools, and an emphasis on sustainability. Support for work-life balance and chances for ongoing education are valued by employees.

Promotion of a Sustainable Culture:

Impact: A culture of environmental responsibility is fostered among Google's employees by the company's dedication to sustainable HR practices. Encouragement of employees to embrace sustainable habits in their daily life is in line with the company's corporate principles and larger sustainability initiatives.

Conclusion:

Google's implementation of sustainable HR technologies serves as an example of how utilizing cutting-edge digital tools in conjunction with creative thinking may result in significant operational and environmental benefits. By implementing green data canters, cloud-based HR systems, digital hiring and onboarding procedures, remote work regulations, employee wellness programs, and environmentally friendly office practices, Google has decreased its environmental impact while simultaneously increasing productivity and worker satisfaction. This case study acts as an example for other businesses looking to include sustainability into their HR procedures, showing the benefits that can be attained by conscientious and proactive management.

12.2 Leveraging Tech for Remote Work and Reduced Emissions

Introduction to leveraging tech for remote work and reduced emissions:

The recent convergence of advanced technology and increasing environmental consciousness has opened up new avenues for creative approaches to work and sustainability. With the development of communication and collaboration tools, one of the most significant shifts that has occurred is the widespread adoption of remote work, which provides businesses and employees with flexibility and efficiency while also offering a significant opportunity to reduce environmental emissions. By utilizing technology to support remote work, organizations can minimize the need for employees to commute, as well as reduce the energy consumption associated with maintaining large office spaces.

Meaning of leveraging tech for remote work and reduced emissions:

Employees can carry out their responsibilities from places other than the typical office environment by leveraging technology for remote work by employing digital tools and platforms. By eliminating the need for daily journeys and the energy used to maintain office spaces, the shift to remote work can considerably reduce greenhouse gas emissions. Technologies like cloud computing, video conferencing, and collaboration software make it easier for distant teams to communicate and work together effectively. Businesses can help achieve wider environmental sustainability goals by lowering their carbon footprints by relying less on physical office facilities and transportation.

- **Concept of leveraging tech for remote work and reduced emissions:**

Leveraging technology for reduced emissions and remote work reflects a sea change in how companies function and engage with their employees, fuelled by the development of digital technologies and a growing consciousness of environmental sustainability. The idea behind this is to reduce the environmental effect of traditional office operations by decreasing the need for daily trips by enabling remote work through the use of various technological solutions. In a larger sense, this strategy is consistent with international initiatives to mitigate climate change and encourage more environmentally friendly corporate practices.

The Evolution of Remote Work:

Although remote work is not a new concept, it has recently gained enormous traction, especially in the wake of the COVID-19 outbreak. The epidemic compelled businesses all over the world to quickly adjust to remote work arrangements, hastening the uptake of digital solutions that facilitate online communication and cooperation. This abrupt change demonstrated how remote work has the potential to become a standard feature of the contemporary workplace.

High-speed internet, cloud computing, project management software (like Asana, Trello, and Monday.com), video conferencing platforms (like Zoom, Microsoft Teams, and Google Meet), and secure virtual private networks (VPNs) are some of the key technologies that have made this shift possible. Employees may work together with co-workers, access job-related materials, and take part in meetings virtually from anywhere thanks to these tools, which do away with the limitations of a traditional office setting.

The advancement of mobile technology, such as tablets and smartphones, has made it easier for people to be mobile and flexible, which is necessary for productive remote work. With gadgets that fit into their pockets, employees can now do tasks, participate in meetings, and connect with their teams, making remote work more comfortable and accessible than ever.

Environmental Benefits of Remote Work:

There are substantial environmental benefits of remote work. The reduction of greenhouse gas emissions as a result of less commuter traffic is one of the main benefits. The International Energy Agency (IEA) reported that transportation plays a significant role in the world's carbon emissions, with personal automobiles making up a sizeable portion of this contribution. Companies can significantly reduce the number of cars on the road, which will reduce emissions of carbon dioxide (CO_2) and other pollutants, by allowing employees to work from home.

Not only may remote work cut down on emissions from commuting, but it can also minimize the environmental impact of office building maintenance. A significant amount of energy is needed in traditional office facilities to operate office equipment and provide lighting, heating, and cooling. Businesses can reduce their overall energy usage by moving to smaller, more energy-efficient hubs or by eliminating the need for huge office premises. This reduction saves money on utility bills in addition to lowering carbon emissions.

Another factor lowering waste output is remote work. Many materials, including plastic and paper, are utilized on a regular basis in a standard office setting. Remote work reduces the need for paper documents because digital solutions are increasingly used, which reduces waste and has a smaller environmental impact.

Technological Solutions and Their Impact:

Numerous technology advancements are essential for enabling remote work and, consequently, cutting emissions. These solutions include:

1. Cloud Computing: Employees can access, save, and share files from anywhere thanks to cloud services. As a result, fewer physical servers and data centres which use a lot of energy are required. Cloud service providers such as Google Cloud, Microsoft Azure, and Amazon Web Services (AWS) have also made progress in utilizing more renewable energy sources and making their data canters more energy efficient. Businesses can extend their operations more effectively and cut down on waste and inefficiency by utilizing cloud computing instead of traditional on-premises IT infrastructure.

2. Video Conferencing: Real-time communication and collaboration are made possible by platforms like Zoom, Microsoft Teams, and Google Meet, which lessen the need for in-person meetings and business travel. Teams can hold meetings, brainstorming sessions, and presentations via video conferencing without having to worry about the carbon footprint of travel. Additionally, cutting-edge tools like breakout rooms, virtual whiteboards, and screen sharing improve teamwork and make remote meetings just as productive as in-person ones.

3. Collaboration Tools: Project management and communication are made easier for teams by software such as Slack, Trello, and Asana, which keeps them linked and organized. As a result of these tools' support for asynchronous work, team members can participate on their own time, increasing productivity and lowering the requirement for physical office space. Furthermore, a lot of collaboration tools include integration capabilities with other programs and software, which helps to create a cohesive ecosystem that facilitates effective workflows and reduces the need for several, energy-intensive systems.

4. Virtual Private Networks (VPNs): VPNs allow employees to securely access company networks remotely, enabling them to work from any location. Maintaining company continuity and safeguarding sensitive data depend on this security. VPNs and other cyber security measures, such multi-factor authentication and endpoint protection, have become indispensable parts of a safe remote work strategy due to the increase in cyber threats.

5. Energy-Efficient Hardware: Compared to earlier models, modern laptops, tablets, and other mobile devices are made with energy efficiency in mind. Companies can further cut down on energy use by providing these gadgets to their employees. These gadgets can operate longer between charges thanks to advancements in power management and battery technology, which lowers the frequency of charging and energy consumption involved.

6. Artificial Intelligence (AI) and Automation: Artificial intelligence (AI) and automation technologies can improve productivity, decrease monotonous work, and streamline workflows to make remote work more effective. Employees can concentrate on more strategic duties by using AI-powered virtual assistants to manage emails, plan meetings, and answer routine questions. Through the intelligent management of device power levels and the adjustment of environmental settings based on usage patterns, automation technologies may also optimize energy use in remote work situations.

Challenges and Considerations:

While using technology to facilitate remote work and cut emissions has many advantages, there are challenges as well that organizations need to be aware of. These include:

1. Cyber security: Threats related to cyber security have increased along with the development in remote employment. To safeguard confidential data and preserve data integrity, businesses need to invest in strong security measures like firewalls, encryption, and employee training. Safeguarding remote work environments also requires the use of advanced threat detection systems, incident response strategies, and regular security assessments.

2. Digital Divide: High-speed internet and dependable technology are not equally available to all employees. To ensure that all employees can work productively from home, organizations need to think about methods to close the digital divide. Some ideas include giving equipment and offering financial assistance for internet connection. Creating an inclusive remote work environment where all employees can thrive requires addressing these discrepancies.

3. Work-Life Balance: The lines between work and personal life may become hazier when working remotely, which increases the risk of stress and burnout. Companies should encourage regular breaks, set clear goals, and provide mental health support in order to foster a healthy work-life balance. Employees can maintain a healthy balance with the aid of flexible working hours, wellness initiatives, and initiatives to promote physical activity and mindfulness.

4. Employee Engagement: In a remote work setting, it can be difficult to maintain business culture and employee engagement. Companies must come up with innovative strategies to encourage communication and teamwork, like frequent check-ins and virtual team-building exercises. A key factor in establishing the culture of remote work is leadership; it should be approachable, open, and encouraging.

5. Compliance and Legal Issues: Regulations pertaining to labour legislation, data privacy, and remote work differ amongst jurisdictions. In order to maintain compliance and safeguard the company and its employees, businesses need to manage these complications. Effective management of these difficulties requires keeping up with legislative changes, consulting with legal professionals, and putting strong compliance structures in place.

6. Technological Adaptation: Although technology greatly facilitates, it also necessitates flexibility and ongoing education. Companies must offer continuing assistance and resources to ease this transition, and employees must receive training on how to use new technologies efficiently. Employees may stay current with technology changes by investing in training programs, producing user-friendly documentation, and promoting a culture of continual learning.

7. Infrastructure and Support: Ensuring that remote workers have access to the tools and resources they need to do their jobs well is essential. This includes having access to technical support, dependable internet connections, and ergonomic workspaces. In addition, companies want to think about offering reimbursements for home offices and formulating policies for preserving a positive and effective remote work environment.

The Future of Remote Work and Sustainability:
Given the advantages remote work has for the environment, this trend is probably just going to get stronger. There's a chance to further reduce emissions and promote sustainability as technology develops and businesses get better at managing remote staff. Several future developments could enhance this trend:

5G Networks: The introduction of 5G technologies is expected to bring quicker and more dependable internet connections, which will facilitate real-time collaboration and smoother video conferencing, thereby facilitating remote work even more. Advanced applications and technologies will be easier to use in remote work environments because to 5G networks' higher bandwidth and lower latency.

Decentralized Workspaces: Decentralized workspaces, in which employees can work from several smaller office hubs or co-working spaces nearer to their homes, are gaining popularity. Long commutes are no longer necessary with this model, which also offers chances for social connection and in-person collaboration.

Sustainable Technology Practices: Employing energy-efficient equipment, establishing sustainable data canter operations, and promoting electronic waste recycling programs are just a few of the green IT strategies that businesses are embracing at an increasing rate. Organizations can further lessen their environmental effect by giving sustainability top priority when selecting technologies.

Hybrid Work Models: A lot of organizations are implementing hybrid work arrangements that blend remote and in-person labour. With this flexibility, the advantages of working remotely can be fully realized while also providing chances for face-to-face teamwork and collaboration. Companies can save even more energy and money by downsizing their actual workplaces thanks to hybrid models.

Environmental Accountability: As stakeholders, such as investors, customers, and regulators, increasingly prioritize sustainability, businesses will be incentivized to implement regulations around remote work that align with their environmental objectives. Demonstrating progress will require open reporting and accountability systems. To demonstrate their dedication to environmental stewardship, businesses can put sustainability reporting frameworks into place and monitor important data such to energy use, emissions reductions, and waste management.

Tele-presence and Virtual Reality (VR): Experiences working remotely can be further improved by new technologies like virtual reality and tele-presence robots. With the use of tele-presence robots, distant employees may engage with co-workers and navigate real office settings just like they would if they were present. When compared to standard video conferencing, virtual reality (VR) can create immersive virtual environments for meetings, training sessions, and collaborative projects that are more dynamic and engaging.

Decentralized Autonomous Organizations (DAOs): The idea of DAOs organizations run by smart contracts and decentralized decision-making processes could revolutionize distant teamwork as block-chain technology develops. With the efficiency, security, and openness that DAOs provide, distant teams may work together and make choices without the need for centralized authority.

Renewable Energy Integration: Renewable energy sources can be included by companies into their infrastructure for remote work. One way to lessen the carbon impact of remote work is to encourage the use of solar panels and other renewable energy sources for home offices. To further lessen their influence on the environment, any remaining office space and data canters can be fuelled by renewable energy sources.

Sustainable Commuting Solutions: Companies can support environmentally friendly commute choices for employees who must work certain days in the office when using hybrid work models. Incentives for biking, walking, carpooling, and public transportation are a few examples of this. Organizations can reduce the environmental effect of transportation even in cases where physical presence is necessary by endorsing these solutions.

Circular Economy Practices: Companies can concentrate on the lifecycle of their technology equipment by adopting the ideas of the circular economy. To cut down on e-waste, this involves techniques for repurposing, recycling, and refurbishing electronic equipment. Reducing environmental damage from end-of-life technology requires collaboration with manufacturers and recycling companies.

Organizational Strategies for Sustainable Remote Work

To effectively leverage technology for remote work and reduced emissions, organizations should adopt comprehensive strategies that encompass various aspects of operations:

Leadership and Vision: The company's mission and basic values must incorporate sustainable remote work, and senior leadership must support this goal. This entails establishing unambiguous sustainability objectives, explaining the advantages of working remotely, and setting a good example.

Policy Development: It is recommended that organizations create and execute policies that facilitate remote work and sustainability. These can include regulations governing technology use, guidelines for working remotely, and sustainability programs that promote waste minimization and energy efficiency.

Employee Engagement: It is imperative to involve employees in sustainability initiatives. Organizations can form sustainability committees or green teams to encourage involvement, solicit input, and promote initiatives. A culture of sustainability can be promoted by regular communication on the effects of remote work on the environment and how employees can help.

Technology Investments: Purchasing the appropriate technologies is essential to promoting sustainability and remote work. This entails utilizing cloud computing, implementing energy-efficient technology, and utilizing environmentally friendly communication technologies. It's important for organizations to keep up with new technology that can improve their capacity for remote work.

Training and Support: It is crucial to offer support and training for technology used in remote work. Workers must be prepared to use digital tools safely and effectively with the necessary knowledge and abilities. Continuous support, such as cyber security training and technical help, makes sure that remote work settings stay secure and productive.

Sustainability Reporting: Gaining the trust of stakeholders can be achieved by open reporting on sustainability initiatives and the environmental effects of remote work. To show their dedication to sustainability, organizations should monitor and report on important metrics including energy savings, carbon reductions, and waste management results.

Continuous Improvement: Sustainability and remote work should be regularly assessed and enhanced. Organizations ought to monitor industry trends, solicit feedback from employees, and evaluate the success of their projects. This iterative process guarantees that tactics stay applicable and efficient in a setting that is changing quickly.

The Role of Government and Policy Makers:

Government and policymakers play a crucial role in supporting the shift toward remote work and reduced emissions. Several measures can be implemented to promote these practices:

Incentives and Subsidies: Governments can offer financial aid and subsidies to companies that implement sustainable practices and policies pertaining to remote employment. Tax benefits, subsidies, and low-interest loans for the purchase of energy-efficient equipment and infrastructure can be examples of this.

Regulations and Standards: Businesses can adhere to a framework by establishing rules and guidelines for sustainability and remote work. Guidelines for data protection, cyber security, and environmental impact reporting are a few examples of this.

Infrastructure Development: Sustainability and remote work can be supported by making infrastructural investments in things like renewable energy sources and fast internet connectivity. To close the digital divide, governments should give priority to building broadband networks in underserved areas.

Public Awareness Campaigns: Campaigns to raise public awareness about the advantages of remote work and environmentally friendly practices can be started by governments. These initiatives can motivate companies and people to embrace eco-friendly practices and technology.

Collaboration and Partnerships: Governments have the power to encourage cooperation between the public and commercial sectors in order to promote innovation and exchange best practices. Collaborations with academic institutions, environmental organizations, and technology companies can hasten the adoption of sustainable remote work solutions.

To sum up, leveraging technology for remote work and reduced emissions is a revolutionary way of doing company that fits in with contemporary social and environmental objectives. Businesses may increase productivity, save operating expenses, and contribute to a more sustainable future by utilizing digital tools and platforms. Even though there are still obstacles, the rapid advancement of technology and growing emphasis on sustainability offer a solid basis for the expansion of remote work. Organizations have the chance to set an example for others to follow as they negotiate this terrain and show that environmental sustainability and economic success are compatible.

Technology improvements have facilitated the shift to remote work, which has practical advantages for both employers and employees. It also marks a significant step towards a more sustainable and egalitarian world. The potential for major environmental impact reduction and a more flexible, adaptive workforce becomes more evident as remote work is woven more and more into the fabric of modern business. Organizations can shape a future in which remote work is not merely a stopgap measure but rather the cornerstone of a long-term corporate strategy by emphasizing sustainability and efficiently utilizing technology.

12.2.1 Role of Technology in Enabling Remote Work and Reducing Carbon Emissions

Technology has become a more potent force in recent years, changing the way we work and solving urgent environmental issues. Technology is playing a more and bigger role in enabling remote work and lowering carbon emissions. It also provides creative ways to boost productivity while lessening the environmental impact of conventional work practices.

Technology development has drastically changed the nature of work, making it possible to work remotely on a never-before-seen scale and simultaneously contributing greatly to the reduction of carbon emissions. In order to solve the problems of environmental sustainability and productivity in the current world, this dual impact is crucial.

- **Enabling Remote Work**

1. Advanced Communication Tools: The foundation of remote work is communication technology. The way teams communicate has been completely transformed by platforms like Zoom, Microsoft Teams, Slack, and Google Meet. These solutions enable real-time communication across geographic boundaries by providing video conferencing, instant messaging, file sharing, and collaborative document editing. These platforms are now essential for remote collaboration because to upgraded capabilities like breakout rooms, webinar hosting, and integrated apps.

2. Cloud Computing and Storage: Robust infrastructure for remote work is offered by cloud services from providers like Microsoft Azure, Google Cloud, and Amazon Web Services (AWS). With cloud computing, companies may host their apps and data on remote servers, giving them safe, scalable access to the resources they need from any location. This makes it unnecessary to physically be present in a central office, allowing for a more adaptable work environment.

3. Project Management and Collaboration Software: Remote team management requires the use of tools like Monday.com, Jira, Trello, and Asana. These platforms include tools for managing deadlines, assigning tasks, monitoring progress, and facilitating team communication. They ensure that projects continue on schedule even when team members are spread out over several locations by supporting the maintenance of accountability, transparency, and coordination within teams.

4. Cyber security Measures: The importance of cyber security has increased with the rise of remote work. Sensitive data is shielded from breaches and unwanted access by technologies like multi-factor authentication (MFA), endpoint security solutions, virtual private networks (VPNs), and encryption. To protect their intellectual property and remote operations, businesses are investing in strong cyber security measures.

5. Virtual Private Networks (VPNs): Employees can safely access their company's network from a distance with the help of VPN services. By encrypting and shielding data from interception during transmission between an employee's device and the corporate network, this technology preserves data integrity and privacy.

6. Remote Desktop Applications: Employees can access their office computers from a distance using programs like TeamViewer, AnyDesk, and Microsoft's Remote Desktop Protocol (RDP). This feature makes sure that employees, whether working from home or other remote locations, may effortlessly use their office programs and data.

7. Digital Workspaces and Platforms: A virtual environment where employees can access their desktop, apps, and data from any device is provided by comprehensive digital workspace solutions like Citrix and VMware Horizon. These technologies replicate the in-office experience by guaranteeing speed and consistency in remote work.

8. AI and Automation: Automation technologies and artificial intelligence (AI) improve remote work by streamlining repetitive operations, delivering insightful analysis, and enhancing decision-making. While automated workflow technologies can expedite corporate operations and free up employees' time for more important activities, AI-driven chatbots, for example, can address customer care concerns.

9. Online Learning and Development: Professional development and ongoing learning are made possible by platforms such as Coursera, LinkedIn Learning, and Udemy. These platforms provide courses that assist employees stay current and competitive because remote work frequently necessitates learning new skills and adjusting to digital tools.

- **Reducing Carbon Emissions**

1. Reduction in Commuting: The considerable decrease in commuting is one of the most obvious environmental advantages of working remotely. Carbon emissions are mostly caused by everyday commutes to and from work, especially in personal vehicles. Because working remotely removes or significantly reduces the need for commuting, fewer cars, buses, and other types of transportation produce pollution.

2. Lower Office Energy Consumption: Companies can drastically cut their energy usage by having fewer employees physically present in their offices. Reduced use of lighting, air conditioning, heating, and office equipment is part of this. To further reduce their energy footprint, many organizations are implementing shared office models or shrinking their office buildings.

3. Decrease in Business Travel: The use of virtual conferences and meetings has decreased the requirement for business travel. Companies can reduce their travel-related carbon footprint by using virtual meetings instead of in-person ones. Air travel is a major source of carbon emissions. High-quality virtual interactions are made possible by platforms such as

Zoom, Microsoft Teams, and WebEx, which effectively replace many in-person meetings.

4. Efficient Resource Utilization: Technologies like virtualization and cloud computing help make better use of server resources. Conventional data canters frequently run on idle servers, which results in wasteful energy use. Cloud service providers ensure greater efficiency and reduced energy consumption per unit of computing by optimizing resource distribution across large networks of computers.

5. Paperless Work Environment: Working remotely promotes the use of digital tools and procedures, which lessens the need for paper. A paperless workplace is facilitated by digital documentation, online collaboration tools, and electronic signatures. This change lowers carbon emissions linked to waste management and paper production while also protecting natural resources.

6. Renewable Energy Integration: Renewable energy sources are rapidly being used to power data canters and many tech enterprises. By 2030, for instance, Google plans to run all of its data canters entirely on carbon-free electricity. These kinds of programs drastically lower the carbon footprint that comes with using electricity to operate remote work infrastructure.

7. Sustainable Work Practices: Reducing the amount of office supplies used, the number of single-use plastics used, and the amount of trash produced are all benefits of remote work. Workers who work remotely are also more inclined to embrace energy-saving habits, such maximizing their houses' heating and cooling systems and utilizing energy-efficient appliances.

8. Hybrid Work Models: The emergence of hybrid work models which blend remote and in-person employment contributes to the ongoing decline in emissions overall. Companies can lessen the environmental effect of daily commutes and office operations while still reaping the benefits of occasional in-person cooperation by enabling employees to work from home for a portion of the workweek.

9. Decentralized Workforce and Regional Development: The concentration of employees in large cities is reduced by remote work, which allows for a more decentralized workforce. This can lessen traffic in cities and lessen the impact that cities have on the environment. Furthermore, it facilitates regional development by enabling skilled individuals from underdeveloped and rural areas to engage in the global economy without having to relocate. This leads to a more equitable distribution of economic advantages and a decrease in the carbon footprint that comes with urban migration.

10. Telecommuting Infrastructure Investments: Governments and organizations are investing in enhancing the digital communication networks and high-speed internet infrastructure that support telecommuting. In addition to enabling remote work, these investments also help other low-carbon projects like Internet of Things (IoT) and smart city efforts.

To sum up, technology has unquestionably changed the way we operate, making remote work practical, effective, and efficient. Businesses can function well in a remote setting by utilizing cloud computing, project management software, sophisticated communication tools, and strong cyber security measures. The environmental advantages of less business travel, less energy use in offices, less commuting, and effective resource management all play a major role in lowering carbon emissions at the same time. The modern world's twin concerns of productivity and environmental sustainability will be greatly assisted by the convergence of technology and remote work, provided that we keep innovating and implementing sustainable methods.

12.2.2 Tools and Platforms for Virtual Collaboration, Communication, and Training

The advent of virtual collaboration, communication, and training tools has completely changed the way that people and organizations connect, interact, and evolve in the dynamic world of modern work and learning. These tools and platforms have grown to be essential resources in the current digital era, from enabling real-time communication and promoting continual skill development to supporting smooth coordination across faraway locations. With the abundance of tools and platforms available in the digital sphere, people and organizations can connect, collaborate, and learn beyond geographical boundaries. These tools and platforms are intended to support virtual collaboration, communication, and training.

❖ **Here are some prominent examples across different categories:**

- **Virtual Collaboration:**

1. Microsoft Teams: This multipurpose platform integrates chat, video conferencing, file sharing, and project management features to function as a focal point for team collaboration. Users of teams can set up channels for particular projects or subjects, which encourages collaboration and targeted conversations.

2. Slack: Slack is a popular tool used by companies of all kinds that provides file sharing, real-time messaging, and connection with a wide range of third-party apps and services. It is an adaptable tool for teamwork and communication because to its user-friendly layout and features that may be customized.

3. Zoom: Zoom, well-known for its dependability and simplicity, has come to be associated with webinars and virtual meetings. Screen sharing, breakout rooms, webinar hosting, and other capabilities make it easy for distant team members to collaborate and organize captivating virtual events.

4. Google Workspace (formerly G Suite): Gmail, Google Meet, Google Chat, and Google Drive are among the cloud-based productivity tools offered by Google. With capabilities like shared calendars, team-based document editing, and video conferencing, these integrated technologies facilitate easy collaboration and communication.

5. Asana: Asana is a collaborative project management platform that facilitates task organization, progress tracking, and workflow management for teams. Teams may easily keep focused on their objectives and organized thanks to its user-friendly design and adaptable project views.

6. Trello: Teams can see their projects and workflows with Trello by using boards, lists, and cards. Trello facilitates efficient team collaboration and organization, whether teams are working remotely or in the office, with features like checklists, due dates, and file attachments.

7. Monday.com: Monday.com is a flexible work platform that facilitates collaborative project, task, and process management. Monday.com provides teams with flexible processes, automation, and connectors that enable them to work together effectively and adjust to shifting priorities.

8. Jira: Software development teams are the main users of Jira, a strong solution for agile project management and issue tracking. It facilitates collaboration and openness throughout the development process by allowing teams to design, monitor, and release software iteratively.

- **Virtual Communication:**

1. Microsoft Teams: Teams provides strong communication options like voice calls, video conferences, and instant messaging in addition to collaborative features. Its smooth Office 365 integration enables users to switch between tasks involving teamwork and communication.

2. Slack: Slack gives team members access to numerous channels for instantaneous communication, including group chats, direct messaging, and channels. Teams can easily access information and work together more productively because to its file sharing and searchable chat history features.

3. Zoom: Zoom provides capabilities that go beyond video conferencing, such as screen sharing, chat, and virtual backdrops, which improve team member engagement and collaboration. Because of its cross-platform interoperability and dependable performance, it is a well-liked option for online gatherings and conferences.

4. Google Meet: Team members may communicate effectively and efficiently by using Google Meet's video conferencing capabilities, which include screen sharing, chat, and real-time captioning. It is simple to arrange and join meetings because to its interaction with Google Calendar and other Google Workspace apps.

5. Skype: Skype, one of the forerunners in online communication, is still a well-liked option for voice, video, and instant message chats. It's a practical choice for both personal and professional communication because of its cross-platform compatibility and user-friendly UI.

6. Discord: Discord, which was first created for gamers, has developed into a flexible tool for team and community collaboration. Discord provides a dynamic environment for interaction and cooperation with features like text chat, audio channels, and server customisation.

7. Cisco Webex: Cisco Webex offers tools for team collaboration, online meetings, and video conferencing to companies of all sizes. Webex makes it possible to collaborate and communicate effectively in virtual settings using features like screen sharing, white boarding, and virtual backdrops.

8. Microsoft Outlook: Outlook is a well-known email client that combines contacts, calendar, tasks, and email into a single program. Team members may communicate and collaborate more easily thanks to its scheduling tools, meeting invites, and Microsoft Teams integration.

- **Virtual Training and Learning:**

1. Coursera: Top universities and institutions throughout the world offer online courses, specializations, and degrees through Coursera. Coursera offers a vast array of courses and adaptable learning choices so that people can learn new things at their own speed.

2. LinkedIn Learning: Offering thousands of courses on subjects like business, technology, creative skills, and professional development, LinkedIn Learning is instructed by professionals in the field. Professionals may easily remain current and learn new skills with its bite-sized classes and individualized recommendations.

3. Udemy: Online courses on a range of topics, such as technology, business, personal growth, and creative abilities, can be found on Udemy. With self-paced learning alternatives and lifetime access to course materials, Udemy provides flexibility for students at every skill level.

4. edX: With the opportunity to pursue certificates and degrees for a charge or audit courses for free, edX provides courses from universities and other institutions throughout the world. For lifelong learners, its demanding academic material and engaging learning activities make it an invaluable resource.

5. Skillshare: Skillshare offers video-based courses in design, entrepreneurship, creative skills, and lifestyle subjects. Discover your passions and unleash your creative potential with Skill share, an online community that emphasizes interactive learning.

6. Pluralsight: Plural sight provides IT professionals with online courses and examinations on subjects like data science, cyber security, software development, and IT operations. Learners can validate their skills and progress in their jobs with the aid of its practical laboratories and skill tests.

7. Codecademy: Programming and coding classes are the focus of Codecademy, which provides engaging projects and lessons for both novice and expert students. Learners may gain practical skills and real-world projects with Codecademy's hands-on practice and fast feedback.

Conclusion:

The abundance of virtual collaboration, communication, and training tools and platforms in today's digital age has completely changed how people and businesses interact, learn, and operate. Through project collaboration, team communication, or skill acquisition, these tools enable people to flourish in remote work settings and adjust to the ever-evolving needs of the contemporary workplace. In an increasingly linked world, people and organizations can overcome geographical boundaries, promote cooperation and creativity, and accomplish their objectives by utilizing technology.

12.2.3 Best Practices for Managing Remote Teams Sustainably and Effectively

A set of best practices adapted to the particularities of virtual work environments must be put into place in order to manage remote teams in a sustainable and productive manner. This means creating an environment of open communication, setting clear expectations for team members, and utilizing technology to facilitate seamless teamwork. Project management tools enable structure and responsibility, while regular check-ins and updates support visibility and alignment. Cohesion and wellbeing within a team are enhanced by prioritizing work-life balance, encouraging skill development, and organizing virtual team-building exercises. It's critical to regularly assess and modify remote work procedures, encourage diversity and inclusivity, and offer mental health assistance. Empathic and compassionate leadership creates a nurturing atmosphere that makes team members feel appreciated and empowered to work from a distance. Managers may effectively lead remote teams, encourage sustainability, and foster a culture of cooperation and well-being in virtual work environments by adopting these best practices.

❖ **Here are some best practices to consider:**

1. Establish Clear Goals and Expectations: Establish clear, quantifiable objectives and goals for remote team members first. Make certain that every team member is aware of their responsibilities, roles, and the overall goals of the work or project. Having clarity up front reduces misunderstandings later on and helps to coordinate everyone's efforts.

2. Develop Robust Communication Channels: For remote teams, communication is essential. Invest in a range of platforms and tools for communication to ensure smooth team member interaction. When it comes to fast questions and updates, use instant messaging apps like Slack or Microsoft Teams in addition to email. For longer talks and brainstorming sessions, save your money on video conferencing services like Zoom or Google Meet.

3. Encourage Regular Check-Ins and Updates: To ensure that everyone is in agreement, schedule frequent check-ins and progress updates. Team members can discuss obstacles, coordinate efforts, and share progress via daily or weekly stand-up meetings. Individualized support and feedback can be provided and a sense of connection can be cultivated through one-on-one sessions between managers and team members.

4. Leverage Project Management Tools: Asana, Trello, Jira, and other project management apps are great tools for assigning duties, managing projects, and monitoring progress in remote teams. These tools help teams stay organized and goal-focused by providing visibility into individual workloads, task dependencies, and project schedules.

5. Promote Accountability and Ownership: Promote an ownership and accountability culture among the team. Assign team members explicit timelines and goals, and hold them responsible for achieving them. Promote autonomy by giving team members the freedom to decide for themselves and accept responsibility for their job, and by offering assistance and direction as required.

6. Provide Opportunities for Skill Development: There are chances for ongoing education and skill improvement when working remotely.

Provide access to webinars, workshops, and online courses that complement team needs and individual career aspirations. Through mentoring or knowledge-sharing sessions, encourage team members to impart their knowledge and skills to others.

7. Prioritize Work-Life Balance: The lines between work and personal life may become hazier when working remotely, which can result in burnout and lower output. Urge your colleagues to clearly define the boundaries between professional and personal time, and set an example by honouring these limits yourself. Promote taking pauses, holidays, and time off to rejuvenate and preserve wellbeing.

8. Emphasize Results Over Hours: Prioritize results and outcomes over hours worked. As long as deadlines are fulfilled and quality standards are maintained, working remotely gives you more flexibility over how and when you complete your work. Put more emphasis on work completed than time spent, and have faith in your team members to use their time wisely.

9. Facilitate Virtual Team Building Activities: Through online team-building exercises and social gatherings, distant workers can strengthen their bonds and sense of togetherness. To promote social engagement and connection building outside of work-related activities, host virtual coffee breaks, gaming nights, or wellness sessions. These exercises can improve morale and cohesiveness within the team.

10. Regularly Evaluate and Adapt: Keep an eye on how well remote work procedures are working and ask team members for their opinions. Surveys, one-on-one conversations, and team retrospectives are effective ways to learn what's going well and where changes may be made. In order to effectively support the dynamics of remote teams, be prepared to modify and refine procedures, resources, and communication techniques.

11. Promote Diversity and Inclusion: Establish a welcoming remote workplace where each team member is treated with respect and feels heard and appreciated. Accept and value the diversity of people's experiences, viewpoints, and backgrounds. Create an atmosphere where everyone is at ease expressing their opinions, participating in conversations, and making decisions.

12. Invest in Mental Health Support: Particularly for team members used to working in an office environment, working remotely might occasionally cause feelings of loneliness or isolation. Provide tools and resources for mental health and wellbeing, like employee assistance programs, mindfulness training, and counselling services.

13. Lead with Empathy and Compassion: Lastly, show compassion and understanding in your leadership. Be mindful of the particular requirements and circumstances of your team members and acknowledge that working remotely has its own set of obstacles. Be understanding of others who are going through difficult times and, when you can, be accommodating.

You may encourage a culture of cooperation, communication, and well-being in virtual work environments, effectively lead remote teams, and advance sustainability by implementing these best practices into your management style.

12.3 Future Trends in Green HR Technology

Future developments in green HR technology herald a significant change in the direction of integrating sustainability ideas into HR procedures and frameworks. These trends cover a wide range of topics, such as monitoring and managing carbon footprints, training and development for sustainability, green performance management, supply chain transparency and sustainability, CSR reporting, ESG integration, remote work optimization, sustainable recruitment practices, employee engagement, and well-being. Through the use of technology, businesses can monitor and assess their carbon footprint, minimize the environmental impact of remote work arrangements, incorporate sustainability standards into hiring procedures, encourage employee involvement and well-being through sustainability programs, offer opportunities for sustainable practice training and development, synchronize performance management with sustainability objectives, encourage supply chain sustainability and transparency, report on corporate social responsibility, and incorporate environmental, social, and governance considerations into HR procedures, and drive continuous innovation in the field of green HR technology through cooperation. These developments point to a comprehensive strategy for sustainability in HR practices, emphasizing the promotion of favourable social, economic, and environmental effects on businesses and their surrounding ecosystems.

❖ **Several future trends are likely to shape the landscape of Green HR technology:**

1. Carbon Footprint Tracking and Management: With continued development, green HR technology will provide all-encompassing options for monitoring, assessing, and controlling an organization's carbon impact. In order to collect information on employee commuting, office energy consumption, supply chain emissions, and business travel, advanced carbon accounting technologies have been developed and integrated with HR systems. Organizations can lower their environmental effect by implementing focused initiatives and identifying opportunities for improvement by receiving insights into the sources of carbon emissions.

2. Remote Work Optimization: Green HR technology will concentrate on optimizing virtual work arrangements to minimize environmental impact as remote work becomes more common. Creating tools and algorithms to optimize remote work schedules in order to lower energy use during peak hours is part of this. Furthermore, as virtual collaboration platforms advance, the necessity for in-person meetings and travel will decrease by offering smooth communication and collaboration experiences.

3. Sustainable Recruitment Practices: The hiring process will increasingly incorporate sustainability criteria thanks to HR technology. This entails creating instruments to evaluate applicants' environmental qualifications and coordinating hiring procedures with sustainable objectives. The increasing prevalence of virtual recruiting alternatives, like online job fairs and interviews, is aimed at mitigating the environmental impact of conventional recruitment techniques.

4. Employee Engagement and Well-being: Through sustainability activities, green HR technology will prioritize fostering employee engagement and well-being. This includes creating tools and platforms that promote environmentally favourable actions among employees, like lowering energy use, cutting trash, and using sustainable means of transportation. Furthermore, wellness initiatives that enhance mental and physical health will be supported by HR technology, resulting in a workforce that is more robust and sustainable.

5. Training and Development for Sustainability: HR technology platforms will provide a broad range of opportunities for training and development with an emphasis on sustainability. This covers the creation of webinars, online courses, and other materials on environmental best practices in addition to instruments for monitoring staff engagement and advancement. Organizations may enable their workforce to adopt more sustainable behaviours and practices by allocating resources towards employee education and development.

6. Green Performance Management: Employee contributions to sustainability goals will be tracked and assessed through the use of green HR technology, which will incorporate sustainability measures into performance management systems. This include establishing goals for sustainability, monitoring employees' progress toward those goals, and recognizing and rewarding employees for their sustainability accomplishments. Organizations can encourage and reward sustainable behaviour among their employees by coordinating performance management with sustainability goals.

7. Supply Chain Transparency and Sustainability: Supply chains will become more transparent and accountable thanks to HR technology, which offers instruments for tracking and documenting vendors' and suppliers' environmental effects. Creating supply chain management systems that monitor sustainability indicators like waste production, water use, and carbon emissions is part of this. Organizations can create responsible sourcing policies and lessen their overall environmental impact by encouraging supplier chains to be transparent and sustainable.

8. Corporate Social Responsibility (CSR) Reporting: Through the provision of tools for gathering, evaluating, and reporting on sustainability data, green HR technology will assist businesses in their CSR reporting initiatives. This involves creating tools for informing stakeholders about CSR performance and CSR reporting platforms that make it easier to collect and evaluate sustainability KPIs. Businesses may show their dedication to sustainability and openness by adopting CSR reporting, which will increase their reputation and trustworthiness among stakeholders such as investors, consumers, and other parties.

9. Environmental, Social, and Governance (ESG) Integration: Environmental, social, and governance (ESG) considerations will be progressively included into HR procedures and decision-making through the use of green HR technologies. As part of this, ESG-focused HR analytics tools are being developed, which offer insights into the social and environmental effects of HR activities like employee well-being programs, diversity and inclusion campaigns, and sustainability initiatives. Organizations can better connect their business strategy with stakeholder expectations and sustainability goals by integrating ESG concerns into HR operations.

10. Continuous Innovation and Collaboration: Green HR technology will keep developing as a result of ongoing innovation and cooperation between industry stakeholders, sustainability specialists, and HR technology providers. This includes collaborations and alliances that promote information exchange and the promotion of best practices, as well as the creation of new instruments, platforms, and solutions to address new sustainability opportunities and challenges. Organizations may generate significant progress towards sustainability and have a positive social and environmental effect by cultivating a culture of innovation and collaboration.

To summarize, the future of Green HR technology will see an increasing focus on supply chain transparency and sustainability, CSR reporting, ESG integration, sustainable hiring practices, remote work optimization, employee engagement, and well-being. It will also see training and development for sustainability, green performance management, and tracking and managing carbon footprints. By adopting these trends and making the most of technology, businesses can create workplaces that are more resilient, sustainable, and socially conscious.

12.3.1 Emerging Technologies Shaping the Future of Green HR Practices

Organizations are realizing more and more how important it is to include sustainability into their human resources (HR) strategies in the quickly changing business landscape of today. HR departments are using emerging technology to support green efforts, enhance employee well-being, and lessen environmental impact as the emphasis on environmental responsibility expands globally.

Green HR practices are undergoing a revolution thanks to emerging technologies, which provide creative ways to improve efficacy, efficiency, and sustainability. Several key technologies are shaping the future of green HR practices:

1. Artificial Intelligence (AI) and Machine Learning: Not only are AI and machine learning algorithms transforming conventional HR procedures, but they are also spearheading corporate sustainability initiatives. Large data sets can be analysed by these technologies to find patterns, trends, and chances to maximize resource efficiency, cut waste, and lessen environmental effect. AI-driven hiring platforms, for instance, can evaluate candidate profiles to find people with experience in sustainability, and machine learning algorithms can optimize office building energy use by taking occupancy patterns and environmental factors into account. AI-driven chatbots can also offer employees customized advice on eco-friendly behaviours like cutting back on paper use or electricity use.

2. Virtual Reality (VR) and Augmented Reality (AR): Employee training and development programs are being revolutionized by VR and AR technology, which provide engaging and interactive learning opportunities on sustainability-related subjects. Employees may practice eco-friendly habits like energy conservation, trash reduction, and sustainable transportation options through VR simulations that transport them to virtual locations. In the meanwhile, augmented reality (AR) apps can superimpose data on actual things to offer contextual advice on best practices for sustainability, such energy- or recycling-related advice. HR departments may provide employees with powerful and engaging training programs that raise awareness of environmental issues and support sustainable practices by utilizing VR and AR technologies.

3. Data Analytics and Predictive Analytics: Data analytics technologies are getting more and more advanced in their ability to analyse HR data and spot trends, patterns, and areas for development. Algorithms for predictive analytics can predict changes in demand, project future labour requirements, and pinpoint areas where corporate value can be generated from sustainability activities. HR departments, for instance, might leverage data analytics to pinpoint high-impact areas for energy savings, such maximizing employee travel schedules or putting in place telecommuting initiatives. Organizations may monitor the success of sustainability projects, make data-driven decisions, and constantly improve their environmental performance by utilizing data.

4. Block chain Technology: Block-chain technology provides a transparent and decentralized platform for monitoring and validating sustainability programs, including supply chain transparency initiatives, carbon offsetting schemes, and investments in renewable energy. Block chain technology has the potential to improve sustainability practices' credibility and accountability by creating an unchangeable and impenetrable ledger of transactions. Block chain-based platforms, for instance, can offer transparent carbon emission data, allowing businesses to track the environmental effect of their activities and confirm the veracity of sustainability claims. Furthermore, transactions pertaining to carbon credits, renewable energy certificates, and other sustainability incentives can be automated using block chain-enabled smart contracts, simplifying procedures and cutting down on administrative burden.

5. Renewable Energy Technologies: Data canters, manufacturing facilities, and office buildings are being powered in large part by renewable energy technologies like solar, wind, and geothermal energy. HR departments and facilities management teams can work together to oversee the installation and maintenance procedures, get funds and incentives, and assess the viability of renewable energy projects. Organizations may lessen their dependency on fossil fuels, cut carbon emissions, and help ensure a more sustainable energy future by investing in renewable energy solutions.

6. Smart Building Technologies: Automation, networking, and data analytics are the three main ways that smart building technologies maximize building efficiency while cutting energy use. These technologies include occupancy sensors, automatic lighting controls, energy-efficient HVAC systems, and building management systems

(BMS). To deploy smart building solutions that produce healthier, more sustainable work environments for employees, HR departments and facilities management teams can work together. Energy-efficient HVAC systems, for instance, can optimize temperature settings to reduce energy consumption, while automated lighting controls and occupancy sensors can change lighting levels based on natural light and occupancy patterns. Organizations may increase employee comfort and productivity, save operating costs, and improve energy efficiency by utilizing smart building technologies.

7. Internet of Things (IoT): Real-time monitoring and management of environmental conditions by enterprises is made possible in large part by the use of IoT devices. These devices can be used to monitor waste creation, water usage, energy consumption, and air quality throughout manufacturing plants, office buildings, and supply chain networks. HR departments may find areas for improvement, put energy-saving measures into place, and guarantee compliance with environmental standards by gathering and analysing data from IoT sensors. Additionally, IoT-enabled wearable's can support worker well-being by tracking steps taken, advocating for breaks, and offering individualised health and productivity reports.

8. Green Certification and Compliance Tools: Organizations can monitor and prove their adherence to industry standards, environmental legislation, and sustainability certifications with the use of green certification and compliance technologies. A consolidated platform for gathering, evaluating, and reporting sustainability data such as energy use, carbon emissions, waste production, and water consumption is offered by these technologies. In order to ensure compliance with green HR practices and foster accountability within the company, HR technology platforms can link with green certification and compliance solutions to improve data collecting, reporting, and certification processes. These tools can also offer perceptions and suggestions for boosting sustainability programs, finding cost-saving options, and strengthening environmental performance.

To summarise, the future of HR practises related to sustainability is being significantly impacted by emerging technologies like AI and machine learning, IoT, block chain, VR/AR, data analytics, renewable energy, smart buildings, and green certification systems. HR departments can encourage environmental responsibility, improve employee well-being, and advance sustainability in businesses by utilizing these technologies. In addition, these technologies facilitate innovation, teamwork, and ongoing enhancement, empowering establishments to build future workplaces that are more robust, sustainable, and socially conscious.

12.3.2 Predictions on the Impact of AI, Block chain, and IoT on Sustainability in HR

There are a lot of big, revolutionary predictions about how AI, blockchain, and IoT will change HR sustainability and how businesses will handle corporate responsibility and environmental stewardship. Let's delve deeper into each technology's potential and how it can revolutionize sustainability practices within HR:

1. Artificial Intelligence (AI):

AI has the potential to revolutionize sustainability by giving HR professionals access to hitherto untapped insights and capabilities. Organizations will be able to anticipate environmental trends, recognize possible dangers, and proactively apply mitigation methods thanks to predictive analytics driven by AI algorithms. Predictive modelling powered by AI, for instance, can examine past data on energy use, trash production, and carbon emissions to forecast trends and maximize resource utilization. This kind of foresight gives HR departments the option to create customized sustainability programs that meet both legal and organizational standards.

HR procedures will be streamlined by AI-driven automation, freeing up important time and funds to concentrate on important sustainability projects. Routine operations like data input, reporting, and compliance monitoring can be automated by machine learning algorithms, freeing up HR experts to focus their skills on creating sustainable initiatives that have a real impact.

Chatbots and virtual assistants driven by artificial intelligence (AI) have the potential to improve employee engagement and raise knowledge of sustainable practices by offering individualized advice, responding to inquiries, and organizing learning opportunities. These virtual assistants have the ability to send out customized messages and prompts to promote environmentally responsible actions, such reducing waste, using less energy, and choosing sustainable modes of transportation.

Through its ability to help organizations find people with excellent sustainability credentials, AI will play a critical role in talent acquisition and retention. Artificial intelligence (AI) algorithms are able to evaluate candidates' environmental understanding, sustainability commitment, and involvement in relevant efforts by examining their resumes, social media profiles, and online behaviour. HR departments may create diverse, environmentally conscious teams that support the organization's sustainability objectives and values by utilizing AI in their recruitment procedures.

2. Blockchain:

Blockchain technology improves accountability, trust, and transparency in HR sustainability policies by providing a decentralized, immutable ledger system. Blockchain allows businesses to safely track and validate environmental indicators like carbon emissions, energy use, and waste management by encoding transactions and data in tamper-proof blocks. Increased accountability and integrity in sustainability reporting are fostered by this transparency, guaranteeing that companies honour their environmental stewardship pledges.

Regulation and standard compliance with sustainability will be automated via smart contracts, which are self-executing agreements with pre-established terms and conditions. Smart contracts, for instance, have the capacity to automatically initiate actions in response to predefined sustainability thresholds, such carbon emissions standards or renewable energy requirements. Organizations may more effectively and transparently show their commitment to sustainability thanks to this automation, which also streamlines compliance monitoring and lowers the possibility of human error.

Blockchain technology allows for the tracking and verification of items and resources, which improves supply chain sustainability and transparency. Organizations may ensure ethical sourcing and responsible production processes by tracking the origin, manufacture, and distribution of commodities through the recording of supply chain transactions on a blockchain ledger. Customers, investors, and other stakeholders will be more trusting of the company as a result of this transparency, which will improve its standing and ability to compete in the market.

Credentialing solutions that are enabled by blockchain technology offer a decentralized and secure means of verifying the sustainability credentials and certifications of employees. Organizations can confirm the legitimacy and integrity of certifications, such LEED accreditation, energy management certifications, or sustainability training programs, by logging credentials on a blockchain ledger. By guaranteeing that employees are capable and qualified to carry out sustainability efforts, this validation improves the legitimacy and trustworthiness of HR procedures.

3. Internet of Things (IoT):

The ability to monitor and optimize environmental performance in workplace operations in real-time is one way that the Internet of Things (IoT) is transforming sustainability in HR. Smart sensors and other Internet of things (IoT) devices gather information on energy use, water use, indoor air quality, and trash production. This data gives businesses important insights to maximize resource efficiency and minimize environmental impact.

IoT sensors are used by smart building technologies to track and manage energy use, HVAC, lighting, and other building functions in real time. Organizations can find ways to enhance building operations and cut down on energy waste by evaluating data on occupancy patterns, temperature fluctuations, and energy use. IoT-enabled lighting systems, for instance, may automatically alter brightness levels in response to occupancy patterns and natural light conditions, saving energy while preserving comfort and productivity.

Through the monitoring of indoor air quality, ergonomic circumstances, and energy-efficient behaviours, Internet of Things devices support employee wellbeing and sustainability. Smartwatches and fitness trackers are examples of wearable technology that tracks employees' stress levels, sleep habits, and physical activity to provide valuable information on their productivity and well-being. Moreover, height, temperature, and ergonomic settings can be changed by IoT-enabled office furniture and equipment to enhance comfort and lessen tiredness.

Analytics platforms backed by IoT make it possible to make data-based decisions and continuously improve HR sustainability initiatives. Organizations can uncover trends, patterns, and abnormalities in environmental performance by compiling and evaluating data from IoT devices. This allows for proactive interventions and optimization techniques. Predictive maintenance algorithms, for instance, can foresee equipment malfunctions and energy inefficiencies, enabling businesses to take proactive measures to address problems before they worsen. With the use of predictive analytics, HR departments are better equipped to make decisions that have a quantifiable impact and advance the sustainability objectives of the company.

In conclusion, technologies like AI, blockchain, and IoT have the potential to drastically change HR sustainability practices by promoting accountability, efficiency, and creativity. Organizations may seize new chances to improve environmental stewardship, motivate employees, and build a more sustainable future for all by using the potential of these emerging technologies.

12.3.3 Opportunity and Challenges in Adopting Cutting-edge Green HR Technologies

The adoption of cutting-edge green HR technologies presents both opportunities and challenges for organizations striving to enhance their sustainability efforts. Let's explore these in detail:

- **Opportunities:**

1. Enhanced Environmental Performance: Green HR solutions, with their real-time data, predictive analytics, and automation capabilities, present chances to improve an organization's environmental performance dramatically. Organizations can decrease waste, maximize resource use, and lower their carbon footprint by utilizing these technologies, which will have a positive impact on the environment.

2. Global Collaboration and Knowledge Sharing: Green HR solutions let companies, sectors, and stakeholders collaborate globally and share knowledge. Organizations can share best practices, lessons gained, and creative solutions to sustainability problems via online forums, networks, and platforms. Through this partnership, companies can take advantage of their combined knowledge, assets, and networks to move closer to common sustainability objectives. Global cooperation also promotes alliances and collaborations that propel group action on urgent environmental problems including resource depletion, biodiversity loss, and climate change.

3. Cost Savings: Using green HR solutions can save money by increasing productivity and optimizing resources. Organizations can enhance sustainability performance and save operational expenses by automating operations, cutting down on paper use, and managing energy utilization. Furthermore, adopting sustainable practices may draw investors and eco-aware consumers, boosting financial gains even more.

4. Supply Chain Transparency: Green HR technology present chances to improve supply chain traceability and transparency. Organizations may track the source, path, and environmental impact of products and raw materials by utilizing blockchain and IoT systems. Because of this transparency, companies are better able to recognize and manage sustainability risks in their supply chains, such as unethical sourcing methods or environmental deterioration. Transparent supply chains can also increase a brand's competitiveness and reputation by fostering trust among stakeholders, investors, and consumers.

5. Talent Attraction and Retention: Using state-of-the-art green HR solutions can improve an organization's employer brand and draw in top talent by demonstrating a commitment to sustainability. Businesses that adopt green HR practices can gain a competitive edge since employees, particularly millennials and Gen Z, place a high value on environmental sustainability when selecting jobs. In addition, cultivating an environment-friendly culture can increase worker retention and engagement.

6. Innovation and Differentiation: Organizations can establish themselves as industry leaders in sustainability and innovation by adopting cutting-edge green HR technologies. By implementing cutting-edge technologies like artificial intelligence (AI), blockchain, and the internet of things (IoT), businesses may stand out from rivals, draw in eco-aware clients, and contribute to positive societal change.

7. Regulatory Compliance and Risk Management: Green HR tools help businesses better manage risks associated with sustainability and comply with environmental standards. Organizations may guarantee compliance with local, national, and international regulations and prevent potential fines and reputational harm associated with non-compliance by accurately recording and reporting environmental data. Proactive sustainability initiatives can also reduce the danger of social instability, resource scarcity, and climate change.

8. Data-driven Decision-making: Data-driven decision-making is made possible by green HR technology, which maximize sustainability performance. Through the collection and analysis of real-time data on operational procedures, employee behaviours, and environmental indicators, organizations may pinpoint areas for improvement and carry out focused interventions. Based on empirical data and predictive modelling, AI-powered analytics solutions, for instance, can discover opportunities for energy savings, waste reduction techniques, and carbon footprint reduction projects. This data-driven strategy improves sustainability initiatives' efficacy and efficiency, producing quantifiable financial and environmental gains.

- **Challenges:**

1. Cost and Resource Constraints: The initial investment needed to implement state-of-the-art green HR solutions is one of the main obstacles. There may be substantial up-front expenses associated with the acquisition, integration, and training of technology when implementing blockchain, AI, and IoT technologies. In addition, companies might not have all the infrastructure, technical know-how, or trained staff needed to implement and manage these technologies.

2. Interoperability and Standards: The lack of established protocols and frameworks, as well as interoperability issues, are problems for green HR systems. Compatibility and interoperability standards are necessary for integrating various platforms, technologies, and data sources in order to guarantee smooth communication and data sharing. Organizations may have trouble integrating blockchain, IoT, and AI technologies with current systems and outside apps if established protocols aren't in place. Disparate data formats and protocols can also make it more difficult for stakeholders to collaborate and share data, which reduces the ability of green HR solutions to effectively solve sustainability issues.

Principles of Green HRM

3. Data Privacy and Security Concerns: Large amounts of sensitive data on employees, operations, and environmental performance are collected, stored, and analysed by green HR systems. In order to guard against data breaches, illegal access, and legal infractions, enterprises need to handle data privacy and security issues. To reduce these dangers, it is crucial to have strong data security measures in place, such as encryption, access limits, and adherence to data privacy laws.

4. Integration Complexity: Modern green HR technology integration can be difficult and complex when integrating into current systems and procedures. Integrating blockchain, IoT, and AI solutions with older HR systems can present compatibility, data silo, and interoperability difficulties for organizations. Furthermore, meticulous planning, coordination, and technical know-how are needed to guarantee flawless data flow and synchronization across various systems.

5. User Adoption and Engagement: One of the biggest obstacles to successfully deploying green HR solutions is user uptake and engagement. Workers may be hesitant to adopt new technologies because they are worried about their usability, their applicability, or whether they will interfere with their current workflows. Organizations must place a high priority on user-cantered design, offer thorough training and assistance, and actively include their employees in the design and implementation process in order to overcome these obstacles. Additionally, encouraging employee engagement and buy-in with green HR technology can help them be successfully adopted and integrated into daily operations. This can be achieved by cultivating a culture of innovation, experimentation, and continual learning.

6. Change Management and Cultural Shift: Implementing green HR technologies frequently calls for organizational change management initiatives and a cultural transformation. Workers may be reluctant to adopt new technologies or resist them altogether; particularly if they feel that they will be disruptive or dangerous. To overcome resistance and encourage the use of green HR technology, effective change management methods are essential. These strategies include communication, training, and stakeholder involvement.

7. Environmental Impact of Technology: Green HR technologies have an environmental impact related to their lifecycle, energy consumption, and development of electronic waste, even though they have the potential to improve sustainability. The manufacture, upkeep, and disposal of IT infrastructure, data canters, and electronic gadgets all contribute to resource depletion, energy usage, and carbon emissions. Companies need to think about how green HR technologies will affect the environment and put plans in place to lessen that impact, like using energy-efficient hardware, sourcing renewable energy, and managing e-waste responsibly. Organizations can also look into ways to reduce their environmental impact by investing in renewable energy, carbon offset projects, and sustainability programs.

8. Ethical and Social Implications: Transparency, justice, and equity are among the ethical and societal issues that green HR technology bring up. For instance, if AI algorithms are not properly created and managed, they may unintentionally reinforce prejudices or discrimination in recruitment procedures. Similar worries over data ownership, transparency, and access rights may be raised by blockchain-enabled systems. Companies need to take these moral issues into account and make sure that green HR technologies are implemented in an ethical and responsible way.

9. Technical Complexity and Expertise: Modern green HR technology implementation and management call for specific technical knowledge and abilities. Employers may have trouble finding and keeping skilled workers with knowledge of blockchain, artificial intelligence, the Internet of Things, and sustainability. Furthermore, continuing education and professional development expenditures are necessary to stay current with technology innovations and green HR best practices.

10. Regulatory Uncertainty and Compliance Burden: The regulatory environment in which green HR solutions operate is complicated and marked by constantly changing environmental standards, rules, and reporting requirements. Regulations pertaining to supply chain transparency, energy efficiency requirements, carbon emissions reporting, and other sustainability programs present challenges for organizations to comply with and manage. To guarantee conformity and reduce legal risks, compliance with a variety of frequently overlapping regulations calls for specialized resources, knowledge, and monitoring capabilities. Furthermore, firms may need to modify their green HR technology and procedures in response to updates and changes in regulations, which would increase their complexity and burden of compliance.

Conclusively, the integration of state-of-the-art green HR technology poses noteworthy prospects and obstacles for establishments aiming to augment their ecological endeavours. In addition to improved environmental performance, there are prospects for cost savings, talent attraction and retention, innovation and differentiation, supply chain transparency, regulatory compliance and risk management, data-driven decision-making, and international cooperation and information sharing. These technologies give organizations the opportunity to use resources more efficiently, increase transparency, and make a quantifiable difference in achieving sustainability goals.

Organizations must, however, also deal with a number of difficulties, such as limited funding and resources, worries about data security and privacy, challenging integration, managing change and cultural shifts, ethical and social ramifications, and technological complexity and competence. In order to successfully implement and integrate green HR solutions, stakeholders must carefully plan, invest, and collaborate in order to overcome these obstacles. Through proactive management of these obstacles and strategic utilization of green HR technology, enterprises can expedite their trajectory towards sustainability and establish a future that is both ecologically conscious and resilient.

www.ingramcontent.com/pod-product-compliance
Lightning Source LLC
LaVergne TN
LVHW061537070526
838199LV00077B/6822